WHEN TECHNOLOGY FAILS

WHEN TECHNOLOGY FAILS

A Manual for Self-Reliance & Planetary Survival

MATTHEW STEIN

Clear Light Publishers
Santa Fe, New Mexico

Clear Light Publishers
823 Don Diego, Santa Fe, New Mexico 87501
Web: www.clearlightbooks.com

First Edition
10 9 8 7 6 5 4 3 2 1

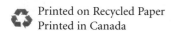 Printed on Recycled Paper
Printed in Canada

Cover photograph "A View of North America from Apollo 16" (NASA photo number: AS16-118-18873) and back cover photograph "A View of 'Africa and Saudi Arabia from Apollo 17" (NASA photo number: AS17-148-22727) from the NSSDC Photo Gallery: Earth (http://nssdc.gsfc.nasa.gov/photo_gallery/photogallery-earth.html)
Cover design by Marcia Keegan and Carol O'Shea
Interior design and typography by Carol O'Shea
Interior illustrations by Merri Mckee, Karen Frances, and Kristen Schwartz

Library of Congress Cataloging-in-Publication Data

Stein, Matthew I.
    When technology fails : the low-tech guide to self-reliance &
planetary survival / Matthew Stein.
        p. cm.
    Includes bibliographical references and index.
    ISBN 1-57416-046-X (cloth)–ISBN 1-57416-047-8 (pbk.)
        1. Survival skills. I. Title.
GF86 .S75 2000
640'.49–dc21

                                                        00-024031

This book is dedicated to my wife Josie, whose deep insight and awesome healing abilities have been a constant source of wonder and inspiration.

Acknowledgments

It is quite a large undertaking to write a book with a huge scope, such as *When Technology Fails*. I would be dishonest if I said that I was an expert on all the varied topics covered by this book. I owe quite a debt of gratitude to the many different experts who reviewed chapters, corrected, suggested, and otherwise contributed their years of experience toward making this book a practical and useful guide for the reader.

First, I would like to thank God, a higher power, the Christ, my spirit guides, or whatever you may wish to call it, for the inspiration to write this book. Shortly before Thanksgiving in 1997, during my daily session of meditation and prayer, I "received" the inspiration for this book in an instantaneous flash. Ideas usually tend to grow slowly, changing and evolving with time. This idea was completely different. From the moment that I received it, the concept and scope have remained unchanged. It is only my execution that has changed, and will continue to change, as I make additions, corrections, and improvements.

Second, I would like to thank my wonderful wife, Josie, for her editing help, clarity, suggestions, and patience putting up with me while I tackled this massive project. Special thanks to my father, Ben, who has given us tremendous support while I focused on this book and let my engineering design business slide. To my sister Jennifer Barker, who has lived a mostly self-sufficient lifestyle for the past fifteen years, and helped me with advice, information, and contacts for several chapters. To my son Joshua, for library research and assistance. To Rick Sylvester whose encouragement and faith in my ability to write helped get this project going. To Carla Emery for her wonderful book that is a great source of information and is recommended in several of my chapters. To Thom Hartman, Lester Brown, Amory Lovins, Richard Heede, and other folks at The Worldwatch Institute and the Rocky Mountain Institute for their inspirational writings and information.

To John Jeavons and the rest of the Ecology Action crew for their assistance and support.

I am very grateful for the assistance of Harmon Houghton, Barbara Kohl, Sara Held, and Carol O'Shea of Clear Light Publishers. Without them, this book would still be just a dream. Thanks to Howard Rheingold and Michael Larsen for giving me the professional encouragement and guidance to keep me going in the early stages of this project. Much credit must go to Merri Mckee (line art technical illustrations), Karen Frances (shaded drawings with people and landscape), and Kristen Schwartz (edible plants) for contributing their artistic talents to the illustrations.

Others who contributed measurably to this project include Dave Ward, Keith Robertson, James T. West, Joseph Nuuanu, Shelly and Phil Rodgers; Andreas Kaupert (emergency preparedness); Dan Vorhis and Howard Backer, M.D. (water); Fred Walters, Richard Nielsen and Amigo Cantisano (food); Glen Nadar (animals); Joe Tibbets, Rick Heede, Will Beemer, Fred Webster, Ph.D., P.E., Michael Frerking, Harris Lowenhaupt, and Joaquim Karcher (green building); Jennifer Lawler, Kimbal Chatfield, O.M.D., L.Ac., and James Duke, Ph.D. (herbs); Hulda Regehr Clark, Ph.D., N.D. (naturopathy and herbs); David Edwards, M.D. (healing and homeopathy); Diane Soucy, Allison Judge, and Carrol Collins (fiber arts); Matt Richards, John McPherson, and Worth Jackson (tanning and leather); Jon Hill, Richard Perez, Windy Dankoff, Don Harris, Paul Cunningham, Chuck Marken, Glenn Rambach, Kevin Cook, Skip Goebel, Ray Darby, Zac Pierce, and Chris Worchester (renewable energy); Hans Standteiner, John Septien, and Stewart Marshall (metals); Pamela Vandiver, Ph.D., and Dan Martinez (ceramics). To the rest of you who contributed measurably, but whose names I neglected to list, thank you for your help and please forgive my oversight.

Table of Contents

Foreword

It is not the strongest of the species that survive, nor the most intelligent, but the one most responsive to change.
—Charles Darwin

When Technology Fails *is a book about our future. On the one hand, it is about preparing for possible future instabilities and failures in technology and the central services that we have come to rely on for our daily sustenance and commerce. On the other hand, it is about awakening to the fact that we are all occupants of a fragile planetary ecosystem that is showing severe signs of strain from expanding global population and the business-as-usual ideal of continuously increasing consumption.* **When Technology Fails** *is a clear, useable, practical handbook. It provides basic information and instructions on widely ranging subjects falling under the loose guidelines of self-reliance, a sustainable future for our planet, and primitive living skills that could come in handy if you should someday find yourself and family deprived of modern conveniences. Since one single book couldn't possibly provide in-depth coverage for all of the relevant subjects, each chapter includes a resource guide to the best applicable literature, web sites, and sources for materials.*

In today's world of global warming, superstorms, record-breaking floods, severe droughts, antiquated and overloaded electrical distribution systems, it is likely that most of us will see significant disruptions in the flow of electricity and goods at some point in our lives. An old Chinese saying asks, "Is it not already too late if one waits until one is thirsty to begin digging a well?" This saying applies equally at both the personal and planetary levels. On the micro level (personal survival), a little planning, training, education, and individual action can significantly reduce one's sense of helplessness. On the macro level (global sustainability), large numbers of people must be awakened to the need for change before governments and the majority of businesses make a sustainable future their number one priority. On both levels, action is required to promote a positive outcome.

We live in the "Information Age" and information is power. **When Technology Fails** *is an exceptional source of information, providing something of value for almost everyone. Whether you wish to cope with possible future instabilities and emergencies, grow your own food in sustainable ways, build an earth-friendly home, develop your own independent power system or expand your alternative healing repertoire,* **When Technology Fails** *provides valuable guidance and instruction. Going far beyond survivalist books, its broadbased appeal ranges from the environmentalist who wishes to reduce humanity's impact on the planet to the average person who simply wishes to provide for friends and family in the event of an emergency. Whoever you are, I hope that you find* **When Technology Fails** *as fascinating to read as I found it to write.*

We are all in this together! Let us create a future that we can all live with.

▮ An Introduction to Self-Reliance

You must be the change you wish to see in the world.

—Mohandas Gandi

AN UNCERTAIN FUTURE

When I was a kid, gasoline pumps and cash registers had hand cranks to dispense gas and receive cash when the power went out. Not so anymore. Modern advances in electronics, coupled with years of a reliably consistent supply of electricity, have turned most appliances and machines into sleek microprocessor-controlled wonders of high technology, which stand mute and motionless when the power goes out. Without electricity, air conditioners, credit card machines, gasoline pumps, and cash registers cease to function. A few hours after the power goes out, most long-distance automotive traffic runs out of gas and comes to a halt.

> In the summer of 1996, a major power outage blacked out several western states for most of one day. Dave and Linda, my brother and sister-in-law, were driving down California's Central Valley on that particular day and remember it well. The heat was a blistering 115°F. It was the kind of day that melts asphalt and could fry an egg in the sun. When their gas tank reached empty, they reluctantly joined long lines of sweating motorists waiting at the pumps for the power to come back on. They waited for five long hours before they were able to buy gas and a cold drink.

What caused this multistate blackout? Was it some terrorist act? Was it a calamitous act of nature? No, it was caused by sagging power lines on a particularly hot summer's day in Oregon (CNN 1996). In the sweltering heat, the lines stretched and expanded, sagging into improperly pruned trees. Because of excessively high demand for electricity from millions of air conditioners, each time the utility tried to restart the West Coast's electrical power grid, it overloaded somewhere and

shut down again. This is one isolated example of the fragility of the complex centralized systems that most of us rely upon for our daily food, fuel, and commerce.

Imagine that you are driving across some desolate part of the western states on your family vacation. You pull up to the pumps at a lonely gas station in the middle of nowhere. As you reach for the gas pump, the attendant says, "Don't bother, the power's out." You ask him, "How long has it been out? Do you know what's going on?" He replies, "I have no idea what's happening. The power's been out for hours. TV and radio don't work and the phones are dead." Hours stretch into days. You are in a desert location. All the drinking water relies on electric pumps to move the water to the surface from deep inside the earth. What do you do? Does this scenario sound farfetched, or does it strike a chord? Do you sense that perhaps this scenario could happen all too easily?

One hundred years ago, most small communities in this country had all the low technology resources necessary to grow, hunt, or fabricate what they needed to live comfortably. Today, our high-tech society is based on a pyramid of very specialized, yet extremely interdependent, industries and technologies. If five or six of your friends were transported to a remote location deep in the heart of a vast wilderness, how much of our technology do you think they could reproduce without assistance or modern tools? If a couple of key cornerstones of our society—such as gasoline and electricity—were knocked out, wouldn't most of us stumble back into the Stone Age?

How well will you fare when a real disaster strikes—like a major hurricane, flood, or severe earthquake? When the Northridge quake destroyed or severely damaged a few hundred buildings and took down several freeway interchanges, traffic was snarled for nine months in the Los Angeles basin.

What if the next Los Angeles quake takes down 600 freeway interchanges? Or what if the nationwide grid of electrical power distribution were shut down for a few weeks instead of a few hours? It could happen and already has happened numerous times across the world, just not in recent U.S. history.

The long-term future of our food supply is increasingly in question. The destruction of native plant cover, monocropping, and sod-busting practices of tilling soil exacerbated the effects of an extended drought to create the Dust Bowl catastrophe of the 1930s, which resulted in the destruction of millions of acres of farmland. Modern chemical-intensive farming continues to deplete the nation's farmlands of topsoil and nutrients. A third of the original topsoil in the continental United States is gone, and most of the rest is significantly depleted of nutrients and degraded by pesticides and chemical fertilizers. Changes in weather patterns may be harbingers of long-term changes in climate that would drastically affect global food production.

Most people agree that our weather patterns seem more erratic now than at any other time in recent history. In 1998, Central America saw the most devastating hurricane in 150 years. It is estimated that it will take Hondurans fully fifty years to rebuild their country. That was also the year of an unprecedented, record-breaking heat wave across the southeastern United States; severe destruction of crops and livestock due to heat and drought in Texas; the worst financial crisis to strike Asian nations since the stock market crash of 1929; and planes crashing in Indonesia because pilots could not see through the dense smoke rising from burning rain forests. The same droughts that allowed the rain forests to burn out of control also brought famine and starvation to many people in Southeast Asia. The past decade has seen record high temperatures over most of the planet—witness Hurricane Andrew's record-breaking destruction in Florida; record high floods along the Mississippi River and in Europe; and deadly earthquakes in Japan, California, China, Indonesia, Pakistan, Peru, Columbia, Turkey, Greece, Taiwan, and the former Soviet Union. People are asking themselves, What is going on with our world? How can we prepare ourselves for the future?

WHY THIS BOOK?

The future belongs to those who prepare for it.
—Ralph Waldo Emerson

With all these future uncertainties and issues and problems competing for attention, it is easy to become confused and paralyzed into inaction. Meanwhile, a little bit of education and preparation can go a long way toward reducing one's personal sense of fear and helplessness. *When Technology Fails* can help you plan and prepare for the possibility of short-term or long-term disruptions in the flow of the goods and services that we have become so dependent on. If you are caught in some natural disaster, this guide can provide you with basic survival information to help you cope with whatever comes your way.

When Technology Fails is more than just a guide for personal survival; it is also a guide to sustainable technologies and a tool for spreading the awareness of sustainable options. We are living in a finite world with growing populations, whose expanding appetites for consuming the world's resources are threatening the quality of life on the planet. We cannot continue to consume resources at our current rate much longer, and certainly can't maintain a continuously increasing rate. Business-as-usual has already taken a severe toll on our planet's major ecosystems and is beginning to reap frightening results, such as global warming, severe weather, crop failures, failed fisheries, and epidemics of modern diseases like AIDS, hepatitis, and cancer. Sustainable technologies can build a positive future for our children and our children's children. Whether you wish simply to weather the storms of short-term emergencies and disruptions, or are concerned about long-term societal conditions, this book can help you plan and prepare for the future.

Perhaps you are simply seeking to change your lifestyle in order to become more self-sufficient. Do you wish to build an energy-efficient home, grow your own food, or live independently from the electric power distribution grid? In this case, *When Technology Fails* can provide you with basic information to help you plan your lifestyle change and guide you to the best resources for accomplishing your goals.

In addition to providing basic practical instructions and guidance on a wide variety of subjects, *When Technology Fails* offers brief descriptions and reviews of several books on each topic, to help you choose the best resources to meet your interests and supply you with reliable up-to-date information. I encourage you to use the recommendations in each chapter to add to your library of resources for personal and planetary survival and self-sufficiency.

Some will want to read this book from cover to cover, but others will focus on a few chapters of primary interest. For those of you who bought this book "just in case," I encourage you to skim the entire book to familiarize yourself with the topics and issues it covers. You may find yourself drawn to chapters that you might think would hold little interest. If you purchased this book to prepare yourself for possible emergencies, you should thoroughly read Chapter 3, *Supplies & Preparations*. At a minimum, I recommend that you follow the guidelines for short-term planning and preparation. I also urge you to read Chapter 2, *Present Trends, Possible Futures*. It will give you a realistic view of future trends and help you decide which preparations and lifestyle changes make the most sense to you. I recommend that all readers familiarize themselves with the principles of first aid (see Chapter 8) and get proper first aid and CPR training. If you are suffering from significant health problems, or have an interest in alternative healing, you should read Chapter 9, *Low-Tech Medicine & Healing*.

If you bought this book for short-term survival skills and emergency preparations, the chapters on planning, survival, water, food, and shelter will be the most valuable to you. If you are concerned with longer-term self-sufficiency and independence from the grid, all chapters will be of interest. If you find yourself subject to a long-term breakdown in central services, your ability to forage and/or grow food will be critical to your success. If you simply want to live a more self-sufficient, planet-friendly lifestyle, the chapters on food, healing, shelter, and energy will probably interest you most.

PREINDUSTRIAL SELF-SUFFICIENCY

For at least 100,000 years, tribal cultures have existed across the planet, living in sustainable harmony with nature. As recently as the 1800s, tribes populated half the earth, but now comprise only 1 to 2 percent of the world's population. Contrary to popular opinion, studies of a number of tribes, such as the Shoshone culture and the !Kung and Hotentots of Africa, indicate that members of many "primitive" tribes spend an average of only two to four hours a day attending to gathering food and other necessities of life. The rest of their time is devoted to family, arts, music, and other leisure activities. Few of us in the western world could claim similar amounts of leisure time. Another common fallacy is that of poor health and short lifespan among hunter-gatherers. Anthropologist Mark Nathan Cohen, in his book *Health and the Rise of Civilization*, points out that the lifespans of agricultural peoples have exceeded those of hunter-gatherers and foragers only during the last 100 years (Cohen 1989, 135). Apparently, most of this gain has been since the introduction of sulfa drugs, penicillin, and other modern antibiotics. Prior to the advent of modern medicine, archaeological records indicate that hunter-gatherers averaged 5 to 6 inches taller, had more teeth left at the time of death, and lived longer than agricultural peoples.

> *The older people used to say that the trees, the rocks, the birds, and the animals used to talk. They had a voice, and today, as I realize it, they still have a voice. My People always say that you have to take care of them in order for you to continue on. If you don't, when they die off, you are going to die off with them.*
> —Corbin Harney, spiritual leader of the Western Shoshone Nation, from *The Way It Is*

Indigenous societies typically honor all of creation as part of their "mother" earth. To destroy their mother would be like cutting off their own hands, an unthinkable act. If we are to survive as a species, it may be critical that we adopt this kind of reverence for our planet and restructure our businesses and industries around planet-friendly priorities. Agricultural practices of many indigenous peoples, such as the Hopi Indians and the Kayapo of Brazil, are wonderful examples of sustainable farming that honors the earth while also providing food for tribal members for hundreds of generations, without destroying the forest or other animal habitats. One of the other benefits of tribal life is a strong sense of community. The tribe cares for each member. Food and responsibilities are shared, such as caring for children and the elderly. There is no fear of retirement, layoffs, orphanages for the young, or isolation for the elderly.

Admittedly, most of us would not willingly give up our modern conveniences for a return to the hunter-gatherer lifestyle of our ancestors. However, if we were to find ourselves in a survival situation, some of their skills could help us to survive and perhaps live comfortably until such time as things returned to normal. Over the past 30 years, there has been a resurgence of interest in traditional tribal skills such as techniques for starting a fire, making stone knives, tanning animal hides, and fabricating utensils, shelters, and crude twine and ropes from foraged plant fibers. There is a sense of trying to recover something important, something valuable that has been lost.

For books on primitive skills, which could make a huge difference in a survival situation, see Chapter 4, Emergency Measures for Survival.

OLD-FASHIONED SELF-RELIANCE AND MODERN SUSTAINABLE TECHNOLOGY

Since before the days of the American Revolution, Americans have admired the ideals of ingenuity, independence, and self-reliance. Much as we admire those ideals, however, most of us have lost our ability to live a truly independent life. Somewhere between the home mortgage, the supermarket, the cost of medical care, the corporate work week, and the video store, the American ideal of rugged individuality has slipped through our fingers. We sense there was a simpler, yet more satisfying lifestyle in the days

of our ancestors. How many of us, after working hard year after year, feel that we have little to show for our work? Or perhaps we have prospered materially yet still feel that our lives lack deep, inner satisfaction or meaning.

My grandmother grew up on a mini-farm in the small town of Chelmsford, Massachusetts. At that time, over half of all Americans lived on farms, but now only 1 percent of the population is engaged in growing food. When Grandma was a little girl in the 1890s, the family's small farm and other small businesses in her community provided practically everything that was needed to lead a reasonably comfortable life. The miller ground the grain, the cobbler made shoes, the tailor made fine clothes. Things like glassware and windows, iron for the blacksmith, plumbing components, and cloth to sew into dresses came from large industrial factories and mills, but almost everything else was made or grown locally. Once every month or two, the family took a trip to Boston to enjoy the city and to purchase supplies that were not as available in their small town. Even though Boston is only 30 miles from Chelmsford, in those days it was a 2-day round trip by horse cart. Today, that same town is part of the giant suburban sprawl on the outskirts of the Boston metropolitan area.

In the event of a breakdown in the centralized systems that we rely upon for our daily needs and comforts, a working knowledge of our ancestors' technologies will go a long way toward helping us to live a comfortable life. Unfortunately, many of the simple technologies of the pioneers are no longer sustainable with today's global population of over six billion.

A typical pioneering family might have cut down thirty cords of wood to burn in fireplaces for heating their home during the long, hard New England winters. A single cord is a considerable amount of wood, measuring a stack 4 feet wide by 4 feet tall by 8 feet long. Is it any wonder that the American pioneers cleared practically all the accessible old growth forests in the eastern United States? Recent design improvements have created clean-burning wood stoves, which heat very efficiently and leave no visible smoke once the stove is warmed up to operating temperatures. These EPA-rated stoves can heat a modern, reasonably well-insulated 2,000-square-foot New England home on only a few cords of wood. A superinsulated home with passive solar collection can make it through a Colorado or Montana winter on the heat given off by the hot water heater and lightbulbs, with a little help from a wood stove on cloudy days.

Using the best of modern technology combined with old-fashioned self-reliance can provide for a comfortable and sustainable lifestyle. Neither the agricultural practices of the 1800s nor today's modern factory farms are sustainable. The good news is that advances in organic and biointensive farming are offering sustainable alternatives to chemical-intensive farming that can actually increase productivity while rebuilding depleted soils. Unfortunately, agribusiness continues to deplete the topsoil and pollute the environment. As consumers, we can do our part by supporting organic farming and other planet-friendly practices.

Standard U.S. agricultural practice today requires at least 45,000 square feet of land to feed a person on a high meat diet, or about 10,000 for a vegetarian.... However, biointensive gardening can provide for a vegetarian's entire diet, plus the compost crops needed to sustain the system indefinitely, on only 2,000 to 4,000 square feet, even starting with low quality land.... This works so well that biointensive agriculture is being practiced in 107 countries worldwide.

—Paul Hawken, Amory Lovins, and L. Hunter Lovins, *Natural Capitalism*

REFERENCES

Even if you have no current plans to buy land and move to the country, you might want to pick up some of the following references. If your supply of food and modern goods were disrupted for an extended period of time, the skills found in the following books could be extremely useful.

Books

***The Encyclopedia of Country Living: An Old-Fashioned Recipe Book,* by Carla Emery.** 1998, 858 pp. (paperback), ISBN 0-912365-95-1. Published by Sasquatch Books, 615 Second Ave., Seattle, WA 98104. Lists for $27.95.

With over 800 pages packed full of useful, practical information, this is the premier reference for making the move from city to the country. If you wish to start growing and preserving your own food, raising your own livestock, and living a simpler more self-sufficient life, there is no better book to start with than this. It will also be useful if you are contemplating a less radical change, such as planting a vegetable garden in your backyard. Carla and her husband Mike moved to the country during the "back to nature" movement in the 1960s. Like many other transplanted city folk, Carla found the transition difficult and genuine practical "how-to" information lacking. She drew heavily on

the guidance, wisdom, and experience of several old-timers. When one of her beloved old-timer friends died, she realized how important it was to record their wisdom and experience before it disappeared forever into an ocean of modern factory farms and high technology. This massive undertaking is a true labor of love, spanning thirty years and nine revised editions.

***Back to Basics: How to Learn and Enjoy Traditional American Skills,* from The Reader's Digest.** 1999, 456 pp. (hardcover), ISBN 0-89577-939-0. Published by The Reader's Digest Association, Pleasantville, NY. Lists for $30.00.

This encyclopedic book is surprisingly good. It covers a wide variety of traditional skills and some new technologies, including adobe, log, stone, and traditional post-and-beam construction; traditional furniture and other woodworking skills; growing your own fruits, vegetables, and livestock; preserving and cooking food; and spinning, weaving, metal-working, and other crafts. It contains many fine illustrations of traditional methods and tools. If you ever need to reconstruct the technologies of our ancestors, this book will give you a good start.

***The Foxfire Books: Hog Dressing, Log Cabin Building, Mountain Crafts and Foods, Planting by the Signs, Snake Lore, Hunting Tales, Faith Healing, Moonshining,* edited by Elliot Wigginton.** 1972, 384 pp. (paperback), ISBN 0-385-07353-4. An Anchor Book, published by Doubleday Division of Bantam Doubleday Publishing Group, Inc., 1540 Broadway, New York, NY 10036. Lists for $15.95.

In the late 1960s, Elliot Wigginton and his students created the *Foxfire* magazine to record and preserve the traditional folk culture, crafts, and skills of the southern Appalachian mountain people. *Foxfire 1*, the first compilation of articles from the magazine, was so popular that it eventually expanded into a series of thirteen books. Very entertaining and informative, these books record traditional self-sufficient living skills and folklore. I recommend that you pick up at least the first book plus *Foxfire 2*. Some folks buy the entire series.

***The Millennium Whole Earth Catalog: Access to Tools & Ideas for the Twenty-First Century,* edited by Howard Rheingold.** 1994, 384 pp. (paperback, large format), ISBN 0-06-251059-2. Published by Harper San Francisco, 1160 Battery St., 3rd Floor, San Francisco, CA 94111-1213. Lists for $35.00.

It's still a great guide to an enormous variety of resources.

Magazines

The following magazines are devoted to the pursuit of self-sufficiency and lifestyles that express cooperation with the earth. They contain excellent "how-to" and "how I did it" articles on a wide range of topics, including a multitude of gardening techniques and

information on animal husbandry, food storage and preparation, alternative energy methods, self-medication, and healing. Each magazine also contains numerous advertisements for the latest products (and catalogs) to assist you in your self-reliance efforts.

Back Home Magazine. Subscription: $18.97 per year for 6 issues. Back Home Magazine, P.O. Box 70, Hendersonville, NC 28793. Call (800) 992-2546 or see their web site at www.backhomemagazine.com. After *The Mother Earth News* was sold and moved to New York City, the magazine's original staff founded *Back Home* magazine. This is a fine magazine, devoted to self-reliance, sustainable living, and ecology. Both the homesteader and the suburban dweller with a backyard garden can enjoy this magazine.

Backwoods Home. Subscription: $19.95 per year for 6 issues. Backwoods Home Magazine, P.O. Box 712, Gold Beach, OR 97444. Call (800) 835-2418 or see their web site at www.backwoodshome.com. My sister has lived off the grid, in remote mountainous locations for the past twenty years, and this is her personal favorite. Lots of practical articles, with the focus on homesteading and self-reliance. The editorial staff's strong libertarian political view and survivalist leanings might be difficult for some folks to handle.

Countryside. Subscription: $18 per year for 6 issues. Countryside & Small Stock Journal, W11564 Hwy. 64, Withee, WI 54498. Call (800) 551-5691 or see their web site at www.countrysidemag.com. User-submitted articles on all aspects of self-reliant country living. Focus is on the serious homesteader.

The Mother Earth News. Subscription: $15.97 per year for 6 issues. The Mother Earth News, 49 East 21st Street, 11th Floor, New York, NY 10010. Call (800) 234-3368 or see their web site at www.motherearthnews.com. Since this magazine was sold to a New York publisher, it has become more citified. Urban or suburban dwellers might find this magazine more to their liking.

II Present Trends, Possible Futures

Survival in the recent past does not predict
survival in an unprecedented future. To realize
this, all you have to do is look at the thousands
of species that survived throughout history only
to be exterminated in this century. To predict
what's needed for the future, we can't just
consider the past—we must look to the future.
—Thom Hartmann, *The Last Hours of*
Ancient Sunlight

What does the scientific community have to say
about the future of the world? Is the weather truly
getting worse, or is it just a lot of media hype? If the
weather is really getting worse, why is this happening
and what might we expect in the next few decades? Is
global warming a real threat, or some environmentalist's fabrication? What about other earth changes, like
major earthquakes? This chapter takes a realistic look
at environmental trends, to help you understand
what to expect in our global future. With education
and an open mind, there is the possibility for us to
create positive change. If we close our eyes and
continue to deny the course we are on, we are like dry
leaves in the wind, with no control over our destiny.

CURRENT TRENDS

The earth is finite. Its ability to provide for
growing numbers of people is finite. Current
economic practices which damage the environ-
ment, in both developed and underdeveloped
nations, cannot be continued without the risk
that vital global systems will be damaged
beyond repair. Pressures resulting from unre-
strained population growth put demands on the
natural world that can overwhelm any effort to
achieve a sustainable future.
—From *World Scientists' Warning to*
Humanity, the Union of concerned Scientists

(UCS), written and signed in 1993 by more
than 600 of the world's most distinguished
scientists, including a majority of the living
Nobel laureates in the sciences

History is full of examples of once great civilizations
that failed to adapt to diminishing resources and
changing world conditions. In most instances their
decline and fall were the result of human behavior
rather than the quirks of nature. The same truth
applies to the contemporary world. It is more likely
that our behavior rather than apocalyptic events will
bring us to the brink of social chaos, mass starvation, and a collapse of our way of life. We must
expect these consequences if population growth and
the consumption of oil and other fossil fuels continue at anywhere near their current rates. An average
high school student with enough knowledge of algebra to plot graphs of population growth, oil reserves,
oil demands, and world production of food can
demonstrate our predicament—and reach some very
discouraging conclusions.

Many believe that science and the free market will
automatically produce technological solutions to our
world energy and environmental problems. The
ecological disasters of the former Soviet Union and in
several African and Asian countries foreshadow
impending global suicide. We cannot continue to
count on reactive politics and technological break-
throughs to bail us out. A wiser approach is to evaluate
current trends and conditions proactively, and develop
plans for attaining a positive, sustainable future. I truly
believe that the people of our world have the capacity
to find positive solutions to our problems. Thus far, we
have inadequately used this capacity. As long as we
collectively continue to pretend there is no problem,
we cannot find or implement the basic societal
changes required to provide a sustainable future for
our children and our children's children.

Sustainability and Limits to Growth

First, when it comes to population growth, what goes up exponentially must stabilize, or it will crash down. Second, with regard to forests and fish and other resources, what gets used up too rapidly and too thoughtlessly will ultimately cease to exist. And finally, as for waste and pollution, what gets dumped—into the water, land, or air—spreads out, hangs around, and creates havoc for generations to come. None of these are desirable outcomes for the human project known as global civilization.

—Alan AtKisson, *Believing Cassandra*

In the early 1970s, a team of young scientists from MIT spent two years developing and working with a world computer simulation program called "World3." They included a multitude of variables in their computer model in an effort to make its output match the real world as nearly as possible. The computer model results were staggering and made quite a stir when first announced to the world, then subsequently published in *Limits to Growth* by Donella Meadows, Dennis Meadows, Jorgen Randers, and William H. Behrens III. In one scenario after another, the computer model invariably predicted that human population would swell to the point where it overshot the planet's capability to support the population, and then come crashing down as one system after another failed in mankind's final attempts to keep people fed, clothed, and housed.

What the computer model made clear was that the unavoidable result of exponential population growth and increasing levels of consumption is a planet-wide crash and burn. Critics have pointed out that the time frame for this crash and burn scenario was way off. The computer model was not perfect. It underestimated the effects of some things, such as global soil losses, while overestimating other factors, such as population growth. Nevertheless, the model does show disturbing trends of apocalyptic proportions, and indicates that we must choose to use our collective powers of free will to change the course of history or suffer the results. From the storm of controversy surrounding *Limits to Growth* emerged the popular term "sustainability," meaning patterns of consumption coupled with population stabilization at a level that the earth can support forever.

For many parts of the planet, disruptions of apocalyptic proportions are already here. From the villages of Rwanda to the streets of Kosovo, their apocalypse is now! Thom Hartmann's book *The Prophet's Way* contains several frightening personal accounts of travels to dangerous areas of overpopulated Third World countries. In his efforts to aid poverty-stricken children, he has traveled where few tourists dare to tread. It is his belief that the almost unbelievable living conditions in the slums of Mexico City and Calcutta, and the lawless horrors of the streets of Bogota, are previews of an all-too-close future in a world with too many people and not enough material goods to go around. The dissolution of the former Soviet Union was once heralded as a giant step forward. The subsequent degeneration of the Russian Federation into a lawless country plagued by economic chaos, black marketeering, and organized crime was certainly neither the Western nor the Russian vision for their future.

The billion or so people severely affected by the spreading desertification of Africa have already reached the threshold of tragic earth changes. Even if the weather stays normal and we can continue to pump oil out of the ground at the current rate forever (which we can't), we will have a hard time providing food and a modest standard of living for most of the planet even during the next few decades. At the 1999 world population growth rate of 1.3% per year, the world's population of 6 billion people will double over the next 54 years. Accounting for a continuation in the current trend of declining birth rates, population experts project that world population will increase to somewhere around 9 billion people by the year 2050 (Brown, et al. 2000b, 98). Most of this growth will be in Third World countries, which are the least capable of handling the burgeoning population.

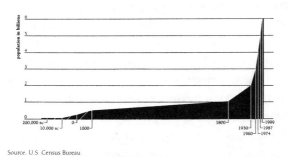

Source. U.S Census Bureau

Figure 2-1. Population growth.
Source: U.S. Census Bureau

The world's oceans are showing alarming indications that we may have passed the level of sustainable environmental impact. A large percentage of the world's coral reefs are now in distress or dying, due to excessive water temperatures (probably from global warming) and pollution. After peaking in 1996, world fish catches have begun to decline. It is estimated that 73% of the world's major fishing areas and 70% of the major fish species are either at maximum production or are in decline (Brown et al., 1999a, 36). According to the United Nation's Food and Agriculture Organization (FAO), 11 of the world's 15 major fishing grounds are seriously depleted.

OIL RESERVES

In 1950 the U.S. was producing half the world's oil....In 1998, America can't produce even half its own petroleum needs.
      —Dr. John Curtis, oil industry expert,
            World Oil Forum (AEI 1999, 6)

Typical estimates for world petroleum reserves, given by oil industry spokesmen, are that we have around 45 years' worth of oil left (estimates range from around 30 years to 100 years). It's hard to say how accurate oil reserve estimates are, because many Oil Producing and Exporting Countries (OPEC) have radically increased their reserve estimates in efforts to increase production and profits. OPEC production limits are based upon each country's estimated oil reserves, so inflating their oil reserve estimates allows individual OPEC countries to ship more oil. Forty years is not a lot of time for scientists and

engineers to implement large-scale oil replacement technologies such as nuclear fusion or massive solar and wind power generators. Estimates from the European Wind Energy Association are that wind power could provide as much as 10% of the world's electrical power generation by the year 2020, which sounds like a lot but is not much for a world running short on oil (AWEA 1999, 1).

Oil will not just run out one day. As reserves and supplies dwindle, maintaining current production rates will become increasingly difficult and expensive. Once production rates fall significantly below global demands for oil, prices will rise at phenomenal rates, as they did during the OPEC oil embargo in the late 1970s. Oil prices rise rapidly even with minor disruptions of supply. For example, following two refinery fires in northern California in 1998, the price of gasoline shot up about $0.60 per gallon higher than prices in the rest of the country, and in the winter of 2000 a minor restriction of oil supplies by OPEC sent gasoline prices over $2.00 per gallon in some areas.

The world currently is consuming 23 billion barrels of oil each year, but discovering only 6 billion barrels. Now that's a recipe for energy bankruptcy and therefore economic bankruptcy.
— Charlie Richardson, ABC-TV, *Over a Barrel*

On October 30, 1998, 200 of the world's top oil experts, including policymakers, scientists, geologists, and oil and gas industry professionals, took part in the World Oil Forum. At this forum, experts gave predictions for the peak in world oil production, which ranged from the year 2000 to the year 2020. According to Franco Bernabe, chief executive of the Italian oil company ENI SpA, as early as the year 2003 and well before the year 2010, the world will probably face 1970s style oil price shocks due to increasing demand and decreasing production (Banks, 6-15-98). Back in 1956, Dr. M. King Hubbert stunned the U.S. government and the oil industry when he predicted that United States oil production in the lower 48 states would peak around 1970 and decline thereafter. At the time, the U.S. was the greatest petroleum producer in the world. Hubbert's prescient proclamation was rejected by the oil industry, but later vindicated when his analysis proved correct. It is predicted that a similar "Hubbert's Peak" in world oil production will arrive shortly due to declining yields from existing oil fields and the fact that in spite of significant technological improvements in oil exploration, discoveries of new oil fields peaked back in the 1960s. In fact, we are now discovering new sources for oil at about one quarter the rate that we consume it.

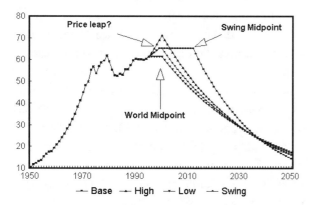

Figure 2-2. The Global Hubbert Peak, forecast of future global oil output. Source: *The Twenty First Century, The World's Endowment of Conventional Oil and Its Depletion,* by Dr. Colin Campbell, 1996

This graph (often referred to as the "Hubbert Curve") is based on an ultimate recovery of conventional oil of 1750 Gb (Giga = billion barrels), and depicts alternative scenarios of production. The swing case assumes a price leap when the share of world production from a few Middle East countries reaches 30%. This is expected to curb demand, leading to a plateau of output until the swing countries reach the midpoint of their depletion, when resource constraints force output to drop considerably.

WATER AND FOOD

The overriding lesson from history is that most irrigation-based civilizations fail. As we enter the third millennium A.D., the question is: Will ours be any different?

—Sandra Postel, *Pillar of Sand*

According to Worldwatch Institute Senior Fellow Sandra Postel, 40% of the world's food comes from irrigated cropland, and this irrigation accounts for two-thirds of the global water usage. So much water is now being used for irrigation and other human purposes that little or none of the fresh water from several major rivers—including the Yellow in China, the Colorado in the American Southwest, the Indus in Pakistan, the Nile in Egypt, the Chao Phraya in Thailand, and the Ganges in India—reaches the sea for significant portions of the year (Postel 1999, 71). Overpumping of groundwater for irrigation is also causing rising groundwater salinity and steadily dropping water table levels in many of the major grain-producing areas of the world. Wherever this trend continues, groundwater eventually becomes unusable or too costly to use for irrigation. Worldwide, one in five acres of irrigated land suffers from a buildup of salt in the soil. Two-thirds of California's rampant groundwater depletion occurs in the Central Valley, which supplies about half the country's fruits and vegetables. Spreading water shortages threaten to reduce global food production by 10% at a time when population could double within 50 years. For a detailed analysis, and possible solutions to the coming irrigation crisis, check out Postel's new book, *Pillar of Sand: Can the Irrigation Miracle Last?*

The giant agricultural businesses that supply most of our food rely heavily on oil to fuel the tractors, transport the food, and produce the fertilizers and pesticides currently used to maintain high levels of productivity. Some experts have said that we are literally eating oil, since it is oil that has fueled the world's dramatic increase in food productivity over the last century. As oil production declines, available water for irrigation decreases, and arable cropland is lost to rising salinity, how will we feed a planet with a population of more than 9 billion people?

WHAT ABOUT THE WEATHER?

Many scientists warn that the planet is warming at a faster rate than at any other time in the last 10,000 years. Some people might say that warmer temperatures could be a good thing, that warmer winters in Maine or Montana might be nice. Our planetary systems are enormously complex, however, and a few degrees of change will have far-reaching effects that will probably severely affect global weather and agricultural output.

> The drought- and heat-damaged U.S. grain harvest in 1988, which fell below domestic consumption for the first time in history, gives us a glimpse of how hotter summers may affect agriculture over the longer term.
> —Lester R. Brown, Christopher Flavin, and Sandra Postel, *Saving the Planet*

There is considerable data to support the finding that weather patterns truly are getting more erratic. It is not your imagination, but an observable, verifiable phenomenon. Since 1983, Planet Earth has experienced its ten hottest years in recorded history. Seven of the ten hottest years on record were in the 1990s. In the summer of 2000, an almost unbelievable event occurred removing most remaining doubts that we are truly in the midst of global warming—for the first time in recorded history, a large hole opened up in the polar ice cap leaving several miles of open water at the North Pole (Brown 2000, 1).

In many respects, 1998 blew the other years off the charts. Not only was 1998 the hottest year in the world's recorded weather history, it also set the record for average temperature *increase*. These unprecedented temperatures may have fueled the record-breaking floods and destructive storms. In 1998, worldwide weather-related damage totaled $92 billion, up a staggering 53% from the previous record of $60 billion in 1996 (Brown et al. 1999a, 15). Even though 1999 showed a slight decrease in global average temperature, attributed to the cooler "La Nina" ocean currents, 1999 was still the seventh warmest year on record (Brown et al. 2000b, 20).

Warmer temperatures are certainly not the only changes in the weather. The recent rise in extreme weather disasters, such as floods, tornadoes, droughts, and hurricanes, has insurance industry executives terribly concerned. According to the large German-based insurance firm Munich Re., insurance industries paid out an average of less than $2 billion a year for weather-related property damage from 1980 to 1989, but from 1990 to 1997, similar weath-er-related losses cost the insurance industry more than $7 billion a year. Estimates of worldwide weather related losses reached a record of $93 billion in 1998. With weather-related losses estimated at $67 billion, 1999 goes down as the second most costly year on record. After including factors for inflation, weather-related losses in the 1990s totaled more than five times as much as similar losses in the 1980s. Within the insurance industry, there is a very real fear that the long-term climactic changes that now appear to be developing could bankrupt the industry (Brown et al. 2000b, 76).

Why is this happening to our planet? Can we expect a return to weather as usual, or will things get worse? I will attempt to explain why the weather is getting more and more erratic, what we might expect in our future, and what we might do to help the situation.

Systems Modeling and Systems Response

The earth is a complex system. There are thousands of different factors ("variables" in systems terms) that contribute to the response of this system. Some factors are major contributors, while others are minor. Right now, we are witnesses to a great experiment that mankind is inflicting on our planet. Modern humankind is radically altering many of the significant variables that contribute to the stability and response of this magnificent system called Planet Earth. No one knows for sure the final outcome of this great experiment, but both the computer model predictions and the preliminary earth changes that we are currently seeing point to very disturbing future developments.

To get some idea of what scientists are talking about when they refer to systems theory, systems modeling, and systems response, let's take a look at a relatively simple system that most of us are familiar with—the automobile. A modern automobile employs shock absorbers and suspension springs to give us a smooth ride. Shock absorbers dampen shocks that the automobile receives to its wheels as it drives over bumps in the road. Without shock absorbers, a car bounces so much that it is almost impossible to control. The automobile system without adequate shock absorbers is "underdamped." The automobile hits a bump and starts bouncing; before it can stop bouncing from the first bump, it hits a second bump, and so on.

In the physical world, there are a few major components to our planetary system that act something like a car's shock absorbers and suspension springs. Changing significant earth variables will have dramatic effects similar to the variations that you might see from worn-out or undersized shocks and springs on a car. The recent rash of severe storms, extreme heat, extended droughts, and record-setting floods are the earth's response—warning signs that we have damaged its "shock absorbers" and are threatening the stability of worldwide ecosystems.

A lot of people think that global warming, the destruction of the ozone layer, and the deforestation of major chunks of the planet will not harm us here in the United States, because we are so technologically advanced and appear to have a sufficient supply of food and natural resources. From the global point of view, this attitude is similar to a first-class passenger on the Titanic saying that the little crease from the iceberg doesn't concern him because he's on the upper deck, not below in third class. If this "ship" (Planet Earth) goes down, any amount of money won't be enough to buy us a seat on a life raft! A series of floods and droughts can alternately rot and parch crops in the United States, just as easily as they do in other parts of the world.

Let's look at the response of some very simple systems to get a graphic idea of what I am talking about. Figure 2-3 is the response of a simple, well-damped car suspension to a sharp bump in the road. Notice that the curve is relatively smooth, with few ripples and bumps. For the earth system, this would correspond to stable, predictable weather. When we change some variables a bit, to simulate a worn or undersized shock absorber, we get a response similar to that depicted in Figure 2-4. This figure corresponds to significantly fluctuating weather, like what we have seen in recent years.

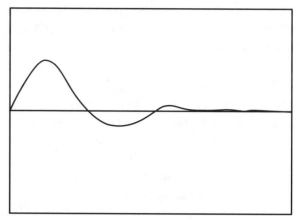

Figure 2-3. Response of a well-damped system (good shock absorbers).

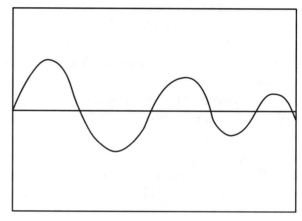

Figure 2-4. Response of an underdamped system (worn-out shock absorbers).

Most real-life systems are a little more complicated than a simple car suspension system and are characterized by "feedback." Feedback causes some portion of the output of the system (average temperature, rainfall, etc.) to input back into the system, with a resulting effect on the output. Feedbacks form loops. The output affects the input, which affects the output, which affects the input, and so on. Too much feedback and the system goes crazy with an unstable response, like the one shown in Figure 2-5. The ear-splitting shriek that an audio system lets loose when a microphone gets too close to a speaker is a result of too much feedback. When you consider the earth's weather as a system with feedback, it's not too hard to see how humankind's meddling with the earth can result in unstable responses ("crazy" weather) and in severe cases, the destruction of entire ecosystems.

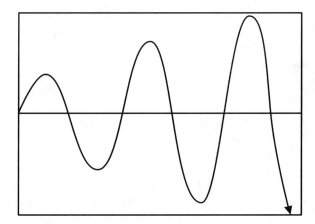

Figure 2-5. Response of an underdamped system with too much feedback (worn-out shock absorbers plus feedback = unstable response).

Traditionally, scientists believed that major climate changes, like the start and finish of ice ages, took place gradually over periods ranging from several centuries to thousands of years. Recently, however, scientists studying ice field corings discovered that climactic changes at the onset of ice ages, on the order of 10°C (18°F), have occurred during a period of time as short as ten years! Apparently, due to some kind of feedback, the earth's climate has shifted radically and abruptly over short periods of time. Scott Lehman, a Woods Hole Oceanographic Institute researcher, announced the Institute's findings in 1993. He stated: "Our results suggest that the present climate system is very delicately poised. The system could snap suddenly between very different conditions with an abruptness that is scary" (Gelbspan 1998, 30).

Humankind's meddling could produce radical, irreversible climate changes over a period of just a few years!

Out of the thousands of different variables influencing earth systems, scientists have identified several major ones. (As our understanding increases, some seemingly insignificant factors will probably also turn out to be very important.) Here are five factors currently recognized as significant climactic system variables:

- Trees of all kinds—not just the rain forests.
- The concentration of greenhouse gases such as carbon dioxide and water vapor in the atmosphere.
- The earth's ozone layer, which acts as a protective blanket, screening out harmful levels of the sun's ultraviolet rays.
- The ocean's plankton production, which is a vital part of both the food chain and the oxygen balance in the atmosphere.
- The size of the earth's polar ice caps.

Each of these significant system factors is interconnected. Major changes in one factor may adversely affect one or more of the others, compounding the overall effects on the system.

TREES

By far the most visible human alteration of the planet has been the destruction of the forests. Almost half the forests that once covered expanses of the earth are already gone.
—Lester Brown et al., *Vital Signs 1998,*
from the Worldwatch Institute

Trees are the great shock absorbers of our planet. They are critical to the carbon/oxygen cycle that maintains breathable air and livable temperatures. Trees also act as giant water pumps, pumping millions of tons of water back into the atmosphere so it can fall back to the earth as rainfall at some downwind location (see Figure 2-6). They stabilize the soils to prevent erosion and build topsoil. They remove minerals from the groundwater and help keep salt levels in the aquifer fit for human consumption and agriculture.

When trees are destroyed, a process called desertification begins. Desertification has occurred all over the world, time and time again, but never in our recorded history on the scale and the rate at which it is happening today.

Trees are the main source of topsoil on the planet. Most shrubs and grasses do not have roots deep enough to work below the top few feet of soil, but the deep roots of trees break up rocks and combine minerals from the rocks with carbon from the air to feed the growth of leaves and branches. As this material falls to the ground and decomposes, it rebuilds and enriches the upper layers of soil, which are vital to agriculture.

It takes from 200 to 1,000 years for nature to generate one inch of topsoil. Modern agricultural practices often flush away inches of topsoil in a

Figure 2-6. Trees and the water cycle.

growth rain forest stores three to five times as much carbon as an acre of mature dry forest and recycles many times as much water back into the atmosphere.

One single rain forest tree will recycle 3 million gallons of water back into the atmosphere during its lifespan. The evaporative surface area of the leaves or needles on one large tree is equal to the surface area of a 40-acre lake (Hartmann 1998, 42). One single acre of rain forest will typically contain over 200 large trees with an evaporative surface area greater than an 8,000-acre lake!

The total amount of rain forest left on the planet is about the size of the continental United States. Every year humankind destroys an area of rain forest about equal to the size of Florida. At the current rate of destruction, 38 million acres per year, the world's last rain forests will be totally eliminated within our children's lifetime. The loss of rain forests is one very big variable with an unknown effect on the system response of our planet. Do we dare risk their destruction without knowing what the effect will be?

single year. That's like borrowing $20,000 on high-interest credit cards each year, without repaying any of the principal. How long could anyone keep that up without going bankrupt?

Trees and shrubby forests still cover about 40% of the world's landmass, but that amount is rapidly shrinking, and the quality of much of that cover has declined. The tropical rain forests are particularly important due to their great density of growth. A young tree or shrub, with a few square feet of evaporative leaf surface area and a few shallow roots, has nowhere near the environmentally stabilizing effect of a mature tree with deep roots. One acre of old-

Archaeologists generally place the dawn of modern civilization in an area known as the "Fertile Crescent," the site of the present nations of Iraq, Syria, and Lebanon. At one time Lebanon, the site of the biblical "Cedars of Lebanon," was 90% forested. The cedars were cut down centuries ago to provide wood to build Phoenician ships, as well as for housing and fuel. Lebanon's forest cover is now a mere 7%. Deforestation has reduced downwind rainfall by over 80%, transforming most of the "Fertile Crescent" into desert and wasteland. The process of desertification continues throughout the world, claiming millions of acres of farmland from the plains of Africa to the eastern slopes of the Rocky Mountains. The famines and extended droughts of North Africa appear to be a direct result of the destruction of Africa's forests.

In both recent and ancient times, humanity has tampered with ecosystems to such an extent that local ecosystems have become unstable and have virtually collapsed. The tropical island of Haiti provides a modern example. When Columbus "discovered" America, he landed on the island of Hispaniola, which is now the country of Haiti. Columbus found a tropical paradise virtually covered with lush, green rain forests and populated by the Taino Indians, who had lived in harmony with the land for thousands of years. Today, not one single Taino Indian has survived, and a radically different sight greets visitors to Haiti. According to Thom Hartmann (1998, 33): "If you fly over the country of Haiti on the island of Hispaniola ..., it looks like someone took a blowtorch and burned away anything green. Even the ocean around the capital of Port-au-Prince is choked for miles with the brown of human sewage and eroded topsoil. From the air, it looks like a lava flow spilling out into the sea."

GREENHOUSE GASES AND GLOBAL WARMING

The "greenhouse effect" is a hot topic for many of the world's scientists. The atmosphere is primarily made up of oxygen (21%) and nitrogen (78%), with the remaining 1% made up of a variety of other gases. Both oxygen and nitrogen allow heat and light to pass through them with minimal resistance. Other gases, such as carbon dioxide, act like an insulating blanket, trapping and holding heat on the surface of the planet and in the atmosphere. These "greenhouse gases" trap heat on the planet similar to the way glass on a greenhouse holds heat inside.

Carbon dioxide is the most prevalent greenhouse gas, with a 1998 concentration of about 367 parts per million (ppm) or 0.037% (Brown et al. 1999a, 58). This seems like a small amount, but it is 30% greater than it was in 1860. Estimates for increases over the next century range from an

optimistic 23% to a rather devastating 173% (ARM 2000, 1).

The percentage of carbon dioxide in the atmosphere has a dramatic effect on the temperatures of the planet. Without any carbon dioxide in the atmosphere, this planet would be a frozen desert, with practically all its water stored in frozen ice caps. Venus, on the other hand, has an atmosphere rich in carbon dioxide. Even though it is only 27% closer to the sun than the earth, it has a surface temperature of a blistering 700°F. The higher atmospheric concentrations of greenhouse gases are a major part of the reason Venus is so much hotter than earth.

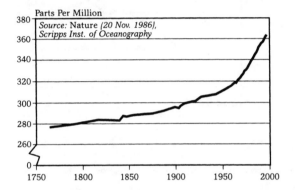

Figure 2-7. Atmospheric concentrations of carbon dioxide, 1764 to 1997. (Brown et al. 1998, 20)

Plants are an important part of the cycle that maintains a healthy atmosphere. When animals breathe, they take oxygen out of the air to oxygenate their blood and digest food for energy. They exhale air with higher levels of carbon dioxide, releasing excess carbon from metabolic processes. For plants, it is the opposite process. Plants absorb carbon dioxide and release purified oxygen into the air. Plants use the carbon from the air to combine with minerals gathered by the roots. Many millions of years ago, earth's atmosphere had much more carbon in it and the planet was much hotter. Coral reefs and forests gradually removed billions of tons of carbon from the air as they grew. Huge ancient forests were fossilized and stored this atmospheric carbon for millions of years as coal, natural gas, and oil, gradually reducing the concentrations of carbon in the atmosphere. That is, until humanity started to liberate ancient carbon by burning coal, oil, and natural gas. Each *gallon* of gasoline burned releases about *19.6 pounds* of carbon dioxide into the atmosphere (CDIAC 2000, 9). Only 5.3 pounds of this is carbon; the rest is oxygen. Burning fossil fuels also releases nitrous oxides and sulfur dioxide, which combine with water moisture in clouds to form acid rains that damage ecosystems. Each year, we release more than 6 billion tons of ancient stored carbon into the atmosphere by burning fossil fuels (see Figure 2-8). Many scientists estimate that global carbon emissions must be reduced to about 30% of current emissions if the world is to avoid dangerous climactic changes (Brown et al., 2000b, 66).

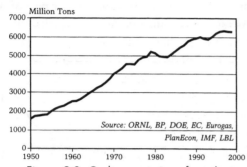

Figure 2-8. Carbon emissions from the burning of fossil fuels. (Brown 2000, *Vital Signs*, 67)

Among the other greenhouse gases, some are naturally occurring, like methane (swamp gas). Some were invented by human beings and are totally new to the planet, like the infamous CFCs (commonly known as freon), which have a greenhouse potential 4,000 to 8,000 times as high as carbon dioxide. Since they are present in much smaller concentrations than carbon dioxide, their greenhouse impact is much less. Methane's greenhouse contribution is second only to carbon dioxide. Even though it is present in far lower concentrations than carbon dioxide, methane is 22 times more effective at trapping heat than an equal amount of carbon dioxide. Decomposition of landfill wastes, coal mining, digestive gases from domestic animals, and the burning of fossil fuels all release methane gases into the atmosphere. Atmospheric concentrations of methane have increased 246% from an estimated preindustrial level of 700 parts per billion (ppb) to a 1998 level of 1720 ppb (ARM 2000, 1). Many scientists now believe that these other gases—natural and manmade—may collectively contribute as much to global warming as does carbon dioxide, effectively doubling the previously predicted warming effect.

Water vapor is a major greenhouse gas that becomes even more significant as warming continues. As the atmosphere warms, it holds more water vapor (at cooler temperatures water vapor condenses into clouds and precipitation). Increased water vapor may become an important factor in system feedback: As the earth warms, the atmosphere holds more evaporated water, which contributes to further warming.

What does all this mean? In Ross Gelbspan's eye-opening book, *The Heat Is On* (1998, 5), he states:

> In November 1995, 2,500 leading climate scientists announced that the planet is warming because all the emissions from coal and oil burning are trapping in more of the sun's heat than is normal for our climate. Even if that warming is not yet obvious, they warned, it is already generating bizarre and extreme changes in the weather. This new period of less stable climate we have entered, the scientists wrote, "is likely to cause widespread economic, social and environmental dislocation." Their report noted that "potentially serious changes have been identified, including an increase in some regions of the incidence of extreme high temperature events, floods, and droughts, with resultant consequences for fires, pest outbreaks and ecosystems.

Ross documents the media campaign that has been successfully waged against the fear of global warming. This campaign is well-funded by the oil and coal industries, which have spent many millions of dollars to persuade Americans that global warming isn't happening, that it is just some environmental hoopla.

With over 90% of the world's climate scientists in agreement that global warming is a concern of extreme urgency, there is a well-grounded fear within the trillion-dollar-a-year gas, coal, and oil industries that the world's governments might band together to limit the use (and profits) of fossil fuels. The opposing views of a well-funded minority of scientists, financially supported by members of the fossil fuel industry, get plenty of press. They do not deny the possible effects of greenhouse gases, but state that the data are not conclusive and things might not be as bad as they look. On the other hand, due to feedback effects that are not fully understood, things could be a lot worse than most scientists project.

DEPLETION OF THE OZONE LAYER

> *I just came home one night and told my wife, "The work is going very well, but it looks like the end of the world."*
>
> —Scientist Sherwood F. Rowland, on his research into the ozone-eating capacity of the chlorine molecule (McKibben 1989, 41)

When the initial scientific discovery of ozone depletion was announced, scientists were very skeptical of the results and were sure that things could not be as bad as preliminary findings indicated. They were wrong. Dr. Michael McElroy, chair of Harvard University's earth and planetary sciences department, explained, "When researchers finally conducted actual ozone measurements in the atmosphere, their findings were far worse than the worst case scenarios of the models. . . . Just because a situation is uncertain does not imply that the underlying reality is benign" (Gelbspan 1998, 31).

Almost everyone has heard that the earth's ozone layer is thinning and has developed holes. What is ozone and why is it important to the planet? Ozone is a molecule made up of three atoms of oxygen, instead of the usual two. At ground level, ozone is very unstable and highly reactive. As it reacts with other substances, ozone's third oxygen atom splits off to oxidize whatever it reacts with, leaving behind an ordinary oxygen molecule instead of ozone. In the upper atmosphere, ozone normally forms a stable, self-regenerating layer that plays a critical part in shielding out harmful concentrations of ultraviolet radiation. Ultraviolet radiation is the part of sunlight that causes sunburn and contributes to skin cancers. Most earthly plant and animal life developed under this umbrella of ozone and, as a result, cannot live without the shielding effects of the ozone layer.

Manufactured compounds—especially CFCs (freon)—have been implicated in the destruction of atmospheric ozone. CFCs are normally very stable, lasting 50 to 100 years before finally breaking down.

Unfortunately, CFCs are lighter than air and slowly migrate into the upper atmosphere, where high-energy rays from the sun blow them apart, liberating a chlorine atom into the ozone layer. Each free atom of chlorine acts as a catalyst, breaking up thousands of ozone molecules before finally reacting with something else, which removes it from circulation. In addition to CFCs, each new launch of America's space shuttle delivers tons of chlorine molecules from burned rocket fuel directly to the upper atmosphere, where they eat away at the planet's ozone shield. Because of the long lifetime of the CFC molecules in the lower atmosphere, the ozone destruction effects are somewhat cumulative.

The good news is that CFC concentrations in the lower atmosphere are gradually decreasing. This is one example of mankind acknowledging a true environmental crisis and taking positive unified international action to remedy the situation. The Montreal Protocol of 1987 introduced international guidelines to control the worldwide phase-out of the production of CFCs. Even though their concentration in the lower atmosphere is now diminishing, they are expected to generate dangerously low concentrations of ozone in the upper atmosphere for roughly the next 50 years and will continue to affect ozone concentrations for at least the next century. For a more complete yet highly informative and understandable description of the ozone problem, its reactions and chemistry, see Bill McKibben's *The End of Nature*.

Since the ozone-eating effects of CFCs and other similar compounds are accelerated at cold temperatures, ozone holes or thinning tends to occur over the poles during winter. Antarctica, with its huge landmass and the coldest temperatures on the planet, generally loses more ozone than the North Pole region. Winds can carry these "holes" away from polar regions. Currently, the ozone depletion over the continent of Australia can be so bad that it is now against Australian law to send children to school without a hat. The Australian government issues constant warnings about the dangers of being outside without the protection of heavy-duty sunscreens. The incidence of skin cancer in Australia has exploded, and many surfers lament about how rapidly they sunburn now compared to earlier decades.

Ozone and Plankton

Unfortunately, applying a little sunscreen does not solve the ozone problem. The outer few layers of human skin filter out most ultraviolet light, but not all of the earth's vital organisms have the protection offered by a multicell thickness of skin. The ocean's phytoplankton are a critical part of the food chain and play a key role in the global carbon cycle. Phytoplankton are mostly single-celled algae that do not have a skin to filter out UV rays. The most productive phytoplankton live in the top layers of the ocean, where they receive the most sunlight. Even with the screening effects of the water, these plankton cannot handle a full shot of UV radiation. Phytoplankton are most prevalent in the nutrient-rich colder ocean waters of the far north and south.

Grey whales have their babies in the warm waters off Baja and Hawaii, but travel thousands of miles to the north each year to feed in the Arctic waters on millions of tons of krill, which in turn feed on the abundant plankton. These whales essentially fast for several months of the year, while traveling and giving birth in warmer waters. Like the whales, most of the other sea animals also feed on a food chain based on plankton as the bottom rung. Like all plants, phytoplankton take carbon out of the environment. If they die, there goes much of the food provided by the ocean as well as a major hedge against an increase in greenhouse gases.

POLAR ICE CAPS

> In January of 1995 a vast section of ice, the size of Rhode Island, broke off the Larsen ice shelf in Antarctica. Although it received scant coverage in the press, it was one of the most spectacular and nightmarish manifestations yet of the ominous changes occurring on the planet.
> —Ross Gelbspan, *The Heat is On*

The melting of polar ice caps and rapid shrinking of most of the earth's glaciers is not a far-off future event. It is happening now. Measurements on the Antarctic peninsula show that its average annual temperature has risen 5°F over the past 20 years. Dr. Rodolfo del Valle, an Argentine research scientist

who witnessed the gargantuan disintegration of the Antarctic Larsen ice shelf, said that he and his colleagues had predicted the ice shelf would disintegrate in ten years, "but it happened in two months." He went on to say, "Recently I've seen rocks poke through the surface of the ice that had been buried for 20,000 years" (Gelbspan 1998, 2). In the north, the area covered by Arctic Ocean sea ice has shrunk by 6% since 1978 and this ice pack has thinned by an almost unbelievable 40% in less than 30 years (Mastny 2000, 3).

The polar ice caps affect the balance of the earth's system in at least two major ways. They store huge amounts of water, and they act as giant reflectors, reflecting the sun's radiation back into space. Archaeological records indicate that the earth's oceans were 500 feet lower during the last ice age than they are now. If significant portions of the polar ice caps were to melt, not only would the oceans rise but the earth would probably warm even more due to increased absorption and decreased reflection of the sun's rays from the polar regions—another potential feedback loop with consequences of unknown magnitude!

EARTHQUAKES AND VOLCANOES

> *I live in the High Sierra mountains, near Lake Tahoe on the California-Nevada border. In February 1998, my family was shaken out of bed by a 5.3 magnitude earthquake centered about seven miles from our home. The quake that shook us out of bed was from a fault that had been labeled "inactive" and caught the geologists totally by surprise. Most people think that California is all sunshine and warmth, but our high mountain town of Truckee is widely known for regularly having record low temperatures. On this particular morning, the temperature was hovering a little below 0°F. Needless to say, we would have had a rough time if our car keys, wallets, and clothes had disappeared in a collapsed house, leaving us standing in our pajamas in subzero weather. Certainly this drives home the importance of keeping an emergency kit, including a few clothes and rations, in the family car.*

Most Americans think earthquakes are only a problem in California and possibly Alaska, but that isn't necessarily the case. Remember, earthquake predictions are based on statistical averages. Living in an area that is not known for earthquakes does not mean you won't ever experience a major earthquake. What it means is that you have a smaller chance of experiencing one. It is a little-known fact that the largest earthquakes on record in the United States did not happen in California but along the Mississippi River in New Madrid, Missouri, in late 1811 and early 1812. The quakes were so powerful that they shook down chimneys 360 miles away in Cincinnati and changed the course of the Mississippi River for more than 100 miles.

Earthquake prediction is based on the study of past earthquake patterns. It generates statistics about the probability of an earthquake within a certain magnitude range occurring in a specified region over a specified period of time. A typical prediction for the San Francisco Bay Area might read something like, "The San Francisco Bay Area is overdue for a significant earthquake. We believe that this area has a 70% chance of having an earthquake in the 7.5 to 9.5 range sometime in the next 30 years." Except in rare instances when undeniable geological signs indicate that a major quake is imminent, modern scientific methods cannot give accurate earthquake warnings. And we think weather forecasters have a hard time being accurate!

Could California fall into the ocean? It is highly unlikely that a quake could accomplish this feat, but it is both likely and probable that California will be struck by violent quakes in the not-too-distant future. It is simply a question of when and how severe they will be. In recent geologic history, smaller chunks of land have fallen into the ocean—part of the island of Crete disappeared under the sea during the time of the Minoan civilization. At no time in recorded history, however, has a physical earth change occurred on the magnitude of California falling into the ocean. There are tales of such disasters, such as the great flood, handed down in the biblical story of Noah and the older epic of Gilgamesh. If disasters on this order of magnitude have already occurred, they may have wiped out civilizations, leaving only legends, like the stories of the fabled lost continent of Atlantis.

Increasing volcanic activity in the Pacific Rim of Fire is one potential sign that the earth is "waking up" from a period of relative calm into a more geologically active period that will bring both earthquakes and volcanic eruptions. Unlike major earthquakes, volcanic eruptions are apt to give distinct warnings, provided the volcano is carefully monitored. I watched a documentary program on the 1994 eruption of dual volcanoes outside the city of Rabaul, the one-time capital of Pau Pau, New Guinea.

The first part of the program showed a beautiful tropical island paradise. The island's main city, Rabaul, was located on a bay formed from an ancient caldera—a huge craterlike depression created by a volcanic explosion or the collapse of a volcano. The islanders had all been evacuated following weeks of increasingly strong and closely spaced earthquakes. Three days later, when the island's two volcanic peaks erupted, cameramen were on location to film the eruption. The film footage captured its violence: plumes of smoke and ash extended miles into the sky from peaks on both sides of the city's bay. Footage of the island, one year after the eruption, looked like film clips from a science fiction movie about the end of the world. An eerie moonlike landscape had replaced the lush, green, tropical paradise. A few old jalopies were seen moving along tracks in the volcanic dust. The stripped remains of palm trees and old buildings dotted the landscape of rolling mounds of ash. According to a geologist quoted in the documentary, California's Long Valley, located near Mammoth Mountain ski resort, is also a caldera and exhibits the signs of increasing seismic activity that this island had shown a few years before the eruption.

Although there is no reason to panic, I suggest that it is reasonable to consider and create a plan for the possibility of a significant earthquake happening in your neighborhood, even if you don't live in an area that is prone to earthquakes. And if you live in an area like the Pacific Coast, where significant volcanic eruptions and earthquakes are a real possibility, you should plan accordingly.

PROPHECIES

*Our prophecies predict a period of 40 years
of pollution of the land, air, and water that is
so severe only a few will survive. We call this
the Day of Purification, and for many white
people it is The Day of Judgment. It's the same
thing and the cycle has already started—four
decades of destruction, natural disasters and
a general breakdown in society. Only a few
places will be safe, and it will be the end of
modern society as we know it....Before
anyone from Europe came to this land it was
written on the rocks that a great gourd of
ashes will drop on this world and pollute
it....I have seen in a vision that survivors will
come walking out of the cities. Thousands of
hungry and cold people will leave California,
walking down I-80 carrying their belongings
on their backs....If spiritual people get together and put things back in their proper order,
the prophecies can be changed.*

—Rolling Thunder, Native American medicine
man, from *Rolling Thunder Speaks:
A Message for Turtle Island*

Quite a number of widely believed gloom-and-doom
prophecies have never come to pass. Before the year
1000 A.D., many Christians believed that the previous
millennium would bring the second coming of Christ
and the battle of Armageddon. In the 1890s, numerous Plains tribal members believed that their partici-
pation in the Ghost Dance would guarantee their
survival and deliver them from the white man.

Most Native American tribes have recorded
prophecies and visions of a coming time of tribulation
and cleansing of the planet, followed by a return to a
long period of peace and harmony. A Hopi prophecy
spoke of a "gourd of ashes, making the rivers boil and
the fish turn up on their bellies" dropped upon the
earth (nuclear bombs?), signaling the approach of
these times. Hopi elders have addressed the United
Nations General Assembly with their concerns.
According to their legends, we are nearing the end of
the "fourth world." Hopi elders say that humankind
has developed three previous highly technological

societies, and that each of these was destroyed in cata-
clysmic earth changes, after these societies fell out of
balance and abused the earth. The last of these cata-
clysms is considered to be the great flood as recorded
in the Bible and the epic of Gilgamesh. Prophecies of
many different tribes speak of a time when indigenous
peoples will unite with white men who are "Indians in
their heart" to revitalize the planet.

In contrast to the deterministic view of a fixed
future, there is the belief that the individual and collective actions of humankind are what determine our
future. Most seers and visionaries, such as Edgar Cayce
and Rolling Thunder, have stated that the future is
constantly in a state of flux and that the collective
consciousness of the planet has a powerful influence
on the timing and magnitude of major future events.
Depending on your viewpoint, you might say that this
is either the excuse or reason for the inaccuracy of the
dates and magnitude of many psychic predictions. The
following biblical selection indicates that even biblical
prophecy is not cast in stone:

*Jonah obeyed the word of the Lord and went to
Nineveh...and He proclaimed: "Forty more
days and Nineveh will be destroyed." The
Ninevites believed God. They declared a fast
and all of them, from the greatest to the least,
put on sack cloth....When God saw what they
did and how they turned from their evil ways,
He had compassion and did not bring upon
them the destruction He had threatened.*

Jonah (3:3-3:10) from
The Thompson Chain Reference Bible,
New International Version, 1983, p. 948.

The sparing of the people of Nineveh indicates
a biblical precedent for the belief in humankind's
potential to change the course of the future. Some
modern prophets are not so sanguine. Thom
Hartmann, in *The Prophet's Way*, describes a chill-
ing vision of the earth that he experienced upon
waking from a sound sleep:

*In the air a few feet in front of me, a globe
materialized, slowly spinning....I immediately
recognized it as the Earth, as seen from*

*space.... It was both real and not-real: like a
hologram projected into the air. As I watched,
the land masses began to darken. Small black
pustules formed, like little blisters or cancers on
the Earth. The blue of the oceans became
brown and muddy around these areas. The
cancers slowly expanded, blackening the Earth
and cracking it in places, until they covered
virtually all the land of the planet. The clouds
turned a death-like yellow-gray, and the waters
no longer sparkled blue but were a dull and
putrid green-brown.*

*A thought came into my mind as if a voice
were speaking to me: "The Earth is a living
thing. It is infected."*

*Then the Earth shuddered as it spun. It
jerked to one side, as if the spin were changing, and the blackened areas split open. The
Earth shuddered again, and the black areas
cracked and shattered into fragments, falling
off into the air around the image and vanish-
ing. The Earth was once again clear and
clean, spinning gracefully, displaying oceans
the color of lapis lazuli and land richly covered
with green. The voice in my mind said, "The
Earth has healed itself."*

*The image vanished and I lay back in my
bed, realizing that the infection in my vision
was humankind....*

*I couldn't sleep, so I pulled out a Bible
from the stack of books next to my bed. I
flipped it open to a random page toward the
end and my eyes looked down at the words of
the Book of Revelation (11:18): "...and I shall
destroy them which destroy the Earth."*

Hartmann interpreted this vision as a warning.
Every major change, he believes, is "preceded by
signs and markers."

WHAT CAN I DO?

*We must do what we can. Always. At night we
must go to sleep knowing that we have done
our best, and there is no more you can do than*

*that. Do not let the problems overwhelm you.
Start somewhere, anywhere, with just the smallest gesture of compassion, and you have made
a dent against the evil of the world.*

—Gottfried Muller in Thom Hartmann's
The Prophet's Way

I sincerely believe that there are solutions with positive outcomes for our planet. It is my hope that, as a
race, we will develop the vision and commitment
needed to find and implement these solutions. When
societies are highly motivated, they can marshal
giant forces to accomplish great things. The threat of
Hitler motivated the world to rise up in unison
against his efforts at world domination. If we could
put humans on the moon, build the Panama Canal,
and rebuild Europe after WWII, why can't we unite
to create a viable planetary culture? We can all take
actions both to prepare for the future and to influence future outcomes. Martin Luther, the founder of
the Protestant movement, was quoted as saying, "If I
knew that the world was going to end tomorrow, I
would still plant my apple tree today." Even if we
can't individually alter the course of the universe,
there is satisfaction, joy, and personal empowerment
in taking action.

A friend of mine once described insanity as
"doing the same thing over and over again and
expecting a different result." This could also serve as
a definition of typical human conduct. As a race, we
continue to do the same thing, over and over again,
refusing to take seriously the results of past actions.
It is clear that new and different actions must be
taken on personal, communal, and global levels if we
wish to provide a positive future for ourselves, our
children, and our children's children.

One might compare humanity's treatment of
our planet to long-term alcoholics' treatment of
their bodies. At first, drinking is fun. They might
suffer from the occasional hangover, but they are
young and their bodies can take it. As time passes,
the detrimental effects of years of heavy drinking
creep up on them. Their faces age prematurely and
they are often sick. Denial is their way of life. "I can
handle it," they say, believing they can quit any time
they want to. One day, the alcoholic awakes in a

hospital bed to be told by a doctor that if he continues drinking, his liver will fail and he will die an early and very painful death. What does the alcoholic do? Does he listen to the wake-up call and finally motivate himself to positive action?

What will the people of our world collectively choose for our future? Will we choose denial right up to the point where we are on our planetary deathbed?

As with alcoholism, positive action to change the present situation is accomplished in steps. The first step is to align our thinking with our goal—to emerge from denial and educate ourselves about the current global situation and prospects for the future. Thom Hartmann's book *The Last Hours of Ancient Sunlight* or Alan AtKisson's *Believing Cassandra* is a good place to start.

Our thinking needs to reflect personal empowerment, the realization that each of us is as powerful as the most powerful human being on this planet. We all have and can use our birthright of conscious awareness and free will. Each of us can make a difference. Our thinking also needs to reflect interconnectedness. Seeing all life as interconnected and sacred helps to dissipate greed—the urge to use, exploit, control, and dominate. Directly experiencing nature—taking walks, camping, or hiking—helps to develop the sense of connection and reverence.

Once our thinking is totally clear, we can act with conviction. Here are a few avenues to explore—individually and collectively—to promote change:

- **Conservation.** Conscientiously conserving, recycling, and reusing resources and products will help to slow the process of planetary degradation. There is a sort of consumption "food chain," where some savings have far more positive impact than others. Consuming fewer goods and improving up-front process efficiencies have the most impact. Reusing goods has a middle impact. Recycling is a relatively easy and painless thing to do, requiring minimal changes in our consumer-oriented lifestyle, and it is usually better than throwing away. However, recycling has the least positive impact of the three options since it is at the tail end of the consumption "food chain" and it takes additional energy and resources to recycle.

- **Planet-friendly diet.** Health and environmental impacts from the agribusiness production of meat range from massive destruction of rain forests for cattle grazing to methane pollution and the consumption of huge amounts of pesticides, oil, fertilizer, water, vegetable protein, and topsoil. Eating less meat benefits the planet.

- **Networking.** Reaching out to like-minded people, to friends, neighbors, and colleagues can generate momentum for change. Great changes begin at the small, personal level before they can branch out to affect the wider world.

- **Political action.** We can join forces with others to promote recycling, clean air, and water, and the preservation of woodlands, wetlands, and forests. We can push for tax reforms and regulations that support planet-friendly practices and eliminate subsidies for businesses that "spend" our natural resources or otherwise hurt the environment. Individually we make a statement by doing business only with planet-friendly companies and voting for candidates with a good environmental record.

- **Personal independence and self-sufficiency.** Developing self-sufficient living skills helps us prepare for the uncertainties of the future.

- **Self-sufficient communities.** There is a growing movement to create small communities based on principles of self-sufficiency and cooperation.

PLANNING FOR THE FUTURE

Planning for the future occurs at multiple levels. On the micro level, we are primarily concerned with planning for personal survival and the survival of our immediate families. This kind of planning involves evaluating local environmental hazards and storing emergency supplies and provisions to deal with these hazards. Does your area have the potential for hurricanes, tornadoes, or earthquakes? For the longer term, micro planning might include growing your own food and becoming energy self-sufficient.

A middle level of planning extends your vision to the community. By banding together with like-minded people, an entirely self-sufficient community might be formed, or perhaps simply a network that shares information, skills, and inspiration and provides needed support. There is strength in both the numbers and the diversity of abilities and resources that a community provides.

The macro level encompasses a more global view. You may think that humanity is not capable of changing its current direction, that human beings have always been selfish and greedy and will never change. The historical record, however, shows us major shifts and changes. Think about it. What happened to slavery, cannibalism, and even human sacrifice? Once common in many parts of the world, they now exist as isolated cases of aberrant behavior. It takes time for a conscious idea to grow to the point where it gains momentum. Sometimes an idea appears to avalanche through the universe, miraculously leaping across oceans and boundaries. This type of event, referred to as "remote shared learning," or "the hundredth monkey phenomenon," has shattered some traditional scientific concepts.

The Hundredth Monkey Phenomenon

"Remote shared learning" among different members of the same species has been observed in the wild and has been demonstrated numerous times in repeatable laboratory experiments. A famous example of remote shared learning concerned the opening of milk bottles by wild birds in England. For nearly a hundred years, milk bottles had been left undisturbed at homeowners' doors. In 1921 it was recorded that a small bird had been seen opening the cardboard tops of milk bottles in Southampton, England. The first species of bird observed opening milk bottles was the blue tit. By 1937, eleven different species of birds had begun opening milk bottles and this activity had spread to 89 English cities. Then the most amazing thing happened. Blue tits in Sweden, Denmark, and Holland began attacking milk bottles. The behavior had leapt across borders and the ocean at a rate far too fast to have been passed from bird to bird as a learned behavior (Hartmann 1997, 107).

An equally famous example concerns a species of Japanese monkeys, Macaca Fuscata. In 1952, scientists studying the behavior of these monkeys on the

island of Koshima provided food for them by dropping sweet potatoes onto the sand. The monkeys liked the sweet potatoes and tolerated the sand that clung to the outside. One day, a bright 18-month-old female monkey named Imo figured out that she could wash the potatoes in the ocean to remove the gritty sand. She gradually taught this brand-new idea and behavior to other monkeys in their group. By 1958, all the young monkeys on the island were washing their potatoes, but only a few of the adults had managed to learn this behavior. Something startling was observed in the autumn of 1958. Suddenly, essentially all of the monkeys in this tribe were observed washing their potatoes, including the older ones who for years hadn't caught on to the behavior of the younger monkeys. Not only did the older monkeys on the island of Koshima start to wash their potatoes, but scientists observed that colonies of monkeys on the other islands and the mainland of Takasakiyama also started to wash their food in the ocean (Keyes 1981, 11-16).

It was proposed that when the knowledge was limited to a few monkeys, the behavior was passed on by observation and learning. But when a significant number of monkeys had learned this behavior—for the sake of simplicity they called it 100 monkeys—it appeared that some critical mass of consciousness had been reached. The new awareness was transmitted mind to mind within the species without being limited by the physical parameters of time and space. The phenomenon of remote shared learning, or the hundredth monkey phenomenon, has also been demonstrated in a number of studies involving learned behavior in laboratory rats. This phenomenon gives evidence of our interconnectedness and lends credence to the belief that positive changes in human consciousness—species wide learning—can occur once a critical mass is reached.

According to my tradition, from the beginning of creation, every morning, when the sun comes up, we are each given four tasks by our Creator for that day. First, I must learn at least one meaningful thing today. Second, I must teach at least one meaningful thing to another person. Third, I must do something for some other person, and it will be best if that person does not even realize that I have done something for them. And, fourth, I must treat all living things with respect. This spreads these things throughout the world.

—Cree storyteller (Hartmann 1998, 205)

Effective Action

The significant problems we face cannot be solved at the same level of thinking we were at when we created them.

—Albert Einstein

If we wish to create a positive future for the human race, we must rise above the level of thinking and doing business that has brought us to today's state of the world. The hundredth monkey phenomenon offers hope that if enough people change their thinking and their actions, the world will follow suit. But, actions alone are not enough. They must be *effective* actions.

Stephen Covey, author of *The 7 Habits of Highly Effective People*, is one of the world's most popular business consultants, nonfiction authors, and inspirational speakers. Studying many of the most successful people on the planet, he has formulated their "habits" of success into simple principles that everyone, in all walks of life, can apply in their own lives.

The first three habits for success form the foundation that the other habits rest upon. Habit number one is to be "proactive" rather than "reactive." Proactive people take the initiative to achieve their goals and know that, in some way, they are responsible for the circumstances of their lives. A proactive person may not always like her outer circumstances but knows that she can consciously choose her response. Covey cites the example of Victor Frankl, who survived several years of confinement in a Nazi concentration camp, which took the lives of almost all of his family. In the midst of torture and physical degradation, Frankl realized that he had no control over what the guards did to his body, but that he did have control over his inner being and mind. No one could take that from him unless he allowed it. Through mental exercises, imagination, and discipline, he developed his internal power and became an inspiration to others, including some of the Nazi guards. Reactive people, on the other hand, are more like leaves blowing in the wind. They are often found in the role of victim or are always fighting fires in their personal life and at work. Proactive people try to plan ahead to avoid the fire.

Habit number two is to "begin with the end in mind." How can you expect to be successful at something if you don't have a vision of where you want to go? Builders must start with a vision in their minds of the building they wish to build. Next, they draw up the plans, typically modifying them a bit here and there. Finally, they build the structure, usually incorporating a few more changes into the process. To successfully navigate our future, it takes vision on all three levels, the micro, middle, and macro levels. Without a vision of the kind of world we hope to create in our future, we cannot plan an appropriate course of action to get us there.

Habit number three is to "put first things first." This habit is about priorities. To be effective, we must devote significant chunks of time to our highest priorities and focus on one thing at a time to avoid becoming scattered and ineffective. This seems so obvious, yet can we honestly claim that we—or our leaders and governments—stick to this habit? Perhaps someday soon we will put our best minds and resources to good use for the benefit of all humanity. Most of us would do everything in our power to help one of our children battle a life-threatening illness. Can we not band together to do the same for our planet?

Mother Theresa once said, "We cannot do great things, only small things with great love." Great world changes start with small, personal internal changes on a one-to-one basis, which blossom into massive movements encompassing much of humanity. The time and place to start is now and with yourself. Remember, the journey of a thousand miles begins with the first step.

REFERENCES

Trends and Solutions

***The Last Hours of Ancient Sunlight: Waking up to Personal and Global Transformation,* by Thom Hartmann.** 2000, 336 pp. (paperback), ISBN 0-609-80529-0. Published by Crown Publishing Group, 299 Park Ave., New York, NY 10171. Lists for $14.00.
"*The Last Hours of Ancient Sunlight* shines like a beacon in the darkness, an education about reality, a needed wake-up call, and a guidebook through the swamps of denial and ignorance into a brighter, sustainable future." (Dan Millman, author of *The Peaceful Warrior* and *Everyday Enlightenment*)

If you read only one book about the future of this planet, this should be the one. It provides us clear insights about how we got to where we are and how we might influence where we are headed. It also offers great ideas and inspiration for finding our way to a positive, better future for our world.

***Natural Capitalism: Creating the Next Industrial Revolution,* by Paul Hawken, Amory Lovins, and L. Hunter Lovins.** 1999, 378 pp. (hardcover), ISBN 0-316-35316-7. Published by Little Brown & Co., Time Life Building, Sixth Ave., New York, NY 10020. Lists for $26.95.
I wish *Natural Capitalism* were required reading for all engineers, businesspeople, and politicians. This book provides a blueprint for a worldwide business revolution that could go a long way toward providing a sustainable future for our children. *Natural Capitalism* explores changes that could reduce our current use of resources (the "natural capital" of the planet) by factors on the order of 10 to 1, without reducing our standard of living, by applying existing technologies and redirecting the way we do business. A rational, well-documented book with many case examples, it was written by three well-respected members of the ecological movement, including founders of the Rocky Mountain Institute.

***Believing Cassandra: An Optimist Looks at a Pessimist's World* by Alan AtKisson.** 1999, 236 pp. (paperback), ISBN 1-890132-16-0.

Published by Chelsea Green Publishing Company, P.O. Box 428, White River Junction, VT 05001. Lists for $16.95.
"Alan AtKisson is the freshest and wisest voice to emerge from the sustainability movement in many years. . . . This book renews our sense of the possible and expands the dimensions of our collective intelligence, transforming our sense of the future from a curse to a blessing." (Paul Hawken, author of *Natural Capitalism*)

Tired of gloom-and-doom outlooks? This author takes a realistic look at where we are heading (which does not look good) and sees it as a wonderful challenge for mankind to wake up and do something really meaningful and worthwhile. In Greek mythology, the god Apollo fell in love with Cassandra, bestowing upon her the gift of prophecy. When Cassandra did not return Apollo's love, he revenged himself by cursing Cassandra such that she would see misfortune before it came, but no one would heed her warnings. In spite of her clear vision and best efforts, all of her warnings were in vain. AtKisson sees the salvation of this world in focusing our attention on current Cassandra-like warnings and awakening to action to prevent ecological suicide from becoming our reality. He challenges us to take the bull by the horns and truly transform our planet by accepting a sustainable future as the only viable option.

***Beyond the Limits: Confronting Global Collapse, Envisioning a Sustainable Future,* by Donella H. Meadows, Dennis L. Meadows, and Jorgen Randers.** 1993, 320pp. (paperback), ISBN 0-930031-62-8. Published by Chelsea Green Publishing Co., PO Box 428, White River Junction, VT 05001. Lists for $16.95.
"This book is essential reading for everybody who is concerned with the central issue of our times: how to achieve a transition to a sustainable global future." (Gro Harlem Brundtland, former Prime Minister of Norway and Chairman of The World Commission on Environment and Development)

Back in the early 1970s, a team of young scientists from MIT spent two years developing and working with a world computer simulation program called "World3," designed to study the potential consequences of current global patterns of growth and consumption. The computer model results were staggering and made quite a stir when announced to the world and subsequently published in *Limits to Growth* by Donella Meadows, Dennis Meadows, Jorgen Randers, and William H. Behrens III. In one scenario after another, the computer model invariably predicted that human population would swell to the point where it overshot the planet's capability to support the population, and then come crashing down as one system after another failed in mankind's final attempts to keep people fed, clothed, and housed. *Beyond the Limits* shows us where we are headed and explores alternatives to change the course from collapse to sustainability. *Highly Recommended!*

State of the World 2000 by Lester R. Brown, Christopher Flavin, and Hillary French. 2000, 276 pp., (paperback) ISBN 0-393-31998-9. Published by W.W. Norton & Co., Inc., 500 Fifth Ave., New York, NY 10110. Lists for $14.95.

Worldwatch Institute comes out with a new edition of their excellent *State of the World* every year. *State of the World* summarizes current trends and includes several excellent informative chapters, contributed by different Worldwatch staff members and guest authors, on topics concerning the state and future of the world. *Fascinating and highly recommended!*

Vital Signs 2000: The Environmental Trends That Are Shaping Our Future, by Lester R. Brown, Michael Renner, and Brian Halweil. 2000, 192 pp. (paperback), ISBN 0-393-32022-7. Published by W.W. Norton & Co., Inc., 500 Fifth Ave., New York, NY 10110. Lists for $13.00.

Each year Worldwatch Institute also releases a new volume of its *Vital Signs* series, which documents global trends in a broad variety of areas. *Vital Signs* provides an excellent bird's-eye view of the state of the world via numerous brief articles on current trends and findings. Articles are heavily supported

through graphical representations of relevant data. *Highly recommended!*

The Consumer's Guide to Effective Environmental Choices: Practical Advice from the Union of Concerned Scientists by Michael Brower, Ph.D., and Warren Leon, Ph.D. 1999, 292 pp. (paperback), ISBN 0-609-80281-X. Published by Three Rivers Press, a division of Crown Publishers, Inc., 201 East 50th St., New York, NY 10022. Lists for $15.00

This book is about doing what counts, doing what matters. As environmentally concerned consumers, many times we are faced with the choice of products and actions that may or may not make a difference in environmental impact. Ever wonder if choosing paper or plastic bags really makes a difference? What about cloth versus disposable diapers? These people have a lot more time and resources than you or I to determine the relative environmental impacts of a huge array of consumer habits and choices. It turns out that a very few things make most of our personal impact on the environment, such as the car we drive, the house we live in, our eating habits, and our travel/recreational choices. Get this book to help you make informed decisions about your everyday habits and major purchases.

The Heat Is On, by Ross Gelbspan. 1998, 278 pp. (paperback), ISBN 0-7382-0025-5. Published by Perseus Publishing, Eleven Cambridge Center, Cambridge, MA 02142. Lists for $13.00.

"Until you've read this book, you are ill-equipped to think about the planet's future." (Bill McKibben, author of *The End of Nature*)

This is a well-documented book about global warming and the coming climate crisis. Frightening, sobering, and illuminating. For those of you who are interested in nitty gritty details, scientific references, and the facts about this No. 1 planetary issue and the megabuck big business and government cover-up, this book is for you.

The Coming Oil Crisis by Colin J. Campbell. 1997, 210 pp. (paperback), ISBN 0906522110. Published by Petroconsultants S.A., P.O. Box

152-24, Chemin de la Mairie, 1258 Perly, Geneva, Switzerland. Lists for $29.95.
Written by one of the world's foremost authorities on world oil resources, this book is a powerful awakening to the very real probability that we shall soon see an oil crisis of a magnitude and permanence that has never been seen before. The author, Dr. Colin J. Campbell, has been involved in all phases of world-wide oil exploration and management. He offers a clear, well-documented explanation of the basic geology of oil and why production is likely to decline sharply in the not-too-distant future. I suggest that you get this book to educate yourself about coming events that will severely affect our society. In America, you can buy this book from EcoSystems, Box 7080, Santa Cruz, CA 95061; phone: (831) 425-8523.

Saving the Planet: How to Shape an Environmentally Sustainable Global Economy, by Worldwatch Institute's Lester R. Brown, Christopher Flavin, and Sandra Postel. 1991, 224 pp. (paperback), ISBN 0-393-30823-5. Published by W.W. Norton & Co., Inc., 500 Fifth Ave., New York, NY 10110. Lists for $8.95.
The authors have assembled an excellent work on turning business-as-usual in new, sustainable directions. It is good companion reading with *Natural Capitalism*, though not quite as current.

Beyond Recycling: A Re-user's Guide, 336 Practical Tips; Save Money and Protect the Environment by Kathy Stein. 1997, 164 pp. (paperback), ISBN 0-940666-92-8. Published by Clear Light Publishers, 823 Don Diego, Santa Fe, NM 87501. Lists for $14.95.
Reusing is a major step above recycling in the ecology efficiency "food chain." Get this guide to assist you in your efforts to reduce environmental impact through reusing products (you can send them on to others even if you do not reuse them yourself).

Pillar of Sand: Can the Irrigation Miracle Last? by Worldwatch Institute's Sandra Postel. 1999, 313 pp. (paperback), ISBN 0-393-31937-7. Published by W.W. Norton & Company, Inc., 500 Fifth Ave., New York, NY 10110. Lists for $13.95.

A sobering look at the world's water usage and growing irrigation crisis, *Pillar of Sand* points the way toward conservation efforts aimed at protecting rivers and vital ecosystems as we work to feed a projected world population of over 8 billion people by the year 2030.

The End of Nature, by Bill McKibben. 1989, 226 pp. (paperback), ISBN 0-385-41604-0. Published by Anchor Books, Bantam Doubleday Dell Publishing Group, Inc., 1540 Broadway, New York, NY 10036. Lists for $14.00.
"McKibben's eye-opening plea ...is likely to prove as important as Rachel Carson's classic *Silent Spring* or Jonathan Schell's *The Fate of the Earth*. *The End of Nature* may convert you, or it may infuriate you. But the world will never look the same to you after you've read it." (*Cleveland Plain Dealer*)
The End of Nature is a groundbreaking piece of compelling and illuminating environmental journalism. Since it was written in 1989, there is mounting evidence to support the real and present dangers of global warming and other major environmental threats.

Diet for a New America: How Your Food Choices Affect Your Health, Happiness and the Future of Life on Earth, by John Robbins. 1998, 423 pp. (paperback), ISBN 0-91581-181-2. Published by H.J. Kramer Inc., P.O. Box 1082, Tiburon, CA 94920. Lists for $14.95.
This is a very powerful, engrossing, and eloquent book about the staggering social, ethical, environmental and health impacts of eating meat. Until reading this book, most people (me included) have no idea of the magnitude of the hidden costs for supporting a heavy meat diet. This book has converted many people to vegetarianism who had not previously given it much thought.

Reworking Success: New Communities at the Millenium, by Robert Theobald. 1997, 119 pp. (paperback), ISBN 0-86571-367-7. Published by New Society Publishers, P.O. Box 189, Gabriola Island, BC Canada V0R 1X0.
Robert Theobald has been on the leading edge of fundamental change issues throughout his 40-year

career as a well-known educator, futurist and world policy specialist. This provocative book urges us to redefine the current definitions of economic and political success that we might stem the tide of increasing consumption and move towards a sustainable future before it is too late.

Rolling Thunder Speaks: A Message for Turtle Island, by Rolling Thunder, edited by Carmen Sun Rising Pope. 1999, 250 pp. (paperback), ISBN 1-57416-026-5. Published by Clear Light Publishers, 823 Don Diego, Santa Fe, NM 87501. Lists for $14.95.

A Native American healer, teacher, and activist, Rolling Thunder is known to millions of people all over the world. *Rolling Thunder Speaks* is a major legacy of his extraordinary life and the summation of his teachings in his own words. This is not as much a "how to" book as it is a book about Native American philosophy, spirituality, and living in harmony with the planet. It delves into sustainable living, visions of the future, healing with medicinal plants, and an earth-honoring spiritual message.

The Way It Is: One Water . . . One Air . . . One Mother Earth, by Corbin Harney. 1995, 232 pp. (paperback), ISBN 0-931892-80-5. Published by Blue Dolphin Publishing, Inc., P.O. Box 1920, Nevada City, CA 95959. Lists for $16.00.

Corbin Harney, the spiritual leader of the Western Shoshone Nation, writes about the future of our world and how we must care for it. He felt obliged by Spirit to become politically active to try to influence people to honor our planet before it is too late.

Prophecies

Black Dawn, Bright Day, Indian Prophecies for the Millennium That Reveal the Fate of the Earth, by Sun Bear with Waban Wind. 1992, 237 pp., (paperback) ISBN 0-671-75900-0. Published by Fireside, Simon & Schuster Building, Rockefeller Center, 1230 Avenue of the Americas, New York, NY 10020. Lists for $12.00.

"One of the most important visionaries of our time teaches people why and how they must heal them-

selves and the earth now. I recommend this book wholeheartedly." (Elizabeth Kubler Ross, M.D.)

This is one of the better books on Indian prophecies, written by a well-known Indian healer and spiritual leader.

Coming Earth Changes: The Latest Evidence, by William Hutton. 1996, 265 pp. (paperback), ISBN 0-87604-361-9. Published by A.R.E. Press, 215 67th St., Virginia Beach, VA 23451. Lists for $14.95.

In the early 1900s Edgar Cayce, the famous American psychic, predicted the stock market crash of 1929, the devastation of WWII, and numerous accelerating earth changes that would lead to a shift of the earth's poles sometime around the new millennium. Geologist William Hutton compares predictions in the Cayce psychic readings with the latest geophysical research findings, and points to patterns predicted by Cayce, as early as the 1930s, which appear to be coming true.

The End Times: Prophecies of the Coming Changes, Including Prophecies and Predictions from the Bible, Nostradamus, Holy Mother, Edgar Cayce, by John Van Auken. 1996, 168 pp. (paperback), ISBN 0-87604-363-5. Published by A.R.E. Press, 215 67th St., Virginia Beach, VA 23451. Lists for $12.95.

An interesting look at biblical prophecies, the prophecies of Nostradamus and Edgar Cayce, and the visions of Mother Mary. For a more traditional gloom-and-doom look at biblical prophecy, consider one of Hal Lindsey's books.

The Millennium Book of Prophecy: 777 Visions and Predictions from Nostradamus, Edgar Cayce, Gurdjieff, Tamo-san, Madame Blavatsky, the Old and New Testament Prophets and 89 Others, by John Hogue. 1997, 400 pp. (paperback), ISBN 0-06-251077-0. Published by Harper San Francisco, 1160 Battery St., 3rd Floor, San Francisco, CA 94111-1213. Lists for $14.00.

Modern prophecy guru John Hogue, featured on the TV series *Ancient Prophecies*, has assembled 777 visions and prophecies from over a hundred of the world's most accurate prophets and seers. This volume is a giant collection of predictions for what may be in store for humankind in the year 2000 and beyond. Beginning some 8,000 years B.C., and ending well into the 38th century, *The Millennium Book of Prophecy* covers aspects of the future—religion, politics, war, and natural disasters—with a breadth unlikely to be topped anytime soon.

RESOURCES

Worldwatch Institute, 1776 Massachusetts Ave., N.W., Washington, D.C. 20036-1904; phone: (202) 452-1999; fax: (202) 296-7365; web site: www.worldwatch.org. The web site contains lots of information and links to other informative sites.

Check out WI's books and web site for some accurate and enlightening information on the state of the world. WI is dedicated to fostering the evolution of an environmentally sustainable society—one in which human needs are met in ways that do not threaten the health of the natural environment or the prospects of future generations. The Institute seeks to achieve this goal through the conduct of interdisciplinary nonpartisan research on emerging global environmental issues, the results of which are widely disseminated throughout the world.

Rocky Mountain Institute, 1739 Snowmass Creek Road, Snowmass, CO 81654-9199; phone: (970) 927-3851; fax: (970) 927-3420; web site: www.rmi.org.

Rocky Mountain Institute is a nonprofit research and educational foundation with a vision across boundaries. Its mission is to foster the efficient and sustainable use of resources as a path to global security. The Institute creates, and helps individuals and private sector businesses to practice, new solutions to old problems—mainly by harnessing the problem-solving power of market economics and of advanced techniques for resource efficiency. These people are real movers and shakers in the movement to create a sustainable future for our planet.

Union of Concerned Scientists, 2 Battle Square, Cambridge, MA 02238-9105; phone: (617) 547-5552; fax: (617) 864-9405; web site: www.ucsusa.org.

UCS is an independent nonprofit alliance of 50,000 concerned citizens and scientists across the country. They augment rigorous scientific analysis with innovative thinking and committed citizen advocacy to build a cleaner, healthier environment and a safer world. Search their web site for numerous well-documented articles on environmental topics, including global warming. They publish a quarterly journal and unite scientists, engineers, and citizens as a positive political force for change.

World Resources Institute, 10 G Street, NE (Suite 800), Washington, DC 20002; phone: (202) 729-7600; fax: (202) 729-7610; web site: www.wri.org.

The World Resources Institute's mission is to move human society to live in ways that protect the earth's environment and its capacity to provide for the needs and aspirations of current and future generations.

Greenpeace USA, 702 H Street, NW, Suite 300, Washington, DC 20001; phone: (202) 462-1177; fax: (202) 462-4507; web site: www. greenpeace.org.

This is one of the oldest and most popular organizations devoted to environmental education, awareness, and activism. Their web site search engine offers access to a tremendous volume of archived environmental information plus a multitude of links to other related sites.

EarthSave International, 600 Distillery Commons, Suite 200, Louisville, KY 40206-1922; web site: www.earthsave.org.

EarthSave is based on the principles developed in John Robbins's book *Diet for a New America.* EarthSave promotes environmental well-being and improved human health through positive food choices. It raises awareness of the vast ecological destruction resulting from the unsustainable production of animal foods, promoting instead a delicious planet-friendly diet.

International Forum on Globalization, Building 1062, Fort Cronkhite, Sausalito, CA 94965; phone: (415) 229-9350; fax: (415) 229-9340; web site: www.ifg.org.

The Forum advocates equitable, democratic, and ecologically sustainable economics. It was formed in response to the current worldwide drive toward a globalized economic system dominated by supranational corporate trade and banking institutions that are not accountable to democratic processes or national governments. These current trends toward globalization are neither historically inevitable nor desirable. The goal of the IFG is twofold: expose the multiple effects of economic globalization in order to stimulate debate, and seek to reverse the globalization process by encouraging ideas and activities that revitalize local economies and communities and ensure long-term ecological stability.

Alternative Energy Institute, Inc., P.O. Box 7074, Tahoe City, CA 96145; phone: (530) 583-1720; fax: (530) 583-5153; web site: www.altenergy.org.

The Institute was organized to educate the public about the impending nonrenewable energy crisis, the search for solutions, and to improve the climate for development of new energy technologies. They are a group of concerned people who believe solutions can be found when people are aware of the problems facing the world. They are focused on finding solutions and encouraging both citizens and public entities to act responsibly for the planet's future. Check out their web site for many informative reports and articles on world energy usage, coal, gas, oil, solar, current trends, new energy technologies, and so forth. This is an excellent source for information and green links to other sites. Sign up for their informative Alternative Energy web-based newsletter (it's free, and it is very good!).

▥ Supplies & Preparations

*Confidence, like art, never comes from having
all the answers; it comes from being open to all
the questions.*

—Earl Gray Stevens

We are living in an era of megastorms, international
terrorism, and increasingly destructive earthquakes.
It would be foolish to assume that there will not be
significant disruptions in the supply of electricity to
your local grid at some time in the not-too-distant
future. Remember, when electricity stops flowing,
furnaces, cash registers, gasoline pumps, phones, and
air conditioners all stop working, except for the rare
facilities that are hooked up to a backup source of
power. Without gas and electricity, most municipal
water treatment and waste removal systems will soon
shut down and emergency medical services are
usually severely limited. If temperatures are well
below freezing, without a backup source of heat (or
winterized plumbing), toilet bowls and pipes can
start to freeze and burst within a day or two after the
power goes out.

ARE YOU PREPARED?

Disturbances such as floods, earthquakes, major
storms, or terrorist acts may disrupt the distribution of electricity, food, fuel, goods, and services for
significant periods of time. In 1998, a severe ice
storm in the northeast knocked out power for periods ranging from three days to several weeks, and
many of the survivors of Japan's Kobe quake did
not receive food or potable water until a week after
the quake.

If a major hurricane or other natural disaster
such as a severe earthquake were to strike your
community, would you be well prepared? Before
the magnitude 6.9 earthquake struck Kobe Japan in
1995, Japanese engineers and politicians had

thought that they were better prepared for earthquake disasters than any other country in the
world. Japan's freeways and buildings are theoreti-
cally designed to handle much stronger quakes
than the one that struck Kobe, yet most of Kobe's
downtown freeways and tall buildings either fell
down during the quake or had to be torn down
afterwards because of structural damage. This
disaster was a harsh blow for hundreds of thousands of survivors who lost friends, family
members, and most of their possessions. How well
would you fare if you could not purchase any food,
water, or gasoline for one week? What about a
month or longer?

No one really knows what the future will
bring. You can't plan for all possible scenarios, but
a wise person plans for several of the most likely
possibilities, and stores at least a few basic supplies
for emergencies. This chapter helps readers to
evaluate their own particular needs and goals, and
offers guidance on planning for both short-term
and long-term situations.

To help you organize your thoughts and guide
your actions, ask yourself the following questions
while making your emergency plans and building
your backup supplies and skills:

- What natural hazards are there in my area? Have
  I taken precautions to protect my home?
- What is my potential for being caught in a
  significant earthquake, flood, hurricane, or
  tornado?
- How long do I anticipate that I might be without access to utilities and supplies?
- If the electricity goes out for an extended period
  of time, how will I cook, and how will I heat and
  light my home?
- Do I have supplies and training to deal with
  medical emergencies if medical help is
  unavailable?

- If I must evacuate my home, do I have portable emergency supplies readily available to bring with me?
- How many people do I wish to store supplies for? What about my friends, neighbors, or relatives?
- Do I have pets that I wish to feed and care for?
- Do I have small children or infants with special needs?
- Do I require prescription medications or are there any addictions I wish to provide for if distribution systems go down for a period of time?

PLANNING FOR THE SHORT TERM

The following information on short-term planning is designed to help you to prepare for emergencies when services are disrupted for periods of up to one week. Everyone should have enough food, water, and other emergency supplies to last for at least three days (72-hour emergency kits), and preferably one to two weeks.

I suggest making these preparations as soon as possible. It is hard to focus on this task when skies are blue and nothing is threatening, but it is usually too late once a disaster strikes or is close at hand. When the tourists come to our town in the High Sierras, just the threat of a major winter storm is enough to send swarms of people to the local supermarkets, where they stock up on food. Once the highway over Donner Summit closes to trucks for one or two days, local market shelves are quickly stripped bare.

Short-Term Preparedness Checklist

- Place 72-hour emergency survival kits in your cars and convenient "grab kits" in your home.
- Determine a local meeting place with a large open area, such as a park or school, where your household can gather if you are separated and do not have access to your home during emergencies.
- Make sure that all capable members of your family know how and where to shut off the water, gas, and electricity for your home in the event of an emergency.
- Stash spare keys to your vehicles somewhere on each vehicle and place an additional supply

of keys somewhere outside of your home (securely hidden).
- Store at least one week's supply of food for your household.
- Store a combination of water, water treatment chemicals, and water-purifying filters to provide for your household for at least a week (see Chapter 5, *Water*, for more information on filters and purification).
- Keep a survival manual in each car with your 72-hour kit.
- Get proper first aid and CPR training for all capable members of your family. See the American Red Cross for first aid training and assistance with local emergency planning.
- Arrange for an out-of-state emergency contact to reach for coordination and communication. After an emergency, it may be easier to call long distance than locally, or your family may be separated and need an outside contact to communicate through.
- Locate your nearest emergency shelter (call your local Red Cross for this information). Practice the route to the shelter, if it's not conveniently located.
- Make sure that you have smoke detectors in your home. Change their batteries at least once each year.
- Store your important papers in one easily accessible location, preferably in a waterproof and flameproof box.
- Discuss your emergency preparedness plans with all members of your household. Keep the discussion light and positive.

72-Hour Survival Kits

These kits, sometimes known as "grab-and-run kits," should be readily accessible and cover the basic daily needs of your family for a period of at least three days. Please note that three days is a minimal time period and that you should have at least one or two weeks' supply of food stored in or around your home. You may purchase ready-made 72-hour kits from various survival supply outlets, or you can put together your own. Large families should probably divide up the stores between several easily grabbed small back-packs or plastic containers. One advantage to building your own kits is that you get to choose foods that you like. Remember that all foods have some kind of shelf life. *Rotate stores and use them or lose them!* Bug infested, rancid, or rotten food doesn't do anyone any good.

Consider placing all of the following items in your 72-hour survival kit:

- Portable radio, preferably one that works with dead or no batteries, such as a hand crank or combination model powered with solar cells (available through survival and surplus outlets).
- First aid kit with first aid and survival handbooks.
- Water, water purification chemicals, and/or purifying filter. Enough to provide one gallon per person per day (see Chapter 5). Retort (foil) pouches can handle freezing in a car trunk, but most other water containers can't handle freezing without the potential for bursting.
- Waterproof and windproof matches in a waterproof container, and a utility-type butane (large, with extended tip) lighter.
- Wool or pile blankets (avoid cotton), because they are warm when wet. Also, a heat-reflective, waterproof "space blanket." Fiber-pile, mountaineering-quality sleeping bags are great, if you have the space.
- Flashlight with spare batteries, or solar recharge flashlight.
- Candles (useful for lighting fires with damp wood) and light sticks.
- Toiletries, including toilet paper, toothbrush, soap, razor, shampoo, sanitary napkins (also good for severe bleeding wounds), several packs of dental floss (for tying things), and so on.
- A Swiss army knife, or a stainless steel multi-tool knife, with scissors, can opener, blades, and screwdrivers.
- Map, compass, and whistle.
- Sewing kit with extra–heavy-duty thread.
- Towel or dishcloth.
- Knives, forks, spoons, and so on.
- Tent and/or roll of plastic sheeting for shelter.
- Extra clothing, such as long underwear, hat, jacket, waterproof mittens, leather work gloves, rain coat or poncho, sturdy boots, and so on.
- Entertainment for kids and other special needs (medicines, diapers, extra glasses, etc.).
- 25 kitchen-size garbage bags and sewage treatment chemicals (powdered type preferred) for garbage and toilet sewage. A few large hefty bags can double for raincoats, ground cloths, and shelter.
- 50 feet of heavy-duty nylon string or light rope.

First Aid Kits

Get yourself a decent first aid kit. Each car should have a kit and your house should have one. Most preparedness/survival suppliers stock an assortment of first aid kits, from simple to field surgical quality. Here are suggestions for a modest first aid kit:

- 2 Ace bandages
- 1 box of adhesive bandages (at least 12 Band-Aids) of varying sizes, with at least two square bandages 2" or larger
- 6 butterfly bandages
- 1 large roll of 2" cloth adhesive tape (may be torn or cut to smaller widths)
- Several 4" x 4" sterile nonadhesive dressings
- Three 3"-wide gauze rolls
- 2 triangular bandages
- *Triple antibiotic ointment
- Mouth shield for mouth-to-mouth resuscitation (precaution against AIDS, tuberculosis, and hepatitis)
- 3 sterile applicator sticks, cotton tipped
- *Alcohol and/or 10 prepackaged alcohol squares
- Instant cold pack/ice pack
- First aid manual
- Thermometer
- Safety pins and sterile needle
- Scissors
- Surgical rubber gloves (several pairs)
- *Pain reliever tablets (aspirin, acetaminophen, etc.)
- *Laxative
- *Antidiarrhea medication
- *Syrup of ipecac (to induce vomiting)

**NOTE: Check expiration dates and try to rotate stock every year.*

Add the following items to prepare a more advanced first aid kit:

- Snake bite kit
- Emergency suture kit
- Splinting material (air splint, traction splint, hard splint, etc.)
- Tourniquet
- Thumb/finger splint
- Burn gel and "second skin"
- Echinacea, colloidal silver, and grapefruit seed extract natural antibiotics (internal)
- Tea tree oil natural antifungal and antibiotic (external only!)
- Single-edged razor blades and surgical scalpel kit
- Kelley hemostats
- Surgical blunt tip and pointed scissors
- Silver nitrate to cauterize bleeding
- Prescription antibiotics and painkillers
- Sterile thread

Earthquake Precautions

When I was living in Santa Cruz, California, a few years before the Loma Prieta earthquake, I experienced my first significant quake. My desk started bumping against my leg and I saw the lights swinging from the ceiling. Most of my coworkers were native Californians. They paused from their work just long enough to say "Earthquake!" Of more than 200 employees, only one other person and I headed out the door. My coevacuee told me that he grew up in Chile, where he experienced a devastating earthquake. He related that he was walking down the street when that earthquake struck. It was one of the most powerful quakes of this century, and was of such magnitude (estimated at 8.5 to 9.5 on the Richter scale), that it immediately knocked him off his feet. Each time he tried to stand, the quake knocked him down again. Unable to do anything more than crawl, he watched as nearly all surrounding buildings tumbled down. After hearing his story, I understood why he had left the building so quickly at the first tremor.

Even though you may not live in an area prone to earthquakes, I recommend that you read this section on earthquake preparedness and follow the guidelines. Several recent significant earthquakes have occurred on faults that were considered inactive or were totally unknown to geologists. Earthquake faults crisscross the entire country. The fact that most of them have not moved significantly in recent geological history does not mean that they can't or won't move within your lifetime.

Because major earthquakes could happen at almost any location, you should take the following precautions:

- Make sure that your home hot-water heater is secured with "earthquake straps" or metal plumber's tape to prevent it from toppling and rupturing gas and/or water lines during an earthquake.
- Store a sturdy pair of shoes and leather work gloves under each bed. Broken glass often covers the floor during quakes.
- If you live in a climate subject to freezing temperatures, store extra antifreeze (preferably the nontoxic RV type) for winterizing your toilet bowls and sink traps.
- Keep a backup propane, kerosene, or wood heater (and fuel) for emergency space heating.
- Store a roll of plastic sheeting, 50 feet minimum (available at hardware or contractor's supply stores).
- Keep well-stocked, 72-hour emergency kits in the car (or other outside location), including spare clothing.
- Use child locks on your kitchen cabinets to prevent your dishes from flying out of the cabinets during an earthquake. Attach heavy bookcases and other tall furniture to the wall. Use Velcro straps to secure computers in place.
- Keep spare car keys stored on your car (or other outside location). If your clothes, wallet, and keys disappear in a collapsed house on a cold winter's day, you will be grateful for a spare key!
- Keep a permanent shutoff wrench attached to your gas shutoff (available at surplus and survival stores).
- If you are an urban dweller and have no car, or store your car under a large building, you might consider arranging with friends or relatives to store some supplies in their garage, garden shed, and so on.

IN THE EVENT OF AN EARTHQUAKE

If you are stuck inside a building during a severe quake, the safest places to be are in doorways or under a heavy-duty desk or table, because these offer some protection from falling debris.

> **CAUTION: If you smell gas, or the quake was severe, immediately turn off the outside electrical and gas utility supply to your house (gas utility personnel may need to turn it back on).**

If a gas leak is suspected, do not light an open flame or turn on an electric switch. All common electric switches arc when turned on or off, and may ignite explosive gases. If you suspect a gas leak and need to turn on a flashlight, turn it on or off outside, in the open air. Glow sticks are a safe light source that will not ignite flammable gases.

A Short-Term Survival Manual

The Emergency-Disaster Survival Guidebook, **by Doug King.** 1994, 100 pp., ISBN 1-883736-10-2. Published by ABC Preparedness Co., P.O. Box 795, Sandy, UT 84091. Lists for $7.95.

An incredibly valuable guide for such a small book, it is clear, concise, practical, easy to understand, and to the point. It contains basic survival instructions, plus many excellent checklists for planning for, and dealing with, numerous potential emergencies and disasters. Not a bad idea to keep a copy of this book in each car.

LONGER-TERM PLANNING AND STORAGE

If you are planning to store food, water, and other items to supply your household for significant periods of time (more than one month), the packaging, preservation, and nutritive quality of your food stores will be vitally important. You can purchase specialty prepackaged bulk foods from preparedness/survival suppliers, or package your own foods. You will probably want to store a significant variety of foods preserved by a variety of methods. Traditional high-heat canning processes destroy 60% to 80% of the food's nutritive value, but low-heat dehydration results in a loss of only about 10%. Many canned foods do have the advantage of providing syrups or juices, which can be a significant source of water if you are experiencing scarcity. If you have access to a source of water, however, it makes better sense to use dehydrated foods. A pound of dry grains or beans will contain many times the calories of a typical pound of canned foods. Each pound of dehydrated fruits or vegetables is equivalent to 10 to 12 pounds of fresh, canned, or frozen produce.

Stored whole grains may be sprouted to give you the nutritive value of fresh, "live" food. Most whole grains and beans can be sprouted. The sprouting process converts proteins in the seeds into different essential amino acids and dramatically increases their vitamin content. For example, sprouted soybeans have 700% more vitamin C than the dry beans. Vitamin C is a natural detoxifier, destroying damaging toxins in the body. It is essential for helping the body maintain an effective immune system and for preventing deficiency conditions, such as scurvy. The downside to whole grains is that unless they are kept cool, they contain oils that can go rancid, thereby ruining them for consumption.

Whole grains last much longer than grains ground into flour, because finely ground particles have far more surface area for oxidation (degradation). A grain mill, preferably hand cranked or combination hand and electric powered, is useful for turning your stored grain into flour as it is required. Most long-term storage programs stress wheat storage, because properly stored wheat has an indefinite shelf life. Some wheat discovered in the pyramids was found to be viable after thousands of years. Brown rice, on the other hand, has a typical shelf life of six months to one year, which may be extended to two to three years with proper packaging and storage.

Basic Supplies and Portable Equipment

- **Water, stored supplies, and treatment.** Water is the most important commodity. You can live for a long time without food, but only three or four days without water.
- **Wheat and other grains, flours, and beans.** The easiest bulk materials to store for calorie, shelf life, and nutritive value.

- **Grain grinder.** Buy a quality grinder for grinding grains into flour. Should be hand cranked or combination hand and power unit.
- **Cooking catalysts and seasonings.** Includes oils, shortenings, salt, leavenings, herbs, and spices.
- **Powdered milk, dairy products, and eggs.** Good for nutritive value and variety in cooking options.
- **Sprouting seeds and supplies.** With a couple of jars, some nylon stockings, and a variety of seeds, you can eat garden-fresh live foods for pennies a day. I suggest alfalfa seeds, any whole grains, mung beans, soybeans, lentils, and cabbage, radish, and broccoli seeds. See Chapter 6 for sprouting instructions.
- **Sweeteners.** Honey, sugar, and maple syrup. Not essential, but may help sweeten an otherwise bitter experience. Honey has the advantage of being a natural topical antibiotic. It has been used for centuries on the battlefield for helping wounds to heal.
- **Canned and dried fruits, vegetables, and soups.** Store a variety of your family's favorites.
- **Canned, dried, or frozen meats and fish.** Store these if you will use them.
- **Dietary supplements.** Vitamins and minerals to supplement the limited nutritional value of stored foods. I suggest using quality supplements manufactured from live foods wherever possible (check your local health food store). Superfood supplements, such as blue green algae and bee pollen, would be a good addition to your emergency food stores.
- **Fuels, lighting sources, camping gear.** Camping gear can provide you with portable shelter and materials for living comfortably if you must evacuate your home (see *Notes on Camping Gear* in this chapter).
- **Medicines and first aid kits.**
- **Pet food and personal items.** Don't forget the things in life that help you stay happy and centered. A deck of cards and a copy of Hoyle's book of card games can bring a lot of laughs when times are tough.
- **Open-pollinated seeds for gardening.** I recommend that you store a variety of seeds for gardening (see Chapter 6). Use open-pollinated seeds, not hybrids, so you can save seeds from your garden for future needs, if necessary. *Do not eat seeds for planting! If they are dyed a bright color, they may be poisonous. Also, they will provide a hundred times more nutrition after the harvest than if eaten first.*
- **Pleasure foods, including snacks, treats, sweets, and beverages.** Not much nutritive value, but great for lifting morale or giving yourself a little reward.

Calculating a Year's Food Supply

> Store what you eat. Eat what you store. Use it or lose it!
> —James Talmage Stevens, *Making the Best of Basics: Family Preparedness Handbook*

Because most stored food has a limited shelf life, you are throwing money away if you do not store food that your family will eat. The chart on the next page shows storage quantities for one typical adult American male, for one year, consuming roughly 2,500 calories per day. Divide these numbers by 12 for a one-month supply and by 52 for a one-week supply. Since not everyone has the same food requirements, refer to the family factors chart to estimate how much food you should store. Totaling the values will give you the equivalent number of typical adult males, which you will multiply by the figures for the various foods (see example below table). Make your own adjustments based on family members, such as counting a teenage female with an unusually large appetite the same as a teenage male (equal to 1.4 typical adult males).

NOTE: For details on canning, drying, and other preservation methods for foodstuffs, see Chapter 6.

FOOD STORAGE QUANTITIES FOR ONE AVERAGE ADULT MALE FOR ONE YEAR

- **Grains–325 lbs.** You will probably want to store a variety of grains, including whole wheat, pasta, oats, corn, rice, barley, and so on. Due to wheat's longevity, most long-term storage plans focus on it. Brown rice goes rancid in six months to a

CALCULATING FOOD REQUIREMENTS (IN TYPICAL EQUIVALENT ADULT MALES)*

Food factor	Equivalent adult males
Multiply the number of adult males X 1.0	_____
Multiply the number of adult females X .85	_____
Multiply the number of teenage males X 1.4	_____
Multiply the number of teenage females X .95	_____
Multiply the number of male children (7 to 11) X .95	_____
Multiply the number of female children (7 to 11) X .75	_____
Multiply the number of children (4 to 6) X 0.6	_____
Multiply the number of infants (1 to 3) X 0.4	_____
Total	_____

*For example, if the members of your family consist of: 1 man (1.0), 1 woman (0.85), 1 boy between ages 7 and 11 (0.95), and 1 other child between 4 and 6 (0.6), your family should store the amount of food needed by the equivalent of 3.4 men. So, 325 lbs. of grain X 3.4 (adult male equivalents) = 1,095 lbs. of grain to feed your family of four for one year. (Adapted from *Making the Best of Basics: Family Preparedness Handbook* by James Talmage Stevens.)

year, but white rice can keep for many years, if stored properly. Whole grains can be sprouted, increasing their food value.

- **Legumes–80 lbs. (dry).** Many different varieties of beans, peas, lentils, seeds, and so on. Soybeans offer very high protein content, but it is a good idea to store several other legumes for taste and variety.
- **Milk, dairy products, and eggs–50 lbs. (dry).** Nonfat dry milk keeps longer than dried whole milk. Dehydrated eggs and powdered milk greatly expand your cooking possibilities. Also, you can make a variety of cheeses from powdered milk.
- **Meat and meat substitutes–20 lbs. (dry).** Dried vegetarian meat substitutes and freeze-dried meats are very light. They are best cooked into stews and soups for extra flavor.
- **Fruits and vegetables–10 to 30 lbs. (dry).** Traditionally, dehydrated fruits and vegetables are much less expensive than freeze dried.
- **Sweeteners–60 lbs.** These include sugar, honey, syrups, and so on. Honey is preferred for its nutritive and antibiotic values.
- **Fats, oils and shortenings–40 lbs. (5 gal).** Includes butter, margarine, powdered butter, shortening, cooking oil, nut butters, and so on. Hydrogenated processed oils are nonnutritive, but last for years (bacteria can't eat them, and

our bodies can't do much with them either). Cold-pressed oils, such as olive and safflower, provide essential fatty acids that your body needs to metabolize foods, but do not last as long. Storing a combination of hydrogenated oils and cold pressed unprocessed oils offers a blend of good nutrition and longevity.

- **Sprouting seeds and supplies–20 to 50 lbs.** Provides live foods and essential vitamins. Great for variety and nutrition. For best results, use untreated organic whole grains, beans, and seeds. I suggest alfalfa seeds, all types of whole grains, mung beans, soybeans, lentils, and cabbage, radish, and broccoli seeds. See Chapter 6 for sprouting instructions.
- **Leavenings–1 lb. (minimum).** Includes dry active yeast, baking powder, and baking soda.
- **Miscellaneous foods.** Includes spices, cocoa powder, seasoning sauces, condiments, vitamins, minerals, other nutritional supplements, and so on. Include at least 5 lbs. of salt.

Storage Tips

The main culprits responsible for destroying your food stores are time, moisture, heat, oxygen, mold, and pests. Poor food selection and improper packaging can compound the problem. Time is always working against you. Try to store what you normally eat, so you can rotate stocks. Do not store dented cans or other goods with damaged packaging. Molds can grow in low-moisture environments and are extremely toxic. *Do not eat moldy foods or food from bulging cans—sickness or death may result.*

Keep stored foods cool, clean, dark, and dry. Try to keep them below 70°F. The optimum storage for most nonfrozen foods is 35 to 40°F. Shelf life decreases by 50% for each 20-degree increase, even for canned foods. Moisture, food, oxygen, and above-freezing temperatures are the key ingredients insects need to grow. A few bug eggs, once they hatch, can rapidly destroy a sealed container of dry food, if they have an adequate supply of oxygen and moisture. Sunlight also contributes to the degradation of many stored foods.

Store foods in manageable sizes of containers. If you are packaging food yourself, I recommend #10 cans (approximately 1 gallon) or the 5-gallon size. Garbage cans will not keep critters out without airtight liners. They are heavy to move, and you risk losing large amounts of food from a single contamination.

Commercial foods are generally free of pests, but paper packaging will not keep pests out for long. All goods packaged in paper, or other flimsy materials, must be repackaged for long-term storage.

Mice, rats, cockroaches, and beetles are "dirty" pests that carry diseases. The foods they have spoiled should be discarded. Weevils, found in many flours and grains, are "clean" pests and are not harmful if consumed.

You can freeze containers of food to destroy living insects, but this will not usually kill their eggs. Refreeze the container after 30 days to destroy bugs that have hatched. Freeze in an upright or chest freezer (not the freezer section of a standard kitchen refrigerator) for 72 hours at 0°F or lower.

You can heat dry food in an oven to destroy living insects, but this method may also kill "live" food. Pour infested foods into shallow pans to a depth of ½ inch and bake for 15 to 20 minutes at 150°.

CAUTION: Foods will scorch if left in the oven for too long.

Do not store food containers directly on concrete floors, due to moisture wicking from the floor. Stack on wood slats for ventilation and reduced moisture.

Use dry ice, vacuum packaging, oxygen absorbers, or nitrogen packaging to reduce oxygen levels, kill pests, and increase the longevity of stored dry foods. You can package foods yourself using these methods (except for nitrogen packing, which requires commercial equipment), or purchase prepackaged foods from preparedness/survival suppliers.

You can dust grains, legumes, and so on with diatomaceous earth to kill bugs when they try to eat your stored food. Diatomaceous earth, available from most garden supply, hardware centers, and building supply stores, is deadly to bugs but nontoxic for humans and animals. It is a good source of silica (helpful for mending bones and joints) and is formed from the shells of single-celled diatoms. These diatom skeletons contain microscopic sharp edges, which wreak havoc with little critters' insides, but have no harmful effects on humans'. Insert 1¼ cups of diatomaceous earth for each 5 gallons of food, then shake, stir, and roll the container until all the contents are thoroughly dusted. Diatomaceous earth is easily rinsed from stored food prior to cooking.

CAUTION: If you rely on frozen food for long-term storage, ensure that you have an adequate source of backup power to prevent losing your food stores to a long-term power outage.

Dry Ice Fumigation

A good way to repackage dry foods and protect them from pests is with dry ice fumigation. Dry ice is frozen carbon dioxide. A properly-sized block of dry ice, placed on the top or bottom of a container of dry foods, will gradually evaporate (dry ice melts straight into gas through a process called sublimation). As it evaporates, the heavier-than-air carbon dioxide floats the lighter air out the top of the container. Bugs cannot live in an atmosphere of carbon dioxide. Dry ice can be stored for a short while in an ice chest (use no regular ice or liquids with the dry ice) and is available at most supermarkets and restaurant supply stores. Wrap it with newspaper for handling. Break it into appropriately-sized chunks with a hammer and chisel or screwdriver.

> **CAUTION: Do not handle dry ice with bare hands! Contact with bare skin immediately results in frostbite!**

PROCEDURE

Place a properly-sized block of dry ice (see chart below) on the top or bottom (preferred for most thorough purging) of a container of dry foods. If frost crystals are present on the surface of the dry ice, wipe clean with a cloth to prevent the introduction of extra moisture into your food. Press the lid down gently, leaving a small gap for air to escape. After 20 to 30 minutes, check to see if the dry ice has fully evaporated. If it has, seal the container. For the bottom-of-the-bucket method, seal the container after 20 to 30 minutes. If the lid pops off, or the container bulges, crack the lid open and try again in five minutes.

> **NOTE: For the dry ice method to be effective for the long term, the container must be airtight.**

BASIC DRY ICE TREATMENT CHART

Container size	Food quantity (lbs)	Dry ice required (oz)	Expansion space
Metal containers			
#10 can	3 to 5½	1	¼"
5 gal	15 to 35	2 to 3	½"
25 to 30 gal	100	8	½"
Plastic containers			
1 gal	3½ to 7	1	¼"
4 gal	13 to 30	4	½"
5 gal	15 to 35	4	½"

Source: *Making the Best of Basics: Family Preparedness Handbook*, by James Talmage Stevens.

Vacuum Packaging

Vacuum packaging removes the oxygen and excess moisture from dry foods, killing critters and extending shelf life. A simple, but only partially effective, vacuum packing method is to pack food in plastic bags and suck as much air out of the bags with a soda straw as you can, prior to sealing the bags. Heat sealers are the most effective vapor barrier, with zip locks a second best. Modestly priced electric and hand-operated vacuum pumps are available for vacuum packing goods in jars, cans, and bags for long-term storage.

Shelf Life Guide

The following list is for foods stored at room temperature (70° F). Shelf life decreases by roughly 50% with every 20-degree increase in temperature. The ideal storage temperature for most nonfrozen foods is around 35° to 40°F. Remember, whenever possible, keep cool, dark, and dry (CDD). Once a container is opened, the contents may not last long. I suggest dating containers with a grease pen, so you can change markings if the container is opened or reused. Many dry or canned foods will last longer than their official shelf life, but *can't be relied on* to last longer.

- **Indefinite.** Indefinite means that under the right conditions, these materials will last a very long time, possibly longer than you live. Honey, sugar, salt, soy sauce, apple cider vinegar, black pepper, Worcestershire sauce, and properly packaged wheat fall into this category.

- **5 to 10 years.** Most dried legumes and most whole grains are in this category, as are dehydrated cheese, instant coffee, vacuum-packed coffee, baking powder, powdered eggs, and frozen butter.

- **Up to 5 years.** Processed (partially hydrogenated) liquid vegetable oils, Crisco shortening, cornmeal and corn flour, and nonfat powdered milk.

- **2 to 3 years.** Bouillon cubes, corn starch, white rice, powdered gelatin, white wheat flour, white flour pasta (dry), tapioca, textured vegetable protein (TVP), hydrogenated peanut butter, catsup, canned salmon and sardines, most other canned foods except for meats, some fish, and fruits. Sprouting seeds, such as alfalfa, mung, soybean, wheat, and so on, will keep for two to three years.

- **Up to 18 months.** Canned meats, canned seafood (halibut, mackerel, tuna, and shrimp), unshelled raw nuts, dry active yeast, bag-packaged snack chips, cake mixes, dry puddings, herb teas, black teas, bottled juices, most seasonings and extracts, jams and jellies, canned noncitrus fruits (blackberries, blueberries, cherries, pears, peaches, plums, etc.), cranberry sauce, pickles, canned rhubarb, and sauerkraut.

- **1 year.** Canned nuts, packaged dry breakfast cereals, rolled oats (oatmeal), bottled dressings, mayonnaise, natural liquid vegetable oils, candy bars, bottled juices (grapefruit, pineapple, apricot, and orange), most dried fruits, canned citrus fruits, and natural nut butters.
- **6 months:** Most store-packaged food in boxes, fresh potatoes (keep cool, dark, and dry), granola, shelled raw nuts, and unshelled roasted nuts (Stevens 1997, 22-34, and Danks 1998, 73).

NOTES ON CAMPING GEAR

If you ever need to evacuate your home, and emergency shelters are either full or unavailable, camping gear can make a big difference in your comfort and mobility. Chapters 4 through 7 each provide additional instructions for getting by with no gear. This section offers suggestions for selecting practical, high-quality camping equipment.

Tents

Your tent is your shelter from the elements. What kind of weather do you anticipate you might encounter? Low-cost dome tents are available from major discount stores and price clubs. They will do an adequate job when the weather is not severe, but will keep you awake in moderate winds due to flapping fabric, and will probably fall apart in winds over 40 mph. Specialty backcountry stores stock four-season tents, which will hold up under significant snow loads and high winds. Expedition tents, proven in arctic conditions and the Himalayan mountains, will hold up under hurricane force winds (provided they are anchored to something that does not blow away), and can provide shelter when roofs are blowing off buildings. Naturally, they cost several times what the cheap discount tents cost. Expedition tents do not have the comfort and head room of low-cost family tents, which are adequate for moderate weather conditions. Several top-quality brands of tents that I can recommend are: Wild Country, Sierra Designs, Bibler, North Face, Gauruda, and Walrus.

CAUTION: *Synthetic materials, such as nylon, have limited resistance to the sun's ultraviolet rays.*

If you are living in your tent for extended periods, pitch your tent in the shade, or shade your tent with a tarp that you are willing to sacrifice. After a couple of seasons in the sun, most synthetic materials will lose their strength and shred easily. With deterioration from the sun, your $600 expedition tent could fall apart even in moderate winds. Natural fibers, such as cotton and wool, will age much better provided that they are protected from mildew and moths and other critters. A UV-protection product, called UV Tech from McNett Outdoor Corp., is available from backcountry suppliers. When applied to plastics and synthetic fabrics, it filters out most UV rays and greatly extends the life of synthetics regularly exposed to the sun.

Clothing

Wool and the new synthetic piles are warm when wet. Synthetic pile sheds water quickly and dries fast. Cotton clothing is terribly cold when wet. A good set of long underwear, made from wool or one of the synthetic moisture-wicking materials, can make a huge difference in keeping you warm. When your body is covered but your head is not, you will lose most of your heat through your head, so get yourself a warm hat that covers your ears. If the weather is severe, you should have a balaclava, which can be pulled over your face and neck. In addition, your head should be covered with a hood or another hat to add an extra layer over the ears. A breathable waterproof jacket or a waterproof poncho is a must for keeping yourself dry. Breathable waterproof fabrics such as Goretex should have factory-sealed seams. Specialty backcountry stores and many camping/surplus stores carry these items.

Sleeping Bags

A good sleeping bag will keep you warm, even in severely cold temperatures. Down has long been known for providing the greatest warmth with the least weight, but it is totally worthless when wet. When used over long periods of time in subfreezing temperatures, down collects frozen condensation from body moisture and gradually loses its insulating value. The new fiber piles, such as Dupont Hollofill, are not as light or resilient as down, but remain warm when wet. You can dunk one of these fiber-filled sleeping bags in an ice cold river, wring it out with your hands, and climb right in to get warm.

CAUTION: Check the temperature ratings on the bag that you are buying and add a 10°-20°- safety margin unless you are a warm sleeper. The ratings are notoriously optimistic.

Mummy-style bags are more constricting, but allow you to cover your head and are much more efficient insulators than traditional, inexpensive rectangular sleeping bags. Discount stores carry fiber-filled bags, but specialty backcountry stores will have the best selection.

Insulating Sleeping Mats

A good insulating pad is important for both comfort and warmth. Without extra insulation under your body, most of your heat will be lost into the ground. Stiff, closed, cell-foam pads are lightweight and excellent for insulation, but are not the best for comfort. Traditional air mattresses are cheap, but not as warm as closed cell-foam and are often unreliable. A great modern invention, developed by Thermarest, is the nylon-covered, self-inflating camping pad with an inner foam layer. The foam gives shape to the air mattress and prevents internal convection air currents from robbing heat from your sleeping body. These mats are comfortable and light, and provide excellent insulation. They are usually available at discount stores and price clubs, but you will find a better selection in specialty backcountry stores.

Backpacks

If the need arises, a large capacity pack (at least 4,000 cubic inches, and preferably over 5,000 cubic inches) can help you transport your gear, food, and water on foot. The traditional frame pack, with a rigid welded frame of tubular aluminum, is best for carrying maximum loads. Personally, I prefer the mountaineering-style soft packs, with internal molded or bendable frames, because they allow more freedom of movement for traveling over rough terrain. Whether you choose an internal or external frame model, a good, comfortable, padded hip belt is essential to take some of the load off your shoulders. Proper fit is also important. If the pack is too long or short for your torso, you will have a hard time adjusting the hip belt and shoulder straps to distribute the load properly. Some recommended manufacturers of mountaineering packs are Osprey, Gregory, Dana Designs, Northface, Arc' teryx, and Lowe Alpine. Specialty backcountry stores will have the best selection.

Stoves

For pure convenience, two- or three-burner Coleman stoves are hard to beat, but they are bulky, heavy, and inefficient. For occasional use, and if you are planning to use your stove inside your house, propane fuel stoves are the most convenient and emit the least fumes. If you use your stove for an extended period, you will find that white gas (Coleman fuel) is much cheaper and more compact than the propane canisters used on propane stoves. For portability, efficiency, and reliability, the hands-down backcountry choice is one of the MSR stoves. Their multifuel models can run on white gas, kerosene, and other fuels. All MSR stoves can be dismantled without tools and can be serviced with simple repair kits. The original MSR patent appears to have expired, since Primus now makes several stoves that are very similar to MSR. Coleman stoves are available at most outlet and surplus stores, but MSR stoves are mostly available at specialty backcountry suppliers. Optimus makes an excellent multifuel stove. It is less compact than the MSR stoves but compact enough for backpacking.

Cookware

Cast-iron Dutch ovens and frying pans are great for cooking over an open fire. Heavy-duty, cast-iron pots spread the heat of a fire evenly, but are too heavy for most backpacking needs. For backpacking, I prefer lightweight spun stainless steel cookware. It weighs about the same as aluminum cookware, but does not leave traces of aluminum in your food (aluminum has been linked to Alzheimer's disease). It's not a bad idea to have both heavy-duty and lightweight cookware on hand.

Footgear

For support, durability, warmth, and heavy-duty use, it's hard to beat a full-grain leather boot with a Vibram-type, rubber-lug sole. These types of boots are heavy and should be worn for several days to break them in (and harden your feet) prior to leaving on a backcountry trip. Leather boots must be preserved and waterproofed with an appropriate boot grease or synthetic sealer. Modern lightweight hiking boots can provide waterproof materials and support with considerably improved comfort and reduced weight, but will not usually offer the durability and protection of a heavy, full-grain leather boot. For protection from extreme cold and travel across snow, the common Sorrel type boot is a good choice. This type of boot has a removable, heavy wool felt liner, an upper of heavy fabric or leather, and a lower outer rubber boot with a steel shank.

I recommend trying on boots and climbing shoes to be sure of a good fit, rather than purchasing them from a mail order catalog. Blisters from badly fitting boots can cripple your attempts to travel on foot. Always bring moleskin and cloth athletic tape along in your pack and, please, *do yourself a favor by dealing with sore spots before they turn into blisters*. Rotate socks to keep your feet dry and comfortable. For multiday snow country travel, I bring along a supply of thin grocery store produce bags. I wear these under my socks to form a vapor barrier and prevent sweat from wetting my socks and causing cold feet. They also help prevent blisters by adhering to your skin and slipping against the socks.

PLANNING FOR THE LONG-TERM FUTURE

Planning for the long haul depends on the possible futures you wish to plan for. If you wish to plan for the possibility that central distribution systems may break down for extended periods, all the chapters of this book will be useful. It will take tools, supplies, skills, hard work, and many spare parts to maintain a some-

what modern existence in the event of the loss of central services. The instructions and illustrations given in this book are basic information designed to get you started and familiarize you with the range of skills and resources needed to create an alternative lifestyle. The suggested readings and resources in each chapter provide the detailed information that will allow you to go into each subject in much greater depth.

When concerned about the long haul, the quality and durability of your tools and other purchases are vitally important. You may not always be able to purchase the items that you need. A few hand tools will allow you to fabricate useful things from abandoned cars and other abandoned materials. Your ability to fabricate spare parts and simple tools will enable you to keep equipment working year after year. If you have access to an alternative power source, shop tools, such as mills and lathes, would be helpful.

Practically all the easily reached metal ores were stripped from the ground many years ago, and our society has dumped tons of these metals back into the ground. Japan has already begun "mining" their older dumps to recapture these materials, and our old dumpsites could be similarly mined as excellent sources of semi-raw materials. It doesn't take much steel to make a simple plow, a few pounds of nails, or a set of horseshoes. See Chapter 12, *Metalworking*, for more details.

Simple things that we take for granted, such as light switches, faucet washers, and heating elements, eventually wear out. Not-so-simple things, such as refrigerator compressors, DC power inverters, transmissions and motors of all kinds, lead acid storage batteries, solar panels, and hot water tanks, also wear out. No one can stock everything, and there are many items we can easily do without. Think carefully about low-cost items that are easy to stock. Also consider the big-ticket items that you really would rather not do without (or that many other items depend on), such as electrical circuit breakers and your main power inverter (if you have a solar or wind system). You can purchase durable traditional hand-operated goods from several supply houses such as Lehman's. Lehman's and others cater to the Amish, who live comfortably without electricity.

REFERENCES

Books

***Making the Best of Basics: Family Preparedness Handbook,* by James Talmage Stevens.** 1997, 240 pp. (plus 120 pages of appendices) (paperback), ISBN 1-882723-25-2. Published by Gold Leaf Press, 14675 Interurban Ave. South, Seattle, WA 98168-4664. Lists for $22.95.

Recently updated and now in its 10th edition, this book has been the family preparedness bible for many years. It contains a wealth of information and many excellent checklists for storing a wide variety of foods and other materials (medical supplies, camping gear, seeds, fuel, etc.) to prepare for long-term supply problems. It includes a huge, cross-indexed "yellow pages" directory of over 3,000 suppliers, but no notes as to recommended suppliers. Several chapters are devoted to cooking with typical stored foods, and there is a good section on nutritional supplementation. I highly recommend this book.

***Building Your Ark: Your Personal Survival Guide to the Year 2000 Crisis,* by Lia Marie Danks.** 1998, 230 pp. (plus about 50 pages of checklists) (paperback), ISBN 0-9671791-0-6. Published by DAL Enterprises, P.O. Box 17, West Fork, AR 72774. Lists for $22.95.

This book is not just about Y2K. It's an excellent resource for self-reliance and personal preparedness planning. *Building Your Ark* does not cover food supply planning as well as *Making the Best of Basics,* but covers other areas better, such as sanitation, lighting, and safety. If you are concerned with planning ahead and preparedness, I highly recommend you pick up a copy of *Building Your Ark* to supplement *Making the Best of Basics.* Available online at www.yourark.com.

Magazines

***Backpacker Magazine*,** 33 East Minor St., Emmaus, PA 18098; phone: (610) 967-8296; fax: (610) 967-8181; web site: www.bpbasecamp.com.

For the latest info on gear, and articles about travel in the backcountry, check out this magazine. Magazine staff regularly test products with field tests by a team of independent backcountry enthusiasts. Their product evaluations are considered the best in the industry and are often quoted by salespeople in backcountry specialty stores.

RESOURCES

This is not a complete list by any means, but it will give you a good start:

***Safety Central*,** 1100 W. El Camino Real, Mountain View, CA 94040; phone: (800) 782-5396; web site: www.safetycentral.com.

The preparedness superstore. This supplier's large catalog offers a wide variety of preparedness/survival goods, including food storage, water filter/purifiers, first aid supplies, survival kits, self-reliance literature, and so on.

Andreas Industries, Inc. For the *Practical Preparedness* catalog, send $3.00 to Andreas Industries, Inc., Dept. B, P.O. Box 70131, Eugene, OR 97401 0107; phone: (541) 746-6828; web site: www.practicalpreparedness.com.

This company prides itself on being the no-frills, low-cost "Costco" of preparedness/survival suppliers. It provides disaster shelters, greenhouses, and alternative energy materials in addition to the usual assortment of preparedness/survival goods.

***Emergency Essentials*,** 165 S. Mountain Way Drive, Orem, UT 94058-5119; phone: (800) 999-1863; web site: www.BePrepared.com.

This company offers one-year food supplies and a variety of other preparedness kits and supplies.

***B&A Products*,** Rte 1, Box 100, Bunch, OK 74931-9705; phone: (918) 696-5998; web site: www.baproducts.com.

Offering an unusual combination of spiritual books and preparedness/survival goods, Byron and Annie Kirkwood (B&A) founded this store after receiving information supposedly channeled by the Mother Mary about the future of the world.

Major Surplus & Survival, 435 W. Alondra Blvd., Gardena, CA 90248; phone: (800) 441-8855; web site: www.majorsurplusnsurvival.com.
This preparedness/survival supplier offers more military surplus than most of the other listed suppliers.

Millennium III Foods, P.O. Box 10010, Bozeman, MT 59719; phone: (888) 883-1603; web site: at www.M3MFOODS.com.
Millennium III is an excellent source for high-quality, nutritious, good-tasting foods preserved for long shelf life. They carry one-year units and other emergency packs.

Food Storage Solutions, 1868 N. 170 W., Toole, UT 84074-9312; phone: (888) 452-3663.
This company carries Perma Pak one-year food storage packages, emergency kits, water filter/storage, grain mills, and so on.

Natural Lifestyle, 16 Lookout Drive, Asheville, NC 28804-3330; phone: (800) 752-2775; web site: www.natural-lifestyle.com
This is a mail order supplier of bulk natural foods, herbs, and so on.

Basco, 2595 Palmer Ave., University Park, IL 60466; phone: (800) 776-3786; web site: www.bascousa.com.
Basco is a bulk supplier of food and water storage containers and seals.

Grain Mills

Grain mills will turn stored grains into flour, cracked wheat, and so forth. There are many grain mills on the market, with a variety of attachments for different tasks. The following grain mills have hand cranks and flywheels for optional motor-powered belt drives, and are recommended for their quality and durability. These products, and less expensive mills, are available through health food stores and preparedness/survival suppliers.

The **Heidelberg** heavy-duty grain mill comes with a 25-year warranty and is available through Family Basics at 817-444-8181 or www.family-basics.net.

The **Country Living** heavy-duty grain mill comes with a 20-year warranty and is available from Country Living, 14727 56th Ave., NW-B, Stanwood, WA 98292. Call 360-652-0761 for free info pack.

The **Diamant** heavy-duty grain mill comes with a 20-year warranty and is available at some preparedness suppliers and health food stores.

Backcountry/Camping Gear Suppliers

Check your yellow pages under backpacking for local suppliers of quality backcountry gear, or shop at the large suppliers listed below.

REI (Recreational Equipment Inc.), 1700 45th Street, East, Sumner, WA 98352.
A user-owned cooperative founded in 1938. If you join the co-op, you will receive a dividend rebate on your purchases of about 8% to 10%. You can shop at over 60 stores or online at their website, www.rei.com, or check the website to locate the store nearest you. For closeouts and discounts, check www.rei-outlet.com. Call 800-426-4840 for a catalog.

EMS (Eastern Mountain Sports), EMS Direct, 327 Jaffrey Road, Peterborough, NH 03458; phone: (888) 463-6367.
A huge selection of outdoor products at 78 stores. Shop online at www.emsonline.com or check the website to locate the store nearest you.

Campmor, Inc., P.O. Box 700, Saddle River, NJ 07458. Not as large as EMS or REI, but offers a good selection of mid-range to high-quality gear, with many significantly discounted items (good deals!). Call 800-226-7667 for a catalog.

Suppliers of Goods for Simple Living

Lehman's, Dept 8-PJB, P.O. Box 41, Kidron, OH 44636; phone: (330) 857-5757; web site: www.lehmans.com.
The classic catalog for simple living. Suppliers of a large collection of nonelectric tools, appliances, kitchenware, and wood stoves. Serving the Amish and similar communities since 1955. For a catalog, send $3 to Lehman's at the above address.

Cumberland General Store, #1 Highway 68, Crossville, TN 38555; phone: (800) 334-4640. Many old-time useful items, such as well pumps, oak barrels, wood stoves, and oil lamps. For a catalog, phone or send $4 to the above address.

The Old Mill Mercantile, Dept. B1, 14580 Wallin Mountain Rd., West Fork, AR 72774; phone: (501) 839-8269; web site: www.oldmillmercantile.com.
Useful items for self-reliant living, including quality tools, wood cook stoves, water heaters, steam engines, and a variety of other alternative energy devices. For a catalog, send $2 to the above address.

IV Emergency Measures for Survival

What another man can do, I can do.
—From the movie, The Edge

In 1943 I was a member of the French Resistance. Using the name Parizot, I had infiltrated an agency of the Vichy government, where I gathered information on German troop movements. Tipped off that the Nazis had just driven up to arrest me, I fled to the attic of my office building. Word came that half a dozen Gestapo men, knowing I was there, were methodically searching the premises. Having been impressed when a friend used Dr. Emile Coué's program of autosuggestion and positive thinking to cure himself of advanced tuberculosis, I quickly calmed myself and took control over my thoughts. I repeated to myself that the situation could be seen as a thrilling adventure, and switched my perspective to a calm, confident, positive state of mind. I told myself that nothing was hopeless and that I must find the one-in-a-thousand chance of escape.

Suddenly I realized that the one thing the Nazis would not expect me to do was to walk downstairs to meet them. By taking off my glasses, slicking down my hair with water, grabbing a file folder from a vacant desk, and lighting a cigarette, I managed to change my appearance somewhat. Walking downstairs I came upon my secretary as she was being interrogated. I asked her what all the excitement was about. Her heart pounding, she managed to maintain an outward appearance of calm, and replied that the "gentlemen" were looking for Mr. Parizot. "Parizot?" I exclaimed, "But I just saw him a few minutes ago on the fourth floor!" The Gestapos rushed upstairs, giving me the break I needed to proceed towards my next obstacle, the guards at the front door. In the main lobby, the concierge informed me that there was another exit, and guided me to the garage, where I stole a bicycle and rode to safety.

—Robert Muller,
Most of All, They Taught Me Happiness

Your personal survival in harsh physical conditions and other emergencies involves more than simply applying the right techniques. A synergistic combination of skill, intuition, action, wisdom, good judgment, training, preparation, and the most important factor of all, the determination to survive, will give you the best chance for success. It pays to be both mentally and physically prepared for survival. The mentally prepared person has a "can do" attitude; she or he sees problems as obstacles to surmount, and has learned basic skills for dealing with survival situations. The common personality traits of survivors are just as useful for adapting and thriving under the changing conditions of modern society, as they are for dealing with emergencies. Physically prepared people have supplies on hand to deal with emergencies and have respected their bodies enough to maintain some kind of physical conditioning, thereby enabling their bodies to perform when needed.

SURVIVAL STRATEGIES

Twenty years ago, I nearly made a tragic mistake while trekking through the High Sierra Mountains during a severe snowstorm. I started this trip dressed in a wool sweater and a pair of pile pants. Heavy snow and high winds settled in about a half hour after leaving the trailhead. I was moving quickly, and my body temperature stayed pretty warm for most of the next hour. Initially, I delayed putting on additional clothing because I wanted to avoid overheating and consequently drenching my clothes with sweat. As I got wetter and colder, I delayed because I knew that as soon as I stopped moving and took my pack off my sweaty back, the icy winds would make me feel miserably cold. I was hoping for a break in the winds, but they only grew stronger. When I finally stopped to put my gloves and coat on, I realized that I had a serious problem. Even though my body core felt just a little cool, I was shocked to find that my hands had chilled to the point where they were numb and nearly useless. They felt like lumps of clay.

The winds had picked up to about 60 miles per hour, blasting snow onto my hands and face. I realized that it was absolutely critical that I get myself into protective clothing, but my fingers were unable to work the zippers, straps, and buckles on my pack. After 15 minutes, using my teeth and near useless hands, I managed to open my pack and remove my mittens and coat. During this time, I started to shiver violently, but I knew that if I gave up, I would lose my fingers to frostbite and might perish in the snow. I managed to slip my coat on, but it took another 10 minutes of warming my hands in my armpits before I could work my mittens over my fingers. I am an experienced mountaineer. It was very sobering to see how close I had come to disaster through procrastination and ignoring a few simple signs!

I committed two common blunders that nearly led to my demise. First, I *failed to react quickly to rapidly changing conditions*, and second, I *failed to conserve my resources*. In emergencies, it is often vitally important to *conserve what you have*. In my case, I failed to conserve body heat. In spite of the wind and snow, I was moving rapidly and felt that I was generating enough body heat from exercise, but I was wrong. Many people facing emergencies squander their resources in the first few hours. Expecting a speedy rescue, they thoughtlessly consume their available food and water supplies before the reality of their situation sets in. Wasted resources can also include fuel, physical energy, health, or dry clothing. It is often easier to conserve the resources at your immediate disposal than to find new ones.

The original 28 survivors of the 1972 airplane crash in the Andes Mountains (made famous by the book and the movie "Alive") also squandered their resources in the first few critical days of their epic struggle to survive. Expecting a speedy rescue, they freely ate and drank from the plane's supplies. Up until the third night, they failed to conserve precious heat and energy, allowing the icy winds to blow unchecked through the plane wreck. It was several days before they decided to ration food and water. Their food ran out on the tenth day, and after that some starved while others resorted to cannibalism.

Rex Lucas, in *Men in Crisis: A Study of a Mine Disaster*, relates similar wasteful actions in the first two days of a mining disaster. Trapped 12,000 feet underground in a major mine collapse and expecting a speedy rescue, the survivors freely drank from their canteens and wasted valuable physical reserves trying to dig themselves out. On the third day, once they realized that rescue might take many days, they began conservation efforts that allowed them to survive for several more days, until rescued.

Basic Strategies
FIRST THINGS FIRST

Quickly scan the situation. If you are in immediate bodily danger, you must deal with this first, and you might have to act with lightning speed. But, if you have the time, don't rush into a decision. In *Survive the Savage Sea*, Dougal Robertson credits his wife's quick thinking with saving his family's life. After whales rammed a large hole in their sailboat, Dougal wasted precious time examining the hole in their hull, but his wife used their remaining three minutes to gather the necessary survival gear into their life raft. Expect that there is some positive action that you can do, and be willing to consider *any* possible action or reaction that might promote your survival.

DON'T PANIC

Try to remain calm, but do not become paralyzed. Action will most likely be required to see you through your ordeal, but it must be the right kind of action. When you are unable to think clearly, it is a poor time to make major decisions. It is important not to waste precious energy and resources doing the wrong things or going to the wrong places. When you are tense and bound by fear, try breathing deeply and repeating a simple word or phrase, such as "stay calm" or "God is good." From many years of rock climbing experience, I have observed that when my breathing is shallow and tense, my muscles are also tense and I waste my energy by fighting one muscle against another. By consciously controlling my breathing, through forcing myself to breathe deeply, I can send a wave of energy and relaxation to my arms and legs, helping me to overcome the debilitating effects of fear.

CONSERVE WHAT YOU HAVE

Assuming that help will be along soon has been the downfall of many. Conservation includes body heat, dry clothing, water, food, fuel, medicine, and so on. Try to tap nature's resources for food and water before using your own reserves. Seek shelter *before* you are cold and wet.

BE REALISTIC

Rambo types are often the first to go. Use a healthy mix of positive attitude and determination to survive, tempered by realistic appraisal of pitfalls and dangers.

USE YOUR INTUITION

Intuitive hunches have been credited with saving many a person's life. That thought or picture that just happens to snap into your mind may be the key to your survival. I remember hearing a powerfully moving account of one woman's survival of the Nazi Holocaust:

> *On a hot summer's day, when she was a teenager in Germany, her father received a strong intuitive message. He told his daughter to wear her ski boots to school that day. Later in the morning, all the Jewish children were rounded up and forced into railroad cars. The following winter, she was marched, along with 800 other children, through heavy snows for several weeks. While many of the other children's feet froze solid, hers were protected by her ski boots. She was one of less than 100 survivors of the march through the snow.*

Compact Survival Kit

Be prepared. The following basic survival kit is small enough to slip into the top pocket of a knapsack or a coat pocket. It fits into a 2-ounce tobacco tin or other small case, and its weight is hardly noticeable. Polish the inside of the case to a mirror finish for signaling.

Check the contents of the case regularly, to replace items that have exceeded their shelf lives. Tape the box seams with duct tape to waterproof the container.

- **Matches.** Fire can be started by other means, but matches are the easiest. Waterproof matches are useful, but bulkier than ordinary stick matches. You can waterproof ordinary matches by dipping them in molten candle wax. Break large kitchen matches in half to save room for more matches. Include a striker torn from a book of paper matches.

- **Candle.** Great for helping to start a fire with damp wood, as well as for a light and heat source. Shave square to save space in your kit.

- **Flint-with-steel striker.** Flint will last long after your matches are used up. You must find very dry, fine tinder to start a fire with sparks from a flint. Solid magnesium fire-starter kits are an excellent improvement on the traditional flint-with-steel.

- **Magnifying glass.** Useful for starting a fire with direct sunlight or for finding splinters.

- **Needle and thread.** Choose several needles, including at least one with a very large eye, which can handle yarn, sinew, or heavy thread. Wrap with several feet of extra strong thread.

- **Fish hooks and line.** A selection of different hooks in a small tin or packet. Include several small split lead sinkers and as much fishing line as possible.

- **Compass.** A small luminous dial compass (for night reading). Make sure that you know how to read it and that the needle swings freely. A string is handy for hanging it around your neck for regular reference.

- **Micro flashlight.** A keychain LED (light emitting diode) type lamp, such as the Photon Microlight II. It is useful for reading a map at night or following a trail when there is no moon.

- **Brass wire.** 3 to 5 feet of lightweight brass wire. Wire is useful for making snares and repairing things.

- **Flexible saw.** These come with large rings for handles that can be removed to allow it to fit into your kit. While using the saw, insert sticks through the end loops for more useful and

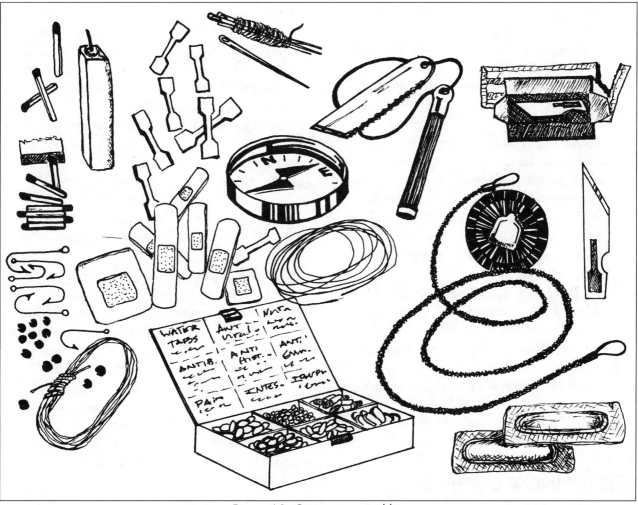

Figure 4-1. Compact survival kit.

comfortable handles. Coat with a film of grease or oil to protect from rust.

- **Survival knife.** For overnight backcountry travel, or as part of your car kit, I would also carry a stout knife with about a 6-inch blade. If the knife has a folding blade, it should have a heavy-duty blade lock. It should be strong enough to use as a pry and to split branches and cut hardwoods without damage. You may need a knife to fabricate crude tools, such as a bow-and-drill for starting a fire without matches. A variety of "survival" knives are available; they are capable of cutting various materials, including thin sheet metal, and will do nicely. If the knife has a fixed blade, it should be covered in a sheath that will not easily cut through. Some knives come with a small sharpening stone in the sheath, which is a nice feature.

- **Condom.** When placed in a sock or other cloth for protection and support, this makes a good emergency water bottle.

- **Compact medical kit.** Vary the contents depending upon your skill and needs. Pack medicines in airtight containers with cotton balls to prevent powdering and rattling. The following list, which is a rough guide, will cover most needs.

  - *Mild pain reliever.* Pack at least 10 of your favorite aspirin, ibuprofen, Tylenol, or other pain reliever.

  - *Diarrhea medicine.* Immodium is usually favored. Take 2 capsules initially, and then one each time a loose stool is passed.

  - *Antibiotic.* For general infections. People who are sensitive to penicillin can use tetracycline. Carry enough for a full course of 5 to 7 days. Use Echinacea or grapefruit seed extract from the health food store, if prescription antibiotics are not available.

- *Antihistamine.* For allergies, insect bites, and stings, use Benadryl or equivalent.
- *Water purification tablets.* Much lighter and more compact than a filter. For use when you can't boil your water.
- *Potassium permanganate.* Has several uses. Add to water and mix until water becomes bright pink to sterilize it, a deeper pink to make a topical antiseptic, and a full red to treat fungal diseases, such as athlete's foot.
- *Salt tablets.* Salt depletion can lead to muscle cramps and loss of energy. Carry 5 to 10 salt tablets.
- *Surgical blades.* At least two scalpel blades of different sizes. A handle can be made of wood, if required.
- *Butterfly sutures.* To hold edges of wounds together.
- *Band-Aids.* Assorted sizes, preferably waterproof, for covering minor wounds and keeping them clean. Can be cut to make butterfly sutures. (Adapted from Wiseman 1996, 16)

DEVELOPING A SURVIVOR PERSONALITY

The best survivors spend almost no time, especially in emergencies, getting upset about what has been lost, or feeling distressed about things going badly.... Life's best survivors can be both positive and negative, both optimistic and pessimistic at the same time.

—Al Siebert, Ph.D., *The Survivor Personality*

The struggle for survival is a fascinating and inspiring subject, forming the basis for many of the most memorable books and movies. Psychologist Al Siebert's personal fascination with survivors began when he received his military training from a group of veteran paratroopers. His teachers were legendary members of the 503rd Airborne Infantry Regiment. They had lost nine out of ten members in combat in the Korean War. Siebert found that these "survivors" were not the crusty, yelling drill sergeants that he had

anticipated. They were tough, yet showed patience. They had a good sense of humor and were likely to laugh at mistakes. They were positive, yet also looked at the downside of things. They didn't act mean or tough even though they could be as mean and tough as anyone. Siebert noticed that each of these men had a type of personal radar, which was always on "scan." He realized that it was not dumb luck that had brought these men through their ordeals, but a synergistic combination of qualities that tilted the odds in their favor. Al believes that we can all benefit in our daily lives by nurturing and developing these positive character traits within our own personalities.

Typical Survivor Personality Traits

- **Flexibility.** The No. 1 trait that many survivors attribute their success to is the ability to adapt to the situation.
- **Commitment to survive.** When conditions are extremely difficult, it takes a strong will and commitment to survive. Jewish Holocaust and Bataan Death March survivors tell tales of watching their friends lose the will to survive. Under these harsh conditions, once the drive to survive was lost, they usually lasted a short while, ranging from a few hours to a few days.
- **Playful curiosity.** Survivors usually like to know how things work. They show a playful curiosity that helps them adapt to changing circumstances.
- **Sense of humor.** The ability to laugh helps people manage under the worst conditions.

My father-in-law, Joseph Jussen, a Dutch resistance fighter and WWII hero, was captured and tortured by the Nazis for weeks before he was freed in a daring escape. Later, as a Dutch Marine in the Indonesian revolution, he survived while most of his company was killed. Throughout his life he maintained a great sense of humor and loved nothing more than to make people laugh. His favorite saying was, "Make you happy!"

- **A mixture of opposites.** The typical survivor is not always either hot or cold. Survivors have the ability to blend optimism with pessimism, so they can see the faults in a plan, but are not paralyzed by negativity. They combine humor with seriousness, self-confidence with a critical eye, and so on.

- **Intuition.** At some point in our lives, we have all had demonstrations of the power of intuition. The rational mind makes decisions based on the available information, which is always imperfect at best. Intuition appears to give us the ability to move beyond the limits of time and space, to "see around corners" that the rational mind can't breach.

- **"Get over it."** Most survivors don't waste a lot of time lamenting mistakes and losses. They move on and deal with the situation, unhampered by paralyzing regrets and disappointments.

- **"Bad patients."** Bernie Siegal, founder of Exceptional Cancer Patients, observed that survivors who beat the odds against cancer and other life-threatening diseases were usually "bad patients." These patients typically questioned their doctors and took an active role in their recovery, whereas "good patients" did just as they were told, questioned very little, and often died right on schedule.

Intuition: A Survivor's Powerful Ally

The intuitive mind is a sacred gift and the rational mind is a faithful servant. We have created a society that honors the servant and has forgotten the gift.

—Albert Einstein

When my boss Jim was the engineering manager of a well-known high-tech electronics manufacturer, he told me this story: Jim and his friend were on their way to Lake Tahoe for a weekend of skiing. It was snowing heavily and Jim's friend was driving. Due to an accident, traffic on the freeway had come to a stop. For a few minutes, Jim's friend pulled up behind the stopped traffic, then he said, "I've got a bad feeling about this." He backed his car up for a several feet and pulled to the side in the breakdown lane. Two minutes later, a car came speeding down the freeway and plowed into the stopped traffic, wrecking about twenty cars and injuring many people. Had Jim's friend not listened to his intuitive guidance, he and Jim would very likely have been among the injured.

Intuition is a powerful ally, especially in dangerous situations. The rational mind is limited by the information at hand, but intuition appears to have the ability to see into the unknown. I'm sure that nearly all of us can remember times when we received strong intuitive guidance about something. If we listened to that guidance, we usually found that we were glad we did. If we didn't listen to the guidance, we usually got "burned" in some kind of painful life lesson.

The difficulty in dealing with intuitive messages is to distinguish between the different inner voices. Which is speaking? Is it the voice of fear, ego, fantasy, or true inner guidance and wisdom? Many times I have allowed my strong rational mind to overrule my inner messages, only to later regret having listened to this mind that thinks it always knows best! In recent years, increasing numbers of businesspeople have found that developing their intuition gives them an extra advantage in today's tough business environment. The authors of both suggested references on intuition (see the end of this chapter) teach high-priced seminars to Fortune 500 business leaders to help them develop their intuitive business skills. You can learn and develop these skills on your own, using the exercises in their books. In addition to boosting your chances of success in emergencies and survival situations, these skills can help you deal more effectively with everyday decision making.

TESTING YOUR INTUITION

My mother-in-law, Jackie Jussen, told me the following story: Orphaned at the age of five, Jackie was raised by her grandmother on a remote coffee plantation on the island of Java, Indonesia. Living far from any sizable community, her grandmother relied on natural herbal medicines. When a neighbor's son was deathly ill with malaria, Jackie's grandmother used her herbs to nurse him back to health. The neighbor was a Japanese immigrant and presented her with the gift of a kimono, which bore the seal of a powerful Japanese family.

Years later, during the World War II Japanese occupation of Java, civilians were forbidden to listen to the radio. All radios were registered with the state and fitted with official seals to indicate whether the radio had been used. Jackie's grandmother broke the seal on her radio so she could hear foreign news. When officials discovered the broken seal, she was ordered to appear in court. To maintain order and obedience, Japanese wartime justice was typically cruel and swift. Infractions, such as breaking the seal on the radio, usually resulted in a public beheading in the square immediately after sentencing. As her grandmother prepared to leave for the court hearing, an inner voice told her to wear the kimono. When the magistrate saw the seal of a royal family on her kimono, he asked her how she had come to own this kimono. Upon hearing her story, he reprimanded her, but spared her life.

I use the following technique for intuitively "testing" the outcome of a potential action. First, take several deep, slow breaths to calm your mind and alter your consciousness. As you do this, offer a simple prayer asking for guidance.

Once you feel that you have calmed and quieted the rational mind, make a mental picture of the potential action, path, or decision. Check for physical reactions in your stomach area. If you have an expanded, relaxed feeling, your pictured action is probably a good path to follow. If you get a clenched, tight feeling in your gut, it's probably a good idea to avoid the pictured action. If you get nothing, either the choice is unimportant, or you simply are not intuitively in touch with it.

WATER

Requirements

Water is essential for survival. Most of us could live for weeks without food, but only about three days without water. The typical adult requires two quarts of drinking water per day under normal conditions and one to two gallons per day in hot-weather conditions. Usually one gallon per adult per day is enough for drinking and some limited washing.

Recommended Emergency Measures

- Any surface water in the United States may be contaminated, and should be boiled or otherwise purified prior to drinking.
- Boil water for at least 1 minute at a rolling boil at sea level. Due to lower boiling temperatures at higher altitudes, boil for at least 3 minutes at altitudes above 6,000 feet.
- Floods and earthquakes often contaminate public water systems. When in doubt, boil or otherwise purify tap water, until authorities say the water is fit for drinking.
- If warned of an impending crisis, store water in as many containers as possible, including sinks and bathtubs.
- Hot water heaters and your home's piping are good sources of stored water. Turn off the gas or electricity to your hot water heater prior to draining it. If the water contains sediment, do not discard it, but allow the sediment to settle. To drain household piping, turn on the uppermost faucet slightly, to release suction in the system, and drain from the lowermost faucet (or other plumbing connection).
- Your body needs water to digest food. If you have little or no water, limit your food intake to the bare minimum.

Dehydration

Avoid dehydration because it will sap your body strength, but ration your water usage if you have a limited supply. Signs of dehydration include thirst, fatigue, dizziness, dry mouth, headache, loss of appetite, dark-colored urine, and sleepiness. If you need physical energy to deal with your situation, you must do your best to find and conserve water.

Conserving Water

- If traveling in hot country, stay in the shade as much as possible. Avoid midday travel. Travel at night, if possible.
- Wear loose clothing because it will provide an insulating layer of air, which will help to reduce evaporative water losses by maintaining high humidity close to the skin.
- *Do not go shirtless!* It will feel cooler, but you will lose more water through evaporation and may sunburn. Severe sunburn can lead to a toxic condition, known as "sun poisoning."

- Move slowly and avoid overexertion. Try to breathe through the nose—you will lose less water than by breathing through the mouth.
- Drink in small sips, not big gulps.
- Sucking on a small pebble, twig, or blade of grass can help generate saliva and minimize the discomfort of thirst.
- The human body seeks to maintain a certain level of humidity at the skin surface. In cold dry climates, this results in the daily loss of significant amounts of water, since the body is slowly pumping water into the air at all times. Mountaineers often use "vapor barriers" to minimize water consumption and the use of fuel to melt snow for water. Vapor barriers are created by wearing waterproof clothing and using plastic bags as inner sock liners. In subfreezing temperatures, and especially when using down sleeping bags, the use of a vapor barrier sleeping bag liner helps to prevent the daily loss of the sleeping bag's insulating value due to the condensation of perspiration into its outer layers.
- Do not waste potable water to cool yourself or wash clothing. Wash in untreated water, if available and not polluted. You can spread clothes out in direct sunlight to deodorize and disinfect, at least to some degree.

For more information on finding, storing, and treating water, see Chapter 5.

FIRE

Your ability to start a fire is important for staying warm in cold climates, for cooking food, and for sterilizing water. I'll start with simple instructions on building a campfire with matches and paper, and then proceed through the more spartan methods, ending with the difficult process of starting a fire by rubbing two sticks together.

Starting a Fire with Matches
MATERIALS

I like to separate my materials into piles by size. Start by gathering with a couple handfuls of tinder, about a third of a shopping bag's worth of kindling, at least a half shopping bag's worth of small sticks (½ to 2 inches thick), and at least a shopping bag's worth of thicker wood (2 to 12 inches thick).

TINDER

Any kind of material that takes very little heat to start it on fire can be used for tinder. Paper makes great tinder, if you have matches. If you don't have matches and are attempting to build a fire with a spark (see *Starting a Fire with Flint and Steel*, below), you will need extra-fine dry tinder. Dry pine needles, fine dry grasses, shredded paper, birch bark, dried moss, bird down, mouse nests, cotton balls, wood shavings, pulverized dry pinecones, and fibrous inner cedar bark make good tinder.

KINDLING

Kindling must catch on fire within a few seconds from burning tinder, yet burns for only a few minutes to ignite the larger pieces of wood. Dry pine needles, still stuck to branches, are perfect. Small twigs, ⅛ to ¼ inch thick, are also excellent. Test the sticks to see if they are dry or wet. If the sticks can be bent and twisted without snapping, they are wet and will not do for kindling. If all available kindling is wet, you can still burn green pine needles or else you must find standing wood, which can be split with an axe, or shaved down to find a dry core. You can make "feather sticks" for kindling from larger sticks of wood by carving many shallow cuts with a knife to create fine curved shavings protruding from the side of the sticks.

POSITIONING THE FIRE

Build your fire in a protected spot, especially if the area is windy. If it is exceptionally windy, you may have to dig a trench for your fire or build it on the leeward side of a fallen tree or large rock. If the ground is swampy or the snow is deep, you may have to build your fire on a platform of green logs covered by dirt.

> **CAUTION: Do not use stones from a riverbed or porous stones around or under a fire. These stones can explode when heated due to internal steam pockets.**

BUILDING THE FIRE

If you have paper, crumple a couple sheets, build a small pile of fine kindling on top of the paper, then light the paper in several places. If you don't have paper, use two handfuls of extremely fine, dry tinder instead. Make sure you don't smother the tiny flames of the beginning fire with a pile that's too big or too tightly packed, or by stacking larger wood too quickly onto the fire. As the kindling catches on fire, pile on more kindling and gradually add thicker chunks of wood. Make sure the fire gets enough air circulating through it. Either build your fire in a crisscross

Figure 4-2. Crisscross- and tipi-style fires.

fashion or lean the wood against itself in a tipi-like cone shape, to ensure that there are plenty of gaps between the wood for air circulation. A well-built fire, with dry wood and plenty of gaps for air circulation, will not smoke much.

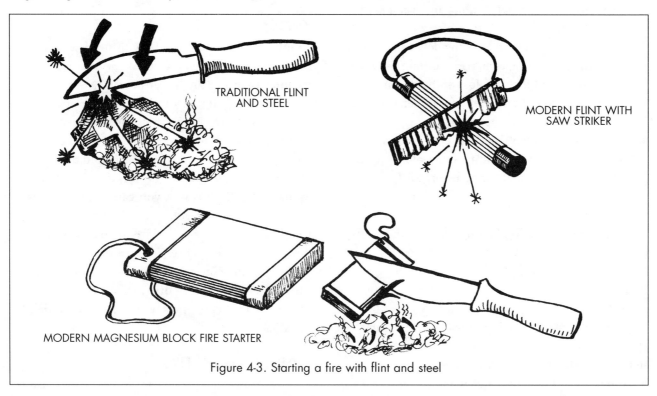

TRADITIONAL FLINT AND STEEL

MODERN FLINT WITH SAW STRIKER

MODERN MAGNESIUM BLOCK FIRE STARTER

Figure 4-3. Starting a fire with flint and steel

Starting a Fire with Flint and Steel

Flint is a naturally occurring stone that yields heavy sparks when struck by a knife or other sharp stones. Artificial flints do the same thing and may come with a saw striker, which creates lots of good sparks. Starting a fire with the spark from the flint requires patience, shelter from wind, and very fine, dry tinder. Strike sparks into your tinder and gently blow on a spark resting in the tinder until it grows

into flames. Continue building your fire following the previous set of instructions. A modern improvement on the flint and steel is a commercial magnesium block with a flint. Using a knife, shave a pile of fine magnesium filings from the side of the block. When struck by a spark from a flint, magnesium filings rapidly burst into a hot flame, easily igniting kindling or tinder.

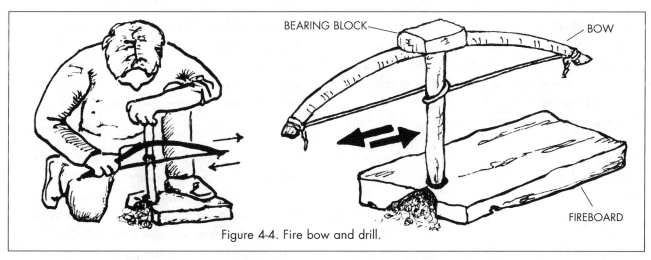

Figure 4-4. Fire bow and drill.

Starting a Fire with Bow and Drill

A fire can be started by rapidly spinning a wooden "drill"—under pressure—against a notch in a board, until enough heat is generated to create a small coal, which is dropped into tinder and fanned into fire. This is not easy, but it's about a hundred times easier than starting a fire with a hand-spun stick.

BOW

Use any stick, preferably curved, and roughly ½ to ¾ inches thick by 30 inches long. With your knife, make a shallow groove around each end, about an inch from the ends, to make a spot to tie your bowstring. Use a hefty, strong string or leather thong (not rope) to tie the bow. Braided leather thongs or ⅛- to ¼-inch nylon cord work well as bow string. Typically, plant fiber cordage must be doubled back on itself and corded a second time to make it strong enough for the bowstring on a fire drill bow. The string may stretch as you work the bow. Tie the bowstring with a little slack to allow for the string to wrap around the drill. Experiment with different string tensions and with using your fingers to tweak the string for more or less tension while using the bow.

DRILL

Usually the drill and the fireboard will be made from the same material, though the choice of wood for the fireboard (also known as hearthboard) is most critical. For a fire drill and hearthboard to make fire, they must be very dry and they must generate an extremely fine powder when spun together. Try to pick freestanding wood with the bark weathered away, as wood lying on the ground usually picks up ground moisture. If your pieces of wood generate coarse, gritty wood shavings, you should find yourself another chunk of wood. The best woods are usually softwoods that are not very resinous. Resins such as those found in most pines, spruce, and firs tend to act like a grease, making it difficult or impossible to get enough friction going to make fire. Some recommended varieties of wood are cottonwood, aspen, sagebrush, yucca, birch, and poplar. Other woods that work, but not as easily, include box elder, elderberry, and willow.

NOTE: Even pieces of the recommended varieties will not work well if they are moist or resinous or generate coarse shavings.

The drill should be about ½ to ¾ inches in diameter and about 6 to 10 inches long. The wood should dent somewhat under your thumbnail, being neither too hard nor extremely soft. Round the drill end for the fireboard and trim the corners of the drill end for the bearing block at about 45 degrees.

FIREBOARD

The exact dimensions of the fireboard are not important but, like the drill, the type and condition of the wood are critical. The fireboard should be long enough to steady with your foot and significantly wider than the drill; about 1½ to 2 inches wide by a couple feet long works well. In a real-life situation, you will use a fireboard many times, until its entire length has been used up. Using your knife, split an appropriate branch for fabricating your fireboard. Shave down the round side until it's about ½ inch thick, and then square up the sides. By rotating your knife tip, make a shallow depression in the fireboard just over one-half the diameter of the drill from the board edge. This depression must hold the drill as it spins. Cut a narrow V notch from the edge of the board to the center of the depression you just gouged into the fireboard. This V notch will collect bits of wood shavings, which eventually smolder as you work the drill.

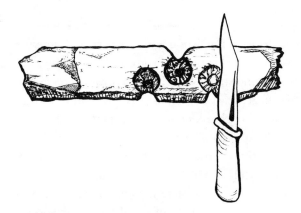

Figure 4-5. The fireboard.

BEARING BLOCK

You can use many different materials for the bearing block. The main requirements are that the materials be hard and slippery. A 1-ounce shot glass, a smooth stone with a depression, a chunk of bone, a knot of resinous softwood, or a knot of hardwood works well. Make a shallow hole in the bearing block to capture the end of the drill. If it's made of wood, a little ChapStick, some Crisco, or animal fat will help to lubricate the bearing block. Make sure you don't contaminate the fireboard end of your drill with the lubricant.

TINDER

Almost any dry, fibrous material will work for tinder. The inner bark of cedar is great, and cottonwood works well as do many dried grasses. Roll these around between your fingers, until they are shredded fine like a cotton ball. Make a small bird's nest out of your tinder, with a depression in the middle to catch the glowing ember. Set it to the side

on a piece of bark, so you can carry it when it bursts into flame, without burning your hands. Make sure that you have kindling and dry wood ready too. Unlike matches, a second chance with a bow drill involves considerable effort.

PROCEDURE

Place a piece of bark under the fireboard notch to catch the ember and to insulate it from the ground. Wrap the bowstring a single full loop around the drill. Kneel down with one foot firmly standing on top of the fireboard next to the V notch. Get comfortable because this will probably take several minutes. Apply pressure with the bearing block and start rotating the drill with a full back-and-forth stroke of the bow. Very little will happen until the drill seats itself into the cavity on the fireboard; at that point it will develop considerably more friction and start to smolder. Once the spark inside the dust pile is clearly smoldering, relax and lift the spark on its bark bed, dumping the spark into your bird's nest of tinder. Blow on the spark until the tinder bursts into flame. Congratulations, you have made fire!

Starting a Fire with a Hand Drill

This is tough, but doable. Prepare the tinder, kindling, and fireboard as above. The fireboard should be a little thinner, perhaps as thin as ¼ inch. The drill should be about ¼ inch in diameter and about 30 inches long. Dried cattails are a favored drill material. Persistence, tough hands, and lots of rapid drilling with steady downward pressure are the keys to success. Use the full length of your hands and apply downward pressure as you spin the drill between your hands. Some people are able to flutter their hands up the drill, while maintaining the drill spin, to prevent it from cooling down as they shift their hands to the top of the drill to begin another round of downward pressure spins. If you find that you must stop drilling to shift your hands, do so as quickly as possible to minimize cooling. Thumb loops of string or a leather thong attached to the top of the hand drill can help you start a fire faster by applying steady downward pressure as you spin the drill.

OPTIONAL FINGER LOOPS
FOR INCREASED
DOWNWARD PRESSURE

Figure 4-6. Using a hand fire drill.

Starting a Fire with a Fire Plough

Cut a lengthwise shallow groove in an 18-inch fire-board made from soft, nonresinous wood, at least 1½ inches wide. Prepare your tinder and kindling in the same way as for starting a fire with a bow drill. Using a hardwood or other nonresinous stick, drive the stick back and forth under considerable pressure to generate friction, sawdust, and eventually a spark.

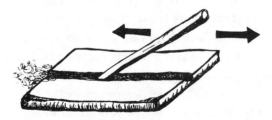

Figure 4-7. Using a fire plough to start a fire.

FOOD

Most people can live for weeks without food, but long-term survival depends upon finding and preparing a variety of foods. If you lived in the middle of a rabbit paradise, or trout heaven, you would eventually starve to death if you just ate either rabbit or trout, since they wouldn't provide you with all the vitamins and minerals necessary for long-term sustenance. This section gives you some basic guidelines and suggestions. See Chapter 6 for more information. If you are stuck without food for extended periods, intestinal cleansing will help you to feel better and to work at a surprising level of functionality. For more information on this subject, see the section on fasting in Chapter 9.

I heard this story from a man who taught survival classes in Arizona. He talked about the experience of a group of college-aged men and women taking part in a wilderness survival class in which they had to forage and hunt for all of their food and water for three days, using their bare hands or what simple tools they could fabricate from found materials. He said that their experience was pretty typical of what most participants experience in their classes. On the first day, the group divided into men and women. They each discussed their game plan. The men's group decided to focus on hunting and trapping to find their daily food, while the women's group chose to pursue foraging for their sustenance. After the first day, none of the men had been successful at hunting or fishing for food, while the women had found a few berries and edible roots. Both groups chose to continue with their individual game plans. By the morning of the third day, the men's group had not managed to kill a single animal for food and hungrily shared the roots and other edible plants that the women's group had to offer them.

Basic Guidelines

- Don't spend more energy looking for food than you get from food.
- Avoid scurvy, caused by vitamin C deficiency. Scurvy is characterized by swollen or bleeding gums, followed by weakness and bruises or wounds that won't heal. For a natural source of vitamin C, chew on wild rose hips or green pine needles (or make a tea out of them). The bright green, fresh pine needle tips are the most palatable. Vitamin C plays an important role in the immune system and is a natural detoxifier.
- If you are dehydrated, do not eat unless the food contains a significant amount of water. Water is required to digest and metabolize food. Eating dry food when severely dehydrated will not give you energy, but will make the dehydration worse.

- In most locations, there will be some kind of vegetation that you can eat to sustain yourself. The trick is to identify and prepare the local edible vegetation.
- Trim moldy areas off food before eating. My mom used to say, "It's just penicillin," but don't you believe it! Molds manufacture aflatoxins, which are extremely toxic substances.

Plants

I highly recommend that you pick up a field guide to edible plants in your area (see *References*). A brief guide to 20 common edible plants is included in Chapter 6.

Edibility is the first consideration when foraging. There are many thousands of edible plants in North America. Since you can't always be sure that you have a field guide in your back pocket, the following test can be used to determine the edibility of unknown plants. Only one person should test each plant. If stomach problems arise, drink lots of hot water for relief. If necessary, induce vomiting by sticking your finger down your throat or swallowing some charcoal.

> **CAUTION: Do not assume that a plant is safe to eat because birds, insects, or animals have eaten it. Many plants that are poisonous for humans serve as food sources for certain animals, birds, or insects.**

EDIBILITY TEST

- *Don't skip a step—go slow and be thorough.*
- Do not use the edibility test for mushrooms. Mushrooms must be positively identified. Improperly identified mushrooms may taste fine but prove deadly in small amounts.
- Do not eat plants with milky sap, except for dandelions.

1. **Smell.** Crush some of the plant. If it smells like almonds or peaches, it probably contains the common plant poison *hydrocyanic acid*. Reject plants with this smell.
2. **Skin irritation.** Crush a small portion and rub some of the juice onto the skin of a sensitive area, such as the inside of your arm or thigh. If you experience any discomfort, rash, swelling, or burning sensations, reject this plant. Oxalic acid, a common plant poison, can be recognized by the sharp dry stinging or burning feeling it leaves on the skin or tongue.
3. **Mouth test.** If the test plant passed the skin test, cautiously proceed with the mouth test. At the first sign of burning, irritation, swelling, stomach ache, nausea, dizziness, or other ill effects, spit it out and reject this plant. First, crush a little bit of the plant and place a small amount on the lips for at least 10 seconds. Next, place a pea-sized portion in a corner of the mouth for 10 more seconds. Move this portion to the tip of the tongue for another 10 seconds. Hold it under the tongue for 10 more seconds. Chew and then hold in the mouth for about 15 minutes total. Spit it out, and then wait for 5 hours.
4. **First swallow test.** If there are no ill effects after 5 hours, chew and swallow one teaspoon-sized bite. Wait 10 hours, drinking and eating nothing else during this period.
5. **Second swallow test.** Eat about ⅓ cup of this plant. Wait 24 hours. If there are no ill effects, consider this plant edible. When in doubt, *go slow!*

TREE BARK

Animals and starving people have survived through the winter months solely by eating the inner live layer of tree bark (cambium layer). You can eat it raw, cook it like spaghetti, or dry and grind it into flour. It can be added to stews for nutrition and to give the stew some body. Peel off a large section of tree bark, keeping the extra for later use. Do not cut bark from more than halfway around the tree, or you might kill it. The light-colored layer of inner bark is the edible portion; sometimes it has a green hue. The more edible barks are aspens, birch willows, slippery elm, tamarack, maples, spruces, pines, and hemlocks. The buds and shoots of these trees are also edible, except for tamarack and hemlock, which are poisonous.

> **CAUTION: All parts of the plant known as hemlock are extremely poisonous, even though it looks very inviting and similar to wild celery.**

The young shoots can look quite a bit like carrot tops. This is not the same plant as the hemlock tree. All contact with the poisonous hemlock plant should be avoided!

GRASSES

Grasses are edible. The best parts to eat are the soft white stems just below the surface of the ground. Make sure it's really grass that you are eating, and do not eat grass that has been sprayed. Some grasses and other plants have tiny hooks on their stems and leaf edges that will irritate the digestive tract and should be avoided.

SEEDS AND GRAINS

All grass seeds are edible, but some other seeds are poisonous. Use the edibility test on unknown seeds. Tasting will do you no harm, but do not swallow any seed that is bitter, burning, or otherwise unpalatable.

CAUTION: Discard all grains from clusters that are blackened or carry black, enlarged bean-like grains. These grains are infected with ergot mold, a powerfully toxic substance.

ROOTS AND TUBERS

The starch granules in most roots and tubers are insoluble in cold water. Most edible roots and tubers should be cooked, since cooking ruptures the starch granules and makes them more digestible.

SEAWEED

Most sea vegetables are edible, except for some thin thread-like seaweeds. Collect seaweed from below the high-water line, and do not eat if from polluted waters. It is rich in vitamins and minerals, but many varieties have a strong fishy taste. Soak in fresh water to remove salt and improve the taste. Eat seaweed raw or cooked into soups and stews, or dry it for later use. Fresh seaweed spoils quickly.

Insects, Grubs, and Worms

Insects can be a valuable source of necessary protein in emergency situations. Pound for pound they have more food value than vegetables and are usually much easier to hunt and gather than mammals. Since they may contain harmful parasites, insects should be cooked before eating. Boiling is the safest method, but roasting in hot coals or on a hot rock will suffice if no pots are available. To make them more palatable, you can chop them finely, or dry and grind them up before adding to soups or stews. Some varieties of grubs can taste like cheese or sweets and are considered delicacies in certain parts of the world. Look for grubs in rotting stumps or under peeling tree bark.

CAUTION: Brightly colored insects, including their caterpillars, are usually poisonous.

ANTS

Most ants have a stinging bite containing formic acid, which is quite bitter and odorous. Cook these ants for at least six minutes to destroy this poison.

CATERPILLARS

If hairy, you can squeeze to remove head and guts. Discard the head and hairy outside. Eat the guts.

GRASSHOPPERS, CRICKETS, AND CICADAS

Remove the head, wings, and legs before roasting or boiling. The legs have fine barbs, which will irritate your stomach. Gather in the morning, when they are cold or sluggish, or trap them by laying out a wool blanket at night in a meadow. Barbs on their legs will catch in the wool, like burrs stuck to a sweater.

WORMS

An excellent source of food for robins and humans. Starve them for a day, or squeeze them to get the dirt out of their bellies. Try drying them and grinding to a powder to make them more palatable.

SLUGS AND SNAILS

Avoid sea snails and any snails with bright shells, especially tropical ones (possibly poisonous). Starve them for a few days to remove any toxins from the food they have been eating.

SHELTER

In severe climates, some kind of fabricated shelter from the elements will be essential for your survival. In more moderate climates, a shelter may not be necessary, but can make your daily life a lot more pleasant and comfortable. This section will cover several rudimentary shelters that you can build from foraged materials. See Chapter 7 for more elaborate, permanent structures. A good shelter can keep you dry and warm, even in torrential rains or subfreezing weather.

Location

- **Water.** Try to locate your shelter near a good water supply, but above high-water marks and never in a dry stream bed or wash. Stay at least 30 yards from your water source to avoid polluting it. If insects are a problem, stay away from stagnant water, especially wet, boggy areas.
- **Building materials and fuel.** Choose a location where you can find building materials and fuel nearby so you are not hauling them a long way.
- **Visibility.** If you are seeking rescue, make sure you are visible and not too near a noisy river that might obscure the sounds of rescuers approaching.
- **Natural shelter.** Utilize natural bluffs, fallen trees, caves, ridges, and so on for protection from the wind and rain.
- **Comfort.** The site should be flat enough and smooth enough for comfortable sleeping. Before pitching a tent, it's a good idea to lie on the ground first to see how the spot feels.
- **Drainage.** Make sure that the site will drain. Avoid hollows that can turn into ponds in the rain. Trenches can help to divert small streams in a downpour, but you can't move a pond.
- **What to avoid.** Don't try to build a shelter on hard, rocky ground. Check the area for stinging ants, bee nests, and so on, and avoid high-wind areas, such as hilltops and ridge tops (unless you want high winds to keep insects away). Avoid areas with danger of falling rocks or large dead branches from overhead trees. Valley bottoms and hollows can collect cold, frosty air at night.

Squirrel's Nest

This is the simplest of survival shelters. It's a drag to get in and out of, so you should really make something else if you will be using it more than once. The basic idea is to heap as much dry debris as you can into a pile, and then crawl into it to stay dry and warm. Use leaves, pine boughs, bark, and so on. The debris is your sleeping bag, so the thicker it is the warmer you will be. To insulate yourself from the ground, make sure you have an insulating layer under you as well as on top. Without a poncho or tarp on top, it won't be very effective at keeping you dry in a rainstorm.

Building on Fallen Trunks and Trees

It is usually easier to start a primitive shelter from an existing feature. A fallen trunk makes an excellent support for a simple lean to. Shingling is an important part of primitive structures, and can be made from any materials that will keep rain from penetrating your shelter. Shingling can consist of thatch, bark, sod, or sticks and dirt. The basic idea is to make enough layers of sloped materials so that water runs down the outside without penetrating the structure and getting you wet.

Figure 4-8. Fallen log shelter.

Scout Pits and Coal Beds

It takes considerable effort, but you can spend a comfortable warm night in a "scout pit," even when it's very cold outside. First, dig a trench about 2 feet deep by 2 feet wide and a few feet longer than your body length. Build a fire in the trench that covers the entire length. After it has roasted the ground for an hour or two, cover the coals with several inches of dirt. Bridge the top of the trench widthwise with a layer of sticks and cover with leaves for insulation, finishing with a layer of dirt. Crawl in and enjoy the warmth of the heated ground. If the trench is big enough, you can use it a second time by heating rocks in an outside fire and dragging them in at night to heat your scout pit. One alternative is to build a fire in a shallower trench, 6 to 12 inches deep. When the fire is down to coals, cover the coals with a few inches of dirt, followed by debris insulation. You can pull some of this insulation over you for a preheated squirrels nest shelter. If you have a tarp, place it underneath your body, to act as a vapor barrier for protection from ground moisture due to steam rising from the heated earth.

Figure 4-9a. Scout pit.

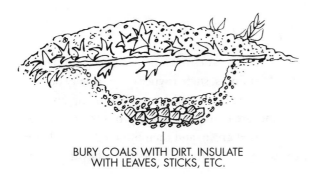

BURY COALS WITH DIRT. INSULATE WITH LEAVES, STICKS, ETC.

Figure 4-9b. Scout pit construction.

Snow Shelters

Snow is a good insulator and can protect you from fierce winds and bitter cold. If your clothing is cotton, or otherwise poorly designed for snow country, beware of getting yourself wet while constructing your snow shelter. Unless you are traveling in the arctic, with wind-packed snow and little contour to the land, you will probably be better off constructing a snow cave or a shelter under the boughs of a tree than trying to construct a traditional igloo. Create a raised platform for sleeping on, with a lower area to collect the coldest air.

> ***CAUTION: You must provide ventilation in snow shelters. Your body heat will eventually raise***

the inside temperature above freezing to the point where it glazes over the inside of a snow cave. You can suffocate without a hole for ventilation (I suggest a fist-sized hole).

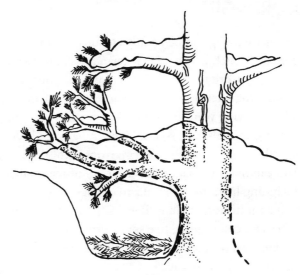

Figure 4-10. Tree-well snow shelter.

If you can't find a firm snowdrift or a suitable tree well for your snow cave, you can pile soft snow into a heap, trample it some, and let it firm up for a couple hours before digging it out to make a snow cave. Make sure that you carve the ceiling into a curved dome shape to prevent sagging and collapse of the ceiling.

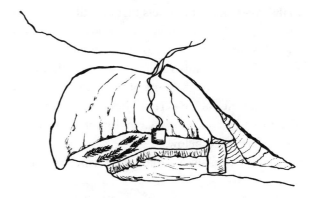

Figure 4-11. Snow cave.

EMERGENCY SNOW SHOES

Boughs of flexible spruce branches with a healthy supply of green needles will suffice for snowshoes in an emergency. Use string or green branches to tie boughs to your feet. Weaving a second or third branch into the boughs ties individual branches together for better flotation and more stability.

CORDAGE

Primitive living can be greatly enhanced with cordage, which is just a fancy term for string, twine, and rope. Cordage is handy for thatching your roof, lashing together branches for your shelter, stringing a bow, sewing your garments, making nets for fish, snaring animals, and so on. Many indigenous societies have been literally held together with string. You can make cordage from a variety of materials, including hair, fur, hides, narrow strips of cloth, and a multitude of plant fibers. Of the recommended references on primitive skills, *Primitive Technology: A Book of Earth Skills* has the best information on cordage.

Recommended Plant Fibers

For many thousands of years, native peoples have gathered and spun plant fibers from thousands of different plants. Their cords have made ropes strong enough to hold elephants and carry suspension bridges across hundred-foot-wide gorges in the Himalayas. Archaeologists have discovered 10,000-year-old fishing nets that are still intact. Any strong flexible plant can make cordage. The following list is for starters, but use the "fiber test" to ensure that the plants you are working with are adequate for cordage. Some of the plants on the list can work well only at certain times of the year or under certain conditions. Common plant fiber sources are listed below.

- **Leaf fibers:** Yucca, cattail, reeds, iris, agave, and palmetto.
- **Dry outer bark:** Bulrush, sage, willow, and cattail.
- **Wet inner bark:** Aspen, cottonwood, sage, juniper, willow, cedar, mesquite, walnut, cherry, slippery elm, and hawthorn.
- **Bast fibers:** Soft fibers located between the outer bark and a woody stem on many common weeds, such as dogbane, milkweed, hemp, stinging nettle, evening primrose, flax, fireweed,

hollyhock, and wild licorice. Dogbane is commonly acknowledged as one of the best fibers for cordage.
- **Roots:** Spruces, poplar, lupines.
- **Whole plants:** Rushes, cattail, sedge, and various grasses (most grasses are weak when dry).

Fiber Test

- Tie a knot in a small bundle of fibers to check for flexibility. If it breaks, the fibers are too brittle.
- Spin a small length of twine. Pull on the twine to check for strength. Good fibers for cordage grip together when spun tightly, but fibers that are too slippery and smooth will not hold together.
- Remember that some fibers are stronger wet, while some are better dry. You may be able to make adequate cordage for a fire drill from green grasses that break once the grasses dry.

Preparing Fibers

Different fiber types must be prepared in different ways. Leaf fibers, such as yucca, are usually best harvested green. Bast fibers, such as hemp and dogbane, are best processed dry, but the plants can be harvested green, and then bundled to dry before processing (allow for ventilation so they don't rot).

BAST FIBERS

Start by trying to scrape off the papery outer bark with a knife held perpendicular to the stalk (if the plant is dry and the outer bark is cracked, skip this step). Buff the stalks over your pant leg to remove what's left of the outer bark. Use a smooth rock or a wooden mallet/chunk to gently crack/split the stalks, without cutting the fibers. You are trying to split the fiber sheath and remove it from the woody core. Using your fingers, bend the fibers and peel out sections of the woody core. Roll the fibers back and forth between the palms of your hands to separate the fibers and clean the remaining bits of bark and woody core out of the fiber bundle. Chunks of this stuff will weaken your cordage and leave it messy looking.

YUCCA AND AGAVE

These and other similar tough leaf fibers are usually processed most easily when green or after they have been soaked for a while. Yucca and agave make very strong cordage and can be used to make packs, sandals, and more. Generally the long leaves need to be pounded to split the fibers from the fleshy parts. Soaking the pounded leaves can remove alkaloids, which can be irritating to the skin. Use a knife or the smooth edge of a stone to scrape the fleshy parts from the fibers. Roll the fibers between the palms of your hands to further clean and separate the fibers.

RETTING

Some plant and bark fibers are most easily processed through "retting"—soaking and letting them partially rot to facilitate separating the fibers and/or their substrates. Retting might take as short a time as one or two days, but can also take as long as two weeks. The retting process uses bacteria in the water to eat away the fleshy binders that hold the fibers together.

Spinning Fibers into Cord

In general, more twists per inch make for stronger and stiffer cordage. For ease of handling, most hand cordage is spun from two strands of fibers at a time, but you can spin from three or more, if you wish. You can spin cords into ropes by the identical process, or you can "plait" (braid) three strands into rope. Since hand twisting makes for the tightest, cleanest, strongest cordage, it is best for things like bowstring, where performance is critical. Leg rolling is faster, but not as tight, so primitive cordage that requires a high volume of spun materials, such as rope and netting, is usually made by leg rolling.

1. **Start.** Tie the end of your fiber bundle in a knot and split the bundle into two roughly equal bundles. Alternately roll both ends of the bundle between your thumb and forefingers until it kinks in the middle.
2. **Spin.** Slip the knotted end over something to hold it or bite the kink in the center of the fiber bundle to hold it in your teeth. Spin two strands of fibers tightly, both in the same direction—either clockwise or counterclockwise.

3. **Spin and twist.** Now twist both of your spun fiber bundles into cord. The direction of twist is critical. Twist the fiber bundles in the *opposite* direction from the way each bundle was spun. Good tension, tight spinning, and the proper directions of spin and twist are what hold the fibers in cordage.
4. **Repeat.** Keep working your way down a few inches of cord at a time. Splice fibers in as you need them.

Figure 4-12. Twisting fibers to make two-ply cordage.

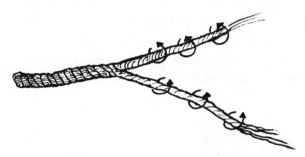

Figure 4-13. Braiding cordage into ropes.

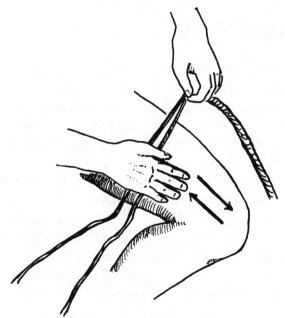

Figure 4-14. Leg rolling cordage.

Splicing

Unless you are making short cords from a long bundle of fiber, you will need to add fibers by splicing. It's best to blend splices in by staggering and thinning the fiber ends in the splice and the ends of the cord bundle so that they blend together well. Unravel the ends of the cordage until the fibers are roughly parallel, and then place the splice bundle next to the cordage ends. Twisting the fibers locks the splice fibers to the existing cordage fibers. Splice fibers to either side of two-ply cordage or bend the splice bundle and splice into both sides of the cordage at the same time. Stagger splices to prevent weak spots in the cordage.

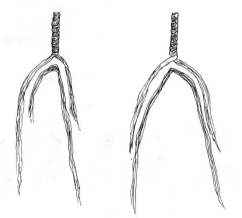

Figure 4-15. Splicing fibers into hand-rolled cordage.

SIMPLE TOOLS

Until recently, scientists and philosophers believed human beings to be the only makers and users of tools. Then anthropologist Jane Goodall discovered that chimpanzees make termite-fetching tools by stripping the bark off properly sized green twigs. The chimps stick their fabricated tools down termite nests, causing the termites to attack the invading stick. The chimpanzees retrieve their "termite tools" from the nest with gobs of attached termites, which provide a delicious treat. Indigenous peoples have fashioned tools since before the dawn of history. Even though monkeys have joined our ranks as makers and users of tools, you may find yourself surprisingly proud of your first efforts to fashion a piece of bone, stone, or wood into a usable tool.

Discoidal Stone Knives

Probably the simplest way to get yourself a knife, without access to modern tools, is to make a discoidal knife. Start with a fine-grained glassy rock, such as quartzite or basalt, preferably oval shaped. Obsidian, which is volcanic glass, breaks into sharper edges than the finest metal scalpels and razor blades. Strike this rock (call it a "cobble") against a larger rock (an "anvil") to bust off a sharp flake or disc of rock from the end. Riverbeds often contain many fine-grained, rounded stones suitable for making into stone knives. Once you have broken one disc off the cobble, it is usually easier to break the cobble into more sharp flakes.

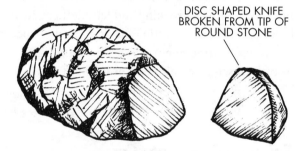

DISC SHAPED KNIFE BROKEN FROM TIP OF ROUND STONE

Figure 4-16. Making a discoidal knife.

CAUTIONS ABOUT WORKING WITH STONE

It is essential to wear safety glasses or goggles when working with stone. Flying shards can damage your eyes or even blind you. Additionally, the dust from stonecutting contains tiny particles with sharp edges that act like tiny knives, settling into lungs and creating scar tissue and cumulative damage. Breathing too much stone dust over a period of years can lead to silicosis (similar to asbestosis). Do your stone cutting and grinding outside, protect your lungs with a dust mask, and wash the particles out of your clothing. Cut stone is sharp, so protect your skin and keep plenty of Band-Aids around when learning these arts.

FLINTKNAPPING

Flintknapping is the art of chipping away at a stone to make it into something useful with a sharp edge. I'm no expert, and will just give you a few guidelines. Both *Primitive Wilderness Living & Survival Skills* and *Primitive Technology: A Book of Earth Skills* have decent sections on flintknapping. John McPherson, author of *Primitive Wilderness Living & Survival Skills*, has a new instructional flintknapping video called *Breaking Rock*. This new video should offer clear, easy-to-follow instructions. For more information on this subject, you might also try *Flintknapping: Making and Understanding Stone Tools* by John C. Whittaker or *Flintknapping—The Art of Making Stone Tools* by Paul Hellweg.

True flints may be hard to find in your part of the country, but most cherts, jaspers, agates, quartz, and so forth will work as long as they are fine-grained and fracture with sharp edges. When flintknapping, the main principle to remember is that stone tends to break into a wide cone, at roughly 120 degrees from the line of impact. Most people would intuitively guess that the stone would break roughly in line with the impact, so you must modify your blows to a shallower angle to account for the breaking angle. Choose a hard, round stone for your hammerstone, which you will pound against the flint to remove flakes. Fist-sized hammerstones are easy to handle.

from your base material, you may need to spend some time squaring the edge of your stock between hammer blows. Stock can be squared by grinding against other stones or lightly chipping the edge. Fine flakes can be removed from flint edges by applying pressure with a sharply pointed stick or pointy bone, such as an antler. Called "pressure flaking," this method is often used for finishing or sharpening up edges. To avoid splitting the brittle flint flakes while pressure flaking, try supporting the flint on a thick piece of leather.

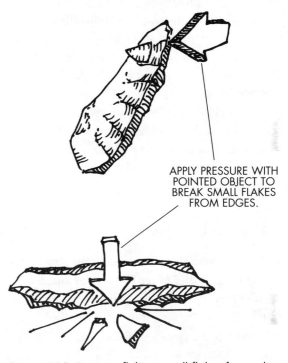

APPLY PRESSURE WITH POINTED OBJECT TO BREAK SMALL FLAKES FROM EDGES.

Figure 4-18. Pressure flaking small flakes from edges.

Bone Tools

Bone is more easily ground and shaped, and is less brittle than stone. Though not as sharp, nor as deadly for bringing down large game, bone arrowheads are more durable and less likely to fracture than flint arrowheads. Antlers and thighbones of larger animals make good stock for bone tools. To use thighbones, start by cutting the heavy ends off with a saw or stone knife, then split the bone lengthwise with a sturdy knife. Grind the bone into the desired shape by abrading it against a rough piece of rock, such as sandstone or granite.

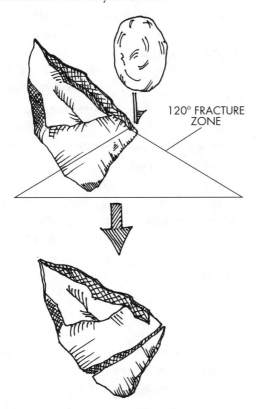

120° FRACTURE ZONE

Figure 4-17. 120° fracture of large flakes.

Because a somewhat squared flat platform is the best edge to impact to remove good, clean flakes

REFERENCES

Mental Strategies

***The Survivor Personality: Why Some People Are Stronger, Smarter, and More Skillful at Handling Life's Difficulties . . . and How You Can Be Too,* by Al Siebert, Ph.D.** 1996, 293 pp. (paperback), ISBN 0-399-52230-1. A Perigee Book, published by The Berkeley Publishing Group, Penguin Putnam, Inc., 375 Hudson Street, New York, NY 10014. Lists for $12.00. This self-help book aims at guiding readers to develop and apply the adaptive and coping skills of survivors in confronting difficult life situations. *The Survivor Personality* provides detailed descriptions of the mental "techniques" of survival, which are just as applicable to thriving in today's rapidly changing world as they are to surviving in emergencies. I found this book a little slow at the start, but fascinating and hard to put down once I got into it. Includes many examples, exercises, and interesting anecdotes.

Developing Intuition

***Practical Intuition: How to Harness the Power of Your Instinct and Make it Work for You,* by Laura Day.** 1997, 192 pp. (paperback), ISBN 0-7679-0034-0. Published by Broadway Books, a division of Bantam Doubleday Dell Publishing Group, 1540 Broadway, New York, NY 10036. Lists for $14.00.
Laura Day is a renowned teacher and business consultant who helps celebrities, scientists, and business leaders to develop their "sixth sense" to improve all aspects of their lives. This book provides a step-by-step program to help anyone unlock remarkable powers of the mind and become productively intuitive. Endorsed by Nobel laureate James Watson, Brad Pitt, Demi Moore, and others.

***Intuition—The Path to Inner Wisdom,* by Patricia Einstein.** 1997, 221 pp. (hardcover), ISBN 1-86204-136-9. Published by Element Books, Inc., P.O. Box 830, Rockport MA 01966. Lists for $24.95.

"Within every human being lie awesome potentials waiting to be realized. In this inspiring work, Patricia Einstein describes how we can allow this power to surface in everyday life." (Larry Dossey, M.D., author of *Healing Words*)
    I suppose you will have to use your intuition to decide whether you want to buy this book or the one by Laura Day. They are both excellent books by famous intuitives with equally impressive clients and credentials.

Survival Handbooks

***The SAS Survival Handbook: How to Survive in the Wild, in Any Climate, on Land or at Sea,* by John "Lofty" Wiseman.** 1996, 287 pp. (paperback), ISBN 0-00-217185-6. Published by Harper Collins Publishers, 77-85 Fulham Place Road, Hammersmith, London W6 8JB. Lists for $24.00. This leading survival manual is authored by John Wiseman, who was a professional soldier for 26 years with the British armed services. John was the survival instructor for the elite unit of the British Army, the Special Air Service (SAS). His book would be an excellent addition to your personal library.

***Camping & Wilderness Survival: The Ultimate Outdoors Book,* by Paul Tawrell.** 1996, 350 pp. (paperback), ISBN 1-896713-00-9. This book is self-published and is available through many bookstores, backcountry specialty stores, and by calling 888-266-5054. Lists for $29.95.
This excellent outdoor travel and survival book is giving *The SAS Survival Guide* some stiff competition. It is copiously illustrated and somewhat broader in scope then the *SAS Handbook.*

***Tom Brown's Field Guide to Wilderness Survival* by Tom Brown, Jr.,** with Brandt Morgan. 1987, 287 pp. (paperback), ISBN 0-425-10572-5. Published by The Berkley Publishing Group, 200 Madison Ave., New York, NY 10016. Lists for $12.95.
This survival book is a cross between the other survival books and the primitive skills books. The

writing is entertaining, though some claim that some of the drawings and instructions are not quite correct or complete. Not as thorough as *The SAS Survival Handbook* or *Camping & Wilderness Survival,* but more readable and entertaining.

***The Emergency-Disaster Survival Guidebook,* by Doug King.** 1994, 100 pp. (paperback), ISBN 1-883736-10-2. Published by ABC Preparedness Co., P.O. Box 795, Sandy, UT 84091. Lists for $7.95.

Nowhere near as comprehensive as the other references, but compact and easy to use. For its small size, this book packs a lot of information. Clear, concise, practical, easy to understand, and to the point. Contains basic survival instructions, plus many excellent checklists for planning for and dealing with numerous potential emergencies and disasters. Not a bad idea to keep a copy of this book in each car.

Basic Skills References

In a survival situation, if one were deprived of access to modern tools, a good knowledge of basic skills could make a huge difference. Even though these skills may seem simple, practitioners will tell you that many of them take work, practice, and patience to yield good results. I have listed several references, which will give you the benefit of their authors' years of practical experience. These books are narrower in scope than the recommended survival handbooks, but offer much more detailed instructions for key skills useful for living comfortably without technology.

> **CAUTION:** It is much easier to perfect the use of basic skills, such as using a bow and drill to make a fire, while in the comfort of your backyard rather than when you are cold and wet and your life depends on it.

***Primitive Wilderness Living & Survival Skills,* by John and Geri McPherson.** 1993, 408 pp. (paperback), ISBN 0-9678777-7-6. Published by Prairie Wolf, P.O. Box 96, Randolph, KS 66554. Lists at $24.95.

Of the many books that I reviewed, this book has the best instructions for the basic skills most closely linked to your survival. If you were to purchase just one book on basic skills, I would buy this one, but each of the recommended books contains information not found in the others. The authors have practiced and lived what they teach for many years. Their book includes excellent sections on primitive tanning of hides, sinew preparation and sewing, bows and arrows, containers, utensils, tools, shelters, pottery, cordage, and fire making. Lacks information on edible plants.

***Primitive Technology: A Book of Earth Skills,* from The Society of Primitive Technology, edited by David Wescott.** 1999, 248 pp. (paperback), ISBN 0-87905-911-7. Published by Gibbs Smith, P.O. Box 667, Layton, UT 84041. Lists for $24.95.

This book contains many excellent articles on a wide variety of subjects. It is the broadest and most interesting of the primitive skill books that I reviewed. The articles are written by members of The Society of Primitive Technology, who each wrote about their personal areas of expertise. The authors stress that "primitive" means first, and not necessarily worse, citing bond strengths of 20,000 pounds per square inch (psi) for some hot hide glues. It includes strong chapters on fire making, building reasonably comfortable and permanent primitive structures, glue, cordage and fibers, stone and bone tools, and various hunting implements. It lacks sections on hides, furs, pottery, herbs, and edible plants.

Participating in Nature: Thomas J. Elpel's Guide to Primitive Living Skills. 1999, 151 pp. (paperback), ISBN 1-892784-04-1. Published by HOPS Press, 12 Quartz Street, Pony, MT 59747-0691. Lists for $16.95.

The author, who runs a school for primitive outdoor living, lives and teaches what he preaches. He includes good sections on tanning hides, primitive cooking, fire making, primitive shelters, and edible plants (this section should be supplemented with books devoted entirely to edible plants, however). Some of the descriptions are not as detailed nor do they cover as many variations as the ones in the other references on primitive skills, but his writing is entertaining and I like his wilderness philosophy.

Earth Knack: Stone Age Skills for the 21ˢᵗ Century **by Bart and Robin Blankenship.** 1996, 192 pp. (paperback), ISBN 0-87905-733-5. Published by Gibbs Smith, P.O. Box 667, Layton, UT 84041. Lists for $14.95.

Of all the different primitive skills books, this one has the clearest illustrations giving particularly good instruction for many skills. The authors own and operate Earth Knack, a school that teaches Stone Age living skills. Excellent instructions for cordage, netting, making fire, primitive tools, baskets, pottery, soap, glue, music and clothing. Lacking in the areas of hunting and edible plants.

Edible Plant References

Edible Wild Plants: A North American Field Guide, **by Thomas S. Elias and Peter A. Dykeman.** 1990, 286 pp. (paperback), ISBN 0-8069-7488-5. Published by Sterling Publishing Co., Inc., 387 Park Ave. South, New York, NY 10016. Lists for $16.95.

Unlike many of the other field guides, this book covers all of North America, not just a specific zone. This is a very thorough guide, with excellent pictures as well as gathering and preparation tips. It includes seasonal photographs for fall and winter identification of certain plants and gives detailed descriptions of poisonous lookalikes. If you were to buy one guide for North America, I would buy this one.

Identifying and Harvesting Edible and Medicinal Plants in Wild (And Not So Wild Places), **by Steve Brill, with Evelyn Dean.** 1994, 317 pp. (paperback), ISBN 0-688-11425-3. Published by Hearst Books, 1350 Avenue of the Americas, New York, NY 10019. Lists for $18.95.

Good recipes and great information from a man who is totally into his subject. The illustrations are beautifully drawn in black and white, which may not be as effective as color photos for identifying plants. A great book for the inexperienced forager, it covers a few hundred of the most common and useful edible and medicinal plants in North America. It is not exhaustive, but very usable and practical. Folk wisdom, firsthand practical experience, and scientific

fact are blended with humorous and interesting anecdotes that help to make this a very readable and valuable guide.

Field Guide to Edible Wild Plants: Eastern and Central North America, **by Roger Tory Peterson and Lee A. Peterson.** 1982, 330 pp. (paperback), ISBN 0-39531-870-X. Published by Houghton Mifflin Co., 222 Berkeley St., Boston, MA 02116. Lists for $18.00.

Many people swear by this guide and claim it is *the* book to buy for edible plant identification. Good for identification, but short on preparation information, it also has a limited geographical spread, which is fine if you are east of the Rocky Mountains.

RESOURCES

Hollowtop Outdoor Primitive School, 12 Quartz Street, Pony, MT 59747-0697; phone: (406) 685-3222; web site: www.hollowtop.com.

Primitive skills allow a person to get closer to nature by experiencing nature directly. Instead of merely hiking through or camping in nature, the skills of primitive living allow one to move in and become part of the process. You learn about nature as you use it to meet your daily needs for shelter, clothing, fire, water, and food. Tom Elpel's Hollowtop Outdoor Primitive School offers classes in brain-tanning hides, edible wild plants, and primitive living "expeditions" where you learn primitive skills on wilderness treks with minimal gear. Staff members maintain an online guide to primitive living skill schools that is helpful for locating one in your area. Lots of interesting articles and links through their web site.

Earth Knack, P.O. Box 508, Crestone, CO 81131; phone: (719) 256-4909; web site: www.earth knack.com.

Owned and operated by Bart and Robin Blankenship, true pioneers in primitive living, and the authors of *Earth Knack: Stone Age Skills for the 21ˢᵗ Century.* They have explored and rediscovered many ancient crafts and skills, which they practice and teach. With the aid of students and interns, Bart and Robin are building a

Stone Age village classroom on the slopes of the Sangre de Cristo Mountains in southern Colorado. The site is bordered by a pristine fish-filled creek that pours off the surrounding 14,000-foot peaks.

Tom Brown, Jr's Tracking, Nature, and Wilderness Survival School, P.O. Box 173, Ashbury, NJ 08802; phone: (908) 479-4681; fax: (908) 479-6867; web site: www.trackerschool.com.
As a child, Tom Brown was mentored by an elderly Native American man who taught him traditional skills including tracking, hunting, fishing, and trapping with homemade implements. At one point, legend has it that Tom disappeared into the wilderness for a period of a year with just his knife and the clothes on his back. This is his school.

Prairie Wolf, P.O. Box 96, Randolph, KS 66554; phone: (800) 258-1232; web site: www.prairiewolf.net.
John and Geri McPherson have lived and taught primitive wilderness living and survival skills for many years. Visit their website to order books and videos or to get an introduction to the primitive lifestyle that they live, love and teach. Their excellent "how-to" videos include instructions in making a composite Asiatic bow, braintanning buckskin, and their new video *Breaking Rock* on the art of flintknapping.

Society of Primitive Technology, P.O. Box 905, Rexburg, ID 83440; phone or fax: (208) 359-2400; web site: www.hollowtop.com/spt_html/spt.html.
The Society of Primitive Technology is a nonprofit organization dedicated to the research, practice, and teaching of primitive technology. Membership benefits include a subscription to *The Bulletin of Primitive Technology* (biannual); networking with practitioners and researchers of primitive skills; notices for workshops and classes; literature reviews; tool and supply sources; and free classified notices in the *Bulletin.*

 # V Water

Ninety-three percent of the surface water in the United States is polluted.... Eighty percent of all disease in developing countries is spread by consuming unsafe water.... By the late 1980s, the water was not fit to drink in at least 33 major U.S. cities.... Ninety-eight percent of China's sewage goes into rivers untreated. ... Waterborne pathogens and pollution kill 25 million people in developing countries every year, accounting for about one-third of all deaths in those countries.... If the world is facing a future of water scarcity, it is also facing a future of food scarcity.... Water scarcity is now the single biggest threat to global food production.

—Worldwatch Institute special reports

WATER REQUIREMENTS

Water is absolutely essential for human survival; it plays a part in all of the body's biochemical reactions. Most of us could survive for several weeks without food, but not for more than a few days without water. Water requirements vary depending on activity level and temperature. When you eat dehydrated foods, you will require more water in any set of conditions.

The absolute minimum for survival is about one quart of drinking water per day, with little or no activity and cool conditions. Two quarts of water per day will usually sustain moderate activity at an acceptable level of comfort, under cool conditions with minimal urination (you will feel somewhat dehydrated). In fact, the standard hospital maintenance level for adults is 2½ liters (roughly 2½ quarts) of intravenous fluids per day to maintain comfort and good kidney function, with no activity. When the weather is hot, just a few hours without water leads to dehydration and fatigue. More than one quart of

water every hour can be required to perform heavy physical labor under extremely hot conditions.

In general, 1 gallon of water per adult per day is enough for drinking and some limited washing (sponge bath style). This is a good figure to use when calculating water for storage.

In 1984, while climbing El Capitan in Yosemite Valley, we hauled the standard two quarts of water, per person, per day for three days of rock climbing. We baked in the sun for three days of a record-breaking heat wave. By the time we drank our last mouthful of water around noon on day three, we were already severely dehydrated. Temperatures on the south-facing rock walls exceeded 100°F, with no shelter or shade. My throat hurt terribly and my mouth and throat were almost as dry as the back of my hand. Whenever I tried to talk, my tongue would stick like glue to the roof of my mouth and I would start to gag and retch. By the end of day three, our need for water exceeded our need for rest, so we climbed into the night. Around midnight, we reached the top and found a mountain stream, where we guzzled water to our heart's content.

STOCKING UP FOR EMERGENCIES

Grocery stores typically run out of bottled water in the first few hours after a public water system fails. I recommend that all households store at least 5 gallons of drinking water to cover short-term glitches in public water systems. An adequate two-week supply of water would be 14 gallons per person. A 55-gallon plastic drum of stored drinking water does not take up much space in the corner of a garage and would provide a family of four with a two-week emergency supply of drinking water in case of an earthquake or other disaster. (Be sure to protect containers from freezing.)

Home-bottled chlorinated tap water should be changed every month or preserved to prevent bacterial growth. Use commercial water preservatives or 2 to 4 drops of household bleach per quart of clean potable water to preserve stored drinking water. If stored water is tightly sealed, taste monthly or chemically test for residual chlorine, and treat again if the chlorine has disappeared. If the container is not sealed, retreat every few days. Preparedness/survival suppliers sell food-grade plastic drums, smaller water containers, and water preservatives such as the Katadyn Micropur products, which preserve home-bottled water for long-term storage.

GUIDELINES FOR COPING WITH DISASTER

Several years ago, my friends David and Nancy flew to the island of Kauai for their vacation. On the first day of their vacation, they went for a walk on the beach. As they gazed out to sea, they watched a dark and sinister looking cloud build and boil on the horizon. When the waterline receded about 20 feet out to sea, they knew that something serious was about to hit. They rushed back to their rented cottage, a mile down the beach and a few houses back from the shore. By the time they reached their cottage, the winds had increased to over 80 miles per hour as Hurricane Iniki approached the Island. Since David was an employee of the public utility district in a mountain community, he knew the importance of preserving a supply of potable water. Immediately, he filled all the sinks and bath tubs in the house with water and instructed the other occupants not to flush toilets or wash with the stored water.

As the day progressed, winds increased to an almost unbelievable 175 miles per hour. The terrified occupants crouched in corners, away from windows, and watched fearfully as large chunks of the neighboring houses blew by. Their house was constantly pelted with flying debris and the roar of the wind was deafening. Hours later, when the storm cleared, there was an eerie silence. Downed trees cluttered the roads, making automotive travel impossible. The stores quickly ran out of food and water. The water that David had stored in the bathtubs and sinks provided drinking water for several households. Electricity and water were restored to most of the island over three weeks later.

In a disaster situation, *conservation counts, as your life may depend on it.* Use rivers, lakes or ponds for washing (provided that they are not severely polluted) to conserve potable water for drinking. If you are aware of an impending natural disaster, such as a hurricane or tornado, or you have just survived a significant earthquake and your house is still intact, take the following precautions.

- **Immediately fill your bathtubs, sinks, and other available containers with water.** This will provide your household with a short-term supply of clean, potable water.
- **Conserve stored water.** There is a supply of clean, potable water in the toilet tanks, hot-water heater, and piping in your house.
- **Tape off all toilets.** When you notice that the tap water has stopped flowing, conserve the water in your toilet tanks (the tanks, not the bowl, contain potable water) and immediately notify the occupants to not flush the toilets.
  CAUTION: Do not drink the toilet tank water if you use an automatic toilet cleaner (turns the water blue).

- **Drain your water heater.** Water heaters are supplied with a vent located near the top of the tank and a drain near the bottom of the tank. Open the top vent (pull on the little lever on the spigot) and drain the tank into containers as needed. If there is dirt and sediment in the water coming out of the tank, *do not discard this water!* Simply allow the sediment to settle and drink the water off the top.
  CAUTION: Turn off the gas or the electric power to your water heater before draining, or you will damage the heater.

- **Shut off the utility water supply to your house if there's reason to believe the public water supply may have been contaminated.** Otherwise, you risk contaminating the usable water in your plumbing.
- **Drain the pipes in your house.** These typically hold several gallons of water, which can be drained into containers by slightly opening a high-point tap and draining from a low-point tap.

WATER POLLUTION

Water systems face...challenges in some of the new, hard-to-kill bacteria that crop up with growing frequency. Among the most feared is Cryptosporidium, the parasite that polluted Milwaukee's water in 1993, killing 111 people and sickening more than 403,000. It was the worst case of waterborne illness in modern U.S. history. The city's treatment system at the time wasn't good enough to kill the bug, which can evade conventional filters and is resistant to chlorine, most systems' main defense.

—Peter Eisler, "Powerful New Pollutants
Imperil Drinking Water Supply,"
USA Today, October 12, 1998

IMPORTANT: All surface water sources in the United States should be considered unsafe to drink without treatment!

Just because water is clear, smells good, and tastes good does not mean that it is safe to drink. When I was a child, I often went hiking in the mountains of New England. We drank eagerly from all the sweet-tasting streams and creeks along the trailside. It was a treat to drink from these unchlorinated, natural water sources, and we never gave it a second thought. Thirty years later, I will not drink from these same sources without first running the water through a portable filter, chemically treating it, or boiling it to remove or kill organisms such as *Giardia* or *Cryptosporidium.* The water still looks and tastes the same, but these organisms can live in clear, clean water. In the High Sierra of California, it is estimated that about 50% of the wild animal feces contain traces of *Giardia.* Lowland waters appear to be even more heavily infected with *Giardia* and *Cryptosporidium,* since cattle are major carriers of these pests.

Western nations have developed vast systems of water purification, storage, and distribution designed to protect us from traditional waterborne diseases, but waterborne diseases and parasites continue to plague most of the population of this planet, particularly in the Third World. In typical disaster situations, modern systems for purifying and distributing clean water often fail. In these situations, to protect your health, you must purify your own water. Basic information on contaminants is presented here so that you will better understand the limitations of particular water treatment options. Subsequently, a variety of water treatment options are presented.

Types of Contamination

BACTERIA

Bacteria, commonly called "germs," are single-celled organisms. They are spread by wind, water, person-to-person contact, animal feces, and contaminated food. You can't be sure that any surface water is free of harmful bacteria, even when it is crystal clear and there are no signs of human habitation. Some examples of harmful waterborne bacteria are *cholera, Campylobacter jejuni, salmonella,* and some varieties of *E. coli.* They multiply by cell division when they are in a "friendly" host environment, which provides them with food and temperatures suitable for growth. Given a positive growth environment, like feces-polluted water or a human body with a compromised immune system, one bacterium cell may multiply into millions within just a few hours. Signs of bacterial infection usually show up from six hours to three days after exposure.

Bacteria are killed by boiling or chemical treatment, provided the chemicals are applied at the proper concentration, temperature, and for the proper length of time. Bacteria are tiny, on the order of 0.3 microns to several microns in size and visible only under a powerful microscope. One micron is a millionth of a meter long. To give you a better idea of how tiny a micron is, realize that a single human hair is about 76 microns thick. Filters, rated at 0.2 microns or less, are usually effective against bacteria, but bacteria can grow through some filter media over a period of time.

CAUTION: Not all filters perform equally well. See the Portable Water Filters section.

PROTOZOA

Protozoa, such as *Giardia* and *Cryptosporidium* are single-celled animals. They are microscopic but relatively large (3 to 10 microns), which makes them considerably easier to filter out of your drinking water. However, they have the capacity to transform themselves into a cyst, which is a form that is very tough to kill, even with traditional iodine and chlorine water treatments. When these little animals get into a harsh environment, such as one that is too cold or has no food (like clean water), they change into cysts. A cyst cannot move itself around or feed itself but it can passively survive in harsh environmental conditions that would kill most bacteria. The cysts remain dormant waiting for a positive growth environment, such as the intestinal tract of an animal or polluted water. In a positive growth environment, protozoa change back to the active form and begin to eat and multiply. Protozoan infections usually take considerably longer to show symptoms—from a week to several months—and they can be extremely difficult to treat, once they have become entrenched in the body. Boiling will kill protozoa and their cysts.

VIRUSES

Viruses are different organisms altogether. They are much smaller than bacteria, on the order of 0.004 to 0.06 microns (Wilkerson 1992, 72) and are much harder to filter out. Viral contamination of drinking water is not as problematic as bacterial or protozoan contamination, but waterborne outbreaks are not uncommon. Viruses are so small that they may be visible only through the use of an electron microscope. Viruses multiply by invading the cells of a host organism and "stealing" some of the genetic material of the host cell to reproduce the virus. This process usually destroys the host cells and reproduces the virus. Some common harmful waterborne viruses are hepatitis A, polio, and Norwalk virus. Proper iodine and chlorine chemical treatments, as well as boiling, will kill viruses. Waterborne viruses are usually spread by human feces. Unlike bacteria, viruses generally do not cross from animals to humans, so the chance of getting viral infections in pristine remote locations is rather small, unless there has been a viral outbreak in the local human population. Viruses usually, but not always, attach themselves to larger particles, which can be effectively filtered out by standard microbial filters, so these types of filters offer some protection against viruses even though their pore size is far larger than the size of the virus.

PARASITES

Parasites live off the bodies of host organisms for at least part of their life cycles. Parasites may be micro-scopic, such as those causing malaria or trichinosis. Single-celled animals, like *Giardia* and *Cryptosporidium* can be considered parasites. Some parasites are several inches long, such as liver flukes, or several feet long, such as intestinal tapeworms. Parasites remain the scourge of many millions of people throughout the Third World and infect a surprisingly large percentage of the Western world. Research scientist Hulda Regehr Clark, Ph.D., believes that twentieth-century solvents tend to collect in some of the organs of our bodies and make them unusually good hosts for a variety of parasites (Clark 1995, 332). According to Clark, these solvents, and the parasites they nurture, contribute significantly to high rates of cancer. In the West, most parasites appear to be picked up through contact with house pets or while preparing raw meat. In the Third World, parasites are often spread by eating raw meat or through poor sanitation and lack of water treatment. Usually parasites do not kill their hosts, but sap health, body strength, and vitality. (See Chapter 9 for low-tech solutions to parasite infections.)

Parasites are killed by boiling, but may survive iodine and chlorine treatments if they are in cyst form. Their relatively large size makes them easy to filter out of contaminated water. All known parasites are filtered out of the water by filters rated at 2 microns or less.

CHEMICAL AND RADIOACTIVE CONTAMINANTS

Potentially harmful chemical contaminants in our drinking water include heavy metals from mining operations, organic compounds from various industries, and nitrates and pesticides from modern farms. In some parts of the world, pollutants also include radioactive contamination from the refining of radioactive materials or industrial accidents, such as the partial meltdown of the reactor at Chernobyl.

Organic compounds are large molecules that consist of chains of carbon and hydrogen atoms with various other atoms attached to them. The modern world has invented huge numbers of organic compounds and refined and concentrated many other naturally occurring organic compounds. Some examples of these are gasoline, solvents, pesticides, latex paint, and plastics. When chlorine combines with organic debris, like dead leaves, it makes carcinogenic (cancer causing) compounds called trihalomethanes (THMs). Boiling your water will kill microorganisms, but will usually have no effect on chemical or radioactive pollutants. Distillation will kill all kinds of microorganisms, but simple distillers will not remove volatile organic compounds since they evaporate and condense along with the water vapor. To remove volatile organic compounds, more advanced distillers include either fractional distillation or an activated carbon cartridge to remove these pollutants. Reverse osmosis and activated carbon filters will remove most organic compounds (see section on *Modern Water Treatment*).

DISINFECTING YOUR WATER

Contrary to popular opinion, clear sparkling water is often unsafe for drinking. Even spring water may not be safe. Deep-water springs from gravel or sand sources are usually safe, but may be contaminated by runoff from agricultural fertilizers, septic systems, sewer lines, and so on. Springs emerging from rock crevices can be exit points for underground streams carrying pollutants from far-off sources. When unsure about the source of your water, it is safest to boil, chemically treat, or filter the water through a certified water filter.

Boiling all your daily drinking water is time and energy consuming. Most chemical treatments leave an aftertaste and should be used with care to ensure the proper concentration and contact time for the temperature of application. Chemical treatments, except possibly for the new Aquamira products, do not provide guaranteed protection from *Cryptosporidium* cysts, which have been found to survive a 24-hour soak in undiluted household bleach! Portable filters can process surface water into potable water, but may not purify as well as their labels lead you to believe. The safest method for portable, fast, reliable water disinfection is a combination of chemical treatment and filtration, though further testing on the Aquamira products may prove that they are reliable chemical treatments for all known microorganisms. Recommended methods for sterilizing and disinfecting water are summarized below.

Heat Sterilization

Water sterilization by boiling is preferred over any method of chemical disinfection. This time-honored method is safe and a sure thing, because disease-causing microorganisms cannot survive the heat of a sterilizing boil. The CDC (Centers for Disease Control and Prevention) recommend that you boil water at a vigorous rolling boil for at least 1 minute at sea level. At altitudes above 6,000 feet, they recommend 3 minutes of rolling boil, since water boils at lower temperatures as the altitude increases. Some references (Wilkerson 1992, 71) state that, regardless of elevation, the boiling temperature and the time to reach that temperature are sufficient to kill all pathogenic organisms (milk is pasteurized at 160°F). Boiled water can be used after cooling (do not add ice).

> NOTE: Boiling usually has no impact on chemical or radioactive pollutants, which must be dealt with by other methods.

Portable Water Filters

There are many different portable water filters on the market. A filter is called a "purifier" if it is certified to remove protozoa, bacteria, and viruses. Other certified filters may remove only bacteria or perhaps just cysts. Many home water filters will remove unpleasant tastes and odors, but will not remove microorganisms. *Read the label, but realize that not all similarly rated filters perform the same*, nor do all filter manufacturers perform the same tests in the same manner. You can tell if a filter's pump is working or if the filter is clogged, but you can't tell if the filter itself is working effectively against organisms. Actual lab tests to verify microbiological filter function are expensive and there is no thorough testing protocol to ensure that all filters are tested in a standardized way by any lab that does the testing. Having personally designed medical IV filters, consumer water filters, and commercial filtration systems, I will give you my opinion and recommendations, but even I find it hard to sort through the different manufacturers' claims for an accurate filter comparison. For more information on this subject, there is an excellent article by Dan Vorhis, "Portable Water Filters: A Designer's Perspective," available on the Marathon Ceramics web site at www.marathonceramics.com.

PURIFYING FILTERS

Almost any backcountry filter, including those not given a "purifier" rating, will do a good job of removing protozoa and their cysts, like *Giardia* and *Cryptosporidium*. Most "purifying" filters have iodine-impregnated resin beads in the filter media, which release iodine into the water to kill viruses and bacteria. These chemically active resins require sufficiently warm water temperatures and contact time to kill bacteria and viruses. Some lab tests indicate that most or all iodine-based purifiers may not pass the EPA "purifier" standard without pumping water through the device more than once or at extremely slow flow rates (Vorhis 1997, 13). If viral contamination is a big concern, I personally would not trust the iodine resin in my purifying filter, but would pretreat the water with a chemical treatment then run it through my filter to remove protozoan cysts and the bad taste of the chemicals. There is one certified purifying filter, the First Need Deluxe Purifier, which uses no iodine to remove bacteria and viruses, and is not as prone to the temperature, flow rate, and usage factors that might allow viruses to slip through most other purifiers.

The new sports bottle type filters are inexpensive, simple, and effective against *Giardia,* and some are certified purifiers. They are extremely simple, using the squeeze bottle as the pump to drive water through the filter. I would exercise extreme caution using any of these filters to purify water from an urban or agricultural area or for treating brackish or foul-smelling water. If you do use a certified "purifying" water filter on these kinds of water, without secondary chemical treatment, I would be extra careful to run the water through the filters at a *very slow rate and run water through the filter twice.* PUR, First Need, and Sweetwater make certified "purifying" filters, which cost on the order of $65 to $130, and have fairly low capacities (on the order of 10 to 20 gallons, if you are treating reasonably clear, clean water).

CERAMIC VERSUS CARBON CARTRIDGE FILTERS

If you might use your backcountry water filter a lot, I would recommend that you purchase a filter with a ceramic filter element, like the Katadyn or MSR units. These units offer far longer life at a much lower cost per filtered gallon than carbon-based or pleated-membrane filter elements. All filter elements have clogging problems that will severely reduce their capacity (useful life), if used with dirty water. Ceramic cartridges will clog faster than the other types of cartridges, but can be serviced fairly easily to remove the outer clogging layer and restore the filter to near its original performance. Some filters have replaceable prefilters, which help somewhat with clogging, but since the pore size of the prefilter is usually much larger then the pore size of the main filter, small particles tend to slip through the prefilter and continue to clog the main filter. Backwashing capabilities can also help extend filter life.

Filters generally work on two principles. The first principle is called "sieving." Sieving is the same as straining particles out through holes in a screen. If the particle is too big to fit through the hole, it doesn't pass through the screen. In addition, most filter media are very thick and create a tortuous path that strains out particles much smaller than the average pore size. Ceramic filter media and most filter membranes work primarily on the principle of sieving.

The second filter principle is called "adsorption." When a particle sticks to the filter media, the way iron filings stick to a magnet, the process is called adsorption. All filters use a combination of sieving and adsorption, but activated carbon filter media are heavy on the adsorption side. Activated carbon has millions of tiny nooks and crannies. A teaspoon of activated carbon has an adsorption surface area about equal to the size of a football field, making it an excellent adsorption material. Carbon is great for sucking up pesticides, iodine, and organic compounds that tend to give water a bad taste. After a while, the sticky adsorptive surfaces of the activated carbon get filled up, so the filter stops removing bad tastes, chemicals, and odors.

My Filter Recommendations

There are lots of filters on the market. In this section I provide my opinions on quality filters to help you decide what to buy. See backcountry specialty stores or preparedness/survival suppliers for the best selection of portable water filters.

> **NOTE: Most filter manufacturers rate their filter life with an "up to" gallon rating based on use with very clean water. Unless you know that you will only use your backcountry water filter with extremely clean water, figure on a realistic life of roughly one third the manufacturer's rated life. Sad, but field tests show that this is generally true.**

OCCASIONAL OR EMERGENCY USE

For simplicity, one of the certified purifiers (PUR, First Need, Sweetwater, etc.) would be a good choice. Independent tests of several different filters indicate that the PUR Explorer, PUR Scout, General Ecology's First Need, and the Sweetwater Guardian (with Viral Guard and Siltstopper) all functioned well at removing bacteria, but the PUR models clogged considerably faster than the Sweetwater and First Need models in actual use.

If viral contamination is a major concern, I would not rely solely on the iodine resin in most purifying filters, but would pretreat the water with a chemical treatment, then run it through the purifier to remove protozoa cysts and the bad taste of chemical treatment. Of course, if you are going to do this, you might as well buy a cheaper, longer-lasting filter and treat the water with chemicals.

I would buy one or two of the sports bottle type filters as a backup in case the pump on the main filter breaks. Also stock at least one spare cartridge, since the cartridges clog quickly with dirty water.

SIGNIFICANT USE, PORTABLE

I would definitely recommend a filter with a cleanable ceramic cartridge, such as the Katadyn Pocket Filter ($250), Katadyn Combi Filter ($220), Katadyn Minifilter ($90), MSR MiniWorks ($60), MSR WaterWorks II ($130), or the Marathon e-water ($34.95), which is a small, pumpless siphon filter.

For reduction of bacteria, tests indicate that the MSR WaterWorks II and the Katadyn Combi Filter perform the best out of the longer-lasting portable filters. Test users liked the Katadyn Pocket Filter and the MSR MiniWorks best for simplicity and ease of use and service. After testing numerous models, the U.S. Marine Corps selected the MSR MiniWorks for use by its Amphibious Raids and Reconnaissance Division. Katadyn has been the Third World traveler's standard for many years, but MSR is giving Katadyn a lot of competition.

The MSR units and the Katadyn Combi Filter have the benefit of activated carbon, which will help remove chemicals, bad tastes, and unpleasant odors until the carbon is used up (the ceramic filter element should continue to provide bacterial and protozoa protection long after the carbon is spent).

Even though these units remove around 99% of most viruses, they are not rated as purifiers, so you should chemically treat your water before running it through one of these filters whenever viruses are a concern.

HEAVY USAGE, NOT SO PORTABLE

If I wanted to provide purified water for several people over a significant period of time, I would buy one of the recommended gravity-fed units. The per-gallon cost of these units is a fraction of the cost per gallon of using a small portable pump purifier, plus you do not have to sit there and pump away for long periods of time to provide a large quantity of purified water.

Gravity-fed units either have a top reservoir that holds the source water while it slowly percolates through the filter media into the bottom reservoir of purified water, or they are siphon-type units designed to siphon water from one container to another. Gravity-fed units require no pumping but cannot produce water nearly as fast as the recommended high-volume, pump-type unit.

Where viruses are a concern, you should chemically treat your water before running it through one of these filters.

Recommended gravity-fed units are the British Berkefeld, the Katadyn Drip Filter, the AquaRain model 200 and model 400 filters, and the Marathon Ceramics siphon units. The big British Berkefeld filter ($280) has a rated capacity of up to 30 gallons per day and a life of up to 60,000 gallons. It comes with a silver-impregnated activated carbon cartridge for removing chemicals and bad taste and odor.

The Katadyn Drip Filter ($275) has a rated capacity of up to 12 gallons per day and a life of up to 26,000 gallons. It does not have any carbon.

The AquaRain models use state-of-the-art, award-winning ceramic cartridges from Marathon (MSR subsidiary) and contain replaceable silver-impregnated activated carbon cartridges for removing chemicals, taste, and odor. AquaRain model 200 ($199) has a rated capacity of 12 to 15 gallons per day and a life of many thousands of gallons. Their model 400 ($260) has twice as many filter elements and can process 24 to 30 gallons per day. The complete AquaRain unit has not been through EPA purifier certification; however, the Marathon ceramic elements used in the AquaRain unit have been thoroughly tested, indicating an excellent microbiological performance.

NOTE: Filter life is dependent on water quality, filter surface area, filter thickness, and ceramic hardness. In actual use, the large-capacity Berkefeld and AquaRain model 400 will probably have about double the useful life of the smaller Berkefeld, the AquaRain model 200, and the Katadyn unit.

The Marathon e-water siphon filter (list $34.95) has a rated capacity of up to 250 gallons of water. The Marathon Group Siphon filter (list $1,500) will filter 1 to 2 quarts per minute with a capacity of up to 16,000 gallons.

The recommended pump type unit is the pricey Katadyn Expedition ($850), which will pump about one gallon per minute (much faster than the gravity-fed units) and has a rated life of 26,000 gallons. Gravity-fed units are considerably less expensive than pump units with equivalent lifetime capacities.

Chemical Sterilization

Various forms of chlorine and iodine chemical treatments are commonly used to disinfect drinking water. Chlorination is the most common method of chemically disinfecting water because it is easy to apply, readily available, and inexpensive. Chemical treatments usually leave an aftertaste that some people may find unpleasant. The taste is caused by traces of chlorine or iodine, which are active halogens that can cause harmful health effects over long periods of time.

CAUTION: Except for possibly the chlorine dioxide solutions (tradename Aquamira), neither chlorine nor iodine disinfection is effective against Cryptosporidium cysts.

If treated water has a strong chlorine or iodine taste, you can improve the taste by allowing the water to stand exposed to the air for a few hours, by pouring it back and forth several times between containers, adding a pinch of salt, or by adding some lemon juice. A pinch of powdered vitamin C (available at health food stores) in a quart of treated water will react with free chlorine or iodine and totally remove the bad taste. Running the water through an activated carbon filter will also remove free chlorine, iodine, and bad tastes.

CAUTION: Do not remove free chlorine or iodine until the water has set for the proper sterilization time (see the following table) and do not remove traces of chlorine or iodine from water that is to be stored for long periods of time.

CHLORINE BLEACH

Liquid chlorine bleaches, such as Purex and Clorox, contain a chlorine compound in solution that will effectively disinfect water. There are some products on the market sold as "bleach" for laundry use that do not contain chlorine and could be harmful. *Read the label!* The procedure for disinfecting drinking water is usually written on the labels of Purex and Clorox brand chlorine bleaches. When the procedure is not given, one should use the percentage of available chlorine as a guide (see the following table). Chlorine bleach is not as stable and reliable as the recommended iodine treatments. Chlorine is very pH sensitive, and alkaline waters significantly reduce its antimicrobial effectiveness (Wilkerson 1992, 72).

CAUTION: Do not use powdered bleach or bleach with conditioning additives, scents, or colorfast additives.

To purify, add 4 drops of standard liquid chlorine bleach (5% concentration) per quart of water, and double that amount for turbid or colored water.

The treated water should be mixed thoroughly and allowed to stand for 30 minutes. The water should have a slight chlorine odor. If it doesn't, repeat the dosage and allow it to stand for an additional 15 minutes. The slight chlorine taste of treated water is additional evidence of safety. Chlorine bleach loses strength over time, so if your bleach is over one year old, the amount used to disinfect should be doubled.

CHLORINE DIOXIDE

With the discovery that *Cryptosporidium* cysts pose a significant health threat and often survive traditional chlorine water disinfection treatments, many municipalities have included chlorine dioxide in their water treatment process. Much like ozone water treatments, chlorine dioxide is a powerful oxidizing agent that can kill *Cryptosporidium* cysts and rapidly purify water. It does not leave the active halogen of free chlorine in the water, so it makes for better tasting water (no aftertaste) than water treated with traditional chlorination.

The Aquamira kit ($12.95) is the first portable water treatment product to utilize chlorine dioxide and will treat up to 30 gallons per kit. Preliminary tests indicate that it may be effective against *Cryptosporidium* cysts, but it has not yet received EPA purification certification.

CHLORINE TABLETS

Chlorine tablets containing the necessary dosage for drinking water disinfection can be purchased in a commercially prepared form. Sources for chlorine disinfection tablets are sporting goods stores, army surplus stores, backpacking stores, preparedness/survival suppliers, and so on. Tablets should be used as stated on the instructions. Chlorine tablets can be stored for years. Their small size and precisely measured amount of chlorine in each tablet make them convenient, accurate, and easy to use. For disinfecting large quantities of water, their cost may be prohibitive, but they are a lot lighter and easier to carry than gallons of pure water.

Redi Chlor tablets, from Continental Technologies, are premeasured tablets of calcium hypochlorite that are handy for disinfecting significant quantities of drinking water. Each tablet treats 5 gallons of water, so a single bottle of 100 tablets treats 500 gallons of water for about $19.95, which is far cheaper than the per gallon cost of purifying filters.

GRANULAR CALCIUM HYPOCHLORITE

Granular calcium hypochlorite is used for chlorinating swimming pools and fairly large quantities of water, and for making stock disinfectant solution. It is best stored in a garage or storage building far enough away from other products that it will not cause pitting and corrosion. Granular calcium hypochlorite is packaged for sale in plastic bottles or drums. Sources of calcium hypochlorite are hardware stores, sporting goods stores, pharmacies, chemical suppliers, and swimming pool supply companies.

> **CAUTION: This chemical is poisonous and extremely corrosive.**

To make a disinfecting solution, dissolve 1 heaping teaspoon of granular calcium hypochlorite (about ¼ ounce) for each 2 gallons of water. This will yield a concentrated chlorine solution of approximately 500 milligrams per liter. To sterilize water, add this chlorine solution in the ratio of 1 part chlorine solution to 100 parts of water to be disinfected (Le Baron 1998, 115). This is roughly equal to adding 1 pint (16 ounces) of concentrated chlorine solution to each 12½ gallons of water. If this seems unnecessarily complicated, use the Redi Chlor tablets as described under *Chlorine Tablets*.

IODINE DISINFECTION

Iodine is one of the best and most dependable germicides and is widely used as a skin disinfectant for the treatment of superficial wounds. You can use iodine to disinfect your drinking water, and it is commonly impregnated into modern water filter media to kill bacteria and viruses inside water filters. However, iodine is not effective against *Cryptosporidium* cysts. Iodine-treated water has a peculiar odor and taste that some people find unpleasant.

> **CAUTION: Pregnant or nursing women, or people with thyroid problems, should not ingest iodine-treated water. The EPA recommends that devices that add iodine to the water should not be used for periods extending beyond two to three weeks at a time.**

DISINFECTION TECHNIQUES AND HALOGEN DOSES (ALL DOSES ADDED TO 1 QT. OF WATER)

Sterilization technique	Qty for 4 ppm (parts per million)	Qty for 8 ppm (parts per million)
Iodine tabs (tetraglycine hydroperiodide; Potable Agua and Globaline products)	½ tab	1 tab
2% iodine solution (tincture)	5 drops (0.2 ml)	10 drops (0.4 ml)
10% povidone-iodine solution	8 drops (0.35 ml)	16 drops (0.70 ml)
Saturated iodine crystals in water (Polar Pure product)	2½ tsp (13 ml)	5 tsp (26 ml)
Saturated iodine crystals in alcohol	2 drops (0.1 ml)	4 drops (0.2 ml)
Household bleach (5% solution sodium hypochlorite)	2 drops (0.1 ml)	4 drops (0.2 ml)

| Halogen concentration | Sterilization time in minutes at various water temperatures | | |
	41°F (5°C)	59°F (15°C)	86°F (30°C)
2 ppm	240	180	60
4 ppm	180	60	45
8 ppm	60	30	15

Note: Recent data indicate that very cold water requires prolonged contact time with iodine or chlorine to kill *Giardia* cysts (both disinfectants are ineffective against *Cryptosporidium* cysts). These contact times in cold water have been extended from the usual recommendations to account for this and for the uncertainty of residual concentration.

Source: Adapted from the *Wilderness Medical Society Practice Guidelines for Wilderness Emergency Care*, 1995.

TINCTURE OF IODINE

Eight drops of 2% tincture of iodine (Salvato 1982, 372) can be used to disinfect 1 quart of clear water (8 milligrams per liter dose). Allow water to stand at least 30 minutes before it is used. Studies of the usefulness of elemental iodine show it to be a good disinfectant over a pH range of 3 to 8. It is effective against enteric bacteria, amoebic cysts, *Cerariae*, *Leptospira*, and viruses within 30 minutes.

IODINE TABLETS

The use of tetraglycine hydroperiodide tablets is an effective method of disinfecting small quantities of water. Tetraglycine hydroperiodide tablets sell under the brandnames of Globaline, Potable Agua, and Coghland's. Iodine tablets are handy, compact, and light. The tablets are very effective as a water disinfectant if directions are correctly followed. If the water to be treated is cloudy, it should be filtered, or treated with double the number of iodine tablets.

You can purchase Potable Agua with vitamin C based taste-neutralizer tablets to totally eliminate the iodine aftertaste. Tablets can be purchased from pharmacies, preparedness/survival suppliers, and sporting goods stores. Once opened, iodine tablets have a shelf life of up to one year.

IODINE CRYSTAL SOLUTION

You can purchase a handy, ready-made iodine crystal water treatment kit from Polar Pure (includes crystals and bottle with thermometer), or you can make your own iodine crystal solution with about 5 g (⅛ ounce) of iodine crystals and a 2-ounce glass bottle. The Polar Pure kit treats about 500 gallons of water for about $10. Cover the crystals with a small amount of water to preserve them from evaporation (sublimation).

When you are ready to use the iodine solution, fill the 2-ounce prescription bottle with water, put the cap on, and shake the bottle for several minutes. Let the heavy crystals settle, then carefully pour out approximately 3 tablespoons (almost all the solution) into 1 gallon of clear water. *Use only the iodine solution: leave the crystals in the bottle.* Stir the water, and let it stand for approximately 30 minutes. If the water is very cold, let it stand for 1 hour.

You can use the crystals up to about 300 times before they completely dissolve. Be sure to label the bottle with "Poison" and keep it out of reach of children. Elemental iodine is poisonous by ingestion (in concentrated form). Elemental iodine crystals are inexpensive and can be obtained at pharmacies and chemical supply companies.

The methods in the table on the previous page have been carefully researched, and are time tested and effective. They are safe when the directions are correctly followed. The raw materials used in purification are inexpensive, but they are *poisonous in concentrated form. Use caution and keep them out of reach of children.*

PRESERVING WATER BY USING SILVER

Improperly stored water quickly grows bacteria, which may have effects ranging from unpleasant to life threatening. In the industrialized nations, our digestive tracts have grown accustomed to water sources free of harmful bacteria. As a result, most of us do not have built-in immunities to common local bacteria, which quickly reproduce in untreated stagnant reservoirs. Many a traveler to Mexico has suffered a bout of Montezuma's revenge, often introduced through seemingly harmless ice cubes made from the local water.

The ancients knew about the antibacterial properties of silver. Alexander the Great used silver urns to store water for his troops on extended sea journeys. The ancients didn't know anything about bacteria, but they knew that drinking "old water" could make them sick, unless it was stored with silver. Solid silver will not usually disinfect water, but putting some of grandma's old silverware or some silver jewelry into a storage container is a good way to prevent the growth of potentially harmful bacteria over long periods of time. The silver introduces metal ions into the water that retard or prohibit bacterial growth. Katadyn makes a variety of commercial silver nitrate products (tradename Micropur) for preserving stored water with silver. There are several nonsilver water preservatives, such as Aerobic 07, for preventing bacterial growth in long-term stored containers of water. See preparedness/survival and surplus stores for these products. Silver-based water purification products are available in Europe, but these are not approved for use in the United States.

You can make your own colloidal silver solution for preserving your water if you have a colloidal silver generator (see Chapter 9). The Environmental Protection Agency has set a limit for the silver introduced into drinking water by bacteriostatic silver-impregnated filters at 50 micrograms per liter (equal to 0.05 parts per million). At this level of silver concentration, several different tests have indicated that silver is only partially effective over periods of time (greater than one hour) against certain bacteria and has little effect against viruses. To obtain these concentrations, you would dilute a 5-parts-per-million (ppm) colloidal silver solution 100:1 with the water to be preserved.

High concentrations of silver, on the order of 5 ppm, might properly purify clear water, but I have no data to support this premise and these concentrations are well beyond the EPA limit. To be safe, I would stick with one of the proven technologies over silver for purifying my water. If I had only a colloidal silver generator, it would be better than nothing, but I would use fairly high concentrations of silver and would let the water sit for at least an hour before drinking.

TREATING AND FINDING WATER THE LOW-TECH WAY

With a few simple materials, if you can dig your way to moist soil or find some healthy green bushes, you should be able to provide yourself with drinking water.

Treating Water
SLOW SAND FILTERS

You can use a slow sand filter to clean and partially purify your drinking water. Sand filtering is probably the oldest public water treatment method. Filtering water through 3 to 5 feet of sand will remove many microorganisms (like *Giardia* and *Cryptosporidium)*, most debris, and most radioactive fallout.

As a sand filter ages, a gelatinous layer forms in the upper layer. The gelatinous layer contains many bacteria, which do most of the processing and filtering. These friendly bacteria will destroy many harmful bacteria, though some harmful bacteria, like *Salmonella paratyhi,* can travel quite a distance through sand filters. The top layer of your sand filter must be cleaned off and replaced regularly.

While sand filters are not as reliable as chemical treatment, they are often incorporated into the primary stages of modern commercial water treatment systems, prior to chemical treatment. One or two layers of charcoal can be included in your sand filter if bad taste, odor, or solvents and other organic chemical contamination is a problem.

CAUTION: Many industrial chemicals and other toxic pollutants will not be removed by sand filters.

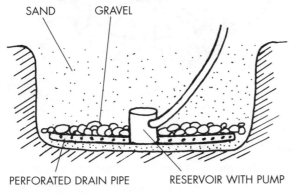

Figure 5-1. Slow sand filter reservoir.

Tips on Creating a Sand Filter

If you have sandy soil near a lake or river, you can utilize this soil to partially filter the water from the lake or river. If you can, it is best to boil, filter, or chemically treat the water from your sand filter reservoir.

For fresh water, you can dig a trench 5 to10 feet from the water's edge. For salt water, the trench should be about 100 feet from shore. Filtered water will gradually seep into your trench.

If you have access to power and modern materials, you can use gravel, drainpipe, sand, and a pump to make a slow sand-filtered water supply (see Figure 5-1). If you have access to a wheelbarrow, it is preferable to wash the sand prior to loading it into your filter bed. Place a few buckets of sand into the wheelbarrow and fill it with water. Swirl the sand and water mixture, and pour off the muddy water. What remains is relatively clean sand.

You can also filter wet and muddy earth through layers of cloth into a suitable catch basin (see Figure 5-2) to collect water from wet earth. Let the water sit for a while to settle out some of the silt.

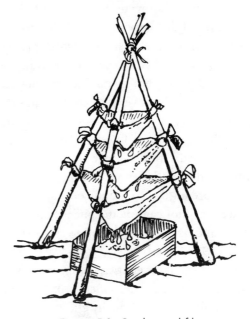

Figure 5-2. Crude sand filter.

CHARCOAL FILTERS

You can make your own crude charcoal filters to remove bad tastes, odors, and some pollutants such as organic toxic chemicals and radioactive fallout. The easiest way to make charcoal is to burn some wood and pick the bigger partially burned chunks out of the fire. Place these chunks into a 5-gallon bucket and pour the water to be treated into the bucket. Shake vigorously for a few seconds then allow to stand for several minutes before filtering this water through a cloth, sand filter, or coffee filter back into a suitable container. If toxic organic chemicals or radioactive fallout are significant concerns, you should filter your water through at least 3 to 5 feet of sand including two 3-inch thick layers of charcoal. A 50-gallon drum filled with sand and charcoal layers, with a few holes punched in the bottom, could do the job nicely. If you crush the charcoal with some rocks, it will do a better job of filtering.

A more efficient way to make charcoal is with an old-fashioned charcoal kiln, which bakes wood in a closed chamber above a fire. This process makes charcoal without burning the wood sealed in the upper part of the kiln, since that section of the kiln does not allow enough oxygen flow to support combustion. Another traditional method for making charcoal is by first covering a huge pile of wood with a layer of straw or pine needles followed by a thick layer of dirt, leaving a small chimney flue in the top center. Vent holes are scratched into the sides of the dirt, and the pine needles or straw are ignited through these vent holes. The chimney and vent holes are partially covered to control the amount of air to insure that the wood chars into charcoal rather than burns into ash. The charcoal mound is watched carefully for several days then the chimney and vent holes are completely plugged for several more until the mound cools down. If the mound keeper is not careful, the pile is built into a roaring fire and burns all the wood to ashes. (Wigginton 1979, 97-99)

If the need should ever arise, common household ion-exchange type water softeners and carbon or slow sand filters are particularly effective at removing radioactive materials from contaminated water sources.

SOLAR STILL

Under a survival situation in dry climates, you can provide yourself with small quantities of pure water with a homemade solar still, using a clear sheet of plastic and a container to catch dripping water. Dig a hole in the ground in an area with wet or moist soil that is also directly exposed to the sun. If the soil is very wet or damp, you may only have to dig a couple of feet. Place a pail or other catch basin in the center of your pit. If you do not have a container, a piece of plastic or waterproof material covering a depression

in the earth will suffice. Cover the pit with the sheet of clear plastic and seal the edges of the sheeting with more soil or rocks (see Figure 5-3). Weight the center of the sheeting with a stick, stone, or some dirt.

The sun's rays passing through the plastic sheet will warm the earth, evaporating water from the moist soil. This water vapor rises until it hits the plastic sheeting, which is cooled by the outside air, causing the water vapor to condense and run down the inside of the sheet until it drips off the low point into the container.

Figure 5-3. Solar still side view.

Figure 5-3. Solar still top view.

PLANT WATER PUMP AND STILL

A variation on the solar still, this technique uses a living plant as a pump to gather water from under the ground with its roots. You must have a plastic bag or tarp to wrap around a leafy, healthy green plant. Pick a plant that is not too big for your tarp. Dig a small hole on one side of the plant. Wrap your bag or tarp around the plant, lining the shallow hole with the bag or tarp. Tie your bag around the base of the plant and arrange the tarp so that condensing water will trickle down the inside of the tarp and collect in the hole (see Figure 5-4).

Water vapor evaporating off the leaves will condense on the inside of your covering and provide a minimal source of water. You may wish to tap several plants to increase your supply.

CAUTION: If the plant receives too much sun for too long, it will cook and die under your plastic cover.

Figure 5-4. Plant water pump and still.

TRADITIONAL WATER DISTILLATION

All kinds of water, from brackish to recycled urine, can be purified with a simple distillation process. Distillation uses a significant amount of energy, because it requires boiling water in one container, capturing the water vapor, and transporting that vapor to a cooler enclosed container where it condenses back into liquid. (See Chapter 14 for more information on distillation apparatus.)

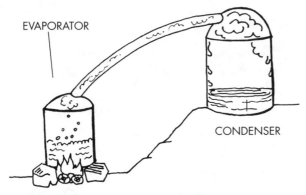

EVAPORATOR

CONDENSER

Figure 5-5. Water distillation.

"Holy Water"

For countless centuries, holy men, priests, and shamans have engaged in the practice of "blessing the water." Perhaps there is more to this than we would care to admit or believe? If I had nothing else with which to treat my water, I would take a moment to invite the Holy Spirit (or other spiritual power that you feel comfortable with) to bless and purify my water before I drank it. Leah told me the following story about drinking "blessed water."

Leah had grown up in a farming community somewhere in California's Central Valley. The water on her farm was terrible. Between the odor and the taste, it made you gag to drink it, so all the local residents relied on bottled water for drinking. Leah had been learning spiritual healing techniques in a class. As one of the recommended class exercises, she had filled a large jug with tap water and placed it by the entrance to their front door. Each time she entered or left the house, Leah would place her hand over the jug of tap water and say a short prayer, asking the Holy Spirit to bless the water.

One day, Leah's brother was terribly ill. He had a very high fever that left his throat parched. At the time, Leah was out of the house, so her niece was attending to the sick brother. He cried out for a drink of water, but the niece could not find any bottled water in the house. Desperate for water, she remembered the jug sitting by the front door. She fetched a glass of water from the jug and gave it to her uncle to drink. The uncle eagerly gulped the water, thanked the niece, and promptly fell into a deep sleep. The next morning, he awoke feeling totally well and amazingly fit. He asked the niece where she had found that water, saying that it was "the sweetest tasting water that I have ever drunk." She replied that he had drunk water from the jug by the front door.

Knowing that this jug contained local tap water, Leah's brother found it hard to believe that the water he drank could have come from that jug. The niece fetched the jug. When he tasted it, he knew it was the same sweet water he had drunk the night before. They asked the local Culligan representative if the taste of their tap water would be improved while standing in a jug for a couple of weeks. The expert replied that they could put their tap water in a jug for years and it would still taste terrible without being run through a special filter to remove several minerals.

Finding Water
PLANT INDICATORS

Look for leafy, green plants that require a lot of water to survive. Cattails, reeds, willows, elderberries, cottonwoods, poplars, and greasewoods all require a plentiful supply of water and indicate a high water table. Dig a shallow well at the base of these plants or trees and you should soon reach wet soil, which will slowly percolate into your pit.

ANIMAL INDICATORS

Animals and insects are very good indicators for water. Most insects require water and live within flying range of surface water. In particular, watch the directions that bees fly. Grazing animals, like deer and elk, will travel to water each day. Look for well-worn animal trails, which will usually lead to water. Most birds, except for birds of prey, require significant water several times a day. Look for water in areas that birds congregate, circle, or roost.

PHYSICAL INDICATORS

Dry riverbeds usually offer areas where water breaks the surface or at least comes close to the surface. Dig for water at outside bends in the river or follow the riverbed to areas where bedrock forces the water to the surface. Look for water at the base of cliffs, where green vegetation suggests a water source.

CACTUS

Some cacti, such as the barrel cactus (but not the giant saguaro), contain a watery pulp that can be crushed or sucked to release a jellylike liquid.

Wells

Modern equipment can drill through hundreds of feet to reach water deep within the earth. The time-honored method of digging a 20- to 30-foot hole by hand is very hard work—a backhoe makes digging a shallow well much easier. However you dig your well, it must be lined with some durable material to prevent the walls from collapsing, and the well should be capped or covered to prevent contamination. Without a cap, everything from bird feces to dead critters will find their way into your well.

For dug wells, the traditional lining was hand-laid stone, but modern concrete well tiles are far easier to lay and do a much better job of sealing the upper reaches of the well tube from surface water contamination. A minimum of one foot of clean, washed gravel should surround and fill the bottom of the well shaft. Drilled wells are typically lined with pipe. See *Cottage Water Systems*, by Max Burns, or *The Home Water Supply* by Stu Campbell for excellent introductions to wells and small water systems for the do-it-yourselfer.

WATER WITCHING (DOUSING)

If you plan to dig a well, and the location of the well is not an obvious water source, do yourself a favor and water witch for the optimal location. There is no definitive scientific explanation for water witching, but many thousands of people swear by it. I have yet to see a successful well-drilling operation that does not use water witching, at least some of the time. Not everyone will be successful at water witching. Some of us seem to have the gift, while some of us don't. Some skeptics have been amazed when they tried it and the forked stick twisted so hard that it felt as if it might take the skin off the palms of their hands. Some true believers don't feel a thing when they try water witching.

There are many different techniques for water witching and no hard-and-fast rules. The traditional water witching tool is a Y-shaped willow branch, with two "handles" about 16 inches long and with a straight section about 12 inches long at the bottom of the Y. Holding your hands palm up and arms bent at the elbows, grasp each side of the forked branch in one hand (see Figure 5-6). The short section should point forwards and slightly upwards. Walk around your land, waiting for the branch to quiver significantly or perhaps take a dive downwards.

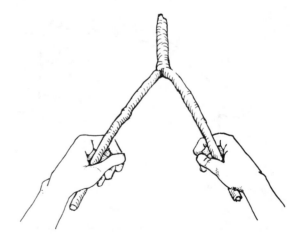

Figure 5-6. The traditional dousing rod.

My father was an architect with a practice in Vermont. He said that whenever road crews were

about to dig in the streets, they would witch for the buried water pipes using bent welding rods or coat hangers. Select two ⅛-inch diameter rods or straightened coat hanger wires two to three feet long. To form the "handles," bend each wire at right angles, 6 inches from one end. Grasp the wire handles loosely in each fist, holding them vertical with the long ends extending horizontally and parallel in front of you (see Figure 5-7). You will probably find the rods crossing dramatically in an obvious X when you pass over water, but may find them spreading apart instead.

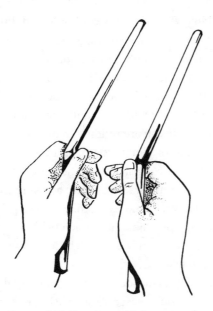

Figure 5-7. Dousing with bent metal rods.

PUMPS

Getting the water out of your well can be a problem, especially if there is a power outage. In addition to the old-fashioned pail, rope, and bucket method, water can be moved by either being pushed or sucked by a pump. Electronic submersible pumps sit near the bottom of deep wells and push the water to the surface. These pumps can pump well water from depths of several hundred feet underground. Many old-fashioned hand pumps (see Figure 5-8), or other surface-mounted pumps, suck the water from a position located some distance above the water source. If these pumps still would develop a perfect vacuum (which they can't), they would only suck water from a maximum depth of 34 feet. Realistically, suction

type surface pumps can't draw water from a source more than 20 to 25 feet below the pump.

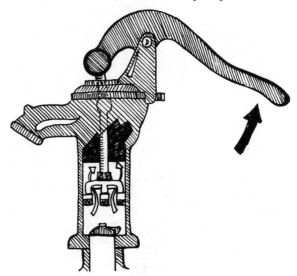

Figure 5-8a. Shallow well hand pump, intake stroke.

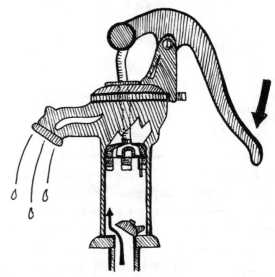

Figure 5-8b. Shallow well hand pump, output stroke.

There are surface pumps, called deep well jet pumps, that get around this 25-foot limit by pumping water down one line to help boost a larger quantity of water up a second line. Deep well jet pumps can lift water as high as 120 feet. There are also hand pumps with long handles and a shaft extending down the well hole to a submerged pump cylinder, which push the water up the well and can pump water from a maximum depth of around 300 feet (see Figure 5-9). For more details on pumps and water systems, see *Cottage Water Systems*, by Max Burns, or *The Home Water Supply* by Stu Campbell.

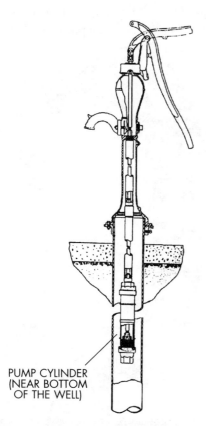

PUMP CYLINDER
(NEAR BOTTOM
OF THE WELL)

Figure 5-9. Deep well hand pump. Illustration courtesy of Baker Manufacturing Company, Monitor Division.

When sizing pumps and water system components, there is a common term called "pressure head" or just "head." This simply refers to suction or output pressure in terms of the pressure (or vacuum) required to suck or push a column of water the specified number of vertical feet. For example, a self-priming pump with a suction head rating of 20 feet and an output head rating of 150 feet could draw water from a source 20 feet below the pump and deliver water to a source 150 feet above the source. For help with figuring out pump and pipe sizing and details like "pressure head," see a reputable plumbing supply house.

When the power goes out, or if there is no readily available power source, a hand pump or a solar-powered pump can provide uninterrupted water service from wells. Solar-powered pumps are typically designed for high efficiency and low output to slowly fill a pressure tank or cistern. The smallest solar pumps require less than 150 watts of power (equal to two 75-watt lightbulbs) and can lift 1½ gallons of water per minute from depths of more than 200 feet.

This doesn't sound like much, but it would amount to 900 gallons of water over a 10-hour sunny day. That's enough water to provide for the needs of several families, 30 head of cattle, or 40 fruit trees. Another solar option is to use a voltage inverter coupled with a solar charged, 12-volt DC battery storage system, to provide 120-volt AC power for a regular jet pump or submersible pump water system (see solar resources section of Chapter 11, *Energy, Heat & Power*).

PROTECTING YOUR WATER SOURCE

Your drinking water source is your lifeblood. Protect it! Dispose of your sewage in a manner that threatens neither your water supply, nor that of your neighbors. The following table provides some general setback guidelines for protecting your water source. (Remember to check with local authorities for codes and approvals.) If you are residing in one spot for a while, some kind of septic system, pit toilet, or outhouse should be constructed. There are lots of alternatives to outhouses if you have access to modern building materials. Composting toilets, electric incinerating toilets, septic tanks, and leach fields are all fine alternatives, its with their own merits and drawbacks. If you need to take care of a large volume of raw sewage, you might consider making an artificial swamp to treat your sewage. As an eco-friendly alternative to modern chemical treatment plants, some cities are resorting to artificial swamps. Apparently, as the light changes with each day and night, plant and bacterial processing of the raw sewage causes the acidity of the treatment swamp to fluctuate drastically, destroying potentially harmful bacteria in the sewage.

A pit toilet can be as simple as a hole 3 feet deep with a couple of logs to sit across, or it can be a beautifully crafted wooden masterpiece, complete with a proper ventilation system, the privacy of four walls, a roof, and a door. The traditional "privy" is about 4 x 4 and 7 feet tall at the front. The seat should be 12 to 16 inches high. A 4- to 5-inch vent pipe should rise from under the seat to about 2 feet above the roof to vent odors. Lime periodically sprinkled into the pit will help reduce odor, especially in the summer months.

Suggested minimum setbacks for wells

Pit toilet from dug, bored, or driven well	100 ft
Pit toilet from well with watertight casing, at least 20 ft deep	50 ft
Septic system absorption area from dug, bored, or driven well	150 ft
Septic system absorption area from well with watertight casing, at least 20 ft deep	100 ft
Vault type outhouse	50 ft
Gravity draining sewer line or building foundation drain	50 ft
Barn housing animals	50 ft
Manure storage site, automobile wrecking yard, and so on	250 ft
Property line, building or driveway	10 ft
Sewage lagoon or landfill/dump site	1000 ft
Cemetery	50 ft

Additional setbacks for drinking water springs

Human habitation/activity downhill from spring	50 ft
Human habitation/activity laterally (sideways) from spring	100 ft
Human habitation/activity uphill from spring	200 ft

Source: Max Burns, *Cottage Water Systems*, 1993.

MODERN WATER TREATMENT
Chlorine Treatment

In the Western world, most potable water systems that purify surface water for the public first filter the water to remove silt and debris, then chlorinate it to kill potentially dangerous organisms. Chlorine in water forms a very active free radical. Free radicals are a hot topic in nutritional literature, but most people do not understand what they are. Free radicals are electrically charged atoms or compounds that are chemically very active. They easily attach themselves to other compounds and react with them, changing the chemistry of both parts. The free chlorine in our water systems reacts with and kills bacteria floating in the water.

Chlorine is also not very good for the human body, since those same free radicals react with our cells. Our bodies have repair and defense mechanisms that help us to deal with chlorine and other free radicals, but over long periods of time exposure to free radicals contributes to aging and many degenerative diseases. Many studies have confirmed that the presence of chlorine in our drinking water has wide-ranging, long-term detrimental health effects, such as the loss of calcium in our bones and significantly increased cancer rates.

Ozone Treatment

To improve the quality of drinking water, some municipal water systems have incorporated ozone generators into their systems. Ozone is an extremely unstable, highly reactive molecule of oxygen. It contains three bonded atoms of oxygen instead of the usual two oxygen atoms that form the more stable regular oxygen molecules in the air. The third oxygen atom of the ozone molecule easily splits off to react with surrounding atoms and molecules, and oxidizing them. These extra oxygen atoms rapidly react with and destroy unwanted bacteria and other organisms floating in the water. Ozone has the added benefit of reacting with heavy metals and other undesirable contaminants, turning them into precipitates or silts, which can be easily filtered out of the water supply. The process of reaction continues until all the ozone molecules have reacted with other substances, leaving only stable regular oxygen and pure, sweet tasting water with no free radicals to cause long-term detrimental health effects.

Most municipal ozone systems also insert a little chlorine into the water to prevent the possibility that stray bacteria start to grow somewhere within the water system. Since ozone treatment leaves the water very pure, not much residual chlorine is required to maintain long-lasting protection against bacterial growth. In traditional chlorinated water systems, the more organic material (food for bacteria) present in the water, the more chlorine is required to safeguard against the survival and growth of potentially dangerous bacteria.

Activated Carbon Filtration

Bad tastes, odors, chlorine, and harmful organic pollutants such as THMs (trihalomethanes) can be removed with activated carbon filters, reverse osmosis filters, ozonation, or distillation of water. Trihalomethanes are common carcinogenic compounds that are created when chlorine reacts with organic material, such as dead leaves. Activated carbon works by a process called "adsorption." Adsorption filter materials have huge amounts of convoluted surface area that attract and trap undesirable pollutants. Activated carbon is formed from carbonaceous materials, such as charred coconut shells, coal, or wood. The carbon base material is typically ground up into fine powder and then either contained loose in a filter bed or combined with a binder and pressed into a porous filter block. Under a microscope, activated carbon looks incredibly convoluted, with millions of tiny nooks and crannies to trap debris and organic compounds. Activated carbon can help remove a wide variety of toxic organic compounds and radioactive contaminants. A single pound of activated carbon can contain 150 acres of adsorption surface area!

By itself, activated carbon is not very effective at removing most forms of heavy metal contamination from drinking water. It usually works well at first, but then dumps high concentrations back into the water. For this reason, many carbon filters have special compounds mixed into the medium to bind specifically to heavy metals. If your local water has a problem with heavy metals such as lead, arsenic, or mercury, make sure your home water filter is designed to remove heavy metals. Except for areas prone to runoff from old mines, backcountry water sources do not usually suffer from heavy metal contamination.

Adsorption filters have a finite useful life and should be replaced when they have been depleted. Testing for free chlorine in chlorinated water that has passed through a carbon filter is one way of determining whether the filter is still effective.

A simple carbon filter will remove chlorine and organic compounds to make your water taste better, but will not guarantee the removal of bacteria and other potentially harmful organisms. Some home water purifiers use carbon filters to remove chlorine, sediment, and various toxic compounds, then pass the water under a high-intensity ultraviolet (UV) lamp to kill any microorganisms. These systems work well as long as the carbon cartridges are routinely changed, the UV lamp is functioning properly, and the lamp's rays are not blocked by dirt or silt.

Carbon filters are usually either made from loose granular activated carbon (GAC) or from solid blocks of carbon that are composed of pressed, extruded, or molded carbon powder mixed with a binding agent. Most carbon block filters are effective at removing larger microorganisms such as *Giardia* and *Cryptosporidium*. Additionally, carbon block filters are usually more effective than GAC filters at removing other contaminants since GAC filters are prone to "channeling," which is where water streams through channels formed in the loose media resulting in less contact with the carbon. The drawbacks to carbon blocks are their lower flow rates and higher costs as compared with similar sized GAC filters.

Reverse Osmosis

Reverse osmosis systems typically incorporate sediment and carbon type prefilters to remove most of the contaminants before passing the water through a micro-porous membrane, which removes almost all the heavy metals, dissolved salts, and other contaminants not picked up by the carbon filters. The disadvantages of reverse osmosis systems are low output (output of average sized units is in the range of 1 to 4 gallons per day) and the fact that the reverse osmosis membrane is kept clean by flushing several gallons of water down the drain for every gallon of processed pure water. Most reverse osmosis systems include an air-charged pressure tank reservoir to store 1 to 2 gallons of pure water for ready use.

REVERSE OSMOSIS FOR DESALINATING SEA WATER

There are several very expensive hand-pump and/or 12-volt-driven reverse osmosis systems for extracting fresh water from salt water. These systems are popular items for life rafts and yachts. PUR has pretty much cornered this market, with a manual unit selling at about $585 and 12-volt units starting at about $2,200. A solar still can be used instead, if you are in a location where you can dig a hole in the ground. Such stills are nowhere near as handy, but a lot cheaper. Check out the PUR web site at www.purwater.com.

Distillation

Distillation systems boil water and then condense it, in the process purifying the water and removing contaminants. Distillation will kill all kinds of microorganisms, but simple distillers will not remove volatile organic compounds since they evaporate and condense along with the water vapor. To remove volatile organic compounds, more advanced distillers include either fractional distillation or an activated carbon cartridge to remove these pollutants. When considering the purchase of a drinking water distiller, insure that the distiller includes at least one of these features to remove volatile organic compounds. Drawbacks to distillation systems include their high consumption of electric power to evaporate the water, the flat taste of distilled water, and low volume throughput in the same range as reverse osmosis systems.

REFERENCES

***Cottage Water Systems: An Out-of-the City Guide to Pumps, Plumbing, Water Purification, and Privies,* by Max Burns.** 1999, 150 pp. (paperback), ISBN 0-96969-22-0-X. Published by Cottage Life Books, 54 St. Patrick Street, Toronto, Ont., Canada M5T 1V1. Lists for $24.95.
Cottage Water Systems is a country-living guide to pumps, plumbing, water purification, and privies (outhouses). It is an excellent source of information for building or maintaining your own water and sewage systems. This book would not be very useful in an emergency situation, but it's a great reference for building or maintaining a country home.

***The Home Water Supply: How to Find, Filter, Store and Conserve It,* by Stu Campbell.** 1983, 240 pp., ISBN 0-88266-324-0. Published by Storey Books, Schoolhouse Road, Pownal, VT 05261. Lists for $18.95.
This book covers much of the same material as *Cottage Water Systems*. It is informative, well written, and has a much better section on water witching than *Cottage Water System*. Besides, the author was one of my ski coaches when I was a kid.

***Don't Drink The Water (without reading this book): The Essential Guide to Our Contaminated Drinking Water and What You Can Do About It,* by Lono Kahuna Kupua A'o.** 1998, 97 pp. (paperback), ISBN 0-9628882-9-X. Published by Kali Press, P.O. Box 2169, Pagosa Springs, CO 81147. Lists for $11.95.
This is the most up-to-date of all the drinking water books that I have seen, providing an accurate representation of the real health threats of different contaminants in public drinking water. It is very readable and gives excellent advice for evaluating your drinking water and treatment alternatives. Has good information about what to look for in the different types of water treatment options, but lacks specific recommendations or testing information about actual brand names and models.

***The Drinking Water Book: A Complete Guide to Safe Drinking Water,* by Colin Ingram.** 1991, 160 pp., ISBN 0-89815-436-7. Published by Ten Speed Press, P.O. Box 7123, Berkeley, CA 94707. Lists for $12.95.
After living in a remote Appalachian community that was besieged with an epidemic of cancer, the author went on a 5-year personal crusade to evaluate and test public drinking water and commercial bottled water, and to test point-of-use treatment options to determine what really worked best in different situations. Back in 1991, when Colin Ingram wrote *The Drinking Water Book,* he had tested and rated most of the drinking water treatment products currently on the market. Not quite as up-to-date as *Don't Drink The Water (without reading this book),* but definitely worthwhile for its practical recommendations and test results.

The New Complete Do-It-Yourself Manual, **from Reader's Digest.** 1991, 528 pp., ISBN 0-89577-378-3. Published by Reader's Digest Association, Inc., Pleasantville, NY 10570-7000. Lists for $35.00. This is a great general reference with good sections on basic plumbing and electrical construction.

Preparation for Nuclear Disaster, **by Wayne Le Baron.** 1998, 387 pp., ISBN 1-56072-557-5. Published by Nova Science Publishers, Inc., 6080 Jericho Turnpike, Suite 207, Commack, NY 11725. Lists for $34.00. This book is a good manual for preparing for potential disasters and interruptions in central services in general, not just the nuclear type. Contains thorough sections on home water treatment and storage in the event of nuclear and nonnuclear disasters. Also covers food storage and air filtration.

RESOURCES
Water Filters & Water Testing

For specific filter recommendations, see "My Filter Recommendations" earlier in this chapter. Municipal water systems are required to test their water regularly and should be able to provide you with a copy of the test results. If you have a well, or don't trust your local water supply, you should have your water tested occasionally. Test results include the EPA's (Environmental Protection Agency) recommended MCL (minimum contamination level) for handy reference. The following companies provide reputable testing services:

National Testing Laboratories, Ltd. The Nation's largest independent drinking water laboratory provides extensive tests at a reasonable price. Call or check their web site for test kits, prices and instructions. 6555 Wilson Mills Rd., Suite 102, Cleveland, OH 44143; phone: (800) 458-3330; web site: www.watercheck.com.

Suburban Water Testing Labs, Inc. Another excellent independent drinking water laboratory. Call or check their web site for test kits, prices and instructions. 4600 Kutztown Road, Temple, PA 19560; phone: (800) 433-6595; web site: www.h2otest.com.

Pumps & Rams

Baker Mfg. Company. These people make the classic long-handled cast-iron well pumps that I grew up drinking from at roadside parks in the White Mountains of New Hampshire and on farms. Baker Mfg. Company, 133 Enterprise St., Evansville, WI 535536; phone: (800) 356-5130.

Rintoul's Hand Pumps. A great source for hand-operated pumps, including old-fashioned deep well pumps. RR#2, Tobermory, Ontario, Canada N0H 2R0; phone: (519) 596-2612; web site: www.handpumps.com.

The Simple Pump Company. A relative newcomer to the hand pump scene, Simple Pump has a great new product for putting a backup hand pump down your well casing right next to your existing electrical submersible well pump. This way, if your power goes out, you can still charge your house's pressure tank with the hand pump. Simple Pump also has a 12-volt gear motor attachment for battery or solar operation. The Simple Pump Company, 1167 Annie Court, Suite A, Minden, Nevada 89423; toll-free phone: (877) 782-0109; web site: www.simplepump.com.

Lehman's. A major supplier of goods for simple living. For a catalog, send $3 to: Lehman's, Dept 8-PJB, P.O. Box 41, Kidron, OH 44636; phone: (330) 857-5757; web site: www.lehmans.com.

Cumberland General Store. Many old-time useful items, including a good selection of hand pumps and well accessories. For a catalog, phone (800) 334-4640, or send $4 to: Cumberland General Store, #1 Highway 68, Crossville, TN38555. Web site: www.cumberlandgeneralstore.com.

Lehman's and the **Cumberland General Store** carry hydraulic rams, or you can buy direct from the **RAM Company**, 247 Llama Lane-BWH, Lowesville, VA 22967; phone: (800) 227-8511. The RAM Company also makes solar pumps.

VI Food: Growing, Foraging, Hunting & Storing

Adequately feeding 8 billion people may be the single most difficult task in building a sustainable world. We are exploring the outer reaches of the solar system, reaping the benefits of the computer revolution, and working wonders in medicine, but as the nineties progress, the ranks of the hungry are expanding. The growth in world output of grain, the staff of life, has slowed dramatically in recent years.

—Lester R. Brown, Christopher Flavin, and
Sandra Postel, *Saving the Planet*

WORLD POPULATION AND FOOD SUPPLY

Over the next 30 years, as weather patterns continue to destabilize due to global warming, population adds another few billion to the planet, and oil supplies begin to lag behind demand, your ability to grow, forage, and hunt for your own food supply may become increasingly important. If long-term disruptions in central services should ever occur, a stored supply of food and the ability to generate more food will be of utmost importance. This chapter will introduce you to a number of practical techniques for food production and preservation, but for detailed and thorough information, do yourself a favor and pick up several of the recommended references.

Two hundred years ago, the British clergyman Thomas Robert Malthus penned his famous essay on population growth and future food shortages. He based his dire predictions on the observation that food production was rising linearly, but population was growing exponentially. One hundred years later, Sir William Crookes warned the British Association for the Advancement of Science that unless science came up with new methods to radically boost grain production, the world would face widespread starvation by the 1930s.

Fortunately, as global population has soared, so has the agricultural output from the world's farms. Over the past century, worldwide grain production has increased by a factor of five. The last 50 years have seen the production of major crops more than double and grain output has tripled. While these gains are truly astounding, they have barely kept ahead of population growth. The population of the planet took many thousands of years to reach its first billion sometime around 1800, but it took only another 130 years to add the second billion. Since I was a small child in 1960, the global population of 3 billion has doubled to 6 billion in 1999 (POPIN, June 7, 1994).

Even though the rate of population growth has shrunk from a high of 2.1% in 1964 to 1.3% in 1998, the world population continues to grow by about 76 million people annually, which is roughly equal to adding one third of the population of the United States every year (U.S. Bureau of the Census, December 29, 1999). At the 1998 rate of growth, global population will double in 54 years, but few scientists believe that the planet will be able to sustain such growth. Most of the world's food supply comes from agriculture, fisheries, and grazing animals. Until recently, food production gains were spread across these three categories, but now it appears that the world's fisheries and pasturelands have reached or exceeded their sustainable loads.

Global fish exports grew fivefold from 1970 until peaking in 1997 but now show disturbing symptoms of impending decline. Starting with the well-publicized collapse of the huge North Atlantic fisheries, the breakdown of large fisheries has now occurred in all of the world's oceans. The United Nations Food and Agriculture Organization (FAO) estimates that 11 out of 15 of the world's most important fisheries are now in decline, and 70% of major commercial fish species are either fully or overexploited (Brown et al., 1999a, 36). The huge growth in the harvest of seafood over the past few decades has resulted in declining fishery populations throughout the world. If the world's fishing fleets continue to harvest the oceans at their present rate, many scientists believe that we will see catastrophic collapses in practically all of the remaining large fisheries. The increasing use of aquaculture fish farms is only a partial solution, because fish farms require grain or high protein feedstock to nurture farmed fish. For example, from 1985 to 1995, shrimp farmers used 36 million tons of wild fish to produce 7.2 million tons of shrimp—not a very efficient use of resources in a world that is having problems feeding the current population.

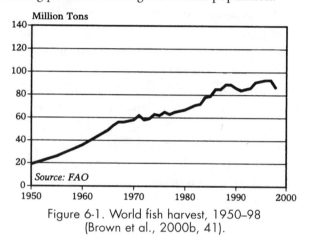

Figure 6-1. World fish harvest, 1950–98 (Brown et al., 2000b, 41).

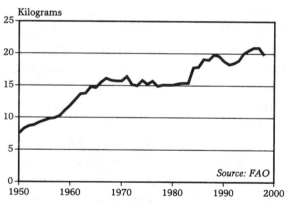

Figure 6-2. World fish harvest per person, 1950–98 (Brown et al., 2000b, 41).

Similarly, poorly managed livestock grazing has caused degradation and decreased output in roughly 20% of the world's pasture and range lands. In all likelihood, due to limits on available land, the number and productivity of the world's livestock herds will not increase significantly in the near

future. Given the state of the world's fisheries, and the lack of new sources for range land, it appears that we must look primarily to significant increases in agricultural output if the world is to adequately feed a few billion more people over the next 50 years.

Agricultural Productivity

Several factors have contributed to the unprecedented rise in the world's agricultural output over the past century. This century has seen the introduction of chemical fertilizers and pesticides, the replacement of beasts of burden by modern farm machinery, the introduction of genetically manipulated strains of high-productivity crops, and the explosion in the use of irrigation both to boost crop returns and expand cropland to areas that do not normally receive enough rainfall. Numerous signs indicate that the period of rapid growth in world food production has come to an end.

Grain consumption directly accounts for about half the calories consumed in the world, and through livestock feed, indirectly accounts for much of the supply of meat, milk, eggs, and poultry. Between 1950 and 1984, world grain output grew at a rate of 3% per year (Brown et al., 1991, 84), which was significantly faster than the population growth rate. This resulted in a 2.6-fold increase in grain output. However, since 1984, increases in grain productivity have slowed to around 1% per year and peaked in 1997. 1998 saw a drop in world grain production by about ½% followed by a drop of more than 1% in 1999. If this disturbing trend continues, the ranks of the hungry and underfed may swell by billions of people throughout the next century. (Brown et al., 2000b, 34)

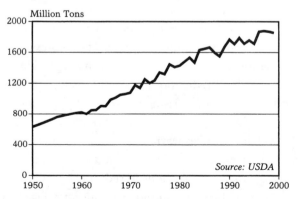

Figure 6-3. World grain production, 1950–99 (Brown et al., 2000b, 35).

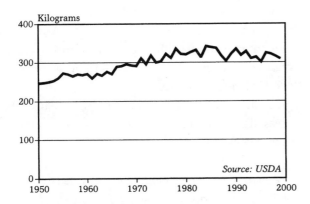

Figure 6-4. World grain production per person, 1950-99 (Brown et al., 2000b, 35).

Of the one-ninth of the earth's land that was considered arable in 1900, little remains really healthy; most is stressed and losses are generally accelerating.

—Paul Hawken, Amory Lovins, and L. Hunter Lovins, *Natural Capitalism*

In the earlier part of this century, acreage devoted to cropland grew dramatically, contributing a healthy share to increasing world food production. For example, cropland devoted to grain grew by 25% from 587 million hectares in 1950 to the all-time high of 732 million hectares in 1981. However, from 1981 to 1999, grain cropland shrank by 6% to 690 million hectares (Brown et al., 1999b, 120). The combination of population growth, desertification, soil depletion, insect resistance to pesticides, overpumping of groundwater, and the drying up of major rivers appears to have caught up with worldwide efforts to pace food production gains with population growth through improved productivity and by farming ever-increasing amounts of land.

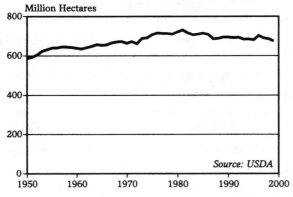

Figure 6-5. World grain harvested area, 1950–99 (Brown et al., 2000b, 45).

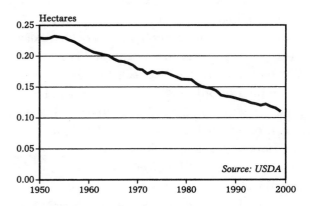

Figure 6-6. World grain harvested area per person, 1950–99 (Brown et al., 2000b, 45).

Irrigation Gains and Losses

Irrigated land comprises only about 16% of the world's cropland, but contributes about 40% of the world's food production (Postel 1999, 5). In 1900, the world's irrigated land was estimated at 48 million hectares of land. By 1960, this amount nearly doubled to 94 million hectares. From 1950 to 1999, the amount of irrigated land first radically increased, then climbed more slowly to 260 million hectares in 1999 (Brown et al., 1999b, 123). In the 1980s, as major rivers began to run dry for parts of the year, and most of the best sites for dams and reservoirs were already developed, the per capita net world irrigated area began to shrink for the first time in the modern era (see Figure 6-7).

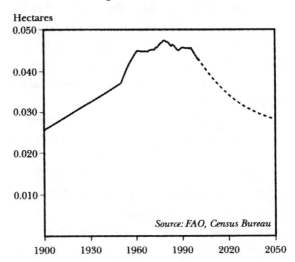

Figure 6-7. Net world irrigated area per person, 1950–98 (Brown et al., 1999b, 124).

In the modern world, downstream farmers are getting an increasingly short end of the stick. China's great Yellow River first ran dry for 15 days in 1972. In 1997, due to droughts and heavy irrigation usage, the Yellow River failed to reach the ocean for a record 226 days out of the year. For much of each year, the Colorado River shrinks to a trickle of polluted, unusable water before it empties into the Gulf of Mexico, depriving Mexican farmers and indigenous peoples of their traditional source of water for drinking and irrigation, and destroying a once-healthy fishery at the mouth of the river. Other large rivers, such as the Nile, the Ganges, the Indus, the Amu Darya, the Syr Darya, and Africa's Chao Phraya face similar problems. In addition, overpumping of groundwater for irrigation and other human needs is resulting in declining water levels, failed wells, and increasing salinity of major aquifers in California's Central Valley, China's grainbelt middle plains, India's principal breadbasket provinces, North Africa, the Arabian Peninsula, and the giant Ogallala aquifer in the south-central United States (Postel 1999, 65–86).

Soil Health and Soil Losses

In addition to increasing the use of irrigation and the physical space allotted to agricultural lands, the introduction of modern chemical-based factory farming has been a major contributor to the tremendous increase in agricultural output over the last 100 years. Although initially dramatic results were obtained using chemical fertilizers and pesticides, today's farms are experiencing diminishing returns in both of these areas. As the long-term depletion of soils continues, due to modern chemical-intensive farming methods, many farmers are finding that they must consume ever-increasing quantities of fertilizers just to maintain current yields. The use of chemical fertilizers and pesticides contributes to killing the natural microbial actions that promote healthy soils and plants. As insects grow increasingly resistant to chemical insecticides, monocropping farming methods provide a haven for exploding

insect populations. In 1948, when the use of chemical pesticides was in its infancy, the United States consumed 50 million pounds of insecticides a year while losing 7% of its crops to pests. In 1999, U.S. crop losses to insects are 13%, now 20% higher than prepesticide days, yet pesticide use has increased twenty times to almost a billion pounds a year (Hawken et al., 1999, 196).

> *A third of the original topsoil in the United States is now gone.*
>
> *It is estimated that the world has from 50 to 100 years of farmable soil, using current farming practices.*
>
> *It takes an average of 500 years for nature to build one inch of topsoil.*
>
> *United States farms have cut soil losses to about 18 times the rate of nature's replacement.*
>
> *Developing nations continue to deplete soil at an average of 36 times replacement, but China currently depletes soil at a rate of 54 times replacement.*
>
> *If used properly, Biointensive farming practices, based on ancient sustainable methods, can build soils at a rate 60 times as fast as nature.*
>
> —Ecology Action, January 2000

It has taken hundreds of millions of years for our planet to develop the thin mantle of topsoil that nurtures plant life on the surface of the earth and grows most of the food that we eat. Modern farming practices, yielding high gains in the short term, are flushing away this precious heritage at an alarming rate.

Healthy soil contains adequate nutrients to sustain plant growth, good structure to hold water and promote root propagation, and a myriad of living organisms. Earthworms, microbes, and fungi are essential for recycling organic material, storing nutrients for slow release to plants, fixing nitrogen from the air, and breaking down soil minerals into forms that plants can utilize. Good soil is 3% humus in tropical areas and 4–6% humus in temperal climates. Humus is decomposed and recombined organic material. Research has shown that simply by increasing poor soil's humus content (typically at about

0.5%) in the upper foot of soil to 2%, rainfall or irrigation requirements can be reduced by as much as 75%. Within one single teaspoon of cured humus live as many as 6 billion microorganisms. That's roughly equal to the entire human population of the planet (Jeavons 1995, 34). These bacteria and fungi release organic acids and other organic compounds into the soil that are an essential part of the food chain for plants. The acids dissolve soil minerals and turn them into a form that is easily used by the plants. Even with lots of chemical fertilizer, plants may still not grow well if there is no organic matter in the soil to sustain healthy microbial action.

In the long run, soil health can only be maintained by recycling organic material back into the soil. Observations of long-term experiments with wheat/fallow systems in the semiarid Northwest found that the soil's levels of organic carbon and nitrogen have been steadily declining since the study was started in the 1930s, except for where manure has been applied. In Asia, where population density is quite high compared to several other world regions, people already recycle most of their own waste to help support agriculture.

About half of good soil's weight is solid matter. Of this, a tenth is organic material, which holds about as much water and more nutrients than the other ninety percent. In addition, the organic matter and the worms and other organisms it supports help to maintain a good soil structure, with millions of tiny nooks and crannies for roots to grow into. Roots do not grow through solid rock, but require spaces and gaps for growth. Healthy soil is not compact, but loose and filled with tiny spaces. Soil that is too coarse, like sand, does not hold many nutrients or water in its matrix. Soil that is too fine, such as clay, compacts easily, can stay wet too long, and is hard to till. Whether the soil is too coarse or too fine, adding decomposed and recombined organic matter (humus) will improve its texture, water retaining-capacity, and fertility.

Sustainable Agriculture

A sustainable agriculture is one that, over the long term, enhances the environmental quality and the resource base on which agriculture depends; provides for basic human food and fiber needs; is economically viable; and enhances the quality of life for farmers and society as a whole.

—American Society of Agronomy

Prior to the recent upheavals caused by humanity's meddling with the earth's magnificent natural systems, our planet was the perfect example of a self-sustaining system. Everything was recycled in an endless circle of birth, consumption, death, and rebirth in the form of a new organism—a fungus, bacteria, plant, or animal form. Modern factory farming methods have been adopted to maximize yields with a minimum of labor, with little regard for the natural systems that have survived on this planet for aeons. On the other hand, sustainable agricultural methods are based upon careful observation of natural systems, mimicking their features in a controlled and nurtured way to produce an abundance of crops without depleting the natural resources (soil, water, purity of the air, etc.) that are so necessary for the survival of humans and millions of other creatures.

Prior to the advent of chemical fertilizers, this country's traditional farming practice was to cut down a chunk of forest (or plow a parcel of prairie), farm the soil for a few years until the soil was depleted, then move on to the next chunk of land, and repeat the same pattern. With growing populations and shrinking sources of arable land, this kind of farming cycle cannot be sustained. When it was discovered that certain essential nutrients could be added back into the soil in the form of chemical fertilizers, yields were maintained over longer periods of time. Unfortunately, these artificial nutrients do not protect or regenerate the topsoil or provide many of the trace nutrients essential to sustain long-term plant and animal health.

"NATURAL" RECYCLING

Forests draw carbon and nitrogen from the air and soil, and water, minerals, and trace elements from the soil, and then harness the power of the sun through photosynthesis to grow branches and leaves.

These branches and leaves eventually fall to the earth, where they are broken down into organic material and recycled back into the soil by the action of worms, insects, and a multitude of microorganisms. The roots of a single plant, often hundreds of twisted miles long, and weighing as much or more than the portion above ground, become another source of organic matter and humus when they die and decompose.

Certain crops, such as corn, millet, wheat, oats, amaranth, and rice, contain a lot of carbon in their stalks. "Grow Biointensive" sustainable farming techniques grow a high percentage of these kinds of crops (grown in roughly 60% of the crop area) to return organic matter to the soil in the form of cured compost, simulating the forest's recycling of leaves, roots, and branches. Deep-rooted crops, like alfalfa and comfrey, that are particularly good at drawing minerals from deeper soils are valuable as "green manures." The root systems of these plants contribute to the depth and structure of the soil. When composted, mulched, or tilled into the soil, green manures provide a source of organic minerals and other nutrients to plant varieties less adept at utilizing raw minerals in the soil. If we focus only on harvesting as much as possible in a short period of time, we will eventually deplete the soil of most nutrients and end up with soil only capable of growing a few weeds. Sustainable agriculture concerns itself with growing soil as well as crops.

PLANT SPACINGS AND COMPANION PLANTING

Nature does not grow plants in neat widely spaced rows. Widely spaced rows are convenient for machinery and harvesting, but provide poor microclimates for nourishing plants. Wide open areas between rows resemble deserts more than nature's gardens. They dry out quickly and provide an ideal space for weeds to grow in. Walking down the rows makes harvesting and weeding easy, but leads to rapid soil compaction. "Grow Biointensive" farming practices and Masanobu Fukuoka's "no till" food-raising methods use closely spaced plantings that resemble natural settings. Closely spaced plants quickly provide shade that helps to reduce weed

infestations. Companion planting of different species that grow well together reduces insect infestations and helps create a synergistic effect that increases crop yields. Simply spacing plants closer together is no guarantee of sustainability or increased productivity. Plants that are spaced too close together will choke themselves, stunting their growth and reducing yields. If care is not taken to replenish the soils with crop rotations, "green manures," and/or cured compost, closely spaced plantings will deplete soils at a faster rate than traditionally spaced plantings.

NATURAL FARMING

After a severe illness culminating in a life changing spiritual experience that he refers to as "the experience of God," Masanobu Fukuoka quit his job as a research scientist specializing in plant pathology and turned to a simple life of farming. Through careful observation of nature, he developed the principles of "natural farming." Even though he sometimes refers to his methods as "do nothing farming" because they eliminate tilling the soil and the use of fertilizers and pesticides, his methods do require work and careful planning. By doing the right things at the right time and in the right order, Fukuoka has continued to improve his yields, soil quality, and topsoil depths over a period of thirty years using natural farming methods. He consistently harvests rice yields equal to those achieved by modern chemical intensive methods, while his winter grain yields are somewhat higher than those on neighboring farms using "modern methods." All of this is done with minimal intervention, minimal labor, and no composting or addition of soil amendments, although the rice and wheat straw from his harvests are all returned to the land as mulch, eventually decomposing to become part of the soil. For more information on his natural farming methods, see *The One-Straw Revolution* and *The Road Back to Nature* by Masanobu Fukuoka. (Both are fine books, but currently out of print. See your local library.)

GRAZING ANIMALS

It is important to note that grazing and other forms of meat production may be managed sustainably, or in ways that are highly detrimental to the environment. When animals graze on grasslands, they turn basically unusable cellulosic materials (grasses) into valuable products like meat, dairy, leather, and natural fibers. On the other hand, when livestock are fed on grain, there is always a loss of food value. For instance, it takes several pounds of grain to grow a single pound of meat. In the case of cattle, it takes an average of 7 pounds of grain to produce 1 pound of beef, but can take as much as twenty pounds. For pork, the food loss is close to 4:1 and for poultry it is just over 2:1. Fish farms lead the pack with a grain-to-feed conversion efficiency of less than 2 (Brown et al., 1999b, 130). Wherever animals are grown in a feedlot, there is the added environmental load from the consumption of water, fertilizer, and petrochemicals used to grow their feed, as well as significant nitrogen runoff into the water table from the resulting giant manure piles.

To maintain the health of grasslands that once evolved with grazing animals (buffalo, wildebeest, gazelle, deer, etc.), it is important to restore and maintain grazing by cattle or other grazing animals. In the wilds, native grazing animals tend to graze heavily in very concentrated areas for short periods of time. When the herd moves on to another area, it leaves behind a heavily churned surface, trapping rain, seeds, and manure to plant and nurture next year's crop of grasses. Modern grazing practices, called management-intensive rotational grazing (MIRG), mimic these natural grazing patterns. Recently, MIRG has spread through the beef, pork, and dairy industries of the U.S. Midwest (Hawken et al., 1999, 208), where it is contributing to the revitalization of the range-fed livestock industry and grasslands. With MIRG, animals are corraled in temporary paddocks where they graze in a concentrated and managed fashion. When they have optimally grazed one area, the paddock is moved on to the next pasture.

"GROW BIOINTENSIVE"

Population will increase rapidly, more rapidly than in former times, and 'ere long, the most valuable of all arts will be the art of deriving a comfortable subsistence from the smallest area of soil.

—Abraham Lincoln, 1857

For the past 30 years, Ecology Action, led by John Jeavons, has conducted research into sustainable farming practices, now known as the "Grow Biointensive" Food-Raising Method. Jeavons's excellent book, *How to Grow More Vegetables: Fruits, Nuts, Berries, Grains, and Other Crops Than You Ever Thought Possible on Less Land than You Can Imagine,* (Ten Speed Press, 1995) summarizes these findings with information on optimal plant spacing, soil preparation, composting, companion planting, seed propagation, and many other topics.

The advantages of "Grow Biointensive" agriculture are listed below:
- Potential to build soil up to 60 times faster than occurs in nature
- Can reduce water consumption by 67% to 88%, energy consumption by 99%, and the amount of purchased fertilizer required by 50% or more per pound of food produced compared with conventional agricultural practices
- Can produce two to six times the yield per unit of area as compared to standard commercial agriculture
- Can reduce by more than half the land area necessary to grow food, compared with standard agricultural methods
- Can produce a 100+% increase in soil fertility while productivity increases and resource use decreases, and a 100+% increase in income per unit of area

The "Grow Biointensive" method is simple to learn and requires no expensive machinery. Based on sophisticated principles dating back 4,000 years in China, 2,000 years in Greece, and 300 years in Europe, it was synthesized and brought to the United States by the English master horticulturist Alan Chadwick. "Grow Biointensive" practices enable a family in the United States to produce an abundant supply of fresh vegetables in a typical backyard. Thousands of Third World farmers on marginal lands have used "Grow Biointensive" practices to turn desperate subsistence farms into successful minifarms that provide a plentiful supply of food for their families and reap substantial profits on as little as one-fifth of an acre of land. For detailed instructions on

"Grow Biointensive" principles, planting charts, and fertilizing recommendations, see *How to Grow More Vegetables: Fruits, Nuts, Berries, Grains, and Other Crops Than You Ever Thought Possible on Less Land than You Can Imagine* by John Jeavons. Important aspects of the "Grow Biointensive" method are summarized below.

- Double-dug, raised beds
- Intensive planting
- Composting, including carbon farming for compost
- Calorie farming for complete diets
- Open-pollinated seeds for genetic diversity
- Companion planting
- A "whole gardening" method

Letter from a Kenyan farmer

I am basically a tiny farmer. I came here to Mabusi village of Kakamega district in 1993 following the clashes that displaced my family from our former home at Chukura in Uasin-Gishu district of Rift Valley province. The ethnic clashes made me lose my 10-acre family land, 5 head of cattle, houses and other property that had taken me years and years to acquire.

The loss of these things caused my hope and that of my children to evaporate from our bodies. I was reduced to nothing. Luckily enough, I managed to purchase 0.3 acres of land here with the help of one of my son's savings...

A year later, towards the end of 1994, a Mr. Eric Kisiangani was introduced to me by one of our neighbors at our newly-found home, Mabusi.... Over the course of time, Eric and I became friends, and my respect for his integrity and ability grew. Each time he visited my family he taught us one or two aspects of Biointensive mini-farming, including double-digging, compost, offset planting, and natural pest control techniques.

On May 13th, 1995, Eric asked me if I could accompany Konambaga Women's Group to Manor House Agricultural Centre for 1-week course. The lessons I had from Manor House and those that I continue to receive from

Eric and his colleagues at Rural Technology Centre have moved my household from misery to normal rich life comparatively. My small "shamba" is producing surplus, which I sell for income. Last season, April to June, I earned Kshs.15,000 (U.S. $268) from sales of Sukuma Wiki (similar to tree collards).

My 0.3 acres of land is producing plenty and healthy vegetables that bring money to knock at my door in the wee hours of the day. I mean, people come knocking at the door of my house before 6:00 AM wanting to buy vegetables....Biointensive farming has recreated hope in me and my household. I can now face the future proudly.

—Susan Wekesa, Kenya

Double-Dug, Raised Beds

At the heart of "Grow Biointensive" is this special soil preparation. Crops are planted in beds that are "double-dug." The soil is loosened "two spades deep" (approximately 24 inches) as compared to modern soil tilling practices, which loosen the soil to a depth of only about 6 inches. The loosened soil enables plant roots to quickly grow deep into the soil, makes weeding an easy chore, allows for good penetration and retention of water, and better utilizes fertilizers and composts. Typical beds are 3 to 5 feet wide and as long as you wish to make them. Double-digging the soil incorporates air into the soil, thereby increasing its volume, and naturally raises the surface of the bed with this extra volume.

Unless you live in an area with high-quality soil, the initial preparation and planting of a 100-square-foot raised bed can take considerable time and effort, on the order of 5 to 9½ hours. Once the bed is established, the soil will have better structure and the next year's preparation will take much less time. Even though initially the raised beds take more time to prepare, the Irish call this the "lazy bed" method, because the beds require less time weeding, watering, and fertilizing than other gardening methods. Because yields average between two and six times those of traditional methods, you need only tend and till about one quarter the area to get the same yield.

With proper crop rotations and composting, soil fertility and crop yields of double-dug beds increase with each successive year. Be patient—it takes five to ten years to build both the soil and one's horticultural skill. Initially, you should test your soil to determine what nutrients are lacking. A professional soil test is best, but a self-test kit (see *Resources* section) is much better than guessing. Testing your soil will save you money by preventing you from under- or over-fertilizing. (It is easy, for example, to add too much nitrogen, which will cause the soil's important organic matter to break down too quickly and lead to insect infestations.) See *How to Grow More Vegetables: Fruits, Nuts, Berries, Grains, and Other Crops Than You Ever Thought Possible on Less Land than You Can Imagine* by John Jeavons or the books by Eliot Coleman for organic fertilization recommendations that will contribute to the long-term health of your soil. With proper nutrient recycling through the compost pile, you may not need to add fertilizers after the first year or two.

THE INITIAL DOUBLE-DIG PROCESS

Prior to double-digging your planting beds, you should perform a soil test to determine optimum fertilization. As mentioned previously, typical beds are 3 to 5 feet wide and as long as you wish to make them. The description of the process here is adapted from John Jeavons, *How to Grow More Vegetables: Fruits, Nuts, Berries, Grains, and Other Crops Than You Ever Thought Possible on Less Land than You Can Imagine.*

1. Soak the planting area with a sprinkler. After soil is lightly moistened 1 to 2 feet deep, pre-loosen the entire planting area 12 inches deep using a spading fork.

2. Spread a 1-inch layer of cured compost (preferable) or aged manure over the entire area to be dug. If your soil has a heavy clay content (fine grain, sticky soil) you should add sand, or if it is high in sand content, you should add clay. In general, you should not add more than a 1-inch layer of clay or sand at one time. Mix thoroughly into the upper 12 inches with a spading fork. Stand on a digging board, roughly 2 feet wide by 4 feet long, to prevent soil compaction and collapsing the edges of your trench as you dig.

3. Dig a 1-foot-wide by 1-foot-deep trench across one end of the area marked out for the planting bed (dig across the short direction of the bed). Place soil removed from this first trench into a soil storage area for use in making compost and flat (sprouting) soil.

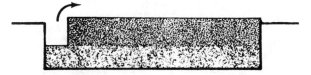

Figure 6-8. Dig first trench and remove soil for compost and flats. Illustration courtesy of *How to Grow More Vegetables, Fruits, Nuts, Berries, Grains, and Other Crops Than You Ever Thought Possible on Less Land Than You can Imagine* by John Jeavons (Ten Speed Press, 1995).

4. Loosen soil ("double-dig") first trench an additional 12 inches deep. In softer soil, loosen by digging with your spade and allowing the dirt to slip off the spade back into the trench. In harder ground, loosen the soil with a back and forth action, using your spading fork. Soil is now loosened to a total depth of 24 inches. If your soil is hard, and you can't loosen the lower layer to the full 24-inch depth, just do the best that you can. With each succeeding year's double-dig, the soil will soften and you will be able to till deeper.

5. Dig out the second one-foot-wide by one-foot-deep trench, and move this soil over to fill the first trench, mixing the layers as little as possible. Do not turn the upper layer over when it is moved from one trench to the next. You are trying to loosen and aerate the soil without destroying the natural soil stratification.

Figure 6-9. Start the next trench and dig over to fill in the top layer of the preceding one. Illustration courtesy of *How to Grow More Vegetables, Fruits, Nuts, Berries, Grains, and Other Crops Than You Ever Thought Possible on Less Land Than You can Imagine* by John Jeavons (Ten Speed Press, 1995).

6. Loosen the lower 12 inches of the second trench (double-dig).

7. Continue the trenching and double-digging process all the way across the planting bed.

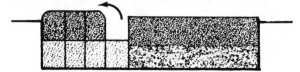

Figure 6-10. Continuing the trenching and double-digging process. Illustration courtesy of *How to Grow More Vegetables, Fruits, Nuts, Berries, Grains, and Other Crops Than You Ever Thought Possible on Less Land Than You can Imagine* by John Jeavons (Ten Speed Press, 1995).

8. Your bed is now a "raised bed" because the soil volume has been increased by the double-digging process. Shape the raised bed by raking. As indicated by your soil test, add organic nitrogen, phosphorous, potash, calcium, and trace mineral fertilizers (such as wood ash, eggshell, or the meals of kelp and alfalfa). Also include the needed levels of pH modifiers, such as leaf/pine needle compost to make the soil less alkaline or lime to make the soil less acid. Sprinkle the fertilizers and modifiers over the surface of the bed and sift in only 3 to 4 inches deep.

9. Plant seeds or transplant seedlings into the raised double-dug bed.

THE ONGOING DOUBLE-DIG PROCESS

The first year, you may not see yield improvements with double-dug raised beds. With each succeeding year, the double-digging process will become easier, the soil quality will improve, and your yields should improve. Start the ongoing double-dig process by removing any remaining bed vegetation for composting. Next, dig the first trench and remove this trench soil, saving approximately one-seventh of this soil for flat soil and six-sevenths for compost. Continue to double-dig across the entire length of the raised bed, as in the initial double-dig process. When the soil is in reasonably good shape (usually after at least two double-digs), you could save time by substituting a U-bar dig to loosen and aerate the soil (see Figure 6-11). If you use a U-bar regularly, double-dig again when you notice increased compaction.

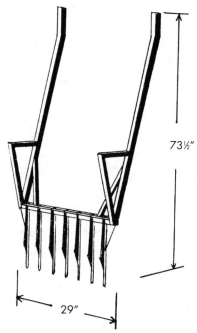

Figure 6-11. U-bar for loosening the soil with less effort. Illustration courtesy of *How to Grow More Vegetables, Fruits, Nuts, Berries, Grains, and Other Crops Than You Ever Thought Possible on Less Land Than You can Imagine* by John Jeavons (Ten Speed Press, 1995).

Level and shape the bed, and then water gently. Sprinkle any fertilizers and pH modifiers, as indicated by the soil test, on top of the bed and spread a 1-inch layer of compost over the bed. Adding compost *after* the double-dig minimizes leaching of nitrogen out of looser soils. Sift in materials 3 to 4 inches deep. Plant seeds or transplant seedlings into the raised double-dug bed (Jeavons 1995, 9).

Intensive Planting

Seeds or seedlings are planted in 3- to 5-foot–wide beds using a hexagonal spacing pattern (see Figure 6-12). Each plant is placed the same distance from the adjoining plants so that when the plants mature, their leaves touch. This creates a miniclimate under the leaves that is similar to natural growth patterns, retains moisture, protects the microbial life in the soil, retards weed growth, and provides for high yields. A partial list of "Grow Biointensive" planting spacings follows:

- Plant on 1-inch centers: radishes
- Plant on 2-inch centers: salsify
- Plant on 3-inch centers: carrots, bush peas, bunching onions

- Plant on 4-inch centers: beets, garlic, kohlrabi, onions, parsnips, pole peas, shallots, turnips, lentils, mung beans, garbanzo beans, and rice
- Plant on 5-inch centers: parsley, barley, oats, rye, wheat, and alfalfa
- Plant on 6-inch centers: basil, lima bush beans, snap bush beans, snap pole beans, celery, leeks, mustard, rutabagas, spinach, kidney beans, pinto beans, red beans, white beans, sesame, and soybeans
- Plant on 7-inch centers: mangels, millet, safflower, and sugar beets
- Plant on 8-inch centers: leaf lettuce (winter), fava beans, lima pole beans, and Swiss chard
- Plant on 9-inch centers: leaf lettuce (summer), Irish potatoes (9 inches deep), sweet potatoes (6 inches deep), peanuts, and rapeseed
- Plant on 10-inch centers: Chinese cabbage.
- Plant on 12-inch centers: collards, cucumber, horseradish, head lettuce, okra, peppers, New Zealand Malabar spinach, and quinoa
- Plant on 15-inch centers: broccoli, cabbage, cauliflower, sweet corn, kale, melons, crook neck squash, and patty pan squash
- Plant on 18-inch centers: brussels sprouts, flour or fodder corn, winter squash, and zucchini
- Tomatoes: 18 inches for cherry tomatoes, 21 inches for regular size, and 24 inches for large ones
- Watermelon: 12 inches for midget varieties, 18 inches for 5 to 7 pounds, 21 inches for 10 to 15 pounds, and 24 inches for largest varieties (Jeavons 1995, 80–108).

See *How to Grow More Vegetables: Fruits, Nuts, Berries, Grains, and Other Crops Than You Ever Thought Possible on Less Land than You Can Imagine* by John Jeavons for complete planting and fertilization charts, orchard and garden layouts, seed propagation, and planting and transplanting techniques.

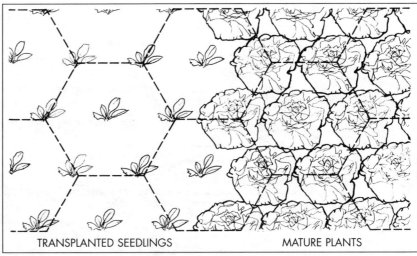

Figure 6-12. Hexagonal spaced planting. Illustration courtesy of *How to Grow More Vegetables, Fruits, Nuts, Berries, Grains, and Other Crops Than You Ever Thought Possible on Less Land Than You can Imagine* by John Jeavons (Ten Speed Press, 1995).

Composting

Well-made compost has been shown to have plant-growing benefits far in excess of its simple "nutrient analysis" and to be an active factor in suppressing plant diseases and increasing plant resistance to pests. . . . [T]he organic matter portion of the soil is more than simply a source of plant food and physical stability. It is also the power supply, so to speak. Organic matter is the engine that drives all the biological (and some of the chemical) processes in the soil. . . . All things being equal, if I were to suggest just one practice it would be to make as much first-class, well-decomposed compost as possible and use it liberally.
—Eliot Coleman, *The New Organic Grower*

The higher yields offered by intensive planting would not be sustainable without a way of maintaining the health and vigor of the soil. Chemical fertilizers, which are derived from increasingly expensive nonrenewable petroleum products, have been shown to deplete the soil over time. As soil quality deteriorates, increasing quantities of chemical fertilizers are needed to sustain yields, causing further harm to soil structure and microbiotic life in the soil. The "Grow Biointensive" food-raising method avoids these problems through recycling organic waste products

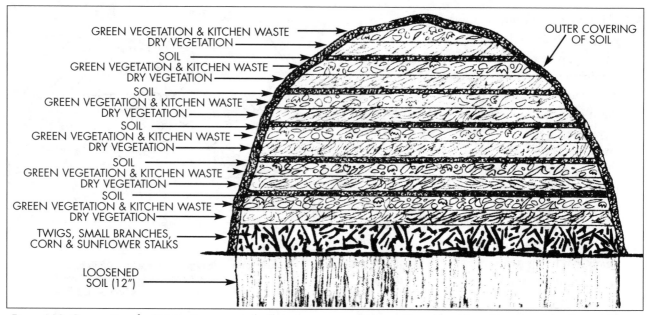

GREEN VEGETATION & KITCHEN WASTE
DRY VEGETATION
SOIL
GREEN VEGETATION & KITCHEN WASTE
DRY VEGETATION
SOIL
GREEN VEGETATION & KITCHEN WASTE
DRY VEGETATION
SOIL
GREEN VEGETATION & KITCHEN WASTE
DRY VEGETATION
SOIL
GREEN VEGETATION & KITCHEN WASTE
DRY VEGETATION
SOIL
GREEN VEGETATION & KITCHEN WASTE
DRY VEGETATION
SOIL
GREEN VEGETATION & KITCHEN WASTE
DRY VEGETATION
TWIGS, SMALL BRANCHES,
CORN & SUNFLOWER STALKS
LOOSENED
SOIL (12")

OUTER COVERING
OF SOIL

Figure 6-13. Cross-section of a Biointensive compost pile. Illustration courtesy of *How to Grow More Vegetables, Fruits, Nuts, Berries, Grains, and Other Crops Than You Ever Thought Possible on Less Land Than You Can Imagine* by John Jeavons (Ten Speed Press, 1995).

in the form of compost. Kitchen scraps, garden trimmings, and many other forms of organic matter, when properly composted, provide the elements necessary to maintain the biological life cycles that exist in the home garden. The structure and the microbiotic life of the soil are improved by compost, which creates better aeration and water retention. As the soil's health improves, optimum plant health is maintained and the garden's yields are maximized.

There are many different styles of compost piles and recipes for composting, but they all try to accomplish the same thing: the decomposition of organic material into humus. A compost pile magically transforms backyard wastes and smelly garbage into dark, rich, sweet-smelling humus with the look and consistency of crumbled chocolate fudge cake. The best times to build a compost pile are in the spring or fall, since too much heat and too little heat are detrimental to the composting process. A spot under the limbs of a deciduous tree provides shade from a hot summer's sun, yet lets the spring sun through to warm the compost heap. Composting is done in a pile to hold internal heat (up to 140°F) and moisture for nurturing the process.

Green plant materials will compost quickly, since they have a high nitrogen content that bacteria thrive on. Carbon-rich low-nitrogen materials, such as straw, sawdust, wood chips, and dry leaves, will decompose

slowly unless combined with high-nitrogen materials, like manure, green grass, or vegetable wastes. The best composts are from a mixture of brown (dry materials like straw and dead leaves) and green (fresh materials like kitchen scraps, grass clippings, and freshly pulled weeds) materials for an optimum mixture of high-nitrogen and carbon-rich materials. Soil is always added to the compost heap to provide a starter supply of microorganisms, improve moisture retention, and absorb smells. Oxygen is the other key ingredient to fuel the bacterial feast, making straw an optimal "brown" material since it provides abundant channels for air infiltration into the pile. If the pile gets smelly, it is could be too tightly compacted (not enough air) loosen the pile with a spading fork. If it has too much nitrogen content, which yields an ammonia smell, add more dry materials to the pile.

Longtime professional organic grower, Eliot Coleman, likes to block in his small-scale compost heaps with straw bales piled two or three high, leaving gaps between bales for air infiltration. The bales usually last for a couple years before becoming part of the next compost heap. His recipe for compost is to alternate 2- to 3-inch layers of brown materials with 1- to 6-inch layers of green ingredients, covering each green layer with a thin layer of topsoil. Since the pile is insulated by straw bales, it decomposes right to the bales and requires no turning. These piles may be used after a few months, but are optimal in about one and a half years. John Jeavons offers a similar recipe for Biointensive compost composed of approximately one-third rehydrated dry vegetation, one third green vegetation (including kitchen scraps) and one third soil, all by weight. Before starting, loosen 12 inches of soil beneath the pile to promote good drainage. The pile should be kept moist, but not wet, like a damp sponge that has been wrung out. You may want to cover the pile during rainy periods to prevent excessive moisture and leaching of nutrients out of the pile. Turning the pile improves aeration and speeds decomposition. Cover kitchen scraps and manure with a ¼- to ½-inch layer of soil to prevent flies and obnoxious odors.

Companion Planting

Research has shown that many plants grow better when near certain other plants. For example, green beans and strawberries thrive better when they are grown together. Some plants are useful in repelling pests, while others attract beneficial insect life. Borage, for instance, helps control tomato worms while its blue flowers attract bees. Additionally, many wild plants have a healthy effect on the soil; their deep roots loosen the subsoil and bring up previously unavailable trace minerals and nutrients. Use of companion planting aids the gardener to produce fine-quality vegetables, reduce pest problems, and create and maintain a healthy, vibrant soil. For more information on companion planting, see Rodale's *Companion Planting* or *How to Grow More Vegetables: Fruits, Nuts, Berries, Grains, and Other Crops Than You Ever Thought Possible on Less Land than You Can Imagine* by John Jeavons.

Whole Gardening

It is important to realize that the "Grow Biointensive" method is a whole system and that the components of the method must all be used together for the optimum effect. For example, if you plant your crops close together, without tending to soil health and fertility, you will reduce your yields and quality while lowering plant resistance to insects and disease.

Seed Propagation

The natural inclination of seeds is to germinate and grow when given the right moisture, soil, and warmth. Whether planting in beds or flats, the seed should be planted in moist, fertile soil (with lots of humus), and two to four times as deep into the soil as the seed's thickness, in the small direction. For most varieties, you will extend the growing season (harvest more times during the year) if seeds are propagated in potting soil within flats or cold frames, then transplanted to the garden. When planting seeds in flats, place them 1 inch apart (2 inches for larger plants such as squash and melon) preferably in a hexagonal pattern, so the seedlings will quickly create a miniclimate of their own.

A classic planting soil mixture for sprouting flats (by weight) is one part compost, one part gritty sand, and one part turf loam. A simpler flat soil mixture consists of equal parts sifted compost and bed soil. If you have double-dug raised beds, combine the soil from the first trench of the double-dig with compost for your bed soil. Gently water seedlings both before and after transplanting, to minimize plant shock. Handle seedlings by the leaves or scoop up with a protective ball of soil to avoid damaging the stem and roots. See the gardening references for more details.

Pest Control

There is a direct relationship between the growing conditions of plants and the susceptibility of those plants to pests. Problems in the garden are our fault through unsuccessful gardening practices, rather than nature's fault through malicious intent. The way to approach pest problems in the garden is to correct the cause rather than treat the symptom.

—Eliot Coleman, *Four-Season Harvest*

A growing number of successful organic farmers agree that insects and disease do not attack healthy unstressed plants, but go for plants that have been compromised in some way. In a healthy ecosystem, nature uses pests to destroy and recycle inferior plants while leaving the hardy plants alone so that they might continue to thrive. Modern scientific research has found that stressed plants have more available nitrogen and less protein, making them ideal feeding grounds for insects and disease. Overfertilizing, especially with chemical fertilizers, supplies excess nitrogen and increases susceptibility to insects.

Your first and best line of defense is therefore soil preparation. Make sure that you provide your crops with lots of composted organic matter. In *The New Organic Grower*, Eliot Coleman tells a story about visiting a German organic farm with a group of U.S. Department of Agriculture researchers in 1979. One member of the group was an entomologist (bug specialist) who was totally amazed by the lack of pests and crop damage in the organic farm's fields stating, "We can't do this well even *with* pesticides."

INTEGRATED PEST MANAGEMENT

For those situations where optimal soil fertility has not yet been established, or where a crop is threatened by blight or insect infestation, integrated pest management (IPM) offers "least-toxic" alternatives to modern chemical intensive pesticides. IPM is a term used to describe a pest control philosophy that focuses on the whole picture of pests, plants, and environment to maximize the effectiveness of natural and nontoxic pest control techniques and minimize the use of toxic chemicals. IPM acknowledges that chemical toxins have detrimental environmental effects, killing natural predators as well as the targeted pests. Throwing natural systems off balance often results in creating long-term problems with increasing numbers of pests. Due to their short life cycles and rapid reproduction rates, insects tend to develop genetic resistance to chemical pesticides faster than we can invent new ones.

For an introduction to IPM and sustainable agriculture, see the ATTRA (Appropriate Technology Transfer for Rural Areas) web site at www.attra.org. ATTRA is a national information service that offers information and technical service free of charge to people and organizations involved in commercial U.S. agriculture.

The Bio-Integral Resource Center (BIRC) is one of the leading organizations in the world providing experience and practical technical and policy infor-

mation in least-toxic urban and agricultural IPM and sustainable agriculture. They have an excellent quarterly publication, the *Common Sense Pest Control Quarterly*, featuring descriptions of the latest research, practical information, products, resources, book reviews, and direct answers to member questions (see *Resources* section). BIRC has also published two excellent books on common-sense pest control.

Nontoxic pest control techniques include the following:

- Supporting and introducing natural predators, such as birds, toads, praying mantises, and ladybugs
- Buying disease-resistant varieties of plants
- Rotating crops to keep from providing multiple years of unrestricted breeding for plant-specific pests
- Using companion planting techniques that have been successful at reducing pests
- Removing insects by vacuuming plants, washing plant leaves, hand picking insects, and so on
- Removing infected plants
- Using various insect baits and traps
- Providing barriers to pests, such as insect screen covers over crops
- Using nontoxic dry materials, such as diatomaceous earth and fine-ground basalt (harms beneficial insects as well as pests)
- Using nontoxic wet sprays, such as plant pyrethrin (harms beneficial insects as well as pests)

Extending the Harvest in Cold Climates

Garden-fresh vegetables can be harvested year-round in harsh climates either by providing them with heated and well-lit greenhouse spaces or by utilizing a variety of low-tech solutions to protect hardy plant varieties from the harsh climate changes of winter. Many crops grown in the late summer and throughout the fall will not grow significantly during the winter months, yet can still provide a delicious harvest of fresh, nutritious vegetables throughout the entire season. In the harsh climate of his farm at Harborside, Maine, organic grower Eliot Coleman has refined traditional techniques for protecting cold-resistant crops throughout the winter months. Eliot explains that he loves fresh vegetables, but is not much of a technocrat, so he prefers the ease and low cost of low-tech solutions over heated greenhouses. To take advantage of Eliot's 35 years of experience and experimentation, pick up his book, *Four-Season Harvest*.

Winter harvesting relies on growing cold-resistant crops in the fall, and then protecting them somewhat from the extremes of winter winds and temperature fluctuations. Many crops can handle freezing temperatures, but do not handle severe fluctuations in conditions, such as wet/dry, hot/freezing, and gale/calm. Simply covering plants will mellow out these conditions significantly by cutting wind, reducing heat loss, and taking advantage of the relatively warm thermal mass of the earth.

COLD FRAMES

A simple cold frame is a traditional method for covering plants to extend both the growing season and the harvest (see Figure 6-14). A cold frame is a shallow wooden box with no bottom and a clear top. Glaze the frame with either double-strength tempered glass or rigid plastic greenhouse material. The top must be removable or hinged to allow for watering and venting. A crop can easily cook inside a cold frame, even on a cold winter's day, when the sun shines brightly. The use of automatic greenhouse vent openers (available at greenhouse and gardener's suppliers) will lift the cold frame cover whenever the internal temperatures get hot, but may not be able to lift a heavy cover glazed with thick glass. Most winter vegetables can withstand freezing and thawing while growing, but may wilt if harvested frozen and then thawed after harvesting. To prevent wilting, do not cut while frozen, but wait until thawed at midday (Coleman 1992, 86).

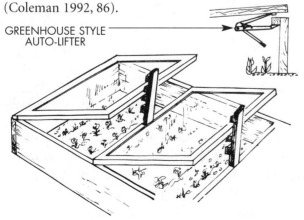

GREENHOUSE STYLE AUTO-LIFTER

Figure 6-14. Cold frames.

OTHER SEASON-EXTENDING METHODS

Plastic tunnels strung over hoops provide another season-extending method. These can be moved to protect different plants. The use of black plastic mulch can hold heat in and help propagate plants outdoors in early spring when the air temperatures are still too cold for normal propagation. Sprouting seedlings indoors in flats or on windowsills can help you get a jumpstart on spring planting, and can be essential when growing seasons are very short. You can make a lazy person's root cellar by placing straw bales over your root crops in the fall. Simply cut off the plant greens about one inch above the soil, prior to covering with bales. The bales will insulate the ground and keep the roots from freezing. Any time of the winter, roll the bales off a section of garden when you want to harvest fresh root crops. Watch for signs of mice and other critters, or you may find that they beat you to the harvest.

SPROUTING: YOUR OWN MINIGARDEN ON A WINDOWSILL

Seeds are one of nature's most perfect foods. They contain all the nutrients necessary to sustain the growth of budding seedlings until the seedling has developed a root system large enough to sustain growth from soil sources. One of the few foods more perfect than raw seeds are sprouted seeds. The sprouting process decreases the carbohydrate and increases the vitamin and protein content in these "live" foods.

Richard Nielsen, owner of Life Sprouts, a large organic seed and sprouting equipment business, tells the following story about an experiment he ran raising chickens.

Richard grew up on a farm. Like his father before him, Richard raised baby chicks on a steady diet of mash, reaching a typical mature weight of 5 to 5½ pounds. After a friend told him that they could increase the weight of their chickens using sprouts, he and his 8-year-old son decided to try feeding some 3-day old sprouted grains to their chickens. That year, their chickens averaged 6 to 6½ pounds. The experiment was such a success that the next year they decided to feed their chickens solely on a "live food" diet consisting of sprouted grains. That year, not one chicken was under 8 pounds, and some were over 8½ pounds. Incredibly, these chickens reached their prize-worthy weights on 25% less grain than consumed in previous years, indicating how significantly the nutritional value of dry grain is increased by the sprouting process.

Sprouting chart

Seed	Quantity per qt. jar	Soak time (hrs.)	Rinses per day	Average number of days to sprout	Harvest length (in.)
Adzuki bean	½ cup	6 to 12	3 to 5	2 to 5	½ to 1½
Alfalfa	2 tablespoons	3 to 8	2 to 5	3 to 6	½ to 2
Almond	1 cup	10 to 12	2 to 3	2 to 5	When split
Amaranth	12 tablespoons	None	3 to 4	2 to 3	¼
Barley	1½ cups	5 to 10	2 to 4	2 to 4	0 to ¼
Cabbage	3 tablespoons	7 to 10	2 to 3	3 to 5	½ to ¾
Cabbage, Chinese	3 tablespoons	4 to 7	2 to 3	3 to 5	1 to 1½
Clover	1½ tablespoons	4 to 8	2 to 3	3 to 5	1 to 2
Corn	1½ cups	8 to 12	2 to 3	2 to 3	¼ to ½
Garbanzo (chickpeas)	1 cup	8 to 12	3 to 4	2 to 4	½
Kidney beans	¼ cup	8 to 12	3 to 4	2 to 4	½ to 1
Lentil	¼ cup	5 to 10	2 to 4	2 to 4	¼ to 1
Lettuce	3 tablespoons	3 to 7	2 to 3	3 to 5	1 to 1½
Millet	1½ cups	4 to 8	2 to 3	2 to 4	⅛ to ¼
Mung bean	½ cup	6 to 10	3 to 4	3 to 5	1 to 3
Mustard	3 tablespoons	5 to 8	2 to 3	3 to 5	1 to 1½
Oats	1½ cups	3 to 5	1 to 2	1 to 2	0 to ¼
Pea (not split)	2 cups	7 to 10	2 to 3	2 to 3	¼ to ½
Peanut	1 cup	8 to 12	2 to 3	3 to 5	¼ to 1
Pinto bean	1 cup	8 to 12	3 to 4	3 to 4	½ to 1¼
Pumpkin	1½ cups	5 to 10	2 to 3	2 to 3	⅛ to ¼
Quinoa	⅓ cup	3 to 5	2 to 3	1 to 2	¼ to 1½
Radish	3 tablespoons	5 to 8	2 to 3	3 to 5	¼ to 1½
Rice	1½ cups	10 to 20	2 to 3	2 to 4	Seed length
Rye	1 cup	6 to 10	2 to 3	2 to 3	¼ to ½
Sesame	1½ cups	6 to 10	3 to 4	2 to 3	Seed length
Soybean	1 cup	10 to 20	5 to 6	3 to 6	½ to 2
Spinach	3 tablespoons	5 to 8	2 to 3	3 to 5	½ to 2
Sunflower (hulled)	1 cup	2 to 6	2 to 3	½ to 3	½ to 2
Triticale	1½ cups	6 to 10	2 to 3	2 to 3	¼ to ½
Wheat	1 cup	6 to 10	2 to 3	2 to 5	¼ to ½

Sources: Stevens 1997, 198; and Emery 1998, 114.

Sprouting is a simple process, and the equipment is very inexpensive. You can sprout seeds in your own home, creating a low-cost source of fresh vegetables all year long. All you need for starting your indoor sprout garden is a 1-quart glass jar, untreated whole seeds, a piece of nylon stocking (or cheesecloth, screen, nylon mesh, etc.) and a rubber-band or canning jar seal to hold the mesh over the jar. Richard Nielsen's company, Life Sprouts (see *Resources*), sells organic sprouting seeds and supplies, including an excellent covered combination crisper and sprouting tray.

Although most nutritious in their raw form, sprouts can be sautéed, stir-fried, boiled, or cooked into almost any dish. In just a few days, sprouts provide a source of garden-fresh vegetables any time of the year. Nearly all seeds can be sprouted, including most whole grains and legumes. Grains and legumes are probably the most compact and inexpensive type of food that can be stored for emergency preparedness.

The Sprouting Process

CAUTION: Potato and tomato sprouts are poisonous. Do not sprout commercial seeds for planting, because these are usually treated with a poisonous fungicide.

1. Measure seed batch according to the sprouting chart below. Use only untreated whole seed, preferably organic (available at health food stores). Inspect and pick debris out of seed.
2. Place seeds in quart jar (or sprouting tray) half filled with warm water (preferably unchlorinated). Cover jar with nylon stocking (or cheesecloth, screen, etc.) and rubberband in place.
3. Soak overnight or as directed in the chart. Drain and rinse with cool water (always rinse with cool water). If you use tap water, let water sit in an open container for a few hours before using, to get rid of the chlorine.
4. Keep warm and covered with a dark cloth, or keep in a cabinet, while germinating. For greener sprouts, give more light as they grow, but usually keep them out of direct sunlight. For whiter sprouts, keep out of the light. Experiment to find how you think they taste best.
5. Rinse and drain well two to three times a day (or as recommended in chart) to keep sprouts from spoiling or souring.
6. Sprouting time is a matter of personal taste but peak nutritive value is reached in two to three days. Sprouts can be kept in the refrigerator for a week. Freeze them if you wish to store for longer periods.
7. Some people recommend that you lightly steam bean sprouts to destroy toxins found in raw beans (Stevens 1997, 198).

FORAGING FOR FOOD

After a long winter, our ancestors usually ran outside and picked a fresh salad from the first green shoots of spring. After living on salt pork, dried beans, and old roots from the root cellar, fresh greens were a welcome change. One spring, I remember going hunting for a wild spring delicacy called "fiddleheads" (young fern shoots). We found what we thought were fiddleheads, brought them home, steamed a batch and gave them a try. They were awful! They made your mouth pucker and your throat gag. Not knowing any better, we had picked the furry kind of fern shoot, instead of the "furless" fern shoots. The next week, we found some of the right kind of fiddleheads, and they were sweet, tender, and delicious.

Carla Emery tells a story about some visitors to her area whose misadventures with wild plants were not as forgiving as mine. She just happened to see a family of three unwittingly dine on a sprig of poison hemlock after a local so-called "expert" on edible plants assured them that it was "Indian celery" (a close look-alike to poison hemlock). Carla rushed them to the drugstore for syrup of ipecac to help them throw up their snack. Unfortunately, one of the three wouldn't throw it up, so she was taken to the hospital for stomach pumping. Wondering if all that fuss was for nothing, one of these unfortunates picked a branch of what they had eaten and took it to the office of a poison weed specialist. The specialist's eyes widened when the visitor said that he had eaten some of this, telling him that he would be dead right now if it weren't for Carla's help. She also relates that both a local forest ranger and a child died from mistakenly eating some wild poison hemlock during the summer of 1975.
Adapted from Emery, *The Encyclopedia of Country Living: An Old Fashioned Recipe Book*, 1998, 401

WARNING: Never eat any wild plant unless you have 100% positive identification that it is edible, or you have taken the time to complete the three-day plant edibility test described in Chapter 4. A small bite of certain plants is enough to kill an adult.

Brief Guide to Wild Edible Foods

There are thousands of edible varieties of plants in North America. Some edible plants are truly delicious, but many that are considered edible taste bad and are primarily useful only in survival situations. A few of the more common and tasty wild edible plants are listed below. I suggest that you pick up one or two "real" guides to edible plants in your geographical region. *Identifying and Harvesting Edible and Medicinal Plants in Wild and Not So Wild Places* by Steve Brill and Evelyn Dean, is an excellent start. It is entertaining, practical, and offers varied cooking suggestions and recipes.

A good plant guide will also warn you about potentially poisonous "look-alike" plants that might be confused with the one that you think you are identifying. Harvesting wild edible plants can be fun and will help you make your diet more complete by adding more vitamins, minerals, and trace elements than are found in typical grocery store veggies. Use caution in your forays into wild edible plants, because nibbling on wild plants can kill you if you make a serious mistake. For a list of recommended edible and medicinal plant guides, see the suggested references in Chapters 4 and 9. In addition, *Foxfire 2* has an excellent section on foraging and cooking with wild greens from the Southern Appalachians.

Acorns. Acorns are the nuts from about fifty-five varieties of native oak trees. Gathered in the fall, acorns were traditional staple foods for several indigenous peoples. They were stored in baskets and crushed or ground into flour for cooking. In my local area, grinding depressions, where indigenous peoples ground their nuts into meal, are a common sight on the granite slabs adjacent to lakes and rivers. Some varieties of acorns are sweet and may be used without special preparation, but bitter varieties require treatment to remove excess tannic acid prior to eating. To remove bitterness, shell the acorns and boil in water until the water turns brown. Drain and repeat until the water stops changing color. If boiling is not an easy alternative, wrap nutmeats in a cloth and soak in a clear running stream for a few days until they taste sweet. Soaking acorn mush to remove bitterness

takes less time than soaking the whole seed. Acorn meal makes excellent pancakes and muffins.

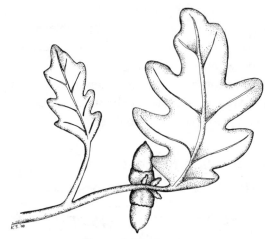

Figure 6-15. Acorns.

Black mustard, field mustard, and others. These weeds grow more or less anywhere in fields and disturbed areas. Most mustard leaves are best when harvested young in the spring, but some in the mustard family are good throughout the summer. Seeds can be harvested, ground, and mixed with vinegar, like commercial mustard. Young basal rosette looks similar to dandelions, only there is no milky sap. This is a tangy treat if you like strong flavors. There are no poisonous look-alikes.

Figure 6-16. Black mustard.

Bulrush. Like cattails, bulrushes provide a source of year-round food. Found in wet marshy areas and shallow waters of lakes or ponds, they are identified by long, non-branching stems, with a spiky cluster of flowers. Young roots and shoots can be used as a vegetable. Older roots can be pounded to remove fibers and then ground into flour.

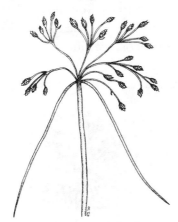

Figure 6-17. Bulrush.

Burdock. Burdock grows throughout the United States on roadsides and in fields and disturbed areas. The large broad leaves look a bit like rhubarb leaves (and rhubarb leaves are poisonous), so be careful. The leaves are bitter tasting, but the first-year plant's long taproot tastes like a delicious cross between potato and artichoke heart. The root may be harvested until the second year flowering, when it becomes inedible. Peel roots, slice to break fibers, and then boil or sauté. Burdock root has excellent nutritional and healing properties for the skin and kidneys, and for overall health. Young flower stalks may be peeled and eaten raw or boiled. Burdock flowers with purple to pink crests grow into sharp, hooked, little burr balls that are either annoying or great toys, depending on your point of view.

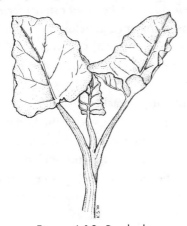

Figure 6-18. Burdock.

Cattail. Another staple of indigenous peoples, cattails are still used for food throughout the world. Find cattails in shallow waters of swampy areas. You can dig up roots in early spring to find delicious sprouts that can be eaten raw. Young summer stalks, up to 2 to 3 feet tall, may be peeled for their tasty core (known as "Cossack Asparagus"), which is eaten raw, steamed, or boiled. Young buds can be picked before pollen ripens and boiled like mini corn on the cob. Roots can be harvested in the fall through spring. Dig, dry, and peel, and then pound into flour. Pounded roots may be soaked and then decanted to render starchy material. Poisonous look-alikes are the stalks and roots of wild irises, so be sure to identify stalks by the presence of old cattails. Pollens can be harvested as a flour or flour extender.

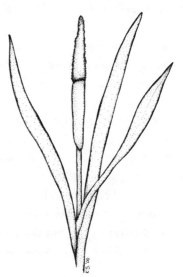

Figure 6-19. Cattail.

Chicory. Like its close relative the dandelion, chicory is a staple green in many countries and has a long taproot. When young, the leaves look like dandelion leaves with the addition of irregular hairs on most of the leaves. When it matures, the resemblance to the dandelion disappears as it grows a tall hairy flower stalk with numerous sky-blue fringed flowers. Widespread, chicory is found in fields and other disturbed areas. Harvest leaves and shoots early in spring. Older leaves may require boiling and water changes, if bitter. The taproot is rather bitter, but makes a good caffeine-free coffee substitute when roasted at 250°F for 2 to 4 hours until brown, and then ground.

Figure 6-20. Chicory.

Curled dock, yellow dock, and sour dock. In early spring, this plant is easily recognized by its rosette of long, narrow leaves—up to two feet long—with curly edges. It grows throughout the country in fields, disturbed soil, and near water. Early spring leaves are delicious steamed and may be acceptable raw, but should be washed first. For later harvests, boil the leaves with multiple water changes to reduce bitterness. In summer, the flower stalk may be peeled and steamed as a vegetable. With much difficulty, the seeds may be threshed and ground into flour. Dock was a staple green during the Depression. The taproot is too bitter for eating, but is a useful medicinal herb for skin and liver conditions.

Figure 6-21. Curled dock.

Dandelion. The common dandelion is quite a versatile and delicious plant. It is found throughout the country in open fields and disturbed areas. The young leaves are excellent as salad greens, and are more nutritious than any you can buy in the grocery store. Peel young roots and eat raw or slice thin and boil. If leaves or roots are bitter, boiling in a couple water changes improves the taste. Dip blossoms in fritter batter and fry in oil, like tempura veggies.

Figure 6-22. Dandelion.

Fiddleheads (bracken and ostrich ferns). Collect young ferns in midspring, before the round "fiddlehead" has started to unfurl (up to about 8" tall). Wash to remove fur or inedible scales. I found the not-so-furry ostrich ferns much sweeter and not bitter like the furry bracken ferns. Perhaps it was just due to local effects or the age of the fiddleheads? Steam or boil fiddleheads to remove mild toxicity. Large quantities of mature bracken have been known to poison cattle. Fiddleheads are an expensive delicacy in upscale restaurants. Please leave a few fiddleheads in every cluster, as they will not return if you harvest the whole lot.

Pigweed (amaranth). Similar to lamb's quarters (which is sometimes also called pigweed), this plant has smoother, more elongated leaves. Use young leaves as a lettuce substitute. Harvest seeds and grind for flour. Seeds have more nutrition and higher protein than grains. Amaranth was a key staple cultivated by the Aztecs for its seeds. Pigweed concentrates nitrates, so use sparingly if taken from fertilized fields.

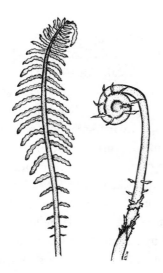

Figure 6-23. Fiddleheads.

Lamb's quarters, goosefoot. "Along with dandelions and watercress, lamb's quarters is one of the most nutritious of foods" (Brill and Dean 1994, 47). Being widespread, tasty, long-seasoned and easily identified, lamb's quarters is a prime candidate for the beginner to learn to identify. This plant has little or no odor, so if the plant you pick has an odor, it's not lamb's quarters and may be poisonous. Leaves are alternating, almost triangular, with a blunt tip and jagged edges. Leaves may develop a white tinge, but they remain perfectly edible. Harvest young shoots up to ten inches tall, or tender new growth until late fall. This plant is a good pot herb, although it shrinks by about two-thirds when cooked.

Figure 6-25. Pigweed.

Pine trees. Harvest pine nuts in the fall from hard, green pine cones. Open the cones in the heat of a fire to reach the pine nuts buried inside. "Open" cones have probably already dropped their nuts. Pine nuts from the piñon pines were once a staple food for the indigenous peoples in Nevada. One of the ways that the U.S. government used to force these tribes to move off their land and onto reservations was to destroy the piñon pines, thereby removing one of their major sources of wild food. Pine needles can be boiled in water to make a tea rich in vitamin C, and in a survival crunch, the inner bark can be eaten.

Figure 6-24. Lamb's quarters.

Figure 6-26. Piñon pine.

Plantain. Plantains are identified by their distinctive parallel veins, running the length of the leaves. This plant is another weed common to fields and disturbed areas. Leaves grow in a basal rosette and the plant grows a long green central flower stalk. Harvest young greens and new growth for salads or as a pot herb. After midspring, the leaves become very fibrous and are mostly good for vegetable stock or as survival food. Harvest seeds for storage and sprouts.

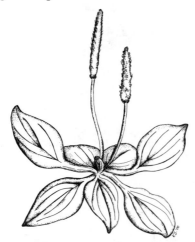

Figure 6-27. Plantain.

Purslane. Cultivated in ancient times, purslane is now mostly seen by gardeners as a pesky weed. Both the seeds and the greens are very nutritious. This plant has succulent-like, smooth fleshy leaves, often reddish-purple, and tends to lie flat in thick mats. Pinch or cut leafy tips June through September. Purslane shoots are excellent cooked or raw in salads. This weed likes fields and disturbed areas, and has spread across the country. It has no poisonous look-alikes.

Figure 6-28. Purslane.

Ramps (wild leeks). Similar to its close cousins, wild onions and wild garlic, ramps are found ranging from the Great Lakes to New England and south to the mountains of Georgia. Wild leeks thrive in partially shaded, moist, rich woodlands, often under maples. They have the long leaves with parallel veins, similar to many poisonous members of the lily family. Crush a piece of one leaf and smell for the characteristic strong onion odor. Plants that smell like onions are not poisonous. In early spring, they look much like smaller versions of grocery store leeks, before the leaves shrivel and are replaced by a slender stalk with an umbrella-like cluster of small white flowers. When a few of the small, three-lobed seed clusters survive the fall, they point to an underground winter supply of delicious bulbs. Harvest green leaves in the spring, or the bulbs any time of the year. Use as flavoring in soups and stews, or sauté like onions.

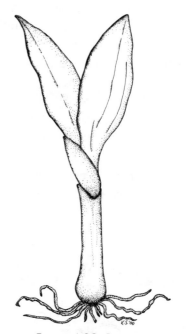

Figure 6-29. Ramps.

Rose hips. Wild roses are found in many different varieties across the United States. Their fruits are a fantastic source of vitamin C. The larger fruits can be quite good raw, although you may want to avoid the bitter seeds. Many people collect rose hips for a delicious tea. Or they may be boiled and strained to make a sauce with the consistency of applesauce.

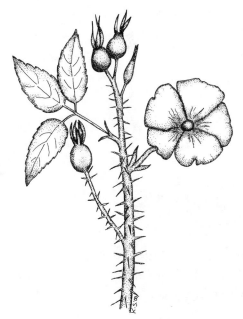

Figure 6-30. Rose hips.

Sheep sorrel. An excellent green, sheep sorrel is one of the few wild plants that does not get bitter as summer comes along. It is distinguished by its elongated arrowlike leaves with "ears" that resemble the front view of a sheep's head, and is found in fields and disturbed areas or areas of poor soil. There are no poisonous look-alikes, but this plant sometimes grows alongside the poisonous vines, nightshade and bindweed, that also have arrow-shaped leaves. Sheep sorrel leaves are tangy and tart, and kind of lemony. Mix in salads with blander greens.

Watercress. "Along with dandelions and lamb's quarters, watercress is one of the most nutritious of foods" (Brill and Dean 1994, 256). Watercress is another Eurasian-introduced, cultivated green-turned-weed that has spread across America. It is usually found in clear running water, such as springs and small creeks. Wild watercress looks like the store-bought variety and is excellent in salads, sandwiches, and cooked like spinach. Collect young growth nearly all year, but it is best in the spring and autumn. Each sprig of leaves grows alternating off the main stalk and contains paired leaves with a single central leaf at the tip. It flowers in clusters of small, white four-petal flowers about ⅓" across and produces slender, capsule-shaped, ¾"–long seeds. The look of the watercress in my local spring varies considerably with the season. In early spring, the leaves sprout with dense closely spaced fleshy leaves that lay on the surface of the water. In early summer, shoots rise up out of the water bearing thin widely-spaced leaves and flowers that look more like the illustration. Very delicious with a slight peppery taste!

Figure 6-31. Sheep sorrel.

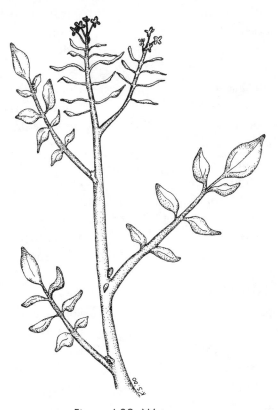

Figure 6-32. Watercress.

Wild onion. Wild onions are found throughout the United States, except in the hot and dry
areas. They are found on the plains, hills, and
mountains, usually in open areas, and all have the
characteristic onion or garlic smell. Its bulb is
usually reddish-purple, and the plant has tall slender stalks with a typical Allium cluster of flowers.
Avoid all onion look-alikes that do not have a
strong onion smell when the leaves are crushed,
because they may be poisonous.

Figure 6-33. Wild onion.

Poisonous Plants to Avoid

Some poisonous plants to look out for are listed below. A few of these plants are also listed as medicinal herbs,
but they are poisonous when eaten in quantity. Both *Edible Wild Plants: A North American Field Guide* by Elias
and Dykeman, and *Edible Native Plants of the Rocky Mountains* by Harrington contain illustrated guides to some
of the common poisonous wild plants.

Common poisonous plants

American false hellebore	Anemone (wind flower)	Angel's trumpet (*Datura*)
Arrowgrass	Azalea	Baneberry (pretty white or red berries)
Bleeding heart	Bloodroot	Bouncing bet
Black locust	Butterflyweed	Castor oil plant
Celadine poppy	Christmas rose	Chokecherry
Cocklebur	Columbine	Corn cockle
Crocus	Daffodil	Daphne
Deadly nightshade	Death camass	Desert rose
Dieffenbachia	Dutchman's pipe	European bittersweet
Foxglove (*Digitalis*)	Frangipani (*Plumeria*)	Horse chestnut
Horsetail	Horse nettle	Hyacinth
Iris	Jack in the pulpit	Jimson weed
Jessamine	Larkspur (annual delphinium)	Laurel
Leafy spurge	Lily, flame	Lily, glory
Lily of the valley	Lobelia	Lupine
Marvel of Peru (*Mirabilis*)	Marsh marigold	Mayapple (except fruit)
Mistletoe	Monkshood	Morning glory
Mountain laurel	Narcissus	Oleander
Poinsettia	Poison hemlock	Poison ivy
Poison milkweed	Poison oak	Pokeweed
Poppy, horned	Poppy, Iceland	Poppy, *somniferum*
Privet	Purple cockle	Rhododendron
Rhubarb (leaves)	Rosary pea	Skunk cabbage
Snowdrops	Solomon's seal	Star of Bethlehem
St. Johnswort	Tobacco	Water hemlock
Wild black cherry	Wisteria	Yew

Sources: Elias and Dykeman 1990, 258–273, Emery 1998, 400; Harrington 1967, 8–52; Runyon 1995, 5.

PRESERVING AND STORING FOOD

Once upon a time, unless you lived in the tropics, one key to living a comfortable life was to preserve and store summer's bounty to carry you through the winter months. Between the food supplies stored in the form of living animals, cheeses, salted and dried meats, grains, root-cellared and dried fruits and vegetables, a typical family stored most of the food that they would need until spring greens began to sprout. With the invention of canning, freezing, and cold storage warehouses, the variety and availability of food stores increased dramatically.

Production, storage, and distribution of the incredible variety of food available today is almost entirely dependent on the plentiful and steady supply of petroleum and electricity. If for some reason these supplies were disrupted, your ability to preserve and store a supply of food would be very important. In addition, if you are producing and storing your own food, you are in control of the quality of that food and the additives and chemicals that go (or don't go) into it. In the following, I provide a few pointers and basic information on food preservation, but suggest that you look to the recommended references for detailed instructions. Keeping written records of what you use and store each year will help you to plan more accurately for the following year. Frozen and canned foods do not last forever, but have a limited shelf life. Try to rotate stocks and use what you store each year to avoid wasting your food stores.

Root Cellars and Other Cold Storage

Light and heat are the enemies of most stored food. A root cellar is the traditional way of storing fresh foods for use throughout the winter. Even canned foods last far longer when stored at lower temperatures. Shelf life of canned foods is doubled for each 20°F decrease in storage temperature (Stevens 1997, 41). Ideal storage temperatures for most nonfrozen foods are 35°-40°F. Most fruits and vegetables shrivel rapidly unless they are kept in a moist environment, so either store them in cartons layered with moist

sawdust, burlap, sphagnum moss, and so on, or keep cold storage areas moist by spraying water on the floor at regular intervals. Too much moisture causes rot, so make sure that moisture is not condensing on the ceiling and produce. Root cellars offer a means of storing "live" food for use throughout the winter. Unlike fresh fruits and vegetables, dry fruits, vegetables, seeds, nuts, and grains must be kept as dry as possible, so they should be kept in sealed containers or in a separate dry cold storage area.

Freezing is simple, quick, and easy, but has higher energy costs than other preservation methods and requires a steady source of power (or an extremely cold winter). Deep freezers can keep food for years, but the regular frostfree home freezer is only good for about six months. Propane refrigerators and freezers are a good option in remote locations, in solar homes to take the load off solar panels, and where power outages are frequent.

You can build yourself an efficient root cellar in the basement of your house, in the outside stairway to your basement, in a pit outside, or above ground in an insulated structure. The keys to success are temperature and moisture control, and effectively keeping critters away from your stores.

A handy basement root cellar can be made by walling off an unheated corner of the basement with insulated stud walls (see Figure 6-34). Building the walls on a double runner of pressure treated wood sills allows for wetting down the floor without rotting the walls. If possible, pick a north wall for one of the walls of the root cellar. A window or some type of screened ventilation pipe is required to vent stale air and allow cooler air into the root cellar. Do not insulate the exterior walls. You are using the thermal mass of the earth (at about 55°F) and the colder north-wall outside temperatures to help keep your root cellar optimally cold. Place a reliable thermometer inside the root cellar and one outside the window or vent. Open and close the vent/window to try and keep the cellar temperatures between 35° and 40°F. Place slats under wooden crates stored on the floor to allow for air circulation and prevent rot.

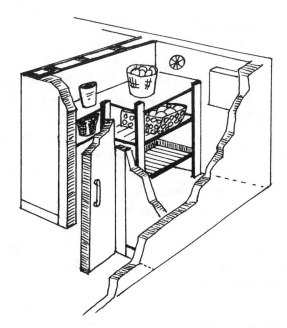

Figure 6-34. In-home root cellar.

You can make an in-the-ground root cellar when a basement is not available. The main things to watch for are water infiltration/drainage, pest barriers, and adequate insulation from the top to prevent freezing. Some people bury garbage cans or old refrigerators. In severe climates, the storage container should be insulated from above with hay bales, rigid styrene foam panels, or at least one foot of loose snow.

Figure 6-35. In-ground food storage.

Low-tech aboveground storage can consist of a hay bale shack or vented "mounds" to keep food stored through the winter months. Both methods rely on the latent heat of the earth and a thick layer of topside

insulation to keep produce cold but not frozen. If vented, the vent should be capped during extremely cold weather. Unfortunately, mice and gophers may enjoy the great nest and food supply that these methods provide, so regular inspection is a must.

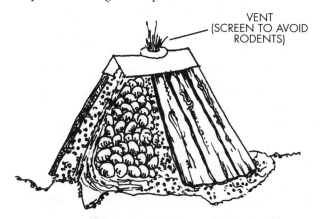

Figure 6-36a. Aboveground storage: vented "mound."

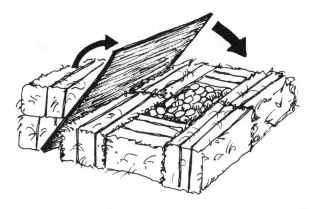

Figure 6-36b. Aboveground storage: hay bale shack.

Drying and Smoking Food

Since prehistoric times, humankind has relied on drying and smoking food to preserve a supply for winter or travel. If you have plenty of sunshine and reliable, hot dry weather, outdoor food drying can be practical and easy. If you have unreliable weather, a commercial or homemade dryer is a lot more practical. Electric thermostatically-controlled food dryers will give you the most consistent results with little fuss and effort. You can dry food in your kitchen oven, provided you keep temperatures below 145°F, the point where nutritional content begins to suffer significantly (Hupping 1986, 145). Where there is a good supply of sunshine, solar dryers can dry large quantities of food quickly while keeping insects off the produce. *Stocking Up III* by Carol Hupping has a good section on drying and illustrates several different plans for homemade dryers.

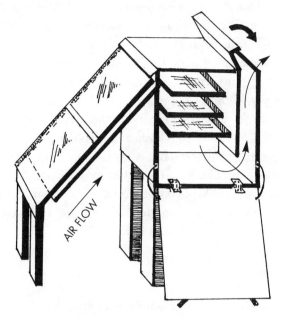

Figure 6-37. Solar dryer.

For outdoor drying, use trays with a nylon mesh screen to lay produce on, which allows for ventilation to all sides of the produce. Cover drying trays with cheesecloth or screen to keep pests off your drying food. Check your dryers with a high-low thermometer. Try to keep drying temperatures between 95° to 130°F.

Figure 6-38. Outdoor drying trays.

Preserving Meat

Traditionally, meats and fish have been preserved by smoking, salting, and drying. The addition of nitrates, often by use of the chemical "saltpeter," is a reliable preservative, but is also a known carcinogen. In addition, smoke tars are known carcinogens. If faced with the necessity to preserve meat, smoking, drying, and salting are all methods that I would use. But, given the health concerns and the hassle, why bother with smoking unless you had no alternative? When available, the freezer is your easiest and cleanest method.

Except for cold storage and canning, meat preservation usually begins with a salt cure. Detailed instructions for curing meat are beyond the scope of this book. To summarize, either submerge meats in a heavy brine solution (about 1½ pounds of salt per gallon of water) or dry pack in pickling salt (not iodized table salt) for several days. Follow this with cold smoking at a temperature of 70° to 90°F for several more days. Smoked cured meats should be stored in cool areas and checked regularly for insect infestation. Non-oily fish can be salt cured for several days and then dried in the sun. Fish spoil quickly, so they should be cleaned and started in the salt cure shortly after catching.

Jerky is dry meat that will keep for months to years, if stored with some ventilation. To make jerky, wet cure 1-inch-thick slabs of meat in pickling brine or dry cure in a heavy salt coating for 3 to 6 days. Then slice into ¼-inch-thick strips and cold smoke for 12 to 36 hours at 75° to 85°F. Alternately, smoke at 100° to 120°F for two to four hours, and then oven dry at 175° to 200°F. For primitive, low-tech jerky, simply cut fresh meat into strips ⅛- to ¼-inch thick and hang on racks or branches in the sun to dry. Jerky is done when it snaps if bent back on itself, rather than folding. Overdrying decreases the nutritional value of the jerky.

DAIRY, TOFU, AND TEMPEH

Before the advent of refrigeration, cheese making was the only way to preserve dairy products for a significant period of time. Warm milk quickly spoils, but cultured cheeses and yogurts spoil milk with "friendly" bacteria that yields a good-tasting product rather than just plain old sour milk. Making butter is one way of preserving cream. The salt in butter helps it to keep for a while, but in hot climates without refrigeration the only solution is to make "ghee" (clarified butter), which keeps well and is used like cooking oil and olive oil. Making your own cheese, butter, and yogurt is a lot simpler than most people think.

Asian peoples make a myriad of healthier low-fat soy products, such as tofu and tempeh. These foods are high in protein and are used much like cheese, although some would say they are a far cry from the flavor of cheese. Most products made from tofu rely on spices and sauces for their flavor, because the soybean base is rather bland. In Indonesia, tasty dishes are made with tempeh, a cultured soy product that is strong flavored and very chewy or crunchy, depending on how it is cooked. Carla Emery's *The Encyclopedia of Country Living* has good instructions and recipes for making quite a variety of cheeses, yogurts, tofu, and tempeh. *Stocking Up III* has good chapters on making cheese, butter, yogurt, and ice cream. If you really get into making your own cheese or tofu, check out one of the recommended specialty books.

Making Butter

Making a pound of butter requires about a gallon of cream. Cow's milk separates pretty easily into cream and milk, but goat's milk does not. If you have goats, or a large number of cows, you should probably get a centrifugal separator to separate the cream for butter, cheese, sour cream, and so on. The simple method for cow's milk is to put it into a tall container in a cool location for 24 to 48 hours, allowing most of the cream to float to the top.

Churning the butter is pretty simple and is accomplished by a variety of methods. Essentially, you are beating the cream until the fat globules stick to each other and separate from what is left of the milk, now called "buttermilk." The old-fashioned wooden butter churns were pretty ineffective and have mostly become museum pieces. The simplest churn, and the one requiring the most work, is to put the cream in a jar and roll it around on the floor

or shake it for about a half hour. Blenders (use low speed), food processors, electric drills with a paint stirring paddle, and butter churns with hand or electric cranked paddles all work well. Lehman's carries all the necessary supplies for efficient butter making.

Once the cream has separated into butter and buttermilk, drain the buttermilk into a separate container through a strainer to catch pieces of butter. Rinse the butter a few times with clean cold water until the rinse comes out clear. Mix about ¾ ounce of salt per pound to help preserve the butter and bring out the flavor. Gather the butter into a ball, then press it out into a thin layer, and keep repeating the process until all the water is worked out and the salt is fully mixed in. Keep the butter cool to store. If butterballs are kept cool and covered by a heavy brine solution (enough salt to float an egg), they can keep for over a month without refrigeration.

Ghee

In hot climates, butter simply will not keep without refrigeration. The Middle Eastern solution is to make clarified butter, known as ghee. Ghee is used just like cooking oil or olive oil, and tastes like vegetable oil with a mild buttery taste. It can keep for months without refrigeration. To make ghee, simmer butter in a pan under low heat for about 30 minutes. Don't let the butter smoke, brown, or burn. Skim off the scum as it forms. When the butter looks totally clear, except for crud that has separated out, strain it through several layers of clean cheesecloth into a scalded container. Scalding kills bacteria in the container and helps keep the ghee from spoiling quickly.

Yogurt

Fresh whole milk and cream spoil rapidly without refrigeration, but by adding cultures of "friendly" bacteria, you can control the way your milk sours and the result is yogurt, which will keep in a cool room for several days. You can start your yogurt with commercial cultures, 3 tablespoons of commercial yogurt containing "live cultures," or some of your last batch of homemade yogurt. To make your own yogurt, take the following steps:

1. Heat the milk to 150°F to pasteurize it (*do not boil*).
2. Cool milk to between 105° and 110°F.
3. Mix in 2 tablespoons of starter yogurt per quart of milk. Add powdered milk if desired for added thickness.
4. Cover and keep warm until thickened. On top of a refrigerator overnight is a good place to keep warm. Wrap in thick towels if there is no warm place.
5. Refrigerate.

Cheese

Cheesemaking is equal parts skill, science, art, environment, and technique. Like making homemade beer, cheesemaking is a traditional craft that more and more people are enjoying at home. Cleanliness, accurate temperature control, basic instructions, a few modest supplies, and lots of milk are the requirements for successful cheesemaking.

Cottage cheese is the simplest cheese to make, but ricotta and cream cheeses are also fairly easy. It is best to start out making these cheeses first, before moving on to more difficult varieties. See Carla Emery's *The Encyclopedia of Country Living, Stocking Up III*, or *Cheesemaking Made Easy* for an excellent introduction to making these cheeses. Because hard cheese keeps longer than soft cheese, and you may need to preserve your milk by making it into cheese, I have included a recipe for a simple semi-hard cheese. Making a pound of hard cheese will require about 5 quarts of milk. A typical small batch of firm cheese starts with 12 to 15 quarts of milk; smaller amounts tend to not work out very well. Use an accurate dairy thermometer. Keep all utensils scrupulously clean and avoid contaminating with dirty fingers and by tasting. Wash hands each time before placing them in the curd or handling the cheese.

1. RIPENING THE MILK

Real cheese is made with the help of bacteria. The wrong bacteria growing in your cheese can ruin it. The sure way to start off right is to use 10 to 15 gallons of pasteurized milk and culture it with ½ cup to 1 quart of fresh cultured buttermilk (with active lactobacillus).

CAUTION: Use large stainless steel or enameled pot, not aluminum or cast iron.

If the milk is already pasteurized, warm to 86°F and then add the cultured buttermilk. Mix thoroughly, and keep covered while holding at 86°F for 30 to 60 minutes, as the culture ripens the milk. If the milk requires pasteurization, heat to 145°F and hold for 30 minutes, cooling rapidly to 86°F. Many people prefer to use raw milk and skip the pasteurization step. A traditional, but less sure, technique is to ripen 11 gallons of fresh milk with 1 gallon of soured milk, mixing thoroughly and allowing it to stand for 15 minutes before adding the rennet.

2. CURDLING THE MILK

Keep milk at 86°F, and add ¼ to ½ teaspoon of liquid rennet diluted in ½ cup cool water. Rennet is a product made from cow's stomach that quickly and efficiently curdles the milk. Bacteria, lemon juice, and several plant products can do the same job as rennet. See Carla Emery's *The Encyclopedia of Country Living* for instructions on making several different rennets, including vegetarian rennet. If using rennet tablets, follow directions on the package, or dissolve roughly ¼ tablet in ½ cup of cool water for every 2 gallons of milk. Stir thoroughly, and then cover and hold at 86°F for about 30 minutes until the curd has formed. Test the curd by inserting your washed finger at an angle into the curd. Lift slowly and see if it breaks cleanly around your finger. If it breaks cleanly, it's done. If it has the consistency of yogurt, it's not done yet.

3. CUTTING THE CURD

Using a long knife, cut all the way through the curd, in a crisscross pattern, spaced about ½ inch apart. Cut the curd horizontally into ½-inch cubes, either with a stiff wire, or by sticking your hand in the curd and using a knife. Alternately, hold the knife at a 45° angle and cut repeatedly in both directions to cut the curd strips into shorter pieces.

4. HEATING THE CURD

Stir the curd gently for a couple minutes, then *slowly* heat to 102°F. Stir constantly to avoid burning the curd on the bottom of the pot. It should take 30 to 60 minutes to heat from 86° to 102°F. During this time, a yellowish liquid, the whey, will start separating from the curds. Hold at this temperature for about a half hour, until the curds reach the desired firmness. To test for firmness, squeeze and quickly release a handful of curds. If the curds are elastic and tend to not stick together, they are done.

5. REMOVE THE WHEY AND ADD SALT

Put cheesecloth over a large colander and pour the curds into the colander. Save the whey for bread, animals, or the compost heap (it's very nutritious). Once the curds are well drained, sprinkle with 2 tablespoons of salt and mix well.

6. PRESSING THE CHEESE

Either tie the ends of the cheese cloth together to make a bag, and hang it where it can drip for the rest of the day, or use a cheese press to squeeze the liquid out of the cheese. You may fashion a crude cheese press from a cylindrical bucket (perhaps a large coffee can?) with holes drilled in the bottom and sides, weighting the top with a bucket filled with stones or water, or a pile of books. To get by with fewer weights, use a long pole as a lever and hang a bucket from the end to weight your home-made cheese press. Press for about a half hour under light weights (approximately 10 to 15 pounds). Then increase the weight to about 40 to 60 pounds and press for 16 to 20 more hours. If you used the hanging method, wrap the cheese bag with a band of cloth, like a headband, and press all night between two paper plates weighted with a heavy flatiron, or something similar. If you plan on making cheese regularly, do yourself a favor and either buy or make a cheese press (see "Resources" section).

7. DRYING THE CHEESE

Remove the cheesecloth and bandage the cheese with a clean dry cloth. Set the cheese in a cool (50° to 60°F) dry place and turn it every day as it dries, until it forms a hard rind. If it shows signs of molding, just rub it with butter and cut the mold away before paraffining.

8. PARAFFINING

Wrap your wheel of cheese in one or two layers of cheesecloth. Melt 1 to 2 pounds of paraffin to almost boiling and dip or brush the wheel in the wax.

9. CURE THE CHEESE

Keep your wheel of cheese in a cool (50° to 60°F) dry place while it cures. Turn it every few days to discourage molding, and wash the shelf to keep it clean and free of mold. A little mold under the wax is okay. If the cheese starts to swell, that means that some of the wrong kind of bacteria invaded it and ruined your wheel of cheese. Cure for six weeks for a mild flavor, or four to six months if you like sharp cheese (Emery 1998, 775; Cobleigh 1996, 53).

Making Rennet for Cheese

If you have to, you can make your own rennet from a suckling calf, pig, or lamb that has not yet eaten solid food. Take the biggest stomach, cut it into strips, salt it, and dry it like jerky. Cut a 1-inch square and add it to milk for the equivalent of two drops of liquid rennet (Emery 1998, 751).

RAISING ANIMALS

We used to live on acreage in the foothills of the Sierra Nevada, where we had a large organic garden and about 15 chickens. Our "girls" would greet us excitedly each day to see what kind of delicious kitchen scraps we had for them. They were especially excited when we gave them the leftover pulp from a batch of fresh carrot juice. In return for our garbage, they rewarded us with wonderful delicious eggs that had bright yellow-orange yolks and were often so big that they wouldn't fit into our leftover egg cartons.

I can't begin to do justice to the broad subject of animal husbandry in the limited space of this chapter, but what I can do is offer you a few words of wisdom and point you in the direction of a number of fine books to help get you started. Carla Emery's *The Encyclopedia of Country Living* is a great all-around reference that will teach you most of what you need to know about raising and caring for animals as well as preparing food from animal products. If you want to know more about raising animals in sustainable ways and maybe even make a healthy profit off of a small farm, check out one of Joe Salatin's books (available from Acres U.S.A., see *References*). Joe has become highly successful using sustainable humane farming practices and capitalizing on the growing market for wholesome nutritious meat, dairy, and poultry products. For an excellent selection of books and videos on horse care and saddlery, see *Centaur Forge*, listed in the Chapter 12 *References*, or see *Small Farmer's Journal* (emphasis on farming with draft animals) listed in the magazine section of this chapter's references. For more books on animal husbandry, see the *References* section at the end of this chapter, the Acres U.S.A. catalog, or the Storey Books catalog.

Raising a few animals alongside your garden can be a great boost to both garden and animal. Chickens love to feast on grubs and other bugs that would otherwise feast on your garden. The carbon rich straw that makes such wonderful bedding for animals also makes great compost when mixed with nitrogen rich manure. Heavy rains carried runoff from our chicken coop directly into our garden, contributing to a particularly rich soil. A word of caution about predators—they can be remarkably persistent in their efforts to feast on your livestock. At one point we found ourselves loosing one chicken a night. It turned out that a raccoon was climbing up the outside 8-foot walls of our chicken coop and squeezing in through a gap between the roof joists where he had peeled back a piece of steel grating that allowed for ventilation. We knew one man who got so tired of a pack of dogs digging under both a fence and the walls of his chicken coop that he eventually trapped six of the marauding dogs with a bear trap. Finally he found a permanent solution to this problem when he poured a cement floor in his chicken coop.

HUNTING AND TRAPPING

Traditional Native Americans respected the spirit and lives of the animals they hunted, killing only as much as they needed for food and utilizing nearly every part of the animal. Using only a primitive bow and arrow, a knife, or bare hands, stalking and hunting larger animals was often a slow, multi-day process. Today, with modern rifles and much larger human populations, wild animals and game would probably grow scarce days after a significant disaster that forced people into hunting for survival. For good instructions on hunting and trapping with primitive tools, check out *Tom Brown's Field Guide to Wilderness Survival*. Tom's childhood mentor was an old Apache scout and medicine man named Stalking Wolf. For a period of about ten years, Stalking Wolf taught Tom and his buddy traditional skills, such as hunting, trapping, healing, and how to travel for days without a tent or sleeping bag.

Animals, like people, have a strong survival instinct and will to live. As a child, I used to like to hunt ducks and deer. The hunt was very exciting, with the "kill" usually pretty clean, leaving an inanimate dead, or nearly dead, animal. One day, we shot a duck that would not die. It was a beautiful young green-winged teal, and she sat in our hunter's blind looking up at us with beautiful, dark, sad eyes. It almost appeared that she was crying. My little brother started crying, and then I started crying, and finally even my dad cried. She had a strong neck that wouldn't break easily, so we ended up shooting her again to end her suffering. The whole experience touched us deeply, leading to the loss of our appetite for hunting as a sport.

I have a good friend, who was really into deer hunting for many years. He was a pretty macho cop, regularly extolling the virtues and excitement of the hunt. One day he told us about a particularly disturbing experience he had on a hunt. The previous fall when he had shot a deer, it let out an audible scream. Upon reaching this deer, he found it lying on the ground looking up at him. Such a beautiful creature, with large tears running down its cheek! The look on his face showed obvious pain and suffering. For the first time, my friend grasped how much these wild animals wanted to live and that they too felt pain. Shortly after this experience, he lost his desire to hunt just for fun.

If I needed the food for my friends or family, I would definitely try my luck at hunting or trapping. Please respect your prey and try to shoot it at close range, or make your traps carefully, to minimize the animal's suffering. In the recommended survival references of Chapter 4, you will find detailed instructions and descriptive diagrams for many more varieties of traps and primitive hunting implements than I can show here. For rudimentary instructions on flintknapping (arrowheads, stone knives, and so on) and bone tools, see Chapter 4. If you want to know how to make traditional flintlock rifles, see *Foxfire 5*, edited by Elliot Wigginton.

Bow and Arrow

The bow and arrow is probably the most effective of the traditional hunting weapons and is not too difficult to make. Seasoned, resilient, long-grained woods are best for bow making. English long bows were traditionally made from yew trees, but fir, cedar, hickory, juniper, oak, white elm, birch, willow, hemlock, maple, and alder will usually do. "Green" wood bows tend to lose their strength or crack after a couple weeks, needing replacement. Traditional crafting of bows often extended for over a year, beginning with the careful selection and curing of wood for the stave.

BOW

For the short term, crude bows of many different green woods will suffice. For durable bows, select strong, straight, resilient, knot-free young saplings such as yew, greasewood, ironwood, hickory, or ash. For the bow stave, select one or two supple limbs, about 1½ to 2 inches thick in the middle, and free of knots and branches. Fire-killed standing wood has already been seasoned. Test the flex of your chosen wood and discard if it shows any signs of cracking. Depending on the stiffness and spring of the wood, either shave flats in the center section of each stave and fasten two curved staves together for a double bow (see Figure 6-39) or shape the stave so that it is about 2 inches thick at the handle, tapering uniformly to ⅝ inch thick at the ends (see Figure 6-40). Notch the ends for the bowstring. Repeatedly greasing and heating a carved bow in front of the fire over a period of several days will deter cracking and make it more durable. The best strings are made from sinew (see Chapter 10 on textiles) or rawhide, but you can use any strong string or make your own cordage from animal fur, hair, or plant fibers (see Chapter 4). Rather than twisting extra thick clusters of plant fibers,

stronger bowstrings are made by braiding or twisting together multiple strands of finer cordage to make thicker cordage. When not in use, loosen the bowstring to save the bow's power, but once a bow has lost its power, throw it away and make another one. A cloth or piece of leather strapped to the inside of your forearm can help prevent chaffing from the bowstring.

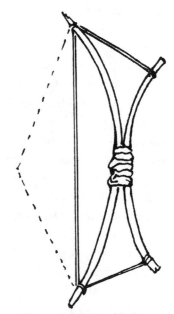

Figure 6-39. Double bow.

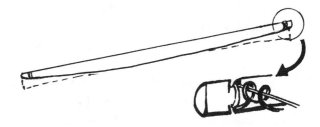

Figure 6-40. Shaping the bow stave.

ARROWS

Any straight wood will do for arrows, but birch and willow sucker branches sprouting from the base of tree trunks work particularly well. Make arrows about ¼ inch in diameter and the length of your arm. Notch one end for the bowstring to catch on (the "nock"). Some type of fletching should be attached about 2 to 3 inches in front of the nock to stabilize the arrow and ensure a reasonably straight and long distance flight. Split feathers work best for fletching, but paper, cloth or even split leaves will do. Attach three or four feathers to the shaft. The simplest arrowhead is a sharpened and flame-hardened wooden point. For larger game and more durability, fashion arrowheads from sheet metal, stone, or bone (see Chapter 4 for basic flintknapping). Attach the arrowheads and fletching to the arrow shaft using fine cordage. Wet sinew works best, because it shrinks and sticks to itself as it dries. Seal binding with boiled pine pitch to prevent unraveling.

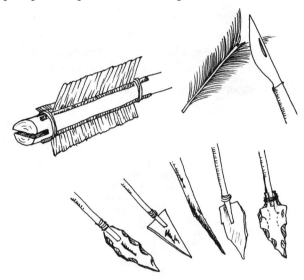

Figure 6-41. Traditional arrow.

Traps

Using traps is a very effective way of catching animals for food, but may result in prolonged suffering for the trapped animal. Traps are not selective. They can kill the neighbor's dog or harm an unsuspecting human who stumbles into them, so use traps only in survival situations and dismantle your practice traps when finished. Set traps in areas near abundant food or a water source that animals frequent. Look for animal scat and signs of feeding to locate a good spot for your trap. Fabricate and test your trap in camp before setting it at the trap location. Disturb the area around the trap minimally and spend as little time there as possible. Animals have a keen sense of smell. You might want to mask your scent by holding your trap materials in the smoke of a fire before setting, or by rubbing them with crushed nonpoisonous leaves. Smoke on your hands can also cover your scent when you handle the traps. Baited traps are usually effective

in semiopen areas. Baitless traps are best set in animal runs where vegetation and natural features force animals to follow a narrow path. Many animals are smarter than you would think, so make traps look as natural as possible. Leave bark on branches and mask carved areas by darkening with smoke or smearing dirt on the fresh cuts.

There are numerous designs for traps and snares, but most are variations on a few basic themes. Traps typically try to strangle, dangle, or mangle the prey. The *SAS Survival Handbook, Camping & Wilderness Survival: The Ultimate Outdoors Book,* and *Tom Brown's Field Guide to Wilderness Survival* (see *References* section in Chapter 4) all have numerous illustrations for traps and snares.

FIGURE-FOUR DEADFALL

This classic deadfall trap does not use cordage and can be made to any size. Three sticks are carved and stacked to support a massive weight, such as a large rock, log, group of lashed logs, and so on. An upright stake is driven into the ground to support the entire mechanism. The bait bar is notched in the center and at the far end. The center notch hooks a flat on the middle zone of the upright stake, while the end notch of the bait bar catches the locking arm. A notch in the locking arm pivots on the chamfered end of the upright stake. The deadfall weight is balanced against the locking arm, dropping the deadfall weight when the bait bar is tugged. To figure the proper spots for notching the various parts, lay them flat on the ground and mark notch locations.

Figure 6-42a. Figure-four deadfall.

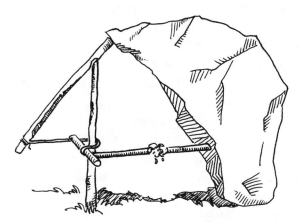

Figure 6-42b. Figure-four deadfall.

ROLLING SNARE

There are numerous variations on this theme. Baitless varieties are placed next to an animal run, where a passing animal will stick its nose through the snare noose and trigger the trap. Baited varieties are set in semiopen areas where passing animals will go for the bait. A forked stake, or notched peg, is driven into the ground for an anchor. A second forked stick, or notched peg, is tied to cordage attached to the top of a springy sapling. The sapling is bent down and the trigger is hooked under the notch in the anchor stake. A loop of cordage makes a loose, wide open noose that is held open across the game run via small twigs stuck in the ground. A passing animal triggers the snare and is held in the air by the noose.

Figure 6-43. Rolling snare.

T-BAR SNARE

The T-bar snare is a baited snare, similar to the rolling snare. Start your circle of stakes by driving two notched stakes into the ground. Form the rest of the circle with plain vertical stakes driven into the ground. The bait bar hooks into the notches on the first two anchor stakes and is tensioned by a bent sapling. Flatten the tops of the bait bar just enough so that it catches in the two anchor stakes and holds horizontal under tension. The vertical stakes force the game to reach its head through the snare noose to reach the bait bar. Carve the notches in the anchor stakes and the flats on the bait bar so that a slight upward tug on the bait bar releases the snare.

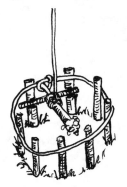

Figure 6-44. T-bar snare.

BOLA

Bolas are a traditional weapon used by Eskimos and many indigenous tribes for hunting birds. Stones are either tied directly to string, or held in circles of material tied to string ends, each string being about three feet long. The bola is twirled around then thrown to tackle birds in flight or on the ground, tangling in their wings.

Figure 6-45. Bola.

Skinning and Cleaning

Mammals should be bled and all animals must be gutted to avoid rapid spoilage. Birds should be plucked, saving their feathers for use as bait, insulation, arrows, or tying fishing flies. You can usually leave the skin on birds, but skin lizards and other animals, being careful to not damage the pelt if it is to be used for something else. Most of the animal can be put to use. Brains can be eaten or used to tan hides (see Chapter 10); hearts, liver, and kidneys can be eaten or used as bait; stomachs and intestines can be used for bottles and containers (turn them inside out and wash them first). Hooves can be used for glue and bones can be split for marrow and used to fabricate a variety of tools. Blood is a rich source of vitamins and minerals and can enrich and thicken stews.

When cleaning an animal, take care not to puncture the entrails or scent glands. Use your eyes and nose to alert you to signs of disease in the organs (funny color and smell) and discard them if there is any question of their quality. If you have any skin cuts, take precautions to prevent infecting yourself from the animal.

CLEANING PROCEDURE

1. Hang larger animals by the rear legs, with ropes tied just above the knees, and cut the large neck vein (jugular) to bleed thoroughly. If blood is not drained, meat will spoil quickly.
2. On males, tie off the penis to avoid getting urine on the meat. Remove scent glands, which might taint the meat. Some deer have scent glands located on their rear legs, just behind the knee.
3. Cut a ring through the skin around each leg and arm by the knee joint.
4. Cut down the inside of the rear legs from the knee to the crotch, making a circle around the genitals.
5. Make a shallow incision through the skin from the tail all the way up the belly to the chin. Pointing the knife's sharp edge outwards and working your fingers behind the blade will help keep it from cutting too deep.
6. Make cuts on the inside of the forelegs to the chin.
7. Peel the skin from the flesh. To keep from damaging the pelt, use your knife minimally while peeling.
8. Pinch the flesh in front of the anus and sex organs, and then make a shallow incision into the abdominal cavity. Using the fingers to guide your knife, open the abdominal cavity all the way to the windpipe and gullet, being careful to avoid piercing the entrails. The bulk of the internal organs will spill out and may be inspected and stored for use. The anus should be clear, showing daylight through it.
9. Provided the weather is cool, hanging the carcass for several days will tenderize the meat and harmful parasitic bacteria will die. Keep flies off meat. Protect your meat from predators and scavengers.

FAT

Fat will go rancid quickly unless it is rendered. To render fat, heat until it turns liquid, and then filter twice through cloth or dried grasses until it becomes pure tallow. Tallow may be used for lanterns, candles, cooking grease, and waterproofing, or may be mixed with equal parts of jerky and dried crushed berries to make a highly concentrated trail food called "pemmican" (the original "trail mix") that can keep for years without spoiling.

FISHING

It does not take fancy fishing gear to catch a fish, but if there are five hundred other fisherman out fishing nearby, chances are slim that you will catch much. My wife was recently talking with a friend of hers who lives on the windward side of the island of Oahu. He was lamenting the fact that as the human population of Oahu exploded, the fish population took a dive. Walter told her, "Forty years ago, when I was a child, I could catch 10 to 20 fish in a single afternoon of fishing out there on the reef. Nowadays, I could fish for two full days and not catch a single fish." Of course, not every place is as densely populated as Oahu, so here are a few techniques that might come in handy sometime.

You will find that fish generally feed the most early in the morning around sunrise, just before sunset, and just before the onset of a storm. On sunny hot days, the fish generally head toward deeper water, or seek shelter in the shade of fallen trees or river-banks. On cold days, they often warm themselves in shallow pools. You can catch fish with your bare hands, nets, traps, baskets, baited hooks, spears, and arrows. Take your time to observe the fish and what they are eating. Bait that is the same as what the fish are eating, or closely resembles it, often works well.

Angling

You can improvise fishing line and hooks from a wide variety of materials. A fishing pole is not required, but a simple young sapling makes an acceptable rod and can help to cast the bait into the water or guide the line. For fishing line, handmade cordage (see Chapter 4) or sinew (see Chapter 10) will do. You may scavenge materials such as electrical wire, or use cordage methods to braid common thread into stronger line. Small hooks can catch large and small fish, but large hooks will only catch large fish. You can improvise hooks from a wide variety of materials, such as bone, pins, nails, thorns, and carved wood (see Figure 6-46). Probably the simplest improvised hook is a sharpened slender piece of stick or bone tied around its middle. The sharpened stick is pushed into the bait so that it is held flush against the line. When the bait is eaten, the stick tends to toggle outwards and stick into the fish's belly or throat.

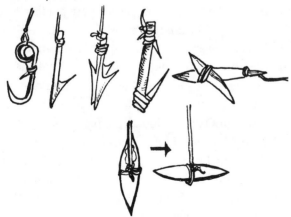

Figure 6-46. Homemade hooks.

For bait, try grasshoppers, flies, meat, berries, fish eggs, worms, minnows, and grubs. If the bait is still alive and wriggling, it is usually more effective.

You can tie bits of feathers and tufts of fur onto hooks to make your own fishing "flies." Artificial lures can be carved from wood to simulate minnows, or you can make your own "spinners" by attaching a shiny bit of foil or metal above the hook in such a way that it moves and reflects light, simulating light flashing off a minnow as it swims. Attach a weight and a float to the line to position live bait at the desired depth, where the fish are hanging out. Lines can have multiple hooks and bait at different depths to improve your chances by fishing several levels at once. Crude floats can be made from some wood or a piece of animal intestine inflated with air.

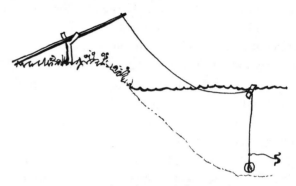

Figure 6-47. Fishing line with float and weights.

Catching Fish by Hand

This takes patience, unless there are tons of fish, such as when the salmon are spawning. Wade into the water and stand very still. Fish will often come up to your legs and nibble on your leg hairs. Slowly lower your hands into the water and allow the fish to come near. Have your hands near the bottom. Try to grasp the fish by the gills and throw it out of the water onto the shore. Late in the summer, in the High Sierra of California, friends of mine have fished like this to their hearts' content when large numbers of fish were trapped in shrinking pools as creeks were running dry.

Spearing Fish

When fish congregate in shallow waters, spear fishing is relatively fast and easy. A barbed, double-prong forked spear is far more effective at catching and holding fish than a single-tipped spear. The addition of a central fork to make a trident spear increases efficiency and is worth the extra effort. Fire harden wooden tips by rotating them in a flame until they sizzle and brown, but do not allow them to char. Check for hardness by creasing with your thumbnail.

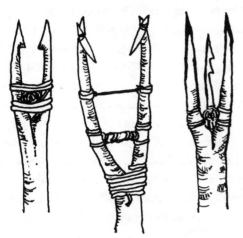

Figure 6-48. Fish spears.

Fishing with Nets

If you have a good source of plant fiber, such as dogbane, milkweed, hemp, or yucca, you can make your own fishing nets. Attach a net to a hoop on a pole, stretch it across a narrows in a fast moving creek, or fish from a boat. Archeologists have found plant fiber fishing nets that are hundreds of years old and are still usable. See Chapter 4 for basic instructions and references for cordage to make fishing nets. Even though hand-twisted fibers make the tightest and strongest cordage, traditionally fishing nets were almost always made from leg-rolled fibers due to the greater efficiency of leg rolling the large amounts of cordage that go into a single net.

CAUTION: Fishing with large "gillnets" stretched across a river can rapidly deplete the local fish population, jeopardizing future fish harvests.

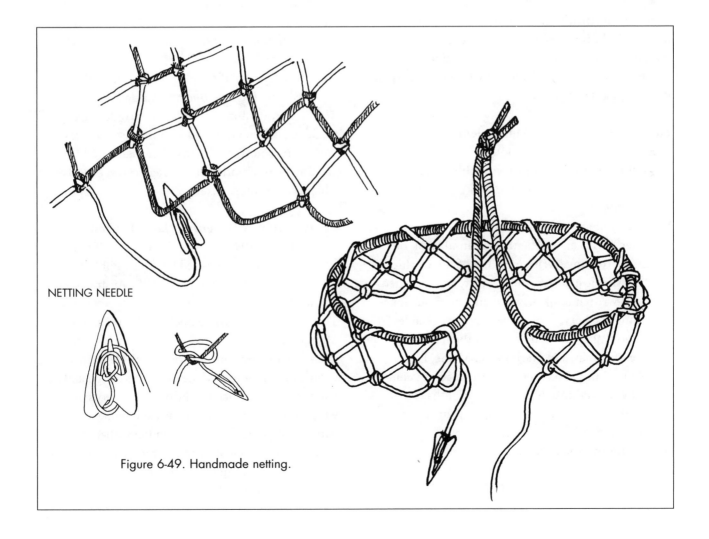

NETTING NEEDLE

Figure 6-49. Handmade netting.

REFERENCES

Growing Food

BOOKS

***How to Grow More Vegetables: Fruits, Nuts, Berries,
Grains, and Other Crops on Less Land than You
Can Imagine,* by John Jeavons.** 1995, 201 pp.
(paperback), ISBN 0-89815-767-6. Published by
Ten Speed Press, P.O. Box 7123, Berkeley, CA
94707. Lists for $16.95.

"The Jeavons approach has done more to solve
poverty and misery than anything else we've done."
(Bob Bergland, former U.S. Secretary of Agriculture)

Truly a landmark book on the "Grow
Biointensive" Food-Raising Method for sustainably
growing high yields of crops on a minimum of land
without machinery and with minimal use of water,
energy, and fertilizers. People in over 110 countries,
in a great variety of climates and soils, are using
"Grow Biointensive" methods to grow food for their
families and communities. Contains excellent information on soil health, fertility, and sustainability.
You might want to supplement it with one or two of
the other gardening references.

***Four-Season Harvest* by Eliot Coleman.** 1992, 212
pp. (paperback), ISBN 0-930031-57-1.
Published by Chelsea Green Publishing, P.O.
Box 428, White River Junction, VT 05001. Lists
for $19.95.

Whether you are a beginner or an experienced
gardener, this is an excellent all-around book on
organic gardening. Written by one of the world's
master organic growers, this beautifully illustrated
and well-written book also explains methods for
extending the harvest of garden-fresh vegetables
throughout the winter months. In the harsh
climate of his farm in Harborside, Maine, Eliot
refined traditional techniques for protecting cold-
resistant crops through the winter months. This
book will show you how to provide your home
with a source of garden-fresh vegetables all year
long, without expensive equipment or a heated
greenhouse.

***The New Organic Grower: A Master's Manual of
Tools and Techniques for the Home and Market
Gardener,* by Eliot Coleman.** 1995, 340 pp.
(paperback), ISBN 0-930031-75-X. Published by
Chelsea Green Publishing, P.O. Box 428, White
River Junction, VT 05001. Lists for $24.95.

"I know of no other person . . . who can produce
better results on the land with an economy of effort
and means than Eliot. He has transformed gardening
from a task, to a craft, and finally to what Stewart
Brand would call 'local science'." (Paul Hawken)

Back in 1965, when Eliot Coleman began farming
organically, the common belief was that organic farming couldn't possibly compete with farms using chemical pesticides and fertilizers. Through hard work,
careful observation, experimentation, and continuous
practical innovation, Eliot proved them wrong. This is
an excellent handbook for the serious gardener or
small-scale grower, filled with practical advice from an
expert who learned by doing, and by doing it well.

***The Encyclopedia of Country Living: An Old
Fashioned Recipe Book,* by Carla Emery.**

This is a great all-around reference, containing a
wealth of information and resource lists for growing
your own food. Voluminous, thorough, and practical. See the description in the *References* section of
Chapter 1 for more details.

***Permaculture: A Designer's Manual* by Bill
Mollison.** 1999, 576 pp. (hardcover), ISBN 0-
908228-01-5. Published by Tagari Publications,
P.O. Box 1, Tyalgum, NSW 2484, Australia. Lists
for $50.00.

This is really a fascinating book! In the 1970s, Bill
Mollison coined the word "permaculture" as a descriptive word for "permanent agriculture." He further
defines permaculture as "the conscious design and
maintenance of agriculturally productive ecosystems
which have the diversity, stability, and resilience of
natural ecosystems." This is a handbook that combines
science, biology, botany, and common sense principles
to form a practical guide for designing sustainable
homes, minifarms, villages, and larger communities.

***Square Foot Gardening,* by Mel Bartholomew.**
1981, 347 pp. (paperback), ISBN 0-87857-341-0. Published by Rodale Press, 33 East Minor St., Emmaus, PA 18098. Lists for $16.95.
An excellent book for intensively planting a small backyard, rooftop, or window garden. An efficient, well-organized, low maintenance gardening method developed by a retired engineer turned famous gardener.

***Rodale's All-New Encyclopedia of Organic Gardening: The Indispensable Resource for Every Gardener,* edited by Fern Marshall Bradley and Barbara W. Ellis.** 1997, 690 pp. (paperback), ISBN 0-87596-599-7. Published by Rodale Press, 33 East Minor St., Emmaus, PA 18098. Lists for $19.95.
This volume contains over 400 entries collected from a national team of gardening experts. Arranged alphabetically by topic, the experienced gardener will easily find answers to most questions or detailed information on most common plants.

***Companion Planting: Rodale's Successful Organic Gardening Series,* by Susan McClure and Sally Roth.** 1994, 160 pp. (paperback), ISBN 0-87596-616-0. Published by Rodale Press, 33 East Minor St., Emmaus, PA 18098. Lists for $14.95.
The complete guide to combining compatible plants for fewer pests and better harvests. An A-to-Z guide for growing over a hundred vegetables, herbs, and flowers using the right synergistic combinations to optimize your gardens.

***Amaranth to Zai Holes: Ideas for Growing Food Under Difficult Conditions,* by Laura Meitzner and Martin L. Price.** 1996, 404 pp. (paperback), ISBN 0-9653360-0-X. Published by ECHO, 17430 Durrance Road, North Fort Meyers, FL 33917-2239. Lists for $29.95.
Published by ECHO, the Educational Concerns for Hunger Organization, for farmers in dry or humid tropical and subtropical areas, this is a collection of practical problem-solving articles from their networking journal. Very good suggestions for crops and techniques to deal with high heat, drought, high humidity, diseases, pests, and so on. If you live in a hot, dry, or tropical climate, this would be a good book to add to your library.

***The Organic Gardener's Handbook of Natural Insect and Disease Control: A Complete Problem-Solving Guide To Keeping Your Garden and Yard Healthy Without Chemicals,* edited by Barbara W. Ellis and Fern Marshall Bradley.** 1996, 534 pp. (paperback), ISBN 0-87596-753-1. Published by Rodale Press, 33 East Minor St., Emmaus, PA 18098. Lists for $17.95.
This book is an excellent source of information for prevention, diagnosis, and treatments that avoid the use of toxic chemicals. Very thorough, it covers many different techniques and has several lists of suppliers of different kinds of natural and nontoxic pest controls.

***The Gardener's Guide to Common-Sense Pest Control,* by William Olkowski, Sheila Daar, and Helga Olkowski.** 1996, 303 pp. (paperback), ISBN 1561581496. Published by Taunton Press, 63 South Main Street, Box 5506, Newtown, CT 06740-5506. Lists for $19.95.
An excellent source of information on integrated pest management (IPM). Here are all the low-to-no toxicity methods for ridding your lawn, garden, and trees of destructive pests without poisoning yourself. They also publish the larger hardcover handbook, *Common-Sense Pest Control: Least-Toxic Solutions for Your Home, Garden, Pets and Community* (1991, 715 pp., ISBN 0-94239-163-2, lists for $39.95), which covers all kinds of pest control, not just for the garden and plants.

***Return to Resistance: Breeding Crops to Reduce Pesticide Dependence,* by Raoul A. Robinson.** 1996, 480 pp. (paperback), ISBN 0-932857-17-5. Published by AgAccess, 603 Fourth St., Davis, CA 9561. Lists for $19.95.
The author of this book has had great success breeding his own pest-resistant crops in Africa and the Americas. Use this book to discover how to breed your own resistant crops that will maintain their pest resistance far longer than genetically engineered, commercially available pest-resistant strains. Past successes show that this horticulturist's techniques

really work! Features an alphabetical encyclopedia of plant breeding techniques and advice, and shows how to organize breeding clubs.

The Humanure Handbook: A Guide to Composting Human Manure, **by Joseph C. Jenkins.** 1996, 198 pp. (paperback), ISBN 096442584-X. Published by Chelsea Green Publishing, P.O. Box 428, White River Junction, VT 05001. Lists for $19.00. The author has been up to his elbows in deep do-do for the past twenty years, since he started recycling and composting his family's "humanure" in 1979. Amusing and well researched, but a bit repetitive, this book includes sections on graywater systems, composting toilets, state regulations, and how to safely compost human waste without significant health risks. Recycling human organic waste is definitely a significant component in building a sustainable society. In Asia, where the pressures of human populations are far greater than in the United States, they already recycle most of their organic human waste.

Sustainable Agriculture Directory of Expertise, 3rd Edition, **by the Sustainable Agriculture Network.** 1996, 220 pp. (paperback), ISBN 1-888626-00-3. Published by Sustainable Agriculture Publications, Hills Building, Room 10, University of Vermont, Burlington, VT 05405-0082. Lists for $18.95.

This is a powerful networking tool for connecting people involved with changing the way America farms using the techniques of sustainable agriculture. This third edition of the *Sustainable Agriculture Directory of Expertise* contains 723 entries that identify and describe nearly 1,000 individuals and more than 200 organizations throughout the United States and two of its territories. The listings have proven to be valuable resources for those seeking information about alternative approaches to achieving farm profitability, resource enhancement and the ongoing vitality of rural communities.

Handy Farm Devices and How to Make Them, **by Rolfe Cobleigh.** 1996 288 pp. ISBN (paperback), 1-55821-432-1. Published by The Lyons Press, 31 West 21st Street, New York, NY 10010. Lists for $12.95.

First published in 1909, this is a valuable little book for the homesteader on a budget. Some of the sketches are for absurd little devices that are more amusing than practical, but most are for handy constructions that could come in useful if one wanted (or had to) do things for oneself. Illustrations include chicken coops, cistern filters, miter boxes, stump pullers, grain bins, cheesemaking, fleecing, farm gates, and more.

Ecology Action Self-Teaching Mini-Series Booklets. Ecology Action (see *Resources*) publishes a series of worthwhile educational books and booklets on a variety of topics concerning sustainable agriculture. Some of their recommended booklets are listed below:

Future Fertility: Transforming Human Waste into Human Wealth, by John Beeby, 1995, 164 pp. On recycling human waste back into compost.

Test Your Soil with Plants! by John Beeby, 1997, 91 pp. On using either wild or cultivated plant indicators for soil testing. This is a useful manual. It allows you to bypass the route of relying on chemical soil tests to discover which nutrients are lacking in your soil.

Learning to Grow All Your Own Food: One-Bed Model for Compost, Diet and Income Crops, by Carol Cox & Staff, 1991, 25 pp.

Growing Medicinal Herbs in as Little as Fifty Square Feet: Uses and Recipes, by Louisa Lenz-Porter, 1995, 40 pp.

Growing To Seed, by Peter Donelan, 1999, 45 pp. On open pollination and saving your own seed from your crops.

The Complete 21-Bed Biointensive Mini-Farm, by John Jeavons, 1986, 39 pp. Gives a step-by-step approach on how to explore sustainably growing all your food, earning a small income, and composting crops on as little as 2,100 square feet per person (versus 10,000 square feet with unsustainable agribusiness farming).

MAGAZINES

Acres USA: A Voice for Eco-Agriculture. Subscription: $24.00 per year for 12 issues. Acres USA, P.O. Box 91299, Austin, TX 78709; phone: (800) 355-5313; web site: www.acresusa.com.

An excellent publication for the serious organic gardener or commercial farmer, Acres USA is devoted to publicizing the latest information on planet-friendly sustainable agricultural practices. Acres USA also has a very extensive mail order book catalog for organic farming, raising chemical-free livestock, homesteading, and natural health.

Organic Gardening. Subscription: $15.96 per year for 6 issues. Organic Gardening Magazine, P.O. Box 7320, Red Oak, IA 51591; phone: (800) 666-2206; web site: www.organicgardening.com. Rodale's classic magazine on organic gardening.

Small Farmer's Journal. Subscription: $30.00 per year for 4 issues. Small Farmer's Journal, P.O. Box 1627, Sisters, OR 97759; phone: (541) 549-2064; fax: (541) 549-4403; web site: www.smallfarmersjournal.com.

This is the magazine to get if you wish to run a small farm with animal power (draft horses, oxen, mules, etc.). Also covers organic farming, sustainable agriculture, livestock, etc. They publish and distribute an excellent selection of books on draft animals, horse drawn carriages, balers, etc.

> **NOTE: See also the magazines listed in the References section of Chapter 1. Each of these has regular articles on growing your own food, herbs and animals.**

Preserving and Storing Food

Stocking Up III: The All-New Edition of America's Classic Preserving Guide by Carol Hupping. 1986, 627 pp. (hardcover), ISBN 0-87857-613-4. Published by Rodale Press, 33 East Minor St., Emmaus, PA 18098. Lists for $26.95.

This is a complete "bible" to preserving and storing foods, including dairy products, fruits, vegetables, seeds, grains, meat, fish, and poultry. This book contains quite a variety of recipes, including stews, soups, pickles, breads, cheesemaking, yogurt, ice cream, jams, jellies, homemade butter, and so on. Has several sketches for homemade food dryers. Highly recommended!

Root Cellaring: Natural Cold Storage of Fruits and Vegetables, by Mike & Nancy Bubel. 1991, 320 pp. (paperback), ISBN 0-88266-703-3. Published by Storey Books, Schoolhouse Road, Pownal, VT 05261. Lists for $14.95

Not nearly as extensive as *Stocking Up III*, but offers far more detailed instructions for constructing a variety of root cellars. Good tips for harvesting and storing produce through the winter.

The Encyclopedia of Country Living: An Old Fashioned Recipe Book, by Carla Emery.

Carla Emery again. Not as thorough as *Root Cellaring and Stocking Up III*, but probably more than adequate for most people's needs. The chapter on food preservation has good sections on root cellaring, drying, freezing, canning, and jams/jellies. Carla has great lists of sources for information and equipment to preserve and store food. See the description in the *References* section of Chapter 1 for more details.

Back To Basics: How to Learn and Enjoy Traditional American Skills, from The Reader's Digest.

Even though it is a broad reference book, *Back To Basics* has decent sections on root cellaring, drying, freezing, canning, jams/jellies, sausage making, smoking and curing meats, and so on. See the description in the *References* section of Chapter 1 for more details.

Basic Butchering of Livestock and Game, by John J. Mettler and Elayne Sears. 1989, 208 pp. (paperback), ISBN 0-88266-391-7. Published by Storey Books, Schoolhouse Road, Pownal, VT 05261. Lists for $14.95.

Everything you need to know for the hunter or do-it-yourself butcher of one's own livestock, plus some tips for preserving meat.

The Canning, Freezing, Curing and Smoking of Meat, Fish and Game, by Wilbur F. Eastman. 1983, 208 pp. (paperback), ISBN 0-88266-045-4. Published by Storey Books, Schoolhouse Road, Pownal, VT 05261. Lists for $12.95.

The title says it all.

Animal Husbandry

***The Encyclopedia of Country Living: An Old
Fashioned Recipe Book,* by Carla Emery.**
Carla Emery again. A great overall reference for raising cows, chickens, sheep, goats, pigs, bees, etc. A
one-stop book that covers everything from birthing
and doctoring to barns, fencing, feed, dairying, and
butchering. A great source for how-to information as
well as lists of other sources for detailed information
and equipment. You may want to start with just this
book then add others on your particular areas of
interest. See the description in the *References* section
of Chapter 1 for more details.

***Small-Scale Poultry Keeping: A Guide to Free-Range
Poultry Production,* by Ray Feltwell.** 1992, 176
pp. (paperback), ISBN 0-571-16699-7. Published
by Faber & Faber, 19 Union Square, West, New
York, NY 10003-3304. Lists for $13.95.
Whether you are a beginner or wish to raise poultry
for profit, this is a fine handbook for raising free-
range poultry the natural way. Covers the type of
poultry to choose, housing selection and construction, feeding, breeding, and general management. A
classic, thorough, and straightforward text.

***A Guide to Raising Chickens: Care, Feeding,
Facilities,* by Gail Damerow.** 1996, 352 pp.
(paperback), ISBN 0-88266-897-8. Published by
Storey Books, Schoolhouse Road, Pownal, VT
05261. Lists for $18.95.
An excellent ABC guide to raising chickens for the
first time. Good solid knowledge includes advice on
choosing stock, housing, feeding, meat bird management, butchering, egg production, breeding, chick
care, etc. The health section is conventional drug-
based farm practices.

***Pastured Poultry Profits: Net $25,000 in 6 Months on
20 Acres,* by Joe Salatin.** 1996, 371 pp. (paperback), ISBN 0-9638109-0-1. Published by Chelsea
Green Publishing Company, P.O. Box 428, White
River Junction, VT 05001. Lists for $30.00.
Joe Salatin will show you how to grow healthy chickens on natural range. Take your tips from a highly

successful farmer who raises livestock with sustainable methods and near zero off-farm inputs. Highly
recommended by professionals.

***Raising Sheep the Modern Way,* by Paula Simmons.**
1989, 288 pp. (paperback), ISBN 0-88266-529-4.
Published by Garden Way Publishing, Storey
Communications, Schoolhouse Road, Pownal,
VT 05261. Lists for $12.95.
Everyone that I know who raises sheep recommends
this book. It is considered the sheep-raising bible from
beginners to small-scale sheep farmers and mini-
ranches. Covers everything from birthing and breeding
to health issues, medication, feeding, and shearing.

***Goat Husbandry,* Edited by David Mackenzie and
Ruth Goodwin,** 1996, 334 pp. (paperback),
ISBN 0-571-16595-8. Published by Faber &
Faber, 19 Union Square, West, New York, NY
10003-3304. Lists for $16.95.
If you want to raise goats, this is the book to get.
Very thorough, it covers feeding, breeding, health
care, milking, leather, fleece, etc.

***A Guide to Raising Pigs: Care, Facilities, Breed
Selection, Management,* by Kelly Klober.** 1998,
352 pp. (paperback), ISBN 1-58017-011-0.
Published by Storey Books, Schoolhouse Road,
Pownal, VT 05261. Lists for $18.95.
An entertaining and comprehensive book about
raising pigs.

***The Family Cow,* by Dirk Van Loon.** 1983, 272 pp.
(paperback), ISBN 0-88266-066-7. Published by
Storey Books, Schoolhouse Road, Pownal, VT
05261. Lists for $16.95.
Even people who grew up dairy farming have said
that they learned something from this book.

***Salad Bar Beef,* by Joe Salatin.** 1996, 368 pp.
(paperback), ISBN 0-9638109-1-X. Published
by Chelsea Green Publishing Company, P.O.
Box 428, White River Junction, VT 05001. Lists
for $30.00.
Let Joe Salatin show you how to grow healthy cattle
on natural range. Take your tips from a highly

successful farmer who raises livestock with sustainable methods and near zero off-farm inputs. Highly recommended by professionals.

***You Can Farm: The Entrepreneur's Guide to Start and Succeed in a Farming Enterprise,* by Joe Salatin.** 1998, 480 pp. (paperback), ISBN 0-9638109-2-8. Published by Polyface Inc., 363 Shuey Road, Swoope, VA 24479. Lists for $30.00.
For those interested in living, loving, and learning on a piece of land, this is a true guide to establishing a small profitable farm. Take your tips from a highly successful farmer who raises crops and livestock with sustainable methods and near zero off-farm inputs. Highly recommended by professionals. Available from Acres U.S.A.

***Small-Scale Livestock Farming: A Grass-Based Approach for Health, Sustainability, and Profit,* by Carol Ekarius.** 1999, 217 pp. (paperback), ISBN 1-58017-162-1. Published by Storey Books, Schoolhouse Road, Pownal, VT 05261. Lists for $18.95.
This is a systems oriented book for helping people to raise and nurture livestock in a planet friendly way. The author has been involved with the sustainable agriculture movement for many years and includes stories and information about other farmers and ranchers from throughout the United States—highlighting the things that have allowed them to be successful.

***Complete Herbal Handbook for Farm and Stable,* by Juliette De Bairacli-Levy.** 1991, 471 pp. (paperback), ISBN 0-571-16116-2. Published by Faber & Faber, 19 Union Square, West, New York, NY 10003-3304. Lists for $21.95.
This fascinating book is a valuable guide for farmers and the general public concerned about the overuse of chemical medicines, herbicides, and insecticides in farm management and animal husbandry. Offers not only an extensive list of plants and their uses, but also specific protocols for a variety of illnesses, all clearly explained. She outlines specific dietary regimens for the purpose of achieving and maintaining maximum health and supporting an ill animal through the healing process.

***Keeping Livestock Healthy: A Veterinary Guide to Horses, Cattle, Pigs, Goats & Sheep,* by N. Bruce Haynes, D.V.M.** 1994, 352 pp. (paperback), ISBN 0-88266-884-6. Published by Storey Books, Schoolhouse Road, Pownal, VT 05261. Lists for $19.95.
Written by a renowned Doctor of Veterinary Medicine (D.V.M.) with over 40 years of private practice, this is an excellent home-care guide to both traditional Western veterinary medicine and preventative health care.

Traditional Hunting, Fishing, and Trapping

***Tom Brown's Field Guide to Wilderness Survival,* by Tom Brown, Jr., with Brandt Morgan.** 1989, 287 pp. (paperback), ISBN 0-425-10572-5. Published by The Berkley Publishing Group, Division of Penguin Putnam Inc., 200 Madison Ave., New York, NY 10016. Lists for $12.95.
When Tom Brown was a child, Stalking Wolf, an old Apache scout and medicine man, took him under his wing. For a period of about ten years, Stalking Wolf taught Tom and his buddy traditional Indian skills, such as hunting, trapping, healing, and how to travel for days without a tent or sleeping bag. At one point, legend has it that Tom disappeared into the wilderness for a period of a year equipped with only a knife and the clothes on his back. His books read well and promote an appreciation for primitive skills and living in the wilderness. He has good advice for tracking, hunting, fishing, and trapping using traditional tools and methods, though the other books on primitive skills (see Chapter 4 *References* section) offer better, more complete instructions for making specific implements.

***Tom Brown's Field Guide to Nature Observation and Tracking,* by Tom Brown Jr.** 1988, 287 pp. (paperback), ISBN 0425099660. Published by Berkley Publishing Group, Division of Penguin Putnam Inc., 200 Madison Ave., New York, NY 10016. Lists for $12.95.
A good guide for tracking and observing animals in the wilderness. For additional sources on this topic, see the *References* section in Chapter 4.

Miscellaneous

Cheesemaking Made Easy, **by Ricki Carroll and Robert Carroll.** 1995, 144 pp. (paperback), ISBN 0-88266-267-8. Published by Storey Books, Schoolhouse Road, Pownal, VT 05261. Lists for $14.95.

This is the "bible" of home-based cheesemaking. Gives step-by-step instructions and easy recipes for 60 different cheeses, instructions for making your own cheese press, equipment lists, and troubleshooting charts.

Book of Tofu **by William Shurtleff and Akiko Aoyagi.** 1992, 336 pp. (paperback), ISBN 0345351819. Published by Ballantine Books, 201 E. 50th St., New York, NY 10022. Lists for $6.99.

This is the book that really brought tofu to mainstream America. Includes 250 recipes for cooking with tofu plus easy-to-follow instructions for making seven different varieties of tofu.

Cooking With the Sun: How to Build and Use Solar Cookers, **by Beth and Dan Halacy.** 1992, 114 pp. (paperback), ISBN 0962906921. Published by Morning Sun Press, P.O. Box 413, Lafayette, CA 94549. Lists for $9.95.

Solar ovens provide a clean, planet-friendly alternative to cooking with wood, gas, or electricity. In Third World nations, much of the deforestation has resulted from foraging for wood to cook with. *Cooking With the Sun* presents detailed, easy-to-follow instructions, accompanied by helpful graphics, on how to build an inexpensive solar oven that can reach 400 degrees and a solar hot plate that can reach 600 degrees. One hundred recipes are included, designed especially for solar cooking. These dishes are simple to prepare and range from "everyday" Solar Stew and Texas Biscuits to tasty exotica like Enchilada Casserole.

The Morning Hill Solar Cookery Book, **by Jennifer S. Barker.** 1999, 101 pp. (paperback), ISBN 0-9642977-1-X. Published by Morning Hill Associates, HC 84 Box 632, Canyon City, OR 97820. Lists for $14.95.

Expand your repertoire of solar recipes with Jennifer's delicious vegetarian recipes. Includes main dishes, breads, muffins, and deserts.

RESOURCES
Growing Your Own Food

American Society of Agronomy, 677 South Segoe Road, Madison, WI 53711; phone (608)273-8080; fax (608)273-2021; web site: www.agronomy.org.

Founded in 1907, the American Society of Agronomy (ASA) is dedicated to the development of agriculture enabled by science, in harmony with environmental and human values. The society supports scientific, educational, and professional activities that enhance communication and technology transfer among agronomists and those in related disciplines on topics of local, regional, national, and international significance.

Acres U.S.A., P.O. Box 91299, Austin, TX 78709; phone: (512) 892-4400; fax: (512) 892-4448; web site: www.acresusa.com.

In addition to publishing the cutting edge magazine on soil-friendly farming technologies, Acres U.S.A. also publishes a terrific catalog containing a very impressive selection of eco-books on sustainable agriculture, animal husbandry, and a host of other self-reliant and sustainable topics.

ATTRA (Appropriate Technology Transfer for Rural Areas), P.O. Box 3657, Fayetteville, AR 72702; phone: (800) 346-9140; fax: (501) 442-9842; web site: www.attra.org.

ATTRA is a national information service dedicated to fostering sustainable agricultural practices. This organization offers information and technical services free of charge to people and organizations involved in commercial agriculture in the United States. Check out their web site for a good introduction to integrated pest management (IPM), holistic farm management principles for improving profitability, and other sustainable agricultural practices.

Bio-Integral Resource Center (BIRC), P.O. Box 7414, Berkeley, CA 94707; phone: (510) 524-2567; fax: (510) 524-1758; web site: www.birc.org.

BIRC is one of the leading organizations in the world providing practical technical and policy information in least-toxic urban and agricultural integrated pest management (IPM) and sustainable agriculture.

BIRC is a nonprofit organization with over twenty-five years of experience and leadership in this area, and has an excellent technical staff to assist professionals with IPM problems and solutions.

Check out the BIRC publication, the *Common Sense Pest Control Quarterly*, which features descriptions of the latest research, practical information, products, resources, book reviews, and direct answers to member questions. It comes highly recommended by a professional grower and consultant to commercial organic farmers. The BIRC has also coordinated two thorough books on common-sense pest control.

Ecology Action, 5798 Ridgewood Road, Willits, CA 95490; phone: (707) 459-0150; fax: (707) 459-5409; web site: www.growbiointensive.org.
The work of Ecology Action has touched, nourished, and enriched the lives of millions of people worldwide. For the past twenty-eight years, Ecology Action has researched, developed, and shared millennia-old techniques for growing more food in a small area, using simple tools and seeds, while maintaining or increasing the health and productivity of the soil. Helping the world to feed more people on less land, growing fertile soil, healthy food, and beautiful gardens is what Ecology Action is all about. Ecology Action publishes numerous small booklets and papers on "Grow Biointensive" topics.

Storey Communications, Inc., Schoolhouse Road, Pownal, Vermont 05261; phone: (802) 823-5810; fax: (802) 823-5819; web site: www.storey.com.
Storey Communications publishes Storey Books, a huge selection of practical books on self-reliance and sustainable living, including quite a number of books on animal husbandry, small farms and gardening.

Sustainable Agriculture Network (SAN), Andy Clark, SAN Coordinator, Room 304, National Agricultural Library, 10301 Baltimore Ave., Beltsville, MD 20705-2351; phone: (301) 504-6425; fax: (301) 504-6409; web site: www.sare.org.
SAN is a cooperative effort of university, government, farm, business, and nonprofit organizations dedicated to the exchange of scientific and practical information on sustainable agricultural systems. Developed by a committee from diverse organizations, SAN encourages the exchange of information with a variety of printed and electronic communications tools. SAN is funded by the U.S. Department of Agriculture's Sustainable Agriculture Research and Education (SARE) program. SAN produces information on sustainable farming practices, principles, and systems. Check out their web site for access to their many publications and links.

TOOLS, GREENHOUSES, SEEDS, AND AMENDMENTS

Bountiful Gardens, 18001 Shafer Ranch Road, Willits, CA 95490; phone: (707) 459-6410; fax: (707) 459-1925; web site: www.bountifulgardens.org.www.bountifulgardens.org
Bountiful Gardens is an excellent source for untreated, open pollinated seeds, gardening tools for the Biointensive Method, soil test kits, a wide variety of books, and eco-friendly pest controls. This organization is a project of the Ecology Action.

Fedco, P.O. Box 520, Waterville, ME 04903; phone: (207) 873-7333; fax: (207) 872-8317; web site: www.fedcoseeds.com.
Fedco is a cooperative operation that offers an excellent variety of untreated hybrid and open pollinated seeds. They also have a tree/shrub division, a bulb division, and divisions called "Organic Grower Supplies" (organic fertilizers and pest controls) and "Moose Tubers" (quite a variety of potato seed stocks). Being a co-op run and owned by growers, their mission is to provide low-cost, high-quality products direct from the growers instead of multinational corporations.

Gardener's Supply Company, 128 Intervale Road, Burlington, VT 05401-2850; phone: (800) 863-1700; fax: (800) 551-6712; web site: www.gardeners.com.
Find a wide variety of special products for the serious gardener at Gardener's Supply. This company offers greenhouses, compost bins, trellises, quality hand tools, various goods for propagating your own seeds, and all kinds of specialty gardening gadgets.

Peaceful Valley Farm Supply, P.O. Box 2209, Grass Valley, CA 95945; phone: (888) 784-1722; fax: (530) 272-4794; web site: www.groworganic.com. Peaceful Valley has been promoting sustainable agriculture for over twenty-three years by providing farmers and gardeners with cost-effective, state-of-the-art organic growing supplies, and the information and tools needed to apply them.

Product lines include fertilizers, weed and pest controls, beneficial insects, vegetable and cover crop seeds, greenhouses and cold frames, row covers and shade cloth, drip irrigation and watering supplies, composting tools, soil testing and monitoring instruments, pruning and gardening tools, and books.

Nichols Garden Nursery, 1190 North Pacific Highway, Albany, Oregon 97321-4580; phone: (541) 928-9280; fax: (541) 967-8406; web site: www.gardennursery.com.
This nursery sells lots of seeds, tea plants, bees and beekeeping supplies, and various gardening implements and books.

Richters, 357 Highway 47, Goodwood, Ontario, L0C 1A0, Canada; phone: (905) 640-6677; fax: (905) 640-6641; web site: www.richters.com.
The site for herbs, both seeds and live, medicinal and flavorful. They also carry quite a variety of organic gourmet vegetable seeds, nontoxic pest controls, essential oils, and books.

Redwood City Seed Company, P.O. Box 361, Redwood City, CA 94064; phone: (650) 325-7333; fax: (650); web site: www.batnet.com/rwc-seed.
An excellent source for open pollinated organic seeds for vegetables, herbs, and flowers, including a huge selection of hot pepper plants.

Seed Savers Exchange, 3076 North Winn Road, Decorah, IA 52101; phone: (319) 382-5990; fax: (319) 382-5872; web site: www.seedsavers.org.
Check out their web site for an eye-opening tour of some of the incredible varieties of heirloom seeds that this organization is helping to save from extinction. Kent Whealy, founder of SSE, made the comment, "Hundreds of years of selective breeding by successful farmers could easily disappear in a bowl of porridge one day." Seed Savers Exchange (SSE) is a nonprofit tax-exempt organization that is saving "heirloom" (handed-down) garden seeds from extinction. SSE's 8,000 members grow and distribute heirloom varieties (you may purchase them from SSE) of vegetables, fruits, and grains. They focus on heirloom varieties that gardeners and farmers brought to North America when their families immigrated, and traditional varieties grown by Native Americans, Mennonites, and the Amish. Since SSE was founded in 1975, members have distributed an estimated 750,000 samples of endangered seeds not available through catalogs and often on the verge of extinction.

Sow Organic Seeds, 1573 Wilson Ct., Eugene, OR 97402; phone: (888) 709-7333; fax: (888) 709-7333; web site: www.organicseed.com.
An excellent source for organic herb, vegetable, and flower seeds. Their web site has good information for saving your own seeds while maintaining the genetic integrity of different species in the same plant families.

Cover-It Inc., 17 Wood St., P.O. Box 26037, West Haven CT 06516; phone: (800) 932-9344; fax: (203) 931-4754; web site: www.cover-it-inc.com.
Cover-It carries a multitude of different sizes and shapes of instant greenhouses, barns, sheds, hangars, and so on.

Miscellaneous Supplies

New England Cheesemaking Supply Company, P.O. Box 85, Ashfield, MA 01330; phone: (413) 628-3808; fax: (413) 628-4061; web site: www.cheesemaking.com.
Cheesemaking at home is easier than you think. This company offers all the ingredients, know-how, cultures, equipment, and other supplies for making your own cheese. Visit their web site for a great introduction to making cheese at home. Informative and delicious.

Life Sprouts, P.O. Box 150, Hyrum, UT 84319; phone: (800) 241-1516.
Life Sprouts carries a wide variety of organic sprouting seeds and quality sprouting supplies to make sprouting easier and sprouts last longer.

VII Shelter & Buildings

Buildings, however much we take them for granted, are where Americans spend about 90 percent of their time. They use one-third of our total energy and about two-thirds of our electricity. Their construction consumes one-fourth of all wood harvested; 3 billion tons of raw materials are used annually to construct buildings worldwide.

—Paul Hawken, Amory Lovins, and
L. Hunter Lovins, *Natural Capitalism*

There is a quiet revolution going on in building design and construction referred to as "green development." Green developments are designed and constructed in ways that use resources efficiently, are environmentally sensitive, energy conserving, and provide pleasant and healthy environments for living, working, and playing. Green building principles employ the *whole building design approach*, which asks members of the design and construction teams to look at materials, systems, and assemblies from different perspectives. The design is evaluated for diverse elements, such as cost, quality of life, energy and resource efficiency, overall environmental impact, productivity, maintenance, and a healthy indoor environment. A huge amount of natural resources goes into purchasing and/or building a home, and houses are the largest single expense in most people's lifetimes. Because we are living in a world that has finite resources and a continuously growing population of humans, it is my hope that the principles of green development rapidly become the rule rather than the exception.

GREEN BUILDINGS

A few facts about and characteristics of green buildings are listed below. Green buildings:

■ Use natural lighting where possible to make for more pleasant living spaces, reduce energy use, and boost productivity.

■ Conserve natural resources in their construction by using locally available materials, or recycled construction materials.

■ Tend to sell or lease faster because they provide a more pleasant living or working space with lower operating costs.

■ Conserve energy. Efficient new buildings conserve around 70% to 90% of traditional energy use. Some green buildings save over 95% of traditional energy use or become net exporters of energy generated by photovoltaic roofing tiles or panels.

■ Are oriented, designed, and constructed in ways sensitive to the local environment.

■ Are well insulated (or superinsulated) to reduce heating and cooling requirements.

■ Often use superwindows (triple pane, gas or vacuum filled, high insulating value, with thermal reflective coatings) to reduce heating and cooling requirements.

■ Use energy-conserving appliances and business machines to reduce heating and cooling requirements.

There is no single "right" way to design a green building. The term loosely applies to quite a variety of design and construction methods that result in comfortable healthy buildings, which use less energy and natural resources. For a good overview of modern green buildings, see the *Green Developments* CD-ROM by the Rocky Mountain Institute (RMI), which provides details on 100 green building case studies, or *Natural Capitalism* by Paul Hawken, Amory Lovins, and L. Hunter Lovins. Here are a few examples of green developments:

■ Village Homes housing development in Davis, California. Passive solar orientation, well-planned design, quality construction methods, and good insulation cut each home's utility bills to roughly a half of the norm. Natural drainage, native landscaping, and cluster housing with abundant green zones all work together to reduce local impact and contribute to making Village Homes a very desirable subdivision. Although modestly priced when originally introduced, these homes now command some of the highest dollars per square foot of any development in Davis.

- Southern California Gas Company Energy Resource Center. An old office building was torn down, and its steel, concrete, and wiring were recycled. The new building was erected on the same site, using 80% recycled materials, superwindows, advanced day-lighting features, and drought-resistant landscaping. The result is a showcase building that's very attractive, architecturally exciting, and physically comfortable and functional, that cost $3.2 million less to build than with conventional construction (40% savings) and uses $21,000 to $31,000 less in electricity annually than typical commercial construction.

- ING bank headquarters, the Netherlands. The design process for this remarkable building complex involved all the employees, the architect, the subcontractors, and the various designers of each of the building's systems to optimize the building features for aesthetics, efficiency, and comfort. The outstanding results far exceeded everyone's initial expectations. Built for roughly the same costs as other similarly sized commercial buildings, the ING headquarters has become a national landmark. The employees enjoy the integrated art, day lighting, gardens, and fresh air so much that absenteeism dropped 15% and they regularly schedule social events at the bank after hours. Energy usage runs at just 8% of average conventional buildings constructed during the same time period and the annual energy savings of $2.9 million paid for the energy-saving systems in the first three months of occupancy. As an added bonus, the publicity gained from their dramatic new headquarters, and their improved public image, have helped

this bank to grow from the fourth largest to the second largest bank in Holland (*Green Developments*, CD-ROM by RMI).

Many green buildings combine enough energy-conserving measures to eliminate or drastically downsize costly mechanical systems, such as central heat and air conditioning. The elimination of these systems can compensate for most or all of the extra costs for superwindows and superinsulation. In the past, photovoltaics and other sources of renewable energy (RE) were usually only cost effective in remote installations where the cost of connecting to the nearest utility could justify paying a large sum for an RE system. However, recent advances in photovoltaics, minihydroelectrics, and wind energy have drastically reduced the cost of RE systems.

For the first time in modern history, RE systems can be cost effective in urban situations as well. When the capital costs for installing a renewable energy system can be included in the mortgage loan for new construction, the monthly mortgage payment increase to build in your own power system may cost less than the monthly utility payments to the power company (see Chapter 11). When generating your own power with photovoltaics, it is almost always cost effective to purchase highly energy-efficient appliances, because the extra cost for purchasing these appliances is generally less than the cost to make your photovoltaic system larger to accommodate appliances with lower efficiencies.

The size of your home also has a direct correlation to its impact on the planet. In an affluent society, where success is often measured in terms of how much you consume and how big you build, it may be hard to adjust to the concept that "small is beautiful." No matter which energy- and materials-conserving methods you choose, when you choose smaller, you make a choice for reduced impact.

When compared to the traditional log home, modern "stick-frame" construction methods cut costs and reduced raw materials usage through the efficient use of lumber cut into standardized sizes. Just 20 years ago, when I was a carpenter, quality redwood decking was readily available. Today, redwood decking is expensive and usually of poor quality due to the logging of most of the old growth redwood forests. Now that old growth forests have nearly disappeared from the continental United States, there is a clear need to further reduce the use of wood in construction, sparking renewed interest in the modern application of ancient building methods utilizing earth, mud, and stone as building materials. Not only do these construction methods save wood and energy during initial building construction, they continue to save more over the lifetime of the building. Stick-frame constructed houses have a typical life span of around 100 years, before becoming just another pile of debris in a landfill site. Well-constructed rammed earth or adobe structures can last for several hundred years.

RAMMED EARTH

Five million years after the evolution of the opposable thumb and 130,000 years after the appearance of the first Homo sapiens, most of the planet's species and 50 percent of the planet's humans still live in shelters made of earth.

—David Easton, The Rammed Earth House

Rick Heede of the Rocky Mountain Institute (RMI) built his rammed earth home in the early 1990s. He hired an experienced rammed earth construction firm to form and ram the walls, but still figures he put in about 3,000 hours of his own time building his 4,100-square-foot home (including 700 feet of solar-heated finished basement). External walls were insulated with four to eight inches of rigid foam, then covered with a stucco exterior finish. Rick used high-efficiency, gas-filled superwindows throughout. The building was oriented for passive solar heating and the roof was superinsulated to R-50. [See page 155 under "Insulation" for an explanation of S-values.] On the occasional winter's day when passive solar heat is not enough to keep his home warm, the propane hot-water system provides radiant hydronic heat by circulating hot water through pipes embedded in the cork-and-carpet covered concrete floors. The net result is a beautiful, solid, supercomfortable, energy-efficient home that should last for centuries. It was built for the low cost of $35 per square foot plus lots of sweat and time.

Rick's home is located at a 7,500-feet elevation in the Rocky Mountains of Colorado, but only uses one-fifth as much energy per square foot as the national average. In 1999, Rick's average electricity bill was $25 per month, which included the use of an electric clothes dryer, and he spent about $550 on propane for space and water heating. He is preparing to hook up several solar hot-water panels that should practically eliminate his propane usage. To get some idea of the scale of Rick's energy savings, I compared it to a 25-year-old, 2,500-square-foot home of average older construction, located at 6,200 feet in California's High Sierra (similar climate to Rick's). Even though this house is almost 40% smaller than Rick's, over the same period of time it cost about five times as much for gas and electricity. Energy bills on this house were $2,500 for a year of natural gas heat (which is about 20% cheaper than propane) and an average of $135 per month for electricity.

For many thousands of years, earth and mud have been traditional building materials. Rammed earth building techniques developed in numerous locations scattered around the globe, where the right combinations of sand and clay are naturally present. Throughout France's Rhone River valley, *pise de terre* (rammed earth) has been a dominant wall-building method for 2,000 years. From the deserts of Yemen, to villages in China, to tall Berber structures in the Atlas Mountains of Morocco, rammed earth has been utilized to build beautiful durable structures that have outlasted many generations of occupants.

Traditional rammed earth structures were built in areas having a natural soil mixture of roughly 70% sand/gravel mixture with 30% of the right type of clay (the wrong kind swells too much when wet, and then cracks when dry). Soil with these proportions has almost magical properties. When moistened and rammed (compressed by thorough tamping of thin layers, one on top of another), the clay and water act like a glue or binder, holding the sand particles together. The result is a hard, durable aggregate material that resembles sandstone. Using soil stabilizers, such as Portland cement, modern rammed earth construction can utilize soils outside of the traditional 70/30 proportion, and can achieve stronger, more weather-resistant results.

To meet stringent earthquake codes, in areas like California's San Francisco Bay Area, rammed earth buildings typically incorporate steel rebar reinforcing and integrally cast concrete beams. This is not to say that traditional construction methods were not strong and durable. French *pise de terre* buildings have survived for hundreds of years in a severe wet climate. Additionally, in California there are about a hundred earth-walled buildings that have survived more than a century of earthquakes—some without foundations and all without the use of cement, steel, or modern fasteners.

The massive walls of rammed earth buildings lend a feeling of strength, quiet, and permanence, as well as being a giant thermal mass, making them cool in the summer and warm in the winter. Even though the walls are thick (typically on the order of 18 to 24 inches), rammed earth is not a particularly good insulator, so an insulating layer is added to either the center or the outside of rammed earth walls when built in cold climates.

In the following, I describe several rammed earth construction basics. For a beautifully illustrated design guide and handbook to building with rammed earth, see David Easton's *The Rammed Earth House*. If you live in earthquake country, or just want to get your rammed earth building past the local building inspector, it is probably a good idea to pick up a copy of *Buildings of Earth and Straw: Structural Design for Rammed Earth and Straw-Bale Architecture* by Bruce King, P.E. This book is written both for the layperson as well as the professional engineer and is surprisingly readable. Even if you do not understand all the engineering jargon, a copy of this book could give your structural engineer just what he needs to get it through the local building department (and make sure it's done right).

The Process

In the Atlas Mountains of Morocco, Berber tribes continue to use methods that are hundreds of years old to make their rammed earth structures. In the traditional process, the outline of the building is traced on the ground or some kind of foundation is constructed. Wooden forms, roughly 2 feet high and 6 or 8 feet long are clamped or tied around two end panels that determine the wall thickness (typically 1½ to 2 feet), while moist earth from on or near the building site is rammed into the form. Loose earth is laid in shallow layers (approximately 4 to 6 inches deep) in the form, and then tamped with about a 10-pound block of wood mounted on a long handle. The

hand rammer is repeatedly lifted 1 to 2 feet in the air and then dropped onto the moist soil layer. The rammer should be heavy enough to ram the earth with its mass, yet light enough for the worker to lift it thousands of times a day. The combination of vibration and compaction helps to solidify the earth into a rock-like aggregate. As the soil becomes compacted, the sound from the rammer changes from a dull thud to a ringing sound, which signals that it's time to add the next layer of soil.

Figure 7-1. Traditional rammed earth forms. Illustration from *The Rammed Earth House* by David Easton (Chelsea Green Publishing Company, 1996).

Traditionally, once the 2-foot–high form has been rammed to the top, the form is moved horizontally along the perimeter of the walls. After the first wall layer is rammed all the way around the perimeter of the building, the form is stacked on the top of the first layer of wall, then worked around the perimeter to form the second layer, and so on. Forms are placed in the wall to block off space for openings such as windows and doors, and the earth is rammed around the forms. Wooden beams bridge across the tops of window and door openings.

Buckets and hand rammers are still cost effective where labor is very inexpensive. Where labor rates are high and construction machinery is available, modern mechanized methods greatly speed the process. Modern rammed earth structures start with a steel reinforced concrete foundation, including a footing and stem wall. In both the Australian form method and David Easton's rammed earth works (REW) method, forms are clamped to the foundation to build full-height wall sections, rather than working round and round while raising the entire walls two feet at a time, as in traditional rammed earth construction. Rototillers, portable batch plants, and cement mixers are effective tools for mixing the soil with stabilizers. Tractor buckets and cranes replace the traditional bucket brigades for lifting the soil into the forms. Pneumatic rammers, run by large air compressors, replace most of the hand tamping except for careful hand tamping around electrical conduit and plumbing.

In earthquake zones, engineered steel reinforced concrete columns are cast as an integral part of the walls between panels of rammed earth, and steel rebar is incorporated into the rammed earth panels as well as connecting the panels to the foundation. An integrally cast, steel-reinforced concrete "bond beam" caps the rammed earth wall panels, providing anchors for a wooden cap and the roof. Piping and electrical conduit are roughed in before the wall forms are placed, essentially becoming "cast in stone" as the walls are rammed around them. If you wish to carve alcoves, niches, or cubbyholes into the rammed earth walls, it should be done in the first few days after the walls are formed. As the walls cure, they become "rock hard" and carving becomes extremely difficult.

Soils

Traditional rammed earth structures were built only in locations with appropriate soils available on site. Using Portland cement as a soil stabilizer has enabled modern builders to use a broader range of soils.

NOTE: Because the manufacturing of Portland cement consumes a considerable amount of energy, contributing significantly towards global warming, it is not a "green" material, but even "green buildings" will usually use at least some cement for building the foundation.

If your soil is not too far from the ideal, adding either sand or clay may make it workable. Begin your quest by making a simple preliminary field test. At several different locations around your building site, dig through the topsoil layer and fill a labeled bucket with soil from each location. Because organic material in topsoil would severely weaken the walls, your soil should be from the lighter-colored, hard subsoil, a foot below the topsoil. Place a couple cups of this soil into a glass jar and fill the rest with water. Shake the jar to thoroughly mix the soil with the water, and then let it sit for a couple hours, until the soil has settled. The fine particles of clay and silt should settle out clearly above the sand. If it is nearly all clay and silt, or all sand, you will have to look elsewhere for your materials (local sand and gravel quarries are a good source). If it is roughly one-fifth to one-third fine particles and the rest is sand (some gravel is okay), then you can probably work with your local soil. In the "jar test," it is hard to tell the difference between clay and silt. Too much silt and your soil will be too weak for rammed earth walls, so lab tests or functional tests will still be required for making the final decision about your local dirt (Easton 1996, 93).

If your soil looks promising, the next step is to make some test blocks to evaluate the material for strength, weatherability, and color. Cylinders can be rammed into concrete-style test cylinders, typically 3 inches in diameter and 6 inches long, for lab strength tests. Like concrete, test cylinders are broken at 7, 14, and 28 days to determine the cured strength. For your personal aesthetic and durability evaluations, ram the moistened earth into a wooden 12-inch by 16-inch form with 2- by 4- spacers, held together with ½-inch bolts. Place the cured slab in the spray from garden sprinklers to determine its moisture resistance. If the building is in a wet climate, and the test slab degrades under a firm hose spray, the soil should be stabilized with Portland cement. Take your time and be very thorough with your soil testing and selection process. The success of your project depends on getting this right. See *The Rammed Earth House* for further soil tests and for advice for working with quarried materials, such as road base, structural backfill, or the less expensive quarry fines. Quarry fines are waste materials that often work well for rammed earth and are usually available for less than half the cost of road base.

Your topsoil is a valuable resource for landscaping and gardening. Prior to the start of construction, scrape topsoil off the building site into piles, including cleared greenery, for composting while the building is under construction. When construction is completed, the composted waste vegetation and topsoil will be a wonderful landscaping aid.

Getting the moisture content right for rammed earth is more of an art than a science. The typical moisture content is a very scientific-sounding 8%, arrived at through very unscientific methods. If it is freshly dug from the ground, it will probably already have about the right moisture content. An experienced builder will take an appropriately sized pile of dry earth and put a garden sprinkler on it overnight to arrive at the 8% moisture content by morning. It is best to add the moisture to the soil from between several hours and a few days before use. It takes time for the moisture to fully wet out the microscopic clay platelets that form the glue in the rammed earth. Stabilizers, such as Portland cement, must be worked into the pile before loading into forms, and the soil must be thoroughly mixed into a homogenous mass before use. Typical cement stabilization is 4% to 6% by weight. One of the easier ways to mix your soil is with the use of a rototiller. Probably the fastest method is for an experienced tractor handler to thoroughly mix the soil by many back and forth sweeps with the tractor bucket.

Moisture Test

The classic test for proper moisture content is the "dirt ball drop." Proper moisture content is a drier mix than the average person would guess. The mixture is damp, but not at all wet or muddy. With both hands, scoop up enough moist earth to gather into a sphere the size of a softball, then firmly pack into a hard ball of earth. The earth ball should be moist enough to hold its shape, even when held by fingers spread widely apart. Drop the ball from a height of about five feet onto the ground. If it shat-

ters into its former loose state, it's fine, but if it does not break or it breaks into clumps, it's too wet (Easton 1996, 141).

The Forms

You can build the forms yourself, hire a rammed earth construction company that has its own forms, or lease them from construction rental companies. As mentioned previously, in both Australia and the United States, modern rammed earth practice is to build full-height walls, a section at a time, rather than the traditional method of building the walls round and round, two feet at a time. The Australians have standardized stackable 2-foot-high by 8-foot-long forms that are easy to handle but require numerous concrete ties to keep the forms from bulging under the pressure of the rammed earth. These ties are tapered and threaded steel rods that are time consuming to install and leave holes that must be patched when removed. David Easton's rammed earth works (REW) form method uses 8- to 10-foot-wide plywood forms with floating stiffening boards (called "walers" in concrete forming terminology) that are 2 inches x 10 inches or 2 inches x 12 inches to allow him to drastically reduce the numbers of required clamps and clamp holes that need to be patched. He uses ¾-inch pipe and quick-action "pony clamps" to rapidly clamp the forms around full-height plywood end plates that set the wall thickness. Pipes are pushed through holes in the forms, and then walers are set on top of the pipes and pony clamps are slid over the pipes to clamp the forms together through the stiffening walers. Hardwood wedges are tapped between the pipes and the end panels to hold the end panels precisely in position, yet allow for removal of the pipes after ramming. The pressure of the rammed earth pins the end panels tightly against the pipes. Tapping the wedges out relieves the pressure on the pipes and allows for their removal. Walers spaced 15 inches apart make a convenient ladder for climbing up and down the form to ram the earth. Easton prefers to use ¾-inch by 10-foot sheets of HDO (high density overlay) plywood for reusable forms, but ¾-inch AC plywood or 1⅛-inch plywood subflooring will do and can be used later for roof sheeting or flooring.

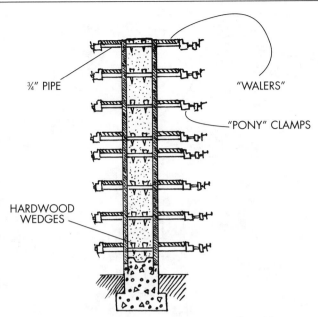

¾" PIPE

"WALERS"

"PONY" CLAMPS

HARDWOOD WEDGES

Figure 7-2. David Easton's rammed earth works forms. Adapted from an illustration from *The Rammed Earth House* by David Easton (Chelsea Green Publishing Company, 1996).

Wall Systems

Typically, the corners are formed first. They are more difficult to form than straight sections, and will define the outline of the building, providing alignment points for each panel. Corners are formed using a roughly 3-foot square form, with a smaller hollow form to make the inside of the corner.

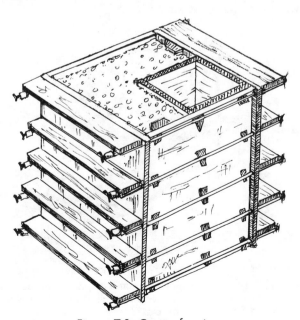

Figure 7-3. Corner forming.

If you have a limited number of forms, the simplest wall system is to form 6- or 8-foot-wide wall panels one at a time. Form every other panel first, allowing the individual panels to cure and harden a couple of days before forming connecting panels. Until the connecting panels are formed, your project will start to look a little like Stonehenge. A keyway is formed into the top of the foundation stem wall and both ends of each individually formed wall panel, so that each wall section locks to the foundation and each other via the keyway (see Figure 7-4). To form the keyway into wall sections, attach a full-length, beveled 2-by-4 to the inside center of each end board in the form. The sides of the keyway 2-by-4s are beveled at a significant taper so that they will release from the rammed earth when the forms are taken down. In the individual panel system, small 45-degree bevel strips are attached to the inside corners of each end board to make for clean expansion joints at each panel junction. The rammed earth walls are either capped with a wooden beam or a reinforced concrete "bond beam" that is cast in place after all wall sections have been rammed. The bond beam is keyed to each wall section, structurally tying them all together and providing steel ties for attaching the roof.

If you have lots of available forms, walls of stepped heights, or a need for a crane, it is cleaner and faster to form entire walls at once. In the continuous wall-forming system, expansion joints are eliminated and there is no need for separate forms to form the bond beam, because it is cast as the top section of the continuous wall. In seismic zones, a freestanding panel system is the norm, with rammed earth panels connected by narrow steel reinforced concrete columns, all tied together by the top concrete bond beam. After the foundation is poured and the corners rammed, each freestanding panel is rammed with keyways formed into both ends. Concrete columns are poured into the gaps between the panels, forming a continuous wall with built-in, post-and-beam style, load-bearing reinforced concrete columns (see *The Rammed Earth House* by David Easton for more detail).

Windows and Doors

With multipanel systems, spaces for windows are often made using short window-width panels rammed to the height of the windowsill, placed between full-height wall panels. Door spaces can be precise gaps between full wall panels. Beam lintels over windows and doors can consist of just the bond beam, cast reinforced concrete, steel, or rot-resistant timbers, such as redwood, cedar, or pressure-treated lumber. In continuous wall systems, strong removable boxes are constructed to the size of the opening. David Easton refers to these forms as volume displacement boxes (VDB). These boxes are precisely dimensioned to allow for sills, trim, and so on. VDBs must be assembled in such a manner that they can be disassembled from the outside, after the form walls have been removed, while under significant pressure from the rammed earth. As is typical of thick-walled construction, most window openings should be formed with an outward bevel to bring more light in and restrict less

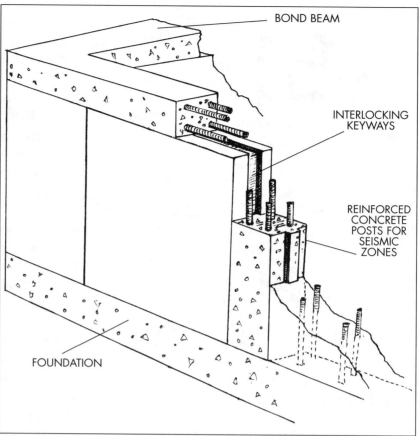

Figure 7-4. Rammed earth wall section (note interlocking keyways).

of the view. VDBs can be used to form bookcases, niches, alcoves, fireplaces, and chimneys directly within the rammed earth walls.

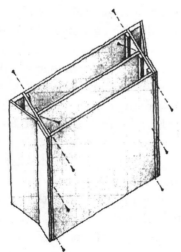

Figure 7-5a. Volume displacement box (VDB) for forming window opening. Illustration from *The Rammed Earth House* by David Easton (Chelsea Green Publishing Company, 1996).

Figure 7-5b. Placement of volume displacement box (VDB) for forming window opening. Illustration from *The Rammed Earth House* by David Easton (Chelsea Green Publishing Company, 1996).

ADOBE

Adobe is a traditional earth wall-building material that has been used for many centuries. The Pueblo Indians of the U.S. Southwest have built passive solar-heated apartment like buildings out of adobe since long before Columbus arrived in the Americas. Traditional adobe is a true "green" building material, being made from local earth and straw. The optimum soil mixture of about one-third sand, one-third silt, and one-third clay is roughly the same as for rammed earth. The soil mixture should have practically no organic content (don't use topsoil), except for optional added straw, which acts as a fibrous reinforcement to deter cracking. For traditional adobe construction, a wet soil and chopped straw mixture is poured into individual wood molds or large, oiled-wood "gang" molds. The earth is wet enough to fill the molds with minimal tamping, yet dry enough to stay put without slumping when the molds are immediately lifted off the bricks so another set of bricks can be cast. When the bricks have dried enough to resist cracking, they are placed on edge to dry completely.

As with rammed earth, the soil composition is critical to the strength of the end product. Stabilizers, such as Portland cement or asphalt emulsion, may be added at roughly 5% of the overall volume to improve the moisture resistance and strength of adobe bricks. Bricks are stacked into thick-walled structures, using adobe mud for mortar between the bricks. Massive adobe walls tend to be warm in winter and cool in summer, although like rammed earth, adobe is not a great insulator. Consequently, for cold climates, modern adobe construction incorporates foam insulation either in the center or on the exterior of the wall. In moderate climates, a double wall of adobe bricks with a 2-inch air gap between the inner and outer walls may add sufficient insulation and provides a convenient space to run plumbing and electricity.

In traditional structures, wooden beams bridge window and door openings, and peeled logs support a flat roof, which is sealed with a thick layer of clay-rich adobe. Adobe mud is smeared over the outside surface walls to give it a stucco-like finish that "breathes." The traditional adobe mud exterior is not waterproof, so a fresh mud coating is typically reapplied every one to five years (depending on rain erosion). When I visited the famous 200-year-old adobe Catholic church in Taos, New Mexico, I was told that 30 years earlier the church had tired of the annual reapplication of a mud adobe exterior finish, so they had applied a Portland cement stucco exterior coating sealed with latex paint. After 20 years, this nonbreathable finish started to cause degradation in the structural walls, so the church had to strip the cement stucco and return to the annual practice of applying an adobe mud surface coat. Since returning to the traditional breathable finish, the structural degradation has stabilized.

Modern Adobe Methods

Most modern adobe buildings start with a steel reinforced concrete foundation, similar to the foundations used for rammed earth. The foundation usually has a short stem wall to protect the adobes from moisture penetration. Like rammed earth, massive adobe walls require adequate support and must be specially engineered for seismic zones. Using Frank Lloyd Wright's foundation system of rubble filled trenches and floating shallow cast footings is a good way to minimize the use of concrete (concrete contributes to greenhouse gases). Similar to rammed earth construction, a wooden or reinforced concrete "bond beam" caps adobe walls, structurally tying the walls together and providing strong attachment points for the roofing system. Designing the roofing system to act like a structural "diaphragm" ties opposing walls together for improved seismic resistance. Building roofs with significant overhangs, although departing from the traditional adobe look, can provide water protection in wetter climates and shade from the high summer sun.

Building with adobe bricks is a labor-intensive process. For the owner-builder with a lot of available time and perhaps an abundance of low-skilled family labor (sweat equity), building with adobe can be one way of providing yourself with a beautiful, energy-efficient home at a very low cost per square foot. If you purchase adobe bricks, the bricks can be pricey due to the labor involved in making them. A time and cost saving device, available to the modern adobe contractor and at some rental yards, is the use of automated hydraulic machines for making pressed adobe blocks from local dirt right on the building site. If the soil is of the right composition, the pressed adobe blocks need no stabilizers and are stronger than traditional adobe. Making the bricks on site saves handling labor, transportation costs, and raw materials expense. Remember, the soil content is important: garbage in equals garbage out.

Building the walls brick by brick is also labor intensive. Traditionally, adobe mud was used as a mortar between the horizontal brick surfaces, but the vertical brick surfaces were left as dry gaps to provide cracks for the plastered mud finish to grip to. Walls are usually plastered with either a Portland-cement-based stucco, gypsum-based plaster, or mud-based adobe plaster. Nowadays, interior walls are often finished with a handcrafted look that leaves the adobe blocks visible to show off the structure of the adobe block walls.

An interesting alternative to adobe bricks was developed in the 1990s by Arizona metallurgist Harris Lowenhaupt and architect/contractor Michael Frerking, who developed a special breakthrough formula and process for "cast earth." Cast earth uses gypsum and a proprietary retardant to stabilize earth mixtures and reduce shrinkage, allowing for the use of standard concrete industry labor-saving machinery, forms, and techniques to make walls of cast earth. Normally, adobe cannot be cast into thick walls, because it would take weeks to dry and would crack from shrinkage as it dried. Cast earth quickly wet hardens to a point where the forms can be stripped and it can support modest structural loads. When fully dried and cured, it has compression strengths that exceed standards for stabilized rammed earth and adobe. Cast earth has the potential to commercially produce earth-walled homes for about the same cost as stick-frame housing (Carpenter 1997, 18). See the next section of this chapter for more information on the cast earth process.

Although it is a bit dated, Paul G. McHenry's *Adobe: Build it Yourself* is still the best practical guide for building with adobe blocks, including code-approved foundations and bond beams. For the latest in up-to-date information on modern rammed earth, cast earth, and adobe building equipment, suppliers, contractors, and methods, check out the Southwest Solar Adobe School's quarterly trade journal, *Adobe Builder*.

Adobe Blocks

Whether you are mixing adobe mud in a traditional earthen pit, or using modern machinery, your adobe blocks should be strong enough to pass the Uniform Building Code (UBC) 300 psi compression strength requirement. Commercial adobes are almost always certified to meet or exceed this specification and their manufacturers should provide material certifications upon request. Cured adobes should be strong enough to survive a five-foot drop without breaking. A crude strength test is to stand in the center of a single adobe block supported by the outer couple inches of two opposing edges. If it collapses under the weight of a 160-pound person, it's probably too weak. If you are making your own adobes, you should cast sample adobe cylinders and have them tested at a local concrete lab for strength (call your building inspector or concrete lab for details).

Begin your quest for adequate soil by checking local soil with the "jar test" as described in the rammed earth section above. Next, mix some adobe mud and cast a sample block in a rectangular wooden form (10 inches by 4 inches by 14 inches is one of the most popular standard sizes). Production adobes are typically made in gang forms of oiled 2-by-4s to make six to sixteen adobes at once. The forms should be placed on dry flat ground on top of a thin layer of sand. Mix the earth with enough water to make a doughy, but not soupy, mass. Traditional mixing was done in an earth pit, but cement mixers work decently and pug mills work best. Make sure that the mud mixture has been worked long enough for moisture to penetrate evenly into all the little balls of earth before pouring into prewetted forms. Scrape across the top of the adobe form with a straight wooden bar ("screed") to make a smooth surface even with the top of the form.

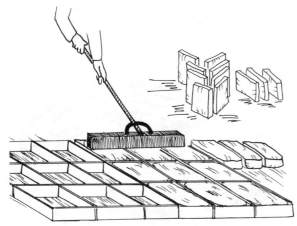

Figure 7-6. Adobe gang molds and hand screed.

After an initial set, the adobe block should be stiff enough to carefully lift the forms off the blocks without slumping. If there is too much clay in the soil (the most common problem), the block will shrink considerably and will usually start to crack within 24 hours. Add more sand or straw if blocks crack. The strongest blocks have the highest clay content without cracking. Too much silt or sand makes for weak blocks. Traditionally, adobes relied on high clay content for moisture resistance. Chopped straw helps clay-rich adobes to resist cracking, but straw also tends to wick moisture into adobes and is considered undesirable in modern adobe construction. Commercial adobes often include stabilizing additives to improve water resistance, which allows for less clay and the elimination of the straw. Adding 2.5% to 5% (by weight) asphalt stabilizer to the adobe mix will make the blocks waterproof. Adding 4% to 6% (by weight) Portland cement will both strengthen and improve water resistance, allowing for use of a greater range of soils, but also increases the cost. Stack adobes on edge to cure for several weeks before using (longer if the weather has been humid). Keep sheltered from rains, and stack in such a way that they do not "domino."

In the 1950s, Colombian engineer Raoul Ramirez invented a simple, long-armed hand press, called a "Cinva-Ram," for compressing moist earth into adobe blocks. The Cinva-Ram speeds the process of making adobes by eliminating the lengthy cure time for cast blocks. Cinva-Rams can be welded from simple steel stock or purchased from a variety of sources. Pressed adobe blocks can be stabilized with Portland cement (4% to 6%), but cannot use asphalt emulsion because the pressed blocks require moist, rather than wet, soil mixes. Modern equipment manufacturers have developed automated machines that hydraulically compress earth into strong and consistent adobe blocks. These machines are expensive ($5,000 for slower, manually operated machines, and up to $200,000 for computerized, high-production models), but they greatly speed up the process for making consistently strong adobes right on the job site or at an adobe factory. Pressed blocks can make high-strength adobes out of soils that do not cast well, but too much clay can cause blocks to splay and crack if they absorb moisture, and too much sand or silt can result in low strength.

CAUTION: Test your blocks!

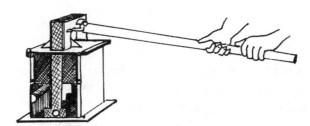

Figure 7-7. Making adobe bricks in a Cinva-Ram.

Adobe Walls

Traditional adobes were built on a stone foundation with mud mortar, or laid directly upon the earth. Modern adobes generally use a cast, reinforced concrete foundation with a concrete block or cast stem wall, raising the adobe blocks above ground level to prevent water damage. Adobe walls must be protected from moisture. If unstabilized adobe blocks become wetted throughout the full thickness of the wall, the massive weight of the upper adobe wall will squirt the lower wet adobes out the side, like toothpaste.

For traditional adobe blocks, spread a layer of adobe mud ½- to 1-inch thick as mortar between the blocks. The mud is the same as that used for the bricks, except that it should be screened through a ¼-inch mesh to remove all stones larger than ¼ inch. If your blocks are stabilized, you should also stabilize your adobe mortar. Score adobes with a hard tool

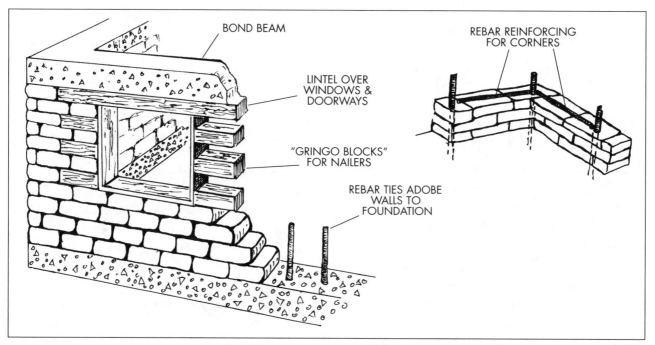

Figure 7-8. Typical adobe wall construction.

and break over a sharp edge to make shorter end blocks for staggering alternate rows. Stagger adobes in the walls by at least 4 inches. Begin laying adobes at the corners and lay toward the middle. Run a tight string from corner to corner to keep the adobe rows level, straight, and even. Thick adobe walls (18 to 28 inches) have better stability in earthquakes than thin (10-inch) walls, have much more thermal mass to store the sun's heat, and use many more bricks.

Doors and windows should be rough framed with timbers or cast concrete frames. For load-bearing lintels across door and window openings, use either heavy timbers or cast reinforced concrete beams. Adobes carry only modest compression loads, so either provide load-bearing posts to support lintels, or extend lintels on both sides of openings to spread lintel loads over several feet of wall (distance varies with loads). In seismic zones, properly engineered reinforced concrete columns and rebar poked through holes in the adobes typically tie the bond beam to the foundation. Traditional adobe construction avoids wall openings within four feet of corners and sometimes adds massive external buttresses to outside corners of buildings to provide extra support. Wooden "gringo" blocks, the same width as adobe blocks, or narrow wooden nailing strips inserted between layers of blocks, are built into

the adobe walls around window/door frames or where shelves are required. Because you cannot nail or screw objects directly to adobe bricks, these wooden inserts provide anchor points.

Adobe plaster will adhere directly to adobe walls, but must be renewed every few years because it erodes with rainfall. Cement stucco is waterproof, but must be applied over stucco wire and expanded metal lath nailed to the adobe walls, wall opening rough frames, and beams. Due to the difference in thermal expansion rates between stucco and adobe, stucco will not adhere directly to adobe over time. Use the expanded metal lath where beams and frames join adobe walls to prevent cracks from forming in the plastered finish.

Adobe Roofs

Traditional adobe structures have massive earth covered flat roofs. The high clay content in the soil roof swells when wet and seals out water, but usually requires annual maintenance to seal cracks in the soil. Heavy log beams or "vigas" provide support for the earthen roof, which may be as much as 18 inches thick and weigh over 100 pounds per square foot. Walls had to be extremely thick to support the massive loads of these roofs.

Modern roofs may be flat or vaulted. The use of modern roofing materials drastically reduces the weight of the roof, which is a big plus in seismic zones. Roofs should be insulated with rigid foam or batt/loose insulation between joist spacers. "Flat" roofs are not entirely flat. They typically have a slope of at least ¼-inch per foot to ensure adequate drainage. Provide roof drainage that won't erode adobe walls. There is quite a variety of modern roofing materials to choose from (see your local roofing contractor). In hot, sunny locations, the use of light-colored roofing materials can significantly reduce your air conditioning bill.

CAST EARTH

An exciting new eco-friendly building process that shows great promise is Cast Earth (patent pending). This process has been used on a variety of residential projects and has the potential to compete favorably with stick-frame construction on a finished cost basis. Traditional earth building methods are extremely labor intensive and usually cost significantly more than stick-frame construction if the labor costs of a construction crew are figured in. Adobe bricks are usually made by labor-intensive processes and adobe buildings require the hand placement of thousands of adobe bricks. Even with modern forms and pneumatic tampers, rammed earth construction also requires a considerable amount of labor.

Cast Earth utilizes gypsum and a proprietary retardant to stabilize earth mixtures and reduce shrinkage, allowing for the use of existing concrete industry labor-saving machinery, forms, and techniques to make walls of cast earth. When walls are poured with the Cast Earth mixture, the forms can be removed on the same day as the pour, since the wet material sets up quickly to the point where it is strong enough to support a complete wall. Lower levels set before the wall height grows significantly, allowing use of lightweight forms and fewer ties than rammed earth requires. Because of the glue-like nature of the calcined gypsum and its slight expansion on setting, shrinkage and cracking are not a problem. With Cast Earth, it is possible to use a much wider range of soils than have historically been employed for earth building, but it does require a mix of about 10% to 15% of gypsum (by weight). In general, steel reinforcing is not used in Cast Earth.

Unlike the manufacturing of cement, which releases large amounts of CO_2 (the major greenhouse gas) directly into the atmosphere as a result of a chemical reaction, the chemical reaction of calcining gypsum directly releases water, but no CO_2 (Lowenhaupt 2000, 9). The burning of fossil fuels to generate the required heat for calcining gypsum does release some CO_2. However, because the calcining of gypsum occurs at much lower temperatures than that required by the cement process, significantly less energy is consumed to make a sack of gypsum than a sack of cement, resulting in far less CO_2 released into the atmosphere. By my calculations, processing gypsum releases roughly a tenth as much CO_2 as processing an equivalent amount of cement. For more information in this new technology, see Cast Earth in the *Resources* section of this chapter.

STRAW BALES

If all the straw left in the United States after the harvest of major grains was baled instead of burned, five million 2,000-square-foot houses could be built every year.
    —Matts Myhrman, founder of Out on Bale

For an excellent introduction to this exciting and versatile "green building" alternative, take a look at *The Straw Bale House* by Athena Swentzell Steen, Bill Steen, and David Bainbridge. Taking advantage of an abundant "waste" material, straw bales provide walls of high insulation value, structure, and form with low environmental impact and low materials costs. Straw is the dry grass left over after the seed has been harvested, whereas hay has higher nutritive value and is usually cut green with the seed attached. Most straw is burned or plowed under, rather than baled. Straw is both cheaper and less nutritious than hay, so it is better for a building material. For thousands of years, straw has been used as a building material to reinforce mud, thatch houses, and insulate walls.

If you are building your own home with a lot of "sweat equity," a straw bale house could be your ticket to a low-cost dream home that is comfortable, durable, energy efficient, and has an old world, hand-hewn, thick-walled look to it. Even though straw bales are cheap, finishing off exterior and interior straw bale walls is a labor-intensive job. Family and friends can rapidly help stack or finish your straw bale walls, further contributing to your sweat equity. If you are hiring a contractor and crew to build your straw bale home, you probably will not save anything in up-front costs as compared to stick-frame construction, but you will save on your energy bills and the end result will be a unique, finely crafted home that goes easy on our remaining forests.

Straw bale building construction originated in Nebraska during the late 1800s. The lack of a good supply of cheap wood, an abundance of straw, and the invention of both horse-powered and steam balers made straw bales a logical building material. Many of those early straw bale buildings are still around today, showing that straw bale construction is durable as well as practical. The early straw bale buildings were typically constructed with bales supporting the entire roof load. This type of construction is commonly referred to as "load-bearing" construction. Because straw bales are not rigid materials (they will settle under load), special design consideration must be given to load-bearing straw bale walls. Although there are many load-bearing straw bale structures built today, most modern straw bale homes are built with some kind of load-bearing post-and-beam construction wherein the bales insulate and give form to the walls, but do not carry structural loads. This type of construction is commonly referred to as "in-fill" walls. With both types of construction, the bales are usually plastered (cement stucco, adobe mud, lime plaster, etc.) but may be covered with sheetrock, wood siding, or almost any other kind of standard wall covering.

In-Fill (Non–Load-Bearing) Straw Bale Construction

If you think you might have trouble getting your straw bale house through the local building inspector, I would stick with "in-fill" straw bale construction.

All structural loads, including roof, seismic, and snow loads, are carried on some form of post-and-beam frame. The straw bales provide insulation and shape to the walls, but carry no load. Due to the wide section of the walls, there are some lumber conserving methods for modified post-and-beam walls that may actually require less lumber than load-bearing straw bale walls. See *The Straw Bale House* by Steen et al. for a wide variety of construction method options, and an interesting case comparison of load-bearing versus non–load-bearing walls constructed by the same builder on two separate jobs utilizing the same floor plan. One method of framing, referred to as "modified post-and-beam construction, utilizes floor-to-ceiling, plywood-sheathed 2-by-4 framed box beams at all windows and doors, and 4-by-4 posts at each corner as the sole support of a glue-lam bond beam support for the roof. This system appears to be easy to construct and uses wood sparingly (see Figure 7-9). The bond beam must be sized to adequately support roof loads across the maximum gap between post supports.

Figure 7-9. Modified post-and-beam, in-fill wall structure. Illustration from *The Straw Bale House* by Athena Swentzell Steen, Bill Steen, and David Brainbridge with David Eisenberg (Chelsea Green Publishing Company, 1994).

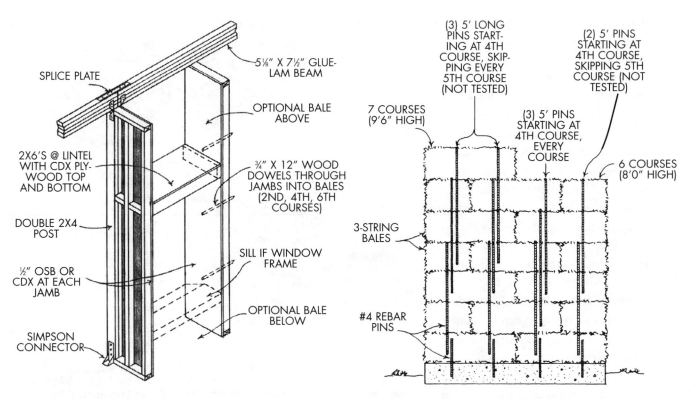

Figure 7-10. Box column detail for modified post-and-beam. Illustration from *The Straw Bale House* by Athena Swentzell Steen, Bill Steen, and David Brainbridge with David Eisenberg (Chelsea Green Publishing Company, 1994).

Figure 7-11. Bale-pinning options. Illustration from *The Straw Bale House* by Athena Swentzell Steen, Bill Steen, and David Brainbridge with David Eisenberg (Chelsea Green Publishing Company, 1994).

The bales in the in-fill wall system are typically pinned or otherwise attached to each other, the foundation, the posts, and the door/window frames. This increases the wall's resistance to shear loads due to wind and seismic loading. Shear loads are sideways loads that effectively try to push walls over rather than compression load that squeeze walls from above. Rebar pins are typically cast into the foundation to pierce through the first 1½ courses of straw bales (see Figure 7-11). Foundation rebar pins are spaced such that two pins pierce each bale. As more courses of bales are added, rebar pins are driven down through the bales to tie all the bales together. One tested system uses 5-foot-long, #4 rebar (½-inch nominal diameter) pins driven down through every course, starting at the fourth. Wooden dowels can attach frames and beams horizontally to end bales. Alternately, expanded metal can be nailed to posts and frames and then bent at a right angle and nailed to straw bales.

Load-Bearing Straw Bale Construction

The use of straw bales as a load-bearing structural material requires paying special attention to both design and construction methods due to the compressible nature of the straw bales. Under loads they will compress and settle over time. Windows, door frames, and stucco wall finishes are relatively rigid materials that do not compress alongside the straw bales. To prevent cracked windows and stucco, or sticky windows and doors, load-bearing straw bale walls must be either precompressed or loaded by the roof and given time to settle before door jams or window lintels are shimmed to the bond beam, and the exterior walls are finished.

It is a good idea to limit the use of load-bearing straw bale walls to fairly small structures utilizing walls with small openings for windows and doors, because large openings require rigid supports that will not settle like the rest of the wall. Gypsum, wood, stucco, and plaster wall finishes are rigid materials. As the bales continue to settle over time, a higher proportion of the roof load will shift from the bales to the rigid exterior wall coverings. Stucco and plaster are weak in tension, so in the case of earthquakes acting on load-bearing straw bale walls, the exterior finish may crack, shifting the loads from the rigid exterior finish back to the straw bales.

In areas with potentially heavy snow loads, I suggest avoiding the use of load-bearing straw bale walls, as the added weight of a heavy snow load could cause the walls to compress further, cracking the rigid external wall facing. When the first load-bearing straw bale structures were built in Nebraska, the walls were left unfinished for months and were not plastered until the weight of the roof had fully compressed the walls and they stopped settling. Additionally, these structures had small window and door openings, and the lintels over doors and windows extended several feet into the straw walls on both sides of the opening to spread the roof load out over several bales.

Due to the possibility that a roof might take off and fly like a bird in high winds, load-bearing straw bale walls require some kind of tie-down system. This has been accomplished by a variety of methods, including threaded steel rods that pierce the straw bales ("all-thread"), steel strapping, steel cables, and polyester strapping (the kind used to strap heavy boxes to pallets for shipping), and some rely just upon the wire stucco netting embedded in stucco. In attempts to shorten the building process, many builders have used these tie-down methods to preload the structure, rapidly compressing the straw bales. The goal is to compress the bales in excess of the combined roof load and dead load (snow, people, furniture, etc.) to cause the structure's straw bale walls to settle in a few days instead of a few months. For a good discussion of this effort and the options with the best success rates, see *Build It with Bales* by Matts Myhrman and S. O. MacDonald.

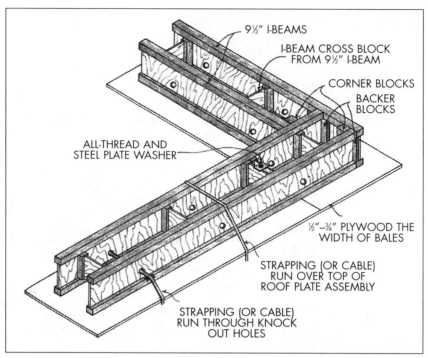

Figure 7-12. Bond beam for load-bearing walls, showing strapping and all-thread options. Illustration from *The Straw Bale House* by Athena Swentzell Steen, Bill Steen, and David Brainbridge with David Eisenberg (Chelsea Green Publishing Company, 1994).

Finishing Straw Bale Walls

The enemy of straw bales is moisture. As long as the moisture content is kept low, rot and vermin will tend to leave the bales alone. Bugs like termites prefer the wooden posts, beams, and window frames to dry straw. A vapor barrier, such as asphalt roofing paper, is typically laid between the first course of bales and the foundation, and then folded upward to cover the exterior of the bottom course. Interior walls should be similarly protected against such common problems as overflowing toilets. The top row of bales is protected from roof condensation and leaks by a drip cap. Some prefer to use clay-based adobe mud or lime-based plasters instead of cement-based stucco, because their manufacture consumes less fossil fuels and they are more breathable, allowing bales to dry over time with less chance for the problem of moisture penetration going undetected.

Plasters are typically applied in at least two or three coats. The first coat, known as the "scratch coat," is a thick layer that typically bonds to the bales and covers all of the expanded metal mesh

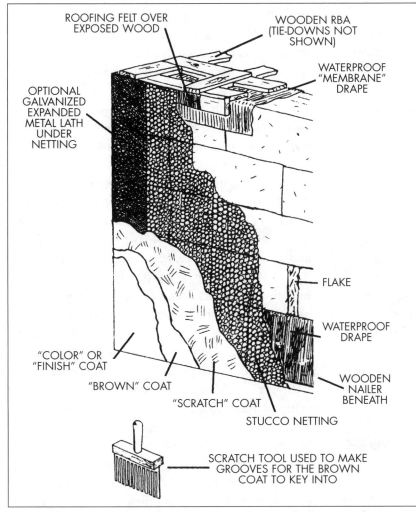

ROOFING FELT OVER
EXPOSED WOOD

WOODEN RBA
(TIE-DOWNS NOT
SHOWN)

WATERPROOF
"MEMBRANE"
DRAPE

OPTIONAL
GALVANIZED
EXPANDED
METAL LATH
UNDER
NETTING

FLAKE

WATERPROOF
DRAPE

WOODEN
NAILER
BENEATH

"COLOR" OR
"FINISH" COAT

"BROWN" COAT

"SCRATCH" COAT

STUCCO NETTING

SCRATCH TOOL USED TO MAKE
GROOVES FOR THE BROWN
COAT TO KEY INTO

Figure 7-13. Plaster finish on a straw bale wall. Illustration from
Build It with Bales by Matts Myhrman and S. O. MacDonald.

and wire stucco netting (if used). The expanded metal mesh is applied to areas particularly prone to stress and cracking, such as window and door-frames, or anywhere else that straw bales attach to rigid wood. Stucco wire netting (chicken wire) covers the rest of the straw walls to provide some internal reinforcement to help prevent cracking. Earth-based plasters are cheap (sometimes free if your site has acceptable soil with lots of clay), eco-friendly, easy to apply, usually eliminate the cost of stucco netting, and have a nice soft feel to them. On the down side, they have poor water resistance, tend to drop fine particles of dust, and are not very hard. For a good discussion of plastering techniques and options, see *Build It with Bales* by Matts Myhrman and S. O. MacDonald.

BUILDING WITH INSULATED CONCRETE FORMS

[O]ne ton of cement produces over one ton of CO_2, and (annual) world cement production was around 1.3 billion tons a few years ago, so we're putting an equal or larger amount of CO_2 into the atmosphere. This is about 8% of CO_2 emissions worldwide, a huge percentage for one industry.... As you know, it (CO_2) is the primary greenhouse gas that is contributing to global warming.

—Scott Shell, Environmental Impacts of Cement and Flyash

Three significant drawbacks to concrete walls are the low insulating value of concrete, the need to either cast concrete within forms or build walls block-by-block from precast concrete blocks, and the huge amounts of greenhouse gases that are released into the atmosphere each year as a result of concrete produc-tion. A relatively new concrete-effi-cient construction technique is the use of insulated concrete forms (ICF), where the walls are built out of Legolike foam blocks that are stacked together to form building walls with hollow channels. Rebar is inserted into the foam blocks, and then concrete is poured into the channels. The result is a well-insu-lated, termite- and rot-resistant wall that uses considerably less concrete than solid wall construc-tion and may even use less cement than cement-stabilized rammed earth walls. Foam blocks have inserts for attaching exterior siding, which may include sheetrock, stucco, wood, and so on. Buildings incorporating ICF can be designed for exceptional earthquake and hurricane resistance.

Cement is fabricated from limestone and clay, which is kiln fired at 2700°F to drive the water out of the limestone. Cement kilns are the largest items of moving industrial equipment in the world. The mining, kiln firing, grinding, and transportation of cement require the consumption of huge quantities of fossil fuels. Cement kilns are mostly fired with coal, which releases large amounts of carbon dioxide (CO_2), nitrous oxides, sulfur oxides, and particulates into the atmosphere. Additionally, the calcining process for cement releases large amounts of CO_2 as a byproduct of the chemical reaction. Concrete is a mixture of cement (usually not from a local source) with sand, water, and gravel (usually locally sourced). The use of cement to stabilize a rammed earth wall, whether for seismic resistance, waterproofing, or simply to strengthen local soil, can rapidly make a "green building" not so green.

Concrete or rammed earth soil-cement mixtures are often referred to by the number of sacks of cement in the mixture to make a finished cubic yard of material. For example, a 6-sack mix of concrete contains sand, gravel, water, and 6 sacks of concrete to make a cubic yard (27 cubic feet) of concrete. One sack of concrete contains 1 cubic foot of material. A common soil-stabilizing mix for rammed earth in earthquake country of 1½ sacks of cement per yard would use as much cement to make a 24-inch-thick, rammed earth wall as a 6-inch-thick, 6-sack, solid concrete wall, and an ICF wall may use considerably less cement.

There are numerous manufacturers of insulated concrete forms. Some well-known tradenames are Blue Maxx, Perma-Form, Polysteel, and Quad-Lock. If you check the Internet under insulated concrete forms, you can find manufacturers of these systems and contractors who do this kind of work. Talk to manufacturers for referrals to local contractors, check your yellow pages, or search the Internet.

PUMICE-CRETE

Pumice-crete is an energy and resource efficient low-density concrete made from pumice aggregate, Portland cement, and water. Pumice is a lightweight volcanic rock that is an excellent insulator and is found in many parts of the world where volcanoes are present. It is a sponge-like stony material formed by expansion of gases when molten lava rapidly

cools. It is found in very shallow deposits in such places as New Mexico, Arizona, California, Oregon, Washington, and Idaho. If you happen to live in reasonable trucking distance from a supply of pumice aggregate, the use of pumice-crete can provide you with a beautiful, functional, super energy-efficient home at a reasonable cost using traditional concrete forming technology.

Typically pumice-crete is poured on site in a wall thickness of 14 inches or greater without additional insulation or structural components (unless you are in an active seismic zone). Wall surfaces are finished by applying plaster coats to the interior and stucco to the exterior. The walls are very durable, fireproof, have good noise resistance, are high in thermal mass, and are aesthetically pleasing. Typical pumice-crete walls have an R-value of at least 1.5 per inch of thickness, giving an R-value of 27 for an 18-inch-thick wall. A mix of about 2 to 2.5 sacks of cement per cubic yard of pumice-crete yields a good balance of strength and insulating value (Berger 2000, 33). Compression strengths for this mix of pumice-crete typically run somewhere around 400 psi, about the same as for good quality rammed earth and stabilized adobe. Increasing the cement content makes the walls stronger and more expensive while decreasing the insulating value. Reducing the cement content weakens the walls. The use of pumice-crete conserves wood and steel, but does not really cut cement usage due to the increased thickness of the walls. For more information on pumice-crete, check out Pumice-crete Building Systems of New Mexico's web site at www.pumicecrete.com.

PASSIVE SOLAR DESIGN

Heat from the sun is free and falls on most homes for a good part of the winter. Even in cloudy parts of the country, most homes could benefit from passive solar design for about half of all winter days. Passive solar design is the use of building orientation, insulation, windows, thermal mass, the right materials, and smart design features to make buildings that heat and cool themselves with minimal inputs of electricity and fossil fuels. Well-designed passive solar buildings are cool in the summer and warm in the winter. Unlike some of the complicated active solar systems utilizing pumps, controllers, and hot-water storage tanks, passive solar designs tend to be simple. They typically require no extra maintenance, are no more complicated to operate than opening a vent or lowering a shade, and can be incorporated into perfectly normal-looking home designs for a modest additional cost.

The principles of passive solar design are fairly simple to grasp. I know of several owner-builders who designed and built beautiful, functional solar homes, without an engineering or design background, and with just a little help from a few books. If the math involved in a detailed solar analysis is intimidating, find yourself an experienced solar designer to help with your project. The use of the sun to heat the home is not a new concept. The ancient cliff dwellings in the U.S. Southwest are some of the oldest surviving examples of passive solar design. These structures are typically oriented in such a way as to catch most of the rays from the low winter sun but are shaded from the high, hot summer sun by rock overhangs. With a little thought, and for the same or slightly more money than you would spend for conventional construction, you can build a home that requires only 10% to 50% of the energy that it takes to heat an average new home.

Passive Solar "Rules of Thumb"

- **Orientation.** Normally, the optimum solar orientation for a building is with the long walls and main windows facing due south. For other reasons, such as to benefit from a nice view, you may choose to vary this orientation from due south (true south, not magnetic south). For modest rotations off true south, you don't lose much solar efficiency. You will lose only about 8% of your solar gain for 22½° off true south, 20% for 45° orientation, and 36% at 67½° orientation (Kachadorian 1997, 18).
- **Minimize north-facing windows.** Placing bathrooms, bedrooms, closets, storage areas, and garages on the north side helps to minimize windows and acts as a thermal block.

- **South-facing glass.** Place most of your glass window surface area on the south side of the home. The square footage of south-, west-, and east-facing windows should equal about 15% of the total surface area of all external heated walls put together. Too much south-facing glass turns a home into a solar oven during the day and a refrigerator on cold clear nights. Too little glass and your house is dark and gains little heat from the sun. The Sustainable Buildings Industry Council (SBIC) suggests limiting the square footage of south-facing glass to 12% of the total square footage of heated floor area (Alexander 1997, 38).
- **Insulation.** Insulate the walls, ceilings, roof, and foundation perimeter. Recommended wall insulation is typically R-19 or better. The "R value" describes the thermal resistance of a wall or material. Higher R-values means better insulation with less heat loss. With conventional stick-frame construction, use at least 6-inch studs with R-19 insulation. A slightly better R-value is obtained using 4-inch studs with fiberglass batts, plus 1-inch rigid foam external insulation that acts as a thermal block over the studs and minimizes air infiltration, for a total wall R-value of about R-21. Insulate under solar slabs with at least 2 inches of rigid foam board, and insulate foundation perimeter with 2 to 4 inches of rigid foam. Because hot air rises, roof insulation should be of a higher R-value, such as R-30 with 9-inch batts. Superinsulated walls are in the R-30 to R-50 range, and superinsulated ceilings may run R-50 and up.
- **Vapor barriers.** All loose insulation, such as fiberglass batts, should have a vapor barrier on its inside wall surface. Warm air holds much more moisture than cold air. If warm moist house air infiltrates exterior walls, moisture will condense against cold wall surfaces, eventually wetting the insulation and causing rot in your walls and ceilings. In addition, wet insulation has lost most of its insulating value.
- **Thermal mass.** Provide thermal mass for heat storage. Thermal mass, typically in the form of a concrete slab floor and/or thick masonry, rammed earth, or adobe walls, absorbs heat from

a day of sunshine and then releases that heat at night to warm the house. Without thermal mass, the house gets uncomfortably hot during the day and uncomfortably cold at night. In the summer, thermal mass helps to reduce cooling requirements. The mass is cooled by venting to outside air at night, and then the cool thermal mass absorbs excess heat during the middle of hot days. When calculating the optimum size of thermal mass, shoot for a daily rise and fall in temperature of no more than 8°F from the solar gain of a full day's midwinter sun and the heat loss from a full night of cooling. In James Kachadorian's *The Passive Solar House*, he uses a 1,900-square-foot, Green Mountain Homes Saltbox design #38, located in Middlebury, Vermont, as an example for solar calculations. This home has R-21 walls, R-32 ceilings, and R-1.92 double-pane windows and patio doors. He has 44 square feet of east- and west-facing glass and 122 square feet of south-facing glass. For this example, James calculated an optimum solar slab of 16-foot x 38-foot by 13-inches thick, containing 548 cubic feet of concrete (15% of the volume lost to ducting) and weighing about 41 tons. He figures that the concrete used to make the solar slab is the same as would be used to make a typical basement (Kachadorian 1997, 85–89).

- **South-facing windows.** South-facing windows naturally have less gain from the summer sun, even without significant roof overhangs, due to the high angle of the sun in the summer sky. Sun at high angles penetrates only a short distance into the room and tends to reflect off the window due to the steep angle of incidence. South-facing solar "collectors" (windows) will turn mostly "off" in the summer months and "on" in the winter months. East- and west-facing windows will have solar gain for half the day. Unless shaded, east and west windows have significant summer solar gain because they catch the lower angled rays directly from morning or afternoon sun. Where summer air conditioning is a necessity, try to minimize areas of east-and west-facing windows to reduce your air conditioning load.

- **Keeping cool when it's hot.** Where summer cooling needs are significant, place properly sized overhangs above south-, east-, and west-facing windows to provide shade from high summer sun, yet allow full solar gain from low winter sun. Solar design handbooks have sun angle charts to assist with sizing roof overhangs at different latitudes. Proper calculations of window and wall overhang size can make a significant difference in your heating and cooling needs, especially with high thermal mass walls like adobe and rammed earth. If you are in a dry climate, swamp coolers that take advantage of the cooling properties of evaporating water use a fraction of the energy of standard air conditioners. With good insulation and orientation, passive solar houses are often very comfortable with a modest swamp cooler when similarly sized neighboring houses require large, energy guzzling air conditioners to stay cool. For example, during multiday 104°F-plus heat storms in Davis, California, when neighbors found that their air conditioned homes couldn't cope with the high heat, they sought refuge in a well-insulated experimental PG&E model tract home that had no air conditioning whatsoever (Hawken 1999, 103).

- **Trees.** Use trees for natural shading and wind breaks. Deciduous trees on the south side provide summer shade and winter sun. Evergreens on the north side provide wind breaks and help slow radiant heat losses in the winter.

- **Ventilation.** In today's tightly built homes, significant ventilation is required both for comfort and to ensure against the buildup of toxic fumes. Ventilation systems that exchange two-thirds of the home's air every hour are recommended. Stale toxic air was never a problem in old, "leaky," energy-wasting homes, but is a common problem in modern "tight" homes. One of the best energy efficient solutions for ventilation is the use of air-to-air heat exchangers that vent warm house air to the outside while drawing cold air inside and simultaneously transferring most of the heat out of the warm exhaust air back into the fresh intake air.

- **Insulated windows.** Use insulated windows with thermal shades or shutters over significant areas of glazing. Single-pane glass is a terrible insulator, having an R-value of about 0.9, which means that one square foot of single-pane glass loses as much heat as 22 square feet of R-20 wall. Typical double-pane windows have an R-value of about 1.9, and standard multi-pane windows with low-e coatings (low-e glass has special coatings that reduce radiant heat loss through windows) have an R-value of 3 to 4.5. Superwindows with low-e glass, thermal breaks, and argon or krypton gas filling can have an insulating value of up to R-12. Superwindows are generally cost effective in cold climates only. Adding a honeycomb opaque shade, such as the Hunter Douglas Duette, raises a double pane R-value to between 4 and 5. When you add interior window shutters insulated with 1 inch of rigid foam, double-pane R-values jump to 11. I highly recommend the addition of insulating shutters to glass patio doors and large windows. The low-e coatings on quality insulating windows can be tailored to either reflect or allow incoming solar radiation. High "solar heat gain coefficient" windows will allow solar heat to pass both in and out of your windows. In hot climates, and on the north walls of homes in cold climates, you want windows with low solar gain coefficients, because they will both hold the heat out when it's hot and in when it's cold. In cold climates, you want windows with high solar gain coefficients on the south walls to let the solar heat pass in through your south windows on cold days.
- **Solar greenhouses.** "Sunspaces" with sloped areas of glass can be a wonderfully warm sunny spot on a cold winter's day, and can be a great place to start your seedlings, but they are usually overglazed, tending to overheat during the day and get very cold at night. Additionally, unlike vertical glass, sloped areas of glass have high solar gain in the summer potentially adding to the air conditioning burden. Make sure you provide solar greenhouse spaces with adequate ventilation and shade for reducing summer heat, thermal mass to prevent nighttime freezing, and doors to close off from the house at night or when the greenhouse is too hot. Data on heavily glazed sunrooms indicates that they tend to lose about as much heat at night as they gain during the day (Kachadorian 1997, 138).
- **Air circulation.** Provide a mechanism for moving your home's air around. Hot air rises. Ceiling fans can drive hot air stuck in the upper reaches of your home back down to where you can feel it (or reverse fan direction for summer cooling). With multistory homes, a small ducted fan can move warm air from the upper level back down to the lower level for a fraction of the energy cost of heating the air. In the summer, a vent damper can switch the flow from the same fan to vent hot air to the outside from the upper areas and insulated attic spaces, keeping the rest of the house cooler.

James Kachadorian's Patented Solar Slab

In the 1970s, James Kachadorian came up with an idea for making a solar slab out of concrete block, with a layer of cast concrete on top. This slab acts as both a thermal mass to store the sun's heat and as an effective heat exchanger to help heat the house in the winter and cool it in the summer. The idea was unique enough that he was awarded a patent for his design. Now that the patent protection has expired, he is telling the world about his idea. Basically, the bottom layer of his solar slab is a layer of hollow concrete blocks turned on their sides and lined up, without staggering, to make a series of air channels running from the back of the first floor to the front. Vents are cut into the front and back of the slab to access the air channels. When the slab surface is heated by the sun, natural convection air currents cause cooler air at one end of the slab to fall into the vents, while warmer air on the other side of the slab rises, sucking air through the solar slab. The holes in the center of the concrete blocks embedded in the slab essentially triple the surface area of the slab. This increased surface area combined with the natural convection currents driving air through the channels in the slab are what makes it into an effective heat exchanger for heating and cooling. Heating and air conditioning units should draw intake air

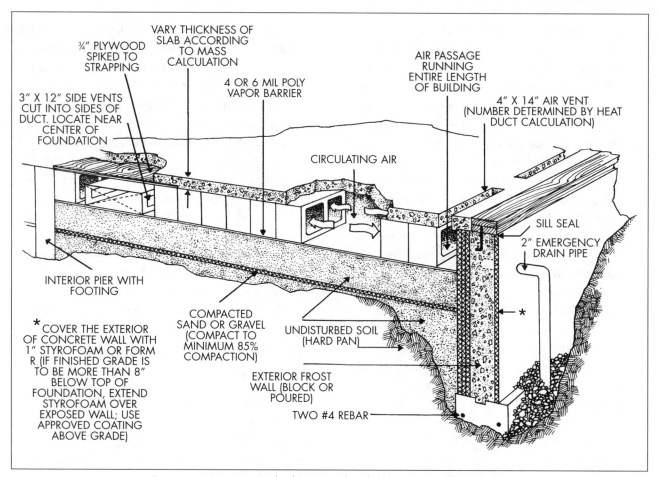

VARY THICKNESS OF SLAB ACCORDING TO MASS CALCULATION

¾" PLYWOOD SPIKED TO STRAPPING

4 OR 6 MIL POLY VAPOR BARRIER

AIR PASSAGE RUNNING ENTIRE LENGTH OF BUILDING

3" X 12" SIDE VENTS CUT INTO SIDES OF DUCT. LOCATE NEAR CENTER OF FOUNDATION

4" X 14" AIR VENT (NUMBER DETERMINED BY HEAT DUCT CALCULATION)

CIRCULATING AIR

SILL SEAL

2" EMERGENCY DRAIN PIPE

INTERIOR PIER WITH FOOTING

* COVER THE EXTERIOR OF CONCRETE WALL WITH 1" STYROFOAM OR FORM R (IF FINISHED GRADE IS TO BE MORE THAN 8" BELOW TOP OF FOUNDATION, EXTEND STYROFOAM OVER EXPOSED WALL; USE APPROVED COATING ABOVE GRADE)

COMPACTED SAND OR GRAVEL (COMPACT TO MINIMUM 85% COMPACTION)

UNDISTURBED SOIL (HARD PAN)

EXTERIOR FROST WALL (BLOCK OR POURED)

TWO #4 REBAR

Figure 7-14. James Kachadorian's solar slab heat exchanger detail.
Illustration courtesy of Chelsea Green Publishing Company (Kachadorian 1997).

through the solar slab ducts to take advantage of preheated or precooled intake air.

TRADITIONAL LOW-TECH STRUCTURES

Traditional low-tech structures range from lean-tos, tents, yurts, tipis, adobe, stone, rammed earth, and sod houses, to log cabins and elegant timber-framed homes. Although lacking the comforts of indoor plumbing and central heating, many old-fashioned homes provided a comfortable, simpler standard of living.

In the 1970s, I visited Frank at his tipi in the Green Mountains of Vermont. For several winters, Frank worked at the Trapp Family Lodge in Stowe, Vermont. They let him pitch his tipi in a thicket of trees where it wouldn't draw too much attention. It was a large tipi, about 20 feet across. Frank spread some straw and carpet remnants

on the packed snow floor and had a fire pit in the middle. After a day of work or cross-country skiing, a few friends would drop by. Gathered around the fire, temperatures quickly rose to the point where we stripped down to tee shirts. Someone brought out a guitar and jug of wine, and we settled in for a comfortable evening of wine, songs and stories, while temperatures outside dropped to well below 0°F on a clear, cold, January night.

Log Cabins

If you want to build a traditional log home without the assistance of modern tools, I suggest that you pick up the first *Foxfire* book (see *References* section in Chapter 1) edited by Eliot Wigginton. *Foxfire* contains a collection of interviews, wisdom, and old-fashioned know-how gleaned from the old-timers of Appalachia, who lived their lives with little or no access to modern machinery. It contains a lengthy

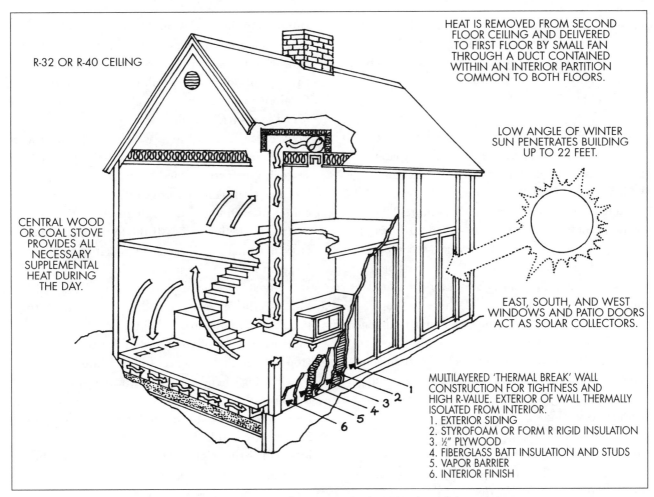

R-32 OR R-40 CEILING

HEAT IS REMOVED FROM SECOND
FLOOR CEILING AND DELIVERED
TO FIRST FLOOR BY SMALL FAN
THROUGH A DUCT CONTAINED
WITHIN AN INTERIOR PARTITION
COMMON TO BOTH FLOORS.

LOW ANGLE OF WINTER
SUN PENETRATES BUILDING
UP TO 22 FEET.

CENTRAL WOOD
OR COAL STOVE
PROVIDES ALL
NECESSARY
SUPPLEMENTAL
HEAT DURING
THE DAY.

EAST, SOUTH, AND WEST
WINDOWS AND PATIO DOORS
ACT AS SOLAR COLLECTORS.

MULTILAYERED 'THERMAL BREAK' WALL
CONSTRUCTION FOR TIGHTNESS AND
HIGH R-VALUE. EXTERIOR OF WALL THERMALLY
ISOLATED FROM INTERIOR.
1. EXTERIOR SIDING
2. STYROFOAM OR FORM R RIGID INSULATION
3. ½" PLYWOOD
4. FIBERGLASS BATT INSULATION AND STUDS
5. VAPOR BARRIER
6. INTERIOR FINISH

Figure 7-15. Heating a house with James Kachadorian's solar slab heat exchanger.
Illustration courtesy of Chelsea Green Publishing Company (Kachadorian 1997).

section devoted to quite a variety of styles and skills for log cabin building, including many photographs and illustrations. Other handy books for building a quick-and-dirty log cabin are the classic *Shelters Shacks and Shanties and How to Build Them* by D.C. Beard and *How to Build This Log Cabin for $3,000* by John McPherson.

If you want to build a beautiful, classic log home and you have access to modern materials, I highly recommend that you pick up the *Log Building Construction Manual* by Robert Chambers. Chambers is a well-known master teacher and builder of log homes. This book will walk you through all of the numerous details that will help make your log building a success. There are many different suppliers of materials, tools, and books for log home building. I think you will find that Schroeder Log Home Supply (see *Resources* section)

in Grand Rapids, Minnesota, is one of the best of the bunch. This supply source stocks an excellent selection of builder's books and tools. In the event you wish to build a log cabin and cannot locate other references mentioned in this chapter, a few guidelines are provided here.

FOUNDATION

If you want your log structure to last, it should be built on a rock or cement foundation at least 18 inches high, to keep the termites away. Peel the bark off your logs, or bugs and rot will infest your structure in short order. Before the advent of cement for mortar, stone foundations were built from carefully selected flat stones, sometimes chiseled or ground to fit. Clay mortar can help hold a foundation together and seal cracks, but you should ensure that your foundation will not fall apart if the clay mortar should wash out in a heavy rain or flood. If you have modern materials, you definitely should take advantage of threaded steel rod and rebar to tie your logs to a reinforced concrete foundation.

LOGS

Using larger logs will reduce the necessary labor and increase the insulating value of your walls, which is only about R-1.5 per inch of dry pine. A good log has an average diameter of more than 14 inches. Building with logs of less than a 10-inch tip diameter is not advised. Have your logs cut, peeled, measured, and marked with measurements before starting to build the walls. Careful thought and planning can avoid lots of headaches and "oops" events. Each log has a fat end (butt) and a thin end (tip). Don't lay crooked logs in the walls; save them for other uses. If your building is longer than your average log, try to use doors and jogs to take full advantage of log lengths without having to hassle with splices.

SILL LOGS

The first layer of logs on top of the foundation are the "sill logs." Proper selection and shaping of sill logs can make or break your walls. When planning how thick your sill logs should be, and how much to cut off their bottoms to make a flat for the wall to rest on, you need to take into consideration the other logs that you will use, and features like windows, doors, and the level of floor joists. You will want a nice fat portion of a log to cross the top of door and window openings. Header logs across door openings will be cut at 88 inches above the floor surface. Try to figure your logs and sills so that the 88-inch header cut will leave about a half to two-thirds of the header log intact. A sliver of a log across a header is not good. At the corners of the house, sill logs should line up "butt to butt" and "tip to tip."

WALLS

All logs are tapered and are laid with alternating tips and butts in the walls, making the top of most courses somewhat sloped. The top log, or plate log,

supporting the roof should be level. Some modern log builders make the centers of each log row level. It is also preferable if the log rows at the tops of doors and windows and the support for floor joists are nearly level. Many old-fashioned log constructions left a significant gap between each row of logs, which was chinked with sphagnum moss, cement mortar, or clay mixed with chopped straw. Modern "scribe-fit" log construction trims a groove into the bottom center of each log to make it closely fit the top surface of the log below. If the log is somewhat curved, or has significant irregularities such as large knots, try to position the log with the straightest sides up and down, and curves and knots to the inside or outside, to minimize fitting problems. If you have a chainsaw to cut grooves into the bottom of your logs to fit the log below (modern method), expect to lose about an inch off each log's height when trimming to fit to the log beneath. The straighter the log the less you lose. In the scribe-fit method, close matching log grooves are chinked with insulation. All green logs will shrink significantly in diameter as they age and dry, so it is a good idea to frame windows and doors with post-and-beam headers leaving about a 2-inch gap on top to the header log to allow for wall shrinkage and settling. Trim over this gap with a wood fascia to weatherproof the gap and hide it.

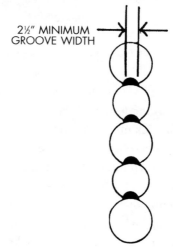

2½" MINIMUM GROOVE WIDTH

Figure 7-16. Custom-cut grooves to fit log rows to each other. Illustration adapted from *Log Building Construction Manual* by Robert Chambers (1999).

There are numerous log end-notching schemes that work well. Whichever method you choose, it is always safest to rough cut notches and saddles first, leaving some extra wood, and then finish cut the excess to make the logs fit.

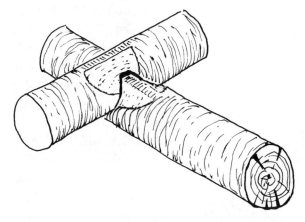

Figure 7-17. Common modern log notch and saddle. Illustration adapted from *Log Building Construction Manual* by Robert Chambers (1999).

Figure 7-18. Dove-tail style log notch and saddle (this method is described in detail in the first *Foxfire* book).

If you are notching the bottoms of logs to fit the row below, rough notch the ends to make the gap between logs even at both ends (widest near the center) leaving a gap between the logs of about 3 inches. Using calipers, find the widest gap between the logs and set a log scriber so that the horizontal distance between scribed lines at this point is about 2½ inches. Holding the scriber plumb, use a scriber (caliper with sharp points) to mark the notch line on the bottom of the new log.

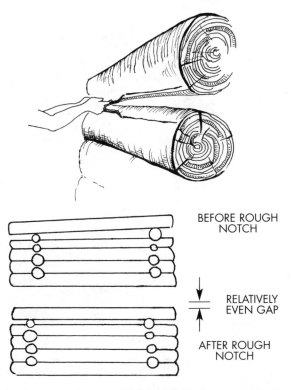

Figure 7-19. Rough notch, then scribe for "scribe-fit" log groove. Illustrations adapted from *Log Building Construction Manual* by Robert Chambers (1999).

ROOFS

Modern building materials will require less maintenance than traditional roofing. Traditional log structures were usually either thatched steep roofs, or low-angle sod roofs. For thatched roofs, space horizontal runners every foot or so (depending on the length of each bundle of thatch) across the roof trusses to tie thatching to. Each thatch bundle should overlap the next lower row by at least 6 inches. Sod roofs are heavy (usually about 8 to 12 inches thick), so make sure they are adequately supported with strong timbers.

Timber Frame Construction

Since the 1970s, there has been a revival in the use of old-fashioned timber frame construction. Traditional timber frames join large timbers together with load-bearing mortise-and-tenon type joints, similar to cabinetry and furniture joints that are pinned in place with hardwood pegs. Three-hundred-year-old timber framed structures that were originally roofed

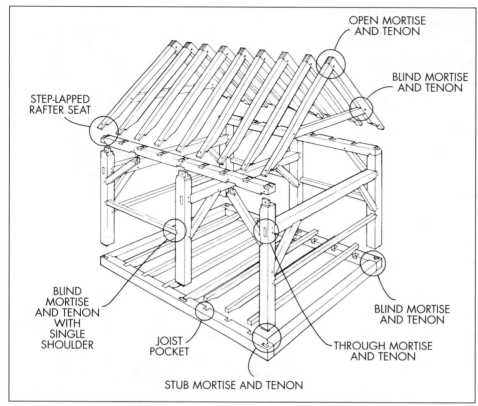

OPEN MORTISE AND TENON

BLIND MORTISE AND TENON

STEP-LAPPED RAFTER SEAT

BLIND MORTISE AND TENON WITH SINGLE SHOULDER

JOIST POCKET

BLIND MORTISE AND TENON

THROUGH MORTISE AND TENON

STUB MORTISE AND TENON

Figure 7-20. Simple timber frame showing several types of joints. Illustration from *Timber Frame Construction: All About Post-and-Beam Building* by Jack Sobon and Roger Schroeder (Storey Books 1984).

guide to tipis. The Laubins were a non-Indian couple who always "felt" Indian. They lived the traditional lifestyle of Native Americans, were adopted by an elderly Indian chief and his wife, and learned traditional crafts and skills from some of the few remaining Native elders who grew up at a time when primitive skills were still a way of life. The Laubins state that the more portable hunting tipis tended to run about 12 feet in diameter while the average family lodge was 18 to 20 feet in diameter, requiring poles about 22 to 28 feet long (Laubin and Laubin 1989, 19).

Beard's *Shelters, Shacks and Shanties* illustrates and describes the construction of several different styles of traditional Indian structures, such as hogans, longhouses, and wigwams. I have not been able to determine the difference between a wigwam and a wickiup, but perhaps they are loose terms that can apply to several different styles of construction. Rolling Thunder describes wickiups in Nevada made by digging the ends of about twenty slender willow poles into a circle. The poles were bent to cross in the center and then tied to make a dome shape. Slender branches were tied in parallel circles around the outside of the frame to provide strength and attachment points for thatching. In the old days, wickiups were thatched with strips of bark or bundles of long grasses tied in overlapping layers. Modern wickiups are usually weatherproofed with tarps. In the dry climate of Nevada, wickiups were often dug a few feet into the ground for natural earth cooling in the summer and heating in the winter.

with thatch are awesome testaments to the strength and durability of this type of construction. Modern timber-frame buildings use energy-efficient, foam-insulated wall panels, have a wonderful airy feel, and handsomely show off large structural timbers and their builders' craft. If you live in an area with a good source of local timber, or if you own a heavily wooded lot, you might be able to skip the commercial lumber suppliers and use local loggers and a portable chainsaw lumber mill to rough cut the timbers for your structure.

Tipis, Yurts, Wickiups, and Wigwams

From the frigid steppes of Mongolia to the plains of North Dakota and the Grand Tetons of Wyoming, tipis, yurts, and wickiups (wigwams) have provided comfortable shelters for indigenous peoples. A great book for building your own tipi is the classic *The Indian Tipi: Its History, Construction, and Use* by Reginald and Gladys Laubin. First published in 1957, and then revised in 1977, this is the definitive

If you want to build yourself a yurt, you might try to find a copy of Len Charney's *Build a Yurt: The Low-Cost Mongolian Round House* (it's out of print).

TIPI TIPS AND PITCHING BASICS

- Poles should be perfectly straight, smooth, peeled, and sharpened to a point at the butts (thick end) so they don't slip on the ground. Poles should extend several feet above the crossing point.

- For portability, light and strong woods are best, such as lodge-pole pine, white cedar, and red cedar. For the 20-foot tipi, poles should be about 2 inches in diameter where they cross and tie (narrower at the tips), no more than 4 to 5 inches at the butt, and about 25 to 28 feet long (no less than 22 feet).

- Cut poles from a thicket of young trees. Do not trim the tips until the poles are nearly finished, or you may cut them too short. You will need 15 strong poles for the 18- to 20-foot tipi frame plus two lighter poles for the smoke flaps. Season your poles before using them; otherwise they will dry with a permanent bend and will not hold the canvas tight.

- Tipi poles are set in a skewed cone shape to make the cross a little behind center so that the smoke flap can be positioned directly above the central fire pit. Start with a tripod of the three strongest poles. Before tying the tripod together, lay the three poles and tipi material flat on the ground, and then mark the poles at the crossing point, allowing extra length if the poles are to be dug into the ground.

- Tie the initial three poles together with a clove hitch followed by several wraps of 1/2-inch, heavy-duty, nonslippery cordage that is about 45 feet long. With the dangling free end of the rope and several pairs of hands, hoist the tripod into position. Position the legs with one leg next to where the door will be.

- Lay the other poles consecutively into the crotches of the tripod, placing about two-thirds of the poles into the front crotch where the smoke hole will go.

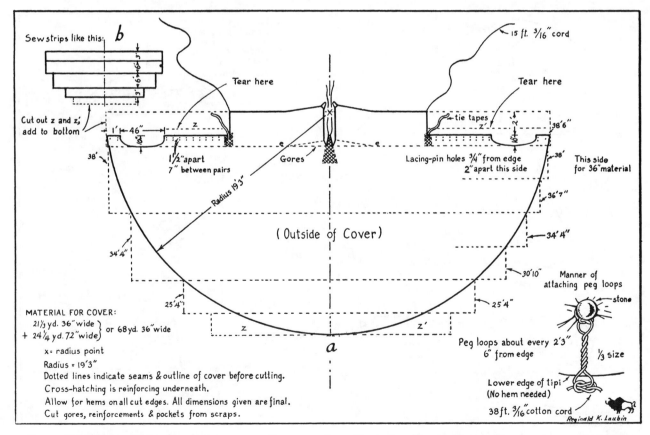

Figure 7-21. Basic 18-foot Sioux tipi pattern. Illustration from *The Indian Tipi: Its History, Construction, and Use* by Reginald Laubin and Gladys Laubin (University of Oklahoma Press, 1989).

- After all the poles are laid into the frame, grab the dangling rope and walk around the tipi frame four times, whipping or snapping the rope upwards as you go, to tightly wrap all the poles together at the narrow neck where they cross. When finished with the wraps, firmly stake the dangling rope end to keep your structure from tumbling if a wind should come up before the tipi is fully set.

- Bundle and tie the tipi canvas onto a lifting pole. Tilt the entire bundle into position on the tipi frame, and then unwrap the canvas from the lifting pole as you wrap it around the tipi frame.

- Traditionally, a cross bar was lashed to the door poles, allowing an adult to stand on it to pin the tops of the

Figure 7-22. Wickiups at Meta Tantay, Nevada. Illustration from *Rolling Thunder Speaks: A Message for Turtle Island,* by Rolling Thunder, edited by Carmen Sun Rising Pope (Clear Light Publishers 1999).

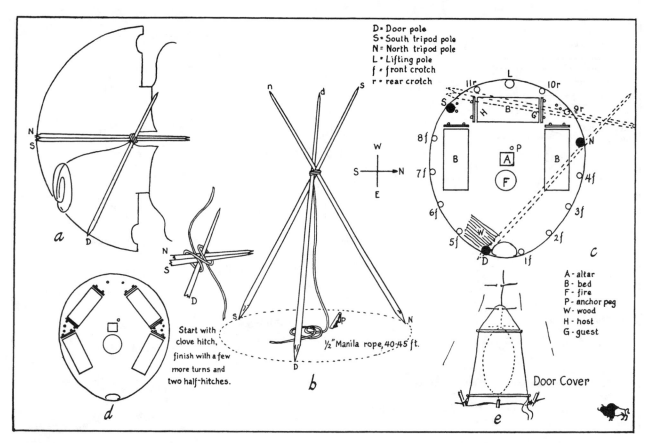

Figure 7-23. Erecting the Sioux tipi. Illustration from *The Indian Tipi: Its History, Construction, and Use* by Reginald Laubin and Gladys Laubin (University of Oklahoma Press, 1989).

canvas together with wooden lacing pins (a ladder will work if available).

■ A tipi liner is important for keeping the heat in during cold weather, for catching drips in wet weather, and for helping the tipi to draft well (Laubin and Laubin 1989, 36–46).

Making and pitching a tipi is not easy. You might do yourself a favor by picking up the Laubins' book *The Indian Tipi* or getting some help from someone who has done this before.

EARTHQUAKE RESISTANCE

We built wickiups that were strong and earthquake proof. . . . I told them that our tipis and wickiups would be standing when their buildings fall to the ground.
—Rolling Thunder, *Rolling Thunder Speaks: A Message for Turtle Island*

Ask anyone who has been through a major earthquake, such as the Loma Prieta or Northridge quakes, and they will tell you that a serious quake can be a terrifying event. Often the main differences between structures that pulled through in relatively good shape and those that got the "bulldozer remodel" (dig a hole with a bulldozer, push the house into it, start over) were whether the building was of older construction, the contractor was sloppy with shear nailing of the building's exterior plywood siding, or there was insufficient use of "hurricane clips" and "Simpson Strong-Ties" to properly brace the frame.

Shelly and Phil Rodgers were in their home in California's Santa Cruz Mountains when the Loma Prieta quake struck. The epicenter was about seven miles from their home. The house shook violently and all of their cupboards opened, throwing every dish, jar, can, bookcase, television, and appliance to the floor. Phil said that the house floors undulated like a snake, appearing to change elevation by more than a foot in different parts of the house as the quake shook through. They were not able to leave the house until the earth stopped moving. Because their car keys and shoes were still inside, Phil had to brave the aftershocks and wade through broken glass to retrieve keys and shoes so they could attempt the drive to town to pick up their kids. He brought a chainsaw with him, which was needed to cut large limbs that had fallen across the road.

On their way to town, they passed the spot where a neighbor's house should have been. It had been built on tall pylons overlooking the hillside. When the quake struck, it slid off the piers and down the canyon. The two occupants on the first floor managed to crawl out the door moments before it took off, but their son, who was sleeping on the second floor, went for the wildest ride of his life. He miraculously rode through it uninjured, as the first floor disintegrated and the roof split away and to the side. Another friend had a home that lacked proper shear wall nailing and adequate attachment to the foundation. This home slid off the foundation and was a total loss, receiving the "bulldozer remodeling job."

Shelly and Phil's home was of post-and-beam construction with massive timbers. Their contractor had paid careful attention to all the exterior plywood shear nailing and steel frame ties. Remarkably, not one window was broken and the house suffered no structural damage even though many of their personal items were destroyed (they cleaned up their dishes and pottery with a shovel). Another friend was not so lucky. This house was of similar design and built by the same contractor that had built Shelly and Phil's, but the framing and plywood sheet nailing had been done by a subcontractor who was not as careful and had nailed at wider intervals than specified. This house suffered severe structural damage, requiring $170,000 to repair the windows and house frame, and resquare the walls, costing more to fix than it originally cost to build.

When an earthquake strikes, the most damaging motion is usually not the vertical, but the horizontal component of the earth movement. The mass of the building tends to want to stay in one place as the earth moves side to side. The resulting sideway forces on the walls, which tend to push the walls into a diamond shape rather than a rectangle, are referred to as "shear forces." As the mass and height of a building increase, the walls will be subject to greater shear forces in an earthquake.

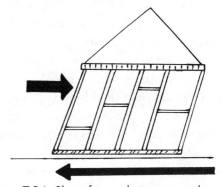

Figure 7-24. Shear forces during an earthquake.

Improving Earthquake Resistance

Recently, through the use of modern analytical tools, and by studying what worked and did not work in actual earthquakes, seismic design has made a lot of progress. Although there is no way to "earthquake-proof" a structure, there are numerous ways to increase its earthquake resistance. At some particular level of severity, all structures will fail. However, good seismic design can dramatically increase the earthquake resistance of a structure. A few factors that affect the earthquake resistance of a building are described below.

Mass and height. The heavier and more massive the walls and ceilings, and the taller the structure, the higher the shear loads will be in an earthquake. Tent-like structures, such as yurts and tipis, have almost no mass. They will usually survive massive earthquakes without failure, but if they do collapse, they are so light that they will probably cause little damage.

Flexibility. If a structure can flex and "give" without failure, it can absorb seismic energy and ride out quakes that might damage or destroy other structures. Fiberglass composites have high strength-to-weight ratios and exceptional flexibility, making them a prime candidate for earthquake resistant structures that are lightweight, strong, and flexible.

Masonry, earth, and concrete. These materials are fairly strong in compression, but notoriously weak in tension. The properly engineered use of reinforcing steel, bond beams, and structural roof diaphragms can drastically improve the earthquake resistance of these types of structures. Most of the stress in the walls is a downward compression from the weight of the building. In an earthquake, shear loads put sections of the walls in high tension, which is the kind of load that masonry and earth handle poorly. Consequently, older masonry and earthen buildings often collapse in moderately strong earthquakes.

Low-tech reinforcing. One low-tech way to improve the earthquake resistance of traditional earthen structures is to incorporate load-bearing post-and-beams into the walls and to thread strong rope through the wall centers to help hold them together (instead of collapsing) when a quake cracks the earthen walls. Another low-tech reinforcing material is bamboo. Some varieties of bamboo are extremely strong and resilient.

Length-to-width ratio. Slender masonry or earthen walls are prone to fracture. Massive, thick walls will usually do better in an earthquake. Sometimes external buttresses are added to building corners to provide extra support.

Isolation design. In the movies, you have probably seen someone attempting to pull a tablecloth out from under a table of dishes. If all goes well, the dishes stay in place as the tablecloth slides from under them. But if the cloth does not slip smoothly under the dishes, they all fall over. Some modern skyscrapers employ huge bearings under the foundation to allow the building to stay somewhat stationary while the earth moves underneath, similar to the action in the tablecloth trick. Massive rubber blocks, or concave bearing supports, act to bring the building back into alignment with the ground once the earthquake is over. These design features are called "isolators" because they try to isolate the earth movements from the building.

Chinese low-tech seismic isolation. Because so many buildings in China are made of earth with little or no structural reinforcement, and most of China is without access to high-tech building materials, low-tech solutions to seismic isolation for active earthquake zones have been developed. Chinese engineer Li Li noted that cracks in the eroded base of an old farmhouse's rammed earth walls allowed that particular farmhouse to slide on its earthen foundation and survive the 1960 quake that destroyed all other buildings in the village of Tuquiao in Jilin province. Based on Li Li's recommendations, numerous buildings that artificially simulate this "cracked wall" design have been erected at a variety of sites. Terrazzo plates are placed, smooth side up, on top of a prepared foundation trench. A thin layer of sand is spread on the plates, then another layer of Terrazzo plates is placed smooth side down on top of the sand. A concrete foundation is poured on top of the second layer of Terrazzo plates, and then the building is constructed as usual. The sand layer acts as a "poor man's" seismic isolation bearing. Engineering shake table tests on large models, and ground blasts next to test buildings, have yielded excellent results, but the true test will come when the next large earthquake strikes China (Tibbets 1997, 34–35).

REFERENCES

Green Buildings

***The Rammed Earth House,* by David Easton.** 1996, 272 pp. (paperback), ISBN 0-930031-79-2. Published by Chelsea Green Publishing Company, P.O. Box 428, White River Junction, VT 05001. Lists for $30.00.

David Easton has been designing and building with rammed earth since the late 1970s, when he stumbled upon rammed earth construction methods while searching for a way to build himself a low-cost, and energy- and materials-efficient home. Since then, his company, Rammed Earth Works, has become one of the major builders of rammed earth structures in North America. This beautiful book takes you through all the steps for building a rammed earth home, from design and planning, through soil evaluation, on to construction details and techniques synthesized from over 20 years of building with rammed earth.

***Buildings of Earth and Straw: Structural Design for Rammed Earth and Straw-Bale Architecture,* by Bruce King, P.E.** 1996, 169 pp. (paperback), ISBN 0-9644718-1-7. Published by Chelsea Green Publishing Company, P.O. Box 428, White River Junction, VT 05001. Lists for $25.00.

A valuable book that provides previously hard-to-find information needed for safe structural design of buildings built with rammed earth or straw bales. It is written for the professional engineer, professional builder, or the layperson seeking to better understand the application of these alternative building techniques. Until now, an engineer had to search far and wide for information that would allow her or him to professionally evaluate, design, and approve the structural design for one of these buildings. Now you can simply provide your engineer with this book and he can do the rest.

***The Straw Bale House,* by Athena Swentzell Steen, Bill Steen, and David Bainbridge, with David Eisenberg.** 1994, 297 pp. (paperback), ISBN 0-930031-71-7. Published by Chelsea Green Publishing Company, P.O. Box 428, White River Junction, VT 05001. Lists for $30.00.

If you are considering a straw bale building project, you should pick up this book. It will give you lots of design options, pretty pictures of a wide variety of straw bale buildings, plus wisdom and advice gleaned from the cumulative experience of numerous builders in several countries. There is no single "right way" to build with straw bales, but this book may help you to find your "right way."

***Build it with Bales: A Step-by-Step Guide to Straw-Bale Construction, Version Two,* by Matts Myhrman and S. O. MacDonald.** 1998, 143 pp. (paperback), ISBN 0-9642821-1-9. Published by Chelsea Green Publishing Company, P.O. Box 428, White River Junction, VT 05001. Lists for $29.95.

Not as broad as *The Straw Bale House,* but more detailed in some respects and offers step-by-step directions. This is a practical guide for the owner-builder. If I wanted to build my own straw bale house, I would pick up both this book and *The Straw Bale House.*

***Adobe: Build it Yourself,* by Paul Graham McHenry Jr.** 1998, 158 pp. (paperback), ISBN 0-8165-0948-4. Published by The University of Arizona Press, 1230 N. Park Ave., #102, Tucson, AZ 85719-4140. Lists for $23.95.

Last revised in 1985, this is still the best do-it-yourself book on adobe construction. In his popular classes, Paul McHenry has taught thousands of people how to build their own adobe homes. This book originally started out as a textbook for his class, and has excellent illustrations for all aspects of building, including foundations, brick making, brick laying, plumbing, roofing, and electrical systems. For the latest in modern labor-saving adobe construction methods, construction technologies, and code changes, see Joe Tibbets's Southwest SolarAdobe School and his *Adobe Builder* magazine (see *Resources* section).

***The Passive Solar House: Using Solar Design to Heat and Cool Your Home,* by James Kachadorian.** 1997, 210 pp. (paperback), ISBN 0-930031-97-0. Published by Chelsea Green Publishing Company, P.O. Box 428, White River Junction, VT 05001. Lists for $24.95

This is an excellent introduction to passive solar concepts and is a good book for helping you to plan and design a passive solar house. It is written by a civil engineer, who also ran a company designing and manufacturing passive solar kit homes for about 20 years. His patented innovative solar slab heat storage system forms the core of numerous comfortable, functional, and modestly priced solar homes. Now that his patent has run out, you can incorporate it into your home, taking advantage of more than 20 years of building experience with this unique solar slab design.

***The Passive Solar Energy Book: Expanded Professional Edition,* by Edward Mazria.** 1979, 687 pp. (hardcover), ISBN 0-87857-238-4. Published by Rodale Press, 33 East Minor St., Emmaus, PA 18098. Lists for $24.95.

To many builders, this is the bible of passive solar design. Unfortunately, it is also out of print, but it is available at most libraries. Many folks are hoping that it will be updated with more recent case studies. The author says a new edition is in the works, but it's probably years away. The engineering information in this book is still correct and has not changed (the sun is still the same sun, and basic building materials are still pretty much the same). For commercial design, you might try to find yourself a used copy. For residential design, *The Passive Solar House,* by James Kachadorian, has all the information, charts, and sample calculations you will need.

***The Alternative Building SOURCEBOOK: Traditional, Natural & Sustainable Building Products and Services,* edited by Steve Chappell.** 1998, 144 pp. (paperback), ISBN 1-889269-01-8. Published by Fox Maple Press, Inc., Corn Hill Road, P.O. Box 249, Brownfield, Maine 04010. Lists for $19.95.

"The *SOURCEBOOK* is unique among green building guides. . . . For builders, architects, and lay people interested in natural building, *The Alternative Building SOURCEBOOK* makes an excellent reference." (*Environmental Building News*)

Over 900 listings of products, builders, and manufacturers for some of the most innovative and creative building resources available for traditional, natural, and sustainable building construction. Includes timber framers, timber suppliers, good wood suppliers, hardwood pegs, natural builders and building sources, tools, sustainable building products and systems, and mechanical systems, all prefaced with editorial and technical information that will help to make your next, or first, building project a successful one.

***Homemade Money: How to Save Energy and Dollars on Your Home,* by Richard Heede and the Staff of Rocky Mountain Institute.** 1995, 258 pp. (paperback), ISBN 1-883178-07-X. Published by Brick House Publishing Company, P.O. Box 266, Amherst, NH 03031-0266. Lists for $14.95.

A practical, clear, well-organized, and very readable guide to saving money, helping the environment, and improving the comfort of your home through increasing the energy and water efficiency of your house. *Homemade Money* walks you through the steps to evaluate your current home and quickly determine which things will make the most difference for the least cost and effort. Some of the suggestions will cost little or nothing, while others require significant capital investment that will be recouped rather quickly due to large monthly savings on energy bills.

***The Natural House Catalog: Everything You Need to Create an Environmentally Friendly Home,* by David Pearson.** 1996, 287 pp. (paperback), ISBN 0-684-80198-1. Published by Simon & Schuster, 1230 Avenue of the Americas, New York, NY 10020. Lists for $23.00.

David Pearson, architect and best-selling author of *The Healthy Home,* created this book after receiving an avalanche of requests to provide information to help people find the resources needed to help them create the environmentally friendly living spaces that he described in *The Healthy Home*. This book is both a design guide to creating people-friendly, environmentally sensitive, healthy living spaces and a resource guide to finding the right materials and products to make it happen.

***The Not So Big House: A Blueprint for the Way We Really Live,* by Sarah Susanka.** 1998, 199 pp. (hardcover), ISBN 1-56158-130-5. Published by Taunton Press, 63 S. Main Street, Newtown, CT 06470-5506. Lists for $30.00.

This book is very popular with owner-builders, architects, professional builders, and designers. From a green perspective, smaller is better for the planet. By downsizing, you can afford to spend more on quality, craftsmanship, energy conservation, and detail. This is a good idea book.

***The Healthy House: How to Buy One, How to Build One, How to Cure a Sick One,* by John Bower.** 1998, 669 pp. (paperback), ISBN 0-9637156-0-7. Published by The Healthy House Institute, 430 N. Sewell Rd., Bloomington, IN 47408. Lists for $23.95.

Twenty years ago the lives of John and Lynn Bower were nearly devastated. They were a young married couple remodeling their first home, a rundown 1850s farmhouse. Every time they fixed up a room a bit of Lynn's health inexplicably deteriorated, until she finally became bedridden. The chemicals in the building materials used for the remodeling efforts had poisoned Lynn, resulting in her developing acquired multiple chemical sensitivity (MCS). Out of necessity, the Bowers became international experts on chemical sensitivity and healthy housing. They authored numerous books on this topic and founded The Healthy House Institute to promote public awareness about the dangers of modern chemicals and indoor air pollution. Use this book to help you avoid the unseen menace of toxic poisoning from chemicals in the modern household and modern building materials.

No Regrets Remodeling: Creating a Comfortable, Healthy Home That Saves Energy,* by the editors of *Home Energy Magazine. 1997, 222 pp. (paperback), ISBN 0-9639444-2-8. Published by Energy Auditor and Retrofitter, Inc., 2124 Kittredge St., #95, Berkeley, CA 94704. Lists for $19.95.

Thinking of remodeling? Thoughtful remodels can deliver big savings on your utility bills and make your house much more comfortable. Before construction gets underway, it's important to take a look at the entire house for energy-saving possibilities. This book covers the house from roof to basement and everywhere in between, and shows you all the possibilities for big energy savings. This is a valuable aid to the commercial contractor or the homeowner considering a remodel. See www.homeenergy.org for energy-saving tips.

***Create an Oasis With Greywater: Your Complete Guide to Managing Greywater in the Landscape,* by Art Ludwig.** 2000, 51 pp. (paperback), ISBN 0-9643433-0-4. Published by Oasis Design, 5 San Marcos Trout Club, Santa Barbara, CA 93105-9726. Lists for $14.95.

"Simply the best book about greywater we've ever seen. . . . The concise, readable format is long enough to cover everything you need to consider and short enough to stay interesting. . . ." (Doug Pratt, Real Goods Renewable Energy Division)

A thorough guide to designing and building greywater systems to effectively utilize your building's usable wastewater for landscape and garden. Covers simple to complex systems, maintenance, health considerations, components, greywater plumbing principles, and so on. If you're planning on integrating a greywater system into new construction or remodeling, you will also want their *Builder's Greywater Guide* (helps to deal with building codes and inspectors) as a supplement to *Create an Oasis with Greywater*. For background information on greywater systems and use, check out the Oasis Design web site at www.oasisdesign.net.

***Composting Toilet System Book: A Practical Guide to Choosing, Planning and Maintaining Composting Toilet Systems,* by David Del Porto and Carol Steinfeld.** 1999, 240 pp. (paperback), ISBN 0-9666783-0-3. Published by Chelsea

Green Publishing Company, P.O. Box 428, White River Junction, VT 05001. Lists for $29.95. For truly sustainable agriculture, we must recycle nutrient-rich human wastes back into the earth. This book describes over 40 different composting toilet systems, both homemade and mass produced. It covers how to choose, install, and maintain these systems.

Traditional Building Techniques and Structures

***Independent Builder: Designing & Building a House Your Own Way (Real Goods Independent Living Books),* by Sam Clark.** 1996, 522 pp. (paperback), ISBN 0-930031-85-7. Published by Chelsea Green Publishing Company, P.O. Box 428, White River Junction, VT 05001. Lists for $30.00. Written and recommended by professional builders, this is probably the best design/build book for the owner-builder seeking to build a mostly traditional home. It covers all aspects of building your own home, including site selection, finance, subcontractors, foundations, plumbing, heating, ventilation, insulation, framing, finish work, roofing, passive solar principles, heat calculations, and so on. The focus is on traditional stick-frame and post-and-beam construction. The writing is easy to understand and the book is filled with clear illustrations.

***Build a Classic Timber-Framed House* by Jack A. Sobon.** 1994, 202 pp. (paperback), ISBN 0-88266-841-2. Published by Storey Books, Schoolhouse Road, Pownal, VT 05261. Lists for $21.95. Jack Sobon is an architect/builder, who has been at the forefront of the revival in timber-framed construction. Several well-known timber-framing teachers have recommended Jack's books as the best how-to books on timber framing. This book walks the owner-builder through the process of building a classic timber-framed house and covers most of the material presented in his earlier popular (also excellent) book, *Timber Frame Construction: All About Post-and-Beam Building.*

***The Timber-Frame Home: Design, Construction, Finishing,* by Tedd Benson.** 1997, 240 pp. (hardcover), ISBN 1-56158-129-1. Published by Taunton Press, 63 South Main Street, Box 5506, Newtown, CT 06740-5506. Lists for $34.95. Tedd Benson effectively started the modern revival in timber framing with his excellent do-it-yourself book *Building the Timber Frame House.* This book is an updated version to include modern developments and energy-efficient construction. It is a beautifully illustrated, "coffee table" design-and-build guide to timber-frame homes that includes all facets of timber-frame building construction. Tedd Benson's books are also highly recommended by timber-framing teachers.

***Timberframe: The Art and Craft of the Post-and-Beam Home,* by Tedd Benson.** 1999 240 pp. (hardcover), ISBN 1-56158-281-6. Published by Taunton Press, 63 South Main Street, Box 5506, Newtown, CT 06740-5506. Lists for $40.00. This is another beautiful "coffee table" book about timber-frame construction. It's not a how-to book, but it does have a wide variety of pictures, several sketches, and rough floor plans to help you design and plan the timber-framed home of your dreams.

***A Timber Framer's Workshop: Joinery, Design & Construction of Traditional Timber Frames,* by Steve Chappell.** 1998, 252 pp. (paperback), ISBN 1-889269-00-X. Published by Fox Maple Press, Inc., Corn Hill Road, P.O. Box 249, Brownfield, Maine 04010. Lists for $30.00. This is the handbook for the Fox Maple School's timber-framing workshop. There was a time when the only way you could get it was by attending a workshop. This workbook contains over 250 pages of in-depth technical information on the joinery, design, and construction of traditional timber frames. Illustrated with over 230 photos and CAD drawings. Included are frame plans, design and engineering formulas, rule-of-thumb guidelines, shop setup, builder's math, joinery design criteria, practical timber-framing tips, and more. If you are a builder, architect, engineer, or an aspiring owner-builder, *A Timber Framer's Workshop* will provide the information you need. This book is also highly recommended by timber-framing teachers.

Log Building Construction Manual, by Robert Chambers. 1999, 153 pp. (paperback), No ISBN. Published by Robert Chambers, N8203 1130th Street, River Falls, WI 54022. Order from Schroeder Log Home Supply (see "Resources" section). Lists for $25.00.

Several professional builders have recommended this book as absolutely the best manual for building a log home. Robert Chambers is an experienced log homebuilder, teacher, and coauthor of *Log Building Standards: The Building Code for Handcrafted Log Homes*. It is filled with helpful photographs and illustrations that guide you through all the steps for making a tight, well-finished, professional style log home, including timber selection, planning, log dressing, roof trusses, special tools, and log treatment. For the latest information on log home building seminars and techniques, check out Robert's log building web site at www.logbuilding.org.

"How-To" Build This Log Cabin for $3000, by John McPherson. 1993, 140 pp, (paperback), ISBN 0-89745-980-6. Published by Prairie Wolf, P.O. Box 96, Randolph, KS 66554. Lists for $24.95.

John's book shows the reader, step by step, how to build a low-cost, two-story log cabin. It is simple and very inexpensive, provided you can log your own timber. Lots of pictures and clear instructions. John's process will not yield slick, professionally finished, log homes like the ones in Robert Chambers's *Log Building Construction Manual*.

Shelters, Shacks and Shanties and How to Build Them, by D. C. Beard. 1999, 243 pp. (paperback), ISBN 1-55821-952-8. Published by The Lyons Press, 123 West 18 Street, New York, NY 10011. Lists for $12.95.

This is a reprint of a classic book, published in 1914, for making your own primitive shelters with no more tools than an axe and a knife. D. C. Beard was an artist, backwoodsman, and one of the two principal founders of the Boy Scouts movement. His book illustrates everything from Indian hogans, wigwams, and lean-tos to modest log cabins, hearths, and chimneys. This is a fun little book to have around, although I would rely upon other references if I was building a real home for myself.

The Indian Tipi: Its History, Construction, and Use, by Reginald Laubin and Gladys Laubin. 1989, 343 pp. (paperback), ISBN 0-8061-2236-6. Published by the University of Oklahoma Press, 1005 Asp Ave., Norman, OK 73019-0445. Lists for $19.95.

This is the definitive book about and for life in a tipi. It offers designs and layouts for a variety of tipi styles, plus pros and cons for different styles. Also has information on brain tanning, moccasins, Indian containers, tipi ceremonies, and so on. In the 1950s, the authors fully embraced the lifestyle and ways of traditional Native Americans, becoming "adopted" by Chief One Bull and his wife Scarlet Whirlwind. At a time when most Indians had lost the knowledge of their traditional crafts, the Laubins sought out Indian elders to learn their skills before they were lost forever.

Magazines

Adobe Builder. Subscription: $19.95 for 4 issues. Adobe Builder, P.O. Box 153, Bosque, NM 87006. Call (505) 861-1255 or see web site at www.adobebuilder.com.

Adobe Builder is the top trade journal for the earth building business, including rammed earth, cast earth, and adobe. Published quarterly, this magazine carries articles written by the shakers and movers in this industry on the latest techniques, materials, and designs. Advertisements in the journal are a "who's who" of builders, designers, and suppliers for building with earth. Good how-to articles and photos for design ideas.

Natural Home. Subscription: $24.95 for 6 issues. Natural Home, 201 East Fourth St., Loveland, CO 80537. Call (800) 340-5846 or see web site at www.naturalhomemag.com.

Natural Home is a magazine focused on bringing earth-friendly, healthy, harmonious homes into mainstream America. Each issue delivers cutting-edge ideas on home building, design, remodeling, and decorating, with additional tips for the kitchen, garden, yard, and personal health.

The Last Straw. Subscription: $28 for 4 issues. The Last Straw, HC 66, P.O. Box 119, Hillsboro, NM 88042. Call (505) 895-5400 or see web site at www.strawhomes.com.

The Last Straw is the grassroots journal of straw bale and natural building, providing up-to-date information on construction techniques, projects, research/testing/code issues, resources, and other information written by and about those who design, build, research, and live in straw bale and natural buildings. The focus is on the owner builder and straw bale contractor.

Joiners' Quarterly. Subscription: $24 for 4 issues. Fox Maple Press, Inc., Corn Hill Road, P.O. Box 249 Brownfield, ME 04010. See web site at www.foxmaple.com.

Although the focus is on joined timber, post, and beam framing, *Joiners' Quarterly* also pays attention to green building practices using natural materials. *Joiners' Quarterly* offers insightful, technical articles about how to make traditional timber framing, combined with natural building systems, to build houses that will last for many generations. Fox Maple Press attempts to provide examples where timber framing and natural building systems, products and resources dovetail seamlessly with modern technology.

RESOURCES

Green Building and Energy Efficiency

Rocky Mountain Institute (RMI), 1739 Snowmass Creek Road, Snowmass, CO 81654-9199; phone: (970) 927-3851; fax: (970) 927-3420; web site: www.rmi.org.

Since 1982, Rocky Mountain Institute has worked with corporations, communities, and citizens to help them gain competitive advantages, increase profits, and create a higher standard of living through

resource efficiency. In 1991, RMI launched Green Development Services (GDS) to help architects, developers, and other real estate professionals to integrate energy efficient and environmentally responsible design into specific projects. GDS has demonstrated significant opportunities for improving the comfort, aesthetics, resource efficiency, and value of properties while reducing pollution and saving money. The RMI's *Green Developments* CD-ROM is an excellent introduction to green building practices and presents a hundred case studies including pictures, mini-videos, development highlights, and project statistics.

Sustainable Buildings Industry Council (SBIC), 1331 H Street, NW, Suite 1000, Washington, DC 20005; phone: (202) 628-7400; fax: (202) 393-5043; web site: www.sbicouncil.org.

The Sustainable Buildings Industry Council (SBIC), previously known as the Passive Solar Industries Council, is an independent, nonprofit organization whose mission is to advance the design, affordability, energy performance, and environmental soundness of residential, institutional, and commercial buildings. Check out the web site for a fine introduction to green building principles.

Environmental Building News, 122 Birge St. Ste 30, Brattleboro, VT 05301; phone: (802) 257-7300, ext.105; fax: (802) 257-7304; web site: www.ebuild.com.

This organization publishes the leading newsletter on environmentally responsible (green) design and construction. The articles, reviews, and news stories are a prime source for information on energy-efficient, resource-efficient, and healthy building practices. Check out the web site for green building definitions, articles, information, and links. They also publish the *GreenSpec Binder,* a comprehensive and up-to-date guide that provides easy access to information on green building products and materials. This two-part tool features the 300-plus-page *GreenSpec Product Directory and Guideline Specifications* plus more than 135 pages of manufacturers' product literature, organized in a large three-ring binder.

Center for Maximum Potential Building Systems,
8604 F.M. 969, Austin, TX 78724; phone: (512)
928-4786; fax: (512) 926-4418; web site:
www.cmpbs.org.

This organization is well known for its development
and promotion of green building technologies. The
Center for Maximum Potential Building Systems
("Max's Pot") is a nonprofit education, demonstration, and research organization with many years of
experience in the application of appropriate technologies and sustainable design practices to meet the
needs of a broad range of users, from individual
home builders to regional planning and natural
resource agencies. The center has helped to develop
several interesting green building technologies.
Check the web site for the *Green Builders Sourcebook*,
which includes information on green building technologies, sustainable sources, and links to numerous
other green web sites.

Energy Efficient Building Association (EEBA), 490
Concordia Avenue, St. Paul, MN 55103; phone:
(651) 268-7585; fax: (651) 268-7587; web site:
www.eeba.org.

The Energy Efficient Building Association promotes
the awareness, education, and development of energy efficient, environmentally responsible buildings
and communities. The strength of the organization
lies in the diversity and talent of its membership,
which includes architects, builders, developers,
manufacturers, engineers, utilities, code officials,
researchers, educators, and environmentalists. The
EEBA's *Builder's Guides* to cold, hot, dry, and humid
climates provide up-to-date professional advice on
optimum building techniques for a variety of
climates and are highly praised by industry professionals. The EEBA has an excellent online builder's
bookstore, which includes energy analysis software,
videos, and a variety of builder's guides.

The Healthy House Institute, 430 N. Sewell Rd.,
Bloomington, IN 47408; phone/fax: (812) 332-
5073; web site: www.hhinst.com.

This organization is dedicated to providing information that will help you to avoid indoor toxic air
problems, identify indoor environmental health

risks, and remedy these problems. For a wealth of
information on these topics, check out the Institute's
web site and bookstore.

Stable Air, Inc., 550 Via Estrada, Unit H, Laguna
Hills, CA 92653; phone: (949) 587-1087; fax:
(949) 587-1093; web site: www.stableair.com.

This company has developed an environmentally
friendly process for making supertough foam to
mix into concrete to produce air-entrained lightweight concrete. By a huge margin, they hold the
world record for high strength lightweight
concrete. This technology has the potential to
reduce the mass of highrise buildings by a third,
drastically reducing the seismic loads and the
resulting structural steel requirements. It does not
reduce cement requirements for structural
concrete, but it does reduce the required sand and
gravel by a third. Air-entrained lightweight
concrete has significantly improved insulating
properties and freeze resistance.

Earth Based Buildings

Southwest SolarAdobe School, P.O. Box 153,
Bosque, NM 87006; phone: (505) 861-1255; fax:
(505) 861-1304; web site:
www.adobebuilder.com.

Founded by Joe Tibbets, a well-known adobe and
rammed earth educator/publisher with over 30 years
of earth building experience, this school provides
classes in modern earth building skills to both
owner-builders and contractors. The School's magazine, *Adobe Builder*, is the top trade journal for the
earth building business. Published quarterly, *Adobe
Builder* carries articles written by the shakers and
movers in this industry on the latest techniques,
materials, and designs. Advertisements in the journal
are a "who's who" of builders, designers, and suppliers for building with earth.

Cast Earth, Harris Lowenhaupt, 4022 E. Larkspur,
Phoenix, AZ 85032; phone: (602) 404-1044; fax:
(602) 404-1134; web site: www.castearth.com.

Check out the web site for a comprehensive introduction to the Cast Earth process (patent pending).

This process has been used on a variety of residential projects and shows great promise. Cast Earth uses gypsum and a proprietary retardant to stabilize earth mixtures and reduce shrinkage, allowing for the use of current concrete industry labor-saving machinery, forms, and techniques to make walls of cast earth.

Traditional Timber Structures

Timber Framers Guild of North America, Timber Framers Guild Office, P.O. Box 60, Becket, MA 01223; phone and fax: (888) 453-0879; web site: www.tfguild.org.
Timber framing is the traditional art of making building structures with large timbers and a minimum of modern fasteners. Check out the web site for information on finding local timber framers, historical timber framing, timber frame events, a bookstore with quite a variety of books on timber-frame construction, green building, and links to related sites.

Schroeder Log Home Supply, Inc., 34810 U.S. Hwy. 2, Grand Rapids, MN 55744; phone: (800) 359-6614; fax: (800) 755-3249; web site: www.loghelp.com.
This company has a great selection of books, tools, sealants, and so forth for timber framing and log home building. Their excellent selection of builder's books extends to all facets of home building, masonry, and furniture making.

Heartwood, Johnson Hill Road, Washington, MA 01223; phone: (413) 623-6677; fax: (413) 623-0277; web site: www.heartwoodschool.com.
Run by Will and Michelle Beemer, this is an excellent hands-on school for timber frame construction, energy efficient homebuilding and design, cabinetry, and finish carpentry. Will is the executive director of the Timber Framers Guild and has taught timber framing workshops worldwide since the late 1970s.

Rocky Mountain Workshops, 505 N. Grant, Fort Collins, CO 80521; phone: (970) 482-1366; web site: www.over-land.com/logbuilder.html.

Rocky Mountain Workshops offer great hands-on classes in a breathtaking mountain setting. Peter Haney teams up with renowned builders, architects, and designers, such as Robert Chambers, Will Beemer, and Catherine Cartrette, to create a series of log building, timber framing, and design workshops.

Fox Maple School of Traditional Building, Corn Hill Road, P.O. Box 249, Brownfield, ME 04010; phone: (207) 935-3720; fax: (207) 935-4575; web site: www.foxmaple.com.
The Fox Maple School of Traditional Building provides hands-on workshops teaching traditional, natural, and sustainable building systems. Workshops begin with a joined timber frame, and then explore the use of natural enclosures such as straw/clay, woodchip/clay, wattle and daub, cob, and straw bales finished with earth plasters. Exploring ways to make traditional systems practical to create high-quality dwellings to meet current building needs is the school's mission. Fox Maple publishes the excellent *Joiner's Quarterly*, which offers insightful, technical articles about how to use traditional timber framing, combined with natural building systems, for building planet-friendly housing that will last for many generations.

Ready-Made Structures

American Structural Composites (ASC), 905 Southern Way, Sparks, NV 89431; phone: (775) 355-4444; fax: (775) 355-4455.; web site: www.asc-housing.com.
ASC makes prefabricated, lightweight, high-strength fiberglass buildings that are flood, hurricane, insect, and earthquake resistant. This company's structural wall and roof panels are made of fiberglass composite layers sandwiched around a foam core, making them extremely strong, lightweight, and well insulated. Panels and floors fit together with a modular connector system. A crew of four unskilled laborers can fully assemble a typical 1,000-square-foot home in a few days without a crane or other heavy equipment. Their homes are attractively designed and look like perfectly normal houses.

Pacific Yurts, Inc., 77456 Hwy. 99 South, Cottage Grove, OR 97424; phone: (800) 944-0240; fax: (541) 942-050; web site: www.yurts.com.

"The best, most satisfying space I've ever lived in." (Gillian C., Vermont)

Pacific Yurts, the original designer and manufacturer of the modern lattice-wall yurt, makes high-quality, four-season yurts certified for snow loads up to 100 pounds per square foot and 100-mph winds. Their products are comfortable, strong, durable, and weather-tight. Easily erected, yurts can be transported in the back of a pickup truck, are nondestructive to delicate ecosystems, and can be adapted to a variety of conventional and alternative energy and water/waste technologies. Yurts make a wonderful camp, low-cost home, studio, guest cottage, or back-up shelter in case of earthquakes. Check out the web site for pictures of these durable, round, timber-framed, tent-like structures based on the traditional nomadic Mongolian round home.

Nomadics Tipi Makers, 17671 Snow Creek Road, Bend OR 97701; phone/fax: (541) 389-3980; web site: www.tipi.com.

This is the largest manufacturer in the world of tipis and tipi accessories. Their standard tipis and tipi liners are made from treated marine cotton duck canvas, but they can custom-make tipis from other materials. Designs are based on the Laubins's designs as illustrated in their book *The Indian Tipi*. Nomadics made all the leather tipis for the movie *Dances with Wolves*, starring Kevin Costner.

Cover-It Inc., 17 Wood St., P.O. Box 26037, West Haven CT 06516; phone (800) 932-9344; fax: (203) 931-4754; web site: www.cover-it-inc.com.

Cover-It carries a multitude of different sizes and shapes of instant greenhouses, barns, sheds, hangars, and so on.

Miscellaneous

The National Information Service for Earthquake Engineering (NISEE), 1301 S. 46th St., Richmond, CA 94804-4698; phone: (510) 231-9403; fax: (510) 231-9461; web site: www.eerc.berkeley.edu.

This web site is a great place to start an investigation into earthquakes and their impacts on buildings and design. This site contains numerous links to other related sites as well as numerous educational articles and papers.

VIII *First Aid*

I can't emphasize strongly enough the value of basic first aid training. You never know when you might face an emergency situation where the knowledge of first aid could make a huge difference in someone's life. This chapter is not intended to replace a first aid manual and first aid training. I recommend that you pick up a copy of *The American Red Cross First Aid & Safety Handbook* and that you take the Red Cross advanced first aid course. I believe that every able-bodied adult should take CPR (cardiopulmonary resuscitation) training, or a more advanced training such as for emergency medical technician (EMT) certification.

A few basic first aid principles and instructions are presented in this chapter, in the event that you find yourself in an emergency and this book is the only text you have. I repeat, *this chapter is not a first aid manual.*

INITIAL EVALUATION

Survey the Scene

The very first thing to evaluate in an emergency is your safety. As a rescuer, it does you and the victim little good if you are injured or killed during the rescue. Assess potential dangers, such as oncoming traffic, rock fall, live downed power lines, poisonous or flammable fumes, and so on, and take adequate precautions to ensure the safety of both rescuers and victim. The general rule is to move a victim only if you absolutely have to. Ask the bystanders or victim(s) what happened.

The ABCs of first aid are airway, breathing, and circulation. If any of these fail, death is certain. *Call for help immediately!* Feel free to ask bystanders for assistance, and don't hesitate to send one of them off to call 911 for emergency medical services (EMS) while you attend to the victim.

In the case of multiple victims, quickly evaluate the status of each victim to determine where to expend your efforts and resources first. Life-threatening injuries require immediate attention, whereas less critical injuries may be able to wait. If someone is obviously fatally injured, spend your time on another victim who might benefit from your efforts, but even when things look terrible, try not to give up. Hypothermic and cold water drowning victims have been revived after unbelievably long periods of time (hours, not just minutes) and many accident victims have been kept alive for hours using CPR.

consciousness, he was surrounded by the paramedics and a group of concerned bystanders. He had broken many bones and suffered serious internal injuries, but still managed to crack a joke, saying, "I suppose you wonder why I gathered all of you here today." The paramedics loaded his swollen and bleeding body into their ambulance and rushed him off to the hospital. At the first hospital they reached, an emergency room doctor told them, "Get the hell out of here. He's going to die anyway. We're too busy to deal with him." Luckily, the medics did not give up, but rushed Eddie to another hospital. Eddie was kept alive with six pints of blood transfusions that replaced the blood he had lost due to internal bleeding. Amazingly, after a long recovery period, Eddie regained full use of his limbs and went on to become a Hollywood stuntman and an inventor.

Consent and Liability

When approaching an accident victim, shout for help, and then identify yourself, quickly explaining that you know first aid and that you are there to help. It can happen that a person just looks like they need help, but may be drunk or simply resting in an unnatural-looking position. Sticking to these procedures can save you embarrassment, justifiable outrage, or a hard fist in the face.

> **NOTE:** *If the victim is aware and mentally capable, you must receive his or her consent before you begin treatment. For minors (under 18), obtain the permission of the guardian. If a parent or guardian is not available, the law says that you have "implied consent," meaning that it is assumed the parents would have wanted you to help their child had they been present.*

If the victim is conscious and aware, talk to her about the extent of her injuries before proceeding. Use your judgment, but always try to do no further harm. For example, using CPR on an injured person whose heart is still beating could cause serious injury; but if the heart is not beating, CPR is probably the victim's only chance for survival. Nearly all states have Good Samaritan laws to protect lay citizens from liability, as long as they did not do something grossly negligent or deliberately harmful.

ABCS OF FIRST AID

Treatment of the trauma victim starts with the ABCs: *airway, breathing, and circulation.* If any of these fail, the victim is in a life-or-death situation and intervention is essential.

- *Airway:* The air passage must be clear of fluids and obstructions so the victim can breathe.
- *Breathing:* To survive, a person must breathe.
- *Circulation:* The blood must circulate for the victim to survive for more than a few minutes. There must be a pulse and severe bleeding must be stopped.

Treatment Priority

Assess the situation and move yourself and the victim(s) out of danger if necessary. Use the following priority list to determine what and whom to treat first.

1. Restore and maintain breathing and heartbeat. Without these, death is certain and quick.
2. Stop the bleeding.
3. Protect wounds and burns.
4. Immobilize fractures.
5. Treat shock.

Unconscious Victim

Follow this sequence to evaluate an unconscious victim's ABCs:

1. **Shake and shout.** Check for consciousness. Tap or gently shake the victim. Ask, "Are you OK?" If not OK, shout for help.
2. **Check for neck or back injury.** If you suspect a neck or back injury, try to evaluate the ABCs without moving the victim. Moving a person with a spinal injury always entails a risk of severing the spine.
3. **Position the victim.** If you do not suspect a spinal injury, carefully roll the victim onto his or her back. Grasp the shoulder and hip, supporting the neck and head as well as you can, while you try to roll the body as a unit.
4. **Open the airway.** Use the "head-tilt/chin-lift" technique. Place one hand on the victim's forehead and two fingers under the bony part of the chin. Lift the chin and push on the forehead to tilt the head back.

   > **CAUTION:** *If a spinal injury is suspected, open the airway with a chin lift only. Do not tilt the head, unless absolutely necessary.*

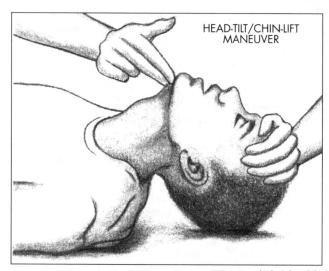
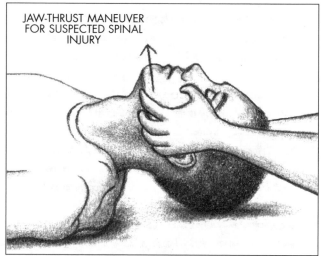

Figure 8-1. Head-tilt/chin-lift procedure for opening airway.

5. **Look, listen, and feel for breathing.** Watch the chest to see if it is rising and falling. Place your ear beside the victim's mouth to listen for the sounds of breathing and feel for breath against your cheek. Chest movement alone does not mean there is breathing.

6. **If the victim is breathing.** Check for bleeding and continue your evaluation.

7. **If the victim is not breathing.** Give two rescue breaths (mouth-to-mouth resuscitation) by pinching the victim's nostrils, taking a deep breath, sealing your lips around the victim's mouth, and giving 2 full breaths. In the case of a small child, it may be easiest to cover both the nose and mouth with your lips. If the breaths do not raise the chest, tilt the head back further and try two more rescue breaths. If the chest does not rise, sweep your finger through the victim's mouth, lift the chin, and tilt the head further back before trying two more rescue breaths. If the head tilt and finger sweep does not clear the airway, begin abdominal thrusts (Heimlich maneuver), to try and dislodge whatever is blocking the airway.

8. **Check the circulation.** Put your index and middle fingers over the windpipe, and slide them down alongside the neck muscle; feel between the windpipe and the neck muscle for a pulse. Check for a pulse for 5 to 10 seconds. *If victim has no pulse, begin CPR.* If there is severe bleeding, it must be controlled. If there is a pulse, but no breathing, continue rescue breathing.

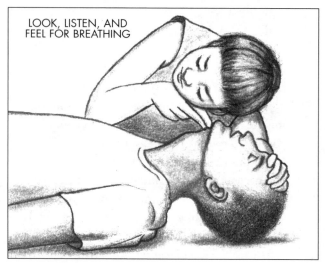
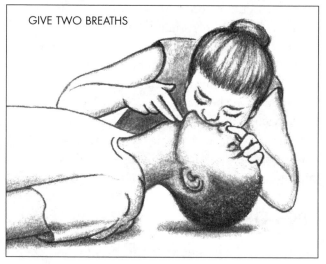

Figure 8-2. Rescue breathing.

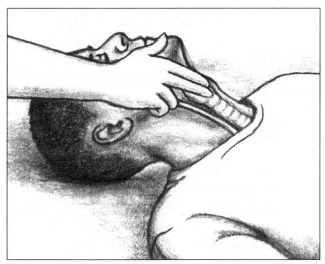
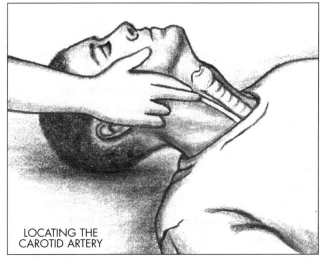

LOCATING THE
CAROTID ARTERY

Figure 8-3. Checking for pulse at carotid artery.

9. **If the victim has a pulse and is breathing.** Continue monitoring ABCs and give first aid for other injuries or illness.

10. **If the victim has pulse, but no breathing.** Continue with rescue breathing, giving one breath every 5 seconds, and checking for pulse once each minute (every 12 breaths). Continue until the patient recovers, you are relieved by EMS, or until too exhausted to continue further.

11. **The recovery position.** If an unconscious victim is breathing and has a pulse and no spinal injury, the safest position is the recovery position. Unconscious victims have little or no control over their muscles and can easily choke on their tongue, vomit, or other fluids. Roll the victim onto his or her side, bending and propping one arm and one leg to prevent the person from lying face down. Keep the head tilted downwards and to the side, allowing fluids to drain, and open the jaw to inspect the mouth to insure that the tongue is lying flat and not against the back of the throat. Loosen tight clothing.

REMEMBER
- Never lay an unconscious victim flat on his or her back, except to begin CPR or rescue breathing.
- Never give fluids to an unconscious victim.
- Never tilt an unconscious victim's head forward with a pillow.

PLACING THE VICTIM IN THE RECOVERY POSITION

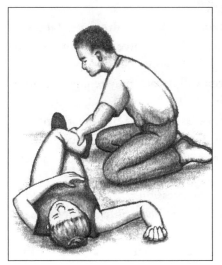
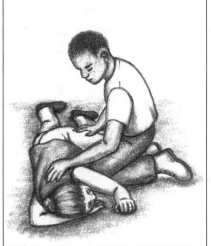

Figure 8-4. The recovery position.

CPR

Cardiopulmonary resuscitation (CPR) is one of those things you hope that you never have to use. When the heart stops, CPR may be the only thing that can prevent death. To properly learn CPR, you must take a course from a certified instructor using a CPR demonstration dummy. Too much force will break ribs or cause other serious internal injuries, while too little force will be insufficient to pump the blood through the victim's heart. The CPR dummy gives feedback to help you get a feel for the proper timing, head tilt, and the amount of force to apply for CPR compressions. Do yourself and your loved ones a favor: get yourself certified in CPR by the American Heart Association or American Red Cross. A summary of the procedure for CPR is included for your reference.

> **CAUTION: Do not attempt CPR solely on the basis of these guidelines (without proper training), unless no CPR-trained person is present and the victim has no pulse—in other words, unless there is no alternative. For a more detailed description of the first five steps, see the previous procedures for "Unconscious Victim."**

1. **Shake gently and ask, "Are you OK?"**
2. **If there is no response, shout for help.**
3. **Position the victim.** Roll the victim onto his or her back on a firm, flat surface. Roll the body as a unit, supporting the head and neck. Try to keep the head at the same level as the heart.
4. **Position yourself.** Kneel next to the victim, halfway between the chest and head.
5. **Check the ABCs:**
   - Open the airway. Use the "head-tilt/chin-lift" technique.
   - Breathing. Kneel alongside the victim and check to see if he is breathing. Look, listen, and feel for signs of breathing.
   - Circulation. Use one hand to keep the head tilted. With the fingers of the other hand (not the thumb), feel between the windpipe and the neck muscle for a pulse at the carotid artery. Check for 5 to 10 seconds. If the victim has no pulse, begin CPR. *Time is critical!*
6. **Call EMS.** If possible, send someone else to call EMS (emergency medical services). Alert EMS to the status of the ABCs.
7. **Position your hands.** Using your fingers, locate the notch at the bottom of the ribs, where they join the sternum (breastbone), a few inches straight above the belly button. Place your index finger on the notch and your middle finger right above it. Using your middle finger and index fingers as a spacer, place the heel of your hand two fingers above the notch, at the center of the breastbone. Remove your two fingers from above the notch, and place the palm of this hand on top of the one on the breastbone.
8. **Chest compressions.** With arms straight and shoulders directly over your hands, lock your elbows and lean over the victim to use your body weight to compress the victim's breast bone 1½ to 2 inches. Keep your fingers raised to compress the breastbone and not the ribs. Compress the chest at a rate of 80 to 100 compressions per minute, stopping every 15 compressions to open the airway and give 2 rescue breaths. Count out loud with each compression, so you do not lose track of the number. Release the pressure, but do not lift your hands between compressions or otherwise allow your hand position to shift. Don't let the heel of your hand slide down over the tip of the breastbone, and keep your fingers away from the chest.

   CAUTION: Excessively forceful or misplaced compressions can cause fractures and injuries to internal organs.

   Special Instructions for Children and Babies. Babies require very little force. Use light pressure with two fingers at about 100 times per minute. Small children will usually only require medium pressure from the heel of one hand, not two as used for adults. Use cycles of one breath and 5 compressions for 10 cycles between pulse checks. Depress the child's breast 1 to 1½ inches per compression. Compress infant's chest only ½ to 1 inch per compression.
9. **2 rescue breaths.** Use head-tilt/chin-lift to open the airway, then give two 2 rescue breaths, watching to make sure that the chest rises with each breath.

10. **4 cycles, then check.** Use the two-finger technique to reposition your hands with each set of compressions. Recheck the pulse after every 4 sets of 15 compressions and 2 rescue breaths.

11. **If the victim regains pulse and is breathing.** Continue to monitor ABCs, while checking for and treating other injuries.

12. **If the victim regains pulse, but is not breathing.** Continue rescue breathing at the rate of one breath every 5 seconds. Listen for breathing and recheck pulse every 12 breaths (count out loud between breaths).

13. **If victim has no pulse, continue CPR until:**
   - Breathing and pulse return.
   - The rescuers are exhausted.
   - The rescuers are in danger.
   - The victim fails to respond to prolonged resuscitation (how you define "prolonged" depends on the circumstances; prolonged CPR is most likely to be successful in hypothermia victims).
   - The rescuers are relieved by medical professionals.

CPR is not magic. There are situations in which it should *not* be attempted, including:
   - A lethal injury (death is obvious).
   - A dangerous setting in which rescuers' lives are in danger.
   - Chest compressions are impossible, such as in cases where the chest is frozen or crushed.
   - When there is any sign of life (breathing, heartbeat, pulse, movement).
   - The victim has stated, in writing, that he does not want to be resuscitated.

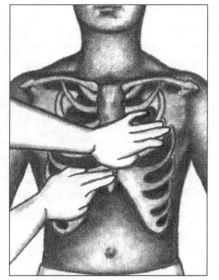
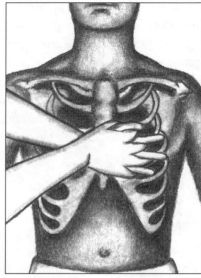

HAND POSITION

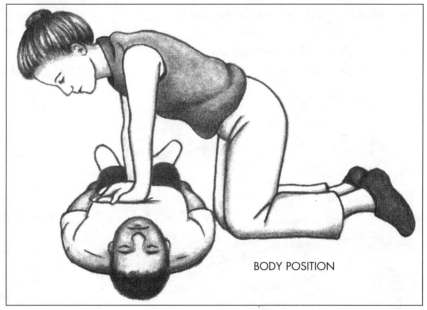

BODY POSITION

Figure 8-5. CPR position.

SURVEY FOR INJURIES AND CONTROL BLEEDING

Do a quick head-to-toe survey for wounds and fractures. Try to control bleeding by applying direct pressure to wounds with any bulky, clean material—use your shirt if nothing else is handy. Use the cleanest material available to reduce the chance of infection, but stopping severe bleeding is far more important than worrying about infection. Elevate the wounded limb to reduce the blood pressure to the wound. Do not change dressings if blood soaked, but add new dressings on top of old ones. Tie dressings in place with strips of cloth or roll bandages to maintain pressure. Bright red blood spurting from a wound is arterial. Oozing, dark blood is probably from a vein. Arterial bleeding, especially from the scalp, neck, groin, or shoulder, can be difficult to control and can rapidly lead to life-threatening shock. If direct pressure and elevation are not enough to stop the bleeding, add pressure point techniques to help control severe bleeding.

Pressure Points

ARM

For arm injuries, the pressure point (for the brachial artery) is located on the inside of the arm, halfway between the elbow and the shoulder, between the upper muscle (biceps) and the lower muscle (triceps). Cup your hand around the arm, applying firm pressure with all four fingers and squeezing the artery against the arm bone.

LEG

For severe bleeding from an open leg wound, apply pressure on the femoral artery, forcing it against the pelvic bone. This pressure point is on the front of the thigh just below the middle of the crease of the groin where the artery crosses over the pelvic bone on its way to the leg. To apply pressure on the femoral artery, quickly place the victim on his back and put the heel of your hand directly over the pressure point. Then lean forward over your straightened arm to apply pressure against the underlying bone. Apply pressure as needed to close the artery. Keep your arm straight to prevent arm tension and muscular strain. If bleeding is not controlled, it may be necessary to compress directly over the artery with the flat of the fingertips and to apply additional pressure over the fingertips with the heel of the other hand. Alternately, to control severe bleeding from a leg wound, push your fist into the abdomen at the level of the navel and press firmly. This

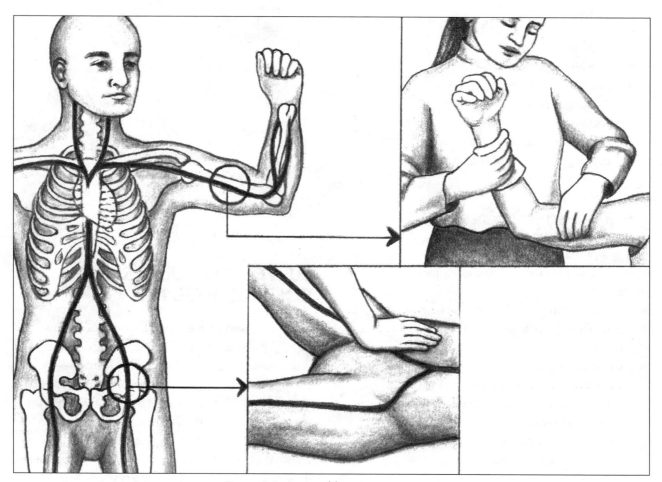

Figure 8-6. Arm and leg pressure points.

compresses the aorta against the spinal column and will control the flow of blood into the legs while you apply a bulky bandage.

Tourniquets

If there is a detectable pulse, severe bleeding must be controlled, but *tourniquets are dangerous and should be used only as a last resort.* Don't use one unless you are willing to write off the limb to save the victim. The only acceptable positions for tourniquets are around the upper arm, just below the arm pit, and around the upper thigh. Tourniquets should be made from material that is at least two inches wide. If string or wire is used, the tourniquet must be padded with a strip of heavy material. If a tourniquet has been applied, loosen the tourniquet every 20 minutes to allow some circulation to the limb (only if this won't cause too much blood loss). Tourniquets should always remain visible, never covered by dressings, blankets, and so on. If a tourniquet is applied, the fingers or toes on the appropriate limb should remain uncovered to allow for visual inspection for discoloration and swelling.

WOUNDS

The danger of infection is always present with any wound. Soap is antiseptic, and it will help to reduce the chance of infection if a wound is washed with soap and clean water. Fresh urine is almost always sterile, and can be used to cleanse a wound in the absence of clean water. Antiseptics are handy to reduce the chance of infection, but will cause further tissue damage if used inside deep wounds. Honey is mildly antibacterial and has been used for thousands of years to prevent infection and speed the healing of battlefield wounds. Silver is also antibacterial and will not harm human tissue.

Abrasions

The main danger from abrasions is the possibility of infection. Clean the wound with soap and antiseptic and cover with a clean dressing. Wash hands in sterile water, and boil nonsterile dressings to sterilize.

Incisions

Incisions, or cuts, generally bleed enough to clean the wound, and are not as prone to infection as abrasions. Minor wounds can be closed with butterfly bandages or stitches (sutures).

If a wound gets infected, it may be necessary to undo some of the stitches or lance the wound to allow it to drain. To stitch a wound, use only a sterilized needle and thread. Draw the edges of the wound together and begin stitching at the center of the wound. Tie off each stitch individually, before moving on to the next stitch.

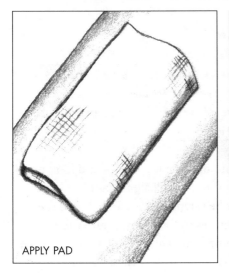
APPLY PAD

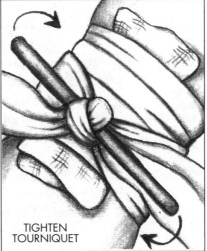
TIGHTEN TOURNIQUET

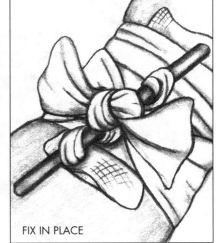
FIX IN PLACE

Figure 8-7. Tourniquet application.

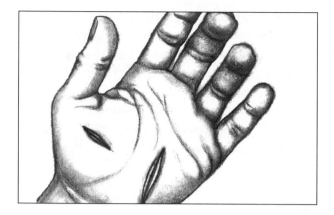

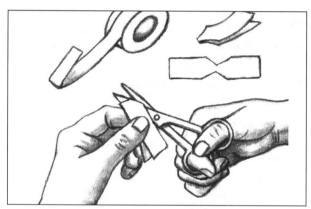

BUTTERFLY
BANDAGES OF
ADHESIVE TAPE

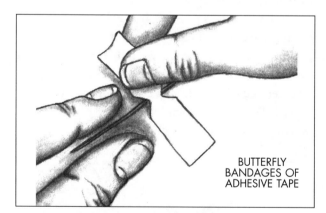

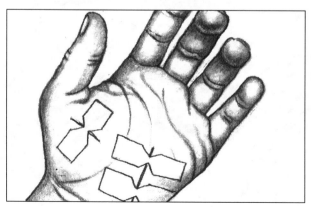

Figure 8-8. Closing wounds with butterfly bandages.

When I was a teenager, I gashed my lip into my teeth while ski jumping. The doctor told me that the shot of anesthetic would probably hurt more than stitching up my lip without anesthesia. He assured me that he could give me anesthesia at any time if the procedure was too painful. To my amazement, he proceeded to stitch my lip without any anesthesia, and it truly didn't hurt much!

Puncture Wounds

Because puncture wounds generally do not bleed enough to flush out dirt and germs, they are prone to infection and should be watched carefully for signs of infection (tenderness, red puffy swelling, discharge with pus, fever). If available, emergency medical personnel should remove foreign material and treat all deep puncture wounds.

Abdominal Wounds

Any deep abdominal wound should be considered serious due to the potential for significant injury to internal organs and internal bleeding. Give no food or water, unless it takes longer than two days to reach medical care. Allay thirst with a damp cloth in the mouth (use IV for fluids, if available). Do not try to stuff bowels back inside the abdominal cavity, but cover with cloths soaked in lightly salted boiled water. Make sure that you keep cloth coverings moist. Seek immediate medical attention.

WARNING: Do not give an enema or purge, because this may cause death.

Head Wounds

In the town I used to live in, a little girl hit her head while playing on a slide in a local park. She went home complaining of a severe headache and went to bed early. To her parents' horror, she never woke up.

Minor head wounds often bleed a lot and look more serious than they are, but all significant head wounds should be examined carefully due to the potential for injuries to the brain. Injuries to the brain can affect breathing and circulation. Any time a person is knocked unconscious, he or she must be observed carefully for at least 24 hours. Dilated

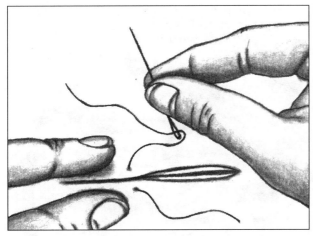

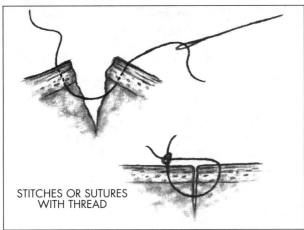

STITCHES OR SUTURES
WITH THREAD

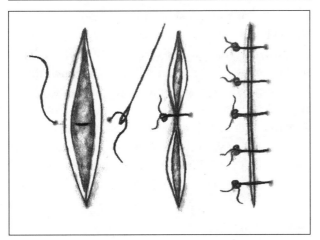

Figure 8-9. Suturing a wound.

pupils, severe and unrelenting headache, nausea, prolonged dizziness, or blood from the ears and nose are all potential signs of serious head injuries. Remove false teeth and carefully monitor the ABCs. Blood or straw-colored fluids seeping from the ear or nose may indicate a skull fracture. Do not block the drainage of these fluids as this may cause brain

damage from internal pressure buildup. If there are no signs of neck or back injury, place the victim in the recovery position, with the leaking side down to help fluids to drain.

Chest Wounds

Puncture wounds in the chest may result in a collapsed lung. If you hear a sucking noise or see bubbles coming from a chest wound, immediately cover the wound with the palm of your hand, then seal around the wound with a dressing made from plastic wrap or aluminum foil. Coat the dressing with petroleum jelly or antiseptic ointment to help it seal to the skin. If available, tape the dressing edges, except for one corner, to improve the seal, yet allow for excess air to vent outwards.

1. Monitor ABCs.
2. Do not give fluids.
3. Call EMS.
4. Do not move the victim unless absolutely necessary.

CHOKING

The symptoms of choking are easily recognized— clutching at the throat, staring eyes, face contorted. If the person is coughing or making significant breathing sounds, his or her own efforts to clear the blockage stand a better chance than your intervention, which might cause the blockage to lodge more deeply. Remember, a person who is choking can hear you even though she or he is unable to speak. Ask the person if he is choking. *If the person is unable to answer, and there are no breathing sounds, or only a high pitched squeaky noise, the blockage is life threatening. Begin abdominal thrusts (Heimlich maneuver) immediately.*

Heimlich Maneuver (Abdominal Thrusts)

1. Stand or kneel behind the victim and wrap your arms around the midsection.
2. Make a fist with one hand and grab the outside of the fist with the other hand. The thumb side

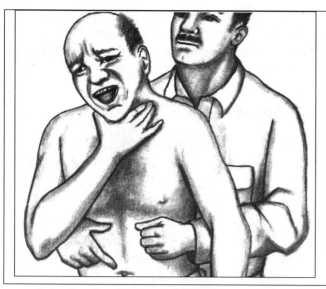

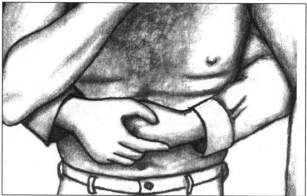

FIST LOCATION IS ABOVE BELLY BUTTON AND WELL BELOW THE BREASTBONE

Figure 8-10. Heimlich maneuver.

of the fist should be touching the victim's belly, just above the belly button and well below the breastbone.

3. With elbows out, vigorously thrust your fist upward into the victim's belly, attempting to force air through the windpipe to blow the obstruction from the windpipe.

4. After four abdominal thrusts, try four sharp blows between the shoulders to dislodge the obstruction followed by more abdominal thrusts. *Do not give up!* Be prepared to give artificial respiration, if the victim passes out.

   NOTE: You can perform abdominal thrusts on yourself with your fists or against an object, such as a chair or stump.

BANDAGES AND DRESSINGS

Dressings are typically sterile, gauze-covered cotton pads placed directly on wounds to stop bleeding and to keep the wounds clean. They often have a shiny protective coating on one side to keep the dressing from sticking to the wound and to facilitate daily dressing changes. Do not touch the surface of sterile dressings before applying to wounds. Roll *bandages* are usually made from gauze, crepe, or stretch material (ace bandage). Bandages can be improvised from any clean cloth material, such as sheets or clothing. Large triangular bandages, with short legs of one yard or more, are versatile. Use large triangular bandages for arm slings, head wounds, binding

splints, and so on. Bandages should be tied just tight enough to hold dressings in place and stop bleeding, but not so tight that they cut into the flesh or restrict circulation. Tie bandages with a square (reef) knot. Check finger tips and toes for numbness or bluish color, which indicates restricted circulation from bandages that are too tight.

SHOCK

Be on the lookout for shock in any accident victim. Virtually any serious injury or illness can lead to shock. When trauma or severe illness threatens the flow of oxygen and blood to the body's tissues, the body responds with a counterattack, known as shock. When in shock, the body constricts blood flow to nonessential organs in an effort to conserve blood and sustain life. Shock can be life threatening, even though the injuries that caused the shock would not normally cause death.

Symptoms

- Skin pale or bluish, cold to the touch, and possibly moist or clammy.
- Weakness, dizziness. Victim may be apathetic and unresponsive due to lack of oxygen to the brain.
- Rapid pulse (usually over 100), often too weak to be felt at the wrist but perceptible at the carotid artery on the side of the neck where the

windpipe joins the muscle, or at the femoral artery at the groin.

- Restlessness, anxiety, or confusion. Decreased alertness.
- Nausea, vomiting.
- Rapid, shallow breathing.
- Intense thirst.

Trauma specialists talk about the "golden hour" in treating shock victims. If shock is not reversed within one hour, the patient may die, no matter what actions are taken.

Treatment for Shock

1. Check the victim's ABCs. Perform CPR or control the bleeding, if necessary.
2. Lay the victim on his/her back in the "shock position": legs flexed at the hips, knees straight, feet elevated 12 inches, and head down. This promotes the return of venous blood to the heart and enhances the flow of arterial blood to the brain.

   WARNING: Do not lay the victim in the shock position if you suspect head, neck, or back injuries, or if the victim is having breathing problems.

3. Give treatment for the underlying illness or injury.
4. Keep the victim comfortable. Loosen tight clothing and conserve body heat by bundling in blankets or a sleeping bag. *Do not add heat from an external source,* as this will swell capillaries in the skin and draw blood from vital organs.
4. *Do not give fluids by mouth.*
5. Move the victim out of danger if you have to, but avoid rough handling. Check vital signs (ABCs) every few minutes, including pulse and breathing rate and pattern. Restlessness and agitation may be signs of worsening shock.
6. Make arrangements for rapid medical evacuation. Time is of the essence!

FRACTURES AND DISLOCATIONS

Dislocations occur when a joint is overstressed to the point where the bone pops out of location (the joint is "dislocated"). Usually dislocations are accompa-

nied by tearing and rupturing of the soft joint tissues. A fracture occurs when a bone is overstressed to the point where it breaks. It is often hard to tell if a bone is fractured or dislocated, but the first aid treatment for both is usually the same. Fractures are divided into two types. In the case of an open fracture (also known as a compound fracture), the broken bone ruptures the skin. The bone may be sticking out of the wound, or it may retract back inside the flesh. Open fractures are very serious injuries, because they are easily infected and can lead to bone infections and gangrene, which are difficult to treat and may result in amputation if treatment is unsuccessful. Injuries that appear to be dislocations may actually be fractures near a joint, and should be immobilized and treated as fractures.

In general, it is recommended that untrained personnel do not try to reposition dislocations or fractures. However, if you are in a remote location, or if you are sure that emergency medical services will not be available for several hours, you should try to pop a dislocated joint back into position, or tension and reposition a fractured limb. You must use your judgment on this one. The Red Cross manuals state that fractures and dislocations should be immobilized in the position they are found in, to minimize the risk of further damage while trying to reposition the joint or break. Wilderness medicine manuals will tell you that you should attempt to reduce (relocate or "pop" back into joint) a dislocated joint as soon as possible after the injury, or swelling and muscle spasms will make this task nearly impossible and will make rescue far more difficult. Similarly, setting a fracture (realigning the break prior to splinting) may cause more damage if done improperly, but if properly handled will reduce the risk of further injury by:

- Preventing a closed fracture from becoming an open fracture
- Reducing bleeding and pain at the fracture location
- Reducing the risk of shock complications
- Making it easier to apply an effective splint

If you do choose to align a fracture ("set" or "reduce" the fracture), you must apply tension to the fractured limb both while the splint is applied and

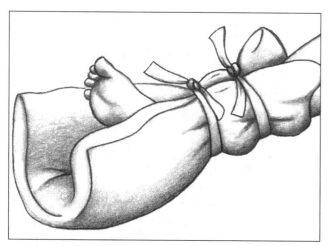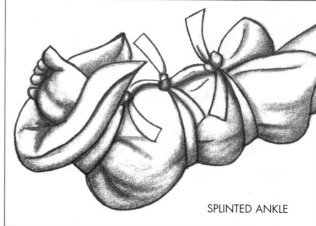

SPLINTED ANKLE

Figure 8-11. Ankle splint.

while in the splint. Without tension, muscle contractions may cause the fractured bone sections to pull beside each other resulting in further injury due to the cutting of internal tissues on sharp bone fragments.

General Guidelines for Treating Dislocations and Fractures

1. Check the victim's ABCs.
2. Keep the victim still. Movement of fractured limbs could turn a closed fracture into a compound fracture or cause damage to internal tissues. *Do not move the limb or attempt to "set" the fracture.*

Movement may cause severe tissue damage from razor sharp edges of fractured bones.

3. If there is an open fracture, or you suspect there may be a fracture below an open wound, take extreme precautions against infection and contamination. Do not wash the wound, but cover the wound with sterile dressings and immobilize the limb. Do not breathe on, or probe, the open wound. Do not try to set the limb (unless you have no access to emergency medical services in the near future).
4. Splint or sling the affected area in the position you found it. Include at least the joint above and below the injury when immobilizing the injured

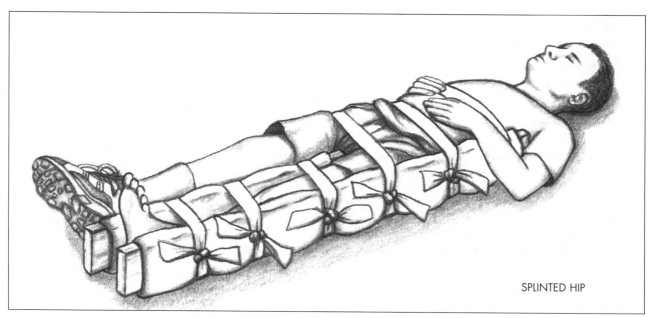

SPLINTED HIP

Figure 8-12. Hip splint.

PREPARE A TRIANGULAR PIECE OF CLOTH APPROXIMATELY 55″ ACROSS THE BASE AND FROM 36″ TO 40″ ALONG THE SIDES

Figure 8-13. Arm sling.

area. Splint the break with some kind of firm material, such as boards, tree branches, ski poles, broom sticks, umbrellas, and so on. If rigid materials are unavailable, you can use rolled-up newspapers or rolled towels, or you can tape or tie a limb to the body or another limb (that is, strap the broken leg to the good leg). Pad the splint with some kind of soft-cushioning material such as towels, moss, or rags between the victim's flesh and hard splints. Tie the splint in at least two places above and two places below the injury, but not directly on top of the injury. Always treat wounds before splinting.

5. Treat for shock. Lay the victim flat, elevating the feet and keeping the head down, *unless you suspect a head, back, or neck injury.*

6. Call EMS.

Special Precautions for Fractures

1. **Pelvis and thigh.** Fractures to the pelvis and thigh are serious injuries that can rapidly turn life threatening. If possible, do not move the victim, but get immediate medical attention. If the victim must be moved, use the clothes drag technique rather than lifting or carrying.

2. **Neck or back.** If a spinal injury is suspected, call EMS immediately and do not move the victim unless in danger. If you must move the victim, use the clothes drag technique. If the neck is injured, it is imperative that the neck be immobilized with a neck collar, sack of earth, or some other obstruction to movement. You may improvise a collar

from a rolled towel, or newspaper, among other items. If a neck fracture is suspected, *do not allow the victim to move her/his neck!* If the victim must be lifted or rolled over, get several people to assist so the victim may be rolled or lifted as a unit, with no twisting to the spine or neck.

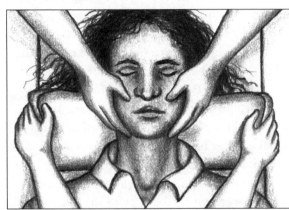

Figure 8-14. Stabilizing the head and neck.

3. **Skull.** Blood or straw-colored fluids seeping from the ear or nose may indicate a skull fracture. Do not block the drainage of these fluids as this may cause brain damage from internal pressure buildup. If there are no signs of neck or back injury, place the victim in the recovery position, with the leaking side down to drain. Cover wounds lightly with sterile dressings if a fracture is suspected. Dilated pupils, dizziness, difficulty breathing, nausea, unclear thinking, vision problems, unconsciousness, and severe unrelenting headaches are signs of potential brain injury. Monitor ABCs and call EMS.

Reducing Dislocations

When traveling in the wilderness, or when emergency medical services are hours away, try to pop dislocated joints back into place ("reduction"). Do not wait too long, or else swelling and muscle spasms will make this task difficult or impossible. Gently probe the area to try to ensure that the dislocation is not actually a fracture.

- **Fingers** are easy. Simply grasp the fingertip and pull steadily outwards until the joint pops back into place. After reduction, tape injured finger to adjacent finger for support.

- For **shoulders**, try to position the victim lying flat on her/his stomach with the arm hanging down over an edge. Either hang a weight of 10 to 15 pounds from the wrist for ten minutes, or pull steadily downwards on the victim's wrist until the shoulder pops back into place. Separated shoulders are often confused with shoulder dislocations. Separated shoulders are usually caused by falls directly onto the shoulder, which tears some of the tissue connecting the collarbone to the shoulder. If you detect a "spongy" feel while gently probing the collarbone, the injury is probably a separation and should be treated by immobilization with a sling. After reduction, support arm with a sling.

- **Elbows** are more difficult and you may not be able to get the elbow to relocate while you are in the backcountry. Check pulse and circulation in the fingers. Have the victim lie on his/her belly, draping the injured elbow over a padded ledge or edge so the elbow bends 90 degrees and the forearm hangs straight down. Grasp the wrist and pull downwards while another rescuer pulls upwards on the upper arm just above the elbow. Rocking the forearm back and forth gently may assist the process. Recheck pulse and circulation in the fingers. After reducing the elbow, splint as if it were fractured.

- **Hips** are tough, but if successfully reduced, will prevent further damage to the hip joint and sciatic nerve. Lay the victim on his or her back and, keeping the knee bent at a right angle, lift the leg until the thigh is pointing straight up.

Have an assistant hold the victim's hips down while you straddle the victim. Grasp just below the knee and pull firmly upwards, slowly twisting the leg a little to the right and left until the hip pops back into place. It takes considerable force to counteract the strong thigh muscles. After relocation, splint the injured leg to the other leg.

Sprains and Strains
SPRAINS

Sprains are injuries to the joints, usually accompanied by soreness and swelling, indicating that internal tissues have torn. Severe sprains can be more debilitating, more painful, and take longer to heal than simple fractures. Standard treatment is covered by the acronym RICE, which stands for rest, ice, compression, and elevation. Stay off the injured limb (rest). Apply cold compresses for the first 24 to 48 hours. Do not apply ice directly to the skin, but insulate ice packs with a towel or folded cloth. After two days, massage and hot soaks (or alternating hot and cold soaks) will boost blood circulation and speed healing. Elevating the limb and compressing the area with a snug ace bandage wrap will help control swelling. Tincture of *Arnica montana* and Traumeel cream, a homeopathic remedy, will usually promote and accelerate the body's natural healing processes. These remedies are also good for bruises and most other traumatic injuries.

Immobilization is key to treating severe sprains and connective tissue tears. It used to be that doctors jumped in right after a serious tearing injury with invasive surgery to reconnect torn ligaments and tendons using pins, stitches, and staples. Years later, these artificial connections tend to cause problems with arthritis and joint degeneration. Researchers have found that the natural intelligence of the body's healing mechanisms usually does a better job of reconnecting these tissues, provided that the injury is immobilized for an appropriate period of time.

In my own case, a severe fall onto sharp rocks caused a compound fracture to my heel and tore most of the connective tissue holding the front two-thirds of my foot to my ankle. The surgeon held together my heel bone fragments and my foot joint with temporary surgical pins, allowing my body to reconnect and regenerate all the severed connecting ligaments and tendons. The initial reconnection process took about ten weeks of immobilization, followed by months of gradual recuperation, but my soft tissues grew back together while immobilized better than the surgeon could have done with pins, screws, and staples, and will hopefully have fewer long-term side effects.

STRAINS

Muscle strains ("pulled" muscles) can be very painful. Apply cold compresses at once and elevate the limb to control swelling. If pain begins to recede, apply heat after 24 hours. If the muscle does not improve in one to two days, seek medical attention.

BITES AND STINGS

Animal Bites

The main concern with animal bites is infection. Thoroughly cleanse the wound and apply disinfectant or antibiotic ointment and dressings. Rabies is always a possibility with animal bites. Felines, canines, apes, raccoons, and other mammals may carry rabies. Always have the victim of a bite examined by the appropriate medical services, even if some time has passed and the wound has healed. Once rabies progresses to the point where there are symptoms of nervousness, light sensitivity, and aversion to water, it is usually fatal.

Snake Bites

Except for the brightly colored coral snake (red, black, and yellow, or white rings with a black nose), all poisonous snakes leave two large holes from their fangs, along with smaller holes from their other teeth. Most snakes are not poisonous, but can generate a significant wound with their bite. Venomous snakebites require first aid and medical treatment.

- Call EMS. Identify the type of snake, if known, so the proper antivenin can be prepared in advance of treatment. Try to kill the snake and take it along for identification.
- Keep the victim calm, quiet, and inactive. Have the victim lie down and keep the bite below the heart.

- Wash the wound and apply antiseptic.
- *Do not* cut the wound and try to suck the venom out. If you have a snake bite kit, you can use the suction cups or suction syringe.
- *Do not* apply a tourniquet or cold compress to the wound.
- Monitor the ABCs and treat for shock if necessary. Remove rings and bracelets that might cause problems if the limbs begin to swell.
- Seek medical treatment.

Spider Bites

Treat spider bites in the same way as snake bites. The most serious spider bites in the United States are from the brown recluse and black widow. Except for the elderly and small children, the bites from these spiders are usually not fatal, but they can make you very sick and lead to flesh loss.

The black widow has a very shiny, black patent-leather look with a large abdomen and a bright red hourglass shaped marking on the underside of its belly. The bite may not even be noticed, or may feel like a small pinprick followed by tingling and numbing of the hands and feet. Symptoms may progress into severe back and stomach cramps, sweating, vomiting, headaches, and seizure. Ice at the wound site can ease the pain somewhat. Seek medical attention as soon as possible; there is an antidote for severe cases. Most people recover within twelve hours without treatment (Weiss 1997, 116).

The bite of the brown recluse spider can cause serious tissue damage if left untreated. The body of the brown recluse is about ½-inch long and has a dark violin shaped marking on the top of the upper section of its body. Initial mild stinging is followed by itching and burning, and then blistering and ulceration at the bite area. Fever, chills, nausea, and vomiting may follow within one to two days. Seek medical attention; there is an antivenin that can halt or prevent tissue damage (Weiss 1997, 117).

Tarantulas are more scary looking than dangerous. Their bites can be painful and should be treated for possible infection.

Tick Bites

Lyme disease is now the most common tick-transmitted infection, with an estimated 5,000 to 15,000 new cases in the United States each year. The majority of people with Lyme disease do not recall the precipitating tick bite.
—Eric A. Weiss, M.D., *A Comprehensive Guide to Wilderness and Travel Medicine*

Ticks typically hang around on blades of grass and other vegetation until a host rubs against them. They crawl onto the host and wander around until they find a spot, then dig their head into the skin for a blood feast (usually when the host is at rest). If you tear a tick off the host, typically at least part of its head is left buried in the skin. Tick bites often lead to infection and may require a quick surgical procedure if a cyst has formed around an imbedded tick head. The preferred removal method is to grasp the tick body with a pair of tweezers, getting as far under the head as possible, without puncturing or rupturing the tick's body. Gently lift upwards and backwards until the tick releases its grasp and pulls free from the host (this may take a few minutes of steady pressure). Traditional methods, such as coating the tick with fingernail polish or petroleum jelly, or burning the tick with a hot object can force the tick to release from the host, but these methods increase infection risk from the tick regurgitating into the host's blood stream. Tick bites can cause infection or introduce diseases such as Lyme disease or Rocky Mountain spotted fever.

The deer tick, which is responsible for the spread of Lyme disease, is so small that it is almost never seen or noticed. The bite is often followed by a flu-like fever and typically develops a "bull's eye" rash up to several inches in diameter centered around the bite, which usually disappears on its own within a month's time. About 20% of Lyme disease victims develop further long-term symptoms, such as severe arthritis, heart problems, and neurological difficulties sometimes resembling multiple sclerosis. Lyme disease is treatable with antibiotics and has been treated successfully with colloidal silver (see the *Micro Silver Bullet* by Dr. Paul Farber).

My friend Eric Perlman, an outstanding athlete, was suffering from painful arthritis in his mid-forties. A blood test uncovered evidence of Lyme disease. Treatment for Lyme disease was able to halt the degenerative destruction of Eric's joints and eliminated most of his arthritic symptoms.

Stings

Bees, wasps, hornets, and scorpions can cause severe reactions in some people. In the case of a scorpion, try to kill the scorpion (and bring it along) for identification, because some varieties can be extremely poisonous. The sting from the small straw-colored bark scorpion (1 to 2 inches in length, with slender pinchers) is potentially lethal. Look for neurological symptoms, such as twitching, drooling, numbness, blurred vision, and seizures. Seek immediate medical attention.

Benadryl can be helpful for reducing the symptoms of swelling and itching associated with many insect bites and stings. Try to remove bee stingers with a scraping action, as pinching a stinger with tweezers may drive more venom into the sting. Multiple stings or allergy to stings can cause a severe reaction, known as anaphylactic shock, a life-threatening conditioning in which the throat swells shut, blood pressure falls, and unconsciousness may ensue. In this case, call EMS and seek immediate medical attention. Check for a medic alert bracelet. A person with severe allergies usually carries a kit with emergency medicine for dealing with this kind of emergency.

EYES

The eye is very delicate, complicated, and easily damaged. When in doubt always seek medical attention. If foreign material is irritating the eyes, try to wash it out with an eyecup, by holding the eye open in a bowl of water, or lie the victim on his/her side and dribble water from a glass across the eye. While washing the eye, use your thumb and forefinger to hold the eyelid open, since the natural reaction is for the eye to clamp shut. Room-temperature sterile saline solution is the best flushing solution for the eyes, but clean fresh water will do if saline solution is

Figure 8-15. Rolling victim onto board.

MOVING INJURED PEOPLE

If the victim is in physical danger, or is in a remote location, it may be necessary to move him or her. Whenever there is a potential spinal injury, the victim must be immobilized and the utmost care must be given to minimize or prevent movement of the back or neck. Ideally, several qualified medical personnel will be available to lift the victim onto a back board or stokes litter, where he will be strapped down to prevent movement. In reality, you may have to improvise and do your best with whatever materials are available. If a spinal injury is suspected, immobilize the head and neck at all times, and always roll or lift the body as a unit.

not available. Use lukewarm or cold water—*never use hot water!* The standard procedure for chemical irritants in the eyes is to flush the eyes for 15 minutes with water, and then seek medical attention. You may be able to dislodge foreign debris by pulling the upper eyelid outward and scraping its inner surface over the short eyelashes of the lower lid. A soft, clean cloth may be gently dragged across the eyeball to snag particles of debris. Do not use cotton or tissue paper.

First Aid for Foreign Object in Eye

- If it does not move freely, do not attempt to remove the object!
- Call EMS.
- Prevent the victim from rubbing the eye and causing more damage.
- Cover both eyes, so the victim will not cause more damage by moving the eyes around.

Clothing Drag for Single Rescuer

If you must move a victim by yourself due to immediate danger, use the clothes drag to drag the person, face down or face up, out of danger. Crouch by the victim's head and grab the clothing by the shoulders, using your forearms to stabilize the head and neck. Keep your lower back straight, to minimize back strain. Walk backwards to drag the victim out of danger. With a helper, you can position the victim on a blanket and use the blanket for a modified clothes drag.

Multi-helper "Stretcher" Rescue

Whenever possible, recruit helpers for moving the injured. The more helpers, the easier it will be. Four people is a good number for moving victims short distances over easy ground. Over rough ground, three per side and one at each end makes the carry less tiring and helps minimize the chance of drop-

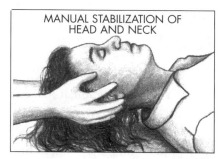
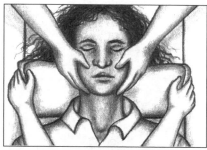

MANUAL STABILIZATION OF HEAD AND NECK

Figure 8-16. Stabilizing head and neck for board carry.

ping the stretcher if one person trips. Rotate crews every 10 minutes over long stretcher hauls. In the event of a suspected spinal injury, the use of a rigid board, such as a door, is preferred over a flexible stretcher made from two poles and a blanket.

If the victim is lying flat, lift the victim as carefully as possible onto the board. Always position one person at the head to cradle the head and neck while lifting. Most of the weight will be in the shoulders and torso, so place most of your strength and attention on these areas.

If the victim is not lying flat, place the board against the person's back, parallel to the body. Roll the victim as a unit, never twisting the spine, onto the board and gently lower the board to the ground. Always have one person attending to the head, cradling the head and neck as the victim is rolled.

In the case of a potential spinal injury, immobilize the head and neck with rolled up towels, blankets, bags of sand, and so on, and strap in place. If you have none of these materials, a helper must stabilize the head with forearms and hands.

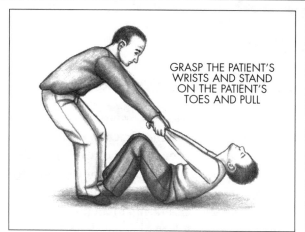

GRASP THE PATIENT'S WRISTS AND STAND ON THE PATIENT'S TOES AND PULL

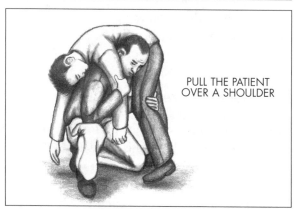

PULL THE PATIENT OVER A SHOULDER

PASS AN ARM BETWEEN THE LEGS AND GRASP THE ARM NEAREST YOU

Figure 8-17. Fireman's lift.

GRIP AS SHOWN: RIGHT HAND ON YOUR LEFT WRIST, LEFT ON THE OTHER PERSON'S RIGHT

Figure 8-18. Two-person wrist-catch seat carry.

One- and Two-Person Carries

Extra help is not always available when it is necessary to move an injured person out of danger or to transport him or her to emergency medical services. In these cases it may be necessary to perform a one- or two-person carry. Use extreme caution with all one- or two-person carries to prevent injuring your back. Try to keep your back relatively straight and lift mostly with your legs. The classic *fireman's lift* is particularly effective where speed is critical, distances are short, and there is no apparent spinal injury.

The two-person wrist-catch seat carry is a comfortable shorter distance carry. Over longer distances, the *backpack* or *sling carry* will be much less tiring and easier on both victim and rescuer than the *fireman's lift*.

CUT LEG HOLES IN THE BOTTOM OF A LARGE BACK-PACK

Figure 8-19. Backpack carry.

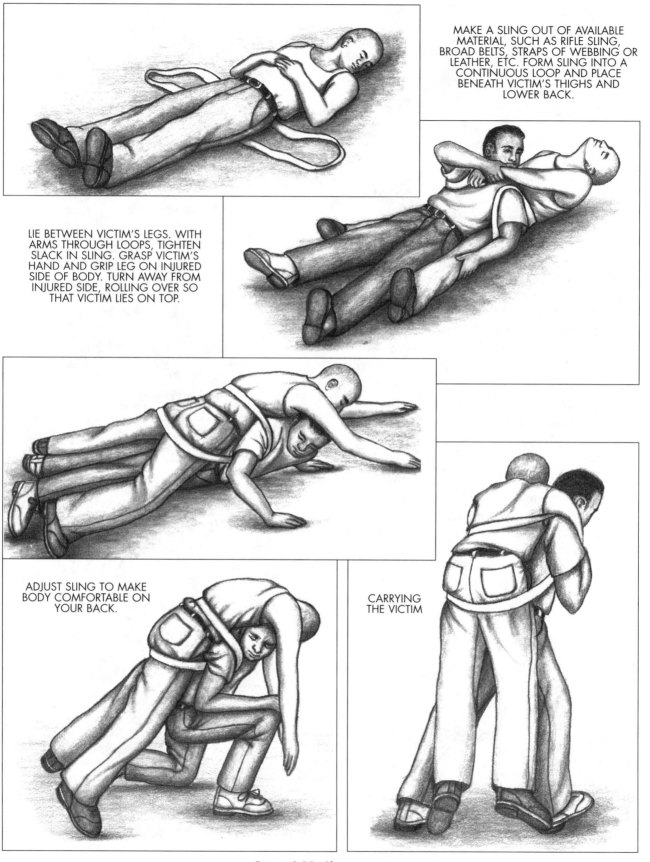

MAKE A SLING OUT OF AVAILABLE MATERIAL, SUCH AS RIFLE SLING, BROAD BELTS, STRAPS OF WEBBING OR LEATHER, ETC. FORM SLING INTO A CONTINUOUS LOOP AND PLACE BENEATH VICTIM'S THIGHS AND LOWER BACK.

LIE BETWEEN VICTIM'S LEGS. WITH ARMS THROUGH LOOPS, TIGHTEN SLACK IN SLING. GRASP VICTIM'S HAND AND GRIP LEG ON INJURED SIDE OF BODY. TURN AWAY FROM INJURED SIDE, ROLLING OVER SO THAT VICTIM LIES ON TOP.

ADJUST SLING TO MAKE BODY COMFORTABLE ON YOUR BACK.

CARRYING THE VICTIM

Figure 8-20. Sling carry.

EMERGENCY CHILDBIRTH

My wife Josie's first child was born in the hospital. She had a very long, difficult labor. Her early labor was slowed down with drugs, because the doctor was not ready. Later, they had trouble getting her labor going again. The whole experience was cold and unpleasant, leaving a bitter taste, so we opted for a home birth the second time around. We chose a registered nurse-midwife to assist at the delivery, and went through natural childbirth classes to prepare us for the event.

Josie's labor started in the midwife's office during a visit for a prenatal exam. When I got there, the midwife exclaimed, "This baby's coming in a hurry! We don't have much time." We drove the midwife to our home where we rushed to get the bed covered and unpack our "birthing supplies." Everything was ready about 15 minutes before my daughter was born. When our daughter passed through the birth canal into my hands, I experienced a powerful sensation—like strong electrical currents flowing through my hands and arms. Our daughter lay quietly on Josie's belly, not crying at all. Slowly she opened one eye and looked around. It was an awesome experience to take such an intimate part in the birthing process. A while later, after the placenta had been passed, the midwife became noticeably concerned. My wife was continuing to bleed heavily from her uterus, but the bleeding should have subsided shortly after passing the afterbirth. The midwife worked her small hands up inside my wife's uterus and removed clots that had not come free with the afterbirth. The bleeding stopped, and we all breathed a sigh of relief. In the old days, with an inexperienced doctor or midwife, those clots could have led to her death from severe hemorrhaging.

This section provides some of the most basic instructions for dealing with emergency childbirth. See Elizabeth Davis's excellent *Heart and Hands: A Midwife's Guide to Pregnancy and Birth*, or David Werner et al.'s *Where There Is No Doctor* for more detailed instruction and advice. When my wife was pregnant with our daughter, we read several books on the subject and found some very interesting statistics. The United States has the highest percentage of hospital births and cesarean sections in the entire world. We also have one of the highest infant mortality rates among the developed countries. Apparently, in most cases, low-risk births happen faster and with fewer complications at home under the care of a qualified doctor, nurse, or midwife, than in the harsh environment of a hospital. Many hospitals have taken this into consideration and now offer "birthing centers" with a more relaxed, homey atmosphere. Whenever possible, enlist the assistance of qualified medical personnel and have the backup insurance of a medical facility available in case of complications.

Signs of Impending Delivery

- Regular contractions, at intervals of two minutes or less between the start of each contraction.
- Strong urge to have a bowel movement.
- Rupture of the amniotic sac ("breaking of the water") may happen while the mother is attempting to go to the bathroom. Usually the baby comes shortly after the sac ruptures, but sometimes may not come for a few days. In this case, it may be best to have the labor induced in a hospital to avoid infection.
- Strong urge to push. Often the mother yells that the baby is coming.

Stages of Labor

The first stage lasts from the beginning of strong contractions until the baby has dropped into the birth canal (launch position). The mother should drink a lot of fluids and try to keep the bowels evacuated. An enema may be helpful to evacuate the bowels. The mother should wash her buttocks and genital area with soap and water. Birthing supplies should be readied, if the birth will be at home. The first stage typically lasts from 10 to 20 hours (but it may last several days) for a woman's first birth and 5 to 10 hours for subsequent births.

CAUTION: Births can happen very quickly, like my daughter's, which took less than two hours from the start of labor.

Make sure you have plenty of clean sheets or other bed coverings (newspaper will do in a pinch) and change them as soon as they get soiled. If the mother has a bowel movement, wipe from front to back. Have a sterile unopened razor blade, or a pair of boiled scissors on hand for cutting the cord. The midwife should not massage the belly and the mother should not push during this stage. Deep, slow breathing can help to ease the pain. Walking helps to speed the delivery and labor.

The second stage starts when the baby has dropped into the birth canal and finishes when the baby is born. This stage is often easier than the first stage and is usually finished within a couple of hours. Cleanliness is of the utmost importance. Hands should be washed frequently in sterile water and surgical gloves should be worn if available. For normal births, the midwife or attendant should never insert hands or fingers into the birth canal, as this is the major cause of severe infections in the mother. The mother should push hard with each contraction until the child's head shows about 3 inches across. At that point the mother should try not to push too hard and should breathe with short fast breaths. This helps to avoid tearing the vaginal opening.

The third stage lasts from the birth until the placenta (afterbirth) has been expelled and bleeding has stopped or reduced to a trickle. This usually happens between five minutes and one hour after the birth.

WARNING: If there is severe bleeding or the placenta does not come out, seek medical attention immediately.

Emergency Childbirth Supplies

- Flashlight in case of poor lighting or power outage.
- Plastic sheet, tarp, or large garbage bags to place under the mother on top of the bedding.
- Clean sheets, towels, newspapers, and so on to place under the mother, and on top of the plastic sheet. Change as soon as soiled. Have at least three extra clean dry towels on hand.
- Sanitary napkins (several).
- A rubber suction bulb for suctioning the newborn's mouth. A turkey baster with a fine tip will do in a pinch.
- Sterile gauze dressings.
- Sterile gloves.
- Sterile razor or scissors for cutting the umbilical cord.
- Two pieces of sterile string, such as shoelace, for tying the umbilical cord. Boil in water for ten minutes to sterilize. *Do not use thread because it will cut through the cord.*
- Receiving blankets and diapers for the newborn.
- A container for the placenta (afterbirth). A plastic bag will do.

Delivery

Keep everything as clean as possible before, during, and after the delivery. Use no antiseptics. Soap and clean water are best. Remove jewelry and watches and scrub hands, including under the fingernails. Wear sterile gloves, if available. Remind the mother to pant or take long deep breaths, because this helps the baby to emerge slowly, with less chance of tearing the vaginal opening.

1. *DO NOT* try to delay the birth in any way, such as by crossing the mother's legs or pushing the baby back inside.
2. *DO NOT* allow the mother to go to the toilet. The sensation of having to have a bowel movement means the baby is coming. Spontaneous bowel movements in the final stages are normal. Wipe the mother front to back (always away from the vagina) and immediately remove soiled cloths.
3. *DO NOT* pull the baby from the vagina.
4. The baby's head usually emerges first, but not always. If something else appears first, the buttocks (breech birth), a shoulder, or a hand, for example, the chances for birthing complications are significantly increased.
5. *To help reduce tearing,* when the crown of the head shows a few inches, have the mother stop pushing. Panting and deep breathing will help her to overcome the desire to push and gives her skin more time to stretch. The midwife can support the skin between the vagina and the anus with the palm of one hand, while gently pressing on the baby's head with the other hand, to keep the head from emerging too fast and tearing the mother's flesh.
6. Tear any membrane covering the baby's face.
7. If the umbilical cord is wrapped around the baby's neck, hook it with your finger and gently but quickly slip it over the baby's head. If it is too tight to flip over the baby's head, it must be tied and cut or the child will suffocate or bleed to death.
8. Support the baby's head in the palm of your hand. Once the head is free, the rest of the body delivers quickly. Be ready for the baby to be extremely slippery. Suction the mouth and nostrils with the bulb, or clean with a clean dry cloth.

CAUTION: Sometimes the baby will have had a bowel movement in the womb. When the water breaks, this will appear as a dark green, almost black liquid. If the baby breathes this material (meconium) into his lungs, he may die. If there is evidence of meconium in the mother's amniotic fluid, or the child's face and mouth, it must be completely suctioned out of the child's nose and mouth before the child begins to breathe. Once the baby's head is free, have the mother proceed very slowly to allow time for suctioning. Seek immediate medical attention, if available.

9. If an arm comes out first, the mother may need an operation to birth the baby.

10. If the buttocks come first (breech), the birth may be easier with the mother in a crouching position on all fours. If the head is stuck, try pushing down on the mother's lower abdomen to help push the head out from the inside. Have the mother push hard, *but never pull on the body of the baby.*

After Delivery

1. Hold the baby face down, with the feet higher than the head, to allow fluids to drain. If you have a suction bulb, gently suction the child's mouth and nose. The baby may be blue but should turn pink a few minutes after he starts to breathe.

2. *If the baby is not breathing,* tap the bottom of the baby's feet a few times and massage his back with a clean towel. If the baby is not breathing within one minute of birth, try a couple of quick rescue breaths then gently begin mouth-to-mouth resuscitation.

3. When the baby cries or is breathing normally, lay the baby on the mother's breast and encourage the baby to nurse. This will help stimulate the mother's uterine contractions for expelling the placenta. Make sure there is no tension on the umbilical cord.

4. The umbilical cord should not be cut immediately. Immediately after birth, the cord is fat and blue. *Wait* until the cord has stopped pulsing and has become thin and whitish in color; then tie the cord firmly in two places using sterile cord (not thread). Tie one spot in the cord about 4 inches from the baby's end, and the other spot about 8 inches from the same end. Cut the cord in between the ties with a sterile razor blade or sterile scissors and immediately cover the baby's end of the cord with clean cloth or sterile gauze. To protect the child from infections, the cord should be allowed to dry and it should be kept dry.

5. Keep the mother and baby warm. The mother will continue to have contractions to expel the placenta, which should happen between five minutes and an hour after birth (but sometimes it takes several hours). If the placenta is slow in coming, feel the womb (uterus) through the mother's belly. If it is soft, firmly massage the womb until it contracts (gets hard) to expel the placenta. Inspect the placenta. If it appears to be missing large chunks, you may be faced with a serious medical emergency due to severe bleeding.

6. Wash the mother and give her plenty of warm fluids.

REFERENCES

The American Red Cross First Aid & Safety Handbook, **by the American Red Cross and Kathleen A. Handal, M.D.** 1992, 321 pp. (paperback), ISBN 0-316-73646-5. Published by Little, Brown & Co., 1271 Avenue of the Americas, New York, NY 10020. Lists for $17.95.
This is *the* standard reference manual for first aid and CPR. It is clear, well illustrated, and concise.

Where There Is No Doctor: A Village Health Care Handbook, **by David Werner, Carol Thuman, and Jane Maxwell.** 1992, 446 pp. (paperback), ISBN: 0-942364-15-5. Published by the Hesperian Foundation, P.O. Box 11577, Berkeley, CA 94712. Lists for $17.00.
This book should be in every home. It was especially designed for people in rural areas without access to a doctor, but the medical information is applicable anywhere. It gives clear and concise directions for many topics, including childbirth, trauma, and the treatment of numerous diseases and parasites. The authors present the information in a way that is easily understood by the layperson who lacks medical training. It includes information on both symptoms and treatment, as well as possible drug side effects, and a good chapter on first aid. It is no substitute for a doctor's services but is indispensable for those situations where no doctor is available. From Peace Corps teams to Hurricane Mitch relief workers, this book has been a valuable resource.

Medicine for Mountaineering & Other Wilderness Activities, **edited by James A Wilkerson, M.D.** 1992, 416 pp. (paperback), ISBN 0-89886-331-7. Published by The Mountaineers, 1001 SW Klickitat Way, Seattle, WA 98134. Lists for $18.95. "Tried and true, the ultimate in take-care-of-yourself instruction by a 'doctor in a box.'"—*American Health*

Medicine for Mountaineering is the definitive guide to providing emergency medical care when a doctor is miles or days away. This book has a list of ten eminent contributors from the medical profession. It is not a substitute for a basic first aid manual or training, but it is a good companion to Werner et al.'s *Where There Is No Doctor.*

Ditch Medicine: Advanced Field Procedures for Emergencies, **by Hugh L. Coffee.** 1993, 216 pp. (paperback), ISBN: 0-87364-717-3. Published by Paladin Press, P.O. Box 1307, Boulder, CO 80306. Lists for $25.00.
A quality text, this book is highly recommended for dealing with significant trauma-type medical emergencies when systems are down and there are no available doctors. For surgical procedures in the field, it goes miles beyond the Red Cross first aid books and well beyond Werner et al.'s *Where There Is No Doctor.* It teaches advanced field procedures for small wound repair, care of the infected wound, IV therapy, pain control, amputations, treatment of burns, airway clearing procedures, and more. This is a book I hope I will never need to use. Containing many graphic photos and illustrations, it is not for the faint at heart.

A Comprehensive Guide to Wilderness and Travel Medicine, **by Eric A. Weiss, M.D.** 1997, 198 pp. (paperback), ISBN 0-9659768-0-7. Published by Adventure Medical Kits, P.O. Box 43309, Oakland, CA 94624. Lists for $6.95.
This is a true "pocket book." It is very precise, concise, and compact. A perfect little book to carry with you on your travels to the backcountry or the Third World. Not only is the author the Associate Director of Trauma at Stanford University Medical Center, he is also a medical officer for the Himalayan Rescue

Association. From National Geographic expeditions in the jungles of Belize to the peaks of the Himalayas, he has done it all. Eric's tidbits of wisdom, called "Weiss Advice," are particularly helpful for improvising during emergency medical situations.

Pocket Guide to Wilderness Medicine & First Aid, **by Paul G. Gill, Jr., M.D.** 1997, 232 pp. (paperback), ISBN 0-07-024552-5. Published by Ragged Mountain Press, a division of The McGraw-Hill Companies. Lists for $14.95.

For those who already have first aid training, this book provides specific information for dealing with illness and injury in a wilderness environment, where you do not have quick access to emergency medical facilities. A compact and practical manual, with good sections on self-rescue, but not as broad as Werner et al.'s *Where There Is No Doctor* or as compact as Weiss's book.

Heart and Hands: A Midwife's Guide to Pregnancy and Birth, **by Elizabeth Davis.** 1997, 287 pp. (paperback), ISBN 0-89087-838-2. Published by Celestial Arts, P.O. Box 7123, Berkeley, CA 94707. Lists for $24.95.

This is required reading at many midwife schools and a textbook for numerous midwife classes. Very comprehensive and beautifully illustrated. Whether you wish to know more about birthing procedures and midwifery, would like to prepare yourself for the possibility of emergency childbirth, or are simply considering the option of a home birth, I highly recommend this book.

IX   Low-Tech Medicine & Healing

Health: 1. Physical and mental well-being; free-dom from disease, pain or defect; normality of physical and mental functions; soundness.
— *Webster's New World Dictionary of the American Language*, Second College Edition

The purpose of this chapter is to provide rudimentary instructions and introductions to a variety of low-tech healing disciplines. Some of these healing traditions are not for everyone. I suggest you read through the descriptions of all of them and keep an open mind. Since at some time you may be in a situation where your preferred choices are not available, it is a good idea to be informed about the alternatives. Even when traditional medicine is available, this chapter may help you find your way to alternative sources or methods for healing modern ailments, such as heart disease, cancer, or AIDS. Some of these healing modalities could help you achieve a higher level of health and a better quality of life. I encourage you to explore the best of both worlds. In some cases, high-tech healing methods will work best, but in other cases alternative methods may work better. Talk to your physician and/or alternative healer. Use wisdom and listen to the voice of your intuition. If your condition is chronic or life-threatening, do some serious research into both high- and low-tech methods. When your life is at stake, there are too many successes within both orthodox and alternative medicine to blindly discount either.

Primitive societies throughout the world have their own healing methods. Most of the oldest societies on the planet are found in the so-called developing or Third World nations and do not have ready access to high-tech medicine. These "low-tech" societies rely on a wide variety of methods and materials that promote the body's natural healing processes. In some cases, these methods may be found to be at least as effective as modern medicine. Sometimes a synergistic combination of Western orthodox medicine and low-tech healing traditions could be just the right recipe for comprehensive healing.

It is often much easier to take an antibiotic or agree to an operation than to pursue an alternative healing method. You may not always have access to modern medical services, however, and there are numerous diseases that do not respond effectively to antibiotics. In times of natural disasters and wars, high-tech medical services and supplies are usually one of the first services to overload or totally disappear. Antibiotics can be extremely valuable in fighting severe infections, but they also tend to disrupt the body's balance and immune systems. In the long run, alternative methods often restore health and the body's overall balance more effectively than antibiotics. The overuse of antibiotics, both in humans and animal feed, has developed new strains of bacteria that are antibiotic resistant and have the potential for exploding into devastating worldwide plagues. For these drug-resistant strains of bacteria, and most viruses, alternative methods may offer the only truly effective treatments.

It is easy to be careless about health, when we know an ambulance is just minutes away and we are "covered" by insurance. Bernie Siegel, M.D., in his wonderful book *Love, Medicine and Miracles*, stated that the death rate has dropped many times during doctors' strikes—for example, in 1976 in Los Angeles and Bogota, and in 1973 in Jerusalem. "Several years ago," he wrote, "there was a strike of ambulance drivers in Cape Cod, where we have a summer house. Panic ensued—what to do in emergencies? Well, the number of emergencies dropped precipitously until the strike was over—another wonderful example of how much control we have."

THE HOLISTIC HEALTH MOVEMENT

Back in the early 1980s, I met Dr. M. O. Garten, an alternative heal-
er who practiced what he preached. At that time, he was in his mid-
eighties and was working full-time helping people to overcome
so-called "terminal" cancers and other serious diseases without drugs
or surgery. He was vibrant, healthy, and strong—he easily turned
patients over to manipulate their joints and spines. He used quite a
variety of methods, lumped under the heading of "naturopathic
medicine." He told me the following story about his youth.

> *When Dr. Garten was in his mid-30s, he ate a typical American*
diet low in fiber, with lots of meat, fat, sugar, and starches. Being
young and generally healthy, he had ignored a slight dull pain in his
chest, which radiated down his left arm until it became excruciating.
In a flash, he lost all strength and slumped to the floor. The diagnosis
was shocking. He had suffered a severe heart attack and was dying
of heart disease. The specialist's estimate was that he had only a few
days left, or perhaps a week or two. Deciding to spend his last few
days in relative comfort, he retired to the beach in Florida. Enviously,
he watched a group of young people playing athletic games on the
beach. One day, they invited Dr. Garten to join in their games. He
explained that he was a very sick man with an incurable heart
disease, and couldn't possibly participate in anything athletic. With
messianic zeal, they practically carried him to their teacher and idol,
Bernard MacFadden, a teacher and promoter of natural healing.
What transpired totally negated the specialist's terminal diagnosis and
resulted in a profound revolution in Dr. Garten's own medical beliefs,
philosophy, and practice.

> *Garten told me, "I underwent a complete fast for 28 days.*
Most surprisingly, at the end of this 'ordeal,' I felt stronger than at
any other time. I could run and play with the younger set, which
they considered 'routine' experience." Not only did he recover
from his "terminal heart disease," he returned to the youthful
vigor and strength of his early 20s. With remarkable vitality and
energy, he continued to work full-time well into his 90s until a seri-
ous mugging fractured his skull and resulted in a loss of memory
and body function.

The modern holistic health movement tries to
combine the best of Western technology with traditional healing arts to treat the whole person and to
promote the body's natural ability to heal itself of
almost any ailment. There are thousands of scientifically documented cases of "spontaneous remissions"
from serious or deadly ailments. "Spontaneous
remission" is the Western term for a healing that
occurs without any rational, scientific explanation of
its cause. These cases include documented spontaneous remissions from AIDS, terminal cancers,
blindness, multiple sclerosis, and other major
diseases. For some difficult-to-heal diseases that the
modern world has labeled "incurable," the success
rate using traditional low-tech healing methods may
be considerably better than that of Western medicine. This is not to say that traditional methods are
always superior to high-tech solutions. Based on
great knowledge of human anatomy and physiology,
Western medicine has developed many life-saving
procedures and medicines plus a battery of techniques for dealing with traumatic injuries.

There are far more low-tech healing systems and
techniques than I could possibly cover in this text. I
have tried to include enough information in this
manual so that in an emergency it may provide some
practical assistance. Look to the recommended
resources for detailed information on each of the
listed healing alternatives. If you are confronted with
a serious illness, I urge you to seek professional help
whenever possible.

THE LOW-TECH MEDICINE CABINET

Here are some of the more effective self-help remedies that I recommend you keep on hand. They are
readily available in your local supermarket, drugstore, or through a health food store. See *Prescription
for Nutritional Healing* by James F. Balch, M.D., and
Phyllis A. Balch or *Food Additives, Nutrients &
Supplements A-To-Z: A Shopper's Guide* by Eileen
Renders for more complete dose and application
information on each remedy or supplement.

> **CAUTION: For serious problems, seek out a
> qualified herbalist, naturopath, or medical
> physician.**

Acidophilus. The use of oral antibiotics kills
the colon's natural bacteria that are an essential
part of healthy colon function. Without these
bacteria, *Candida albicans* (yeast) tend to breed
like wildfire, throwing off the balance of the entire
body. This usually causes fatigue and a general
sense of malady while opening up the body to

further bacterial or viral infection and another round of antibiotics. Take acidophilus in liquid or capsule form or eat yogurt with active cultures twice a day after taking oral antibiotics. For more information, see *The Yeast Connection* by William G. Crook.

Aloe vera gel. The juice from the aloe vera plant has been scientifically proven to improve the healing of burns. It is also good for healing cuts and scrapes (it is not antibiotic or antiseptic) and as a nutritional supplement. Use the live plant by cutting off a leaf and squeezing the gel from the leaf directly onto the wound. Alternatively, buy the gel or juice at a health food store.

Arnica montana. Arnica is an herbal remedy available in a tincture or extract or in homeopathic preparations. It is a useful remedy for boosting the body's healing response to traumatic injuries, such as sprains, fractures, bruises, and so on.

Astragalus. One of the most highly regarded herbs used in Chinese medicine, astragalus is an efficient immune system booster. Recommended dosage is 10 drops of the extract taken in water daily (Renders 1999, 203). Taking it during the flu season is recommended if there is something "going around" or if you are suffering from cancer, AIDS, or other immune deficiency diseases. Do not take astragalus if you are already suffering from a fever. Many immune system booster combinations, available at health food stores, are based around astragalus.

Calendula cream. An effective salve for skin irritations and rashes, including eczema, this cream can promote the healing of stubborn skin splits and wounds that are not responding to normal treatment.

Coffee. Not generally perceived as a healing herb, coffee does have healing applications. Use it in enemas (see the *Naturopathic Healing* section for details) to promote healthy liver function. Use the grounds as a poultice to combat fungal infections, such as athlete's foot.

Colloidal silver. Colloidal silver is effective against harmful protozoa, bacteria, and viruses. It can be used topically on wounds (applied to dressings) or internally to fight infection. The 2-ounce bottle available at most health food stores is proba-

bly only strong enough to act as an immune booster or as a mild topical antiseptic. For use against serious illnesses, you should purchase or build your own colloidal silver generator so you can make more concentrated solutions in higher volumes and at lower cost. See the *Colloidal Silver* section for details.

Colostrum. Colostrum has been called "Nature's Healing Miracle." Medical research shows that colostrum is one of the few supplements that can help nearly everyone who's ill. It is a powerful immune system booster, supernutrient, and anti-aging supplement. Colostrum is a thick, yellow pre-milk substance that is produced toward the end of a female's pregnancy by her mammary glands and during the first 48 hours after giving birth. Humans produce small amounts of colostrum, but a cow produces approximately 9 gallons during the critical first 36 hours after giving birth. Each drop contains immunoglobulins, growth factors, antibodies, vitamins, minerals, enzymes, amino acids, and other special substances designed to give the body a head start in a lifetime of invasion by various microorganisms and environmental toxins. Numerous testimonials indicate that colostrum significantly improves general health, wound healing, allergies, diabetes, hepatitis C, immune deficiencies, bowel problems, chronic infections, fibromyalgia, cancer, chronic fatigue syndrome, severe allergies, and a host of other maladies. They also indicate that the quality of colostrum varies significantly between suppliers and that it is important to use colostrum that has been processed correctly to retain its biological potency. Avoid colostrum from cows nurtured with antibiotics, hormones and on feed grown with pesticides. For information on dosages, choosing a brand of colostrum, and the efficacy of colostrum for specific problems, see *Immune System Control: Colostrum and Lactoferrin* by Beth M. Ley, *Colostrum, "Nature's Healing Miracle"* by Donald R. Henderson, M.D., M.P.H. and Deborah Mitchell or check out the CNR (Center for Nutritional Research) web site at www.bovinecolostrum.com.

Echinacea. A traditional Native American medicinal herb, echinacea has become a part of mainstream self-help medicine. It is now available at most drugstores, since its antiviral and antibacterial properties have been scientifically documented. Take a dropperful of the extract twice daily for short-term use or use as directed in one of the many different commercial healing herb combinations (Renders 1999, 212). Echinacea is often combined with goldenseal for fighting flu. Do not use echinacea for over three weeks at a time, due to potential bladder irritation.

Enema bag. An enema is useful for far more than just relieving constipation. Coffee enemas are a powerful aid to healing because they stimulate and boost liver function. If you have been fasting, cleansing the toxins out of your colon will improve your energy and vitality, enabling you to function at surprising levels of activity (see the section on fasting).

Epsom salts. Epsom salts are useful for adding to water for hot-soak infection treatments, the liver cleanse (see section on liver cleanse) and for adding to enema water. A low-cost material, Epsom salts are available at all drugstores and many supermarkets.

Garlic. A true "wonder herb," garlic has powerful antibiotic and antibacterial properties as well as tremendous nutritional antioxidant value. Crush the whole cloves and use directly on fungal infections and on wounds to prevent infection or gangrene. Taken internally, it has been found effective against various tumors, tuberculosis, cholera, typhus, and amoebic dysentery. It has been used effectively against many different viruses and antibiotic resistant bacteria, as well as intestinal parasites. Use raw, fresh cloves, as powdered garlic loses most of its potency.

Grapefruit seed extract (GSE). Like garlic, GSE is another true "wonder herb," exhibiting powerful antibiotic, antiviral, and antibacterial properties. It has been used successfully to battle numerous diseases and ailments, including Lyme disease, *Candida*, *Giardia*, amoebic dysentery, many kinds of parasites, athlete's foot, ringworm, gum disease, herpes, colds, flu, and some forms of arthritis. The liquid form is bitter and may be diluted in juice to make it more palatable. The typical treatment is 10 to 15 drops of GSE liquid concentrate diluted in juice, taken 3 to 4 times daily (Sachs 1997, 78). Its high antibacterial action combined with low toxicity makes GSE a great alternative to regular antibiotics as a topical treatment for wounds. Mix ½ ounce GSE with 8 ounces of distilled water and apply to wounds with a spray bottle. Drinking water may be disinfected using 10 drops of GSE concentrate per 6 ounces of water. Allow water to stand for 15 minutes before drinking. For more information on specific treatments and the efficacy of GSE, see *The Authoritative Guide To Grapefruit Seed Extract* by Alan Sachs D.C., C.C.N.L.

Honey is a natural antiseptic. It has been used on the battlefield for treating wounds since ancient times and as recently as WWI. Some physicians claim that wounds treated with honey heal faster than with modern antiseptic treatments.

Joint health. The efficacy of the combination of glucosamine sulfate and chondroitin sulfate for helping the body to regenerate joint tissue has been well documented (see the book *The Arthritis Cure* by Jason Theodosakas, Brenda Adderly, and Barry Fox). You can pick up this combination in most drugstores, but Costco carries it under the name "Pain Free." About a third of all arthritis sufferers do not improve with glucosamine and chondroitin, but may improve with the addition of MSM (methyl sulfonyl methane), a naturally occurring organic nontoxic compound that supplies the body with readily assimilated sulfur for joint regeneration. In addition to daily supplements of glucosamine with chondroitin, you might try adding 10 to 20 grams per day (4 grams equals 1 teaspoon) of MSM spread throughout the day for the first couple weeks before tapering off to between 2 and 10 grams per day on a long-term basis (Ley 1998, 34). Since MSM is very bitter, mix powdered MSM with juice to make it more palatable, or dilute ½ teaspoon in 12 ounces of water to make it nearly tasteless. Only recently approved for sale in America, SAM-e (S-adenosylmethionine) has been available in Europe for many years. SAM-e is another scientifically documented joint care supplement. SAM-e users often report improvements in joint mobility and reductions in joint pain within the first two weeks of usage, whereas users of glucosamine with chondroitin usually do not experience significant improvement over the first two months of usage.

Neem oil. The National Research Council (NRC), Washington, D.C., considers the neem to be "one of the most promising of all plants. . . . It] may eventually benefit every person on this planet." Like garlic, neem appears to be another "wonder herb" with tremendous antiviral, antifungal, and antibacterial properties. It is used in herbal cosmetics, medicines, shampoos, and for organic pesticides/fungicides. Check it out at www.neemon.com.

Parasite herbs. Take black walnut tincture, clove capsules, and wormwood capsules to deparasite yourself and your pets. See the herbal section of this chapter for more details.

Parasite zapper. Build yourself a low cost electronic "zapper" or buy one from the Self-Health Resource Center (see *References and Resources* section). Searching the Internet for "zapper" combined with "Hulda Clark" will turn up several different suppliers, since Dr. Clark did not patent this technology, but gave it to humankind as a gift. See the herbal section of this chapter for more details.

> **CAUTION:** *If you plan to build your own zapper, check the internet for a correction to the wiring connections described in Dr. Clark's* **The Cure for All Diseases.**

St. John's wort. Sometimes called "nature's Prozac," St. John's wort is mostly known for its antidepressant and mood-enhancing properties. It is also an immune system booster with antiviral properties. A typical dose is 10 drops of the liquid extract once daily (Renders 1999, 242). Do not take if pregnant. It may cause increased photosensitivity and can have adverse reactions with some prescription drugs. (Contact your physician before combining it with drugs.)

Super-antibacterial/antifungal lotion. I found this combination works well against toenail fungus that no longer responded to over-the-counter medications. It is very powerful, very effective, and very malodorous. First, mix equal parts of tea tree oil and neem oil. Next, crush an equal part of fresh garlic cloves and throw into the solution. The tea tree oil keeps the neem oil liquid and preserves the crushed garlic cloves, drawing active components out of the cloves and into the oil.

Tea tree oil. A powerful antifungal and disinfectant. Use topically (do not take internally) for skin infections, itchy scalp, and fungal infections such as athlete's foot. This oil is very penetrating and will penetrate through the skin to heal sealed-over infections and pimples. Tea tree oil is one of the few liquids that can seep through toenails.

Tiger Balm. A soothing balm for easing the pain of sore muscles, stiff necks, bruises, and so on. Do not use with homeopathic remedies, because the camphor in Tiger Balm may counteract ("antidote") many homeopathic medicines.

Traumeel cream. This homeopathic ointment is great for speeding the healing of bruises, muscle aches, and sprains. Rub the ointment into the affected area. It is based on *Arnica montana* and combined with about a dozen other homeopathic remedies. Also comes in liquid and tablet form.

Usnea. Another powerful herb with antibiotic, antiviral, and antibacterial properties. Use internally or externally against bacterial, fungal, or viral infections. Usnea is often combined with echinacea. Apply tincture directly to external infections or take 5 to 10 drops of the tincture with water.

Vitamin C. Vitamin C is a powerful antioxidant, immune system booster, natural detoxifier, and necessary body nutrient for tissue health and wound healing. Nobel Prize winner Linus Pauling suggested daily ingestion of 2 to 9 grams (spread into several doses throughout the day) for cancer prevention and optimum health. A more conservative daily dosage is 500 to 1000 mg (Renders 1999, 197). Powdered vitamin C is handy for sprinkling in foods and liquids to detoxify mold aflatoxins and many other toxic substances.

Vitamin E. Vitamin E is a powerful antioxidant useful for maintaining the health of the circulatory system and the skin. The benefits of vitamin E could fill several pages. I like to break open capsules to spread on healing wounds to help speed the healing process and minimize scar tissue. A dose of 400 IU is good for combating the effects of toxins in everyday foods (Renders 1999, 114).

THE ESSENCE OF HEALING

The natural healing force within each one of us is the greatest force in getting well.

—Hippocrates

What is healing? What do we know about the body's different mechanisms for healing? *Webster's New World Dictionary of the American Language, Second College Edition*, defines "heal" as "1. to make sound, well, or to make healthy again; restore to health 2. a) to cure or get rid of (a disease); (b) to cause (a wound, sore, etc.) to become closed or scarred so as to restore a healthy condition."

We all know the feeling of a healthy body and a good state of health. In one sense, "dis-ease" or "poor health" helps us to define the "healthy" state. We do not usually notice a state of good health, but we immediately notice a state of disease by how lousy we feel. Over the past few decades, Western science has made tremendous progress in understanding the body's biochemical mechanisms for communication between the cells and some of the body's internal mechanisms for responding to health threats. A whole new field of research, called "psychoneuroimmunology" (PNI), has developed to research the complex interconnections of mood, attitude, and mind on the body's defense systems and biochemistry. However, modern science has a long way to go to fully understand the complex control systems that actually govern the healing process. The effectiveness of these control systems determines the final outcome of the healing process.

Many doctors will agree that they do not really heal people. They do their best to facilitate healing, but the body—and the life energy within it—does the actual healing.

Genetics and Cellular Growth

Although the scientific understanding of genetics, DNA, and the body's biochemical message transmitters and receptors has grown tremendously over the past 20 years, we still do not understand how the body governs the growth of new cells. We know that DNA contains the information that determines hair color, body size, and many other characteristics, but we do not understand how that information is transmitted to control the growth of cells. All the cells in one body contain the same DNA, the same genetic code. All humans start out from one fertilized egg cell, which receives half its genetic code from the mother and half from the father. As the fertilized egg grows, the cells multiply by splitting in two. One cell becomes 2, then 4, then 8, then 16, then 32, and so on. At some point in time, the cells start differentiating. Egg cells slowly change to become skin cells, bone cells, muscle cells, nerve cells, and so forth. Each type of cell has the same genetic information, yet the cells of each organ are significantly different in appearance and function. How does this happen? What controls this process? With all its magnificence and advances, Western science still does not understand this process. Why can a lizard grow a new tail, but a human cannot grow a new arm? Why does this control system go crazy sometimes and allow tumors and cancers to grow in an otherwise healthy body? In every epidemic, why do some people remain healthy while others succumb to disease? Among the low-tech healing traditions of the world, there are many different explanations for these processes, but there are a few recurring themes.

Body Energy

Numerous traditions from around the world refer to some kind of nonphysical energy system that governs the growth and health of the body. There appears to be a complex web of interconnections between the physical systems of the body and the nonphysical aspects of the being. Western science is just beginning to explore the effects upon physical healing of many different nonphysical influences. There is a growing body of scientific evidence showing conclusive correlation between healing success and such intangibles as mood, thoughts, remote prayer, and therapeutic touch, among others. Some of these data derive from carefully controlled, scientific double-blind studies.

The Asian healing disciplines of acupuncture and shiatsu both deal with some kind of energy distribution system within the body. In the ancient Chinese system of health, it is the proper flow and distribution of chi or life energy that is responsible for maintaining physical health and vitality. The Indians speak of prana—or the breath of life or life energy. Hatha yoga from India uses various postures and stretches combined with mental imagery and controlled breath concentration to stimulate the proper circulation of prana throughout the body to help it maintain perfect health. In shamanistic cultures throughout the world there is a common thread of belief in the soul or spirit that is responsible for distributing the healing life energy throughout the body. In these cultures, a shaman travels into nonordinary reality to retrieve parts of the sick person's soul and accumulates personal power that is then reintroduced back into the patient's being to help restore physical health and spiritual harmony. Recently, scientists have documented many cases of shamans healing people suffering from serious disease and illness, even those deemed incurable by Western doctors.

Kirlian photography, a method of photography that captures energy fields, yields scientific evidence supporting the existence of some kind of bioenergy field around living things. The Armenian electrician Semyon Davidovich Kirlian discovered that he could make photographs of an apparent aura around objects (such as a hand or a leaf) by electrically charging an object and placing the charged object on top of a photographic plate. Because the color and shape of the apparent aura vary dramatically with the health of the subject, Kirlian photographs seem to show more than just an electric field. Researchers discovered another startling feature: if the tip of a leaf is cut off, the missing portion shows in a Kirlian photograph as a phantom outline! Likewise, a Kirlian photograph of a man's hand that is missing a finger will show the phantom outline of the missing digit. One explanation is that each organism projects a blueprint of itself into a bioelectric field. It is hypothesized that this field may provide the basic pattern that controls the growth of individual cells. If the projection of this field is weak or nonexistent, disease-causing organisms can easily multiply within the body, or the

growth of individual organs may not be controlled properly, producing tumors and cancers.

The bioelectric fields hinted at by Kirlian photographs have not been scientifically measured; that does not mean they do not exist and won't be scientifically verified at some future date. Two hundred years ago, the existence of radio waves had not yet been discovered. If you were to describe today's phenomena of cellular phones and satellite television to George Washington or Thomas Jefferson, they would probably think you were crazy. There is a small segment of the population who do see "auras" around people and other living things. According to interviews with these people, the colors and intensities of these auras vary depending on such factors as mood and health.

Perhaps the consciousness of an individual is just as strong a factor in the health of an individual's field as are environmental factors, such as diet, exercise, and toxic pollutants. It is possible that the influence of our thoughts and beliefs upon this field explains some of the scientifically documented influence of mood, attitude, and remote prayer upon the probability for success and the rate of healing from serious illnesses and surgery. Perhaps many traditional healing modalities might be just as successful as or even more successful than the materialist medical system at stimulating this field and promoting good health. An antibiotic can be a great help for attacking an invading germ, but it does nothing to stimulate the body's natural defense mechanisms for maintaining long-term health. Some of the low-tech healing disciplines covered by this chapter deal with the mind, spirit, and subtle energies of the body. Through their application, you may be able to facilitate healing and promote long-term health and longevity.

COLLOIDAL SILVER

Imagine a powerful antibiotic agent that attacks over 600 harmful bacteria, protozoa, and viruses that you can make yourself any time and any place for just pennies a day. This is what proponents of colloidal silver claim it to be. They tout it as a solution to antibiotic-resistant bacteria and possibly devastating future plagues. Silver has been used medically for over a hundred years, and the medical use of colloidal silver is approved by the FDA in a grandfather clause. Because it is not patentable, and therefore has no economic value to pharmaceutical companies, there is little money available for thorough scientific research of the medical effectiveness of colloidal silver for fighting various diseases. My personal experience with colloidal silver is rather limited. I find that it is not as fast acting as antibiotics (when they are working right) and requires consumption of significant amounts of the liquid to be effective.

Many claim to have used colloidal silver to cure themselves of serious diseases like Lyme Disease, AIDS, a variety of cancers, Hepatitis C, *Candida albicans*, and the flu. Because there are no good data on dosages, people suffering from serious diseases have been experimenting on themselves. Typically, these people have been finding positive results drinking about 8 to 32 ounces per day of 40 part-per-million (ppm) colloidal silver (Metcalf 1998, 18). You can drink more at lower concentrations or less at higher concentrations to get the same effect. When you start drinking colloidal silver, you may find yourself feeling a little weak, with flulike symptoms. This is explained as the result of your body dealing with toxic wastes from organism die-off. If this happens, drink lots of pure water to flush your system, and reduce the dosage for a few days before resuming a higher dose. Improvement is generally seen in a few days, but cures of serious diseases may take weeks to months. A single 8-ounce glass of 5 ppm colloidal silver appears to be a reasonable daily dosage for immune system boosting for healthy persons. You can make a low cost silver solution using a colloidal silver generator or you can buy 2-ounce bottles of 10 ppm colloidal silver at health food stores for about $15.00 each. You would have to drink 24 of these bottles each day, at a daily cost of $360, to equal the dosage of a single 12-ounce glass of 40 ppm colloidal silver per day (made for pennies with your own colloidal silver generator).

There is a rare medical condition, known as Argyria, which is caused by the ingestion of large amounts of silver, typically in the form of the silver salts and nitrates that were common in patent medicines of the 1800s and early 1900s. Argyria is a cosmetic condition that is physically harmless, but results in an undesirable bluish tint in some parts of the body. To my knowledge, there has not been one reported case of Argyria due to the ingestion of colloidal silver, but I suggest that you proceed cautiously when ingesting large quantities of high-concentration colloidal silver.

MAKING YOUR OWN COLLOIDAL SILVER GENERATOR

In the early 1900s, colloidal silver was very expensive, but in recent years a physicist (Bob Beck, D.Sc.) came up with a simple method for making it. A modern colloidal silver generator is about as complex as a flashlight. Making colloidal silver simply involves placing a DC voltage across two chunks of pure silver (a cathode and an anode) immersed in pure water. Supposedly, 30 volts is the optimum voltage, but 27 volts from three 9-volt batteries works fine. If these are not available, you could get by with two 12-volt solar panels wired in series for a total output of 24 volts. This setup would generate colloidal silver at a slower rate.

See Figure 9-1 for a sketch of how to hook up your own colloidal silver generator. Connect three 9-volt transistor radio batteries in series (+ terminal to – terminal to + terminal, etc.) using readily available 9-volt battery clip-on terminals. Wire a 24-volt light bulb in series with the batteries, then connect to a minijack for easy use. The light bulb performs two functions. First, it is your battery indicator, which should shine brightly when you touch the two alligator clips or silver wires to each other. Second, it provides a load to the battery, so you don't drain your batteries dead after a minute or two if the silver wires accidentally touch while making solution. Connect one wire from your battery pack, and one from the light bulb to a minijack socket. Tape your battery pack together and mount your lamp, battery pack, and minijack socket into an appropriate box. Split the wires from the minijack plug and connect to two alligator clips. Cut two 6-inch lengths of 99.99% pure silver wire (14 or 16 gage works well) and bend the ends into ½-inch hooks for hanging over the edge of a glass. Purchase electrical materials at Radio Shack, Wall Mart, Intertan, etc. Silver wire of 99.9% purity is available from jewelry supply stores and some craft stores or you may purchase the pure silver wire, silver generator kits, and complete silver generators from Silver Solutions (see *References and Resources* section at the end of this chapter).

USING YOUR COLLOIDAL SILVER GENERATOR

- Pour distilled water into a glass (do not use plastic). Reverse-osmosis filtered water will do. For animals or plants, tap water is okay.

- If using distilled or reverse osmosis water, increase the conductivity by adding one drop of saline solution for every 4 ounces of water. Make a saline solution by adding ½ teaspoon of sea salt (do not use table salt, because it contains additives) to 2 ounces of distilled water and shake to dissolve.

- Hang the two pure silver wires over the edge of your glass into the water, and clip the two alligator clips to the outside ends of the wires (see Figure 9-1). Plug the minijack connector into your box. The light bulb should be dark, or glowing faintly. If glowing brightly, either the wires are touching or the water contains a lot of impurities. Separate the wires in the solution by 1 to 2 inches.

- If the generator is working properly, after a minute there should be clouds of charged silver particles coming off one of the silver wires while tiny bubbles form on the other wire. If these clouds of particles are not visible, then the batteries need to be replaced, there is a bad connection, or you forgot to put the 4 drops of sea salt solution in. Touch wires together to check battery and/or connection (bulb should shine brightly).

- Dosage is a matter of personal preference and experience. Some people suggest drinking a daily

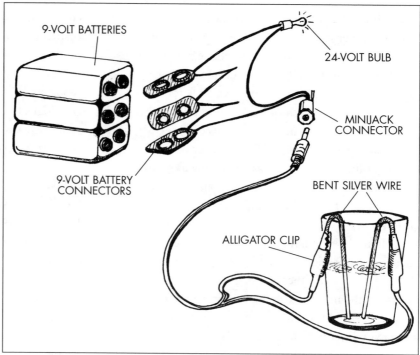

Figure 9-1. Colloidal silver generator.

16 oz glass of solution generated for 15 minutes at room temperature (roughly 10 ppm). Others suggest drinking a daily 8 oz glass of 5 ppm solution. To make a roughly 5 PPM solution using 72°F water, run the generator for four minutes with 8 ounces, six minutes with 12 ounces, or eight minutes with 16 ounces of water. More time provides a proportionate increase in solution strength. The silver generator will produce silver colloids at a faster rate at higher solution temperatures. According to Mark Metcalf, solution strength roughly doubles with each increase of 10°F (not yet verified by tests) above 72°F solution temperature. (Metcalf 1998, 3)

- After each use, clean the silver wires with a harsh plastic pot scrubber.

- For external use, silver solution may be applied to Band-Aids and compresses, or sprayed onto burns and affected skin areas.

- Best quality 9-volt batteries will last a very long time. It is preferable not to use rechargeable batteries as they only produce 7.6 volts. An alternative to using three 9-volt batteries is to purchase a 30-volt converter that can be plugged into a wall outlet.

■ Storing colloidal silver solution: Silver colloidal solutions are light sensitive. Store in brown glass bottles (beer, wine, root beer, or prune juice bottles) out of sun and florescent light, or in a dark cabinet. Do not store in refrigerator or near microwave or magnetic fields. Do not store in plastic or metal containers. Wash and rinse bottles thoroughly, with a final rinse using colloidal silver solution. If capping bottle with plastic or metal, be sure the cap does not touch the colloidal silver solution. If put into eyedropper bottle, the dropper stem must be glass.

In a pinch you could use silverware, old silver coins, or jewelry for your colloidal silver generator, although you would get other nonsilver materials in your solution because of impurities.

HEALING WITH HERBS

To take medicine only when you are sick is like digging a well only when you are thirsty—is it not already too late?

—Ch'I Po, c. 2500 B.C.

Herbs have been used for maintaining and restoring health since the dawn of civilization. Herbal healing is very easy for most westerners to accept, since it is close to the style of medicine we are accustomed to for treatment of common ailments. In fact, the Western systems of oral and topical medicine developed and evolved from herbal medicines. About one quarter of today's high-tech medicines contain active ingredients produced from herbal extracts or are chemically synthesized versions of active chemicals first identified within traditional healing herbs. For example, salicin, identified as one of the active ingredients in willow bark, was synthesized and later modified to become aspirin. Other examples include the many different ephedrine pharmaceuticals for coughs, hay fever, and asthma that are derived from active ingredients in the traditional Chinese herb, ma huang.

In some studies, herbal products clearly perform better [than their synthesized pharmaceutical counterparts]. Ginger, for example, has

been clearly shown to be superior to pharmaceutical dimenhydrinate (Dramamine) as a preventative therapy for motion sickness. I'm not saying that pharmaceuticals are bad. I'm saying that we need more research that tests herbs against pharmaceutical drugs. . . . The Green Pharmacy with its herbal remedies may, in many cases, prove to be more economical, more effective and safer—all with fewer side effects—than the pharmaceuticals.

—James A. Duke, Ph.D. *The Green Pharmacy*

Indigenous peoples across the planet continue to rely on herbs for much of their healing, just as they have for thousands of years. Traditional herbalists have found that certain combinations of herbs have synergistic effects: the beneficial effect of some combinations far exceeds the sum total effect if each herb is taken individually.

Herbs can be applied for specific diseases and symptoms; however, their benefits are often much broader and less specific than traditional pharmaceutical medicines. Many herbs are rich in antioxidants and other nutrients that boost the immune system and help the body to regenerate tissues. Some herbs, such as *Ginkgo biloba* and ginseng, have scientifically verified positive effects on overall health, vitality, brain functions, and so on, yet are not usually prescribed for specific illnesses or symptoms.

Most herbs contain numerous potentially beneficial substances. Dr. Alejandro Zaffaroni, pharmaceutical innovator and founder of a large and successful pharmaceutical company, once commented to me about the incredible complexity of these substances. "Our current understanding of their molecular chemistry is in its infancy," he said. "With today's level of technology, we can only fully understand and synthesize a tiny portion of the potentially medicinal compounds found in herbs."

The form and potency of herbal remedies varies considerably. Most remedies use chopped or ground leaves, flowers, stems, bark, seeds and/or roots blended into a tea, ointment, or powder or distilled into some liquid form. Some herbs, like ginkgo leaves, must be highly concentrated to be effective. It takes many pounds of ginkgo leaves to make a single dosage. On the other hand, medicinal factors in many herbs are so concentrated that they require small doses or must be significantly diluted. For example, a simple teaspoon of powdered echinacea or Cascara sagrada is too large a dose for most needs.

As the U.S. public has become increasingly enamored with herbal remedies, to the point where numerous herbal formulas are now available in major chain drugstores and supermarkets, the medical industry has been fighting back by promoting rather biased newspaper articles focusing on the "dangers of herbs." One such article, "Health Concerns Grow Over Herbal Aids," by Guy Gugliotta (*Washington Post*, March 19, 2000) drew a scathing reply from renowned herbalist, James A. Duke, Ph.D. According to Dr. Duke, "Two of my good friends are so alarmed by such negative press on herbs that they are stopping. That means that they and their kids, if they must medicate, will take pharmaceuticals that are at least 1000 times more likely to kill the patient. . . . The growing health concerns from Gugliotta's title are being planted and fertilized by trigger-happy journalists, pharmaceutical manufacturers and promoters, and physicians who know so little about herbs that they don't realize their pharmaceuticals are killing 140,000 Americans a year, while herbs (usually through abuse or exceeding recommended dosage) are killing fewer than 100" (Duke, April 18, 2000).

A really good herbalist might know 1,000 to 2,000 herbs, which is far more than I can describe in this text. The table on the facing page lists proven herbal remedies for common problems. For herbal dosages, preparation, and application, see the recommended literature or consult a trained herbalist/naturopathic physician.

Types of Herbal Preparations

Appearing below are general guidelines for the different methods of making herbal preparations. The amounts of herbs used, however, will vary for certain plants. For more specific information, as well as for dosage and applications, see the recommended references or consult a reputable herbalist/naturopathic doctor.

Infusions. Infusions are made by steeping herbs in near boiling water. Use this method with the delicate parts of herbs, like flowers and leaves, which contain volatile oils that may be lost if the herbal preparation is boiled. The usual proportion is 1 ounce of dried herb, or 2 ounces of fresh herb, to 1 pint of water. Steep the herbs in a glass or ceramic container (metal containers may react undesirably with the herbs) for 10 to 20 minutes. Strain and drink ½ cup three times daily (Brill and Dean 1994, 9).

Decoctions. Twigs, bark, and roots are often prepared by decoction. This method uses roughly the same proportions and dosages as infusions, and is used to extract the active components from these coarser materials. Heat the herbs in cold water and simmer in a covered glass or ceramic pot for about an hour.

> **NOTE: Consulting an herbal reference is advised because the twigs, bark, and roots of some plants should not be boiled.**

Tinctures. Tinctures are made by extracting vital components of the herbs using alcohol and water.

> **CAUTION: Never use industrial alcohol, methyl alcohol, or isopropyl alcohol (rubbing alcohol), because all three are poisonous.**

To make a tincture, combine 4 ounces of cut or powdered herb with one pint of distilled liquor. Vodka seems to be the purest liquor of choice, but rum can mask the unpleasant flavor of some herbs. Store in a tightly covered glass container and shake daily for a period of about two weeks. Strain through a fine cloth or filter and store in a tightly covered glass container. Tinctures will keep for long periods of time, as long as the alcohol is prevented from evaporating to less than 30% concentration. Dosage is typically about 1 teaspoon taken three times a day, but varies from a few drops to 2 tablespoons depending on the herb (Brill and Dean 1994, 9).

Compress. A compress is simply a dressing soaked in a hot herbal extract, such as an infusion or decoction. Compresses are typically applied to painful areas to ease discomfort and accelerate the healing of wounds, bruises, or muscle injuries.

Poultices. Poultices are herbal preparations consisting of warm, moist, ground or powdered herbs applied directly to the affected area and

HERBAL SUBSTITUTES FOR COMMON PHARMACEUTICALS

Ailment	Pharmaceutical	Herbal options
Acne	Retin-A, Tetracycline	Tea tree oil (external), calendula
Allergies	Synthetic antihistamines	Garlic, stinging nettle, *Ginkgo biloba*
Anxiety	Ativan, Xanax, Klonopin	Hops, kava-kava, valerian
Arthritic pain	Tylenol and other NSAIDs*	Cayenne (external), celery seed, ginger, turmeric
Athlete's foot	Griseofulvin	Tea tree oil, garlic, coffee grounds (all external)
Boils	Erythromycin	Tea tree oil, slippery elm (both external)
BPH (benign prostatic hyperplasia)	Hytrin, Proscar	Saw palmetto, evening primrose, stinging nettle, *Pygeum africanum, Serona repens*
Body odor	Commercial deodorants	Coriander, sage
Bronchitis	Atropine	Echinacea, garlic
Bruises	Analgesics	Arnica, St. John's wort, yarrow, plantain (all external)
Burns	Silvadene Cream	Aloe vera gel (external), calendula
Colds	Decongestants	Echinacea, ginger, lemon balm, garlic
Constipation	Laxatives	Flaxseed, psyllium, cascara sagrada
Cuts, scrapes, abscesses	Topical antibiotics	Tea tree oil, calendula, plantain, garlic (all external)
Depression (mild)	Prozac, Elavil, Trazodone, Zoloft	St. John's wort
Diarrhea	Imodium, Lomotil	Bilberry, raspberry
Dysmenorrhea (painful menstruation)	Naprosyn	Kava-kava, raspberry
Earache	Antibiotics	Echinacea, garlic, mullein
Eczema (itchy rash)	Corticosteroids	Chamomile
Atopic eczema (allergy-related rash)	Corticosteroids, sedatives, antihistamines	Evening primrose
Flu	Tylenol	Echinacea, elderberry
Gas	Mylanta, Gaviscon, Simethicone	Dill, fennel, peppermint
Gingivitis (gum inflammation)	Peridex	Chamomile, echinacea, sage
Halitosis (bad breath)	Listerine	Cardamom, parsley, peppermint
Hay fever	Antihistamines, decongestants	Stinging nettle
Headache	Aspirin, other NSAIDs*	Peppermint (external), feverfew, willow bark
Heartburn	Pepto-Bismol, Tums	Angelica, chamomile, peppermint
Hemorrhoids	Tucks	Plantain, witch hazel, calendula (all external)
Hepatitis	Interferon	Dandelion, milk thistle, turmeric
Herpes	Acyclovir	Lemon balm
High cholesterol	Mevacor	Garlic
Hives	Benadryl	Stinging nettle
Indigestion	Antacids, Reglan	Chamomile, ginger, peppermint
Insomnia	Halcion, Ativan	Chamomile, hops, lemon balm, valerian, evening primrose, kava-kava
Irregularity	Metamucil	Flaxseed, plantain, senna, psyllium
Lower back pain	Aspirin, analgesics	Cayenne (external), thyme
Male pattern baldness	Rogaine	Saw palmetto
Migraine	Cafergot, Sumatriptan, Verapamil	Feverfew
Motion sickness	Dramamine	Ginger
Nail fungus	Ketoconazole	Tea tree oil, garlic (both external)
Night blindness	Vitamin A	Bilberry
PMS	NSAIDs*, diuretics, analgesics	Chaste tree, evening primrose
Rhinitis (nasal inflamation)	Cromolyn, Vancenase	Echinacea
Shingles	Acyclovir	Cayenne (external), lemon balm
Sprain	NSAIDs*	Arnica, calendula
Stress	Diazepam	Kava-kava, valerian
Tinnitus (ringing ears)	Steroids	Ginkgo
Toothache	NSAIDs*	Cloves, willow bark
Urinary tract infection	Sulfa drugs	Cranberry, stinging nettle
Vaginitis	Clindamycin, Flagyl	Garlic, goldenseal

*NSAIDs are nonsteroidal anti-inflammatory drugs.
Source: Adapted from "Nature's Medicine—The Green Pharmacy," *Mother Earth News* (Dec/Jan 2000): 22-33, by James A. Duke, Ph.D.

covered with a linen or other cloth wrapping. Poultices are typically applied to draw out infections or irritants. Moisten the herbs with hot water or tincture. You can mix with clay or cornmeal to improve absorption.

Ointments. Cook a handful of herbs in 1 quart of light oil, such as sunflower or safflower oil. Start by cooking roots and bark (if any) for about an hour. Keep the herbs at a simmer, just below bubbling. Add leaves and flowers, cooking for another 20 minutes. Add melted beeswax, at a ratio of about 1½ ounces per pint of oil, to thicken the mixture to the desired consistency. Add the contents of a capsule of vitamin E oil, or about a teaspoon of tincture of benzoin per quart of oil, to preserve the ointment. Strain hot mixture into clean glass storage jars (Brill and Dean 1994, 9).

Gelatin capsules. For bitter herbs, or herbs that must be taken in small doses, you can choose to pack them into gelatin capsules. Empty capsules may be purchased at health food stores. Fill a bowl with powdered herbs and scoop the capsule halves through the herbs to fill. Tap the filled capsules to remove powders from the outside.

Powerful Herbal Combinations for Better Health

The following formulas have been shown to possess exceptional healing properties. The anticancer formulas can be great for restoring the body's overall level of health and vitality and should not be restricted to just fighting cancers and tumors. Many herbal combinations have synergistic effects, providing far greater benefits than the same herbs taken separately and at different times.

The parasite, liver, and kidney cleanses described below can be extremely beneficial for improving and maintaining health. The liver, kidneys, and colon are the body's main organs for purifying the blood, processing chemicals and drugs, and eliminating toxins. We are surrounded by toxins. Common chemicals, such as antifreeze, rubbing alcohol, and paint thinner are easily absorbed through our skin, yet difficult to purge from the body. We produce an average of about 9,000 new chemicals each year.

These new molecular combinations do not exist in nature, and 90% of them are carcinogenic. Herbal remedies can give your body a badly needed boost in its fight against chemical invaders.

Rene Caisse's "essiac" (also known as Caisse's tea), Jason Winters's herb tea, and Harry Hoxsey's herbal cancer treatments are well-known herbal formulas credited with thousands of cases of recovery from cancer. These herbal remedies work primarily by cleansing the body of toxins and restoring its natural balance, so that the immune system can heal tumors and other illnesses. Current research indicates that they may also contain compounds that target cancerous cells and tumors. Thousands of personal testimonials make it clear that the regular use of these herbal formulas can be extremely beneficial for helping the body to maintain health or heal from serious illnesses like cancer. Because herbs cannot be patented, several companies package and sell similar herbal combinations that may, or may not, work equally well.

John Robbins's book, *Reclaiming Our Health: Exploding the Medical Myth and Embracing the Source of True Healing*, contains an excellent account of the systematic persecution (including multiple arrests and a public slander campaign) of both Rene Caisse and Harry Hoxsey for helping people to heal cancer using their herbal formulas. This persecution was primarily funded by major pharmaceutical corporations, which have billions of dollars invested in selling patented (both toxic and expensive) chemotherapy drugs.

> In 1953, Benedict F. Fitzgerald, Jr., special counsel to the U.S. Senate Commerce Committee, conducted an in-depth investigation to determine whether a conspiracy existed to suppress Hoxsey's and other innovative cancer treatments. The Fitzgerald report, released on August 3, 1953, declared that a conspiracy had indeed been undertaken by the AMA, the National Cancer Institute, and the FDA to suppress a fair investigation of Hoxsey's methods.
>
> —John Robbins, *Reclaiming Our Health: Exploding the Medical Myth and Embracing the Source of True Healing*

Caisse's Tea (Essiac)

Dr. Charles Brusch, M.D., President John F. Kennedy's personal physician, wrote, "I endorse this therapy even today, for I have in fact cured my own cancer, the original site of which was the lower bowel, through essiac alone."

In 1922, Canadian nurse Rene Caisse obtained an Ojibwa medicine man's herbal formula. It was given to her by an 80-year-old patient who claimed that it had healed her of advanced breast cancer 30 years earlier. The formula, which was subsequently named essiac (essiac is Caisse spelled backwards) or Caisse's Tea, was described as, "A holy drink that would purify the body and place it back in balance with the Great Spirit." Caisse did little with the formula until 1924, when her aunt developed stomach and liver cancer and was given six months to live. Caisse received permission from her aunt's physician to administer the herbal formula. Rene later said, "My aunt lived for 21 years after being given up by the medical profession. There was no recurrence of cancer."

Essiac is not just an herbal treatment for cancer, but has been credited with restoring health for a variety of ailments. For example, Cynthia Olsen, author of *Essiac: A Native Herbal Cancer Remedy*, participated in a Native American program to administer essiac to Hopi Indians suffering from a variety of ailments. Two testimonials from her book regarding the effects of essiac in treating other illnesses are reproduced below.

> *Hopi Grandmother: She is in her late fifties and was recently diagnosed with diabetes. She is on the doctor's medicine. She started taking essiac several months ago. One of her daughters prepares a tea with essiac and distilled water in the morning and at bedtime. When the doctor tested her blood sugar recently, it had gone from over 300 to 130. Her energy is good. She enjoys taking the essiac because it makes her feel better. Her legs get swollen at times, so she elevates them during the day and when she goes to bed. She feels the essiac helps to keep the swelling down (Olsen 1998, 119).*

> *R.M.: "In August of 1993, I was diagnosed with chronic late stage hepatitis C. I was constantly fatigued and suffering chronic pain in the liver region. I lost 30 pounds and my eyes were dull and sunken back into my head. The doctors knew how to treat hepatitis 'A' and 'B', but knew very little about 'C'. They tried experimental drugs that were of little success. They told me my only alternative was a liver transplant. A friend of mine suggested I try essiac tea. I tried it and noticed an immediate reduction in pain. As I continued to take essiac, I began to regain my weight and feel less depressed. My pain did not disappear, but was reduced 90%, and my health improved overall with lab results to prove it. I still have the virus, but my immune system is stronger, which gives me a quality of life I would not have had if I hadn't tried essiac" (Olsen 1998, 28).*

You can purchase essiac tablets, premixed essiac tea or the bulk essiac herbs from many health food stores. Alternately, you may harvest your own herbs, and prepare the tea following Rene Caisse's instructions appearing in the next section.

ESSIAC RECIPE

Yield: 8 cups of dry mix.

- Thoroughly mix 6.5 cups of burdock root (cut), 16 ounces (scale weight) of powdered sheep sorrel, 4.0 ounces (scale weight) of powdered slippery elm bark, and 1.0 ounce (scale weight) of turkey rhubarb root (powdered).
- Presterilize storage containers. Boil the containers for ten minutes in water with a little food-grade peroxide or Clorox bleach.
- Measure one gallon of pure, nonchlorinated drinking water for each four cups of dry mix to be prepared. Bring the water to a rolling boil in a clean stainless steel or glass pot.
- Stir dry ingredients into boiling water. Replace lid and continue boiling for ten minutes at reduced heat.
- Remove from heat. Scrape down herbs stuck to sides of pot and stir thoroughly. Cover pot and allow to cool at room temperature for six hours.

Stir thoroughly and let sit for another 6 hours (total of 12 hours sitting).

- Bring mixture to the boiling point, and then remove from heat.
- Strain mixture through a sterile strainer into a sterile pot. Clean first pot and strainer. Strain mixture a second time back into first pot.
- Immediately pour hot liquid into sterile containers. Allow containers to cool, and then refrigerate.
- Discard tea if mold starts to grow inside the container.

(Olsen 1996, 59)

USING ESSIAC TO TREAT CANCER OR AIDS

- Take 2 ounces, twice daily, at least two hours before or after eating. Tea may be diluted with 2 ounces of pure water. Ideally, take tea in the morning, at least two hours prior to eating, and take at bedtime on an empty stomach (at least two hours after eating). Do not microwave.
- Before pouring tea from container, shake gently to mix any sediment that has settled in the container.

(Olsen 1996, 61)

USING ESSIAC AS AN HERBAL SUPPLEMENT AND PREVENTATIVE

Take 2 ounces, once daily. Tea may be diluted with two ounces of pure water. Take at bedtime on an empty stomach (at least two hours after eating) or take in the morning at least two hours prior to eating. Do not microwave.

Before pouring tea from container, shake gently to mix any sediment that has settled in the container (Olsen 1996, 60).

SIDE EFFECTS

Side effects are rare. Nausea and indigestion are generally caused by eating or drinking too soon after taking essiac. Sometimes severe intestinal or digestive discomfort is caused by the body's rapid elimination of toxins into the colon. If this occurs, stop taking the tea for several days, and then begin taking it again in ½-ounce doses every other day. Gradually decrease

the interval and increase the dosage to the standard treatment levels (Olsen 1996, 61).

Jason Winters' Herbal Tea

An example of the synergistic effect of herbs is related in *Killing Cancer: The Jason Winters Story* by Benjamin R. Smythe.

Jason Winters lived life on the edge. He was an adventurer, Hollywood stuntman, and womanizer. Jason loved to party, confessing to consuming a pint of whiskey on a typical day. In 1978 a large, cancerous growth appeared on the side of Jason's neck. Normal cancer treatments, including radiation and chemotherapy, were not successful in eliminating the cancerous growth and Jason was given 90 days to live. When he was told that his only chance was radical surgery that would remove his tongue and much of his jaw, Jason became despondent and desperate. Winters said he sat on the edge of his London hospital bed and sobbed. It was then that he received a most unexpected visitor, Prince Charles. Winters said, "He was there visiting a friend, and when he passed by my room, he found me crying. I was completely terrified of dying."

With the help of Prince Charles and the Archbishop of Canterbury, Winters identified healing herbs mentioned in the Bible and the Hindu Bhagavad Gita, which he hoped would heal his cancer. When these herbs failed to heal his cancer, he remembered that the American Indians he had met on the set of Hollywood Westerns had used sage for cleansing and healing. Unfortunately, the sage also failed to heal his cancer. In desperation, Jason mixed all of these herbs together in a tea. As his tumor began to shrink in size, Jason consumed "buckets" of his new formula. The cancer left his body and today he is in perfect health. Jason considers his daily consumption of this herbal tea formula a major factor in maintaining outstanding health, claiming not to have had as much as a cold in the past 15 years.

Jason Winters credits his recovery from terminal cancer and his subsequent return to a state of exceptional health to the daily consumption of his herbal tea formula. Winters's tea consists of red clover flowers, gotu kola, Indian sage leaves, and an Asian herb he refers to as "herbalene." Even if cancer does not run in your family, I would recommend making essiac tea and/or Jason Winters's tea a part of your regular diet. Personally, I have started to use essiac tea for two-week periods of self-cleansing and the milder, more pleasant tasting Jason Winters tea as a daily beverage. His tea is available, along with other healing herbs, from his web site at www.sirjasonwinters.com.

Dr. Clark's Herbal Parasite Cleanse

A couple of years ago, my cat was dying. She was nothing but skin and bones. I had taken her to the vet and she was diagnosed with a thyroid condition and probably had worms. We bought some pills from the local vet to try deworming her, but the vet's worm pills contained a highly toxic substance, toluene. These toxic pills were supposed to kill the worms before they killed the cat. My cat was too sick to take the pills, so we decided to try Hulda's herbal pet parasite program instead. It worked beautifully, returning my cat to more than double her weight in just two weeks' time. After the outstanding results with our cat, we decided to try the parasite program on ourselves. My wife had undergone extensive medical tests for colon problems. The diagnosis was not clear, but the symptoms indicated a potentially serious situation. Using Hulda's parasite program, her condition cleared up completely within a couple of weeks. My mother-in-law, who was born in the highlands of Indonesia, had been in and out of hospitals and medical clinics for two years, trying to diagnose severe heart palpitations combined with digestive problems. When she tried the parasite program, her condition also cleared up! In my own case, even though I felt perfectly healthy, when I used the parasite herbs, a tapeworm appeared in my stools.

I once believed that parasites are just a health problem in Third World countries. The research of Hulda Regehr Clark, Ph.D., presents compelling evidence linking the presence of parasites with numerous Western diseases, including cancer and AIDS. Her tests indicate that roughly two-thirds of Americans, and nearly all people with pets, have parasites in their bodies. Dr. Clark has helped many patients improve or cure a wide variety of diseases ranging from AIDS and arthritis to cancer, by using various herbal remedies and eliminating toxins from the patient's diet and environment.

Dr. Clark studied biophysics and cellular physiology at McGill University and the University of Minnesota, receiving her doctorate degree in physiology in 1958. For specific details on her research, or if you are currently suffering from a serious illness, I highly recommend that you pick up a copy of Dr. Clark's book *The Cure for All Diseases* or her new book *The Cure for All Advanced Cancers*. I do not believe that her program will cure all diseases in all cases (it neglects the mind-body factor), but I do believe that she has uncovered a number of extremely significant factors that could benefit the health of many people. Her most recent book, *The Cure for Advanced Cancers*, boasts a 95% success rate treating advanced cancers (so-called "terminal" stage four and five cancers).

The following herbal parasite cleanse, kidney cleanse, and liver cleanses are from Dr. Clark's books. Clark does not claim credit for inventing these formulas, which were developed by herbalists. From her practical experience using hundreds of different herbal formulas, she has found that the following are particularly effective. The kidneys, colon, and liver are the body's primary organs for processing and removing toxic wastes from the blood. Keeping these organs healthy and clean are critical for maintaining optimum health. I cannot do justice to Dr. Clark's work in the few pages that follow, so I urge you to pick up one of her books to assist you in your pursuit of good health.

If you are unable to find the listed parasite herbs, fasting or eating several crushed raw garlic cloves each day for one or two weeks will also help the body to purge parasites. By consuming parasite herbs on an empty stomach, the parasites are forced to feed on the herbs instead of food in your system.

Dr. Clark's program is a great herbal treatment combined with eliminating toxins from your environment and food, which may restore balance in your body's immune system, helping it to fight more effectively against almost any disease. The parasite program consists of taking gradually increasing dosages of black walnut tincture, ground clove capsules, and wormwood capsules over a two-week period followed by regular doses of these herbs to keep from becoming reinfected with parasites. She also recommends the use of an electronic device, which she refers to as a "Zapper," which electronically destroys parasites living in different parts of the body. Her book contains basic instructions for building a low-cost Zapper and summarizes research that she has completed with herbs, the Zapper, and other devices. You can purchase these materials from health food stores, herbal suppliers, Dr. Clark's web site (www.drclark.ch), or the Self-Health Resource Center. Zappers are available from a variety of sources found on the Internet.

CAUTION: If you plan to build your own zapper, check the internet for a correction to the wiring connections described in Dr. Clark's **The Cure for All Diseases.**

PARASITE PROGRAM QUICK REFERENCE CHART

Day	Black walnut hull tincture — Drops 1 time per day on empty stomach (before a meal)	Wormwood capsule (dose, 200–300 mg) — Capsules 1 time per day on empty stomach (before a meal)	Clove capsule (dose, size 0 or 00) — Capsules 3 times per day (at mealtimes)
1	1	1	1,1,1
2	2	1	2,2,2
3	3	2	3,3,3
4	4	2	3,3,3
5	5	3	3,3,3
6	2 tsp.	3	3,3,3
7	(Now once a week)	4	3,3,3
8		4	3,3,3
9		5	3,3,3
10		5	3,3,3
11		6	3,3,3
12		6	(Now once a week)
13	2 tsp.	7	
14		7	
15		7	
16		7	
17		(Now once a week)	
18			3,3,3

You may wish to take ornithine (available at most health food stores) at bedtime for insomnia. Even if you do not suffer from insomnia now, you may when you kill parasites. If you have pets, I recommend that you refer to Dr. Clark's book for the pet parasite program (the doses are significantly different). You will be continually reinfected with parasites from your pets, unless you get yourself and your pets on the parasite maintenance program.

BLACK WALNUT HULL TINCTURE RECIPE

- Use your largest enamel or ceramic (not stainless steel, nor aluminum) cooking pot, preferably at least 10 quarts.
- Black walnuts in the hull, each still at least 50% green, enough to fill the pot to the top.
- Grain alcohol (or vodka), about 50% strength, enough to cover the walnuts. (*Never use rubbing alcohol—it's toxic!*)
- ½ tsp. powdered vitamin C.
- Plastic wrap or cellophane.
- Glass jars or bottles.

The black walnut tree produces large green balls in the fall. The walnut is inside, but you will use the whole ball, uncracked, since the active ingredient is in the green outer hull. Rinse the walnuts carefully, put them in the pot, and cover them with the alcohol. Sprinkle with half the vitamin C. Seal with plastic wrap and cover. Let sit for three days. Pour into glass jars, discarding walnuts, and divide the remaining vitamin C amongst the jars. If the glass jar has a metal lid, first put plastic wrap over the top before screwing on the lid. The potency of the tincture remains strong for several years if it is unopened, even if it darkens. The alcohol is a preservative, preventing bacterial growth. (Adapted from *The Cure for All Diseases* by Hulda Regehr Clark, Ph.D., N.D., 1995: 338–344, 543.)

Kidney Cleanse

Dr. Clark recommends that you clean your kidneys at least twice a year. The following recipe dissolves crystals and stones inside the kidneys and boosts kidney function. The kidney cleanse should be started after the initial two-week period of the parasite program, to ensure that parasites are eliminated from the kidneys prior to starting the cleanse.

KIDNEY HERBS

- ½ cup dried hydrangea root
- ½ cup gravel root
- ½ cup marshmallow root
- 4 bunches of fresh parsley
- Goldenrod tincture (leave this out of the recipe if you are allergic to it)
- Ginger capsules
- Uva ursi capsules
- Vegetable glycerin
- 8 ounces black cherry concentrate
- Vitamin B6, 250 mg
- Magnesium oxide tablets, 300 mg

PROCEDURE

Measure ¼ cup of each root and set them to soak together in 10 cups of cold tap water, using a nonmetal container and a nonmetal lid (a dinner plate will do). After four hours (or overnight) add 8 ounces of black cherry concentrate, heat to boiling, and simmer for 20 minutes. Drink ¼ cup as soon as it is cool enough. Pour the rest through a bamboo strainer into a sterile pint jar (glass) and several freezable containers. Refrigerate the glass jar.

Rinse the fresh parsley, and boil in 1 quart of water for three minutes. Drink ¼ cup when cool enough. Refrigerate 1 pint and freeze 1 pint. Throw away the parsley.

Save the roots after the first boiling, storing them in the freezer. After 13 days when your supply runs low, boil the same roots a second time, but add only 6 cups water and simmer only 10 minutes. This will last another eight days, for a total of three weeks. You can cook the roots a third time if you wish, but the recipe gets less potent. If your problem is severe, cook them only twice.

DOSE

Each morning, pour together ¾ cup of the root mixture and ½ cup parsley water, filling a large mug. Add 20 drops of goldenrod tincture and 1 tablespoon glycerin. Drink this mixture in proportionate doses throughout the day. Keep cold. *Do not drink it all at once:* you will get a stomachache and feel pressure in your bladder. If your stomach is very sensitive, start on half this dose.

Also take:

- Ginger capsules: one with each meal (3 per day)
- Uva ursi capsules: one with breakfast and two with supper
- Vitamin B6 (250 mg): one a day
- Magnesium oxide (300 mg): one a day

Take these supplements just before a meal to avoid burping.

After three weeks, repeat with fresh herbs. You need to do the kidney cleanse for six weeks to get good results, and longer for severe problems.

This herbal tea, as well as the parsley, can easily spoil. Heat it to boiling every fourth day if it is being stored in the refrigerator, because boiling resterilizes it. If you sterilize it in the morning (in a glass container), you can take it to work without refrigerating it. When you order herbs, be careful! Herb companies are not all the same! These roots should have a strong fragrance. If the ones you buy are barely fragrant, they have lost their active ingredients and you should switch to a different supplier. Fresh roots can be used. Do not use powder. (Adapted from *The Cure for All Diseases* by Hulda Regehr Clark, Ph.D., N.D., 1995: 549–551.)

Liver Cleanse

Many naturopaths believe that using this program to cleanse the liver bile ducts is one of the most powerful methods that you can use to boost your health. Dr. Clark stresses that the first two weeks of the parasite program should be completed prior to starting the liver cleanse. For best results, you should also complete the kidney cleanse and any needed dental work prior to starting the liver cleanse. Cleanse your liver twice a year for health maintenance.

The liver is full of bilary tubes that channel bile to a large tube called the common bile duct. Bile is essential for proper digestion and assimilation of food. Over time, these tubes get choked up with various deposits and chunks of debris, much like a garden hose filled with gravel. Eventually, these deposits may calcify into "stones." Naturally, the liver can't perform its function properly when it is all choked up with debris. This program flushes out the debris from the liver ducts. It accomplishes this feat through three separate phases. First, eat no fat on day one of the program to force the liver to store up a considerable amount of bile. Second, drink the Epsom salt solutions to make the liver bile ducts swell to a larger size and release their stranglehold on the debris stuck inside. Third, drink an olive oil and grapefruit juice mixture; the high fat content in the olive oil causes the liver to dump the stored bile, flushing the stones and other debris from the bile ducts.

PROCEDURE

Day 1: Choose a day such as Saturday for the cleanse, because you should rest the next day. Take no medicines, vitamins, or pills that you can do without: they could prevent success. Stop the parasite program and kidney herbs, too, the day before. Eat a no-fat breakfast and lunch such as cooked cereal with fruit, fruit juice, bread and preserves or honey (no butter or milk), baked potato or other vegetables with salt only. This allows the bile to build up and develop pressure in the liver. Higher pressure pushes out more stones.

2:00 p.m.: Do not eat or drink after 2 p.m. If you break this rule you could feel quite ill later. Get your Epsom salts ready. Dissolve 4 tablespoons in 3 cups water and pour mixture into a jar. This makes four servings, ¾ cup each. Set the jar in the refrigerator to get ice cold (this is for convenience and taste only).

6:00 p.m.: Drink one serving (¾ cup) of the ice-cold Epsom salts. If you did not prepare this ahead of time, mix 1 tablespoon in ¾ cup water now. You can add ⅛ tsp. vitamin C powder to improve the taste. You can also drink a few mouthfuls of water afterwards or rinse your mouth. Get the olive oil and grapefruit out to warm up.

8:00 p.m.: Drink another ¾ cup of Epsom salts. You haven't eaten since two o'clock, but you won't feel hungry. Get your bedtime chores done. The timing is critical for success; don't be more than 10 minutes early or late.

9:45 p.m.: Pour ½ cup (measured) olive oil into the pint jar. Squeeze the juice of one fresh grapefruit into the measuring cup. Remove pulp with fork. You should have at least ½ cup. A little more (up to ¾ cup) is best. You can top it up with lemonade. Add this to the olive oil. Close the jar tightly with the lid and shake hard until watery (only fresh grapefruit juice does this). The purpose of the grapefruit juice is to help the olive oil go down. It does a surprisingly good job of making the olive oil palatable. Now visit the bathroom one or more times, even if it makes you late for your ten o'clock drink. Don't be more than 15 minutes late.

10:00 p.m.: Drink the olive oil and grapefruit juice mixture. Take 4 ornithine capsules with the first sips to make sure you will sleep through the night. Take 8 if you already suffer from insomnia. Drinking through a large plastic straw helps it go down easier. You may use ketchup, cinnamon, or brown sugar to chase it down between sips. Take it to your bedside if you want, but drink it standing up. Get it down within 5 minutes (15 minutes for very elderly or weak persons). *Lie down immediately.* You might fail to get stones out if you don't. The sooner you lie down, the more stones you will get out. Be ready for bed ahead of time. Don't clean up the kitchen, for instance, before you go to bed. As soon as the drink is down walk to your bed and lie down flat on your back with your head up high on the pillow. Try to think about what is happening in the liver. Try to keep perfectly still for at least 20 minutes. You may feel a train of stones traveling along the bile ducts like marbles. There is no pain because the bile duct valves are wide open (thank you, Epsom salts!). *Go to sleep*; you may fail to get stones out if you don't.

Next morning: Upon awakening take your third dose of Epsom salts. If you have indigestion or nausea wait until it is gone before drinking the Epsom salts. You can go back to bed if you wish. Don't take this potion before 6:00 a.m.

2 hours later: Take your fourth (the last) dose of Epsom salts. Drink ¾ cup of the mixture. You can go back to bed.

After 2 more hours: You can eat now. Start with fruit juice. Half an hour later eat fruit. One hour later you can eat regular food but keep it light. By suppertime you should feel recovered.

Expect diarrhea in the morning of day two, so do not stray too far from a toilet. You may find gallstones in the toilet with the bowel movement. Look for the green kind since this is proof that they are genuine gallstones, not food residue. Only bile from the liver is pea green. The first cleanse may rid you of allergies or bursitis or upper back pains for a few days, but as the stones from the rear travel forward, the same symptoms might return. You can repeat cleanses at two-week intervals. Never cleanse when you are ill. Sometimes the bile ducts are full of cholesterol crystals that did not form into round stones. They appear as a "chaff" floating on top of the toilet bowl water. It may be tan-colored, harboring millions of tiny white crystals. Cleansing this chaff is just as important as purging stones.

How safe is the liver cleanse? In Dr. Clark's opinion, it is very safe. Her opinion is based on over 500 cases, including many persons in their seventies and eighties. None went to the hospital; none even reported pain. The cleanse made some people feel quite ill for one or two days afterwards, but in every one of these cases the maintenance parasite program had been neglected. This is why the instructions direct you to complete the parasite and kidney rinse programs first. (Adapted from *The Cure for All Diseases* by Hulda Regehr Clark, Ph.D., N.D., 1995: 553-558.)

DETOXIFICATION

Naturopathic Healing

When I met Jackie, she was often bedridden for days at a time. She suffered from severe allergies and asthma. She had spent many days at the local hospital and relied upon a high-tech machine, called a "nebulizer," to treat the air in her bedroom. She spent huge amounts of time in her bedroom, afraid to leave the proximity of her nebulizer. A friend told her about a naturopathic doctor, named M. O. Garten, who had worked wonders with many patients suffering from severe medical problems that were not responding to standard medical treatments. Dr. Garten started Jackie on a regimen of cleansing fasts, chiropractic manipulation, and massages. Within a few weeks, Jackie felt like a new person. The debilitating asthma attacks and severe allergies had totally disappeared.

Many different healing philosophies point to a build-up of toxic compounds within our bodies as one of the primary factors contributing to a compromised immune system and the inability to fight off invading diseases. The modern world is filled with thousands of carcinogenic chemicals and pollutants that did not even exist a century ago. Cancer rates now grow nearly exponentially. Why do some people succumb to these carcinogens while others do not? It appears to be a combination of many different factors, such as diet, genetics, environment, and mental disposition. According to naturopathic doctors, many "inherited" conditions may be improved or totally eliminated through diet, exercise, body manipulation, and fasting.

Naturopathic medicine includes a wide variety of techniques and therapies designed to cleanse the body of toxins and help restore the body's natural immune and healing mechanisms. Among these therapies are fasting and organ cleanses for detoxification, herbal remedies, massage, osteopathic and chiropractic manipulation, diet and nutrition, and stretching and exercise. This section focuses on the use of fasts for internal cleansing and rebalancing of the body.

Fasting

The theory behind fasting was explained to me as follows: When a body is digesting food, it does a poor job of cleaning toxic wastes and deposits out of its different systems. A fast gives the autonomic nervous system, which controls digestion and other automatic processes, the chance to focus on internal cleansing. A fast gives the body a chance to "spring clean" and helps it to return the immune system to peak performance. In addition, the fasting body scavenges raw materials from places such as cholesterol deposits, tumors, and calcified deposits in the joints for use in other parts of the body. Normally the body's natural cleansing cycle dumps toxins into the colon in the morning. In the afternoon, if you are fasting, the body will be hungry and will try to absorb what it can from the colon. Unless the colon is cleansed, the body will reabsorb toxins, which may produce headaches and nausea. Because you are not eating anything to push the toxins out of the colon, you should do an enema or drink some bulk nonnutritive fiber, like psyllium, to cleanse the colon.

Medical practitioners from Hippocrates to modern "Medical Deities" (M.D.) have advocated the health benefits of the fast. In Western medicine, a systematic fasting cure was first developed by the Austrian farmer Johann Schroth (1798–1856). Schroth developed an enlarged and crippled knee as a result of being kicked by a horse (Garten 1967, 60). The farmer had observed injured animals refusing all food until cured. Using fasting and the application of hot packs, Schroth rapidly restored his crippled leg to its former healthy condition. The Schroth fasting cure became famous, and the country of Austria currently maintains a state-supported Schroth Institute. Fasts tend to dissolve fatty cholesterol deposits from artery walls, help to remove arthritis-causing uric acid and calcium deposits from joints, and boost the immune system by lowering the levels of toxins in the body.

In August of 1954, ten members of the Swedish Vegetarian Society marched 325 miles from Goeteburg to Stockholm to publicize the health benefits of the fast and to demonstrate its relative safety. After marching an average of 32.5 miles per day for ten days straight, eating no food and drinking nothing but spring water, the fasters arrived in Stockholm in excellent health and remarkable physical condition (Garten 1967, 83). If you are ever stuck without food for a prolonged period of time, remember these results! Cleanse your colon and you may be able to perform remarkably well for prolonged periods without food.

FASTING GUIDELINES

Water fasts, with nothing taken in except for water or herb teas, seem to have the best and quickest long-term health effects. For the first fast, it may be easier to complete a juice fast than a water fast. Up to 3 quarts a day of fruit or vegetable juices may be taken to help maintain energy levels. Dr. Garten advises against extending juice fasts beyond a few days for two reasons. First, because juices are partial foods, the stomach continues to manufacture secretions such as hydrochloric acid. In the absence of solid foods, the acid might begin to digest the stomach wall itself, resulting in ulcers.

Second, because digestive secretions (even partial) are present, hunger sensations are apt to be prolonged. The drinking of juices will actually contribute to the continuance of hunger pangs!

Underweight people should not fast for more than 3 days at a time, with intervals of constructive diets between fasts. Underweight people often find that a fast restores balance to the body and actually enables them to gain weight after the fast is over. A typical shorter fast is 5 or 6 days. Prolonged fasts, on the order of 14 to 30 days, are most effective for treating serious disorders. Successive shorter fasts can be used to obtain similar results, if necessary. The European Fasting Institute tries to limit fasts to periods of no more than 21 days. I like to do one or two 5-day juice fasts each year to maintain my health, but have found the most significant improvements when I did a 14-day fast.

If the fast is of short duration, up to six days, don't be too concerned over the details of breaking the fast, but try to avoid heavy foods like meat or dairy products. The breaking of longer fasts, especially water fasts, is more important since the body has fully shut down the digestive processes. As a general rule, each five days of complete food abstinence requires one day of fruit or vegetable juice consumption before taking solid foods. Start your first day on solid food with some fruit for breakfast. Include generous portions of raw vegetables with your noon and evening meals and try to avoid heavy foods such as meat and dairy products. There are no hard and fast rules, but following these guidelines should help make your fasting experience a positive one.

ENEMAS

This is not everybody's favorite topic, at least not mine! If you find enemas distasteful, you may substitute the use of a bulk intestinal cleanser, such as psyllium seed, to purge your colon during a fast (see a natural healing book or the cleanser's package for instructions). During a fast, if you are not using an herbal colon cleanse, an enema should be taken once a day at the beginning. Gradually it may be reduced to once every two days, then twice a week until no longer needed. A standard 2-quart enema bag, available at any drugstore, is fine. Use bottled spring water if your tap water is heavily chlorinated. Dissolve 2 tablespoons of molasses, honey, or Epsom salts in 2 quarts of warm (body temperature) water, then fill your enema bag with this mixture. Some naturopaths recommend adding ½ cup pineapple juice or the juice of three lemons to this mixture.

Hang the bag about 2½ feet above where you will be positioned. Lubricate the tip with some vitamin E oil, aloe vera juice, or vegetable oil, then gently insert the tip into the rectum and lie on your back on the floor, on your side, or kneel with your head down. Most enema bags will have a clamp to control the rate of fluid entrance into your colon. If not, you can fold the tube or pinch it with your fingers. Breathe deeply as you allow the fluid to enter your colon slowly. If the pressure is uncomfortable, temporarily shut off the fluid flow and continue to breathe deeply. Resume the fluid introduction when you feel the pressure subside. There are many pockets and convolutions in the colon. To help the fluid work around the kinks in your intestine, try firmly massaging your stomach, while both legs are raised against an object or simply in the air. At the start, a 2-quart enema may be too much to handle, but should be no problem once most of the fecal matter has been evacuated.

COFFEE ENEMA

A variation on the standard enema is the coffee enema. During WWI, a nurse discovered that patients who received coffee grounds in their enemas recovered from serious wounds at a much faster rate than those who received regular enemas. Scientific research has found that the coffee enema stimulates the liver and the gall bladder to dump their toxins into the colon, where they are flushed away. A healthy, fully functioning liver is important for proper digestion, assimilation of food, and for detoxifying the body. Coffee enemas have been employed to help heal cancer patients and sufferers of many degenerative diseases.

To make the coffee enema, boil 6 heaping tablespoons of ground coffee (do not use instant) in 2 quarts of water (spring, filtered, or distilled) for 15 minutes. Cool to a comfortable temperature and strain. Use only 1 pint at a time and refrigerate the rest for later use. The best position to assume when receiving the enema is "head down and tail up." After the liquid has been received, roll onto your right side and hold the solution in your body for 15 minutes before allowing the liquid to be expelled. Do not be concerned if the liquid is not expelled after fifteen minutes. Simply stand up and move around as usual until you feel the urge to expel the fluid.

CAUTION: Do not use coffee enemas for more than six weeks at a time.

SUPPLEMENTS AND FOOD

One positive feature of the heavily centralized modern business of food production and distribution is the fact that we now have access to fresh fruits and vegetables during all seasons, not just when they are in season in our particular local area. However, when you ask any older person if the fruits and vegetables we buy in the supermarket taste as good as the fresh produce they used to buy direct from farmers, you will usually get a definitive "No!" The giant agribusinesses responsible for producing most of the food found in our supermarkets are primarily concerned with productivity and profit margins, not optimum nutrition. There are many different trace minerals and other nutrients that contribute to the composition of healthy, nutritive, natural soil. Profit-centered agribusiness usually concerns itself with replacing nitrogen, phosphorous and potassium in the soil to keep up maximum vegetable production, but does not concern itself with replenishing dozens of other micronutrients. These nutrients are essential for maintaining healthy bodies, and are often lacking in fresh fruits and vegetables due to soil depletion. When crops are grown with modern chemical intensive methods, the natural microbial action in the soil is either destroyed or severely hampered. In natural systems, these microbes (numbering as many as six billion in a single teaspoon of healthy humus) release organic acids that dissolve the minerals and other micro-nutrients in the soils into a form that is readily assimilated by growing plants. Without a healthy microbial presence in the soil, plants will be lacking in micro-nutrients, even when provided with chemical fertilizers. For these reasons, I highly recommend the use of dietary supplements and/or a wide variety of organic produce to ensure that you get proper nutrients in your diet.

For the better part of this century, scientists have studied geographical groups of people who exhibit norms for excellent health in their 70s to 90s and include productive elders in the 100- to 120-year-old range. These people tend to live in dry climates, at high altitude, and downstream from glaciated peaks. Their fields are irrigated with water called "glacial milk," because of its milky color due to ground-up rocks (minerals) from the grinding action of the glaciers. This glacial milk constantly replenishes the minerals in the soil. Due to modern hydroelectric and flood control dams, huge tracts of fertile farmland that used to receive mineral replenishment from yearly floods, no longer flood. The food we buy as "fresh" not only lacks these minerals, it is stored for months in cold warehouses, heavily sprayed with pesticides and fungicides, and genetically selected for durability over taste and nutrition. It is no wonder that the nutritive value of today's average supermarket produce is not up to par.

Not all supplements are created equal! In order for our bodies to take advantage of the nutritive value of a supplement, it must be in a form that our body can assimilate. Our bodies are designed to receive sustenance from food, not rocks. Human beings cannot survive eating ground up rocks. Most vitamins, minerals, and other nutrients must be absorbed from food or food-based supplements. Many multivitamin and mineral formulations contain synthetic vitamins and ground-up minerals, which pass through the body without doing much

good. The best supplements use food-based nutrients, that is to say, that the supplements were made from plant or animal sources grown on highly enriched soils and feeds, to create vitamins and minerals in easily assimilated forms. Talk to your local health food expert, nutritionist (choose one who is familiar with alternative healing), or naturopathic doctor for recommendations on specific brands and supplements for particular uses.

HOMEOPATHY

Since croup is thought to be viral in origin, there is no conventional pharmaceutical treatment for this illness. However, there are several homeopathic remedies that can alleviate the symptoms of croup, often within 1 to 5 minutes. Indeed, one of the most skeptical parents I have known, a pediatrician, became an instant convert to homeopathy after seeing his child respond immediately to Aconite for croup.
—Wayne B. Jonas, M.D., and Jennifer Jacobs, M.D., M.P.H., *Healing with Homeopathy: The Doctor's Guide*

Homeopathy is a system of healing based on the principle of stimulating the body's natural healing processes. Unlike most allopathic medicines, which chemically target specific diseases or symptoms, homeopathy appears to enhance healing responses from within the body's own immune system. Homeopathic remedies are useful for treating a wide variety of illnesses and symptoms. After waning in popularity during the earlier part of this century, homeopathy has seen a resurgence of popularity, especially in Europe, Latin America, and parts of Asia. For example, in France, Germany, and Great Britain, most pharmacies stock homeopathic medicines, roughly one third of the populace uses them, and about one third of physicians refer patients for homeopathic treatment. The low cost of homeopathic medicines and the ease of self-medication have contributed to the high growth rate of homeopathy in many developing countries where there is limited access to high-tech, Western-style medicine.

The Origins of Homeopathy

The original system of homeopathy was developed by Samuel Christian Hahnemann, between 1790 and his death in 1843. It was the most scientifically developed healing system of its day, relying on systematic observation and experimentation to develop the series of homeopathic remedies. Samuel had stumbled on one of the foundations of homeopathy while attempting to disprove a British herbalist's claims that quinine was an effective antimalaria drug because it was "bitter and astringent." He reasoned that he knew of several other drugs that were far more bitter and astringent than quinine, yet were of no value against malaria. He devised an experiment in which he medicated himself with quinine to study its effects, even though he had never been exposed to malaria. What he found was that the quinine produced symptoms similar to malaria when taken by people who did not have malaria.

Based on his initial experiments, Hahnemann hypothesized that a drug is therapeutic if it produces symptoms in a person without the disease that are similar to those in a person suffering from the disease. Using the best available scientific methods of his day, Hahnemann experimentally "proved" numerous remedies by observing their effects on patients. In an effort to reduce the toxic effects of some of the remedies, he began diluting remedies and discovered, much to his surprise, that the heavily diluted remedies often worked better and the effects lasted longer than the full-strength remedies. In keeping with alchemists' traditions of the day, Hahnemann began to shake or "success" the dilutions as they were made. When prepared in this fashion, which Hahnemann called "potentizing," the effects of the remedies were further enhanced.

Homeopathic "Potencies"

In the late 1800s and early 1900s, the idea of potencies and the use of high dilutions brought homeopathy into disrepute with many scientists and medical practitioners. Based on the physicist Avagadro's discoveries, it was calculated that after twelve serial dilutions at ratios of 1:100, there are probably no remaining molecules of the original remedy. Since homeopathic practitioners have reported remarkable results at these or higher dilutions, most scientists could not comprehend how such diluted remedies could still be effective.

Over the past 20 years, there have been numerous randomized clinical trials of homeopathic medicines. A summary of these trials, published by some very skeptical researchers, found that over 80% of the studies showed positive effects from homeopathic treatment. Wishing to avoid the "publication bias" of positive studies, these authors went out of their way to find all reports of homeopathy research, including unpublished reports and negative reports. The authors of this study stated that, based on this research, they might be willing to accept homeopathy as legitimate therapy if the way it worked could be explained. I find it amusing that doctors could use aspirin and penicillin for many decades without knowing how they work, but most doctors refuse to accept homeopathy because they do not understand how it works. Perhaps the scientific discovery of exactly what happens when a homeopathic remedy is made, and how this remedy affects the body's immune system, will revolutionize our understanding of cellular physiology, biochemistry, and immunology. Recent advances in the fields of solution dynamics, bioelectromagnetics, and chaos theory show promise of shedding some light on the mystery behind the healing mechanisms of homeopathy.

Effectiveness of Homeopathy

Many people turn to homeopathic medicine for chronic illnesses that have failed to respond to more traditional medicines. Because homeopathic medicines are nontoxic and highly diluted, they can be used in conjunction with allopathic medicines to help boost the healing response, without fear of chemical complications due to mixing medicines. Scientific studies indicate that homeopathic medicine may be particularly effective for treating upper respiratory problems with flu-like symptoms, physical traumas like sprains and bruises, digestive tract problems, and migraine headaches. The remedy *Arnica montana* is helpful for accelerating the healing of trauma injuries like bruises and sprains and is a valuable addition to any first aid kit.

For the healing of chronic illnesses that are not responding to allopathic medicine, I would seriously consider the use of homeopathy, but recommend consulting an experienced and trained homeopathic medical practitioner. The medical practitioner that we use for our family doctor is a homeopathic M.D. who had been head of cardiology at a major hospital. After many years of practicing orthodox Western medicine, he became disillusioned when he realized that modern technology and his best efforts, although usually effective in the short run, often failed to generate long-term health and vitality. He has found that by combining traditional healing herbs, acupuncture, and homeopathy with orthodox medicine, he is able to promote long-term healing and a state of good health in many patients who had failed to thrive when limited to allopathic medicine.

Prior to the introduction of modern antibiotics, homeopathic treatments proved far safer and more effective than the prevailing orthodox medicines. Death rates during epidemics of serious infectious diseases, including scarlet fever, cholera, yellow fever, and diphtheria were reported to be significantly lower in homeopathic hospitals than in their orthodox counterparts. For example, statistics compiled during cholera epidemics of the 1800s claimed that 3% to 30% of patients cared for with homeopathic treatment died as compared to a death rate of 50% to 60% under regular care (Jonas and Jacobs 1996, 35). With the outbreaks of some new diseases and antibiotic resistant strains of common illnesses, homeopathic medicines may once again provide more effective healing rates than those of orthodox medicine. For an excellent discussion of when homeopathy is appropriate and what homeopathy might truly heal, see *Healing with Homeopathy: The Doctor's Guide* by Wayne B. Jonas, M.D., and Jennifer Jacobs, M.D., M.P.H. Homeopathic self-care kits are available from many health food stores and on the Internet.

Homeopathy Practices

Three fundamental ideas separate homeopathy from other health care systems. The first premise is that the choice of remedy is based on matching a specific set of symptoms to a single "similar remedy" to bring about improvement or cure. The second premise is that the minimum dose is needed to stimulate the natural self-healing process. Much like allergy shots, which rely on minute amounts of allergens to stimulate the body's immune response, homeopathic medicines rely upon minute amounts of ingredients that would normally stimulate similar symptoms to bring about improvement or cure. The third premise is that the process of cure should occur in a global way with more serious and central problems improving first.

A skilled homeopathic practitioner will typically spend far more time with a patient during the initial interview than a conventional doctor. The homeopathic system assumes that all symptoms are related, regardless of diagnosis. When selecting the remedy, it is the exact relationship of symptoms, signs, and life experiences that are used to help select the best medicine. A wide variety of information may come into play, such as how well the patient sleeps, whether he or she perspires or not, state of mind at different times of the day, and so on. Once the remedy is selected, it is given in the appropriate dosage and interval. It may be given several times a day to once every few months. Most of the time, symptoms will not worsen, but will gradually improve. However, with homeopathic medicine, it is not unusual to experience a "healing crisis" or temporary aggravation when the symptoms actually degrade before improving significantly. This is seen as part of the body's self-healing mechanism and is usually followed by considerable relief. Once the healing response has begun, no further doses are required. After a few hours, if a remedy does not appear to have any positive effect, a different remedy should be tried.

Certain materials are considered "antidotes" for specific homeopathic remedies, as they appear to interfere with the homeopathic properties of those remedies. Coffee, camphor, menthol, and eucalyptus are considered antidotes for numerous homeopathic remedies and should be avoided while using remedies.

HEALING WITH ENERGY

When I met Karen, she was a gymnastics coach at a well known training center in Palo Alto, California. A few years earlier, Karen had been a top-notch gymnast, competing at the junior national level, until she broke her back in competition. She recovered from the broken back and resumed a healthy, active lifestyle. One day, Karen leapt off a couch and "landed funny." She twisted in agony. Unable to move her legs, she feared she must have rebroken her back. She was brought to the hospital, where x-rays confirmed that she had fractured one of her vertebrae. Her legs were paralyzed and it was not known whether or not she would regain the use of her legs. A few months earlier, Karen had been introduced to Madhusudandasji, a powerful 108-year-old Indian yogi. The yogi visited Karen in the hospital and gave her energy healing treatments. Holding his hands on various parts of her body using special techniques, the yogi transmitted healing energy into Karen's body. There was a strong feeling of electricity, as if thousands of volts were traveling through her veins. She felt tremendous heat, as if the temperature in the room had suddenly jumped to 120°. One day later, Karen had regained feeling and movement in her legs. Within an astounding two-week period, Karen was fully recovered from a fractured spine and paraplegic paralysis! Several other students of this yogi have told me similar stories about miraculous healings and spontaneous remissions of serious diseases, such as terminal cancers and tumors.

The practice of "laying on of hands" and other forms of therapeutic energy healing are as old as recorded history. The Christian Bible, Hindu Bhagavad Gita, and other holy writings from around the world contain numerous references to this kind of healing. It is easy to be skeptical as there are no visibly measurable ways to judge the effectiveness (or integrity) of a healer other than the healer's reputation and personal testimonials. Numerous charlatans have preyed upon innocent and desperate people willing to give anything to be healed. As a scientifically trained and educated person, I used to get upset by the way the term "energy" was commonly used. I thought it extremely overused and misused. Once I personally experienced the transmission of some kind of extremely powerful spiritual healing energy (I felt like I was on fire and ready to explode), I realized that simply because scientists had failed to measure or detect spiritual healing energies, didn't mean that they do not exist. After all, the stars had transmitted X rays and radio waves for billions of years prior to humanity's discovery of their existence.

There are many different healing traditions that incorporate some type of nonphysical healing energy. I cannot do any of them justice in the short space of this section, but you may find the following guidelines useful if you have an interest in the subject. If you are very sensitive, you may feel the energy as soon as you begin to work. As with most healing arts, however, the best way to learn is directly from someone who is already proficient and to practice what you learn on a regular basis. In the case of the reiki healing tradition, an "attunement" by a reiki master opens the student as a channel for greatly magnified manifestations of some kind of universal healing energies, which are independent of religious beliefs.

The first and foremost requirement is your intention to heal. It is your intention that will help to bring the healing energies through. I find that a good way to start is with a simple silent prayer asking for help and stating your intention to bring in the light (holy spirit, Christ, divine mother, higher power, etc.). Many practitioners start at the head and work toward the feet, although there are no hard and fast rules. Some simply hold their hands above or touch various parts of the body and ask the light to heal the patient, consciously doing nothing but allowing the light to do as it may. Other traditions use visualization or the breath to help guide, direct, and focus the healing energies. If the healing session leaves the healer feeling tired, drained, or sick, the healer should try to see the healing energies as passing through the healer from a higher power and not as coming from the healer's own energy. Some find it helpful to feel or visualize the energy coming in from above with the healer's inhalation and flowing out through the hands to the patient with the exhalation. Included below is a chart of the bioenergy centers known to the Hindus as chakras. Chakra charts can provide varying colors and locations for the energy centers. These differences need not concern you; you can simply use the chart to help you visualize and move healing energies in the body, letting your experiences and intuition guide you in your work.

A FEW USEFUL GUIDELINES (NOT RULES)

Take off watches and rings. Wash hands before and after treatment. Loosen tight belts, clothing, and neckties on patient and healer. The patient should remove shoes and lie or sit in a relaxed position with uncrossed legs.

Begin by making the connection between your spirit and the universal life force, using your intention to bring in the light (Holy Spirit, Christ, divine mother, etc.). You may wish to offer a silent prayer.

At the start, stroke the aura several times with your hands, to balance it a bit. Stroke from head to the feet, lifting your hands from the patient's body while returning from feet to head. On the down stroke, hold the hands a few inches from the patient's body, letting your intuition determine the actual distance. You may use your intention and breath to help direct the waves of healing energies through your hands.

Hold your hands on or above the body for several minutes at each location, until the feelings of energy become calm and even. Start at the head and work toward the feet, paying particular attention to "hot spots" and trouble areas. Follow your intuitive guidance. "See" the energy as flowing from a universal source into the patient and not as your own energy.

Before ending the session, ask the receiver (and the universal energy) if there is a place that still wants to be treated. End with a few more smoothing aura strokes, perhaps a "grounding" exercise (touch the soles of the feet and "see" the energy connecting to the earth's center) and a prayer of thanks to the healing energies for their blessings. (Adapted from *A Complete Book of Reiki Healing* by Brigitte Muller and Horst Gunther.)

Once a practitioner has become proficient in one of the different energy healing arts, the healer and/or the patient will probably begin to feel manifestations of the healing energies. These may be experienced as elevated body heat, tingling, trembling, vibration, sound, lights, or other unusual sensations. Occasionally, the patient may feel cold or pain. I have found that sometimes my own healing work has been most effective when my mind has been totally quiet. In these instances the "small me" seems to have gone away and something greater has taken over. I did not consciously "do anything" but simply had the intention to assist with a healing.

THE POWER OF PRAYER

Prayer is not an old woman's idle amusement. Properly understood and applied, it is the most potent instrument of action.

—Mahatma Gandhi

I met a man who had been deaf for twenty years. He had been in and out of hospitals for years and had several operations, none of which was successful at restoring his hearing. One day, a friend suggested he try a healer he knew, who practiced Christian Science and was known to have facilitated many miraculous healings. He was skeptical, but willing to give it a try. He met with the Christian lady, who agreed to do her prayer-based healing work. That night, he was mildly hopeful and optimistic when he went to sleep. The next morning, he awoke to the sounds of passing traffic. Not only could he hear traffic for the first time in 20 years, but he could hear the sound of a pin drop!

Years later, he was approached by a Native American man walking with the aid of crutches. The Indian explained that he had fallen and broken his leg. Since he had no money, he had not seen a doctor to have his leg set properly. The broken bone became infected and gangrene had set in. The Indian asked, "Could you get that Christian lady to pray for me? I'm going into the hospital tomorrow. They are going to cut my leg off and I'm real scared." They contacted the Christian Science lady, who then did her prayer healing work for the Indian. The next day, the Indian walked into the hospital and amazed the doctors. On the day scheduled for his amputation, his leg was fully healed with no signs of either the broken bone or the infection.

Numerous scientific studies now confirm that prayer does, indeed, have a positive effect on healing (Dossey 1995, 233–271). Similar to the case of homeopathic medicine, scientific analysis of data gathered in carefully controlled, double-blind studies indicates that there are positive healing effects from prayer, but science can offer no clear explanation. Experiments indicate that the healing powers of prayer are not limited by time, space, or any type of material barrier. Prayer is not a particularly easy healing tradition to study in the laboratory. Applying the same technique may result in a miraculous healing effect on one subject while producing no noticeable positive effect

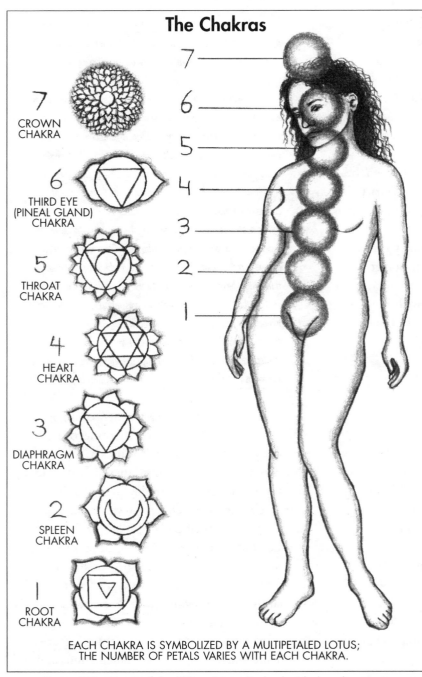

The Chakras

7 — CROWN CHAKRA

6 — THIRD EYE (PINEAL GLAND) CHAKRA

5 — THROAT CHAKRA

4 — HEART CHAKRA

3 — DIAPHRAGM CHAKRA

2 — SPLEEN CHAKRA

1 — ROOT CHAKRA

EACH CHAKRA IS SYMBOLIZED BY A MULTIPETALED LOTUS; THE NUMBER OF PETALS VARIES WITH EACH CHAKRA.

Figure 9-2. Circuit of the ki (or chi) in the body (chakra diagram).

people with so little faith that they turned to prayer only after all orthodox medical procedures had failed to heal, yet these "of little faith" received a miraculous healing when they finally did resort to prayer. In my experience, it is the faith of the healer doing the prayer work that seems to matter more than the faith of the patient, but even great spiritual healers are not always successful. Perhaps there are other factors, such as personal growth, subconscious choice, life path, karma, and divine grace that all bear on the outcome of spiritual healing. There appear to be no hard and fast rules, but experience indicates that if the patient totally disbelieves in the power of prayer, he or she greatly reduces the probability of receiving a healing through prayer. I do not believe that healing by prayer is limited to any particular religion or denomination, but can work for Hindus, Christians, Muslims, and those of other faiths.

For over a century, Christian Scientists have relied on prayer for their physical healing. In 1875, Christian Science founder Mary Baker Eddy published *Science and Health.* One of the preeminent works on spiritual healing, it remains in print today. Eddy claims that human beings are made in the likeness of God, so our true nature is spirit and perfection. By truly "seeing" this as fact, health is restored. Her "Scientific Statement of Being" summarizes the basic postulates upon which the Christian Science method of spiritual healing is based:

There is no life, truth, intelligence, nor substance in matter. All is infinite Mind and its infinite manifestation, for God is All-in-all. Spirit is immortal Truth; matter is mortal error. Spirit is the real and eternal; matter is the unreal and

on another. Additionally, even though it is often referred to as "faith" healing, the faith of the patient does not always bring the expected result.

There are many people with such strong religious faith that they refuse all healing from any source other than prayer and "God" and are willing to die before seeking medical attention. In spite of their great faith, some of these people are not healed of their afflictions. On the other hand, I have personally witnessed *temporal. Spirit is God, and man is His image and likeness. Therefore, man is not material; he is spiritual.*

A common belief (I must admit that I used to buy into this one) is that Christian Scientists are religious fanatics who would rather die than go to a medical doctor. In reality, they rely upon a system of prayer-based healing that has proven, on thousands of occasions, to work. When a Christian Scientist's personal prayers for healing are not garnering the desired result, they call on "Christian Science Practitioners," specially trained spiritual healers who can perform their prayer-based healing work at any distance from the patient. Practitioners will often work with non-Christian Scientists, and may be found in the Yellow Page listings under "Christian Science Practitioners."

SHAMANIC HEALING

A shaman is a man or woman who enters an altered state of consciousness—at will—to contact and utilize an ordinarily hidden reality in order to acquire knowledge, power, and to help other persons. The shaman has at least one, and usually more, "spirits" in his personal service.

—Michael Harner, Ph.D.,
The Way of the Shaman

For at least twenty-thousand years, and possibly for hundreds of thousands of years, indigenous peoples have relied on the extraordinary powers of shamans for spiritual and physical healing. Widespread similarities in shamanic techniques, beliefs, experiences, and results have been extensively documented in Mircea Eliade's classic work, *Shamanism.* Michael Harner suggests that the remarkable similarities between shamanic knowledge in such wildly separate cultures as the Amazonian Conibo, Siberian native cultures, and the Australian aborigines is due to the fact that it is experientially gained knowledge and is based on "real" principles.

A Catholic monk, who grew up in Hawaii, told me the following story: Brother Anthony was teaching at an all-Hawaiian Catholic school, where many considered the success of their football team a high priority. In the middle of an important game, one of their star football players broke his leg. He was in severe pain and the bone was sticking out through his shin. Being the school official in attendance at the game, Brother Anthony accompanied the injured football player inside the ambulance. The ambulance driver and attending EMT were native Hawaiians. Knowing how much their star football player meant to the success of the team, the ambulance driver and the EMT entered into a rather heated debate. Finally, they resolved to take the player to a well-known Hawaiian "Kahuna" (the Hawaiian term for shamanic healers), rather than the Honolulu hospital. Some Kahunas are rumored to have extraordinary powers. One week later, at the very next football game, Brother Anthony was amazed to see the same football star playing ball with a fully healed leg. He said, "If I had not seen the whole thing with my own eyes, I would never have believed the leg could have healed so quickly. The injury was very serious. There was no question that the leg had been severely broken."

Shamans traditionally alter their consciousness, either with drumming, dance, chanting, or herbal concoctions, to travel in their minds to other "realities." In these alternate realms, they "journey" to meet spirit guides (often in the form of animals), gain knowledge, and retrieve power for their personal use or to help their patient. Whether the "shamanic state of consciousness" (SSC) is drug induced by herbal concoctions or induced by the shaman's drumming or rattle, the results and experiences gained from "journeying" in the SSC are very similar in widely varying cultures spread across the planet.

It would be easy to attribute fantastic stories of shamanic journeys to simple hallucinations and overactive imaginations, but the powerful healing results and detailed information received from the shaman's "guides" go far beyond idle imaginings. Sandra Ingerman, in her book *Soul Retrieval*, cites numerous examples of receiving detailed personal information pertinent to the healing of her patients. Often this information was not even known by her patient, but was later verified by an older family member or relative. Lewis Mehl-Madronna, M.D., in his book *Coyote Medicine*, relates a story about a Native American healing ceremony he took part in for the benefit of a young Indian woman. In the darkness of this sweat lodge ceremony, a giant eagle's wings brushed against Madronna and the visiting spirits "told" Lewis about the incestuous abuse of this young woman by her uncle. This was critical information to the case. When Lewis confronted the uncle, he angrily confessed to his sins and accused the young woman of telling her story (which she had not) to Madronna. Sometimes a shaman's spirit helpers will provide detailed medical diagnosis or suggest healing herbs or other ceremonies to facilitate healing. Many shamans claim that indigenous peoples' in-depth knowledge about medicinal herbs has been gathered directly by shamans from plant spirits and other helpers in nonordinary reality, rather than through the dangerous and tedious process of simple trial and error.

If shamanism intrigues you, I suggest that you read Michael Harner's *The Way of the Shaman* and attend an introductory workshop on shamanism. The *Way of the Shaman* includes fascinating stories as well as detailed exercises for experiencing the SSC and exploring alternate realities for knowledge and healing, without the use of drugs of any kind. As with any new skill you learn, practice, a natural inclination, and the tutelage of an experienced teacher will help you achieve positive results more rapidly. Some will be called to this path, most will not. Even if you are not called to practice shamanism, you may wish to visit a shaman someday for help and healing.

One way to begin exploring shamanism is to attempt what is known as the First Journey, which begins with envisioning an opening in the earth and entering it. The journey is done lying on the floor with eyes shut and covered, while listening to drumming—live or recorded—at a rate of about 205 to 220 beats per minute. During the journey, after entering the opening, you traverse the tunnel, see what is beyond it, and return through the tunnel. The initial journey and return take about ten minutes, but advanced journeys may take several hours in "earth time" while days pass in the SSC.

When I took a "Core Shamanism" workshop, I anticipated that my years of meditation would make it easy for me to enter the SSC. As the first day progressed, many people shared fantastic experiences

from their first journeys, but I joined a silent, discouraged group who obviously felt like we were getting nowhere fast. The workshop teacher encouraged those who were unsuccessful in their journeys to "Keep trying! Imagine you are traveling down the tunnel, even if you don't believe you are." We were assured that most of us would eventually experience the SSC if we stuck with the different workshop exercises. On day two of the workshop, I noticed a significant portion of my discouraged comrades had not returned. As the day progressed, I still experienced nothing more than idle daydreams and imaginings, until we reached the last exercise, "retrieving a power animal for another person." The teacher mentioned that this exercise is often more successful than journeying for yourself, since the power animals have more compassion for a shaman seeking to help another being. Even though things were a bit fuzzy and unclear, for the first time it actually felt like I had journeyed down the tunnel into the lower world. I remember no distinct images of this world, but I did clearly see a giant eagle appear several times at different angles and positions. Following the workshop leader's instruction, I grasped this animal to my chest (don't ask me how I could grasp a six-foot eagle in the palm of my hand), returned through the tunnel to my partner, cupped my hands on my partner's breastbone and "blew" the eagle into her chest, and then into the top of her head. Her body jumped visibly when I did this. I still was not totally convinced that I hadn't imagined the whole thing, but my partner explained that she felt a burst of energy in her chest, like a small explosion of light, when I blew the giant eagle into her. She then journeyed for me, returning with a power animal, and I too experienced a burst of light and energy in my chest. Although certainly not a natural shaman, I was glad I had stayed through the entire workshop. From watching 95% of the participants enthusiastically "dance their animal" after the last journey, it was clear that this exercise had been a powerful experience for nearly all of the workshop participants.

HYPNOSIS FOR PAIN CONTROL AND HEALING

When my wife took her professional hypnotherapist training, one of the other students in her class related this remarkable story: Patty and her husband, Joe, were cutting firewood in a remote location. Joe's chain saw slipped and cut deeply into his thigh, severing a major artery. Blood was spurting everywhere and they were many miles from any medical services. Maintaining a cool head, Patty decided to try a hypnosis technique that she had heard about. Speaking in a soft monotone, she quickly induced a light trance in Joe, then gave him the hypnotic suggestion that the severed arteries in his leg were squeezing shut and that the blood flow was turned off, like the flow of water from a faucet. Amazingly, the leg stopped bleeding! They were able to walk to their truck and drive for half an hour until they reached the hospital. When they arrived at the hospital, the surgeon expressed concern that the wound had not bled enough to cleanse the chain saw gash and therefore left a significant chance for severe infection. At his recommendation, Patti removed the hypnotic suggestion to allow the wound to bleed. Immediately, the wound began spurting startling amounts of blood. The surgeon said that he had never seen anything like that in all his years of medicine. Normally, without a tourniquet, this kind of severe bleeding would have cost the life of her husband before they could have reached the hospital. The other amazing thing about this story is that Patty had no training in hypnotic techniques at the time of the accident.

Hypnosis has been employed for healing since "temple sleep" was used in the healing temples of Greece and ancient Egypt. Hypnosis is not a sleep state, but an altered state of mind in which the subject is in a heightened state of awareness, with exceptional concentration, similar to a state of focused daydreaming. Contrary to popular opinion, the subject will usually remember what happened during the hypnotic trance and cannot be forced to say or do anything that goes against his or her will or personal moral ethics. Typically, the subject will snap out of the trance state if asked to see or do something he is not ready or willing to see or do. Hypnosis is a natural state of mind that most people slip in and out of several times a day. The mind will accept positive images and suggestions far more easily under hypnosis than in the normal waking state of consciousness.

Hypnosis can be a valuable tool for pain control and relief from allergies, stomach problems, skin problems, migraines, and other conditions. In the 1860s, the British surgeon James Esdaile reported that he had performed hundreds of successful, pain-free surgeries using hypnosis for anesthesia. The journalist F. W. Sims once watched Esdaile amputate the leg of a woman using no anesthesia. Amazed by how little the wound bled and how still the conscious woman lay, Sims wrote, "During the whole operation, not the least movement or change in her limbs, body, or countenance took place: she continued in the same apparently easy repose as at first, and I have no reason to believe she was not perfectly at ease."

Currently, hypnosis is occasionally used for operations where the use of anesthesia might cause severe complications. Experiments with the medical use of hypnosis for burn patients indicates that the use of positive mental imagery in the hypnotic trance can stimulate the self-healing response and accelerate healing. The use of creative healing visualizations combined with relaxation exercises is essentially the same thing as self-hypnosis. As an adjunct to standard cancer therapies, Carl and Stephanie Simonton, authors of *Getting Well Again*, recommend a program of relaxation, attitude change, and mental imaging. Many of their patients have successfully used imagery, such as Pac Mans gobbling up tumors, to help their bodies eliminate cancers and tumors.

Because hypnosis gives conscious access to the normally subconscious mind, it can also provide valuable insights into the subconscious roots of disease or blocks to healing. Hypnosis may be used to access memories, even those from infancy and early childhood. Additionally, when in the trance state, some patients appear to have the ability to access some kind of higher source of wisdom or knowledge, providing self-diagnostic or therapeutic information for themselves that they normally could not access.

The best hypnotic subjects tend to be people who can easily focus their minds and are able to visualize well. Children over the age of eight tend to make excellent subjects. About 95% of the public can achieve at least a light trance, and roughly 70% are capable of a medium-level trance, where much of the most powerful hypnotic work is done. In one sense, all hypnosis is self-hypnosis, because it takes the trust, consent, and relaxation of the self to allow the mind to enter the hypnotic trance.

The typical hypnosis session is divided into three parts. The first part, the "induction," is the process for initiating the hypnotic trance. There are many different types and styles of inductions. The second part of the session is where the work is done. If it is a self-hypnosis session, positive suggestions are repeated in several different ways. This is referred to as "auto-suggestion." In a session with a hypnotherapist, the patient will be given positive suggestions during this part of the session or possibly "regressed" to a time when the problem originated, so that it may be examined from a detached perspective and then remedied. Painful memories may be made easier to review by the suggestion that they will be viewed on a screen and the patient will not feel any pain or trauma. The third part of the session is the "waking up" or "coming back," when suggestions are given to return the patient to a normal state of mind. Suggestions such as "At the count of five, you will be wide awake, alert, and feeling fine" help the patient to emerge fully and clearly from the hypnotic trance.

The induction should be read slowly and in a medium monotone. Gradually slow down more and more, pausing often between sentences. You should feel as if you are talking too slowly. The pace and tone should pick up somewhat for the suggestion or regression part of the session and should pick up significantly for the awakening part. Even though the last part of the session is referred to as "awakening," remember that the patient is not asleep during the hypnotic trance. For self-hypnosis, the easiest method is to make yourself a tape recording to be played back on a regular basis; it should include the induction, auto-suggestions, and the awakening suggestions. If a tape recorder is not available, you can write the script for a partner to read to you. Due to common misconceptions fostered by movies and stage acts, many hypnosis subjects will find it hard to believe that they were actually hypnotized. Time distortion, rapid eye movement, and very deep rhythmic breathing are frequently noted signs of a hypnotic trance.

Fractional Relaxation Induction

(Tape or use this entire induction, except for what is in parentheses. This is an excellent induction for beginners.) Lie down on your back, arms parallel to your body, fingers loosely outstretched and palms downward. Separate your feet by eight or ten inches so that your thighs are not touching. Use a pillow if you wish, and make yourself as comfortable as possible. Remove or loosen clothing that binds you in any way and remove your shoes if they are tight. The idea is to get comfortable and relaxed.

Fix your eyes on a spot on the ceiling and take three long, deep breaths. Inhale, hold the air in your lungs for three seconds, and as you exhale slowly, you will relax all over. Now let's take the first breath. Inhale. (Pause) Exhale. — Sleep now. (Pause) Now another deep breath, even deeper than before. Inhale. (Pause) Exhale. — Sleep now. (Pause) Now a third deep breath. Inhale. (Pause) Exhale. — Sleep now. (Pause) Now as your whole body begins to relax, and as every muscle and nerve begins to feel loose and limp, your eyelids also become heavy and tired. They grow heavier and heavier and will close now. The lids have become so tired and so heavy, it would be difficult to open them. But you have no desire to try because you want them to remain closed until I tell you to open them. (Pause)

Now I want you to concentrate all of your attention on your right foot. Relax the toes of your right foot. Imagine they are like loose rubber bands dangling from your foot. (Pause) Let this loose feeling spread back through the ball of the foot and then all the way back to the heel. (Pause) (Drag out the word "all" and speak very slowly from this point on, pausing between all sentences.)

Now let this relaxed feeling go up into the calf of the leg. Let the calf muscles go loose — and limp — and LA-A-A-ZY. (Long pause) And now, while your muscles and nerves are relaxing, let your mind relax also. Let it drift away, to pleasant scenes in your imagination. Let your mind wander where it will, as you go deeper — deeper — in drowsy relaxation. You are breathing easily like a sleeper breathes. All of your cares and tensions are fading away, as you go deeper — de-e-e-per into drowsy slumber. Every breath that you take— every noise that you hear — makes you go deeper, deeper, in pleasant, comfortable relaxation.

Now let the wonderful wave of relaxation move from your right calf up into the large thigh muscles. Let them go loose and limp. The right leg is now completely relaxed and comfortable. (Pause) Now the left foot. The toes relax, the whole foot relaxes just as the right one did — limp and lazy. Let the feeling of pleasant relaxation go up into the left calf. Let the calf muscles go. Your legs are feeling heavy like pieces of wood. As you relax the left thigh muscles, they feel heavier and heavier, and you become more and more drowsy. Now as the wave of relaxation moves upward through your hips and abdomen, you let go more and more. Think of your abdomen as an inflated ball. You are letting the air out of the ball and it spreads out and relaxes completely. Stomach and solar plexus relax. Let them go — as you go further into deep — deep slumber. (Pause)

(Slowly) The fingers in your right hand are now relaxing, and so is your wrist. Now your forearm relaxes. On up to your right shoulder — your whole right arm is relaxed and numb. You probably feel your fingers or your toes tingling. This is a good sign, so continue to go deeper. And now, just go on over, into a deep, deep hypnotic sleep. (Pause)

The fingers on your left hand are completely relaxed. Your hand and forearm are letting go. Up, through your elbow, to your upper arm, relax. Now the left shoulder, let that go, too. Loose, limp, and lazy. Now relax all the large back muscles, from your shoulders all the way down to your waist — let them all go limp and loose. (Remember, plenty of pauses. Continue to speak softly and very slowly.)

Relax the muscles in your neck. Let your jaws separate and let the chin and cheek muscles go loose and rubbery. (Pause) Now let your eyes go. Let them go completely — relax and feel comfortable and good. Relax the eyebrows, too, and the forehead. Let the muscles rest. Back across the scalp — let the entire scalp relax — from the forehead all the way back to the back of the neck — all relaxed — all resting — all loose. You are now completely relaxed. You are going deeper and deeper into restful hypnosis. Your mind is experiencing a wonderful feeling of tranquillity. Your subconscious is now receptive to the helpful suggestions I am now

going to give it. (At this point the suggestion is given to the subconscious mind.)
  —From *Self-Hypnosis and Other Mind-Expanding Techniques* by Charles Tebbetts

There are many different forms of inductions and hypnotherapy scripts. Milton Erikson, a psychiatrist and master hypnotherapist/counselor, developed a radically different approach that uses metaphors and a wide variety of inductions, some designed to trigger trance by confusing the conscious mind. Eriksonian hypnotherapy can be especially effective with people who do not easily go into trance. *My Voice Will Go With You: The Teaching Tales of Milton H. Erikson*, edited and commentary by Sidney Rosen, provides an excellent introduction. *Hypnotherapy Scripts: A Neo-Ericksonian Approach to Persuasive Healing*, by Ronald A. Havens and Catherine R. Walters, offers an excellent variety of Eriksonian hypnotherapy scripts. For the serious hypnosis student, a rather expensive, thorough and clinical text is the *Handbook of Hypnotic Suggestions and Metaphors* edited by D. Corydon Hammond. If you are interested in the techniques of regression therapy for deep emotional healing and to explore forgotten or submerged memories and past lives, I highly recommend *Regression Therapy, a Handbook for Professionals: Volume I* and *Volume II* by Winafred B. Lucas.

Hypnotic Suggestion

By its very nature, the subconscious mind seeks to obey suggestions as if they were orders. By properly structuring your hypnotic suggestions, you can put your subconscious mind to work, carrying out your orders without conscious effort and will power. The following guidelines will help you design positive, powerful suggestions for your own use.

Make sure motivation is strong. There should be good reason for wishing to carry out the suggestion. Hypnosis can help you to change or heal if you really want to, but it can't make you do something you really don't want to do. You can start your suggestion with your motivating suggestion, such as "Because I am a child of God and a healthy individual, my broken leg is healing rapidly and perfectly."

Frame the suggestion positively. If you say, "I will not be angry," you are reinforcing to the subconscious mind that you have a problem with anger. Never mention the negative idea you are trying to eliminate. Instead, repeat and emphasize the positive idea you are trying to manifest. For the anger example, think of twenty or thirty different ways of saying how you wish to be. You might start with, "I am a relaxed and calm person. No matter how anyone behaves towards me, I stay calm and centered, acting with compassion and wisdom." Expand on this.

Use the present tense. It may sound strange, but instead of saying "next week I will be totally healed," try saying "next week I am totally healed." The subconscious mind is the feeling, emotional mind and responds to the present.

Say and visualize your suggestion. The more vividly you can "see" your suggestion, the more real it is to the subconscious mind.

Set a time limit. In one sense, you must see your goal as being accomplished, but your subconscious mind may rebel if given a time limit it believes is unachievable. Even though there are cases of broken bones mending overnight, probably this will be too much for your subconscious to accept. Try starting with half the normal healing time. Your subconscious mind is a goal-oriented mechanism. Set a reasonable time limit, see your goal clearly, and you will be amazed at how fast you can achieve it!

Be specific and use repetition. Don't suggest too many things at once. Focus on one area in each session, though you should think of as many different ways of saying and picturing what this one area is. The more often you are exposed to an idea, the stronger it will influence you.

Keep it simple. Speak as if you are talking to your ten year old.

Emotionalize. *Your* subconscious mind is the seat of your emotions. Say and think descriptive, vibrant words with strong feeling and emotion. (Adapted from *Self Hypnosis and Other Mind-Expanding Techniques* by Charles Tebbetts)

The suggestions should be repeated in a crisp, businesslike tone. To design a suggestion for pain control, you might find it useful to use the metaphor of switches and knobs controlling the level of pain transmitted by the nerves. By turning these switches "off" or the knobs "down," the patient can control his or her own pain level from within the hypnotic trance. Similarly, to control bleeding, the image of faucets or valves attached to the blood vessels will cause the blood vessels to constrict and stop or reduce the blood flow when given the positive suggestion. Use whatever image you wish to vividly convey the image of what you want to accomplish. I definitely recommend that you practice these techniques before trying them out in an emergency situation.

Awakening Technique

Record the following or have your partner say it to you to bring you out of the hypnotic trance. Even without the awakening procedure, you would eventually awaken yourself from the trance state. The awakening should be spoken louder, with enthusiasm and a forceful tone.

> *Now it is time for you to return to normal consciousness. You feel wonderfully rested. I will count to five, and as I do, you feel vitality and energy surging through your body. You are wide awake at the count of five.* **One**. *You are waking up now. When you awaken, you feel full of pep and energy.* **Two**. *More and more awake! More and more awake! You feel refreshed and perfect from head to foot, normal in every way.* **Three**. *You feel as though your eyes have been bathed in cool spring water. You feel physically perfect and emotionally serene.* **Four**. *You feel wonderful in every way! Refreshed and full of vigor, but perfectly relaxed and calm. You feel good all over!* **Five**. *Eyes wide open! Wide awake now. Take a deep breath, stretch and feel good!*
> —From *Self Hypnosis and Other Mind-Expanding Techniques* by Charles Tebbetts

VISUALIZATION AND MIND-BODY HEALING

Even though the distinction among self-hypnosis, guided visualizations, and waking dream therapy is at best a blurry line, it is results that matter, and the results with these similar techniques can be mind boggling. Dr. Gerald Epstein relates the case of a friend who used waking dream therapy techniques to fully mend a fracture within a three-week period after it had been diagnosed by two doctors as requiring three months to heal (Epstein 1989, 13). Science does not yet understand the exact mechanism that the mind uses to translate mental images into physical body changes. With the combination of intention, focus, and the consistent daily application of your mental visualization exercises, each lasting for about five minutes, you may find profound results. I suggest that you seek regular medical attention for all serious conditions, but supplement and speed your healing with these techniques. The following guidelines and exercises are adapted from Epstein's excellent book, *Healing Visualizations: Creating Health Through Imagery.*

General Guidelines

- Sit comfortably in a chair, spine straight, legs and arms uncrossed, arms resting on arm rests with palms either up or down.
- State your intention to yourself for doing the exercise.
- Close your eyes and breathe several deep breaths to relax, calm, and focus your attention. Place your attention on long, slow, deep out-breaths followed by regular relaxed in-breaths.
- Do your specific imagery exercises for three to five minutes.
- Consistently repeat your exercises several times a day, perhaps every three to four hours while awake. Suggested times are upon waking, at dusk, and before retiring at night.

Visualization for Mending a Broken Bone

Close your eyes and focus your attention on your deep out-breaths. Make a mental picture of the broken bone. Visualize the ends of the bone breaks cleanly touching each other. See the white marrow flowing from one bone end to the other, carried

along by a blue channel of pulsating light. See and feel the ends of the bone meshing together until the break can no longer be seen. Know that the bone is healed into one solid unit, and then open your eyes (Epstein 1989, 12–13).

Egyptian Healing Visualization

Use this technique to mentally probe, diagnose, and heal a variety of physical conditions. Close your eyes and focus on several long out-breaths, while imagining that you are standing peacefully in a field of tall green grass. See yourself stretching your hands, palms outward, up toward the sun on a bright clear blue day. See the sun entering the palms of your hands and circulating throughout your palms and fingers, and then extend a ray out each fingertip. If you are right-handed, see a small hand sprout from the ray extending from each fingertip of the right hand, so that there are five small hands extending beyond each of your fingers on this hand. If you are left-handed, start with the left hand. On the opposite hand, visualize one eye sprouting from each of the rays extending from each finger, so that there are five eyes attached to the fingertips of this hand. Turn these hands and eyes towards your body and enter the body using the eyes to guide and direct the miniature hands to the area in need of healing. With the eyes you may see into the organs to diagnose problems. Use small scalpels and lasers in the miniature hands to cut and scrape as required. Stitch and mend with golden thread where necessary and apply blue or blue-golden ointments for healing. Exit the body by the same route that you entered and throw any wastes behind yourself. Stretch your hands toward the sun and retract the miniature eyes and hands back into your fingers for future use. (Adapted from *Healing Visualizations: Creating Health Through Imagery,* by Gerald Epstein, M.D., 1989, 45.)

SOME NOTES ON DEATH AND DYING

All of us are destined to die someday. Sometimes our healing work may eliminate a so-called terminal disease, but if it does not avert death, it should not be seen as failure. If all sincere prayers to prolong the lives of our loved ones were answered, the world would rapidly overpopulate with decrepit bodies of tortured beings, held earthbound long past their time. I have heard many stories of healing work improving the quality and duration of life during a terminal illness, helping the patient to achieve a graceful death with dignity.

After my father-,in-law was diagnosed with terminal cancer, the use of herbs and other alternatives, combined with endoscopic clearing of a tumor blocking his bile duct, helped him to live the last two years of his life in surprisingly good health, with joy,

mobility, and little pain. In the end, he died at home, with dignity and love, surrounded by his family. The last week of his life was very difficult. We gave him round-the-clock personal care, as his body's systems started to shut down. This was a tough time, but I would not trade the experience for anything. It was magical, horrible, painful, and wonderful, all at the same time. In our society, we are so terrified of death that we usually thrust this responsibility onto the "experts," estranging our loved ones during their final hours and missing a great opportunity for experiencing the miracle of life's full circle.

REFERENCES & RESOURCES

Holistic Healing and Natural Health—General

Colostrum, "Nature's Healing Miracle" **by Donald R. Henderson, M.D., M.P.H. and Deborah Mitchell.** 1999, 60 pp. (paperback), ISBN 0-9676514-0-9. Published by CNR Publications, 4700 S. 900 E. Ste 30-257, Salt Lake City, UT 84117. Lists for $4.95.

This is an informative and well-referenced book about colostrum, a natural pre-milk super nutritional substance produced by mammary glands during the first 48 hours after birth. Colostrum has been credited with boosting the body's immune system and helping it cope with a wide variety of ailments (practically a panacea) including diabetes, hepatitis C, immune deficiencies, bowel problems, chronic infections, fibromyalgia, cancer, chronic fatigue syndrome, severe allergies, etc. Colostrum is nature's way of jump starting a newborn's immune system and appears to have similar beneficial effects on our immune systems when used as a dietary supplement. This book will help you to understand everything you need to know about colostrum.

Deep Healing: The Essence of Mind/Body Medicine, **by Emmet E. Miller, M.D.** 1997, 401 pp. (paperback), ISBN 1-56170-336-2. Published by Hay House, Inc., P.O. Box 5100, Carlsbad, CA 92018-5100. Lists for $12.95.

Deep Healing awakens even the most skeptical among us to the miraculous, inborn, self-healing capacities of one's own mind-body. Dr. Miller presents eye-opening research, fascinating healing stories, advanced new skills in affirmative mental imagery, the transformation of disease-oriented perceptions, the writing of positive life scripts, and much more. This is a practical book with an effective mixture of science, information, skills, and exercises that can help establish the mind-body connection and put the magic of healing back into your own hands.

Eight Weeks to Optimum Health: A Proven Program for Taking Full Advantage of Your Body's Natural Healing Power, **by Andrew Weil, M.D.** 1997, 276 pp. (paperback), ISBN 0-679-44715-6. Published by Alfred A. Knopf, Inc., Division of Random House, 201 E. 50th St., New York, NY 10022. Lists for $13.95.

This excellent general reference was written by one of the gurus of alternative medicine. In this book, Dr. Weil outlines an easy, eight-week course for gradually introducing changes for improving one's health through proper diet, herbs, supplements, exercise, and mental imagery. Recipes are provided to make it easy and delicious to follow Weil's recommendations.

The Encyclopedia of Natural Medicine, revised 2nd ed.,
**by Michael T. Murray, N.D., and Joseph E.
Pizzorno, N.D.** 1997, 960 pp. (paperback), ISBN 0-
76151-157-1. Published by Prima Publishing, P.O.
Box 1260, Rocklin, CA 95677-1260. Lists for $24.95.
Written by naturopathic doctors, this voluminous
book is an exhaustive and detailed reference.
Drawing on the best of centuries-old wisdom and
modern knowledge, it explains the principles of
natural medicine and outlines their application
through the safe and effective use of herbs, vitamins,
diet, lifestyle, and nutrition.

*Food Additives, Nutrients & Supplements A-To-Z: A
Shopper's Guide,* **by Eileen Renders, N.D.** 1999,
265 pp. (paperback), ISBN 1-57416-008-7.
Published by Clear Light Publishers, 823 Don
Diego, Santa Fe, NM 87501. Lists for $14.95.
This easy-to-use reference by a naturopathic doctor
takes the mystery out of a bewildering array of food
additives, herbs, and supplements. The book is a
valuable guide to help readers make healthy choices
in eating and dietary supplementation.

*Food and Healing: How What You Eat Determines
Your Health, Your Well-Being, and the Quality
of Your Life,* **by Annemarie Colbin.** 1996, 352
pp. (paperback), ISBN 0-345-30385-7. Published
by Ballantine Books, a division of Random
House, 201 E. 50th St., New York, NY 10022.
Lists for $12.95.
"An eminently practical, authoritative, and supportive
guide. ...*Food and Healing* is a remarkable achieve-
ment." (Richard Grossman, director, The Health in
Medicine Project, Montefiore Medical Center)

If you wish to really understand optimum diet
and the effects of different foods on your health, this
is the book for you.

The Heart of Healing, **from The Institute of Noetic
Sciences, with William Poole.** 1993, 192 pp.
(hardcover), ISBN 1-878685-80-5. Published by
Turner Publishing, Inc., 1050 Techwood Drive,
NW, Atlanta GA 30318. Lists for $24.95.
A fascinating, entertaining, and well-written survey
and introduction to the world of mind-body healing

and medicine. This book is a companion to the PBS
television series *The Heart of Healing,* and grew out
of Brendan O'Regan's (V.P. for the Institute of Noetic
Sciences) hope to increase public awareness of mind-
body health. This six-year project organized and
simplified volumes of research data and anecdotes
into a very readable, illuminating narrative.

*Immune System Control: Colostrum and
Lactoferrin,* **by Beth M. Ley.** 2000, 200 pp.
(paperback), ISBN 1-890766-11-9. Published by
B L Publications, 14325 Barnes Drive, Detroit
Lakes, MN 56501. Lists for $12.95.
This well-researched book will help you make
informed decisions about using colostrum, a natural
product credited with boosting the body's immune
system and helping the body to heal from a wide
variety of ailments. Individual testimonials credit
colostrum with helping them to recover from
diabetes, hepatitis C, immune deficiencies, bowel
problems, chronic infections, fibromyalgia, cancer,
chronic fatigue syndrome, severe allergies, etc.
Colostrum is a natural pre-milk supernutritional
substance produced by mammary glands during the
first 48 hours after birth. Colostrum is nature's way
of jump starting a newborn's immune system and
appears to have similar beneficial effects on our
immune systems when used as a dietary supplement.

*The Immune System Cure: Optimize Your Immune
System in 30 Days—The Natural Way!* **by Lorna
R. Vanderhaeghe and Patrick J. D. Bouic, Ph.D.**
1999, 250 pp. (paperback), ISBN 1-57566-486-0.
Published by Kensington Publishing Co., 850
Third Ave., New York, NY 10022. Lists for $14.00.
"For decades we have been searching for a cure for
cancer, arthritis, the common cold and now AIDS. A
magic drug, antibiotic or vaccine has been the focus
of this research. Yet we have the most powerful
curing machine hardwired into our body—the
immune system. Nature eloquently designed the
human body with the tools needed to prevent and
fight most diseases. It is only through neglect, abuse
and overuse that we have altered the ability of the
immune system to function optimally. This book is
not about a magic cure; it is about treatments that

boost and balance the immune system to give it the support it needs." (Lorna R. Vanderhaeghe and Patrick J. D. Bouic, Ph.D., from the preface to *The Immune System Cure)*

This is an excellent book based on the latest scientific research into the immune system. Very readable and informative. It contains many testimonials and examples plus enough science to hold up under the scrutiny of a medical doctor. It combines the best of natural healing, supplements, and modern chemistry to help you design an effective program to fight AIDS, herpes, hepatitis, allergies, chronic fatigue syndrome, etc. Whether you simply want to improve your health, stave off potential plagues, or are fighting a debilitating disease, I highly recommend this book.

Love, Medicine & Miracles: Lessons Learned about Self-Healing from a Surgeon's Experience with Exceptional Patients by **Bernie Siegel, M.D.** 1986, 243 pp. (paperback), ISBN 0-06-091983-3. Published by Harper Collins Publishers, Inc., 10 East 53rd St., New York, NY 10022. Lists for $14.00. "One of the most wonderful books I have ever read."—Karl Menninger, M.D.

This book really is terrific. Bernie Siegel practiced general and pediatric surgery in New Haven, Connecticut, until he retired in 1989. He founded Exceptional Cancer Patients, based on "carefrontation," a loving, safe, therapeutic confrontation that facilitates personal change, empowerment, and healing. *Love, Medicine & Miracles* is filled with wisdom, love, and many case examples of the mind-body connection to healing. It is not about abandoning Western medicine, but empowering the mind and body to make the most of healing, whether it is from within the structure of traditional Western medicine or alternative healing practices.

The Miracle of MSM: The Natural Solution for Pain by **Stanley W. Jacob, M.D., Ronald M. Lawrence, M.D., and Martin Zucker.** 1999, 272 pp. (paperback), ISBN 0425172651. Published by Berkley Publishing Group, Division of Penguin Putnam, 200 Madison Ave., New York, NY 10016. Lists for $12.00.

MSM is a naturally occurring organic sulfur compound that plays an important factor in providing usable sulfur for growing healthy connective tissue in joints and muscles, and is a key component in many important amino acids. The body can assimilate sulfur only when it has been incorporated into an organic compound by a plant or an animal (we cannot eat sulfur rocks). Both in the literature and on the Internet, you can find a huge number of personal testimonials as to the effectiveness of MSM for reducing arthritis and allergies, healing scar tissue and contributing to an improved overall level of health.

Prescription for Nutritional Healing: A Practical A-Z Reference to Drug-Free Remedies Using Vitamins, Minerals, Herbs & Food Supplements, by **James F. Balch, M.D., and Phyllis A. Balch, C.N.C.** 1997, 600 pp. (paperback), ISBN 0-89529-727-2. Published by Avery Publishing Group, 120 Old Broadway, Garden City Park, NY 11040. Lists for $19.95.

A very thorough reference volume on drug-free remedies using vitamins, minerals, herbs, and food supplements, this book is arranged alphabetically to provide easy access to cures for a wide variety of ailments. My family uses this reference on a regular basis.

Reclaiming Our Health: Exploding the Medical Myth and Embracing the Source of True Healing by **John Robbins.** 1996, 416 pp. (paperback), ISBN 0-91581-169-3. Published by H.J. Kramer Inc., P.O. Box 1082, Tiburon, CA 94920. Lists for $14.95.

A scathing review of the current medical profession in the United States and the powerful for-profit alliances between the AMA, FDA, and pharmaceutical giants. It provides highly recommended reading with well-documented reports on the systematic persecution of several successful alternative therapies. These therapies have been attacked simply because they provide competition to the ultra-lucrative, high-tech medical industry. John Robbins advocates a very sane combination of the best that both alternative medicine and high-tech medicines have to offer. This book is a real eye-opener, with some good general practical advice, although it's more on the political than the instructive side of medical issues.

***Why People Don't Heal and How They Can,* by Caroline Myss, Ph.D.** 1997, 263 pp. (paperback), ISBN 0-609-60090-7. Published by Harmony Books, 201 East 50th Street, New York, NY 10022. Lists for $14.00.

Caroline Myss is a medical intuitive and an immensely popular author of books on the mental, spiritual, and psychological aspects of healing. In the late 1980s, she started running into a lot of people who were doing "all the right things," yet still not healing. Her book offers deep insights into the nature of healing, numerous case history examples, and mental/spiritual exercises for removing the inner roots of disease. If you like this book, you will probably also like her bestseller, *Anatomy of the Spirit*.

***Women's Bodies, Women's Wisdom: Creating Physical and Emotional Health and Healing,* by Christiane Northrup, M.D.** 1998, 906 pp. (paperback), ISBN 0-553-37953-4. Published by Bantam Books, 1540 Broadway, New York, NY 10036. Lists for $17.95.

"A masterpiece for every woman who has an interest in her body, her mind, and her soul." (Caroline Myss, Ph.D., author of *Anatomy of the Spirit*)

This voluminous book offers the most up-to-date information on the entire range of women's health problems. Dr. Christiane Northrup provides sound advice for helping women to heal faster, more completely, and with far fewer medical interventions. She combines mind-body wellness with nutrition and sound medical advice.

Magazines

Natural Health. Subscription: $23.95 per year for 9 issues. Natural Health, P.O. Box 37474, Boone, IA 50037-0474. Call (800) 526-8440 or see their web site at www.naturalhealthmag.com.

This magazine is devoted to optimizing your health through fitness, supplements, herbs and other forms of natural healing. Interesting monthly articles on the latest anti-aging compounds, natural supple-

ments, health research and natural forms of healing. Advisory board and regular contributors include Andrew Weil, MD, James Duke, Ph.D., Dean Ornish, MD, Christiane Northrup, MD, Dana Ullman, MPH, Jennifer Jacobs, MD, etc.

Alternative Medicine. Subscription: $20.00 per year for 6 issues. Alternative Medicine, 1640 Tiburon Blvd. Suite 2, Tiburon, CA 94920. Call (800) 333-4325 or see their web site at www. alternativemedicine.com.

This magazine is dedicated to providing educational and informative articles on alternative medicine that are neither too technical nor just a bunch of "fluff" without any real substance. Check out their web site for valuable information on the health benefits of specific alternative medicines and their effectiveness for healing certain ailments.

Herbs for Health. Subscription: $24.00 per year for 6 issues. Herbs for Health, P.O. Box 7708, Red Oak, IA 51591-0708. Call (800) 456-6018 or see their web site at www.discoverherbs.com.

An excellent magazine devoted to promoting health through the use of medicinal herbs. They enlist the help of a very impressive list of expert advisors and contributing authors.

Yoga Journal. Subscription: Yoga Journal, 2054 University Avenue, Berkeley, CA 94704. Call (800) 600-9642 or see their web site at www.yogajournal.com.

For thousands of years Far Eastern peoples have practiced Hatha Yoga to promote physical and spiritual well being. Yoga Journal is not just about yoga, but also includes interesting and well-written articles on natural healing and diet.

Colloidal Silver & Grapefruit Seed Extract

***The Authoritative Guide to Grapefruit Seed Extract: A Breakthrough in Alternative Treatment for Colds, Infections, Candida, Allergies, Herpes, and Many Other Ailments,* by**

Allan Sachs. 1997, 125 pp. (paperback), ISBN 0-940795-17-5. Published by LifeRythm, P.O. Box 806, Mendocino, CA 95460. Lists for $10.95. The author of this book is a certified clinical nutritionist and chiropractor. He is recognized as a leading authority on the use of grapefruit seed extract, and has successfully employed this amazing new herbal-based remedy to heal a wide variety of ailments.

***Colloidal Silver: Making and Using Your Own,* by Mark Metcalf.** 1998, 92 pp. (paperback). Self-published by Silver Solutions, P.O. Box 923, Forest Grove, OR 97116. Lists for $12.00. Call toll free (888) 505-6005 for price list and free reprints of articles on healing with colloidal silver.

This book provides detailed instructions for making your own colloidal silver solution generator and for making solutions of different concentrations. It also contains many testimonials and interesting information on the applications, history, and research concerning the use of colloidal silver. Mark's company, Silver Solutions, manufactures silver generators and sells the raw materials to make your own generators. His mission is to empower people to take control of their own health with low-cost medical alternatives to high-priced pharmaceuticals. Visit his web site at www.silversolutions.com.

***The Micro Silver Bullet,* by Dr. M. Paul Farber.** 1998, 664 pp. (paperback), ISBN 1-887742-01-8. Published by Professional Physicians Publishing & Health Services Inc., Houston, TX. Lists for $29.95.

This book is rather poorly organized but offers a considerable amount of data and anecdotal stories that support the use of colloidal silver (and its adjunct, mild silver protein) for curing numerous severe ailments, including AIDS, Candida albicans, multiple sclerosis, and Lyme disease. I suppose that time will tell if Dr. Farber is an eccentric genius or simply just an eccentric. If you are searching for a cure for a serious disease, this book is definitely worth reading. It documents his personal battle overcoming Lyme disease and multiple sclerosis using silver, plus his successful efforts to help a number of AIDS victims. Dr. Farber has numerous

academic degrees and is both a naturopathic doctor and a doctor of chiropractic. Visit his web site at www.silverbulletgold.com.

***Colloidal Silver: The Natural Antibiotic Alternative,* by Zane Baranowski, CN.** 1995, 17 pp. (paperback), ISBN 0-9647080-1-9. Published by Healing Wisdom Publications, 2067 Broadway, Suite 700, New York, NY 10023. Lists for $3.50.

This small health store booklet contains excellent background information on colloidal silver that I did not find in the other recommended books, plus a good bibliography in case you want to do some research on your own.

Death and Dying

***On Death and Dying: What the Dying Have to Teach Doctors, Nurses, Clergy and Their Own Families,* by Elizabeth Kubler-Ross.** 1997, 286 pp. (paperback), ISBN 0-684-83938-5. Published by Simon and Schuster, 1230 Avenue of the Americas, New York, NY 10020. Lists for $12.00.

A brilliant book by a woman who has dedicated her life to researching and serving the needs of terminally ill patients and their families. Elizabeth Kubler-Ross pretty much founded the conscious dying movement, which has brought a great deal of compassion and understanding into a modern world where the dying are often thrust into cold, compassionless institutions. Written in 1969, this is a classic book that still holds tremendous value after all these years.

***Transcending Loss: Understanding the Lifelong Impact of Grief and How to Make It Meaningful,* by Ashley Davis Prend, A.C.S.W.** 1997, 280 pp. (paperback), ISBN 0-425-15775-X. Published by The Berkley Publishing Group, 200 Madison Ave., New York, NY 10016. Lists for $12.95.

This is one of the best books out there for dealing with grief. *Transcending Loss* is a compassionate, poignant, and practical guide that not only covers the short-term crisis of dealing with the loss of a loved one, but the long-term process of living with and transcending grief. We found this book very helpful for dealing with the loss of a beloved family member.

Who Dies? An Investigation of Conscious Living and Conscious Dying, **by Stephen and Ondrea Levine.** 1989, 317 pp. (paperback), ISBN 0-385-26221-3. Published by Anchor Books/Doubleday, 1540 Broadway, New York, NY 10036. Lists for $12.95. Stephen Levine has worked with the pain and suffering of terminally ill and dying people for more than twenty-five years. This is a wonderful book, which compassionately shares some of the wisdom and experiences that Stephen has garnered through his work. Highly recommended both for personal growth and if you wish to prepare yourself to assist others with pain, suffering, or dying. Stephen describes several excellent mental techniques for dealing with chronic pain.

Energy Healing

The Complete Book of Reiki Healing, **by Brigitte Muller and Horst Gunther.** 1995, 185 pp. (paperback), ISBN 0-940795-16-7. Published by Life Rhythm, P.O. Box 806, Mendocino, CA 95460. Lists for $15.95.

This book is an excellent introduction to reiki, which is a healing system for both self-healing and the healing of others. Even though reiki was "discovered" by a Christian monk, it is nondenominational and operates totally independent of religious beliefs. Written by well-known, experienced reiki masters, the excellent illustrations make this a useful "how-to" book. In order to practice true reiki, however, one must receive "attunements" and instruction from a certified reiki master.

Essential Reiki: A Complete Guide to an Ancient Healing Art, **by Diane Stein.** 1995; 156 pp. (paperback), ISBN 0-89594-736-6. Published by The Crossing Press Inc., 97 Hanger Way, Watsonville, CA 95019. Lists for $18.95.

In this book, Diane Stein provides a good introduction to reiki energy healing. *Essential Reiki* is not strictly about reiki, but combines several other aspects of Asian bioenergy healing traditions with traditional reiki. Excellent illustrations make this a true "how-to" book. In order to truly practice reiki, however, one must receive "attunements" and

instruction from a certified reiki master. If Diane's feminist language or nontraditional approach bothers you, try the other reiki reference instead.

The Therapeutic Touch: How To Use Your Hands to Help or Heal **by Dolores Krieger, Ph.D., R.N.** 1992, 256 pp. (paperback), ISBN 0-671-76537-X. Published by Simon & Schuster, Rockefeller Center, 1230 Avenue of the Americas, New York, NY 10020. Lists for $12.00.

Shortly after receiving her Ph.D., Dolores Krieger was asked to participate in a research study concerned with scientifically evaluating the techniques and effectiveness of several well known healers who employed the "laying on of hands." The unmistakable feelings of warmth and energy felt during a healing session combined with startlingly positive effects on the patients profoundly effected Dr. Krieger's foundational beliefs and future work. The researchers found that not only can some kind of healing energy be felt and transmitted but that a process for doing this can be taught to most people. This excellent book started a revolution in western medical belief and practice known as therapeutic touch. Dolores Krieger has taught therapeutic touch to many thousands of medical professionals all over the world.

A Gift for Healing: How You Can Use Therapeutic Touch, **by Deborah Cowens and Tom Monte.** 1996, 256 pp. (paperback), ISBN 0-51788-651-0. Published by Crown Publishing Group, 201 E. 50th St., New York, NY 10022. Lists for $17.00.

This is a good companion book to *The Therapeutic Touch: How You To Use Your Hands to Help or Heal* by Dolores Krieger. Written by a natural born healer who is also a registered nurse, nutritionist and herbalist, it is a comprehensive guide to this system of bioenergy healing that is used successfully by a growing number of medical professionals and holistic healers. This text offers many interesting case examples of the use of therapeutic touch plus helpful illustrations and easy visualizations that enable readers to master these techniques for themselves.

Hands of Light: A Guide to Healing Through the Human Energy Field, **by Barbara Ann Brennan.** 1993, 294 pp. (paperback), ISBN 0-55334-539-7.

Published by Bantam Doubleday Dell Publishing Group, 666 Fifth Ave., New York, NY 10103. Lists for $23.95.

This is a well-written and beautifully illustrated book about the human aura and healing with bioenergy. Barbara Brennan is an atmospheric physicist and former NASA scientist turned author, healer, and teacher. She also operates the renowned Barbara Brennan School of Healing. I highly recommend this book, if you have any interest in this area of healing.

***Joy's Way: A Map for the Transformational Journey: An Introduction to the Potentials for Healing with Body Energies,* by W. Brugh Joy, M.D.** 1979, 290 pp. (paperback), ISBN 0-87477-085-8. Published by J. P. Tarcher, Inc., 200 Madison Ave., New York, NY 10016. Lists for $12.95.

In 1974, when W. Brugh Joy, M.D., was diagnosed with a terminal illness, he was a distinguished and respected member of the Los Angeles medical community. Later that year, he experienced an illuminating meditation, which caused him to give up his medical practice. Six weeks after leaving his practice, he discovered that his illness was completely cured. These experiences compelled him to further his exploration of the healing process in connection with body energies, meditation, and higher levels of consciousness. This book is a fascinating exploration into the nature of healing and offers practical exercises and techniques for working with the body energy fields.

Herbal Remedies and Naturopathy

***The Complete Medicinal Herbal,* by Penelope Ody.** 1993, 192 pp. (hardcover), ISBN 1-56458-187-X. Published by Dorling Kindersley, Inc., 95 Madison Ave., New York, NY 10016. Lists for $29.95.

This is a very practical guide to the use and preparation of herbs for natural healing. It contains many photographs of herbs, which may be useful if you wish to collect your own. Ody includes a good section on preparing your own medicines from herbs and includes specific dosage and type of remedy for each of about 120 herbs and for about 250 different home remedies.

***The Complete Illustrated Holistic Herbal: A Safe and Practical Guide to Making and Using Herbal Remedies,* by David Hoffman.** 1996, 256 pp. (paperback), ISBN 1-85230-758-7. Published by Element Books, Inc., P.O. Box 830, Rockport MA 01966. Lists for $24.95.

This new full-color edition of Hoffmann's highly acclaimed herbal is an A-to-Z compendium of more than 200 herbs. In it, Hoffmann provides extensive information about the uses, actions, dosages, and cautions for each herb, as well as instructions for gathering and preparing herbal remedies. It contains full-color photographs of herbs, which are useful if you wish to collect your own. Good information on herbal preparations. The folks at Ecology Action refer to this as their favorite herbal reference.

***The Cure for All Diseases,* by Hulda Regehr Clark, Ph.D., N.D.** 1995, 604 pp. (paperback), ISBN 1-890035-01-7. Published by New Century Press, 1055 Bay Boulevard, Suite C, Chula Vista, CA 91911. Lists for $21.95.

This excellent book contains many case histories and a wide variety of techniques/recipes for improving one's health. Dr. Clark stresses parasite elimination and toxic cleansing that allow the body's natural healing systems to respond to chronic and short-term diseases. She describes some of her research and the development of electronic devices for self-healing and diagnosis. Check out the rave reviews on Amazon.com, including personal testimonials about cancer cures using the information in her books. Her recent arrest for practicing medicine without a license indicates that Dr. Clark, like many others who threaten the profits of large pharmaceutical companies, has been targeted for persecution. To check out this story, order products online, or take a fascinating look into an alternative health revolution, visit her web site at www.drclark.ch.

***The Cure for All Advanced Cancers,* by Hulda Regehr Clark, Ph.D., N.D.** 1999, 610 pp. (paperback), ISBN 1-890035-16-5. Published by New Century Press, 1055 Bay Boulevard, Suite C, Chula Vista, CA 91911. Lists for $21.95.

This is Hulda Clark's latest book. It contains new

information from her ongoing research and many new case studies from her clinic. It claims a 95% success rate for treating advanced cancers (so-called "terminal" stage four and five cancers). If I were diagnosed with cancer, I would certainly consult this book right away. Contains fascinating information and many valuable self-help procedures. *The Cure for All Advanced Cancers* can help you to improve your health, even if you are not suffering from cancer, and if you wish to avoid cancer, it will tell you how.

The Edgar Cayce Handbook for Health Through Drugless Therapy, by Harold J. Reilly D. Ph.T., D.S., and Ruth Hagy Brod. 1975, 348 pp. (paperback), ISBN 0-87604-215-9. Published by A.R.E. Press, 67th Street and Atlantic Avenue, P.O. Box 595, Virginia Beach, VA 23451. Lists for $14.95.

"Medicine and most doctors aim at curing a specific ailment. The Cayce 'readings' and the Reilly therapy aim at producing a healthy body, which will heal itself of the ailment. We try to understand Nature and work with Nature. Then the body cures itself." (Harold J. Reilly, D.Ph.T., D.S.)

Edgar Cayce was likely the most famous U.S. psychic of all time. Known as the "Sleeping Prophet," he found that he could enter a sleeplike state in which he had access to detailed information for diagnosing and healing persons whom he had never met. Never having heard of the naturopathic healer and physical therapist Harold Reilly, the "sleeping" Edgar Cayce started referring cases to Dr. Reilly for treatment. In one of the most bizarre medical alliances of modern history, Dr. Reilly eventually became the dispenser of the mystical healing knowledge transmitted through the medium of Edgar Cayce. The amazing accuracy and effectiveness of the information received by Cayce has been thoroughly studied and documented by numerous scientists and physicians. These healing principles, techniques, remedies, and dietary suggestions, which are basically naturopathic in content, are very well-organized in Reilly's book. The Reilly Health Institute, which was located in the Rockefeller Center until Dr. Reilly retired, was made famous by the nonstop flow of celebrities who raved about the health benefits of

Reilly's treatments. Regular patients included Bob Hope, Nelson Rockefeller, the Duke and Duchess of Windsor, and Mae West.

Essiac: A Native Herbal Cancer Remedy by Cynthia Olsen. 1996, 119 pp. (paperback), ISBN 0-9628882-5-7. Published by Kali Press, P.O. Box 2169, Pagosa Springs, CO 81147-2169. Lists for $12.50.

This book provides information on the preparation and use of Essiac, many personal testimonials, and several lists of herbal sources and alternative medical treatment centers. It also tells the story of Rene Caisse's work and struggles with the government and the medical industry.

A Field Guide to Medicinal Plants: Eastern and Central North America (Peterson Field Guide Series), by Steven Foster, Roger Torey Peterson, and James A. Duke, Ph.D. 1990, 384 pp. (paperback), ISBN 0-39592-066-3. Published by Houghton Mifflin Co., 222 Berkeley St., Boston, MA 02116. Lists for $18.00.

One of the better field guides for identifying over 500 medicinal plants. Line drawings for each and color photographs for about half of them. Includes where the plants are found and detailed descriptions of their uses, both folk remedies and scientifically proven uses.

The Green Pharmacy: New Discoveries in Herbal Remedies for Common Diseases and Conditions from the World's Foremost Authority on Healing Herbs, by James A. Duke, Ph.D. 1997, 507 pp. (paperback), ISBN 1-57954-124-0. Published by Rodale Press, Emmaus, PA. Lists for $17.95.

James A. Duke, Ph.D., author of *The Green Pharmacy*, is recognized as the world's foremost authority on healing herbs. This book is a useful, entertaining, well-written, A-to-Z guide for using herbs to heal common ailments. James spent more than thirty years interviewing thousands of folk healers and scientists while compiling a unique database of the medicinal compounds found in common and exotic plants. This book is organized alphabetically by ailment. Dr. Duke offers multiple herbal remedies for each ailment, with useful notes concerning both scientific and folklore support for each remedy's effectiveness. Even though it is short on instructions for the preparation of herbal remedies, I recommend this book for its wealth of information on the use of specific herbs for specific ailments.

Herbal Antibiotics: Natural Alternatives for Treating Drug-Resistant Bacteria by Stephen Harrod Buhner. 1999, 135 pp. (paperback) ISBN 1-58017-148-6. Published by Storey Books, Schoolhouse Road, Pownal, VT 05261. Lists for $12.95.

This book explains how and why bacteria are becoming increasingly resistant to modern antibiotics and how herbal remedies offer hope for combating new supergerms and viruses, while maintaining effectiveness without developing bacteria resistant to these herbs. *Herbal Antibiotics* is an excellent little book that presents current information about antibiotic resistant microbes and the herbs that are most effective in fighting them.

Herb Contraindications and Drug Interactions, by Francis Brinker, N.D. 1998, 263 pp. (paperback), ISBN 1-888483-06-7. Published by Eclectic Medical Publications, 14385 S.E. Lusted Road, Sandy OR 97055. Lists for $19.95.

This is an excellent reference for the serious herbalist or physician seeking to integrate herbs and modern medicine, or for anyone seeking significant self-treatment with herbs. It exhaustively covers potentially harmful herbal interactions with other herbs and medical conditions, and with modern pharmaceutical drugs.

Identifying and Harvesting Edible and Medicinal Plants in Wild (And Not So Wild) Places by Steve Brill and Evelyn Dean. 1994, 317 pp. (paperback), ISBN 0-688-11425-3. Published by Hearst Books, William Morrow & Co., 1350 Avenue of the Americas, New York, NY 10019. Lists for $18.95.

This is a great book for the inexperienced forager. It covers a few hundred of the most common and useful edible and medicinal plants in North America. It is not exhaustive, but very usable and practical. Folk wisdom, first-hand practical experience, and scientific fact are blended with humorous and interesting anecdotes that help make this a very readable guide.

Indian Herbalogy of North America, by Alma R. Hutchins. 1991, 382 pp. (paperback), ISBN 0-87773-639-1. Published by Shambala Publications, 300 Massachusetts Ave., Boston, MA 02115. Lists for $19.00.

Considered the bible of Native American healing herbs, this is a great guide to finding, preparing, and using traditional American Indian herbal remedies. Covers all of North America. Highly recommended! Exhaustively researched, with black-and-white drawings for each herb, plus notes on domestic use, preparation, dosage, traditional application, homeopathic applications, and foreign uses.

Medicine from the Mountains: Medicinal Plants of the High Sierra Nevada, by Kimball Chatfield, O.M.D., L.Ac. 1997, 219 pp. (paperback), ISBN 0-9658001-0-5. Published by Range of Light Publications, P.O. Box 2000153, South Lake Tahoe, CA 96151. Lists for $17.95.

"A smooth-reading medicinal flora for the Sierra Nevada. The author skillfully relates it to Eastern American and European plants as well. I certainly want this compact volume next time I travel to the Range of Light" (James A. Duke, Ph.D., economic botanist, USDA, retired)

This is a beautifully illustrated guide to common medicinal plants in the High Sierra and other mountainous areas of the western states. Well researched, it includes preparation and doses.

The Way of Herbs, by Michael Tierra, L.Ac., O.M.D. 1998, 375 pp. (paperback), ISBN 0-671-02327-6. Published by Pocket Books, a division of Simon & Schuster Inc., 1230 Avenue of Americas, New York, NY 10020. Lists for $14.00.

This was recommended to me by an herbalist as her favorite all-around guide to herbal medicine. If you were to buy only one book on herbal medicine, this would be an excellent choice. The author, Michael Tierra, has studied and practiced herbal medicine for over thirty years. He has studied with traditional healers of Native America, India, and China. Tierra incorporates his broad knowledge into this book, offering healing philosophies and formulas that can make herbal healing far more effective than simply applying individual herbs to treat specific symptoms and diseases. The book includes information on herbal preparations and dosages, but provides no visuals for identifying herbs in the wild.

***The Way of Chinese Herbs,* by Michael Tierra, L.Ac., O.M.D.** 1998, 474 pp. (paperback), ISBN 0-671-02327-6. Published by Pocket Books, a division of Simon & Schuster Inc., 1230 Avenue of Americas, New York, NY 10020. Lists for $15.00.

For over 3,000 years, Chinese people have relied upon a wide variety of herbal concoctions for their health and longevity. In 1982 Michael Tierra, one of the nation's most respected herbalists, was chosen to be a part of the first group of Americans to travel to China specifically to study herbal medicine. Tierra's extensive knowledge of Chinese medicine is now available through this book to help readers access the healing power of Chinese herbs.

RESOURCES FOR HERBS AND SUPPLEMENTS

AllHerb.com, 14900 Sweitzer Lane, Laurel, MD 20707; phone: (877) 255-4372; fax: (301) 483-6800; web site: www.allherb.com.

This is truly a great herbal resource. The family of the founder of Allherb has been in the herbal business for more than fifty years, starting when his grandfather was in the ginseng trade in Asia in the 1940s. Allherb offers a huge variety of herbs, vitamins, and books, many at a significant discount. Tour their web site for numerous current articles on herbs by internationally renowned herbalists, such as James Duke Ph.D., Christopher Hobbs, and Steven Foster.

MotherNature.com, 1 Concord Farms, 490 Virginia Road, Concord MA 01742; phone: (800) 517-9020; fax (877) 355-1144; www.mothernature.com.

This is a great source for herbs, supplements, and other natural products for healthy living. Good online articles and information. Wide variety of products.

Self-Health Resource Center, 1055 Bay Blvd. #A, Chula Vista, CA 91911; phone: (800) 873-1663; Fax: (619) 409-9501.

This center sells the herbs, amino acids, supplements and other materials described in Dr. Clark's books, including the kidney cleanse, parasite program, liver cleanse, and her parasite "Zapper" and "Syncrometer" products. The Resource Center also offers nontoxic household products, such as deodorant without propylene glycol and baking powder without aluminum.

Sir Jason Winters's Products, Tri-Sun International, Inc., 2230 Cape Cod Way, Santa Ana, CA 92703; phone: (800) 387-4786; fax: (714) 835-4948; web site: www.sirjasonwinters.com.

Jason Winters's herbal teas, books, and other medicinal herbs are available, both online from his web site or by phone from Tri-Sun International.

Homeopathy

***Everybody's Guide to Homeopathic Medicines: Safe and Effective Remedies for You and Your Family,* by Stephen Cummings, M.D., and Dana Ullman, M.P.H.** 1997, 375 pp. (paperback), ISBN 0-87477-843-3. Published by J. P. Tarcher, 200 Madison Ave., New York, NY 10016. Lists for $16.95.

This is an excellent guide to homeopathy, including advice on strengthening the immune system, individualizing homeopathic treatment, and accessing homeopathic resources. The primary author is a physician and the leading homeopathic educator in the United States.

***Healing with Homeopathy: The Doctor's Guide,* by Wayne B. Jonas, M.D., and Jennifer Jacobs, M.D., M.P.H.** 1996, 349 pp. (paperback), ISBN 0-446-67342-0. Published by Warner Books, Inc., 1271 Avenue of Americas, New York, NY 10020. Lists for $14.99.

This is an excellent introduction to homeopathy written by two physicians. In addition to being a practical guide for self-medication with homeopathy, it includes very interesting information on the history, foundations, scientific studies, and case histories of homeopathic healing.

Hypnosis

The Art of Hypnosis: Mastering Basic Techniques, by Roy C. Hunter. 1996, 224 pp. (paperback), ISBN 0-7872-2524-X. Published by Kendall/Hunt Publishing Co., 4050 Westmark Drive, Dubuque, IA 52004-1840. Lists for $21.95.

This book provides numerous techniques for beginners to professionals. It comes highly praised by both hypnotherapists and psychologists. If the narrower focus of self-hypnosis is what interests you, try Roy Hunter's *Master the Power of Self-Hypnosis*. For information on the broader topic of hypnotherapy, try *The Art of Hypnotherapy* by the same author.

Hypnosis for Change, by Josie Hadley and Carol Staudacher. 1996, 294 pp. (paperback), 1-57224-057-1. Published by New Harbinger Publications, a division of Random House, 1540 Broadway, 11ᵗʰ Floor, New York, NY 10036. Lists for $15.95.

This practical and inspiring handbook will show you how to begin today to use hypnosis to change your life, including habit control, physical and emotional healing. Step-by-step explanations and case-histories will teach you about the different trance states, the effective use of treatment scripts, and the best use of these and other techniques to bring you success. My wife uses some of Josie Hadley's hypnosis scripts in her hypnotherapy practice.

Odyssey of the Soul, A Trilogy: Book I, Apocatastasis, by Pamela Chilton, C.H.T, and Hugh Harmon, Ph.D. 1997, 271 pp. (paperback), ISBN 0-965989-100-0. Web site: www.odysseyofthesoul.org. Published by Quick Book Publishing, 10 Venus Drive, Rancho Mirage, CA 92270. Lists for $15.00.

The authors are both certified hypnotherapists, who work in private practice and their own hypnotherapy school. This book blends personal stories with practical details and case examples of the application of hypnotherapy for a wide variety of applications. Includes neuro-muscular response (NMR) techniques for bypassing the conscious mind to gain insightful information on health problems, toxic sensitivity to certain materials, optimal paths, and so on. Also contains information on spirit possession, past-life regressions, and "channeled" information. Not as traditional as the other references, but very interesting and informative.

Self-Hypnosis and Other Mind-Expanding Techniques, by Charles Tebbetts. 1997, 141 pp. (paperback), ISBN 0-930298-18-7. Published by Westwood Publishing Co., 700 S. Central Ave., Glendale, CA 91204. Lists for $9.95.

This is a classic text on self-hypnosis. It is a clear, simple manual, written by a master hypnotist and well-known teacher of hypnosis. Short and sweet.

My Voice Will Go With You: The Teaching Tales of Milton H. Erikson, edited and commentary by Sidney Rosen. 1991, 256 pp. (paperback), ISBN 0-393-30135-4. Published by W. W. Norton & Company, 500 Fifth Avenue, New York, NY 10110. Lists for $13.95.

This fine book gives an excellent introduction to the brilliant, highly successful, and uncommon approach to counseling and hypnotherapy as practiced by Milton Erikson. It is highly recommended, whether you are a professional therapist or simply struggling with the problems of raising children or dealing with difficult people.

Spirit Releasement Therapy: A Technique Manual, by William J. Baldwin, D.D.S., Ph.D. 1995, 456 pp. (paperback), ISBN 0-929915-16-X. Published by Headline Books, P.O. Box 52, Terra Alta, WV 26764. Lists for $39.95.

"A brilliant, daring tour de force by one of the pioneers of Spirit Releasement Therapy: Dr. Baldwin has painstakingly integrated an enormous range of techniques as well as much wisdom gleaned from Past Life Therapy, spirit releasement, soul retrieval, inner child work, and traditional psychotherapy. With his abundance of case studies, highly practical differential diagnosis outlines and therapeutic strategies, his book is invaluable as both a manual and a sourcebook. . . . I predict it will be referred to and argued about for years to come." (Roger J. Woolger, Ph.D., Author of *Other Lives, Other Selves*)

A practical and fascinating modern therapist's manual for using hypnosis to deal with many different psychological problems, including multiple personalities and spirit possession. These therapies are powerful tools for spiritual and emotional healing. They even have the capacity to return apparently "crazy" people from insanity to fully functional "normal" human beings.

Prayer and Healing

Healing Words: The Power of Prayer and the Practice of Medicine, by **Larry Dossey, M.D.** 1995; 320 pp. (paperback), ISBN 0-06250-252-2. Published by Harper San Francisco, 1160 Battery St., 3rd Floor, San Francisco, CA 94111-1213. Lists for $14.00.

Capturing the attention of the American Medical Association (AMA) and the presidential task force on health care, Dr. Dossey's provocative book shares the latest evidence linking prayer, healing, and medicine. Calling for a bold new integration of science and spirituality, Dossey shares case studies and anecdotes that illustrate those methods of prayer offering the greatest potential for healing. In addition to summarizing a convincing array of scientific tests and studies that support the power of prayer to positively affect healing, Dossey blasts the idea that illness is the patient's fault and that physical health always reflects spiritual health. He points out that many saints and holy men have suffered from terrible physical maladies, including some of the same illnesses that they reportedly healed in others.

Science and Health: With Keys to the Scriptures, by **Mary Baker Eddy.** 1991, 700 pp. (paperback), ISBN 1-87864-100-X. Published by Aequus

Publications or The First Church of Christ Scientist, Boston MA. Lists for $9.95.

Originally published in 1875, this is one of the preeminent books on spiritual healing. When her own prayers and the prayers of her congregation had failed to heal Mary Baker Eddy of a chronic illness, she turned repeatedly to the Bible. Seeking solace and understanding, she feels that she received divine inspiration for a deeper spiritual interpretation of Jesus' words and the process that he used to heal without material medicines or manipulations. Many thousands claim to have been healed by reading her book and applying its spiritual healing principles. Her book supports her beliefs with selections from the Bible, offers a deeper explanation of her spiritual healing methods, and gives numerous testimonials to the effectiveness of these methods of healing.

Shamanic Healing

Coyote Medicine: Lessons from Native American Healing, by **Lewis Mehl-Madrona, M.D.** 1998, 304 pp. (paperback), ISBN 0-68483-997-0. Published by Fireside Books, a division of Simon & Schuster Inc., 1230 Avenue of Americas, New York, NY 10020. Lists for $13.00.

Stanford-trained physician Lewis Mehl-Madrona has written an outstanding book about his struggles with integrating his Native American roots, traditional Indian healing practices, and Western style medicine. Half Cherokee, Mehl-Madrona is a survivor, not fully comfortable in either world. His accounts of Native American shamanic healing and ceremonies are fascinating glimpses into another world. This book is well written, entertaining, illuminating, and informative. However, this is not a "how-to" book.

Shape Shifting: Shamanic Techniques for Global and Personal Transformation, by **John Perkins.** 1997, 172 pp. (paperback), ISBN 0-89281-663-5. Published by Destiny Books, One Park Street, Rochester, VT 05767. Lists for $12.95.

"Only a handful of visionaries have recognized that indigenous wisdom can aid the transition to a sustainable world. John Perkins's wonderful story of life among the shamans brings great insight for an industrial civilization consuming and polluting itself towards catastrophe." (Edgar Mitchell, Sc.D., Apollo astronaut and founder of the *Institute of Noetic Sciences)*

Since 1968, master shamans in Africa, Asia, the Middle East, and the Americas have been training John Perkins to teach the industrialized world about the powerful techniques involved in shape shifting. Shape shifting is more than just a shamanic trick—it is a tool for personal healing and transformation that we may collectively apply toward shifting the future of our planet. This is a fascinating book.

***Soul Retrieval: Mending the Fragmented Self,* by Sandra Ingerman.** 1991, 240 pp. (paperback), ISBN 006250. Published by Harper San Francisco, 1160 Battery St., 3rd Floor, San Francisco, CA 94111-1213. Lists for $15.00.
This excellent book covers the traditional shamanic practice of soul retrieval as taught and practiced by many shamans from different cultures around the world. Ingerman, like her mentor Michael Harner, is a practicing Western shaman and teaches workshops around the world on this subject. The ancient practice of soul retrieval can yield powerful, permanent, profound, psychological, spiritual, and physical benefits after only a single session.

***The Way of the Shaman,* by Michael J. Harner, Ph.D.** 1990, 171 pp. (paperback), ISBN 0-06250-373-1. Published by Harper San Francisco, 1160 Battery St., 3rd Floor, San Francisco, CA 94111-1213. Lists for $14.00.
This classic work is a fascinating, informative, and practical introduction to shamanism. The author is one of the world's foremost academic authorities on shamanism and has been a practicing shaman since his initiation by an Amazonian native shaman around 1960. Harner has worked directly with numerous shamans across North and South America, and has researched shamanic cultures throughout the world. Harner insists that shamanism is an experiential system, not based upon religious or scientific beliefs, and offers exercises to help the reader explore alternate realities and states of consciousness, without the use of drugs. He also

established The Foundation for Shamanic Studies, which offers practical, experiential workshops on various aspects of shamanism at several locations around the country. If you are intrigued by shamanism and the possibility of experiencing it for yourself, I highly recommend this book. It contains numerous exercises and references for exploring the shamanic state of consciousness (SSC) on your own.

RESOURCES FOR SHAMANISM

The Dance of the Deer Foundation: Center for Shamanic Studies, P.O. Box 699, Soquel, CA 95073; phone: (831) 475-9560; web site: www.shamanism.com.
This organization offers experiential courses in traditional shamanic healing and other practices. The foundation is directed by Brant Secunda, who completed a twelve-year apprenticeship under Don José Matsuwa, the renowned Huichol shaman. Later he became the adopted grandson of Don José, who left Brant in his place to carry on the Huichol shamanic practices and traditions.

Dream Change Coalition, P.O. Box 31357, Palm Beach Gardens, FL 33420; phone: (561) 622-6064; web site: www.dreamchange.org.
The Dream Change Coalition is a grass roots movement dedicated to encouraging sustainable lifestyles for the individual and the global community. They offer trips to visit and work with master native shamans for personal healing and transformation. Their objective of inspiring earth-honoring changes in consciousness is accomplished through forest conservation projects that support and apply indigenous wisdom, and programs that educate and foster environmental and social balance. The Shuar Indians of Ecuador believe that "the world is as you dream it." Through the encroachment of the modern world into their realm, they have come to realize that their contemporaries have been busy dreaming an environmental nightmare of conquering and controlling nature's resources. They asked their friend of three decades, author John Perkins, to help birth a new vision for the industrialized societies.

The Foundation for Shamanic Studies, P.O. Box 1939, Mill Valley, CA 94942; phone: (415) 380-8282; web site: www.shamanism.org.

This foundation offers numerous experiential workshops on various facets of shamanism. The Way of the Shaman Basic Workshop is a prerequisite class for all of the Foundation's more advanced workshops. Classes are offered at a variety of locations across the country. They also sell drumming tapes and CDs that are helpful for experiencing the shamanic state of consciousness on your own.

Visualization

***Healing Visualizations: Creating Health Through Imagery,* by Gerald Epstein, M.D.** 1989, 227 pp. (paperback), ISBN 0-533-34623-7. Published by Bantam Doubleday Dell Publishing Group, 666 Fifth Ave., New York, NY 10103. Lists for $13.95.

Dr. Gerald Epstein has written an inspiring and practical guide to utilizing the powers of your own mind for promoting rapid and effective healing. A psychiatrist and pioneer in waking dream therapy, Epstein shows the reader how the mind can help to heal the body through the power of "imaginal medicine." Containing numerous case examples and more than seventy-five specific exercises, this guide covers suggested imagery therapies for ailments ranging from the rapid healing of fractures, to arthritis, AIDS, and cancer.

"Western" Medical Model

***The Pill Book: The Illustrated Guide to the Most Prescribed Drugs in the United States,* edited by Harold M. Silverman, Pharm.D.** 1996, 1241 pp. (paperback), ISBN 0-553-57452-3. Published by Bantam Books, 1540 Broadway, New York, NY 10036. Lists for $6.99.

This is a great reference for anyone who relies on traditional western medicines for healing. Compiled by a team of eminent pharmacologists, *The Pill Book* provides excellent information on specific medicines, including side effects, interactions, effectiveness on specific ailments, and cross-references to other generic or more effective medicines. Most doctors only know what the drug companies tell them and do not read the multiple pages of fine print that come with each of the thousands of different medicines. If you use pharmaceutical drugs, buy this book and educate yourself about what you put into your body!

***Healthwise Handbook: A Self-Care Guide for You,* by Donald W. Kemper.** 1999, 372 pp. (paperback), ISBN 1-877930-71-7. Published by Healthwise Publications, P.O. Box 1989, Boise, ID 83701. Lists for $9.95.

The award-winning *Healthwise Handbook* is the best-selling self-care manual ever printed. This book contains family guidelines on prevention, home treatment, and when to call in a health professional. Visit the publisher's web site at www.ivillage.healthwise.com to search the *Healthwise Knowledgebase* medical information database about virtually every health topic. Purchase of this book gives you free access to the medical information database.

Where There Is No Doctor: A Village Health Care Handbook

See the description in the *References* section of Chapter 8.

Ditch Medicine: Advanced Field Procedures for Emergencies

See the description in the *References* section in Chapter 8.

***Where There Is No Dentist,* by Murray Dickson.** 1999, 195 pp. (paperback), ISBN 0-942364-05-8. Published by The Hesperian Foundation, P.O. Box 11577, Berkeley, CA 94712-2577. Lists for $9.00.

Designed for village health care workers in Third World settings, *Where There Is No Dentist* provides basic dental health educational guidelines for promoting good dental hygiene, even where there is no access to simple tools like the modern tooth brush. Covers temporary fillings, extractions, and cleaning, in addition to diagnosis and treatment recommendations for quite a variety of medical and dental problems in and around the mouth. I would rather go to the dentist, but if one was not available, this book could be a big help.

X Clothing & Textiles

No one knows when spinning began—10,000 BC? 15,000 BC? The oldest fabric we know of so far shows that its maker already had remarkable skill. It was found in Turkey and is believed to have been made around 6300 BC. Far newer fabrics, almost 4,500 years old, were made with such precision and skill that they have yet to be duplicated by hand or machine. These are the Egyptian "transparent" linens (there is some dispute over the actual fiber used) with more than five hundred threads to the inch. These and countless other striking textiles all began with yarns spun on a hand-spindle. Spinning wheels wouldn't be seen for another 3,500 years.

—Lee Raven, *Hands On Spinning*

In many primitive cultures, spinning, weaving, dyeing, knitting, sewing, and otherwise fabricating textiles and clothing occupies a large chunk of time, often second only to farming. Luckily for modern people, these traditional crafts can now be enjoyed as relaxing artful pastimes rather than never-ending chores. Hopefully, things will remain this way and you can use this chapter to acquaint yourself with the way things used to be done, or to help you find your way to sources for learning these fine traditional crafts.

Preindustrial peoples probably first clothed themselves with skins and furs from animals or woven coverings from local grasses and plants. Native Americans created beautifully woven cloth long before the Europeans brought spinning wheels and shuttle looms to America. Remarkably effective Eskimo clothing was skillfully crafted from elk, deer, and seal skins that protect the wearer from the most extreme arctic conditions, exceeding ultramodern high-tech expedition clothing in some aspects of durability and function.

FIBER ARTS

Since before recorded history, indigenous peoples have spun threads, yarn, and cordage from thousands of native plants at locations spread across the globe. Wool remains a favorite of many spinners and weavers. Wool has the benefit of natural water repellency that helps it retain insulating value even when wet. Cotton, on the other hand, although comfortable against the skin, is a poor insulator when wet. Linen was once one of the most important fibers in the world for cloth production. Due to the lengthy processes involved in extracting linen fibers from flax stalks, it now occupies a minor position far below cotton. Hemp was once the premier plant fiber of choice in America for making paper and cloth, but due to political forces and the development of the cotton gin, it was preempted by cotton and wood pulp. Hemp is making a comeback, although the United States remains one of the few nations to suppress the farming of hemp for fiber. Thousands of other perfectly usable plant and animal fibers have faded into obscurity because, for one reason or another, they have not been economically adapted to modern machinery-intensive textile processes.

Preparing Fibers

Most plant and animal fibers must be cleaned, untangled, and oriented prior to spinning into thread and yarns. When working with wool, spinners usually prefer to work with washed (or "scoured") wool. A "fleece" is the shorn coat of a furry animal. Wool fleeces usually contain a quantity of animal grease, insecticide from "dips" to kill pests, dirt, and debris. Washed wool may weigh 20% to 50% of what the raw fleece weighs, so take this into consideration when buying a fleece.

Animal fibers are typically further cleaned and oriented by "teasing," "carding," and sometimes "combing." The simplest method, which requires no tools, is simply to "tease" the fibers. While holding a lock of wool in one hand, pinch some of the fibers with the fingers of the other hand and gradually draw the fibers into elongated parallel strands. This works best with the long fibers from the prime parts of the fleece.

Figure 10-1. Teasing fibers.

If wool is spun unwashed, which some spinners like to do (in Australia and New Zealand it is the preferred method), it must be skeined (wound into a large loose bundle, rather like a coil of rope) and washed after spinning. Tie the skein, hand wash it in soapy water, and then rinse, towel, and hang with a small weight that roughly matches the weight of the skein.

CARDING

Carding fibers is the traditional method that the pioneers used to open, clean, and align fibers before spinning. The carding process uses two paddles, about 4" x 9", with hundreds of fine wire teeth mounted on the face of the card, like a wire brush for combing a dog's fur. Wool is first loaded onto one carder, and then gently brushed with the other carder via a rocking stroke action. The wool is transferred a few times between carders, the fibers becoming more oriented and combed with each transfer. Most books on spinning provide a detailed well-illustrated explanation of this process. If you are too vigorous in your carding actions, you will create lots of small tangles called "neps," which will make lumps when spun into yarn or thread. For best results, card

gently with no more wool than it takes to just cover all the teeth of your carder. Hand carding is a time-consuming process. It has been reported that it takes 17 people hand carding wool to keep up with one weaver (Brown 1983, 223). Many spinners, who only wish to spin for themselves and their families or friends, find a 4"-wide, hand-operated drum carder a worthwhile investment.

Figure 10-2. Carding wool.

COMBING

Combing is a far older process than carding, probably because it employs a simple and logical tool consisting of one to eight rows of long, slender pointed teeth. Drawing the wool through the comb removes all the short fibers and tangles from the wool. Spinning with combed wool yields a "worsted" yarn, which is stronger, smoother, and more lustrous than the softer and more "wooly" yarn produced from carded wool. Combing wool can result in the loss of as much as half of the fleece, depending on the breed of animal and quality of the fleece.

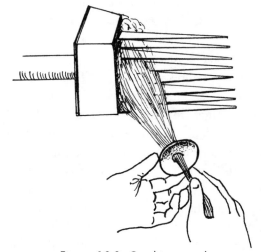

Figure 10-3. Combing wool.

PLANT FIBERS

Plant fibers are usually in the form of *bast* fibers, leaf fibers, or a hairy clump of fibers that surround the seeds or fruit of the plant. Bast fibers are long tough fibers that form a sheath in the plant stalk surrounding a woody core, such as in flax, hemp, and jute. Leaf fibers are tough fibers extending the length of the leaf, such as in sisal, yucca, and agave. Some examples of plant fibers surrounding seeds and fruit are cotton, kapok, and milkweed pod. With all plant fibers, some form of processing is required to remove the fibers from the rest of the plant material.

Bast fibers typically go through a process called "retting," which involves partially rotting the plant stalks to loosen the bond between the fibers and the bark and central core, without destroying the fiber's strength. Too much rotting, and the fibers lose their strength or fall apart. Modern manufacturers use harsh chemical baths for quickly retting plant fibers, but traditional methods relied on water, time, and bacterial action for retting plant stalks. Stalks were either retted in running water, stagnant water, or dew. For running water retting, the fibers are bundled into crates weighted with stones, and then placed in a river or creek for 10 to 20 days (the time period depends on plant type and water temperature). When plant stalks are retted in stagnant water, fermentation and bacterial action are greatly accelerated quickening the process, but care must be taken to not weaken or destroy the fibers by overretting. The simplest and longest process is "dew retting." In this process, the plants are laid out on a grassy field and turned every week or so for a period of 6 to 8 weeks (Leadbeater 1983, 60–61). Regardless of the method used, the retting process is complete when the bast fibers separate easily from the woody core.

After retting, bast type stalks are dried in preparation for the next step, called "breaking," where the woody cores and unretted hulls are broken out of the stems while leaving the long bast fibers intact. The crude method is to simply beat the stalks with a wooden mallet. A more effective low-tech breaking method is the use of a wooden flax break.

Figure 10-4. Flax break.

The next step, called "scutching," consists of beating the fibers against a board with a wooden knife driven at an angle to the fibers, to remove all the broken crud ("boon") from the bundle of fibers. The last step is to comb the fibers through a circular pattern comb, called a "hackle," to remove tangles and shorter fibers, and smaller bits of debris. The shorter fibers may be twisted into coarse yarn, rope, or twine, while the longer fibers are spun into thread or yarn. See *A Weaver's Garden: Growing Plants for Natural Dyes and Fibers* by Rita Buchanan or *Handspinning* by Eliza Leadbeater for more complete information on low-tech methods for preparing plant fibers.

Sustainable Fibers

Half of all textile fibers come from cotton, whose cultivation uses one-fourth of all agrochemicals and of all insecticides.
—Paul Hawken, Amory Lovins, and L. Hunter Lovins, *Natural Capitalism*

The production of fibers for human use takes its toll on the environment. Consuming about 25% of the world's agricultural use of petrochemicals, fertilizer, pesticides, and herbicides, cotton clearly holds the dubious honor of having the highest global impact of any processed fiber. A small, but growing percentage of the world's cotton is now grown organically. Overgrazing of goats and sheep has also contributed significantly to the desertification of millions of acres of range land around the world.

On the one hand, the petrochemical industry is a known polluter and uses nonrenewable resources to supply the world with synthetic fibers for clothing, cordage, and composites. On the other, the use of synthetic fibers has probably saved millions of acres of trees from being cut down for their fibers, and for acreage to grow additional cotton. One part of the sustainable fiber solution is to recycle rags back into cloth, and plastic waste into synthetic fibers.

Patagonia, a $165-million-a-year clothing company, has used only organically grown cotton in its products since 1996 and is dedicated to reducing its impact on the planet by using planet friendly fibers, processes, and products whenever possible. This company has converted most of its entire Synchilla line of fleece clothing to PCR (post-consumer recycled) fleece, fibers spun from recycled soda bottles (Patagonia, 2000). Hopefully, other major manufacturers will follow their example by changing their product lines over to the use of recycled fibers and organically grown natural fibers.

Another part of the solution is to replace cotton with less environmentally taxing fibers. Hemp is one plant fiber that has a fraction of the environmental impact of growing cotton, and has the added benefit of producing highly nutritional foods and valuable industrial products from hemp seed and hemp oil. Hemp is one of the strongest plant fibers, and can be used to make cloth that lasts two to three times longer than cotton, or paper that lasts several times as long as wood pulp paper. George Washington and Thomas Jefferson both grew hemp. They wore clothes woven from hemp fiber and wrote the Declaration of Independence on paper made from hemp. Hemp is a naturally pest-resistant plant that acts as a weed killer. When farming hemp, one can practically eliminate the need for herbicides and pesticides. Hemp can yield three to eight dry tons of fiber per acre, roughly four times the average fiber yield from 20-year-old forests grown for pulp (NAIHC, 2000).

Unfortunately, due to political maneuvering by wood pulp and synthetic fiber industrial giants, combined with unwarranted fears about marijuana and hemp, hemp farming was banned from U.S. soil in the 1950s. Hemp strains grown for fiber have almost none of the psychoactive components (THC) of marijuana. Additionally, hemp farming practices for optimum fiber growth require close-packed plantings to maximize tall stalks and minimize leaves and flowers, which is the exact opposite of agricultural practice for farming marijuana, making it impractical to hide marijuana cultivation within hemp farms. Hemp requires far less water than cotton and can be grown in much colder climates. In 1997, Canada repealed its ban on hemp farming and is actively supporting the return of its hemp farming industry. The United States is one of the few remaining industrialized nations where it is still illegal to grow hemp for fiber.

Spinning

The act of twisting a stream of fibers from a loose bundle interlocks the individual strands to make strong continuous threads and yarns that resist pulling apart. The fibers should be teased, combed, or carded so that they are mainly free from each other and only loosely interlocked. The crudest method for spinning fibers is to hand roll the fibers on your leg with one hand while loosely grasping a bundle of teased fibers with the other hand.

DRAFTING

By controlling the tension on the bundle of fibers with your fingers, you can allow a controlled amount of fiber to gently and slowly slide through your fingers, feeding the growing thread or yarn that you are twisting with the other hand. This controlled feed of fibers is called "drafting." Too much tension on the fingers of the drafting hand, and your yarn will not pull enough fibers from the clump. Too little finger tension and your yarn will be thick and lumpy. Test your yarn's strength by pulling on it. If there is too little twist, the yarn will be weak and will pull apart easily. Practice goes a long way toward improving your comfort and ability with this skill. Be patient with yourself.

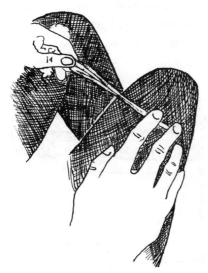

Figure 10-5. Drafting and hand rolling fibers.

SPINNING WITH A HOOKED STICK

A simple tool for primitive spinning is the "hooked stick." A 12" length of coat hanger will do. Run the hook through some of the fibers from your bundle, and then draw out a few inches of fibers and start spinning your hooked stick along your thigh. As a section of your yarn gets wound adequately, pinch the yarn next to the drafting zone to keep it from unwinding, and then wind the yarn around the center of your hooked stick, finishing with a loop through the hook, before drafting and spinning another section of yarn.

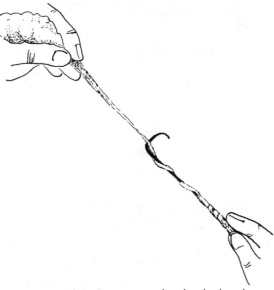

Figure 10-6. Spinning with a hooked stick.

JOINS

When you run out of fibers in the bundle in your drafting hand, you need to "join" or splice in a new bundle of fibers. A proper join is an invisible overlapping of fibers that is as strong as the rest of your yarn. To make a join, untwist and fluff up a few inches of fiber from the end of your yarn. Tease a fluffy section from the end of your next bundle of fibers and overlap this with the fluffed up end of your yarn. Hold this overlapped section of fibers in your hand and draft together while you continue spinning your yarn. This technique applies to all hand-spinning methods.

SPINNING WITH A HAND SPINDLE

The next step up the evolutionary ladder of spinning is the hand spindle, which is still used throughout the world for spinning yarn. There are many different variations on this theme, but all basically have a long dowel-like stick with a weight, called a whorl, which gives some mass to the spindle and helps it to keep spinning for awhile after each time it's given a quick hand spin. The process is much the same as for the hooked stick, but the process is sped up significantly because the spindle keeps spinning on its own for a short time after each flick of the hand. Start by hand rolling a yard of two-ply yarn on your leg and tying it to the spindle next to the whorl. This is called the "leader." Two-ply yarn holds the twist, whereas one-ply yarn tends to untwist and break. To make two-ply yarn, pinch a section of yarn in its middle and twist the two half-sections of yarn together in the opposite direction of the twist from that which they were spun. See the two-ply cordage illustration in Chapter 4 for more details.

Suspend the spindle and give it a quick spin with one hand as you draft the fibers with the other hand. Alternately, some designs of spindles may be rolled against your thigh or spun like a top in a shallow dish. As with the hooked stick, when the yarn stretches out uncomfortably long, pinch the yarn below the drafting zone and wind the yarn around the spindle shaft. If the spindle shaft has a hook or T-slot, spiral the yarn up the shaft and run it through the hook or slot before starting to spin on the next length of yarn. If the end of the spindle shaft does not have a hook or T-slot, secure the yarn with a half hitch around the tip of the spindle. Even when there is a notch near the top of the spindle, you might find the use of a half hitch helpful.

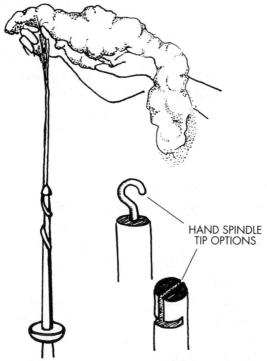

Figure 10-7. Spinning with a hand spindle.

HAND SPINDLE
TIP OPTIONS

SPINNING WITH A SPINNING WHEEL

India is credited with developing the first spinning wheel known as the *charkha* around 500 BC. In 1530, the German woodcarver Johann Jurgen is credited with adapting a scheme from Leonardo da Vinci's sketchbook to make the first modern spinning wheel that incorporated spinning and winding into one operation with a U-shaped arm (called a "flyer") spinning around a bobbin. Leonardo's ingenious concept became the foundation for all modern spinning and sewing machines. The center of the flyer has a hole in it to allow the yarn to feed into one end of the spinning flyer, getting twisted as it goes, and then feeds out the side of the flyer through a series of hooks where it is wound onto the bobbin. The spinner pauses now and then to position the yarn through a different hook for winding on a different section of the bobbin. There are many different styles of spinning wheels, but most involve similar hand techniques where one

hand holds and drafts the fiber supply while the fingers of the other hand gently pinch the yarn to control the tension of the twist.

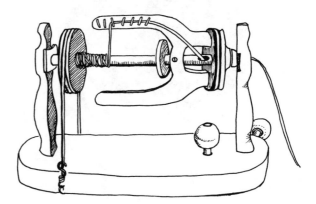

Figure 10-8. Spinning wheel flyer and bobbin.

Figure 10-9. Spinning wheel.

Weaving

For thousands of years, people have woven beautiful carpets and cloth on simple handmade looms. Numerous loom designs are used across the planet, but they all work on variations of the same principles. In woven fabrics, two sets of yarns cross perpendicular to each other. One longitudinal set of yarns, called the "warp," is first strung across some kind of loom. Then a second set of yarns, called a "weft" or "woof," is woven repeatedly back and forth through the warp.

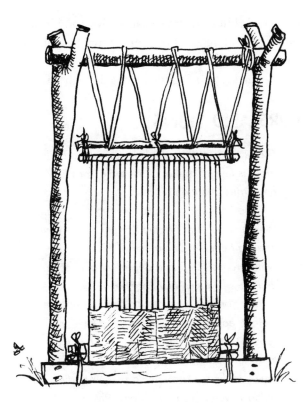

Figure 10-10. Navajo loom.

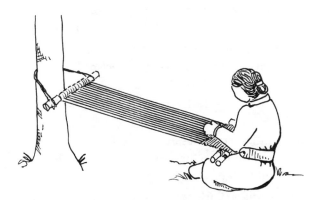

Figure 10-11. Backstrap loom.

To manually weave the cross threads (weft) over and under each individual thread of the warp would be a time-consuming and tedious job for all but simple narrow belts with only a few threads in the warp. Ages ago, people figured out that there was a better way to weave than this tedious manual method. They found ways to grab and lift, or lower, whole sets of alternating threads utilizing loops or slender shafts called "heddles," making a wide tunnel (called a "shed") that a wooden yarn carrier (called a "shuttle") could be easily tossed through. When loading the warp onto the loom, the warp threads

are fed through the heddles, which are attached to a shaft to allow an entire set of alternating threads to be raised or lowered with a single motion. With flexible string heddles strung from a heddle stick, a spacer, called a "shed stick" is required to bias the shed open in one direction.

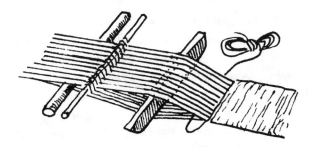

Figure 10-12. Primitive stick loom shed, heddles "down."

To switch the warp threads for the next shuttle pass, the heddle stick is raised or lowered after each pass of the shuttle. Raising or lowering the heddles causes the warp threads to cross over the weft thread before the shuttle is passed through the shed again. In this way the weft thread is woven alternating above and below the warp threads without having to tediously thread it manually. Rigid heddles work similarly to string heddles, except that they eliminate the need for the shed stick because they can push a set of warp threads down, as well as pull a set up, to form sheds in either direction. Rigid heddles are often called "reeds" since they were originally made from slender reeds.

Figure 10-13. Primitive stick loom shed, heddles "up."

Shuttles typically are carved to allow a significant amount of yarn to be wound onto the shuttle, so that a long weft thread can be handled without tangling.

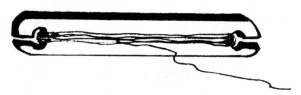

Figure 10-14. Stick shuttle.

Modern looms basically do the same thing as these primitive looms, but they have multiple heddle bars and other features to deal more efficiently with larger weavings and complex patterns. For an excellent introduction to a wide variety of simple traditional looms, see *The Weaving, Spinning and Dyeing Book* by Rachel Brown. For outstanding instructions on learning how to weave using a modern loom, see *Learning to Weave* by Deborah Chandler.

Knitting and Crocheting

Knitting and crocheting use needles and a continuous long strand of yarn to produce garments through a series of repetitive interlocking loops of yarn. Crocheting uses a single needle with a hook in the end, but knitting uses two or more smooth-tipped needles. My mother spent countless hours knitting hats, mittens, sweaters, shawls, and socks, often from yarn that she had spun herself. These garments contained quite a variety of stitches and patterns of colored yarn. Every year she usually won several prizes at the county fair, but I'm afraid that few of her award-winning skills rubbed off on me.

Knitting and crocheting are a bit complex for me to provide you with any kind of a practical introduction in this short chapter, but I can steer you in the right direction for several wonderful books that can take you from beginning steps through advanced techniques. The number one overall knitting book for beginners through experts is *Vogue Knitting*. It is a clear, well-illustrated, encyclopedic volume. *Knitting in Plain English* by Maggie Righetti is a nice companion to *Vogue Knitting*, being more verbal in its descriptions and not as copiously illustrated. Master knitter Elizabeth Zimmerman is credited with coming up with simple mathematical formulas that opened up a new world of sweater design and flexibility. Her book, *Knitting Without Tears*, is not a standalone knitting

handbook, but provides valuable advice and instructions for knitting items of clothing that fit well. For basic crocheting instructions, you might try *Crocheting in Plain English* by Maggie Righetti.

FURS AND SKINS

The real home of the Ihalmio (an inland Eskimo tribe) is much like that of the turtle, for it is what he carries about on his back. In truth it is the only house that can enable men to survive on the merciless plains of the Barrens. It has central heating from the fat furnace of the body, its walls are insulated to a degree of perfection that we white men have not been able to surpass, or even emulate. It is complete, light in weight, easy to make and easy to keep in repair. It costs nothing, for it is a gift of the land, through the deer....Most white men trying to live in the winter arctic load their bodies with at least twenty-five pounds of clothing, while the complete deerskin home of the Innuit (inland Eskimos) weighs about seven pounds....If he must sleep out, without shelter, and it is fifty below, he has but to draw his arms into his parka, and he sleeps nearly as well as he would in a double-weight eiderdown bag.

—Farley Mowat, *People of the Deer*

For countless centuries, American Indians have made beautiful, soft, durable, clothing from brain tanned hides, called "buckskin." Unlike leather, which is stiffer, fairly waterproof and holds up poorly under repeated washings, buckskin is soft, breathable, and very washable. Leather was traditionally processed by soaking in bark-derived, acidic tanning solutions, but this has been almost entirely replaced by modern chromic acid solutions, which act much more quickly but are highly toxic and harmful to the environment if not contained and 100% recycled. Some examples of bark-tanned leather are traditional saddles, holsters, belts, and boots. Making buckskin relies on lots of hand manipulation and is not a process that has adapted well to modern mechanization. Commercial so-called buckskins are often soft chrome tanned leathers lacking the breathable and

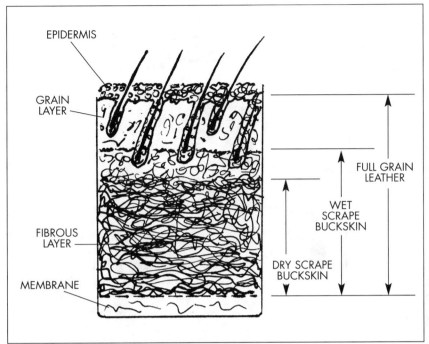

EPIDERMIS

GRAIN LAYER

FIBROUS LAYER

MEMBRANE

FULL GRAIN LEATHER

WET SCRAPE BUCKSKIN

DRY SCRAPE BUCKSKIN

Figure 10-15. Hide structure.

washable qualities of real buckskin. Transforming a raw animal hide into a soft chamois-like buckskin is a time-consuming but rewarding affair. Buckskin clothing is truly a delight to wear.

The following is a quick summary of the steps involved in the process of wet-scraped brain tanning of a hide that Matt Richards describes in far greater detail in his book *Deerskins into Buckskins*. If some of the steps are not properly completed, the result of your hours of hard work might be a tough leathery hide with unusable rock-hard sections, that must be reworked and rebrained. To improve your chances for success, I encourage you to pick up one of the recommended references, which gives a more complete description than I can give you here. Making your own buckskin is not a difficult process, but it does require patience, attention to detail, practice, sweat, and perseverance.

Brain Tanning Overview

Because deer hide is similar to the hides of most other hoofed animals (goat, sheep, cattle, buffalo, etc.), is a good practical size to work with, and is readily available from road kills or as free giveaways during hunting season, we are going to discuss it

here. The same techniques can be used with other hides, varying things a bit to take into account thicker or thinner skins. Making buckskin from small fur-bearing animals isn't very practical. Their hides are best utilized with the fur left intact.

A deerskin is made up of several layers. On the outer furry side, the first layer is the epidermis, a thin protective layer of mostly dead skin cells. Under the epidermis is the grain, where most of the active skin cells lie. Under the grain is a fibrous layer, which is what buckskin is made from. On the inside of the fiber layer is a membrane (hypodermis) that separates the flesh and fat from the hide.

The fibers in the fibrous layer will make glue if boiled down. The trick to making a buckskin out of an animal hide is to coat these fibers with an oil and work the fibers as the hide dries so that they do not "glue" themselves together into a hard lump of rawhide rather than a soft supple buckskin. Because oil and water don't normally mix, in order for the oil to adequately penetrate and coat the moist fibers of a wet hide, it must be "emulsified." Traditionally, brains were squished and mixed with water to provide an oily water emulsion that would penetrate the hide and coat the fibers. There is an old saying that each animal comes with enough brains to tan its own hide. Either use the brains from your animal's carcass, or purchase them from your local butcher.

Because both the inner membrane and the outer grain are barriers to the penetration of the brain mixture (oil-water emulsion), both must be removed prior to "braining," leaving just the bare fibrous layer. Traditionally, these layers were removed by either a "wet-scrape" or a "dry-scrape" process. In the dry-scrape process, a raw hide is strung to a frame and stretched while it dries. A sharp scraper is used to scrape the membrane off the flesh side of the hide, and the grain and fur from the outside. In their book *Primitive Wilderness Living & Survival Skills*, John and Geri McPherson provide clear, well-illustrated directions for the dry-scrape process.

In the wet-scrape process, the wet hide is laid on the smooth curved surface of a scraping beam, and is then scraped with a slightly dull scraper to remove the grain, hair, and membrane. Presoaking the hide in a caustic wood ash or lime solution, known as "bucking" the hide, makes the wet-scraping process easier. *Deerskins into Buckskins* by Matt Richards is a good book on the wet-scraping process for buckskins. For an excellent introduction to a variety of buckskin processes and options, see Matt Richard's web site at www.braintan.com. Choosing wet scraping or dry scraping is a matter of personal preference. Having done both processes, and made a living by tanning hides, Matt Richards prefers the wet-scrape process, saying that it requires considerably less effort and yields a superior product. John McPherson prefers dry scraping saying, "With the dry-scrape process, you can skin your deer in the morning and have a finished buckskin that same evening. You can't do that wet scraping." Traditionally, dry scrape was used on thicker hides such as buffalo, which needed thinning. Wet scrape was used on thinner hides, such as deer, which did not require thinning.

Simply applying the braining mixture is not enough to make a soft buckskin. It also must be stretched and worked repeatedly as it dries, to prevent the fibers from interlocking and hardening the hide. The last step in the process is smoking the hide, which chemically changes the proteins in the fibers and permanently binds the emulsion, making the hide washable. Without the smoking step, a good soaking could return your buckskin to a hardened "rawhide" state. Buckskin "breathes," allowing sweat to pass through, but it will also soak up water like a sponge.

THE WET-SCRAPE BRAIN TANNING PROCESS

1. **Skinning.** Hides should be skinned with minimum use of the knife, to prevent cutting and nicking the inside of the hide. Cuts and nicks

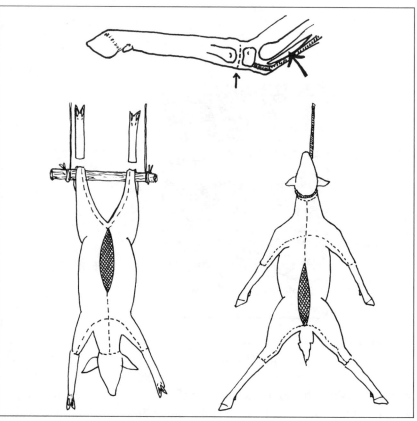

Figure 10-16. Knife cuts for skinning.

will often turn into holes in the hide when the hide is worked and stretched after braining. Hides are skinned most easily when the animal is freshly killed. Free or cheap hides are often available from butchers and hunters during hunting season, but most hunters and butchers will seriously damage the hides while skinning. You might try talking to them first to see if you can persuade them to pull the hides off, rather than cut them off, when skinning animals for your use. Matt Richards says that once you get the technique down, it is actually much faster to pull hides off, rather than to cut them off. Cut the hide around the elbows, knees and neck, and split it up the belly and inside of the arms and legs. After this step, put your knife down and try to peel the hide from the animal with your hands, using the knife minimally or not at all.

2. **Fleshing.** The purpose of this step is to remove the hunks of meat and fat from the inside of the hide. Don't worry about getting all the membrane, as it will come off in a later step. For the wet-scrape method, you will need a broad double-

handled scraper with a semidull blade that will tend to peel layers off the hide without cutting the hide surface. The scraper edge should be either beveled or square, with no chips or peaks and valleys. The edge should be slightly dull. If it is sharp enough to shave your thumbnail, it is too sharp and you might cut your hide while scraping. Traditional scrapers were made from hardwoods, stone, or sharpened pieces of large bones. Most modern tanners prefer hardened steel because it requires sharpening far less often.

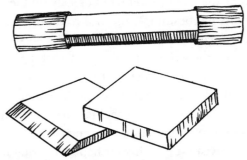

Figure 10-17. Scraper for wet scraping.

Lay the hide flesh side up on a curved smooth surface, such as a 6"- to 8"-diameter log about 6' long, or a section of 6" PVC pipe. This process is messy, so you should wear old clothes and cover yourself with something like an apron or garbage bag. Depending on how you brace your scraping beam, either pin the hide between the beam and your hips, or pin it between the beam and what it leans against. Hides are tough, so you can really lay your weight into it, except for around holes, cuts, and edges.

SCRAPING BEAM

Figure 10-18. Fleshing and scraping.

3. **Bucking.** This step soaks your hide in an alkaline bath to clean the protective mucous out of the hide and swell the hide making the grain easier to see and remove. You make the solution with wood ash or hydrated lime. For hydrated lime, mix 1 pound of lime with 2 gallons of water to soak one hide. If you use wood ash for bucking, make your solution differently depending on whether you use the ash from hardwood or softwood, because the ash from softwoods has a lot less caustic material than most hardwood ashes. With softwood ash, mix about 3 gallons of ash with enough water to make a solution at the consistency of a milkshake.

When using hardwood ash the pioneers used the floating egg trick to determine if the ash solution was of the right strength. Mix a couple gallons of white hardwood ash with at least a gallon of water, and then allow it to settle for at least 15 minutes. Drop a raw egg into the solution. If it sinks or barely floats, the solution is too weak. Add more ash, stir, and allow to settle, and then test as before. If the egg floats high and turns on its side, the solution is too strong. Add some water, stir, allow to settle and then retest. The egg should float showing an area at the tip roughly the size of a quarter to a half-dollar.

Pick out pieces of floating charcoal from your solution. Soak the hide in this solution for three to four days, until the hide is no longer blue-white in color, but is swollen and tawny colored (Richards 1998, 45–49).

CAUTION: The caustic solution is irritating to the skin. Use rubber gloves or wash hands thoroughly after contact. Rinse hides thoroughly when you are finished.

4. **Graining.** Lay your hide on your beam, like you did for "fleshing," except hair side up. Firmly push or pull your tool down and forward into your hide in one continuous stroke to dig through the grain and skate along the hide's fibrous layer. Removing the grain is work and requires patience and careful attention. Before moving on to another area, work one area at a time with overlapping

strokes until all the hair, epidermis, and grain are removed. The grain will look darker than the fibrous layer. Unless your scraper is too sharp, you will not hurt the fibrous layer by bearing down extra hard. Periodically, grain as hard as you can to make sure that you got all the grain. If you dig up sheets of stuff, you missed some of the grain, but if you just get little bits of hide, you got all the grain. Be careful around the edges, holes, cuts, and armpits. Graining is the hardest step to learn from a book. If you failed to remove all of the grain, as you work the hide while it dries, it will stiffen in those areas that still have some grain. To soften further, you must remove the remaining grain and rebrain. If your hide is drying out while graining, wet it to keep it moist.

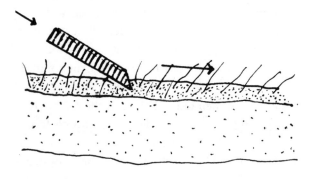

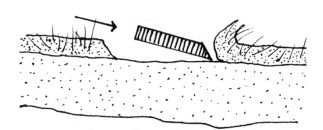

Figure 10-19. Scraping to remove the grain.

5. **Membraning.** Turn your hide over and systematically scrape the membrane side to break up and remove the membrane. Keep the hide moist and supple through this step. It can be hard to see the membrane, but it is not as critical that all of it is removed as it was with the grain.

6. **Rinsing.** You must rinse all the alkaline bucking solution out of the hide. Do this in a river, pond, or a tub of water with a hose in it. The best

method is to weight or tie the hide in a creek overnight. Rinsing takes at least 12 hours in moving water and up to 48 hours in still water. When it is fully rinsed, the entire hide will have lost its swollen tawny look and will have returned to the earlier supple bluish-white appearance. Check the neck and rump to make sure that they feel limp and supple again, like they did before bucking.

7. **Wringing.** You must remove all excess water before proceeding to the next step. Spots of the hide that are too wet will not soak up the dressing (braining), and will result in a stiff or hard section on the hide. John McPherson likes to use the wringer from an old washing machine for this step, but the traditional method uses a stout stick (an axe handle works great) and a tree branch. First, lay your hide over a smooth section of branch or a sturdy bar and twist it up with your hands to wring much of the excess water from it. Untwist it and lay it out flat, and then loop it over the branch so that one end overlaps the other end by several inches. Roll your hide from each side in towards the middle to make a thick loop of hide, still wrapped around the branch. Insert your stout stick into this loop and twist it firmly, wringing as much water as you can from the hide. Unroll the hide and spread it out flat. Inspect it for spots that are too wet. The color should be white to tawny. Bluish areas, or areas that show surface water when scraped from below with your thumbnail, are too wet. Use your scraping beam and scraper to squeegee excess water out of wet areas.

8. **Dressing (Braining).** This is the step where the hide is soaked in an oil-water emulsion to coat all the individual fibers in the fibrous layer. The traditional dressing is made from mashed animal brains and water, but you can also make your dressing from beaten eggs, or soap mixed with oil. Make a brain dressing by mashing ½ to 1 pound of fresh or thawed raw brains with a cup of hot water. Some folks like to liquefy this mixture in a blender. Some people use brain dressings raw, while others suggest that you add

Figure 10-20. Wringing the hide.

the water from the next step and cook it for about ten minutes. It works fine either way, but the cooked brains seem a little more sanitary and probably reduce the chance of infection. Make an egg dressing by beating a dozen raw eggs. For soap-and-oil dressing, mix ¼ bar of grated soap with ¼ cup of neat's foot oil (many other oils will do) (Richards 1998, 66).

Dump the dressing into a 2- to 5-gallon bucket and mix with ½ gallon of hot water, no more than 120°F (over 120°F will cook your hide, ruining it). The water is right when it is about as hot as you can stand to hold your hand in it for a couple minutes. Cold water will work, but hot water is faster and easier. Place your hide in the bucket and work the dressing into all areas of the hide, paying particular attention to holes, edges, and thick sections. Cover tightly and leave to soak in the dressing from 20 minutes to overnight. You can't get too much dressing into the hide, but too little will result in a stiff hide in the drying stage and you will have to dress the hide all over again.

Unfold your hide and lay it over a branch with the neck hanging down. Stretch it in all directions and inspect it for stiff and puckered areas. Except for scarred areas the hide should stretch evenly and lay smooth and flat. If you find stiff or rippled areas, wring and then repeat the dressing application. Both Matt Richards and John McPherson suggest wringing and dressing hides at least two times to ensure complete dressing. Thoroughly wring out the hide. Stretch it out on your beam and squeegee any wet spots with your scraper, to remove excess moisture.

9. **Sew Holes.** It is a good idea to stitch up any holes in your hide before continuing on to the stretching and softening step, or else small holes may turn into major tears. Pinch the edges of holes together from the back former flesh side of the hide and whip stitch with small needles, tight stitches, and strong thread or sinew. Holes stitched at this stage will lay flat and effectively disappear from the skin side during the next step.

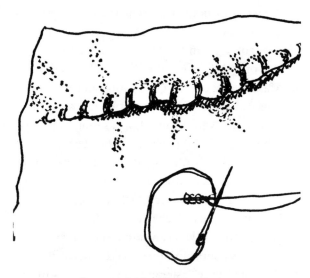

Figure 10-21. Stitching holes.

10. **Softening and Stretching.** This is the most physically demanding, but rewarding step in the process. It turns your squishy wet mass of a hide into a supple beautiful buckskin. You can choose to hand stretch your hide or frame stretch it as you work it throughout the drying process. If hand stretched, the hide can be wrapped in a plastic bag and stuck in the refrigerator midstream to take a break. If frame stretched, the process must be carried out to completion in one session. Whichever method you choose, the idea is to keep the fibers stretched and moving in all directions until the hide is dry, so that the individual fibers do not glue themselves together to make hard spots in your hide.

For hand stretching, most tanners stretch and abrade the hide by pulling it back and forth around a steel cable or a stout rope attached to a tree or pole, performed in conjunction with hand stretching and working the hide over your knee and thigh, or stretched between people. Initially, when the hide is still pretty wet, you can take breaks and only work the hide about half the time. As the hide starts to dry in the thinner sections, work it nearly continuously. If some areas start to stiffen up, abrade them vigorously several times. If they don't soften, go back to the dressing stage before the hide dries further.

Figure 10-22. Hand stretching over a cable or rope.

Frame stretched buckskins will be thinner and cover more area, but will also be more prone to shrinkage from washing. Build a strong frame from notched branches or 2-by-4s. Using a sharp knife, cut slots around the perimeter of your hide every 3 to 4 inches and ¼ inch from the edge. Cut the slots parallel to the edge so they won't tear out too easily. String the hide loosely to the frame, starting at the neck area, followed by the rump, and then the sides. Tighten it evenly, all the way around. Using a beveled pointed stick (dull any sharp edges and points), roughly the size of an axe handle, deeply stroke the hide to work and stretch the entire surface. Periodically pull and stretch the hide's edges with your fingers. Use care around holes and cuts. Focus on the thinner drier sections first, and then shift your focus to the thicker sections when the thinner ones are completely dry.

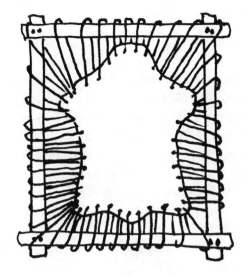

Figure 10-23. Frame stretching.

11. **Smoking.** By now your buckskin looks and feels like a real buckskin. As long as it's kept dry and away from critters and insects, you can store it for a long time. The last step is to permanently seal the fibers with wood smoke, making your buckskin washable and rot resistant.

The quick way to smoke one or two skins is to stitch them together, or bond with wood or hide glue, to form a hide sack, leaving the neck area open as a mouth for smoke to enter. It is safest to stitch a denim or canvas skirt around the opening to prevent scorching and possibly ruining your hide. The sack is either hung over a smoky fire to catch heavy smoke inside the sack, or smoke is piped from a wood stove into the sack. Smoke this side for about 20 minutes (longer if you want a darker hide). Pull the sack and skirt inside out and smoke the other side.

To make a smoky fire that smokes for a long time without flaring up requires punky rotten wood, not wet wood. Collect a few armfuls of this kind of wood, and then break it into small chunks and keep it next to your fire. Build a decent-sized fire with dry wood and burn it until there is a bed of coals several inches deep. Cover the bed of coals with a layer of punky wood and you will generate a lot of smoke.

CAUTION: Pay attention and check your fire every few minutes. A minute of inattention could send your hide up in flames if the fire flares up. If the skirt catches on fire, tear it off the hide immediately to save your hide.

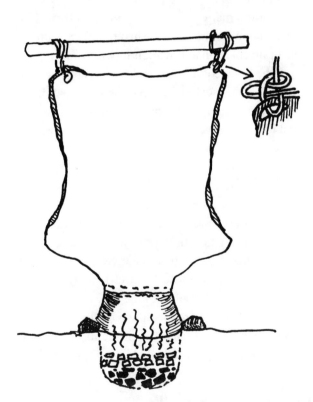

Figure 10-24. Smoking a hide over a pit.

If you have many hides to smoke, some people prefer to hang them in a tipi or smokehouse and smoke them all at once, although they will need to stay in the smoke much longer, typically all day.

Dealing with Furs

You can also make a beautiful fur out of a road kill or hunting trophy, using mostly the same methods as used for making a buckskin. The main difference is that you don't remove any of the grain and fur, so your braining solution must soak through the entire hide thickness from just the flesh side.

SKINNING AND FLESHING

After skinning the animal, as described in step 1 of the previous section, stake the pelt out flat or throw it over a curved scraping beam. Give your pelt a thorough fleshing and scraping to remove all the membrane and flesh from the inside of the hide. Stitch up any holes in the hide. Buff the surface with a pumice, sandpaper, or a rough stone.

BRAINING

At this point, many people prefer to brain their skins stretched in a frame. Soak the inside surface with your brain solution and work it in with your fingers. Apply the brain solution several times, scraping and buffing the hide surface between each application. Drench the skin in brains and wrap it up in a hot moist towel for several hours, until the pelt is wet and flexible.

SOFTENING

As the pelt dries, stretch it and work it over a cable, rope, or edge, such as the back of a chair. If some areas start to dry too stiffly (except for the edges, which you may want to trim off anyway), reapply the brain solution and continue to stretch and work the pelt until dry. Don't wait until the hide is totally dry before reapplying brains, because a totally dry hide will not soak up the brains as well. Continue rebraining and resoftening until the hide is acceptably soft.

Bark Tanning Leather

> No leather is better than good bark tanned
> and no other processes require as many
> months to produce it.
>
> —A. B. Farnham, *Home Tanning
> and Leather Making Guide*

This is one of the oldest methods for making leather, and involves considerable time and effort, but does yield an exceptional product if done properly. The active process ingredient is tannic acid from tree bark. Some acceptable tree barks are the hemlock, Spanish chestnut, Jack red, and most oaks. The *Home Tanning and Leather Making Guide* by A. B. Farnham offers good instructions for both bark tanning and more chemically oriented tanning processes. There are many different variations on the process, but in the event that you have no other books or tanning chemicals, the following should work in a pinch.

1. Bark for the tanning solution is usually gathered when the sap is running. It is peeled from the tree, stacked to dry, and then stored until ready for use. The bark solution should be started about 20 days prior to use. Place 30 to 40 pounds of finely ground bark in a barrel and pour 20 gallons of boiling water over the bark (use soft water or rain water). Cover, stirring every day or two, until ready for use.

2. Skin and flesh as in the wet-scrape process.

3. Buck as in the wet-scrape process, but leave the skin in the solution for 6 to 10 days until the hair pulls easily from the hide. Keep the barrel covered except for when you stir the solution and plunge the hides to the bottom (three to four times each day).

4. Remove the hair, grain, and flesh as in the wet-scrape process (should come off easily if soaked for several days).

5. Rinse the hides 12 to 48 hours as in the wet-scrape process.

6. Neutralize the caustic bucking solution remaining in the hides, so that it won't neutralize your tanning acids. At one time this was done by fermenting with animal bacteria, but it is accomplished more quickly with an acid solution. To make your neutralizing solution, add a half gallon of vinegar or 3 ounces of USP grade lactic acid per barrel of clean water. Soak the hides in this solution for 24 hours.

7. As in the wet scrape process, wring and then squeegee the excess solution out of the hides using your scraper and beam.

8. Strain the tanning solution through a coarse cloth into the tanning barrel. To extract more of the tannin from the ground bark, add another 10 gallons to the moist bark and stir. Strain this 10 gallons through a cloth into the tanning barrel.

9. Add 2 quarts of vinegar to the tanning barrel. Plunge the hides into the tanning solution and work hides to thoroughly soak in the tanning solution. Hang hides over sticks inside the tanning barrel to give the solution clear access to all parts of the hide (hides will stay in the tanning solution for a total of 4 to 7 months).

10. As soon as the hides have been placed into the tanning solution, prepare a second barrel of fresh tanning solution, just like the first. Ten to 15 days after starting the hides in the first solution, take 5 gallons of used solution from the tanning barrel and replace it with 5 gallons of fresh solution plus 2 quarts of vinegar. Stir the tanning barrel solution.

11. Every 5 days, replace another 5 gallons from the tanning barrel with 5 gallons of fresh solution (add no vinegar) until the fresh barrel of solution is used up.

12. About 35 days after starting the hides in the tanning barrel, weigh out 40 more pounds of ground bark. Place in a tub or barrel and moisten with just enough hot water to saturate the bark.

13. Pull the hides out of the tanning barrel and cut a small piece off one hide to inspect for tanning progress. The cut edge should show a brown streak or line extending in from the surface toward the center.

14. Dump the moistened bark into the tanning barrel, retaining as much as you can of the old tanning solution. Replace the hides in the tanning solution, burying the hides in the bark mixture.

15. Leave hides in this mixture for 6 more weeks, stirring occasionally.

16. Remove hides a second time. Remove about half of the tanning solution. Return the hides to the barrel and fill the remaining space with freshly ground bark.

17. Leave hides in tanning barrel for about 2 more months. Stir occasionally and add more water and bark as necessary to keep hides covered with solution.

18. When a slice through a thick section of hide shows that the tanning solution has penetrated the full hide thickness, you can remove hides from the solution. Scrub and rinse thoroughly to remove the acid from the tanning solution and to prevent long-term weakening of the fibers. Thick sole hide may take as long as 7 months soaking in the tanning solution.

19. Slowly dry the leather, and then oil or grease to waterproof. If you wish to soften the leather somewhat, work it as it dries. Softening begins when the hides are partly dry, and continues until hides are completely dry and sufficiently soft. (Adapted from the *Home Tanning and Leather Making Guide* by A. B. Farnham.)

PATTERNS AND CUSTOM-TAILORED CLOTHING

You can purchase ready-made patterns from a variety of sources (see *Resources* section below) or tailor your own clothing. The easiest way to make your own pattern is to split the seams of an existing article of clothing and use that for your pattern. If you stretched your buckskin on a frame, you should wash and dry it to preshrink the material before cutting your pattern into the hide. At this point, you have invested a lot of time into the process, and your buckskin clothing should last for many years, so go slow and pay attention to detail.

I have designed and made a variety of articles of clothing and gear. It is a better idea to design your own pattern by starting out with a sacrificial material that you don't mind throwing away, rather than to cut and hack at your precious buckskin as you figure out the proper dimensions. Start by cutting your material pieces oversize, and then drape them over your body and pin or tack-stitch together. Mark, trim and re-tack the pieces back together until you're happy with the way the garment fits. It's much easier to cut off excess material than to piece in patches where you cut too much off. When your tacked together article of clothing feels, looks, and

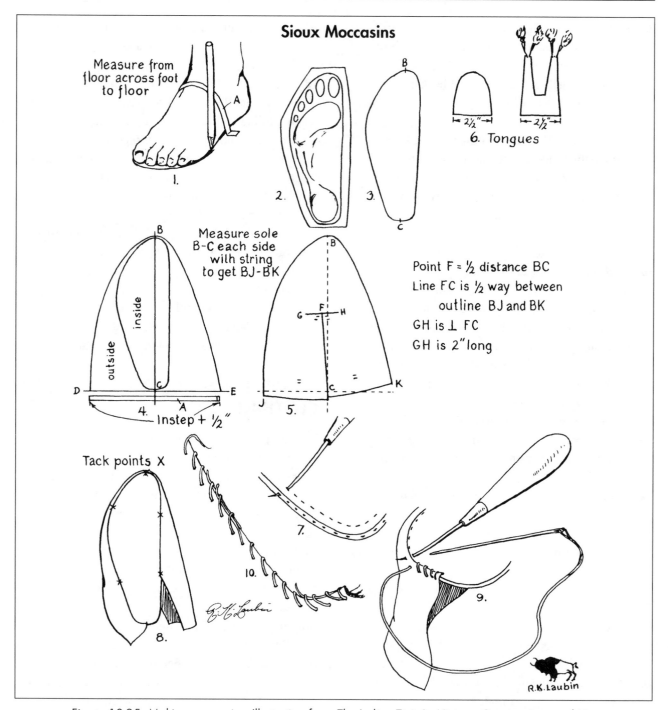

Figure 10-25. Making moccasins. Illustration from *The Indian Tipi: Its History, Construction, and Use* by Reginald and Gladys Laubin (University of Oklahoma Press, 1989).

hangs right, undo the pins or tack stitching, lay it out flat on the buckskin, and mark the outline. After cutting out the buckskin pieces, stitch the pieces together with leather thongs, sinews, or strong thread. Glover's needles are sharp needles with a triangular shaped tip that are specifically designed for sewing leather. They will pierce through buckskin rather easily, though the use of a thimble or a tough leather finger ring will help push the needle through the buckskin without the head of the needle piercing your skin. Artificial Sinew (heavy-duty waxed nylon thread) and a Speedy Stitching Awl (available at leather-work outlets and many backcountry suppliers) work well for stitching together shoes, gear, and rugged clothing.

SINEWS

Larger animals, such as deer and elk, contain a supply of sinews, which are large flat tendons that can be split into tough threads for sewing articles of clothing and shoes. Useable sinews are loin sinews located in the back, and leg sinews. Loin sinews are much longer and easier to work with than leg sinews. Loin sinews are a thin silvery band running from the shoulder to the hip along both sides of the backbone.

After skinning, make a cut about ¼" deep along the length of the backbone. Peel the outer layer of fat back to expose the shiny sinew lying along the top of the meat. Using a rounded knife, such as a butter knife, work it under the sinew, and then work it back and forth to separate and lift the sinew from the meat. While still attached to the ends, run the knife back and forth on both sides of the sinew to clean off all the pieces of meat and fat. Cut the ends to remove the sinew from the animal, and then clean it again by scraping before laying flat to dry. Once dry, roll the sinew band lengthwise and twirl tightly between the fingers and hands for a couple minutes, until it splits into individual threads. When sinew dries, it shrinks, so it is often a good idea to wet the sinew thread before sewing, so that it will tighten the stitching as it dries (McPherson 1993, 52).

FOOTWEAR

In pioneering days, a good-fitting pair of shoes was a truly valuable possession. Often, when shoemakers passed through a village, they would make several pairs of shoes for each person who could afford them as it might be years before they could purchase another pair of good-fitting shoes. Making your own traditional boots is not easy, but sandals and moccasins are easy and rewarding leather craft projects for the beginner.

Soles can be attached with stitching, primitive hide glues, more modern glues such as Barge Cement, or nailed in place (cobbling). McNett Corporation makes an excellent urethane shoe repair cement, called Freesole, which can be used to repair holes in shoes and worn soles, or glue new soles in place. Freesole is available through backcountry

suppliers and shoe repair shops. It is reportedly much stronger than Barge Cement and withstands much higher temperatures, but I have not tried it yet for gluing soles in place. See Chapter 14 for instructions on how to make your own glues.

Sinews, heavy waxed nylon thread, or multi-strand wire are all good strong materials for stitching together footwear. If you scavenge wire for thread, make sure that the strands are fine, or else constant flexing will cause the metal to fatigue and the wire to break. Shoe soles and straps can be nailed together by a process called "cobbling." Shoe soles that were attached by simply nailing short nails through the soles into the mid-sole would soon work loose and fall off. Traditional cobblers use nails with slender tapering tips that are nailed through the straps and soles against a metal anvil, bending the nail tips backwards so that they form into a hook shape. In this way, the sole or strap is captured in such a way that the nails can't easily work their way back out.

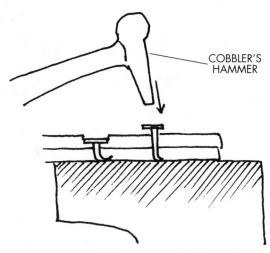

COBBLER'S HAMMER

Figure 10-26. Cobbling to attach soles and straps.

Cast-off rubber tires make great sandals and soles. Thomas J. Elpel, author of *Participating in Nature*, believes that the best all-around homemade footgear is a tire sandal worn over a moccasin. You can wear holes in a pair of moccasins in less than a day of rough travel, and tire sandals can wear a hole in your feet (blisters) in a few hours. When you wear the two together, you get the comfort of moccasins combined with the durability of tire sandals. Around camp you can wear just the moccasins. When fording rivers, wear just the sandals. Using a band saw, sharp knife, chisel, hacksaw or coping saw, cut tire sandals and buckles from older style tires that don't have steel belts.

Use the pattern shown in Figure 10-27 as a rough guide. Start by tracing the outline of your foot on a piece of paper. Add about ⅜" to the front and sides, but not the heel area. Make two marks at the centers of your ankle bones (A) and a mark at the side of the ball of your foot, directly behind your big toe (B). Draw lines through these points, as shown in the pattern, to help you locate the strap loops. The strap loops are designed for ¾"-wide webbing. If you use a different size of strap material, adjust and customize your pattern as necessary to fit your foot. Cut out your pattern as you would a paper doll and lay it on the tire to mark the outline for cutting the rubber (Elpel 1999, 134).

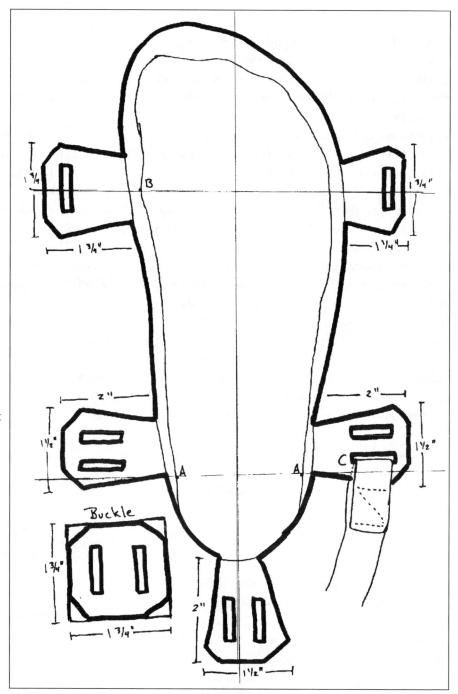

Figure 10-27. Tire sandal pattern. Source: Illustration from *Participating in Nature,* 1999, by Thomas J. Elpel.

REFERENCES

Fiber Arts

Hands On Spinning, by Lee Raven. 1987, 120 pp. (paperback), ISBN 0-934026-27-0. Published by Interweave Press, Inc., 201 East Fourth Street, Loveland, CO 80537. Lists for $16.95.

This is an excellent introduction to spinning. It covers everything from simple hand spinning with crude handmade instruments (or no instruments) to spinning with traditional spinning wheels. It is well written and illustrated with clear simple drawings, and includes instructions for several projects. Active spinners' guild teachers, on opposite sides of the country, have recommended this book as the single best introduction to spinning. The author helped found the Bay Area Spinner's Textile Study Group and is a former editor of *Spin-Off* magazine.

Learning to Weave, by Deborah Chandler. 1995, 232 pp. (hardcover), ISBN 1-883010-03-9. Published by Interweave Press, Inc., 201 East Fourth Street, Loveland, CO 80537. Lists for $24.95.

This is an excellent introduction to the art and craft of weaving on a treadle or table-top loom. Several weaving guild teachers have recommended it as the single best reference for learning how to weave. It is well illustrated and guides the beginner through a variety of exercises designed to teach weaving, as if the reader were taking part in a comprehensive class.

The Weaving, Spinning and Dyeing Book, by Rachel Brown. 1983, 430 pp. (paperback), ISBN 394-71595-0. Published by Alfred A. Knopf, Division of Random House, 201 E. 50th St., New York, NY 10022. Lists for $40.00.

This excellent book illustrates quite a variety of weaving methods and equipment, including simple Navajo and Hopi looms. If you wanted a single comprehensive backup book in case you needed to spin a skein of yarn, weave yourself a bolt of cloth, or perhaps fashion your own simple equipment, this would be an excellent reference. The other recommended books provide clearer learning instructions for their covered topic, but this is a good all-around guide. This book is well illustrated, lists many different sources for materials (though it hasn't been revised since 1983 so it's somewhat out of date), and provides reasonably clear instructions.

Foxfire 2: Ghost Stories, Spring Wild Plant Foods, Spinning and Weaving, Midwifing, Burial Customs, Corn Shuckin's, and Wagon Making, edited by Eliot Wigginton. 1973, 410 pp. (paperback), ISBN 0-385-02267-0. Published by Doubleday division of Bantam Doubleday Publishing Group, Inc., 1540 Broadway, New York, NY 10036. Lists for $15.95.

This is the second in Elliot Wigginton's excellent series of books chronicling the old-timer's ways of doing things in Southern Appalachia. It has a decent section on spinning and weaving, including details for how to make your own simple spinning wheel and loom. The title lists some of the other things that are also covered by this book. The section on wagon making provides details and instructions that I have not seen anywhere else, related by an old-timer who actually made wagons for a living when he was a young man.

A Weaver's Garden: Growing Plants for Natural Dyes and Fibers, by Rita Buchanan. 1999, 240 pp. (paperback), ISBN 0486407128. Published by Dover Publications, 31 E. 2nd St., Mineola, NY 11501. Lists for $8.95.

This is really a fascinating little book about many useful plants and plant applications. In addition to plants for natural fibers and dyes, it covers plants for soaps, scents, insecticides, and useful textile tools. Buchanan is also the author of *A Dyer's Garden: From Plant to Pot, Growing Dyes for Natural Fibers.*

Hands On Dyeing, by Betsy Blumenthal. 1988, 111 pp. (paperback), ISBN 093402636X. Published by Interweave Press, Inc., 201 East Fourth Street, Loveland, CO 80537. Lists for $16.95.

An excellent book for the fiber artist using chemical dyes. Covers batik, dip dyeing, overdyeing, color gradations, fabric painting, and more.

Vogue Knitting, **by the editors of** ***Vogue Knitting Magazine.*** 1989, 240 pp. (hardcover), ISBN 039457186X. Published by Pantheon Books, Division of Random House, 201 E. 50th St., New York, NY 10022. Lists for $37.50.

This encyclopedic guide to knitting contains 1,600 full-color illustrations and covers all basic techniques, a stitch dictionary, correction of errors, following patterns, knitting supplies, and so on. To many it is the knitter's bible. Beginners can teach themselves how to knit, while experienced knitters use it as a reference for unfamiliar stitches and techniques.

Knitting in Plain English, **by Maggie Righetti.** 1986, 241 pp. (paperback), ISBN 0312458533. Published by St. Martin's Press, 175 Fifth Ave., New York, NY 10010. Lists for $14.95.

This is an excellent companion to *Vogue Knitting*. It is more verbal, but with fewer clear illustrations. Combining the text of this book with the pictures from *Vogue Knitting* can help clarify confusing techniques.

Homespun Handknit: Caps, Socks, Mittens & Gloves, **edited by Linda Ligon.** 1988, 160 pp. (paperback), ISBN 0934026262. Published by Interweave Press, Inc., 201 East Fourth Street, Loveland, CO 80537. Lists for $19.95.

This is a collection of projects from fifty expert knitters and spinners, ranging from simple beginner projects to advanced designs. Filled with instructions, tips, helpful hints, and techniques. If you wish to try your hand at knitting practical items with homespun, get this book.

Knitting Without Tears, **by Elizabeth Zimmerman.** 1995, 120 pp. (paperback), ISBN 0-684-13505-1. Published by Fireside Books, Simon & Schuster, Rockefeller Center, 1230 Avenue of the Americas, New York, NY 10020. Lists for $16.00.

Master knitter Elizabeth Zimmerman is credited with developing simple mathematical formulas that opened up a new world of sweater design and flexibility. Her book *Knitting Without Tears* is not a stand-alone beginner's knitting handbook (I would

be totally lost if I only had this knitting book), but it is a valuable addition to a knitter's reference library. It contains techniques and directions for knitting garments to fit all sizes.

Complete Guide to Sewing: Step-By-Step Techniques for Making Clothes and Home Furnishings, **by Reader's Digest.** 1995, 432 pp. (hardcover), ISBN 0-88850-247-8. Published by The Reader's Digest Association, Pleasantville, NY 10570-7000. Lists for $30.00.

This encyclopedic volume is a true sewing bible. Copiously illustrated it covers everything from beginning techniques and learning how to sew, to advanced seamstress tips, tricks, and techniques. From bachelors to dress designers and county fair prize winners, this is a great reference to have on hand.

Crocheting in Plain English, **by Maggie Righetti.** 1988, 244 pp. (paperback), ISBN 0312014120. Published by St. Martin's Press, 175 Fifth Ave., New York, NY 10010. Lists for $15.95.

Crocheting resembles knitting, only you use a single needle with a hooked tip rather than two or more smooth-tipped knitting needles. This book offers clear instructions for beginning to advanced crocheting. Very readable and accessible, even if you have never crocheted before.

Hemp: Lifeline to the Future, **by Chris Conrad.** 1994, 314 pp. (paperback), ISBN 0-9639754-1-2. Published by Creative Xpressions Publications, P.O. Box 1005, Novato, CA 94948 Lists for $13.00.

Written by the president of the Hemp Industries Association, this is a well-documented study of hemp issues, uses, history, and politics. Includes the uses of hemp as fiber, food, medicine, raw material for plastics production, and alternative fuel. Hemp is portrayed as a sustainable answer to many current nonsustainable industrial and agricultural practices. Presents evidence that the prohibition of hemp was based on profit-motivated political maneuvering and false representation engineered by a few powerful greedy industrialists, who were protecting their non-hemp oil and fiber interests.

MAGAZINES

Spin-Off. Subscription: $24 per year for 4 issues. Interweave Press Inc., 201 E. Fourth St., Loveland, CO 80537; phone: (800) 767-9638; fax: (970) 667-8317; web site: www.interweave.com.

A favorite among spinners and knitters, each issue is devoted to the history, techniques, equipment, supplies, and meaning of the spinner's craft.

Shuttle Spindle & Dyepot. Subscription: This quarterly magazine is included in the $35 per year annual dues to the Handweavers Guild of America, Two Executive Concourse, Suite 201, 3327 Duluth Highway, Duluth, GA 30096; phone: (770) 495-7702; fax: (770) 495-7703; web site: www.weavespindye.org.

An award-winning magazine with articles on design, history, wearable art, shows, books, techniques, product and equipment reviews, and reports from museums, guilds, and members all over the world.

The Leather Crafters & Saddlers Journal. Subscription: $26.00 per year for 6 issues. *The Leather Crafters & Saddlers Journal*, 331 Annette Ct., Rhinelander, WI 54501-2902; phone: (715) 362-5393; email: journal@newnorth.net.

This is the journal to get for serious leatherworking. Each issue is a comprehensive guide to sources for tools, leather, machinery, and patterns. Journal articles include step-by-step instructions and full-size patterns for leather projects.

Skins, Furs, and Leather

Deerskins into Buckskins: How to Tan with Natural Materials, by Matt Richards. 1998, 158 pp. (paperback), ISBN 0-9658672-0-X. Published by Backcountry Publishing, P.O. Box 967, Weaverville, CA 96093. Lists for $14.95.

This is an excellent guide to the wet-scrape process for making buckskin. It contains step-by-step instructions for brain tanning and over 130 photos and illustrations. Includes a resource guide and a nifty section on making your own buckskin clothing. The author has made his living by tanning buckskins, so he definitely knows what he's talking about. Excellent tips and hints for the beginner to expert tanner.

Primitive Wilderness Living & Survival Skills, by John and Geri McPherson. When John McPherson started brain tanning buckskins in the late 1970s, he found that none of the available books gave accurate and complete information. Through trial and error, and by making many mistakes, he discovered what was missing from these books, and then wrote his own guide to help others brain tan without having to learn the hard way. McPherson's original booklet, *Brain Tan Buckskin,* has probably taught more people the art of dry-scrape brain tanning than any other book, and is now Chapter 1 in *Primitive Wilderness Living & Survival Skills.* It provides clear, practical, well-illustrated instructions for dry-scrape brain tanning of hides. See Chapter 4 references for a more complete description of this book.

Home Tanning and Leather Making Guide, by A. B. Farnham. 1959, 176 pp. (paperback), ISBN 0936622113. Published by Fur-Fish-Game, 2878 E. Main, Columbus, OH 43209-9947. Lists for $4.95.

Leather is more abrasion resistant and waterproof than buckskin, but not as washable and breathable. This guide is a good start for home tanning leathers either with chemicals (faster and more toxic) or by traditional bark tanning.

Leather: Preparation & Tanning by Traditional Methods, by Lotta Rahme. 1996, 112 pp. (hardcover), ISBN 1-887719-00-8. Published by Caber Press, 7549 North Fenwick, Portland, OR 97217. Lists for $24.95.

The author of this book is a well-versed tanner who has studied traditional tanning methods with Native Americans in northern Canada, and the Sami (Laplanders) in northern Sweden. Lotta has combined her extensive tanning experience with research into the history and science of these methods. She includes many details, recipes, tools, and methods for traditional tanning, most of which she has used, or at least tried, herself. Not the best how-to book for a beginner, but combined with a book such as *Deerskins into Buckskins,* you will probably do fine. There is more information in this book on a diverse selection of primitive tanning methods, than in any other book that I know of.

The Leatherworking Handbook: A Practical Illustrated Sourcebook of Techniques and Projects, by **Valerie Michael.** 1995, 128 pp. (paperback), ISBN 0-304-34511-3. Published by Cassell Wellington House, 125 Strand, WC2 0BB, UK. Lists for $19.95.

This is a clear, informative, well-illustrated book on basic leatherworking techniques. An excellent practical guide, with tips on tools, techniques, and setting up a simple home workshop for leatherworking. It includes several interesting and beautiful starter projects.

Saddlemaking: Lessons in Construction, Repair, and Evaluation, by **Dusty Johnson.** 1993, 100 pp. (paperback), ISBN 0-9639164-0-8. Published by Saddleman Press, P.O. Box 909, Loveland, CO 80539. Lists for $19.95.

If you think you may want (or need) to make or repair a saddle someday, this book is for you. If you really want to go all out, you can also purchase the three-volume *Stohlman Encyclopedia of Saddle Making* for $59.95 per volume.

Dictionary of Leather-Working Tools, C. 1700-1950: And the Tools of Allied Trades, by **R. A. Salaman.** 1996, 377 pp. (paperback), ISBN 1-879335-72-7. Published by Astragal Press, P.O. Box 239, Mendham, NJ 07945. Lists for $37.50.

For those who want to know how to make everything themselves, here is a marvelous collection of British leatherworking tools, about 1,100 in all. Covered here are tools of the bookbinder, boat and shoe maker, clog maker, driving belt maker, furrier, glove maker, handbag and purse maker, harness maker and saddler, and hat maker.

Encyclopedia of Rawhide and Leather Braiding, by **Bruce Grant.** 1972, 556 pp. (hardcover), ISBN 0-

87033-161-2. Published by Cornell Maritime Press, P.O. Box 456, Centreville, MD 21617-0456. Lists for $28.95.

A voluminous work dedicated to illustrating and documenting a myriad of fancy horse tack and leatherwork that few remaining craftsman remember how to make.

How to Make Cowboy Horse Gear, by **Bruce Grant.** 1956, 193 pp. (paperback), ISBN 0-87033-034-9. Published by Cornell Maritime Press, P.O. Box 456, Centreville, MD 21617-0456. Lists for $8.95.

Instructions for crafting saddles, bridles, reins, and quirts. Includes a section on how to make a Western saddle by Lee M. Rice. Much of the material in this book is covered by Grant's larger *Encyclopedia of Rawhide and Leather Braiding.*

RESOURCES

Fiber Arts

Handweavers Guild of America, Inc. Two Executive Concourse, Suite 201, 3327 Duluth Highway, Duluth, GA 30096; phone: (770) 495-7702; fax: (770) 495-7703; web site: www.weavespindye.org.

If the fiber arts are what turns your spindle, you might want to join the Handweavers Guild of America (HGA). HGA is a nonprofit, international, membership organization of weavers, spinners, dyers, basket makers, bead weavers, felters, and fiber artists in the related crafts. Membership in HGA includes a subscription to their award-winning quarterly magazine, *Shuttle Spindle & Dyepot,* featuring a broad spectrum of articles about the fiber arts, including design, history, shows, education, products, books, textile news, and updates about HGA programs.

Interweave Press Inc. 201 E. Fourth St., Loveland, CO 80537; phone: (970) 669-7672; fax: (970) 667-8317; web site: www.interweave.com.

Interweave Press publishes seven magazines and over a hundred high-quality books about things created, grown, or nourished by hand, including fiber, thread, crafts, beads, herbs, natural health, gardening, and cooking. One of their magazines, *Spin-Off*, is a favorite among spinners and knitters. Their web site is an online source for fiber craft information.

Yarn Barn. 930 Massachusetts, Lawrence, KS 66044; phone: (785) 842-4333; fax: (785) 842-0794; web site: www.yarnbarn-ks.com.

The Yarn Barn offers a wide selection of supplies for knitting, weaving, spinning, and other textile crafts, including looms, spinning wheels, and books. Their employees are knitters, weavers, or spinners, so they can answer your questions and provide good advice.

Woodland Woolworks. 262 So. Maple St., P.O. Box 400, Yamhill, OR 97148; phone: (800) 547 3725; fax: (503) 662 3641; email: woolwrks@ teleport.com.

An excellent source for fibers at reasonable prices, in addition to spinning wheels, books, and supplies.

Vermont Department of Agriculture, Foods & Markets. 116 State St., Montpelier, VT 05620-2901; phone: (802) 828-2416.

Call for a free copy of the Department's *Vermont Fiber Producers Directory*. With this directory you can buy fleeces, homespun, patterns, tools, and so on direct from the producers themselves.

Skins and Furs

Braintan.com. 10398 Takilma Rd., Cave Junction, OR 97523; phone (541) 592-3693; web site: www.braintan.com.

A great source for books, supplies, buckskins, and general information on making your own buckskin, furs, and leather. This company stocks hard-to-find tools and books. Check out their web site for an extensive selection of interesting how-to articles and book reviews written by backwoods mountain residents who know their subjects well.

The Leather Factory. P.O. Box 50429, Ft. Worth, TX 76105; phone: (800) 433-3201; fax: (817) 496-9806; web site: www.leatherfactory.com.

This is an excellent source for all your leather-working needs. The Leather Factory carries a wide selection of leathers, hand tools, books, saddle and tack hardware, shoe repair goods, and so on.

Tandy Leather Company. P.O. Box 2934, Fort Worth, TX 76113; phone: (808) 890-1611; fax: (817) 551-9624; web site: www.tandyleather.com.

Another excellent source for all your leather-working needs. Tandy carries a wide selection of leathers, hand tools, books, hardware, dyes, and so on. This company offers the full line of Stohlman's encyclopedic books on the art of leather craft, all at 20% off the listed retail prices.

Hanson's Leather. 6900 Andressen Road, Sheridan, CA 95681; phone: (530) 633-0844; fax: (530) 633-0193; web site: www.hansons.net.

When it comes to leather and old-fashioned western clothing, Hanson's does it all. This shop sells a wide variety of leather-working tools, patterns, and supplies. Hanson's carries an excellent selection of books on leather working, traditional crafts, and the old west. They make a line of traditional clothing and have supplied old-west clothing and Native American dress for Hollywood movies.

Eagle's View Publishing. 6756 North Fork Road, Liberty, UT 84310; phone: (801) 393-4555; fax: (801) 745-0903; web site: www.eaglefeathertrading.com.

Eagle's View publishes authentic patterns for pre-1800 clothing, which are great for homemade buckskins. They also sell books on Native American arts and crafts.

Buckaroo Bobbins. P.O. Box 1168, Chino Valley, AZ 86323-1168; phone: (520) 636-1885; fax: (520) 636-8134; web site: www.buckaroobobbins.com.

Buckaroo sells authentic vintage western clothing patterns, related books, and sewing accessories such as beads and buckles.

XI Energy, Heat & Power

Humankind, at the end of "The Century of Oil,"
teeters on the brink of the third millennium. On
one side of our perch stretches bountiful oppor-
tunity, and an abundant, fulfilling future based
upon the principles of sustainable living. If we
look closely here, we see that the stage is set
for a rapid conversion from a fossil fuel-based
economy to a lifestyle based on renewable
energy. On the other side, looms the destruc-
tion of Homo sapiens' natural habitat, obstruc-
tionist government policies, and big business
threatening to engulf us in a deathly haze of
greenhouse gases. Our generation is the first in
the history of our species to be offered the
opportunity for a conscious choice: exploitation
or stewardship; devastation or sustainability.
Will we have the foresight to take heed of our
natural limits, or continue down the slippery
slope of unfettered consumption until it is too
late to correct our course? Our fate is in our
own hands.

> —John Schaeffer, founder and CEO of Real
> Goods, from the introduction to the 10th edition
> of *The Real Goods Solar Living Sourcebook*

Essentially, except for geothermal and nuclear power, all other sources of power and energy on planet Earth come from the sun. It is the sun that grows the plants we burn for fuel and eat for food. It is commonly believed that decayed vegetation from giant prehistoric forests formed the subterranean beds of coal, gas, and oil that have fueled the unprecedented growth of the industrial revolution and modern society. When we burn these fuels, we are burning the stored energy of millions of years of ancient sunlight. When these fuels are gone, it will take millions more years for sunlight and plant growth to recreate them. On the other hand, renewable energy (RE) sources are renewed on a daily basis by the powers of the sun or the heat stored within the earth. The great wind and ocean currents swirling around our planet are driven by thermal differences powered by the sun. Every day, the sun evaporates water from the oceans and continents, forming clouds and bringing the lifeblood of rain to the soil and water to the rivers. For centuries, wind and waterpower have been harnessed by humankind as clean, natural sources of power. Our ancestors used waterwheels to power their lumber and grain mills. Hundreds of years ago, the Dutch people were known for their use of windmills to pump water.

Wood has been a valuable source of heat and energy for countless millennia, although declining forests and expanding populations clearly indicate that most of the world can no longer consume wood at anywhere near the current rates, without devastating what remains of the last half of the world's forests. Coal has been used for hundreds of years, but it was not until the nineteenth century that efficient machinery was developed to extract significant amounts from the earth. Experts estimate that the world has somewhere around 250 years worth of coal reserves left in the ground, but there are major environmental drawbacks to mining and burning coal. In some parts of the world, where coal is a primary industrial fuel, the air is thick with smoke that burns the eyes and chokes the lungs, making the sky a muddy gray color on days that should be a clear blue.

Humankind has now consumed nearly half of the world's oil reserves, including projections for new discoveries. Even though we have been using petroleum since 1850, half of the oil consumed thus far has been since 1970, a mere 30 years ago. After peaking in the mid-1960s, discoveries of new oil fields have dropped to the point where we are now consuming oil six times as fast as we are discovering new reserves (Campbell 1996, 8). As we begin to draw on the second half of the world's oil reserves, we will see increasing amounts of energy required to extract oil from deposits that are deeper in the ground or harder to refine. At a given depth, it takes as much energy to extract oil as one gets from burning the oil. As an oil-hungry world competes for dwindling reserves, there will be increasing financial costs and environmental tolls. Now that we are seeing both a decline in world oil reserves and the beginning of dramatic climactic changes resulting from the burning of fossil fuels, it is becoming clear that we must shift our global energy economy away from burning hydrocarbons.

SHIFTING TO RENEWABLE ENERGY (RE)

[S]tabilizing earth's climate now depends on reducing carbon emissions by shifting from fossil fuels to a solar/hydrogen economy. Solar is here defined broadly, including not only direct sunlight but also indirect forms of solar energy—wind power, hydropower, and biological sources such as wood. Fortunately, the technologies for tapping this enormous source of energy already exist. We can now see electricity generated from wind being used to electrolyze water and to produce hydrogen. Hydrogen then becomes the basic fuel for the new economy, relying initially on the distribution and storage facilities of the natural gas industry. Put simply, the principles of ecological sustainability now require a shift from a carbon-based to a hydrogen-based energy economy.

—Lester R. Brown et al., *State of the World, 2000*

Making the shift from burning nonrenewable fossil fuels, and our last remaining forests, to harnessing renewable sources can be an exciting and prosperous venture for humankind. The wind power industry is growing by leaps and bounds. From 1995 to 1998, total worldwide wind energy capacity increased rapidly at an average growth rate of 27.75% per year, and then in 1999 capacity leapt by a whopping 36% (AWEA 1999, 1). Sales of solar cells grew at an average annual rate of 16% during most of the 1990s, but jumped to 21% in 1998 (Brown et al. 1999a, 54).

Increasing awareness of global warming from burning fossil fuels coupled with decreasing RE costs have contributed to the strong growth in the use of renewable energy. It will take a more explosive growth rate, similar to the recent exponential growth in Internet use, to radically reduce our dependence on fossil fuels and shift towards true sustainability. In spite of years of record growth, wind and solar power only accounted for less than 1% of the world's total energy consumption in 1999.

No one needs to suffer by changing to RE. My sister and her husband have lived comfortably off the grid for many years. She has written the following description of their RE lifestyle.

I live in a cabin in the Ponderosa Pine forest in the Blue Mountains. Our alpine valley holds the record for being the coldest place in Oregon. When my husband started building our house in 1979, the nearest power line ended 2 miles down the road. After a year of living with kerosene lamps, he bought one solar panel and a 12-volt light, and hooked them up to an old auto battery. He never had to fill a lamp by flashlight again.

Our house was one of the first solar-powered homes built in Oregon. Now we have 32 solar electric panels on our roof, which produce all the electricity we use. We still haven't bothered with a backup generator, mostly because we don't like the noisy smelly things. The power produced by the panels, which is stored in batteries at 24 volts, is converted to 110 volts AC by an inverter. The system runs our deep-well pump, which irrigates a large garden where we grow all our vegetables. It also runs a refrigerator and a small chest freezer where we store perishable produce from the garden. We have a clothes washer, computer, stereo, TV, VCR, and power tools just like most American families.

We don't have to do without anything we really want. We enjoy the benefits of the electronic age. What we do differently is to look at power usage ratings when we buy any new item that uses electricity. We used to depend on the information plate on the back of appliances, but now we have a new meter that makes power measurement a snap. We just plug it in, plug the appliance into it, and read the usage off the display. When you live with a limited supply of something like electricity, knowledge is power.

As I look at my daily calendar, I also plan my day's power usage. If I look at the sky and see the sun, I observe the battery meter to check how close we are to fully charged, and I plan to do laundry or vacuum the house. I do my writing on a laptop computer because it takes such small sips of power that its usage is never an issue. When winter weather is howling outside, I like to cozy up to the computer with a cup of tea and write. It doesn't matter how dark the weather is when I am using only 18 watts.

I don't worry about my computer crashing from a power glitch, because my whole house is running on an uninterruptible power supply! When the wind blows and the power flickers and goes out in our valley, my husband Lance and I don't even notice. Essentially, we own our own power company, which means we are responsible for solving any problems with the system. It's up to us to make sure everything works the way we need it to.

After a long day's work, we turn out our compact fluorescent lights and slip outside for a starlit soak in our wood-fired hot tub. As we listen to the sandhill cranes chirping along the river meadows, and their voices come clearly through the silence, I have a hard time believing that we are suffering!

—Jennifer Barker

Why Renewable Energy?

- **Economics.** If you live more than a third of a mile from your nearest power line, it may be cheaper to buy your own RE system than to hook into the grid. In addition, you will have no electricity bills. When you buy a piece of land that does not have an easy grid connection, you may save a huge chunk of money on a beautiful piece of property that will cover the extra cost of adding an RE system.

- **Independence.** Having your own renewable energy system makes you independent from large corporate power generation and distribution systems. You are your own uninterruptible power supply. Acts of god, nature, and terrorists will probably not affect your source of power while disrupting the lives of those who are hooked to the grid. Some people who are hooked up to the grid add an RE system to supply part of their home's energy needs. They feel good about reducing their environmental impact and enjoy the security of having a back-up power system in their home, in the event of grid power outages.

- **Hedge on inflation.** Installing an RE system now can provide you with insurance against escalating energy costs. You may be more comfortable paying for planned RE system costs than being stuck with potential energy crisis cost escalations as global energy sources become less stable.

- **Environmental.** We live in a country that uses far more than its share of the world's resources. With less than 5% of the world's population, the United States accounts for 28% of the world's oil consumption. As the world seeks to "catch up with the Joneses" (the USA), it has become increasingly clear that the planet cannot possibly support U.S. lifestyles everywhere. A personal switch to renewable energy is one way of saying that we care about the environment and our children's future. When we consider the astronomical health and environment costs from acid rains and global warming caused by burning fossil fuels, it is clear that we are not paying for the full cost of energy with our utility bill. If we were to factor in the hidden costs, I believe that RE would be immediately cost effective in most situations.

Energy Conservation, "Negawatts," and RE

Amory Lovins, a well-known ecologist and cofounder of the Rocky Mountain Institute (RMI), first coined the term "negawatts" to describe one effect of energy conservation. He calculated that it actually costs less to fund energy conserving technologies and practices than to build new power plants to generate more power for increasing populations and industrial needs. This same philosophy applies equally well to small-scale RE systems as to large-scale power producers.

Photovoltaics (solar cells) are the backbone of most common small-scale RE systems, but they are not cheap. A single 100-watt solar panel, costing over $500 in the year 2000, provides only enough power from 5 equivalent hours of sun (average available standardized hours of sunshine for a typical winter day in Phoenix, Arizona) to run a single 75-watt bulb for about 6½ hours. Yet, if you replace two 75-watt incandescent bulbs with compact fluorescent bulbs, which produce equivalent lighting and last more than 10 times as long, you will save over 100 watts of power, and will have spent only $30 to $50 up front. This is a tiny fraction of the cost for the solar panel it would save, plus it will recoup more than twice this amount over the average life of a single compact fluorescent by cutting your utility bill and saving the expense for 13 replacement incandescent bulbs. *Homemade Money* by Richard Heede and the staff of RMI is an excellent book about energy conservation within the home, outlining numerous cost-effective energy solutions. I highly recommend that you pick up a copy to help you plan your new home or improve the energy consumption of your existing home, especially if you are considering the addition of an RE system (see the description of *Homemade Money* in the *References* section of Chapter 7).

> By replacing a single 75-watt incandescent light bulb with an 18-watt compact fluorescent bulb, you will save yourself about $37.06 in combined utility and bulb costs, over the lifetime of one fluorescent bulb. These energy efficient bulbs produce the same quantity and quality of light as a regular 75-watt bulb and last about 13 times as long. Over the life of one compact fluorescent, you will save yourself the hassle of buying and replacing 13 incandescent bulbs. The energy savings from a single bulb will accomplish one of the following:

> Spare the earth more than 1,500 pounds of carbon dioxide and about 20 pounds of sulfur dioxide spewing from the stack of a coal-fired power plant.
>
> Avoid the production in a nuclear plant of half a curie of high-level radioactive waste (which is a lot) and two-fifths of a ton of TNT-equivalent of plutonium.
>
> Keep an oil-fired power plant from burning 1.25 barrels of oil—enough to run a family car for a thousand miles or to run Honda's new hybrid car from Los Angeles to New York and on to Miami before it needed more gas.
>
> —Adapted from *Homemade Money*, by Richard Heede and the staff of Rocky Mountain Institute

RE SYSTEMS

Easy-to-use and highly efficient "power centers" are finally bringing RE into mainstream America. These power centers are the heart of modern RE systems. They are smart systems that connect and seamlessly integrate the various components of modern renewable energy systems to create your own independent home power supply that keeps you powered with a little attention, maintenance, and energy usage planning.

The modern RE system typically consists of a source of direct current (DC) energy, such as a solar panel and/or wind turbine, a battery system for storing DC energy, an optional backup generator, and a device known as an "inverter" for converting battery power into standard household alternating current for powering common appliances. Cars and RVs typically operate on 12 volts DC, but most common household appliances run on 110 to 120 VAC (volts alternating current). High-power-consuming electric household appliances, such as electric dryers, stoves, and baseboard heaters, usually require 220 to 240 VAC, and are best replaced with nonelectric appliances if you are not hooked to the grid. If you are confused by the use of these electrical terms, skip ahead to the *Energy, Power, and Electricity Primer* at the end of this chapter.

Electrically, it is a simple thing to convert alternating current to direct current (wall chargers for modern phones do this all the time), but it is a far more complicated process to convert direct current to alternating current. Twenty years ago most RE-powered, off-grid households ran strictly on 12 volts DC (direct current), drawing from a limited selection of rather expensive 12 VDC appliances. Trace Engineering really helped to change the popularity of RE with the introduction of their efficient and highly reliable solid-state inverters that convert DC electrical power from batteries, solar panels, wind turbines, and so on, into 110 and 220 VAC. Using inverters, RE powered houses can be built with standard wiring that supports regular power tools and appliances such as TVs, washing machines, dishwashers, and stereos.

Trace inverters and others like them often combine several functions into a single box, turning the inverter into a true power center. Multifunction inverters may include the following facilities:

- Multistage battery charging for extended battery life
- Automatic control of a backup generator to cover short-term high power demands or kick in when batteries are low
- Low battery cutout to prevent costly damage to your battery storage system caused by discharging your batteries too low
- Automatic integration of various RE sources such as wind turbines, photovoltaics (solar panels), and micro-hydro turbines
- Utility Interactive Mode, which allows grid-tied systems to run your utility meter backwards (where allowed by law) when your system is producing more energy than the batteries can store, or allows your system to use the grid as its battery backup—pumping excess power into the grid when generating capacity is higher than loads, while drawing power from the grid when demand is higher than generating capacity. Because batteries are the weak link in RE systems, having high initial cost, significant maintenance, and shorter lifespans than the rest of RE system components, grid-tied RE systems can reduce or eliminate the need for batteries. (Some batteries or a generator are needed if you wish to maintain backup power protection.)

WARNING: *Inverters are usually specified as "square wave," "modified sine wave," or "full sine wave" inverters. These terms describe the shape of the "wave" of alternating current that the inverter makes out of the input direct current. Most motors and appliances are designed to run on standard household current, which is full sine wave alternating current. Square wave inverters are lowest in cost, but will only run certain types of electronic equipment. Light bulbs, simple heating elements, and some small appliance motors run well using square wave inverters. Modified sine wave inverters are significantly more expensive, and will run most appliances, but even modified sine wave inverters can harm larger motors, such as those on washing machines, and some electronic equipment, such as computers and quality stereos. Richard Perez, editor of* Home Power Magazine, *used to post a rather lengthy list of items that had been reported as ruined by modified sine wave inverters. For household usage, I suggest you play it safe, by spending more and getting yourself a full sine wave inverter. The folks at Home Power tested a number of popular sine wave inverters for total harmonic distortion (THD) and found only three acceptable manufacturers: Trace Engineering, Statpower Technologies, and Exeltech, with 5% to 20%, 2%, and .3% THD, respectively.*

Net Metering

"Net metering" essentially means that you can use the grid as a battery source for grid connected systems, by running your meter backwards when your system is producing more energy than you need, offsetting your meter bill for those times when you draw power from the grid. Since 1978, a federal law known as PURPA (Public Utilities Policy Regulation Act) has required all publicly owned electric utilities to buy power produced by its customers. However, PURPA only requires the utilities to pay the "wholesale avoided cost," or in plain terms, the rate that they pay to other utilities when they buy power. Not surprisingly, this rate is far lower than the retail rate that normal customers (you and I) are asked to pay. In some cases, they pay only about 25% of what they charge their customers.

Recently, many states have enacted "net metering laws." This means that they are required to offset the customer's bill at the full retail rate for power fed

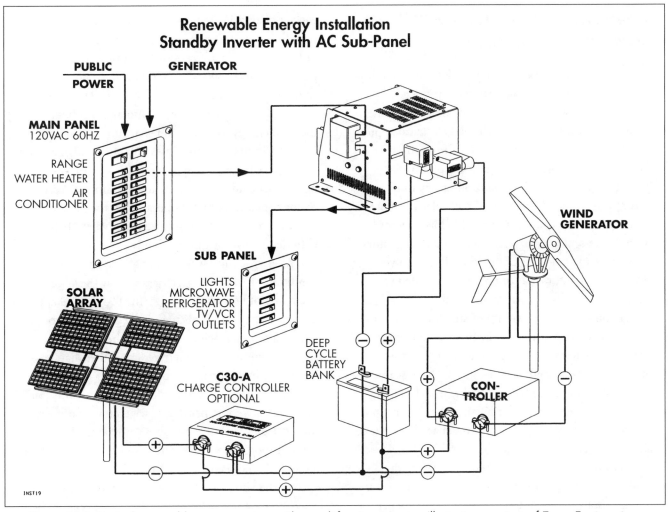

Renewable Energy Installation
Standby Inverter with AC Sub-Panel

PUBLIC
POWER

GENERATOR

MAIN PANEL
120VAC 60HZ

RANGE
WATER HEATER
AIR
CONDITIONER

SUB PANEL

LIGHTS
MICROWAVE
REFRIGERATOR
TV/VCR
OUTLETS

WIND
GENERATOR

SOLAR
ARRAY

DEEP
CYCLE
BATTERY
BANK

C30-A
CHARGE CONTROLLER
OPTIONAL

CON-
TROLLER

INST19

Figure 11-1. Typical renewable energy system with a multifunction inverter. Illustration courtesy of Trace Engineering.

back to the utility. While all state programs accept solar power, many also accept wind and other renewables. As of spring 2000, thirty states allow some form of net metering, and conditions vary from state to state. In general, you must use approved inverters that produce AC power synchronized with your grid hookup, your system must include appropriate electrical disconnects, and systems must be approved by a local building inspector. Check with your local RE dealer to determine which conditions apply in your area.

REBATES

Utility rebates and tax credits are now available in several states. You could save a hefty chunk of money from the cost of your new RE system through a variety of rebates. Check with your local RE dealer to determine the conditions that apply in your area.

AC Versus DC

Small simple systems, such as most dedicated water pumping stations and small cabin installations, are usually best left as DC-only systems that skip the extra cost and efficiency losses of an inverter. Even with inverter systems, some circuits may be best left as DC. For example, high-efficiency electrical refrigerators that run on AC consume about twice as much power as their DC versions, and DC, solar-powered submersible pumps consume less than half as much power as standard AC submersible pumps. In AC systems, it is also a good idea to leave at least a few lights on a DC circuit, especially one in your battery/power-system area, so that you still have some light when your inverter is not functioning properly or you need to service the system.

Alternatives for High-Energy-Consuming Appliances

Unless you have a steeply falling creek to drive a mini-hydro system, or steady high winds to run a good sized wind turbine, your RE system will get extremely expensive if you try to run high-load electrical appliances for more than short periods of time strictly with RE. The highest energy loads in the typical U.S. household are for heating and cooling. Try to use natural gas, wood, propane, or direct solar heating to power your large heating and cooling loads. Items like water heaters, clothes dryers, stoves, and refrigerators consume large amounts of power and can run very efficiently on natural gas or propane, provided you have access to these items at your location.

If you have a fair amount of sunshine, solar hot water and space heating can be immediately cost effective. Solar panels can directly heat either water or air at far greater efficiencies and for far less initial cost than trying to convert sunlight into electricity, and then convert that electricity into heat. For more information on solar hot water and space heating see later sections in this chapter.

Two things count most when considering the loads from different appliances. The first is the power that an appliance needs to run. Power is energy per time unit and is usually measured in watts (see the *Energy, Power, and Electricity Primer* at the end of this chapter for more information) for electrical appliances and Btus (British thermal units) for gas appliances. The total number of watts consumed at a given moment gives you an idea of your maximum peak load, which helps you decide how big your wires should be and the size of the inverter or backup generator you need. Electrical appliances usually have a label that tells you how much power (watts) they draw, but you may wish to purchase a small plug-in meter that connects between an appliance and an outlet to give you a more accurate power consumption reading.

The second item of major importance is how much time an appliance is used every day. The total energy consumed on a daily basis by all of your appliances combined helps you to decide how many solar panels, wind generators, storage batteries, and so on you will need. Total daily energy consumption for each appliance is the power (watts) multiplied by the time that the appliance is expected to be on (number of hours). A toaster, for example, consumes a lot of power (around 1500 watts), but for only a few minutes a day. Thus, a toaster requires a fair-sized inverter, but only a fraction of a solar panel because the total energy for six minutes of run time is only 150 watt-hours (1/10 hour times 1500 watts). Unless you have a very large (and expensive) RE system, you may need to schedule your power usage so that several major appliances are not operating at the same time and you may need to minimize usage when the batteries are low or during cloudy periods.

After space and water heating (and sometimes air conditioning), the refrigerator is usually the largest consumer of household energy. In 1993, federal appliance efficiency standards mandated greatly improved refrigerator efficiencies, so it makes the best energy sense to junk your older refrigerator rather than leave it running in the garage. Typical 1970s to mid 1980s household 120 VAC refrigerators consume from 2,500 to 6,000 watt-hours per day. Refrigerators that meet the 1993 standards average about 1,900 watt hours per day, but those meeting the proposed 2001 standard are about 35% more efficient. Ultra-efficient refrigerators, such as the Sun Frost 16-cubic-foot model, consume only about 540 watt-hours per day. Solar cells are now available for about $5 per watt, but figure that the cost for the solar panels is only part of the cost for a complete photovoltaic RE system. With three standard hours of sun (typical average January sun in middle America, equal to three noontime hours of unobstructed sun at the equator), the year 2000 cost for a midrange comprehensive photovoltaic-based RE system (including storage batteries, inverter, etc.) is roughly $3.50 per watt-hour. At this rate, it would cost a whopping $12,250 for the system to run just one older 3500 watt-hour refrigerator, but only $1,890 to run a 540 watt-hour, ultra-efficient refrigerator! Propane operated refrigerators, 12-volt DC appliances, super-efficient appliances, and design assistance are available from most RE dealers.

Large compressor-style air conditioners consume too much power to run off of anything but extremely large RE systems, a good-sized backup generator, or a grid hookup. If your climate is typically below 70% relative humidity during hot weather, evaporative coolers can be a good match for an RE system. Given low humidity, they can effectively utilize the cooling power of evaporating water to air condition your house for a fraction of the power consumed by compressor-based systems. Proper home design and insulation can work together to passively cool homes in hot and humid climates so they do not need any air conditioning. RMI's *Green Developments* CD-ROM (see Chapter 7 on shelter and buildings) illustrates examples of successful passive cooling design in a large Taiwan home that needs no air conditioning in spite of high humidity and air temperatures, plus an air-conditioner-free home in Davis, California, that neighbors escaped to when their own air conditioners failed to keep up with a 104°F plus heat wave.

Photovoltaics Versus Wind Versus Micro-Hydro

No single RE source works best all the time in all situations. Hybrid systems often yield the best year-round performance. Wind and micro-hydro usually perform well during stormy periods while photovoltaics work best in dry summer conditions with long sunny days. Photovoltaics have the benefit of no moving parts, no maintenance, high reliability, and a long life averaging about 25 years for solar panels. The current (year 2000) solar panel cost of about $5 per watt (remember that batteries and inverters will add significantly to this cost) has been steadily dropping as sales of solar cells have doubled every few years. The recent invention of solar roofing panels and the introduction of major PV incentives in several countries are expected to continue to boost sales and significantly reduce prices over the next decade.

Worldwide wind energy sales have increased at a faster rate than any other source of power, and for good reason. If your area is subject to consistently windy conditions, you can generate electricity with much less initial investment than for photovoltaics. At roughly $1.50 per watt, a small wind generator can produce far more power for far less money than the equivalent wattage of solar panels, when you consider that a wind generator operates day and night. The downside to wind generators is their need for maintenance (they do have moving parts), mounting expenses (they are usually mounted on towers to catch the best wind), annoying noise in high winds, and they have little or no output in low winds. Don't be seduced by a wind turbine's high wattage rating if you really don't have enough local wind to make it worthwhile. See the *Wind Power* section later in this chapter for more details.

Micro-hydropower is the way to go if you have the right conditions for it. Hydropower requires two things: first, you must have a good source of running water, and second, that water should drop from a significant vertical height. Micro-hydro has the advantage of running 24 hours a day, 7 days a week, as long as your water supply holds out. Given a water source with adequate flow and pressure (head), micro-hydro will generate far more power than a photovoltaic system of equal cost. The downside is regular maintenance to clear debris from intake screens, service for generator brushes and bearings, and the need for a water source with adequate flow and head pressure. See the *Micro-Hydropower* section later in this chapter for more details.

Batteries

Nearly all RE systems rely on a sizeable bank of heavy-duty batteries to store energy both for when the system is not producing much energy and to cover short-term high capacity loads that draw more power than the system can instantly generate. A battery bank is often the weak link in an RE system, requiring regular maintenance. Improper charging and repeated deep discharging will rapidly destroy a hefty investment in batteries.

BATTERY POINTERS

■ *Battery type.* Use heavy-duty, "deep cycle," lead antimony batteries. Six-volt electric vehicle type batteries, such as those made by Trojan, U.S. Battery, and Surrette, are good for small- to mid-size RE systems. They have thick lead plates that hold up well to repeated charging. For medium- to large-sized PV systems, super heavy-duty, 2-volt industrial batteries, such as those made by IBE, are recommended.

DO NOT use regular automotive batteries unless you are hooked into the grid and draw on the batteries only for occasional backup during power outages. Automotive batteries are not meant to regularly discharge to below 80% of their capacity and will quickly wear out under typical RE system cycling.

- **Venting.** Place battery bank in a well-vented, preferably heated, area. Charging batteries can release hydrogen gas. A spark from a light switch or motor could cause an explosion if the battery area is not properly vented.

- **Temperature.** Cold batteries have significantly reduced capacity (roughly 50% at 0°F) and hot batteries have significantly reduced life. Optimum battery storage temperatures range from 55° to 80°F. If your batteries are stored in an unheated area, take reduced capacity into consideration when sizing your battery bank.

- **Battery bank.** Batteries should be on shelves with easy access for cleaning and maintenance. On most batteries, the charging cycle will cause some battery acid to collect on the top of the battery where it will lead to corrosion of the contacts. Keep battery terminals and jumpers clean and greased or coated with special terminal coatings to prevent corrosion. Bad connections can ruin your batteries in a short period of time.

- **Discharge cycle.** Even deep cycle batteries will not last long if repeatedly discharged below 50% capacity. Try to keep normal daily cycling above 80% charge and multiday cloudy cycles above 50% charge, with only occasional discharge to 20% of capacity. Multifunction inverters will often have a battery cutoff safety feature that prevents discharging batteries below 20% of capacity.

- **Charging.** Use a multistage battery charger that "floats" fully charged batteries at a lower voltage than the primary charging voltage to prevent excessive gassing and shortened battery life. Temperature compensation is a valuable charger feature that must be included with your charge controller if batteries are to be stored in an unheated area. Battery capacity and optimum charging currents are affected by temperature. Sophisticated charge controllers offer both temperature compensation and multistage battery charging.

- **Protect your investment.** A considerable chunk of your RE system cost is for batteries. Proper charging, maintenance to ensure proper fluid levels, mostly shallow cycle discharges, and never fully discharging your batteries will help to ensure long battery life.

- **Backup generator.** For mid-range and large RE systems, a backup generator probably costs significantly less than your battery bank and will help prevent excessively deep battery discharges during periods of cloudy weather or low wind.

- **Metering.** For less than $200, you can buy a nifty amp-hour battery meter that will accurately tell you how much capacity you have left in your batteries as well as provide you with instantaneous load information for evaluating and diagnosing your system. This meter acts like a car fuel guage, but actually provides you with more information that makes good battery care much simpler for the average user. Recommended models include the TriMetric units by Bogart Engineering and E-Meters from Cruising Equipment. A meter of this kind is cheap insurance to help protect your battery investment. Check out "A TriMetric User's Manual" online at www.bogartengineering.com for an excellent introduction to battery basics and care.

- **Discharge rate.** Battery storage capacity is expressed in amp-hours at the rate that the battery was designed to deliver its maximum capacity. If the battery is discharged faster than this rate, it has reduced capacity. For example, the Trojan L-16, deep cycle 6-volt battery is rated at 360 amp-hours with a 20-hour discharge rate. Divide 360 amp-hours by 20 hours to get a recommended maximum discharge rate of 18 amps.

- **Charge rate.** Most batteries can be safely charged at a fifth of their amp-hour rating, but a charge rate of a tenth of their amp-hour rating will give you longer life and the batteries will require maintenance less often. For example, the Trojan L-16, deep cycle 6-volt battery is rated at 360 amp-hours, and can be charged at a maximum rate of 72 amps, but a better charging rate would be 36 amps maximum. Industrial batteries can handle higher charge rates (see manufacturers' recommendations).

- **Battery bank wiring.** You should use batteries of the same voltage, capacity, and model within each battery bank. When batteries are hooked in series, the output voltage is the sum of all the battery voltages, but the maximum amperage is only that of the single lowest-capacity battery in the series. When batteries are hooked in parallel, the output amperage is the sum of all the battery amperages, but the output voltage is only that of the single lowest battery voltage. Never mix voltages in parallel-wired batteries, or the higher voltage batteries will overcharge and ruin the lower-voltage batteries.

Backup Generators

Generators are noisy, smelly, inefficient, and require regular maintenance, including full rebuilds after surprisingly low numbers of hours of use. In spite of these drawbacks, most RE systems designed for homes will include a backup generator. The generator provides power for short-term periods when high loads exceed the capacity of your RE system, such as when running large electric motors, or when batteries run low due to cloudy weather or excessive drain. When friends or relatives visit, they might not be used to living with reduced energy consumption, so they will tend to drain your storage batteries. The extra PV and battery expenses to size a system to cover all possible loads and extra-long cloudy periods will usually cost far more than a backup generator.

Generators typically run on gasoline, propane/natural gas, or diesel. If available, propane/natural gas is usually the fuel of choice for RE home systems, since it burns cleanly and quietly and stores easily. Gasoline must be stored somewhere safe and needs special treatment to prevent it from going "stale" after a period of a few months. Some of the new generators are multifuel units that are easily converted among propane, natural gas, or gasoline. For heavy-duty continuous operation, diesel fuel generators are the most economical and longest lasting choice, but for occasional battery charging and backup use, they are not usually worth the hassle, smell, and expense. Additionally, diesel fuel does not do well in extremely cold temperatures.

Generators should be sized to exceed by about 10% to 25% the maximum power draw of the battery system charger plus any AC loads that may be running at the same time. Typical household backup generators are sized in the 4 to 10 kW range. It usually takes about half as much fuel to run small loads, such as a single 100-watt light bulb, from a generator as it takes to run at full load. Low-load operation can actually cause more wear and tear on some generator systems than operating under full load. Both from a fuel economy and generator life perspective, it makes much more sense to run a generator intermittently to charge battery banks and cover short-term peak loads, then to run it continuously.

System Sizing

Most RE systems are sized at a compromise between what you want and what you can afford. Luckily, so long as you allow for extra heavy gage wiring and extra space for future components (such as more batteries and a second inverter), it is usually fairly simple to expand your system size in a modular pay-as-you-go fashion. As mentioned earlier, the total energy consumed on a daily basis by all of your appliances put together is the major factor in determining how many solar panels, wind generators, storage batteries, and so on you will need. Average daily energy consumption for each appliance is the power (watts) multiplied by the time that the appliance is expected to be on (number of hours). For items that are used very intermittently, estimate how many hours they will be used each week and divide by seven for average daily usage.

> *CAUTION: You must estimate your average daily energy load very accurately. Undersized estimations will result in a frustratingly undersized system whereas an oversized installation will be excessively expensive. Use the following table as a preliminary guideline, and then follow up with actual numbers taken from your own appliance tags or use amp meter readings (most accurate) taken while operating the appliances.*

LOAD CALCULATION

1. List all AC appliances and multiply their number of watts by average daily usage (in hours) to get the average daily load for each appliance in watt-hours. Add all loads together for the average daily AC energy load.

2. Multiply the average daily AC energy load (from step 1) by 1.15 to account for energy losses from the inverter. This is your adjusted average daily load from all AC appliances.

3. List all DC appliances and multiply the number of watts by average daily usage (in hours) for each appliance to get the average daily load for each appliance in watt-hours. Add all of these loads together for the average daily DC load from DC appliances.

4. Add the average daily DC load due to DC appliances plus the adjusted average daily load from the AC appliances (add steps 2 and 3). This is your total average daily load (in watt-hours).

5. Divide the total average daily load (step 4) by .7 to account for system losses and inefficiencies (roughly 30% loss). This is your adjusted total average daily system load, in watt-hours. You will use this number to help you calculate how big your solar panels, wind generators, inverter, wiring, and battery banks should be.

6. Look over your appliance list and estimate what your maximum total wattage might be for all AC appliances that you will run at the same time. This figure will determine the minimum size for your inverter (number of watts).

After running the above calculation for the first time, and pricing out an RE system, most people go back and sharpen their pencils to see how they might conserve energy in order to reduce the size of their system.

SIZING YOUR BATTERY BANK

The size of your battery bank is dictated by how much storage capacity is desired, the temperature at which the batteries will be stored, the maximum battery charge rate, and the maximum battery discharge rate. Your battery bank should be the largest size dictated by any one of these factors. Battery capacity is specified in terms of amp-hours.

The total energy stored in a battery is the number of amp-hours multiplied by the battery voltage, which will give you the watt-hours stored in a battery. Since batteries waste some power when they are charged, and have reduced storage capacities at lower temperatures, these factors must be taken into account.

1. Determine total adjusted average daily load (step 5 in the load calculation) in watt-hours.

2. Determine the maximum number of cloudy days in a row (or low-wind days if you have a wind turbine) that you wish to store energy in your batteries to provide for (typically 3 to 10 days). If you have a good generator backup, and don't mind using it a lot, you can shoot for the lower number. It may be easiest to start low, adding more panels and batteries as you go.

3. Multiply step 2 by step 1.

4. For reasonable life, deep-cycle batteries should not be discharged more than 80%. For optimum life, it is better to keep them charged to at least 50% of capacity. Depending on your choice, divide line 3 by either .8 or .5 to maintain at least 20% or 50% charge in the batteries, respectively.

5. If your batteries will be stored below 80°F, adjust for reduced battery storage capacity by multiplying step 4 by the following temperature/capacity factors (use lowest expected battery storage temperature): 1.04 for 70°F; 1.11 for 60°F; 1.19 for 50°F; 1.3 for 40°F; 1.4 for 30°F; 1.59 for 20°F; 2.0 for 0°F. The result is your temperature adjusted battery storage load.

6. Calculate the watt-hour storage capacity for your selected battery. This is the battery spec sheet amp-hour capacity times its voltage, for a single battery.

7. Divide step 5 by step 6 and round up to the nearest whole number. The result is the minimum number of storage batteries you should have in your battery bank.

8. Battery bank amp-hour rating should be at least 5, and preferably 10 times the maximum amperage of the largest appliance draw, the PV array output, or the generator-driven battery charger output, whichever is larger. Adjust your number of batteries upwards if load rating is too low.

Typical appliance power consumption

Appliance	Watts/hour	Appliance	Watts/hour	Appliance	Watts/hour
Coffee pot	200	Ceiling fan	10 to 50	Compact fluorescent incandescent equivalents	
Coffee maker	800	Table fan	10 to 25	40 watt equiv.	11
Toaster	800 to 1500	Electric blanket	200	60 watt equiv.	16
Popcorn popper	250	Blow dryer	1000	75 watt equiv.	20
Blender	300	Shaver	15	100 watt equiv.	30
Microwave	600 to 1500	Waterpik	100	Electric mower NA	1500
Waffle iron	1200	Computer		Hedge trimmer	450
Hot plate	1200	laptop	20 to 50	Weed eater	500
Frying pan	1200	pc	80 to 150	¼" drill	250
Dishwasher	1200 to 1500	printer	100	½" drill	750
Sink waste disposal	450	Typewriter	80 to 200	1" drill	1000
Washing machine		TV		9" disc sander	1200
automatic	500	25" color	150	3" belt sander	1000
manual	300	19" color	70	12" chain saw	1100
Vacuum cleaner		12" b&w	20	14" band saw	1100
upright	200 to 700	VCR	40	7¼" circ. saw	900
hand	100	CD player	35	8¼" circ. saw	1400
Sewing machine	100	Stereo	10 to 30	Refrig/freezer, conventional	
Iron	1000	Clock radio	1	20cf (pre 1993)	145 to 250
Clothes dryer		AM/FM car tape	8	20cf (post 1993)	60 to 100
electric NA*	4000	Satellite dish	30	Sunfrost	
gas heated	300 to 400	CB radio	5	16cf DC	22.5
Heater		Electric clock	3	12cf DC	14
engine block NA	150 to 1000	Radiotelephone		Vestfrost refrig/freezer	
portable NA	1500	receive	5	12cf	30
waterbed NA	400	transmit	40 to 150	Freezer, conventional	
stock tank NA	100	Lights		15cf ff (post 1993)	88
Furnace blower	300 to 1000	100w incandescent	100	15cf (post 1993)	61
Air conditioner NA		25w compact flour.	28	Sunfrost freezer	
room	1000	50w DC incandescent	50	19cf	50
central	2000 to 5000	40w DC halogen	40		
Garage door opener	350	20w DC compact flour.	22		

Note: *NA denotes appliances that would normally be powered by nonelectric sources in an RE-powered home.
Source: Adapted from *Solar Electric Design Guide* by Golden Genesis Corporation.

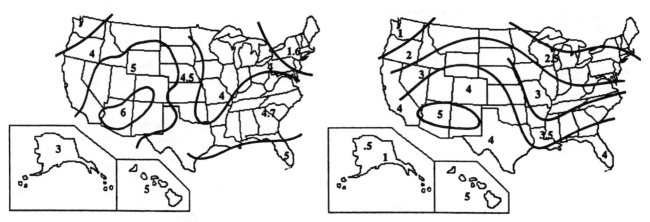

Figure 11-2. Yearly average equivalent sun hours per day. Illustration courtesy of Sierra Solar Systems.

Figure 11-3. December/January average equivalent sun hours per day. Illustration courtesy of Sierra Solar Systems.

PHOTOVOLTAICS

Banks of solar modules are the backbone of most residential RE systems. They are reliable and have no moving parts to wear out or require maintenance. Output from solar panels is dependent on the amount of available sunlight (insolation), orientation towards the sun, and shading of the modules. Properly sizing your PV (photovoltaics) system requires attention to each of these factors as well as system loads.

Insolation

Insolation is a measure of average sunlight intensity and is specified in equivalent hours of full sunlight. The standard of one equivalent hour is based on one hour of sunlight at the equator when the sun is directly overhead. Insolation figures account for cloudy days and the angle of the sun to come up with an average figure for a specific location and time of the year.

The appendix at the back of *The Solar Electric Independent Home Book* contains a detailed list of insolation figures for solar panels tilted to three different angles for numerous North American cities at different times of the year. Use figures 11-2 and 11-3 for a rough estimate of your insolation, but contact your RE dealer or check out *The Solar Electric Independent Home Book* for more accurate figures.

Solar Array Sizing

In northern and cloudy locations, available winter sunshine can be radically less than what is available in the summer. Rather than size a PV system based on minimum winter insolation, many people prefer to size their systems based upon average annual insolation, and to use a generator and/or a small wind turbine to make up the difference during the winter months.

1. Locate your site (or one near you) in Figure 11-2 or 11-3 and list the figure for average equivalent daily hours of sunlight.

2. Take the adjusted total average daily system load (in watt-hours) from step 5 of your load calculation worksheet (system losses are already included).

3. Divide the figure in step 2 by that of step 1. The result is the total number of watts your system should produce in an hour of direct sunlight.

4. Calculate the actual number of available watts for your selected solar module. Solar modules produce constant amperage in full sun at a voltage somewhat higher than your battery charging voltage. For example, a 100-watt Siemens module has a 17-volt output at 5.9 amps. With a battery charging voltage of 13 volts (4 volts not used), available power to charge the batteries is only 76.7 watts (13 volts times 5.9 amps).

5. Divide step 3 by step 4, and then round up to the nearest whole number. This is the minimum

number of solar modules that you will need. Remember that 24-volt systems require pairs of modules and 48-volt systems require modules in sets of 4.

Panel Orientation

Panels can be mounted in fixed orientations or on frames that allow for orientation adjustment. Optimum panel orientation is to face directly into the sun at all times. You may choose to purchase automatic tracking frames, which keep a cluster of modules pointed toward the sun. These trackers can increase the efficiency of your system by up to 40%, but the efficiency gain is mostly during the summer and is highest at tropical latitudes. If your peak loads are in the summer, a tracker will cost less than the modules it saves through increased efficiency. If you live in a northern climate and you have plenty of summer power, then your money is better spent on more modules than on trackers.

ORIENTATION RULES OF THUMB

- **Fixed orientation.** Orient panels due south (not magnetic south) and tilt to latitude plus 15° for winter optimization. This is not the best angle for summer sun, but the extra sun in the summer will make up for the less-than-optimum angle.
- **Adjustable orientation.** Orient panels due south (not magnetic south) and tilt to latitude plus 15° for winter optimization. Adjust the tilt angle to latitude minus 15° for summer optimization. It is generally not worth the effort to manually shift panel orientation more than twice a year (once in the spring and once in the fall).
- **Tracker orientation.** Two-axis and one-axis trackers are available. Two-axis trackers will automatically track the sun east to west and adjust the vertical tilt angle to optimize efficiency. Single-axis trackers track the sun east to west, but the vertical tilt angle should be manually set to the same seasonal angles as regular adjustable frames (see tracker manufacturer's instructions).
- **Shading.** Even partial shading can make a huge difference in the output from your solar

modules. Shaded cells become loads instead of power sources, and rapidly reduce module output. Make sure that your modules have the critical 6 middle hours of the day clear of all shading, both for summer sun and winter sun. See your RE dealer or a good solar design handbook for seasonal sun angles in your area, to help you determine potential shading during different seasons at possible panel locations.

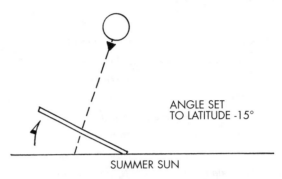

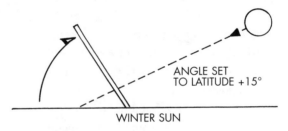

Figure 11-4. Panel seasonal orientation.

Maximum Power Point Trackers

The name for this ingenious and worthwhile electronic device is somewhat misleading. It is not a physical tracking device that points your panels toward the sun, but an electronic "black box" that optimizes the power output from your solar modules. As mentioned in step 4 of the solar array sizing guidelines, your solar panels usually put out a constant current (amperage) at a higher voltage than is required by your battery charger, wasting a significant portion of available power. Maximum power point trackers (MPPT) track the output voltage from your solar modules and convert the DC module voltage to a lower voltage at a higher current to match the input battery charging voltage to optimize power output. *Home Power* magazine has tested several MPPT devices and found the Solar Boost models from RV Power Products to work exceptionally well. Although advertised as increasing system efficiencies up to 30%, I would expect an average improvement of around 20%. In all but very small systems, a 20% improvement will probably save you considerably more money than the cost of the appropriately sized MPPT, by reducing the number of required solar modules.

WIND POWER

There are currently over 150,000 small-scale RE systems in America, and this number grows by 30% annually. The small-scale use of wind power is growing at twice that rate—over 60% per year. What Americans and folks all over the world are finding out is that wind power is an excellent and cost-effective alternative to utility line extensions, utility bills, and fossil fuel generators.... According to our research at Home Power, 82% of the small wind turbines work in systems that also contain photovoltaics. This is a marriage made in heaven: in most locations, when the sun doesn't shine the wind most certainly blows.

—Richard Perez, publisher of *Home Power* magazine, from the introduction to *Wind Energy Basics* by Paul Gipe

If you live in a high wind area, a wind turbine could provide you with far more energy at far less investment cost than a bank of solar modules. Current prices (spring 2000) on small wind turbines start at about $1.50 per watt as compared with solar panel prices of around $5.00 per watt. Wind turbines operate day and night, so a wind turbine generating its rated power over 24 hours will produce 8 times as much power as a bank of solar panels with equal wattage receiving only 3 equivalent hours of winter sun (typical for the Midwest United States). Of course, these great prices per watt do not mean a thing without adequate wind. Unless you live in an area with reliable high winds, you will probably want to build yourself a hybrid wind and PV system, so that for most of the days either the wind turbine or the solar modules (or both) produce a fair amount of energy.

Wind Energy Tips

- Check out your local average wind speeds to help you size your wind system. An RE dealer, the *Home Power* web site, local weather stations, or the National Climactic Center in Asheville, NC (see *Resources* section in this chapter) should be able to give you a good idea of local wind velocities, but the best way to evaluate your site is with an anemometer-based wind speed totalizer. This gadget is sold and sometimes rented by RE dealers.

- Available wind power increases with the cube of the wind speed. This means that if you double the wind speed, it has the potential for 8 times the wind power.

- In areas with inconsistent wind, a low-cost micro wind turbine to supplement your PV system is a lot easier to justify than a larger turbine.

- Check manufacturer specifications and power curves carefully. Some models maintain power output in high wind while others drop off radically. Low turbine power output in high winds is fine for most areas, because they are subject to high winds (above 35 MPH) only for short periods of time, but will not work well in areas with consistently high winds. If you live in an area characterized by low average winds, the low-speed section of the turbine power curve will be the most important.

- Most turbines are rated at around 28 MPH wind speed, which is a very windy condition. At 15 MPH, which is moderately windy, available wind power is only about 15% of what is available at 28 MPH. At 6 to 8 MPH (light winds), wind turbines have little or no output. For realistic expectations, you should know your available wind speed or rely on the experience of others in your area that already use wind energy.

- Wind generators should be installed at least 20 feet higher than any obstructions closer than 500 feet, and mounts should be well grounded. Prefabricated towers and roof mounting kits are available from RE dealers and wind turbine manufacturers. Some towers have tilt features that allow you to lower the turbine to the ground in the event of approaching severe weather, such as tornadoes and hurricanes. (Protect your investment!)

MICRO-HYDROPOWER

If your property contains a creek with a significant drop to it, micro-hydropower could provide you with a terrific source of electricity for an investment far less than an equivalent sized PV system. The vertical distance that your water supply drops from the source to the turbine is known as the pressure "head." Available water power is a function of the volume flow rate (how much water is flowing) multiplied by head feet (head relates directly to available water pressure). Micro-hydro turbines can operate with as little as 5 feet of head if you have a high flow rate, but are usually operated with heads of 25 feet or more. Good water flow rate can compensate for less head, but head tends to be the more important factor.

Micro-hydro, like most PV systems, generates electricity at modest rates that are far below most residential peak demands, but because it generates electricity day and night, it adds up to quite a bit of energy every day. This energy is accumulated in batteries where it is available to drive high loads when required.

Micro-Hydro Considerations

- **Head.** What is the vertical drop (head) from your water source to your micro-hydro generator? This is the most important factor in determining whether micro-hydro is feasible and how much power you will be able to extract. If you have a fast-flowing creek with less than 5 feet of head, you will not be able to use a jetted turbine, but you may get a worthwhile amount of energy from your creek using a propeller-type turbine from Jack Rabbit Energy Systems.

- **Flow rate.** How many gallons per minute can you provide to your micro-hydro turbine? This factor combined with head determines your potential available power. For small flows, time the flow of your supply into a 5-gallon bucket to estimate flow rate. For larger flows, civil and mechanical

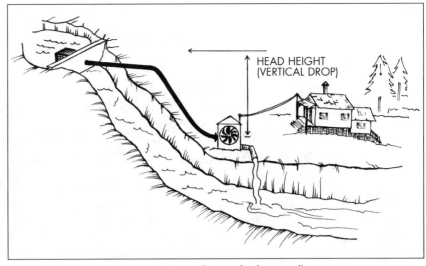

Figure 11-5. Typical micro-hydro installation.

engineering books or the *Micro-Hydropower Sourcebook* show you how to build a simple "weir" to accurately estimate stream flow rates.

- **Available power.** A good rule of thumb for determining available power (in watts) is to multiply the flow rate in gpm (gallons per minute) times the head (in feet), and then divide by 10. The maximum theoretical power is actually divided by only 5.3, but a factor of 10 accounts for efficiency losses in the turbine, the alternator, and some in the piping. For example, a head of 25 feet with a flow rate of 100 GPM would provide you with somewhere around 250 watts of continuous power (100 x 25/10). In general, a value of 1000 or more for the flow rate (GPM) multiplied by the head (feet) is the point where micro-hydro turbines become worthwhile.

- **Pipe head loss.** The flow rate, length, size, and type of pipe will determine how much pressure and power are lost due to the friction of water flowing through your pipe. Friction through a pipe decreases with a cube of the diameter; thus, a pipe that is twice as big has one-eighth the friction loss. Fire hoses are big fat hoses, because you can't squirt a lot of water through a small hose. The same is true for your micro-hydro supply piping. Water pipe sizing charts (see Figure 11-6) will help you to size your piping by estimating how many feet of pressure head are lost flowing through the length of pipe. Losses are typically given in feet of head

Water Pipe Sizing Chart

Friction Loss in Plastic Pipe with Standard Inside Diameter (SIDR)

THIS CHART APPLIES ONLY TO: PVC pipe, Schedule 40 (160 PSI) and to
PE (polyethylene) pipe with SIDR designation (most common 100 PSI black pipe)

HEAD LOSS in VERTICAL FEET per HUNDRED FEET of pipe or VERTICAL METERS per HUNDRED METERS of pipe

Nominal Pipe Diameter (Inches)

FLOW RATE		1/2 *	3/4	1	1 1/4	1 1/2	2	2 1/2	3	4	5	6
GPM	LPM	.662	.82	1.05	1.38	1.61	2.07	2.47	3.07	4.03	5.05	6.06
										actual Inside Diameter (inches)		
1	3.8	1.13	0.14	0.05	0.02	.	.	.	.	.	.	.
2	7.6	4.16	0.35	0.14	0.05	0.02	.	.	.	.	.	.
3	11	8.55	2.19	0.32	0.09	0.05	.	.	.	.		
4	15	14.8	3.70	0.53	0.16	0.09	0.02	.	.	.		
5	19	22.2	5.78	0.81	0.25	0.12	0.04	.	.	NOTE: Shaded values are		
6	23	31.0	7.85	1.00	0.35	0.18	0.07	0.02	.	at velocities over 5 feet per		
7	27	.	10.6	1.52	0.46	0.23	0.08	0.03	.	second and should be		
8	30	.	13.4	1.94	0.58	0.30	0.09	0.05	.	selected with caution.		
9	34	.	16.9	2.43	0.72	0.37	0.12	0.06	.	.	.	.
10	38	.	20.3	2.93	0.88	0.46	0.16	0.07	0.02	.	.	.
11	42	.	24.3	3.51	1.04	0.53	0.18	0.08	0.03	.	.	.
12	46	.	28.6	4.11	1.22	0.65	0.21	0.09	0.04	.	.	.
14	53	.	.	5.47	1.64	0.85	0.28	0.12	0.05	.	.	.
16	61	.	.	7.02	2.10	1.09	0.37	0.14	0.06	.	.	.
18	68	.	.	8.73	2.61	1.34	0.46	0.18	0.07	.	.	.
20	76	.	.	10.6	3.16	1.64	0.55	0.21	0.08	0.02	.	.
22	83	.	.	13.3	3.79	1.96	0.67	0.25	0.09	0.03	.	.
24	91	.	.	14.9	4.44	2.31	0.79	0.30	0.11	0.04	.	.
26	99	.	.	.	5.15	2.66	0.90	0.35	0.14	0.05	.	.
28	106	.	.	.	5.91	3.05	1.04	0.42	0.16	0.05	.	.
30	114	.	.	.	6.72	3.46	1.18	0.46	0.18	0.06	.	.
35	133	.	.	.	8.94	4.62	1.57	0.62	0.23	0.07	.	.
40	152	.	.	.	11.0	5.91	1.99	0.79	0.30	0.09	0.02	.
45	171	.	.	.	14.2	7.37	2.49	0.97	0.37	0.12	0.04	.
50	190	.	.	.	17.3	8.96	3.03	1.20	0.46	0.14	0.05	.
55	208	.	.	.	.	10.7	3.60	1.43	0.55	0.16	0.06	.
60	227	.	.	.	.	12.5	4.23	1.66	0.65	0.18	0.07	0.02
65	246	.	.	.	.	14.5	4.90	1.94	0.74	0.22	0.08	0.03
70	265	.	.	.	.	16.7	5.64	2.22	0.85	0.25	0.09	0.04
75	284	.	.	.	.	19.0	6.40	2.52	0.97	0.28	0.10	0.05
80	303	.	.	.	.	.	7.21	2.84	1.09	0.32	0.12	0.06
85	322	.	.	.	.	.	8.06	3.19	1.22	0.37	0.13	0.07
90	341	.	.	.	.	.	8.96	3.53	1.36	0.39	0.14	0.08
95	360	.	.	.	.	.	9.91	3.90	1.50	0.44	0.16	0.09
100	379	.	.	.	.	.	10.9	4.30	1.66	0.49	0.18	0.12
150	569	.	.	.	.	.	23.1	9.10	3.51	1.04	0.37	0.16
200	758	.	.	.	.	.	.	15.5	5.98	1.76	0.62	0.28

*NOTE: 1/2"
data applies to
PE pipe only.
PVC has smaller
ID of .612"

Figure 11-6. Water pipe sizing chart. Illustration courtesy of Dankoff Solar.

per 100 feet of pipe length, so you must factor in the length of your pipeline. For high flow/ low head systems, a friction loss of more than 1 or 2 feet of head may be unacceptable.

- **Distance to batteries.** Squeezing electrical current through wires is a lot like squeezing water through pipes. Long distances between generator and batteries can result in excessive power losses. Thicker wires and higher micro-hydro output voltages (24V, 48V, or higher) can help reduce power transmission losses between generator and batteries. (See the *Energy, Power, and Electricity Primer* at the end of this chapter for more information.)

- **Custom systems.** Micro-hydro alternators and water jets are custom matched for each application. See your RE dealer for assistance in evaluating your site and choosing among different micro-hydro options.

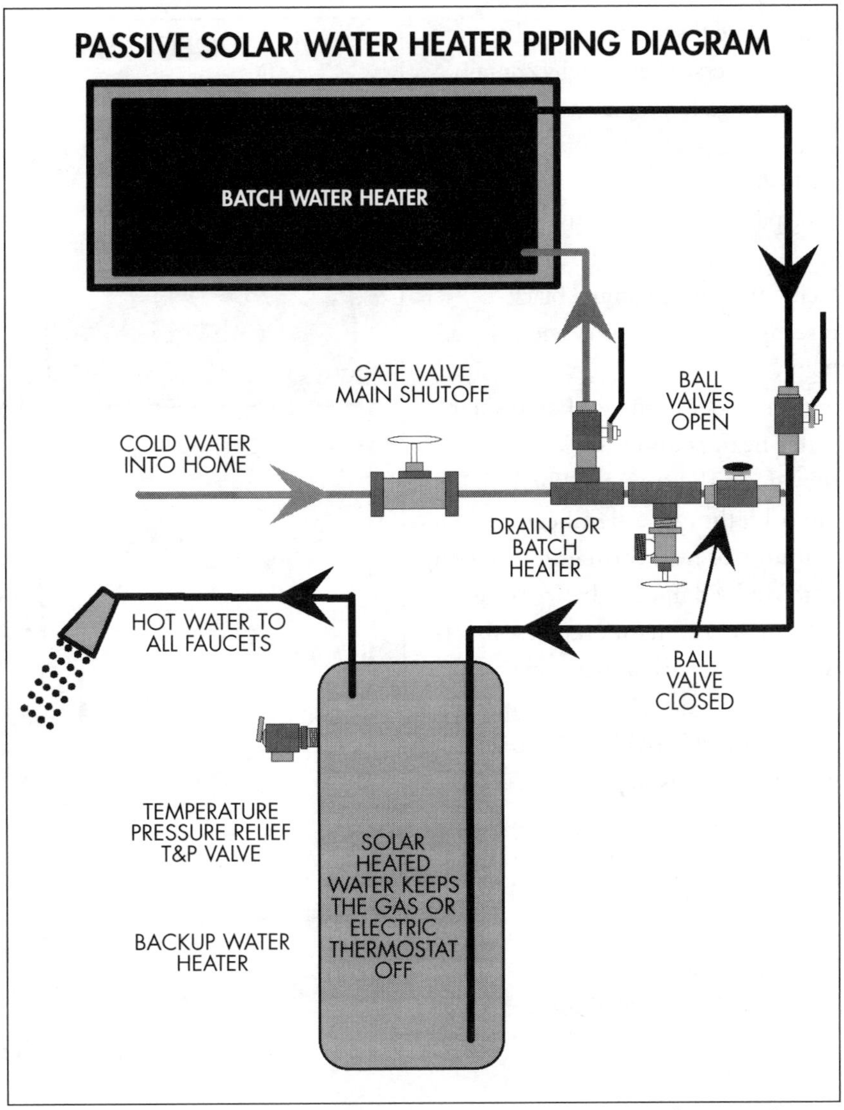

SOLAR HOT WATER

In addition to reducing global warming and the use of fossil fuels, solar hot water heating for your home probably makes good economic sense, provided you have good sun exposure and live in a climate that is sunny for at least a third of all days throughout the year (most of North America). The basic concept of solar hot-water heating is pretty simple. A solar hot-water heater acts like a car with black upholstery sitting in the hot sun. Sunlight enters through clear glass and hits a blackened plate, dumping heat into the black plate, which is in contact with water, so the water gets hot, while the glass and insulation on the back side of the solar panel keeps the box from losing much of its heat. Simple! Well, it's very simple in warm climates, but a bit more complex in

Figure 11-7. Solar batch water heater. Illustration courtesy of AAA Solar.

climates where the solar panels are subject to freezing temperatures. Solar collectors should face within 30° of true south (true south is the optimum orientation) and be tilted at an angle of latitude plus 15° (optimized for winter sun). For more complete information than provided in this section, see AAA Solar's excellent online design guide to solar heating at www.aaasolar.com.

Passive Solar "Batch" Heating

In places like Hawaii, where fuel costs are high and it's warm all year round, solar batch water heaters on the roofs of homes are a common sight. Batch water heaters, also known as integral tank and collector heaters, are the simplest of all solar water heaters. They usually contain 30- to 80-gallon tanks. The tank is placed in a weatherproof, insulated enclosure with one side having a transparent or translucent glazing (usually double-glazed). The tank side facing the sun is painted black to directly absorb the sun's energy. (See Figure 11-7, p. 293.)

In colder climates, batch solar water heaters don't work as well as they do in the tropics. When nights are cold, they lose significant amounts of heat through the glazing and can be damaged by freezing in extremely cold temperatures. Batch water heaters are inexpensive, simple, reliable, and easy to install. They usually provide 50% to 90% of hot water needs depending on usage and climate. The piping to and from the heater is the weak link in the chain. It should be well-insulated and heat tape should be installed in harsher climates.

CAUTION: DO NOT use batch type solar water heaters in extremely cold climates.

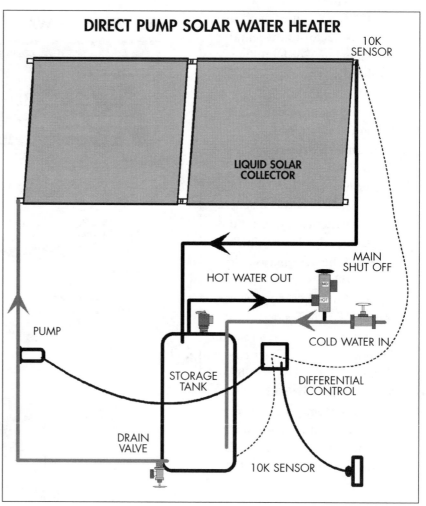

Figure 11-8. Direct pump type solar wate heater. Illustration courtesy of AAA Solar.

Direct Pump Solar Water Heating

Simple direct pump systems were first developed in the late nineteenth century and were in wide use up to the 1920s in Southern California and Florida. These efficient and reliable systems use a low-power pump to circulate tap water through a loop containing the solar collector(s) and a storage tank. This type of system tends to be more efficient than the batch system, because only a small volume of water is exposed to cooler nighttime temperatures.

In AC systems, a differential controller monitors the tank temperature and the collector temperature, turning the pump on only when the collector is hotter than the tank. In PV-powered DC systems, when there is enough sunlight for the PV module to run the pump, then the collector is usually hot enough to heat the tank water, so a controller is not needed. The panels must not be exposed to freezing temperatures since they contain potable water at all times.

CAUTION: These systems are appropriate for use only in warm climates.

Active Solar Hot Water

Most people in North America live in climates where freezing temperatures are at least a possibility. Different types of solar systems have been designed to prevent solar collectors from being damaged by water freezing within the panels. Two of the more common systems for these locales use heat transfer fluids and a drain-back mechanism.

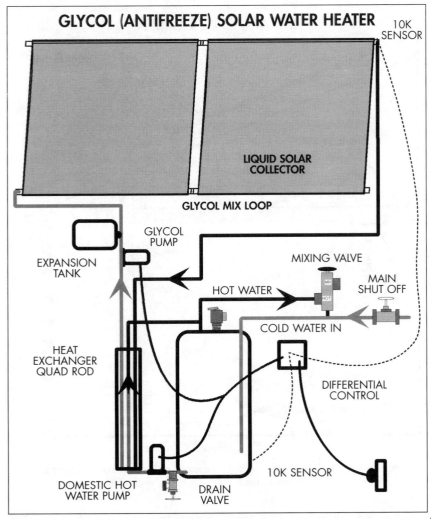

GLYCOL (ANTIFREEZE) SOLAR WATER HEATER

10K SENSOR

LIQUID SOLAR COLLECTOR

GLYCOL MIX LOOP

GLYCOL PUMP

EXPANSION TANK

MIXING VALVE

MAIN SHUT OFF

HOT WATER

COLD WATER IN

HEAT EXCHANGER QUAD ROD

DIFFERENTIAL CONTROL

10K SENSOR

DOMESTIC HOT WATER PUMP

DRAIN VALVE

Figure 11-9. Glycol (antifreeze) solar water heater for freezing climates. Illustration courtesy of AAA Solar.

water is pumped at low pressures through the panel and a water-to-water heat exchanger. When panel temperature cools below the storage tank temperature, the pump is switched off and the panel water drains back into the indoor heat exchanger reservoir, leaving no water in the panel to freeze.

SOLAR SPACE HEATING

Solar panels can heat your home, using either fluids or air as the heat exchange medium. In the case of fluids, either water or a nonfreezing heat exchange liquid is circulated through solar panels, then run through a heat exchanger to heat a large insulated tank of hot water. This is essentially the same as for a regular solar water heating system, except it is separated from your household potable water piping. Upon demand, hot water is circulated through hydronic radiators or piping embedded in the house flooring to provide radiant heat to the house. Hydronic heating fluid is typically treated with chemicals to prevent corrosion and scaling inside the piping. *This water is not potable*, and must be kept in a closed loop isolated from your regular house water system. Solar collectors should face within 30° of true south (true south is the optimum orientation) and tilted at an angle of latitude plus 15° (optimized for winter sun).

When air is the heat transfer medium, fan circulated air is blown through hot air solar panels and then circulated throughout the house. The principal niche for air collectors in the solar industry is supplying 25% to 50% of required energy for space heating. The thermal mass of a typical modern well-insulated house will hold heat for a few hours after the sun stops heating the panels before requiring backup heat. More massive thermal storage, such as from adobe, brick, or concrete

- **Heat transfer fluids.** Panels can be filled with a nonfreezing fluid (not plain water) that is circulated to a heat exchanger, which transfers heat from the nonfreezing panel fluid to your potable stored hot water. Ethylene glycol, propylene glycol, silicone fluid, and a variety of oils have been used as heat transfer fluids, but most installers prefer a nontoxic solution of equal parts of propylene glycol and water. Double-walled heat exchangers should always be used in these systems to prevent the possibility of contamination of your potable water supply with the heat transfer fluid.

- **Drain back.** A drain-back system uses water as the heat transfer fluid. In this case, when panel temperatures are hotter than the storage tank, walls and/or flooring provides improved heat storage to help prevent the house from overheating during the day and getting very cold at night. Supplementary water and rock thermal storage systems are generally not economically competitive with solid thermal masses. For the most part, basic passive solar building principles apply, even when active solar panels provide supplemental heating. Active solar heating panels can help make up for a house orientation where it is not practical to place a lot of south-facing windows, such as when the view is to the north, or to lower heating bills when retrofitted into older houses. For more information on energy-saving principles in home construction, see Chapter 7, with special attention to the *Passive Solar* section.

SOLAR WATER PUMPING

One of the best applications for solar energy is solar water pumping at locations without easy grid access. Solar pumps offer a clean and simple alternative to fuel-burning engines, generators, and windmills. They require no fuel deliveries and very little maintenance. A solar pump produces the most water when it is needed the most—when the weather is sunny and dry. Solar pumps are often used for livestock watering, irrigation of crops and orchards, and for providing a residential water supply to off-grid homes and cabins.

Solar water pumps are specially designed to utilize DC electric power from photovoltaic panels. They must work during low-light conditions at reduced power, with-

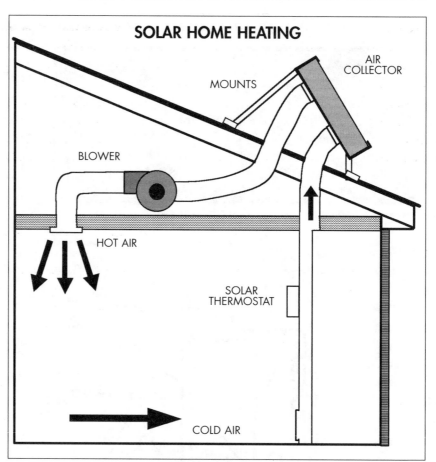

Figure 11-10. Active solar space heating with hot air solar collectors. Illustration courtesy of AAA Solar.

Figure 11-11. A herd of American bison roam the great plains in Nebraska, with the help of a SunRise Submersible pump (installed by Northwest Rural Public Power). Illustration courtesy of Dankoff Solar.

out stalling or overheating. A pump controller (current booster) is an electronic device used with most solar pumps. It acts like an automatic transmission, helping the pump to start and avoid stalling in weak sunlight. Most submersible AC well pumps draw a lot of power and are designed to pump a high volume of water in a short period of time, and then shut off. Solar pumps are designed to pump slowly, efficiently, and steadily, drawing a modest amount of power while the sun is shining. They can pump from well depths of 600 feet and tend to be most competitive in small installations where combustion engines are least economical. The smallest solar pumps require less than 150 watts, and can lift water from depths exceeding 200 feet (65 m) at 1.5 gallons (5.7 liters) per minute. You may be surprised by the performance of such a small system. In a 10-hour sunny day it can lift 900 gallons (3400 liters). That's enough to supply several families, or 30 head of cattle, or 40 fruit trees! Larger solar pumps can pump much larger volumes (Dankoff Solar 2000, 2).

In some RE system applications, a traditional AC submersible pump is better suited than a DC solar pump. If your system already has a large inverter (most AC submersible pumps draw considerable current and require a large inverter) and you have modest water demands, it is probably not worth the extra cost to purchase a solar pump. According to Windy Dankoff, founder of Dankoff Solar Products (a major solar pump manufacturer), with modern appliances and attention to water conservation, the average home will consume only around 25 gallons of water per person per day. However, if you have substantially higher water demands, such as watering a large garden or fruit trees, the extra cost for a high-efficiency solar pump is probably justified, since it will save you far more than the pump cost simply by reducing the number of required solar panels. Solar pumps save about 60% of the energy required for running an AC submersible pump. If you are seriously considering the application of a DC solar pump, contact your RE dealer to help size and specify the pump. Pump voltage and capacity must be matched both to water requirements and electrical system voltage

and wattage. See Dankoff Solar's web site at www.dankoffsolar.com for an introduction to solar pumping plus a number of technical articles authored by Windy Dankoff on several RE subjects.

STEAM ENERGY

Outside of animal power (real horsepower) and water power, steam energy was the major source of power that ran this country's factories, heavy machinery, and trains throughout much of the nineteenth century and the first part of the twentieth century. Many farms and factories used a single steam engine as a "prime mover," which ran a variety of equipment through belts and pulleys (balers, lumber mills, stamp mills, etc.).

The primary advantages of steam power are that it is not dependent on high-tech refined fuels, such as diesel fuel or gasoline, and it can run off locally available materials, such as wood or coal. Whenever the old-fashioned steam locomotives of the 1800s "ran out of steam," they simply needed to fill a car with wood and a tank with water, and then they would be off and running again.

Modern steam power is very economical for large industrial applications where both the mechanical energy of the steam and the waste heat of the steam are harnessed. Quite a number of hobbyists and a few small manufacturers are building steam engines for prime movers and to generate electricity for residential or factory use. If you are concerned about the long-term availability of gasoline, or the stability of governments, you might want to look into steam power. Sensible Steam Consultants make, sell, and install steam engines and steam-powered electrical generating systems (see the *Resources* section below). Check out their web site for a good introduction to steam and numerous pictures of small modern steam engines and installations. For people who wish to build their own steam engines, Lindsay Books sells quite a variety of reprinted engineering manuals and other texts on steam engine design.

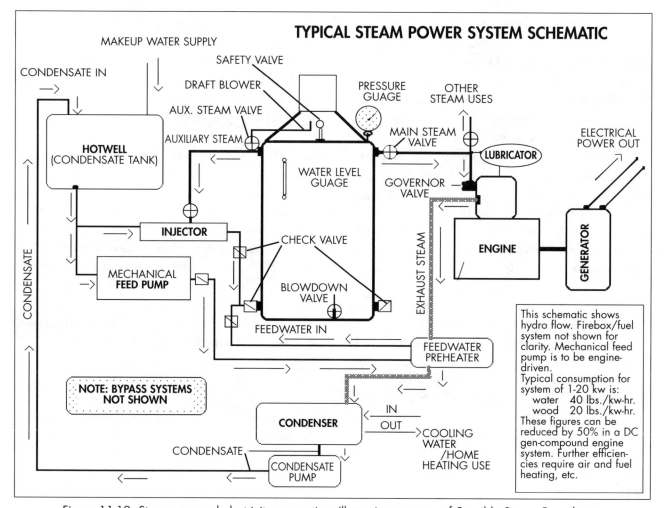

Figure 11-12. Steam-powered electricity generation. Illustration courtesy of Sensible Steam Consultants.

FUEL CELLS

The fuel cell has recently been termed the "micro chip of the energy industry"....The fuel cell may well go down in history as one of the most important technological developments of the coming century, just as the airplane, automobile and computer were for the last one.

—Glenn D. Rambach, fuel cell research engineer, Desert Research Institute

Fuel cells are receiving considerable press these days, being heralded as a major part of the solution to global warming and fossil fuel depletion. A fuel cell is an electrochemical device that is two to three times more efficient than an internal combustion engine at converting fuel into power. Fuel cells produce electricity, water, and heat by combining hydrogen with oxygen from the air. A fuel cell only produces electricity while fuel is supplied to it. The reaction occurs at relatively low temperatures, and no combustion takes place in the fuel cell.

Even though the first fuel cell was demonstrated by British amateur physicist William Grove in 1839, it took the space program to focus attention and development money on the creation of efficient fuel cells to provide safe, clean electrical power for moon shots. After the patents ran out, General Electric (the developer of the space program fuel cells) mostly lost interest in fuel cell technology. Geoffrey Ballard, an idealistic former geologist, persisted through years of financial hardship to spearhead research into economically feasible fuel cells that could power cars, homes, and industry. Starting in a makeshift lab in Arizona, Ballard Power Systems has brought fuel cell technology to the point where fuel-cell driven vehicles and fuel-cell powered skyscrapers are now a reality. For a fascinating look at the technical and human story behind the Ballard fuel cell, see *Powering the Future* by Tom Koppel.

How Fuel Cells Work

Like a battery, fuel cells convert chemical energy into electricity. In the case of a battery, when the battery has discharged its available power and the electrochemical reaction is all used up, the battery is thrown away if it is not reusable. If it is reusable, it is "recharged," which reverses the electrochemical reaction to separate the chemicals back into a state where they are ready to create more electricity. Unlike batteries, fuel cells use external fuel to convert chemical energy into electricity, so they don't need recharging, but they do need a steady supply of fuel. Fuel cells generally work by separating an oxygen source from a hydrogen source using a nonconducting permeable barrier, called an "electrolyte." Oxygen or hydrogen ions flow through the electrolyte to the other side of this barrier where they are encouraged by a catalyst to combine chemically to form water. To restore electrical balance, the resulting excess electrons left on one side (electrons can't pass through the nonconducting electrolyte) are transported around the electrolyte through wires and a load, such as an electric motor.

There are five primary types of fuel cells, each distinguished by the type of electrolyte used to carry charge between the fuel and the oxygen. Sharon Thomas and Marcia Zalbowitz of the Los Alamos National Laboratory have written "Fuel Cells: Green Power," an excellent comprehensive introduction to fuel cells. "Fuel Cells" covers fuel cell history, basics, chemistry, applications, and potential impact on global warming and pollution. You can download it for free from www.education.lanl.gov/resources/fuelcells.

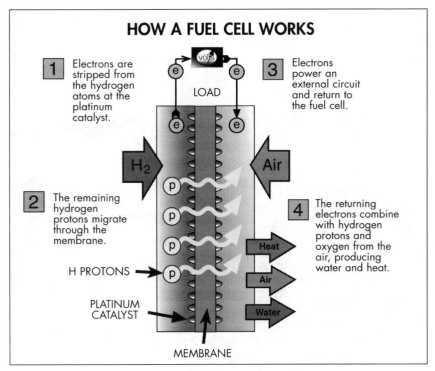

HOW A FUEL CELL WORKS

1 Electrons are stripped from the hydrogen atoms at the platinum catalyst.

2 The remaining hydrogen protons migrate through the membrane.

3 Electrons power an external circuit and return to the fuel cell.

4 The returning electrons combine with hydrogen protons and oxygen from the air, producing water and heat.

H PROTONS

PLATINUM CATALYST

MEMBRANE

Figure 11-13. How a fuel cell works. Illustration courtesy of *Home Power Magazine*.

A more basic introduction to fuel cells is available from Desert Research Institute's Energy and Environmental Engineering Center. See the "Featured Projects" section of their web site at www.dri.edu.

Efficiency and Environmental Considerations

Today, only about one-third of the energy consumed reaches the actual user because of the low energy conversion efficiencies of power plants. In fact, fossil and nuclear plants in the U.S. vent 21 quads of heat into the atmosphere—more heat than all the homes and commercial buildings in the country use in one year! Using fuel cells for utility applications can improve energy efficiency by as much as 60% while reducing environmental emissions.

—Sharon Thomas and Marcia Zalbowitz,
"Fuel Cells: Green Power"

Fuel cells are considerably more efficient than internal combustion engines. Gasoline engines in automobiles are approximately 13% to 25% efficient. That means that 75% to 87% of the gasoline you put in your tank is wasted as unburned fuel or excess heat. Fuel cells convert fuel directly into electricity through a chemical reaction and already have efficiencies of 45% to 58%. Fuel cells attached to an electric motor can have system efficiencies of more than 40%, including motor losses (DRI 2000, 1). If the excess heat generated by the fuel cells is captured and used for hot water or space heating, overall system efficiency can rise to over 80% (Plug Power 2000).

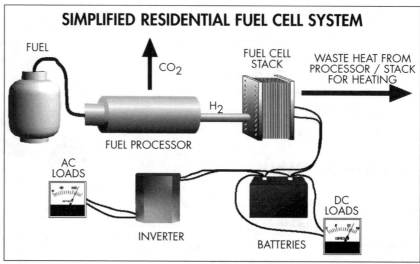

Figure 11-14. Simplified residential fuel cell system. Illustration courtesy of *Home Power Magazine.*

Fuel-cell powered vehicles are no longer just a dream of the future. Most major automobile manufacturers have active fuel-cell powered vehicle programs. Today, you can take a ride in fuel-cell powered taxis in London or ride fuel-cell powered city buses in Vancouver or Chicago. Because a fuel cell produces electricity directly from hydrogen fuel, its application can be for anything that requires power in the form of electricity, rotary power, or heat. Currently, worldwide over 200 mid-scale, 200-kW fuel-cell power plants are supplying quiet, clean, efficient electrical power to office buildings and industrial plants.

Fuel cells require hydrogen for fuel. At the present time, all fuel-cell driven automobiles have some kind of system to break down liquid hydrocarbon fuels into hydrogen-rich fuels to drive the fuel cell. A fuel cell that operates on pure hydrogen and air has absolutely no harmful emissions (the byproduct is simply water vapor), but a fuel cell system that uses hydrocarbon fuels (gasoline, methanol, natural gas, etc.) does have some emissions, although they are significantly less than emissions from internal combustion engines. For example, General Motor's Opel Zafira, an experimental fuel cell car that runs on methanol, has nearly zero sulfur dioxide and nitrogen oxide emissions, and only about 50% of the carbon dioxide (a greenhouse gas) emission from a comparable internal combustion engine.

Currently, hydrogen to power fuel cells is most economically created by breaking down hydrocarbon

based fuels, such as natural gas or methanol. In the future, if renewable energy sources are sufficiently developed to generate most of the world's electricity, it may become economical to use electricity to crack water molecules into hydrogen and oxygen, producing hydrogen gas to power zero-emission fuel cell cars. Currently, due to electrical generation inefficiencies in fossil fuel power plants, using electricity to generate hydrogen for fuel cell cars causes more harmful emissions and greenhouse gases than simply burning gasoline in an internal combustion engine does.

Fuel Cells in the Home

Fuel cells produce quiet, clean electricity, on demand, at about twice the efficiency of burning fossil fuels, and they give off clean, usable, low-grade heat as a byproduct. They are a natural match for home cogeneration systems that provide both electricity and heat. Currently, several companies are working on residential fuel-cell powered cogeneration systems. Demonstration units have been built, and commercially available residential systems are scheduled for release in 2001 (see Resources). Home systems rely on a fuel processor to transform hydrocarbon fuels (typically natural gas or propane) into hydrogen for the fuel cells. Although the main emphasis of government-financed research has been on automotive applications, the technical problems for producing fuel processors for stationary systems are actually much simpler. For an excellent survey of the status of fuel cell packages for residential use and current major players, see "Residential Fuel Cells: Hope or Hype?" by Russ Barlow, in *Home Power Magazine*, issue #72, August/September 1999.

HEATING WITH WOOD

Humanity has kept itself warm with wood heat for unknown millennia. When Benjamin Franklin invented the first enclosed wood stove, he felt it was too important an invention to patent, so he gave the design for his "Franklin Box" to the world. Prior to this time, people kept themselves warm by standing in front of open fireplaces that send most of their heat up the chimney and only radiate a small portion of this heat back into the room. An open fireplace constantly sucks large volumes of cold outside air into the house to replace the hot air that flows out the chimney. Heating a home with 30 cords of wood each winter was not uncommon for fireplace-heated homes. A single cord of wood measures 4 feet wide by 4 feet tall by 8 feet long, so you can imagine what a huge pile 30 cords of wood makes. What a waste of good forests!

The Franklin Box probably cut wood consumption by three-quarters and made for better-heated homes with fewer drafts. Modern EPA-rated wood stoves have considerably improved burning efficiencies beyond that of the Franklin Box. Rather than dumping a significant portion of your energy up the chimney in the form of thick wood smoke, new stoves encourage secondary burning processes in different areas of the combustion chamber. In each of these combustion zones, some of the heat that would have escaped up the chimney of conventional wood stoves is instead captured and transferred to your home. In this way, the maximum heating value is extracted from your fuel with a minimal environmental impact.

FORCED (FAN DRIVEN) OR NATURAL CONVECTION

INSULATE BAFFLE PLATE WITH ROCK WOOL TO KEEP PLATE HOT

SECONDARY AIR JETS PROMOTE COMBUSTION OF UNBURNED HOT GASES AS THEY HIT THE HOT BAFFLE PLATE

INSULATE WALLS AND FLOOR WITH FIRE BRICK

CLEAN-BURNING WOOD STOVE

Figure 11-15. Clean-burning wood stove features. Illustration courtesy of Aladdin Hearth Products, manufacturers of Quadra-Fire wood stoves.

EPA-rated, highly efficient wood stoves burn roughly one-half the fuel of noncertified wood stoves.

We live in the mountain town of Truckee, situated near Lake Tahoe at 6,000 feet above sea level. We have had a Quadra-Fire wood stove for over ten years. It is rated by the EPA as the cleanest burning, noncatalytic wood stove on the market. Once it heats up, it burns so clean that you can't see any visible smoke coming from the chimney. Unfortunately, many of the wood stoves in town are older models that do not have modern clean burning features. On clear, cold windless winter nights, a thick blanket of wood smoke settles into many of our town's neighborhoods. It is a shame that for many days every winter, our pristine mountain community has worse air quality than downtown Los Angeles.

Do yourself and your neighbors a favor and replace your old wood stove with a modern, clean-burning EPA-rated model. The bottom line is that efficient wood stoves keep your air cleaner, minimize chimney maintenance, and require far fewer trips to the wood pile!

Efficient Stove Features

- **Baffle plate.** At the top of the combustion chamber, a horizontal metal plate, called a "baffle plate," performs two functions. First, it retards the flow of hot smoky combustion chamber air as it rises toward the chimney. Second, an insulating layer (usually rock wool) on top of the plate helps to keep this plate extremely hot so that it can ignite unburned gases for secondary burning before they flow up the chimney as smoke.

- **Secondary air jets.** A set of secondary air jets provides a regulated flow of air to the area under the baffle plate to encourage complete secondary burning of the smoke in the top area of the combustion chamber. This smoke mixes with the fresh air from the secondary jets and ignites as it hits the hot baffle plate. If done right, all the visible smoke is burned within the wood stove.

- **Ducted outside air intake.** A significant amount of air is required to burn wood. This air has to come from someplace. The most efficient wood stoves allow for ducting the air intake to draw air directly from outside your home. If your stove draws air from inside your home, cold outside air will filter through the windows, doors, and cracks to replace the heated house air that flows up your chimney.

- **Catalytic secondary combustion.** Some stoves rely on a catalytic element in the top of the stove to accomplish secondary burning. Although catalytic stoves can burn with excellent efficiencies, most folks prefer high-efficiency, noncatalytic models because they tend to require less maintenance and are not prone to smoky backdraws when starting a fire, which can be a problem with some catalytic models.

- **Convection fan.** The efficiency of most stoves is improved by adding a blower system to transfer more heat from the stove to your home. Long turbine-type fans quietly move more air than the noisier and less expensive propeller-type fans. A nifty recent invention, which is particularly handy in homes with a limited supply of power, is a fan attached to the wood stove and powered by a thermoelectric generator that uses the heat from the wood stove to generate electricity to drive the fan.

ENERGY, POWER, AND ELECTRICITY PRIMER

Energy

Energy is often defined as the capacity for doing work. There are many different forms of energy, and many different machines and processes that transform one form of energy into another. In fact, most machines transform energy in some way shape or form. Chemical reactions can release energy in the form of heat, radiation (light), electricity (batteries), or mechanical energy (expansion, such as in an engine cylinder). A moving object has *kinetic energy* due to its mass and velocity (momentum). When a vehicle crashes into a wall, the rapid release of its kinetic energy is devastating. Electric motors transform electrical energy into mechanical energy. When you lift a mass within a gravitational field, you increase its *potential energy*. When you lower the mass, you can extract the work that it took to raise it. An example of potential energy is using a waterwheel to extract energy as water is lowered a certain distance. Another example of potential energy is a spring. When a spring is compressed, energy is stored in the spring that can be extracted when the spring relaxes back to its free state. Last, but not least, is *nuclear energy*. Physicists discovered that tremendous amounts of energy can be released by nuclear reactions that transform relatively tiny chunks of matter directly into energy.

Energy units include calories, foot-pounds, watt-hours, and Btus (British thermal units). Some of these units are metric and others are English. A Btu is the amount of energy that it takes to raise one pound of water by 1°F in temperature. A calorie is the metric unit similar to a Btu. It is the amount of energy that it takes to raise one gram of water by 1°C in temperature. A foot-pound is the amount of energy (work) it takes when a force of one pound is applied through a distance of one foot (or ½ pound through 2 feet, etc.). A watt-hour is the amount of energy used when one watt of electrical power is expended for one hour. These are all different terms for describing energy, and there are multiplication factors that allow you to convert from one unit to the other. Energy is energy, no matter which unit is used to describe it. For example, 1 Btu equals 778.3 foot-pounds, equals 252 calories, equals .29 watt-hours. Home electrical energy consumption is generally measured in kilowatt-hours (1 kilowatt = 1000 watts).

Power

Power is the *rate* at which energy is used, transmitted, transformed, and so on. The *horsepower* was one of the first units of measurement for power. Prior to defining a horsepower as 550 foot-pounds per second, it was just some vague notion equal to the power available from one average horse to pull a load for a while. A watt is a unit of electrical power. It is equal to the number of volts (electromotive force) multiplied by the number of amps (electrical current). All power units can be converted. For example, one horsepower equals 550 foot-pounds per second, equals 745.7 watts, equals 10,680 calories per minute, equals 42.44 Btus per minute. The amount of work, or energy, is the power times the time that the power is consumed. In electrical terms, the number of watts (power) multiplied by the time (number of hours) that the watts are used gives you the watt-hours, or the amount of energy consumed.

Electricity

Because electricity is one of those things that you can't see, touch, or hold in your hand, it can be difficult to understand. The easiest way to grasp electricity is usually to draw an analogy between electrical characteristics and something physical that's familiar to most of us, such as water. Electricity is measured in terms of watts (power), volts (electrical potential, also known as electromotive force), amps (electrical current), and watt-hours (total energy).

VOLTS

Voltage, also known as *electrical potential*, is similar to the pressure that pushes electricity through a wire or some kind of load. Imagine a tall tank of water that is open to the air at the top. At the surface of the water, there is no water pressure. If you poked a hole in the side at a level equal to the surface of the water, at most the water would only dribble out through the hole. If you moved down a few feet and poked a hole in the tank, water would start to run out at a much faster rate. If you went to the bottom of the tank, where the water pressure is really high, and poked a hole in the tank, the water would spurt out at a very fast rate. The number of volts is the electrical equivalent to the water pressure in the tank. It is the driving force behind the electricity that does work in our electrical machines.

One of the confusing things about voltage is that it is always measured between two points as a voltage differential. There is no universal voltage reference point, but the earth is often referred to as the zero voltage reference point. For instance, if you placed two identical tanks of water side by side and hooked a pipe between the bottoms of both tanks, there would be no flow of water between the tanks because there is no pressure differential to drive a flow. With respect to each other, there is no pressure differential (voltage drop), but with respect to the outside air there is significant pressure (voltage with respect to the earth). However, if you lower the level in one tank, water will begin to flow from the tank with a higher level into the tank with a lower level, because there is now a differential (voltage drop) between the two tanks.

AMPS

Amperage, also known as *electrical current*, is measured in the unit known as an *amp*. It is a measure of the amount of electricity that is flowing or discharging at a given moment in a given device. Returning to the analogy of the water tank, the physical analogy to electrical current is how much water is flowing out of a hole in the tank at a given time.

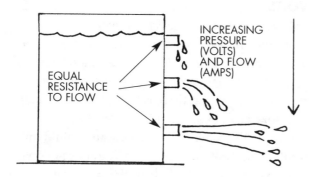

Figure 11-16. Water tank analogy to volts and amps.

RESISTANCE

The resistance to electrical current flow is measured in terms of *ohms*. Let's return to the water tank analogy. If you welded a short wide pipe onto the bottom of the water tank and opened it to the air, water would gush out through that opening. Because the water had a lot of pressure behind it (volts), and the big hole had little resistance to it (ohms), there is a strong current flow (amps). If you welded a long skinny pipe onto the tank instead of the short fat one, the flow would be drastically reduced, because the long skinny pipe has a lot of resistance to flow. This electrical relationship is described by Ohm's Law as voltage equals current times resistance. In symbolic terms it is $V = I \times R$, or $I = V/R$. Both equations mean the same thing. Don't ask me why they always call current "I" instead of "A". I didn't invent the standard, so it's not my fault.

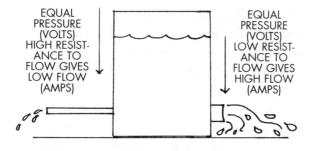

Figure 11-17. Resistance versus flow.

ELECTRICAL POWER

Electrical power is defined as the number of volts multiplied times the number of amps, and is measured in terms of watts. You can have a huge number of volts, such as the 20,000 volts typical of a static

charge from rubbing your feet on the carpet on a dry winter's day, but with almost no current so you get very little power (a mild shock). If you were unfortunate enough to pick up a downed high voltage power line, it would probably kill you with a combination of high voltage and high amperage (high power) flowing through your body to the ground. On the other hand, a car battery can store a lot of energy at a low voltage (12 volts). A typical car battery voltage is so low that it is not usually dangerous to human beings. The low voltage does not have enough push to drive a significant current through human skin to cause bodily harm (because of the high resistance of our skin). However, if something with low resistance, such as a metal wrench, is shorted across the two terminals of the battery, enough current will flow to melt the ends of the wrench onto the battery terminals (low voltage times very high current equals high power). Even though batteries have low voltage, you should approach them with caution. Mechanics have been known to fry the nerves in their arm when they made a particularly good connection between a battery and a ground, dumping high current into their bodies.

Because Ohm's Law defines the relationship between volts, amps, and resistance (ohms), it also defines power in the same terms. According to Ohm's Law, $P = V^2/R$ or $P = I^2 \times R$. In the case of power losses when power is transmitted over wires, the power loss is not the voltage with respect to ground, but the voltage *drop* from one end of the wire to the next. For example, if your wall socket provides 110 VAC, but by the time it runs through a 100-foot extension cord to a table saw it has dropped to 100 volts, the voltage drop of 10 volts is what is used to calculate the power loss through the extension cord.

AC VERSUS DC

Batteries always generate electricity pushing the current in one direction. The electrical push from a battery, known as its voltage, stays fairly constant, dropping somewhat whenever a high current is drawn or the battery begins to discharge a significant percentage of its capacity. This type of current is known as *direct current*. Cars, boats, RVs, batteries, and photovoltaic (PV) solar panels operate on direct current (DC).

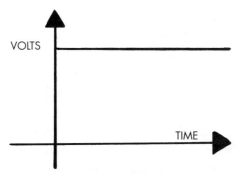

Figure 11-18. Direct current.

The other type of current that is commonly talked about is *alternating current* (AC). The voltage for alternating current flips back and forth, first pulling electrons in one direction, and then pulling them in the other direction. Common household current is AC. Standard electrical AC produced by rotating electrical power generating equipment, such as power plant steam-driven turbines, has a smooth sinusoidal wave form (see Figure 11-19). When you measure AC voltage using a voltmeter, you do not measure the peak voltage, but the root-mean-square (RMS) voltage, which is the average voltage under each alternating current "wave."

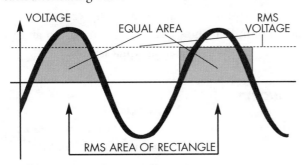

Figure 11-19. Sinusoidal alternating current (AC).

You might wonder why the world would standardize on AC power when it seems so much more complicated than DC power, but there is an excellent reason for this. About 100 years ago, a great debate raged between Thomas Edison and Nikolai Tesla over the merits of AC versus DC. Edison believed that DC was the way to go, but Tesla argued that AC was better for long-distance power transmission. Tesla was right and won the battle. According to Ohm's Law, the power lost to resistance while transmitting power long distances through wire is I² x R. Thus, in order to minimize power losses, the lower the current, the better.

Because power is the amount of current multiplied times the amount of voltage (P = V x I), to transmit high power at low current requires very high voltages. Standard car batteries have a DC voltage of only about 12 volts. To transmit significant household quantities of power at only 12 volts requires thick, expensive, hard to handle wires (like a fat pipe to carry a lot of water). Household voltage is 110 to 120 VAC, which works fine for most appliances; but heavy-duty appliances, such as electric clothes dryers and electric stoves, use so much power that they usually run off of 220 to 240 VAC to keep their wire sizes reasonable. Power transmission lines, such as the ones that you see strung from the huge towers, transmit tremendous amounts of power over long distances. To keep power losses to a minimum, power is transmitted over these lines at extremely high voltages, on the order of 100,000 volts (to keep the current reasonably low).

Now we come to the real reason why AC became the grid standard instead of DC. Until recently, there was no efficient way to transform DC voltages from a low voltage to a high voltage and back again. An electrical device, called a transformer, can simply and efficiently transform AC from low voltage to high voltage or vice versa, but transformers do not work on DC. When you turn a low voltage signal into high voltage, you don't get something for nothing—the power remains nearly the same. When low voltage AC is transformed to a higher voltage, the current is proportionately lowered. The new high voltage AC has slightly less power because some power is lost in the form of excess heat in the transformer. The transformer power losses are miniscule compared to what the losses would be if you tried to transmit lots of power long distances at low voltages. Modern "inverters," which efficiently change DC into AC, have finally made it practical to store DC power in large battery banks, and then convert it into AC for use in powering standard AC appliances or for transmitting significant power across the grid.

Proper Wire Sizing

From the previous discussion, you can begin to see that wires must be properly sized to match the voltage and power requirements of your system. Wire size is typically a function of the amount of current that is trying to squeeze through the wire, and not the voltage that is driving that current. Wire resistance is inversely proportional to the square of its diameter, so fatter wires will cause less voltage and power loss than skinnier wires (just like pushing water through a bigger pipe). Because typical household wiring is designed to run on 110/120 VAC, if you try to drive significant loads through the same wire at 12 VDC (common battery voltage), you will be running 10 times the current and will overload your wiring. In severe cases, your wires could get so hot that they could start a fire. The National Electrical Code (NEC) has standard guidelines to cover wire sizing and other facets of wiring to ensure that buildings are wired properly and safely (if wired according to code). Certified electricians are required by law to wire according to the NEC. Figure 11-20, developed by Dankoff Solar, is a simplification of NEC wiring size specifications appropriate to residential RE applications.

Battery Voltage: 12 volts versus 24 volts versus 48 volts?

Now that you understand a little about power, current, and wire sizing, I'll talk briefly about choosing the DC voltage for your battery banks and inverter. By choosing a DC voltage that's higher than 12 volts, you can run thinner wire for longer distances between your solar panels, wind turbines, water turbines, battery bank, and/or inverter. Especially in large RE systems, or in cases where for one reason or another significant distances separate major system components, the high currents involved in transmitting power at 12 VDC can mandate thick, unwieldy, expensive wiring. Each time you double the system voltage, you cut the current in half and cut the power losses through a given wire size by a factor of four. Remember that 12-volt batteries and solar panels must be hooked in series in sets of 2 for 24 VDC and sets of 4 for 48 VDC. Most inverters are field switchable to different DC voltages.

> **CAUTION: Your system components must be set to match system voltage or wired to match system voltage. If you attempt to run a component at voltages other than what it is designed for, system components will probably be ruined.**

Capacitance

Capacitance is an electrical quality that describes an electrical component's capacity to store a charge. Do not confuse electrical capacitance with battery capacity, because they are different. (Batteries produce energy by electrochemical reactions, not capacitance.) The unit of measure for capacitance is a *farad*. A single farad is a very large capacitance. Electrical components, called capacitors, are usually sized in "micro-farads" or smaller. A micro-farad is a millionth of a farad. Capacitors store small amounts of electrical energy similar to the way a spring stores mechanical energy. A voltage drives a certain amount of charge into a capacitor. If the voltage lowers, some of this charge is released from the capacitor. Another physical analogy is a pressure tank on a home water system. If the pump pressure increases, more water can be pumped into the storage tank that then becomes available for later use. Under a constant voltage, once the capacitor is charged, current ceases to flow through a capacitor (kind of like how a pressure tank stops filling once it reaches the same pressure as the pump cutout setting). This explanation does not indicate how a capacitor is used, but at least it gives you some idea about what it does.

Inductance

Inductance is an electrical quality that describes an electrical component's capacity to store electrical energy in the form of a magnetic field. Transformers use the magic of inductance to "induce" a voltage and current in one set of transformer windings (the "secondary" coil) by the action of the magnetic field created by current flowing through a different set of windings (the "primary" coil). Inductance works on changing currents (AC) and has little or no effect on constant currents (DC). "Inductive loads" are loads that usually have a high starting current, such as in starting most larger electric motors, and then settle down to a considerably lower power draw once they get going. The "surge capacity" on your inverter tells you how large of a short-term inductive load your inverter can handle.

Dankoff's Universal Wire Sizing Chart

©2000 by Dankoff Solar Products, Inc.

This new chart works for any voltage or voltage drop, American (AWG) or metric (mm²) sizing.
It applies to typical DC circuits and to some simple AC circuits (single-phase AC
with resistive loads, not motor loads, power factor = 1.0, line reactance negligible).

STEP 1:   CALCULATE THE FOLLOWING:

$$\frac{\text{AMPS X FEET}}{\text{\% VOLT DROP X VOLTAGE}} = \text{VDI}$$

VDI = Voltage Drop Index (a reference number based on resistance of wire)
FEET = ONE-WAY wiring distance   (1 meter = 3.28 feet)
% VOLT DROP = Your choice of acceptable voltage drop (example: use 3 for 3%)

STEP 2:   DETERMINE APPROPRIATE WIRE SIZE FROM CHART

Compare your calculated VDI with VDI in the chart to determine the closest wire size.
Amps must not exceed the AMPACITY indicated for the wire size.

WIRE SIZE	area	COPPER		ALUMINUM	
AWG	mm²	VDI	AMPACITY	VDI	AMPACITY
16	1.31	1	10		
14	2.08	2	15		
12	3.31	3	20	*not recommended*	
10	5.26	5	30		
8	8.37	8	55		
6	13.3	12	75		
4	21.1	20	95		
2	33.6	31	130	20	100
O	53.5	4 c	170	31	135
OO	67.4	2	195	39	150
OOO	85.0	78	225	49	175
OOOO	107	99	260	62	205

METRIC SIZE	COPPER	ALUMINUM
by cross-sectional area	VDI X 1.1 = mm²	VDI X 1.7 = mm²
Available sizes: 1 1.5 2.5 4 6 10 16 25 35 50 70 95 120 mm²		

EXAMPLE   20 Amp load at 24V over a distance of 100 feet with 3% max. voltage drop

VDI = $\frac{20 \times 100}{3 \times 24}$ = 27.78   For copper wire, the nearest VDI = 31.
This indicates #2 AWG wire or 35mm²

NOTES: AWG = American Wire Gauge. Ampacity is based on the National Electrical Code (USA) for 30°C (86°F)
ambient air temperature, for no more than three insulated conductors in raceway in free air of cable types AC, NM, NMC
and SE; and conductor insulation types TA, TBS, SA, AVB, SIS, RHH, THHN and XHHW.
For other conditions, refer to National Electric Code or an engineering handbook.

Figure 11-20. Dankoff's universal wire sizing chart. Illustration courtesy of Dankoff Solar.

REFERENCES

Photovoltaics and RE Systems

Independent Energy Guide: Electrical Power for Home, Boat and RV, **by Kevin Jeffrey.** 1995, 280 pp. (paperback), ISBN 0-9644112-0-2. Published by Orwell Cove Press, P.O. Box 126, Ashland, MA 01721. Lists for $19.95.

This is a good all-around guide to renewable energy systems. It will educate you about all the major system components and help you perform your initial system planning. Not as detail- and hardware-oriented as *The Solar Electric Independent Home Book.* You will need supplementary design guides and manufacturers information available from RE dealers when you get down to your system design.

Practical Photovoltaics, **by Richard J. Komp, Ph.D.** 1995, 197 pp. (paperback), ISBN 0-937948-11-X. Published by Aatec Publications, P.O. Box 7119, Ann Arbor, MI 48107. Lists for $18.95.

If you really want to understand photovoltaics, and not just how to build them into a system, you should get this book. Contains good information on photovoltaics, making your own solar panels from individual solar cells, and the care and use of batteries in photovoltaic systems. However, this is not a how-to book on RE system design.

The Real Goods Solar Living Sourcebook: The Complete Guide to Renewable Energy Technologies and Sustainable Living, **edited by Douglas R. Pratt, introduction by John Schaeffer.** 1999, 562 pp. (paperback), ISBN 0-916571-03-3. Published by Chelsea Green Publishing Company, P.O. Box 428, Whiter River Junction, VT 05001. Lists for $30.00.

An excellent introduction to solar living and sustainability. Use this book to help plan your new home or improve the environmental impact of an existing one. It contains quite a variety of product catalog information, introductions to concepts, and design guidelines. Covers everything from composting toilets and energy-efficient appliances to solar panels and wind turbines.

The Solar Electric House: Energy for the Environmentally Responsive, Energy-Independent Home, **by Steven J. Strong with William G. Scheller.** 1993, 276 pp. (paperback), ISBN 0-9637383-2-1. Published by Sustainability Press, but distributed by Chelsea Green Publishing Company, P.O. Box 428, Whiter River Junction, VT 05001. Lists for $21.95.

Steven Strong is a pioneer in the design and construction of photovoltaic and environmentally responsive homes. Since 1981, Strong and his company, Solar Design Associates, have been designing homes with RE systems. This book is a good combination design handbook and introduction to RE systems. It combines basic RE educational information, similar to that given by *Practical Photovoltaics,* with handbook type information. It is not as hardware specific and generous with practical how-to information as *The Solar Electric Independent Home Book.*

The Solar Electric Independent Home Book, **by New England Solar Electric Inc.** 1995, 174 pp. (paperback), ISBN 1-879523-01-9. Published by New England Solar Electric Inc., 3 South Worthington Road, Worthington, MA 01098. Lists for $16.95.

This is an excellent how-to book put together by people who have designed and built numerous PV systems. They wrote it to help others learn from their experience and avoid mistakes. They offer good advice on specific brands to trust and those to avoid. Because technology and equipment are constantly changing, I suggest supplementing this information with the latest up-to-date advice from a reputable RE dealer. If you wish to design and install your own RE system, I highly recommend this book.

Wind Power

Wind Power for Home and Business: Renewable Energy for the 1990s and Beyond, **by Paul Gipe.** 1993, 413 pp. (paperback), ISBN 0-930031-64-4.

Published by Chelsea Green Publishing Company, P.O. Box 428, Whiter River Junction, VT 05001. Lists for $35.00.

This is still the bible for small to mid-size wind power applications. Very detailed and comprehensive, it has excellent engineering and educational information on all aspects of wind energy. If you are considering buying a used wind turbine or rebuilding an old one, Gipes provides good advice on which brands are worthwhile and which should be avoided.

***Wind Energy Basics: A Guide to Small and Micro Wind Systems,* by Paul Gipe.** 1999, 122 pp. (paperback), ISBN 1-890132-07-1. Published by Chelsea Green Publishing Company, P.O. Box 428, Whiter River Junction, VT 05001. Lists for $19.95.

This is a scaled-down version of Gipe's *Wind Power for Home and Business,* tailored for the home RE system, and including some more recent information on rebate programs and newer hardware. Coupled with some of the latest manufacturers' spec sheets from your local RE dealer, this book should provide you with what you need to know for purchasing and installing a small wind system. If you are excited by wind energy in general, and want to know as much as possible about this subject, buy *Wind Power for Home and Business* instead.

Micro-Hydropower

You can get pretty good micro-hydro installation and system design guidelines both from Harris Hydroelectric Systems (see *Resources* section) or from Energy Systems & Design's web site at www.microhydropower.com (see their online "owner's manual"). If you want more information than either of these sources offer, the following two books are really the only sources available.

***The Residential Hydropower Book,* by Keith Ritter.** 1986, 152 pp. (paperback), No ISBN. Published by Sierra Solar Systems, 109 Argall Way, Nevada City, CA 95959. Lists for $15.00.

This book covers system design, sizing, selection, placement, and maintenance. It is a practical handbook for the folks with some property and a creek with at least 6 feet (preferably more than 25 feet) of elevation drop from the water source to the generating area. Not available from most sources, your best bet is to purchase this book directly from Sierra Solar Systems (see *Resources* section).

***Micro-Hydropower Sourcebook: A Practical Guide to Design and Implementation in Developing Countries,* by Allen R. Inversin.** 1986, 285 pp. (paperback), No ISBN. Published by NRECA International Foundation, 4301 Wilson Blvd., Arlington, VA 22203-1860. Lists for $22.00.

This book is geared towards AC electrification from dams and mini-hydro facilities that might supply electricity to a small community or factory. The focus is not on small homestead applications, but if you are engineering oriented and want to build yourself a rather large RE system, you will probably get a lot out of this book. Not widely available, your best bet is to purchase this book directly from NRECA at (703) 907-5637.

Fuel Cells

***Powering the Future: The Ballard Fuel Cell and the Race to Change the World,* by Tom Koppel.** 1999, 288 pp. (hardcover), ISBN 0-471644-21-8. Published by John Wiley & Sons, 605 Third Ave., New York, NY 10158. Lists for $29.95.

Ballard Power Systems is the world leader in developing commercial fuel cell technology that will soon drive our cars and power clean, efficient electricity generation facilities around the world. Ballard Power Systems is poised to literally change the way we live. Along the way, founder Geoffrey Ballard and his engineers had to cajole government agencies for grants, keep creditors at bay, and line up private sector investors. This book tells their fascinating story based on extensive interviews with Geoffrey Ballard, his early partners, and the hands-on technologists who built and perfected the cell.

Solar Hydrogen Chronicles, **edited by Walter Pyle.** 1999, 118 pp. (paperback), ISBN 0-9663703-0-9. Published by H-Ion Solar Inc., 6095 Monterey Avenue, Richmond, CA 94805. Lists for $28.00.

This is a compilation of interesting and practical articles about the production, purification, storage, and use of hydrogen produced by energy from RE systems. If you are a hands-on kind of person, you can start using hydrogen today with help from this book, using currently available technology. Walter Pyle, editor of the *Solar Hydrogen Chronicles,* is a regular contributor of articles to *Home Power Magazine.* His company, H-Ion Solar, sells products for making, storing, and using hydrogen, and is the best source for this book (see *Resources* section).

Miscellaneous

Producer Gas for Motor Vehicles, **by John D. Cash and Martin G. Cash.** 1997, 194 pp. (paperback), ISBN 1-55918-187-7. Published by Lindsay Publications, P.O. Box 538, Bradley, IL 60915-0538. Lists for $12.95.

This reprint of a 1942 manual shows you how to make special gas generators and modify automobile systems to operate on gas generated from coal, charcoal, and wood. The process was developed in Australia and Europe during WWII to allow motor vehicles to operate (with some modification) on fuels other than gasoline, due to wartime restrictions on importing and refining of oil. Could be useful again at some point in our future, but implementation of this process will require significant fabrication capability (access to a machine shop).

House Wiring with the National Electrical Code: Based on the 1999 National Electrical Code, **by Ray C. Mullin.** 1999, 352 pp. (paperback), ISBN 0-8273-8350-9. Published by Delmar Publishers, P.O. Box 15015, Albany, NY 12212. Lists for $25.95.

If you plan on wiring your own house or RE system, do yourself a favor and pick up a copy of the NEC for about $50, or this clearer, simpler, less expensive manual on house wiring per the code.

Lindsay Publications Inc., P.O. Box 538, Bradley IL 60915; phone: (815) 935-5353; fax: (815) 935-5477; web site: www.lindsaybks.com.

Lindsay Publications reprints and distributes a huge variety of older manuals on how to make and build almost anything, including numerous books on old-fashioned steam engines. Skip Goebel, owner of Sensible Steam Consultants, highly recommends *Steam Engine Design,* ISBN 0-917914-10-4, available from Lindsay Publications.

Magazines

Home Power Magazine. Subscription: $22.50 per year for 6 issues. Home Power, P.O. Box 520, Ashland, OR 97520; phone: (800) 707-6585; web site: www.homepower.com.

Home Power is the premier magazine for people interested in residential-size renewable energy systems. *Home Power* publishes numerous informative do-it-yourself articles on all aspects of small- to mid-scale RE. Check out their incredibly useful web site for solar insolation and seasonal wind energy maps or to search the *Home Power* database for RE manufacturers, suppliers, and dealers, either by name or location. They also post practical and informative articles, a system-sizing workbook, and numerous green links to other related sites. A set of CDs covers all past issues of *Home Power* plus audio interviews and useful RE sizing and applications programs.

Solar Today. Subscription: $29.00 per year for 6 issues. American Solar Energy Society (ASES), 2400 Central Avenue, Unit G-1, Boulder, CO 80301-9880; phone: (303) 443-3130; web site: www.solartoday.org.

Solar Today is the award-winning magazine of the American Solar Energy Society. It covers all solar technologies, from photovoltaics to climate-responsive buildings to wind power. Regular topics include building case studies, energy policy, and community-scale projects.

RESOURCES

See also the *Resources* section of Chapter 7 for energy-efficient building resources, and the *Resources* section of Chapter 2 for major organizations devoted to sustainable technologies, including renewable energy.

Renewable Energy Dealers

> NOTE: *This is by no means a complete list, but will provide you with several large dealers that can help you figure out what you need/want and who can be of significant assistance when designing your RE system. Most of the following dealers offer design guides and design consultation, but don't forget to check out your local dealer, who may be able to offer you better service.*

AAA Solar Service and Supply Inc., 2021 Zearing NW, Albuquerque, NM 87104; phone: (800) 245-0311; fax: (505) 243-0885; web site: www.aaasolar.com.

Most RE dealers are very knowledgeable about electrical energy systems, but not great on solar hot water, which is often delegated to the plumbing contractors. This dealer does an excellent job with solar hot water and space heating, as well as solar electric applications. AAA's web site has a good online design guide and educational introduction to a variety of RE topics.

The Alternative Energy Store, 43 Almont St, Medford, MA 02155; phone: (877) 242-6718; fax: (877) 242-6718; web site: www.altenergystore.com.

This dealer advertises itself as a discount online RE dealer. The Store's web site has a section called "Alt-E University," which contains a series of educational articles on various aspects of renewable energy.

Atlantic Solar Products, 9351-J Philadelphia Rd., P.O. Box 70060, Baltimore, MD 21237-6060; phone: (410) 686-2500; fax: (410) 686-6221; web site: www.atlanticsolar.com.

Atlantic Solar Products (ASP) is an international distributor of photovoltaic (PV) components and packaged power systems. ASP's web site has particularly good solar insolation maps for most of the world, and a section titled "Info Corner" that has good information on system sizing and troubleshooting.

Applied Power/Alternative Energy Engineering. P.O. Box 339, Redway, CA 95560; phone: (800) 777-6609; fax (800) 777-6648; web site: www.solarelectric.com.

Alternative Energy Engineering is now a division of Applied Power, making them a part of one of the nation's largest RE companies. Since 1981, Applied Power has installed thousands of solar electric systems worldwide, from complete PV/hybrid systems powering remote sites in national parks and mountaintop telecommunication systems in the United States, to solar homes and village water pumping systems in South America and North Africa. Alternative Energy Engineering is one of the world's largest distributors of photovoltaic, wind, and small hydroelectric equipment. Applied Power offers an excellent design guide to help you plan your system.

Backwoods Solar Electric Systems, 1395-in Rolling Thunder Ridge, Sandpoint, Idaho 83864; phone: (208) 263-4290; fax: (888) 263-4290; web site: www.backwoodssolar.com.

Backwoods Solar Electric Systems is a favored supplier among many off-the-grid backwoods types. They specialize in solar generated home electricity, dedicated to serving homes located beyond the reach of utility lines. The company's own home and business location is two miles from the closest utility lines, and has been powered entirely by equipment in their catalog for the past 20 years. Backwoods has an extensive catalog that includes a modest section devoted to design guidelines.

Real Goods. 200 Clara Ave., Ukiah, CA 95482; phone: (800) 919-2400; fax (707) 462-4807; web site: www.realgoods.com.

Real Goods sells far more than just RE products. They have an RE catalog, a gift catalog with nifty eco-friendly gifts, an eco and RE consulting business, and a bookstore. Real Goods has teamed up with Chelsea Green to publish a series of books on green building, RE, and other green topics.

Sierra Solar Systems, 109 Argall Way, Nevada City, CA 95959; phone: (888) 667-6527; fax: (530) 265-6151; web site: www.sierrasolar.com.

Sierra Solar Systems is a full-service RE supplier. For 20 years, they have been designing and supplying solar, wind, and micro-hydro electric systems all over the world. The owner, Jon Hill, has a BSME degree from NYU, and has been working and living with RE since he first lived off-grid in the late 1970s. Sierra offers an extensive catalog, which includes an excellent design guide to help you plan your system. Check out Sierra's comprehensive "Design Center" on its web site for RE information and design assistance and guidelines. The online system sizing guide is particularly helpful. In addition to the catalog, this web site also contains interesting and practical RE articles plus links to other RE/green sites.

Sunelco, 100 Skeels St., P.O. Box 787,Hamilton, MT 59840-0787; phone: (800) 338-6844; fax: (406) 363-6046; web site: www.sunelco.com.

Sunelco, another full-service RE supplier, has an excellent combination catalog and design guide to help you plan your system. You can shop online, order their design guide, or access the *System Planning Center* via the web site.

Sunweaver, 1049 1st NH Turnpike, Northwood, NH 03261; phone: (603) 942-5863; fax: (603) 942-7730; web site: www.sunweavers.com.

Since its founding in 1987, Sunweaver has earned national recognition for its pioneering work in incorporating innovative technologies for water, power, and heat, especially its mechanical system designs for independent "off-grid" buildings. This company offers a wide range of products plus expert design and engineering services.

Wind Turbines

NOTE: Wind energy is a fast growing field, and the technology is constantly changing. I am listing a few of the well-known manufacturers and one new player who is developing a promising new technology. Just because a manufacturer is not listed does not mean that it does not provide quality products and service. See a reputable RE dealer for the latest technology, reliability statistics, costs, system design assistance, and information on other players in the field of wind energy.

Bergey Wind Power, 2001 Priestly Ave., Norman, OK 73069; phone: (405) 364-4212; fax: (405) 364-2078; web site: www.bergey.com.

Bergey WindPower Company has been manufacturing wind turbines since 1980 and is considered by many to make the "cadillac" of small wind turbines. Bergey wind turbines are well built and extremely rugged. Bergey's web site is an excellent source for information on wind energy, containing a large selection of articles and information on wind energy and wind systems.

PrimeEnergy, 1320 Freeport Blvd., Suite 101, Sparks, NV 894311; phone: (775) 782-8471; fax (775) 782-4171; web site: www.powerjet.com.

This newcomer in the wind energy business has been developing a promising new wind turbine that is both highly efficient and extremely quiet. Time will tell whether or not PrimeEnergy becomes a major player.

Southwest Windpower, Inc., 2131 N. First Street, Flagstaff, AZ 86004; phone: (520) 779-9463; fax: (520) 779-1485; web site: www.windenergy.com.

After Southwest Windpower introduced its sleek, small wind turbine model AIR-303 in 1996, the company quickly became a major contender in the small-scale wind business. Now, the 400-watt (rated at 28 MPH) model AIR-403 has become the best-selling wind turbine in the world. Priced about the same as a 100-watt photovoltaic module, it produces four times the power, day and night, for a total of more than seven times the potential energy output in a 24-hour period (with optimum wind conditions). In May 2000, Southwest Windpower purchased a leading competitor, World Power Technologies, manufacturer of the Whisper line of 900 to 3000 watt wind turbines. This move will almost certainly seal their position as the leader in low-cost small wind turbines.

Micro-Hydropower

Harris Hydroelectric Systems, 632 Swanton Road, Davenport, CA 95017; phone/fax: (831) 425-7652.

Don Harris provides mini-hydro systems that work with water having heads of 10 to 600 feet and flows from 2 to 250 GPM. Call for catalog and applications manual. He also puts out an excellent video about working with micro-hydro systems.

Energy Systems and Design, P.O. Box 4557, Sussex, NB Canada E4E 5L7; phone: (506) 433-3151; fax: (506) 433-6151; web site: www. microhydropower.com.

Energy Systems and Design's Stream Engine can operate at heads as low as 6 feet. Check out the company's web site for a good introduction to mini-hydro, and applications and installation information. Energy Systems makes its own highly efficient brushless DC alternator, which requires almost no maintenance and has at least 20% better efficiency than a standard automotive type alternator.

Jack Rabbit Energy Systems, 425 Fairfield Ave., Stamford, CT 06902; phone: (203) 961-8133; fax: (203) 961-0382; web site: www. jackrabbitmarine.com.

Jackrabbit makes a propeller-type, submersible micro-hydro generator that was developed for sailboats but will work in any fast moving creek or river. To see if this will work in your creek, use the ping pong ball test. Toss a ping pong ball into your creek and run along beside it. It will produce only a modest supply of electricity at a very fast walk, but if you have trouble keeping up with it, this could provide you with a reasonable source of power. If you have more than 10 feet of head, I would go with a system from one of the other two micro-hydro suppliers instead. Jackrabbit also sells quite a variety of RE products focused on the marine business, including wind turbines.

Fuel Cells and Hydrogen Systems

Ballard Power Systems, 9000 Glenlyon Parkway, Burnaby, BC V5J 5J9; phone: (604) 454-0900; fax: (604) 412-4700; web site: www.ballard.com.

These are the people who brought fuel cells down to earth. They transformed rocket science into a product that is currently showing up in commercial buildings and vehicles, and will soon be seen powering consumer automobiles. Check out their web site for a look at this emerging technology.

Dais-Analytic, 11552 Prosperous Drive, Odessa, FL 33556; phone: (727) 375-8484; fax: (727) 375-8485; web site: www.daisanalytic.com.

Formerly known as American Fuel Cell Corp., this company has had developmental co-generation, residential fuel cell modules running since 1998. Dais-Analytic expects to have commercially available residential power packages sometime in 2002. They are working to perfect a fuel cell power pack that can put out 3 KW of continuous power and stores excess energy in the integral battery bank for powering short-term loads greater than 3 KW. The system's 5 KW inverter can handle surge loads of up to 11 KW.

H-Ion Solar Inc., 6095 Monterey Avenue, Richmond, CA 94805; phone: (510) 237-7877; fax: (510) 232-5251; web site: www.hionsolar.com.

H-Ion's primary focus is renewable and sustainable energy production, hydrogen and oxygen technology for small-scale systems, and environmental improvement. They actually produce commercial products for generating, handling, and using hydrogen in small RE systems. The founder, Walter Pyle, is a regular contributor of articles to *Home Power Magazine* and editor of the *Solar Hydrogen Chronicles*.

Idatech, 924 S.E. Wilson Ave., Suite F, Bend, OR 97702; phone: (541) 383-3390; fax: (541) 383-3439; web site: www.northwestpower.com.

Northwest Power is now officially called Idatech. Northwest is developing a promising new fuel processing technology to provide very clean hydrogen to fuel cells. Look for the company's residential fuel cell power packs in 2003. They are currently selling a significant quantity of fuel cell system components to their strategic partners.

Plug Power, 968 Albany-Shaker Road, Latham, NY 12110; phone: (518) 782-7700; fax: (518) 782-7914; web site: www.plugpower.com.

At this time, Plug Power is probably today's leader in the race to provide simple, economical fuel cell residential power systems. Plug Power is building and testing hundreds of systems over the next year to ensure their product is ready for the marketplace, and expect to sell thousands of systems in 2001.

Steam Power

Sensible Steam Consultants, 152 Von Goebels Lane, Branson, MO 65616; phone: (417) 336-2869; fax: (520) 244-1028; web site: www. sensiblesteam.com.
Sensible Steam makes, sells, and installs steam engines, and steam-powered electrical generating systems. If you have a good source for something that will burn (wood, coal, oil, etc.), you will be able to generate all the electricity you need for a fraction of the initial cost of an equivalent-size PV system. Steam systems work when it's cloudy and the wind doesn't blow, but you do have to feed them fuel. Sensible Steam's web site is very informative and has links to related sites.

Solar Pumping

Dankoff Solar Products, Inc., 2810 Industrial Road, Santa Fe, NM 87505-3120; phone: (888) 396-6611; fax: (505) 473-3830; web site: www.dankoffsolar.com.
Dankoff Solar has been manufacturing high-efficiency DC solar pumps since 1983. Founder Windy Dankoff has authored numerous technical articles on a wide variety of RE topics, many of which are available on the company's web site. The web site also includes an excellent introduction to solar pumping and a technical design guide.

Organizations

Alternative Energy Institute, Inc., P.O. Box 7074, Tahoe City, CA 96145; phone: (530) 583-1720; fax: (530) 583-5153; web site: www.altenergy.org.
The Institute was organized to educate the public about the impending nonrenewable energy crisis, the search for solutions, and to improve the climate for development of new energy technologies. The Institute is comprised of a group of concerned people who believe solutions can be found when people are aware of the problems facing the world. They are focused on finding solutions and encouraging both citizens and public entities to act responsibly for the planet's future. Check out the web site for many informative reports and articles on world energy usage, coal, gas, oil, solar, current trends, new energy technologies, and so on. This is an excellent source for information as well as for links to other green sites. Sign up for their informative *Alternative Energy* web-based newsletter (it's free, and it is very good!).

American Wind Energy Association, 122 C Street, NW, Suite 380, Washington, DC 20001; phone: (202) 383-2500; fax (202) 383-2505; web site: www.awea.org.
AWEA is a national trade association that represents wind power plant developers, wind turbine manufacturers, utilities, consultants, insurers, financiers, researchers, and others involved in the wind industry. Check out the web site for publications and some good wind information, including the *Global Wind Energy Market Report* and wind expert Mick Sagrillo's articles on a variety of wind energy topics.

Danish Wind Turbine Manufacturers Association, Vester Voldgade 106, DK-1552 Copenhagen V, Denmark; phone: +45 3373 0330; fax: +45 3373 0333; web site: www.windpower.dk.
The Danish wind turbine industry is huge. With strong public and government support of privately owned, grid-tied wind power, Denmark now generates over 10% of its electricity with wind, and they export over 75% of their wind turbine manufactures. The web site is excellent, providing an in-depth introduction to many facets of wind energy.

Energy and Environmental Engineering Center, Desert Research Institute, 2215 Raggio Parkway, Reno, NV 89512; phone: (775) 673-7300; fax: (775) 674-7060; web site: www.dri.edu.
The mission of the Energy and Environmental Engineering Center (EEEC) is to conduct high-qual-

ity research to understand current and future human impacts on the environment, especially air quality, and the technology that can be applied to mitigate these impacts. For an introduction to fuel cells and current fuel cell research, check out the "Featured Projects" section of DRI's web site.

Energy Efficiency and Renewable Energy Network, web site: www.eren.doe.gov.
This web site is a comprehensive source for the Department of Energy's energy efficiency and renewable energy information, in addition to access to more than 600 links and 80,000 documents on energy related topics.

National Climactic Data Center (NCDC), Federal Building, 151 Patton Avenue, Asheville NC 28801-5001; phone: (828) 271-4800; fax: (828) 271-4876; web site: www.ncdc.noaa.gov.
The NCDC keeps meteorological data, including wind speed data for numerous locations, which may be helpful for sizing a wind turbine and determining its effectiveness and feasibility. For a modest fee, they can provide you with thorough wind data for your area, or for one close by.

National Renewable Energy Laboratory (NREL), 1617 Cole Blvd., Golden, CO 80401-3393; phone: (303) 275-3000; web site: www.nrel.gov.
As the nation's leading center for renewable energy research, NREL is developing new energy technologies to benefit both the environment and the economy. See the web site for information on current research and renewable energy basics, as well as access to related data and documents.

Renewable Resource Data Center (RReDC), web site: www.rredc.nrel.gov.
The RReDC provides information on several types of renewable energy resources in the United States (wind, solar, geothermal, bio-mass, etc.) in the form of publications, data, and maps. The web site includes an extensive dictionary of renewable energy related terms. The "News" section announces new products on the RReDC. For very detailed solar radiation data for locations across the country, customized for month and orientation, see the Center's web site at www.rredc.nrel.gov/solar.

The Energy Guy, web site: www.theenergyguy.com.
Ray Darby, "The Energy Guy" maintains this terrific web site. Ray is a mechanical engineer who has been active in renewable energy since the late 1970s when he started designing solar systems and analyzing buildings for energy efficiency. For more than a decade he has been involved with the State of California as an energy specialist and is currently Energy Specialist and Mechanical Engineer with the Non-Residential Efficiency Services Group within the Energy Efficiency Division of the California Energy Commission. Check out his web site for information on a wide variety of energy related topics and links to many related web sites.

XII Metalworking

My grandfather, like many blacksmiths of yesteryear, brings to mind an image of robust and independent craftsmen who were a main force in the early history of our country. They were central figures in the life of the villages, because they provided most of the tools and implements that were needed for the life of the community. The scale of work was small, personal and communal. These men were also forceful in the development of new industrial processes and the invention of tools and products. They widened the range of goods and products that this newly created force brought about. They were part of the industrial revolution and helped spur it on.

—Jack Andrews, *New Edge of the Anvil*

Today's giant steel mills and fabrication plants are a far cry from the village blacksmith shops of our forefathers. The modern blacksmith creates individually crafted one-of-a-kind objects that can provide a wonderfully personal touch to a striking entryway, hand tool, fireplace door, or sculpture. In the days of my grandfather, a "mass produced" item may have been made in a local foundry in quantities of ten to a hundred—a miniscule fraction of today's common production quantities ranging from a few thousand to many millions.

Crafting your own piece of art or a useful item from a simple lump of metal can be a very rewarding experience. In this chapter I provide a brief introduction to some of the metalworking processes that are applicable to backyard operations. Should you wish to expand your knowledge of the metal crafts, the recommended references will give you an excellent start. With luck, the course of our future will maintain these time-honored crafts in their current position as hobbies and artful occupations, rather than returning to their prior position of communal necessity.

CAUTION: *The tools and temperatures required for working metal can be very dangerous. The best way to learn these skills is under the tutelage of an experienced craftsman. Use caution and proceed carefully. Most older instruction manuals do not stress safety. Safety glasses, high temperature gloves, leggings, forearm protectors, and a heavy face shield are cheap insurance when compared with the loss of an eye, arm, finger, or even a visit to the emergency room.*

Metal is commercially available in a bewildering variety of different alloys, finishes, hardnesses, and forms. The Yellow Pages in most cities contain listings for suppliers of metal stock, or you can ask your local machine shop where they purchase their supplies. A metal scrap heap can also provide a bountiful supply of raw materials for the home forge or foundry. Nearly all of the easy-to-reach sources for high-grade ores have been mined long ago. If you are ever in a situation where central services are down for a considerable period of time, and you wish to fabricate useful items from metal, junkyards and garbage dumps will provide you with a source for raw materials far superior to the best ore that you could find. I have heard that certain Japanese companies have begun to mine old landfill sites, but I do not believe that this practice has spread to Western Europe, United States, or Canada.

A BRIEF INTRODUCTION TO METALS

There are a myriad of metal fabrication techniques, but most of these fall into four broad categories: casting, forging, machining, and sheet metal. Forging is probably the oldest metal fabrication method. In the forging process, a piece of metal is beaten and worked to "push" the metal into a desired shape. Usually the metal is heated in a furnace until it softens somewhat before it is worked. This process is repeated until the desired shape is obtained. The village blacksmith is the most well-known example of common low-tech metal forging. Sometimes the metal is "cold forged" without any heat. Pure silver, gold, and copper deposits were probably first cold worked into useful and decorative shapes.

The next metalworking skill to develop was probably the casting of metal. In the casting process, metal is heated in a furnace until it liquefies, and then poured into a mold to produce the desired shape. Silver, gold, and copper were mined, forged, and cast thousands of years ago. These metals were found naturally in fairly pure states. They are processed at considerably lower temperatures than iron or steel. Copper artifacts first showed up around 6500 BC. Bronze, originally an alloy of copper and tin, was used in Greece and China before 3000 BC, but did not show up in Britain until around 1900 BC. Bronze melts at around the same temperature as silver and gold (1760° to 1945°F), but has superior strength for use in tools and hardware.

Iron began to replace bronze as the metal of choice for many tools and weapons around 1200 BC in the Middle East and southeastern Europe, but not until 600 years later in China. Iron is far stronger than bronze, but requires considerably higher temperatures (2800°F) to melt fully and more sophisticated methods for refinement and fabrication. The crude predecessors to the blast furnace could only reach temperatures of about 2100°F, so instead of producing liquid iron for casting, they produced a solid chunk of low carbon iron called a "bloom," which was then heated and hammered into various wrought iron objects. Around the fifteenth century, blast furnaces appeared and iron making split into a two-stage process. The first stage created a string of brittle high carbon cast iron billets called "pigs" because they resembled a cluster of suckling piglets. The second stage consisted of running a plentiful supply of air through the iron to oxidize some of the carbon, resulting in a lower-carbon cast iron, called malleable iron, which is much less brittle and far more manufacturing-friendly than pig iron. England's magnificent forests were decimated to make sailing ships and the charcoal that fueled the blast furnaces of the Iron Age. The use of charcoal to

fuel furnaces continued well into the nineteenth century, long after the establishment of coal and coke as foundry fuels. It was during the second half of the seventeenth century that Englishman Dud Dudley first demonstrated the use of coal for melting metal. Not long afterward, foundries extended the charcoal making process (turning hardwoods into charcoal) to charring coal to make "coke," a hotter and cleaner burning material than regular coal (Marshall 1996, 7–14).

Steel is made by either forging and reheating low-carbon blooms to introduce more carbon, making wrought iron stronger and harder, or by refining high-carbon cast iron to reduce its carbon content to less than 2%. Egyptian artifacts indicate that Egyptian metallurgists had a knowledge of heat treatment and forging techniques to make steel products as early as 900 BC. It takes around twenty cycles through the carburizing, hammering, and reheating process to make a good sword from low carbon "bloom." In 1751, Englishman Benjamin Huntsman established a steelworks that developed the crucible process for making large quantities of steel from cast iron melted in crucibles. This significantly lowered the cost of steel production and improved the ability to alloy the steel and control the process.

The machining process takes raw metal stock, typically in round or rectangular shapes, and cuts away excess metal until you end up with the shape you want. Machining metal is kind of like carving wood, only it's done on rugged industrial machines, like mills and lathes, utilizing hardened steel cutters. The development of machine tools in England during the late1700s led to the Industrial Revolution of the 1800s.

Sheet metal is made on machines with heavy-duty rollers that transform thick cast metal stock into large sheets of metal ranging from only a few thousandths of an inch thick to around 3/16 of an inch thick (thicker plates of steel can be cast and hot rolled to virtually any thickness). Car bodies and tin cans are made out of sheet metal. Sheet metal is either "hot-rolled" or "cold-rolled." To make common sheet metal, thick plates are first hot-rolled to significantly thin the plates. Often hot-rolled sheet is thinned further by the cold-rolling process. Hot rolling leaves a "scale" on the surface that requires extra finishing steps. Cold rolling improves the workability of the steel and leaves a fairly clean surface finish. The cold rolling process tends to work harden steel. Cold-rolled steel is often thinned until it hardens significantly, and then "annealed" (baked in an oven) to remove hardening residue from the rolling process and make it ready for another stage of rolling to thin it further. In ancient times, a metal worker might make thin metal plates by repeatedly heating, hammering, and peening a chunk of bloom until it spread out into a thin sheet.

Casting and forging lend themselves to do-it-yourself, low-tech processes, provided you have some ingenuity and a few tools. For an investment of less than $100, you can build yourself a small backyard forge or foundry that can turn old pistons, aluminum cans, or brass plumbing fixtures into useful tools or objects of art. Scrap sheet metal can be transformed into useful containers, and pots and pans, but you won't be able to turn a chunk of iron into a piece of sheet metal without an industrial rolling mill.

CASTING METAL

I don't remember the artist's name, or what his college major was, but I can't forget his work. He had a sort of mad-scientist crazed look in his eye as he focused 100% of his attention on the project at hand. He carved 3-foot-long graceful flower petals from giant chunks of Styrofoam. Large casting frames were custom built from scrap lumber to contain the black sand that was carefully pounded around each foam petal. Once a petal was fully encased in casting sand, a funnel shaped cut was carved into the sand to channel the flow of metal to one corner of the petal. When the time came for pouring the molten aluminum, the casting lab buzzed with excitement so thick you could taste it. Ed, a maintenance man, barked orders as the filled crucible was hoisted from the furnace. Ed was a true "foundry-man," having worked for several years in a pre-automation production foundry, and was the undisputed king of this dirty little room tucked away in the maze of basements below MIT's main building complex. Ed was in his glory as the shimmering silvery liquid poured into the black sand funnel, burning its way through the Styrofoam. Days later, after all of the petals had been cast, removed from the black sand, cleaned up, and assembled, the finished product was awesome indeed. It was a stunning 3-foot-tall by 5-foot-wide
aluminum orchid. News spread quickly of this casting lab beauty, drawing the attention and admiration of the chancellor's office. At the chancellor's request, the giant orchid was proudly displayed in his office for all to see. When asked where the idea came from and what he was going to sculpt next, the artist only shrugged and answered, "I don't know the answer to either."

The basic idea behind casting metal is pretty simple—you melt some metal and you pour it into a mold, generally made from a pattern and some sticky sand. When I was a boy, you could usually find at least one small-time foundry within a couple hours' drive of most towns in America. With increasing safety concerns, foreign competition, and the advent of large computerized foundries, most of the small American foundries have disappeared. Much of what remains from hundreds of years of hands-on metal casting experience lies in the hands of hobbyists, old-timer foundry workers, and Third-World foundry workers.

Sand Casting

The use of damp sand to make molds for casting metals has been utilized for thousands of years. In essence, dampened sand is rammed into two or more interlocking frames (called "flasks") encircling a pattern for the part that is to be cast from metal. When the frames are parted, a depression is left in the rammed sand that is a mirror image of the part to be cast (a "female" impression). A channel is formed to funnel molten metal into the cavity within the rammed sand. After the metal has been poured and cooled, the sand is broken away from the metal casting and the rough casting is cleaned up. Sometimes a little sanding, filing, and brushing is all that's necessary to clean the raw casting, but usually secondary machining is necessary to add threads or make precision surfaces for mating the casting to other parts. The following illustrations and descriptions are provided to help you understand the basic processes involved with casting metal. For detailed instructions that can provide you with a practical knowledge of sand casting, I suggest you pick up some of the recommended references.

PATTERN

To make a sand casting, you must start with a pattern for the part you wish to cast. If it weren't for three factors called "shrinkage," "undercuts," and "draft," it would be a simple matter to take almost any existing part and copy it by using the part as a pattern in a sand casting. Most patterns are made from wood, but they can be modeled in clay or wax or carved/machined from almost any hard material. Useful materials for pattern making include moldable auto-body putties that can be sanded or carved after curing. Varnish protects wood patterns from moisture in the casting sands and helps to facilitate a clean release from the sand.

Lost wax castings use patterns made from wax. The wax is either melted or burned out of the mold, leaving its shape in a cavity for the liquid metal to flow into. A variation on lost wax is to carve the pattern out of plastic foam. When the metal is poured into the mold, it burns its way through the foam, leaving metal in the shape of the foam pattern.

SHRINKAGE

When molten metal cools, it shrinks a significant amount. The amount of shrink varies with the type of metal. Even metals of the same type will shrink a little differently depending on wall thickness and overall size of the part. Mold shrinkage is usually specified as inches per inch or as inches per foot. For parts under 24 inches long, mold shrinkage per foot of length is figured at ⅛" for cast iron, ¼" for steel, ⁵⁄₃₂" for aluminum, and ³⁄₁₆" for brass. For example, if you wish to make a 12"-long brass candlestick, the pattern for this part would be shaped just like the candlestick, but would be 1.6% larger to account for shrinkage and would measure 12³⁄₁₆" in overall length (U.S. Navy 1958, 27).

DRAFT

A pattern must be tapered slightly on the sides to allow for the rammed sand to release from the pattern when the pattern is withdrawn from the rammed sand. If the pattern has totally square sides, the casting sand will stick to the pattern and will not leave a clean impression in the sand. Rounded corners and edges also help the pattern to release

cleanly from the sand. Typically, outside surfaces need less draft than inner surfaces and thin delicate cores, such as those that make holes in the castings, need the most draft. The more tapered a pattern is, the easier it will release from the rammed sand. A good general draft allowance is ⅛" per foot of length, which works out to be about 1° of taper. Holes might require 2° to 3°. You may be able to get away with as little as ¼° to ½° draft for long flat surfaces.

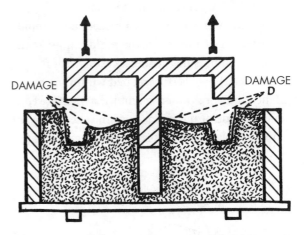

MOLD BROKEN DUE TO A LACK OF TAPER

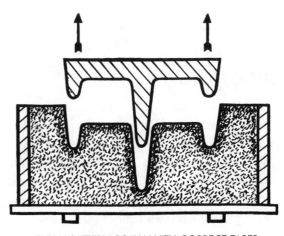

CLEAN PATTERN DRAW WITH CORRECT TAPER

Figure 12-1. Pattern draft (taper) for releasing from the sand. Illustration courtesy of *U.S. Navy Foundry Manual* (Lindsay Publications, 1989).

UNDERCUTS AND CORES

An undercut is an area of the part that the two mold halves would not pull straight away from, without damaging the mold impression. For example, the mold cannot simultaneously release from both the outsides and the center of the hollow ornamental column of Figure 12-2. The inside area of this column is called an "undercut" because it cuts underneath the outer sides. To sand cast this hollow column requires making a pattern for the inside shape of the column and using this pattern to cast a "core" using a sand mixture formulated with special binders. Before it can be placed into the sand mold that contains the impression of the column's outer surface, this core must be baked to harden the binders. After the core has been placed in the mold, and the part is cast in metal, the mold's moist sand is removed from outside the metal casting, but the hardened sand core is still trapped within the casting. The sand core is then crumbled and removed from the inside of the metal column. The end result is a hollow column that uses far less metal than if it were solid.

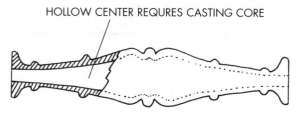

Figure 12-2. Hollow column requiring a core to form the undercut center.

CASTING FLASKS

The forms for containing the rammed casting sand are called "flasks" and they are usually rectangular forms that have open tops and bottoms. The top flask is called a "cope" and the bottom flask is called a "drag." The cope and drag are keyed with tapered offset pins or interlocking pegs for precise alignment after the pattern has been removed from the rammed sand. The taper provides accurate alignment when the mold halves are fully closed, yet makes it easy to split the mold halves apart. The "leader pins" or other aligning features are offset from the center to insure against assembling the cope and drag backwards. Commercial flasks are usually metal, but you can make your own flasks from wooden frames. If you make your own, insure that they are square, the corners are strong, and the tops and bottoms are flat.

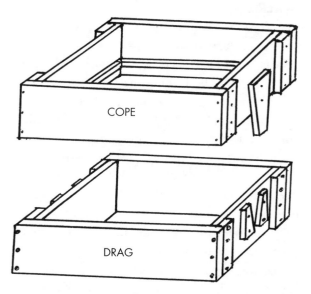

Figure 12-3. The casting flasks. Illustration courtesy of *The Charcoal Foundry* by David J. Gingery (Gingery, 1983).

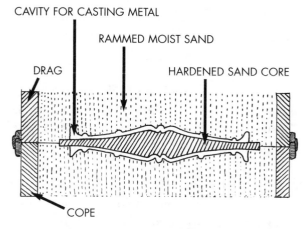

Figure 12-4. A sand mold with a baked sand core to cast a hollow column. Adapted from an illustration courtesy of *Metalworking: A Book of Tools, Materials and Processes for the Handyman* by Paul N. Hasluck (Lindsay Publications, 1994).

For simple forms with a flat bottom, the drag is rammed full of sand flush with its top edge. The pattern is placed on a flat smooth surface. A round smooth pin (called a "sprue bushing") is placed next to the pattern to provide an opening for metal to enter the mold, and then sand is rammed around the pattern and sprue bushing.

When the pattern will extend both into the cope and the drag, the simplest way to accomplish this is by first ramming the drag full of sand and scraping it off flush with the top edge of the drag. Next, the pattern is laid on top of the drag and tapped until it sinks into the drag. The mold must split at the widest point of the part, so the sand in the drag is carefully carved at a smooth taper until this point is reached (called the "parting line"). Next, dust the top of the rammed moist sand with fine dry "parting sand" that will prevent the sand in the cope from sticking to the sand in the drag. Position the drag on top of the cope and place a sprue bushing next to the pattern (for metal to flow into the mold). Now ram moist sand into the cope until it is flush with the top edge of the cope.

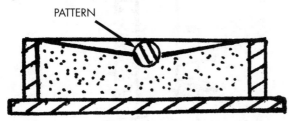

PATTERN

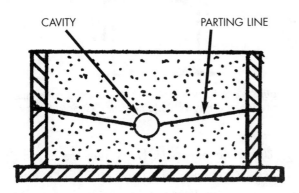

CAVITY   PARTING LINE

Figure 12-5. "Coping down" to match the parting line. Illustration courtesy of *The Charcoal Foundry* by David J. Gingery (Gingery, 1983).

Once the cope is rammed full of sand, lift the cope from the drag and carefully remove the pattern from whichever half it remained stuck to. Using a spoon or small trowel, carefully patch minor imperfections in the cavity surfaces with casting sand. The *sprue* is the large hole that the metal is poured into. As a rule of thumb, the sprue must be larger in diameter than the thickness of the part that it feeds. The size of the sprue depends on the size of the part. A *runner* is a horizontal channel that is carved along the parting line of the mold to carry metal from the sprue to the part. In the case of multiple parts being cast in a single mold at the same time, the runner

connects the sprue to several different parts, rather like branches on a tree connecting to a central trunk. The "gate" is where the runner narrows before entering the part, to minimize the area that must be trimmed and finished where the hot metal enters the part. "Risers" are tubular holes that are carved into the cope to feed extra metal to thick sections of the casting as it cools. Risers help prevent wrinkles or voided areas from forming as the metal inside the cavity shrinks while cooling.

A pattern is often split into two halves, each half being attached to a plate, to facilitate repeated use of the pattern for production casting. To prevent undesirable mismatches at the parting line, *match plates* are keyed to ensure that the cavity rammed into the cope mates precisely with the cavity rammed into the drag when the cope is placed on top of the drag.

CASTING SAND

Green sand castings are not made with green-colored sand, but with sand that has not been cured into a hardened state. Casting sand is typically made from silica sand mixed with bentonite or fire clay and a small amount of flour. The flour and clay, combined with a small amount of water, are "binders" that help the casting sand mixture to stick together. The mixture should be moist but not wet. Properly moistened casting sand is referred to as "tempered" sand. If there is too much clay in the mixture, or too much water, the casting sand will not allow escaping steam to pass through the sand and this will cause major problems. A stiff wire or rod is poked repeatedly into the cope's sand, forming vent channels for steam to flow into after it has filtered through the first layer of sand. The vent channels must not pierce into the mold cavity or they will fill with metal. Too little moisture or binding material and the sand will crumble and not retain the pattern's shape. David Gingery suggests a mixture of 85-mesh sand with 8% bentonite and 1% wheat flour (Gingery 1983, 13). To make baked cores, a binder must be added to the sand that will hold the core together after baking, yet will not harden so hard that the core cannot be easily crumbled and removed from the part after casting. *The U.S. Navy Foundry Manual* provides a good discussion of the merits of various core binding materials and offers several recipes for both core sands and regular casting sands.

Furnace

The heart of a backyard foundry is its furnace. The small foundry is faced with two choices of basic furnace styles—"crucible" or "cupola." Crucibles are containers of heat-resistant material (refractory materials such as graphite, silicon carbide, or fire clay) that chunks of the casting material are placed into for melting in the furnace. Crucible furnaces melt metal in a batch within the crucible. When casting lower melting temperature metals, such as tin, lead, and aluminum, you can use steel or cast iron containers for a crucible. If you are going to cast only one or two items in a firing, a crucible furnace is the way to go.

In a cupola furnace, the furnace itself becomes the chamber for both the combustion of the fuel and the melting of the metal. Metal is melted continuously in cupola furnaces, as long as they are stoked with fuel and metal, resulting in a much higher potential throughput and fuel efficiency than a small crucible furnace, but with less control over pour temperatures and alloy composition. If you wish to cast a number of items and significant quantities of metal, a cupola furnace is probably your best option. For a collection of articles on making a variety of low-cost backyard furnaces, and other forging/casting topics, see *Emile's Blacksmithing Links* at www.anvilfire.com/links/hotlinks.

SMALL CUPOLA FURNACES

Figure 12-6 shows the typical layout for a small cupola furnace. The cupola has a small cylindrical chimney-like bore that is lined with a refractory material. The casting metal is placed directly on a bed of fuel. When it melts, it flows through the glowing coals, superheating as it goes, until it collects at the sloping sand bottom off the cupola (A). On demand, a moldable refractory plug (called "botting") is dug out from the taphole at the spout (B) and liquid metal is drawn off into a waiting ladle or directly into a mold placed below the spout. The inlet for the air blast (C) is called a "tuyere"

(pronounced "tweer"), the same as a blast inlet in a blacksmith forge. Slag floats to the top of the molten metal and is drawn off through the small spout (D). A relatively modern improvement is the drop door (E), which is opened at the end of the heat to clean out the slag and remaining fuel.

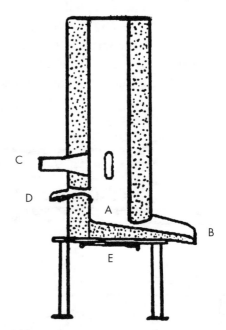

Figure 12-6. Basic construction of a small cupolette. Illustration courtesy of *Building Small Cupola Furnaces* by Stewart Marshall (1996).

The beauty of cupolas is that they are amazingly inexpensive to build and provide an almost continuous supply of molten metal for as long as you keep recharging it with fuel and iron. The initial layer of fuel and iron is followed by more layers of fuel and iron for as long as you wish to keep melting iron. You get ladles of iron every 5 to 10 minutes instead of waiting for 45 minutes to an hour for a crucible of iron to melt in a crucible furnace.

CONSTRUCTION OF A SMALL CUPOLA

In *Building Small Cupola Furnaces*, Stewart Marshall provides detailed instructions for building and using several different sizes of small cupola furnaces. He starts with a 7"–inside-diameter "baby cupolette" furnace made from welding two 5-gallon steel buckets, one on top of the other, and then lining them with a refractory material. From there Stewart moves on to a 10"–inside-diameter cupola furnace made from two 30-gallon steel drums, and follows with several variations for Great Depression-style cupolas made from two or three 55-gallon steel drums. The information that I provide here is very minimal and may be enough to help you build a cupola in a pinch, but do yourself a favor and get Stewart's book if you have a genuine interest in this subject. Cupolas are simple enough that it could be possible to make yourself a small cupola on a deserted island with scraps of steel and local clay, and then fire it with charcoal.

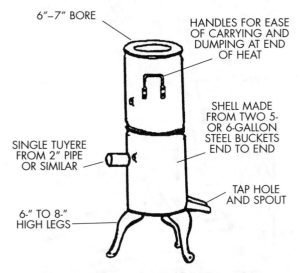

Figure 12-7. Small portable cupolette furnace for iron castings up to 10 lbs. or bronze to 20 lbs. Illustration courtesy of *Building Small Cupola Furnaces* by Stewart Marshall (1996).

After the tuyere and the two drums are welded in place, the cupola is lined with a suitable refractory material. The tuyere must extend through the refractory layer. Make a form for the 7" inside diameter of the cupola out of sheet metal wrapped around discs of wood, cardboard filled with sand, or any other suitable material that may be burned out or disassembled once the refractory material is rammed in place. There are numerous recipes for refractory material, but most involve a mixture of clean coarse silica sand (typical construction grade) and fire clay (usually available from ceramics suppliers). The finished lining must withstand 3000°F of sustained heat, so a quality fire clay is essential.

Start with a small test batch consisting of about one-third fire clay and two-thirds coarse sand. Mix a little water into the sand before adding to the fire clay. Add just enough water to make a stiff mixture,

about the consistency of modeling clay. Wrap your refractory mixture in a plastic bag and let it set overnight to fully absorb the moisture into the clay platelets. Ram a large handful of this test mixture into a small can or tray and bake at around 400°F for an hour until dry. If the baked mixture shrinks significantly from the edges, try a mixture with more sand. If it is crumbly, try more clay or more water. Strength is more important than shrinkage, as cracks can be repaired with clay slurry but a lining that falls apart is no good at all. Potters use a material called "grog" to reduce firing shrinkage. Grog is made from ground prefired clay. It is available at ceramics supply houses and can help reduce shrinkage in refractory materials.

When you are satisfied with your test mixture, mix about a half wheelbarrow full of stiff mixture (mixtures with too much water shrink excessively). Put into buckets or cover with plastic and let sit overnight or longer to fully absorb the water. Ram this mixture into your cupola stack, encircling the core form. Lay a couple of inches at a time, using an axe handle or similarly sized stick to firmly tamp each layer. Be extra careful to ram firmly round the tuyere. Once it is fully dry, fire the stack to cure the refractory material. Put a couple inches of sand in the bottom of the stack (you will be rebuilding the bottom with sand every time you fire the cupola) and start with a small wood fire. Build the fire slowly until it is burning very hot, and then add some charcoal or furnace coke. Over a period of several hours, slowly fill the furnace with fuel until it is filled to the top with glowing coals. After it has burned very hot for a few hours under natural draft, hook up the blast blower to the tuyere and run it extremely hot for about 5 to 10 minutes. Shut down the blast, plug the tuyere, and cover the stack with a plate or fire bricks. Slowly cool the cupola overnight.

In the old days, the blast was often provided by a large bellows driven by a horse, water wheel, or helpers. A large vacuum cleaner or a small shop-vac will work fine for the blast. In a pinch, a 12-volt DC ducted fan salvaged from an automobile would probably do.

Cut a hole in the center of the bottom steel drum of your cupola to match the inside stack diameter and weld on a hinged plate for a bottom trap door. Cut a 1½" opening for the tap hole, about ½" above the bottom. Line this hole with some furnace daubing or refractory mud, leaving about a ½" opening for the tap hole. The outside of the tap hole is tapered so that a relatively short neck presents itself to the molten metal to minimize the chance that metal will freeze in the neck and block the flow through the tap hole (see Figure 12-8). After each firing, you will probably need to rebuild this opening. A coating of "plumbago" wash to blacken the surface of ladles and the tap hole helps to keep molten metal from sticking to the lining. Make plumbago wash by mixing 1 part powdered graphite with 2 parts alcohol or "molasses water." Molasses water is 1 part heavy black molasses mixed with 8 parts water. Ladles for pouring liquid metal can be homemade from steel cans lined with refractory material. Punch holes in the cans and squeeze a bit of the moist refractory mixture through the punched holes to improve lining adhesion to the cans. Bake the ladles to cure the lining (Marshall 1996, 20–28).

OPERATING THE SMALL CUPOLA

The coke consumption in an ordinary cupola of just about any size is about one pound per hour for every square inch of bore area.

—Stewart Marshall,
Building Small Cupola Furnaces

Every time you fire up a melt, you must close the cupola's bottom trap door, pack in a new sloped sand bottom to funnel the molten iron to the spout, and reshape the spout and tap hole with some fresh refractory mixture of furnace daubing. After the furnace is fired up to heat and then charged with a load of fuel and iron, the tap hole is temporarily closed up with a material called "botting." There are many different recipes for botting. The botting mixture must be friable and easily dug out for fast tapping. For the small cupolas, a botting mixture of fire clay with some sand and about one-third sawdust should work well (Marshall 1996, 41).

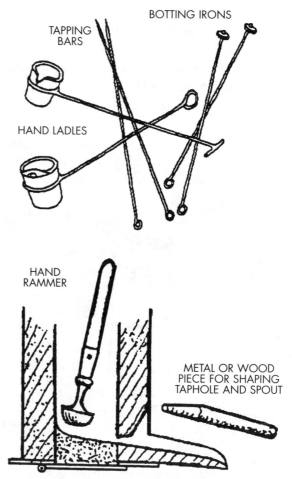

Figure 12-8. Tools for making up the bottom and operating the cupola. Illustration courtesy of *Building Small Cupola Furnaces* by Stewart Marshall (1996).

Fire the furnace starting with a wood fire lit off a match or torch held to the tap hole. Once it is burning real hot, start adding charges of coke or coal. Once this is glowing, add coke to well past the tuyere. When all has caught fire and is glowing red, add the rest of the fuel bed. Minimum bed height for cupolas to properly heat the drops of molten iron as they fall through the coke is 15" to 18". Throughout this period, the tap hole has been left open to fully dry and preheat the entire area. The tap hole is not plugged until the furnace has been charged with iron and a steady trickle of melted iron has run out of the spout, further preheating the area. Have a couple bott irons readied with golf-ball sized wads of botting material on hand. Jam one into the tap hole, hold it for a couple seconds and then with a twist remove the bott iron, leaving a plugged hole. Your first charge of iron

Figure 12-9. David Gingery's charcoal-fueled mini blast furnace. Illustration courtesy of *The Charcoal Foundry* by David J. Gingery (Gingery, 1983).

small cupola furnace. You can make the refractory mix yourself or buy a ready-made castable refractory mix from a ceramics or foundry supply house. Remove the core form and roughen the bottom couple of inches up to the level of the bottom edge of the tuyere hole. Ram refractory mix into the bottom, until it meets the level of the bottom edge of the tuyere hole. Check the lining for voids and patch with refractory mix (Gingery 1983, 38–46).

Make a lid for your furnace by ramming the same refractory mix into a 2"-high sheet metal form that is riveted or screwed at the ends to make a hoop slightly larger than the outside circumference of your 5-gallon furnace bucket. Poke about 12 evenly spaced ⅛" holes into the sides of this form. Place a glass or can in the center to form the vent hole in your furnace cover, and then string bailing wire in a crisscross fashion around the vent hole and through the ⅛" holes in the form. Cut a round hole in a piece of stout cardboard to support the outside shape of the form while you are ramming it full of refractory material. Ram it full of refractory mix, making sure that the sand is rammed firmly beneath and around the wires.

will probably be too cold to be of much use, so drain it into a "pig" mold to make an ingot for reuse, and then bott the tap hole again and repeat the process to get suitably hot iron for quality castings. Once the metal starts flowing, you will tap a new charge of molten iron every 5 to 6 minutes, so there will be very little time between pours. Make sure that plenty of botting and all the tools you will need for tapping and pouring are already prepared and easily accessible before you tap the first charge of molten iron.

> **CAUTION: These instructions are just enough to give you a basic understanding of the procedure. Before trying this yourself, I suggest you consult a manual for building and using small cupola furnaces.**

CHARCOAL FURNACE FOR CRUCIBLES

David Gingery has written a valuable book for the backyard foundry worker called *The Charcoal Foundry*, which shows you how to build and operate your own small, low-cost, crucible-type blast furnace that is fueled with regular charcoal and air charged by a vacuum cleaner blower. Dave suggests using a 5-gallon pail for the outer wall of the charcoal furnace. Much like in the construction of a small cupola, a collapsible form is made about 7" in diameter to pack refractory material around, leaving a hollow central core. Pack a moist (not wet) refractory sand/clay mix around the outside of this form as described in the section on making the

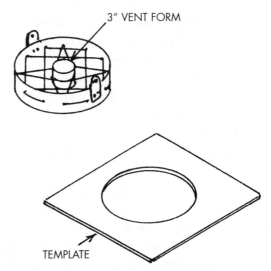

Figure 12-10. Lid form for the charcoal furnace. Illustration courtesy of *The Charcoal Foundry* by David J. Gingery (Gingery, 1983).

Partially cure the lid in a conventional oven before curing the main lining of your charcoal furnace. Bake the lid at 250°F until the steam has been driven off, and then continue to bake for another couple of hours at about 500°F. Cure the main furnace refractory in pretty much the same manner as for the small cupola furnace. Fill the bottom of the furnace with a double layer of charcoal, saturate it with lighter fluid, and start the charcoal burning. Fill the furnace with charcoal and place your cover on top. Let all of the charcoal catch fire before turning on the air blast. Continue firing until the inside of the walls and lid are glowing brightly and the charcoal is mostly burned up. Cover the vent and the tuyere with bricks and allow your furnace to cool slowly. After cooling, cracks in the lid and furnace walls can be patched with some of the moist refractory mixture.

Dave suggests getting used to using your furnace by starting with aluminum, which pours at around 1400°F, before trying brass, which pours at over 2000°F. A heavy steel pot is fine for melting aluminum, but a silicon carbide crucible is best for melting brass, bronze, or iron. See *The Charcoal Foundry* by Dave Gingery for casting basics plus numerous tips, tools, and other details pertaining to the construction and use of the charcoal foundry.

Precautions for Foundry Safety

- It is extremely dangerous to spill hot metal on a damp surface, such as concrete (hot metal may sputter, which sends small globs flying). Spread a 2"-thick layer of sand several feet around your foundry. Do all your pouring and handling of molten metal over this layer of sand.
- Wear glasses when you look into the vent hole. When adding metal to the crucible or pouring into a mold, it's a good idea to protect your entire face with a welder's face shield.
- Use dark welder's goggles or a face shield when working with metal over 2300°F to protect your eyes from excessive infrared radiation.
- Protect yourself with flameproof chaps and gloves.

- Work in a well-ventilated area. Carbon monoxide from charcoal is toxic, but odorless and invisible. If you overheat zinc (a common die-cast material), it burns and makes poisonous smoke.
- Wear stout leather or fireproof shoes to protect your feet. Ensure that you can strip them off quickly (no laces) if molten metal should drop onto your feet.
- Keep a large bucket of water handy for dousing burning clothing or skin.

BACKYARD FOUNDRY AND ENVIRONMENTAL CONSIDERATIONS

We are living in an era of greenhouse gases, toxic waste dumps, limited resources, and a record rate of species extinction. Please try to work as energy-efficient and environmentally conscious as possible by adhering to the following recommendations:

- Use as much exhaust heat as possible (e.g., preheating metal molds).
- Combine as many batches of metal melting as possible. Reheating a cold furnace takes much more energy than filling a still-hot crucible with cold metal and putting it in a hot furnace.
- Take all fluxes, slag, and dross skimmed off the metal bath to a local hazardous waste collection point and do not dump them into the trashcan or the sewer. Metal oxides are hazardous waste and should be recycled to reclaim the metals.
- Avoid use of cadmium, lead, or mercury in your alloys. These metals are very toxic and may be hazardous to your health. For making hard solder for silver or gold, zinc is a less toxic additive than cadmium for lowering silver or gold solder's melting point.
- Pickle (a solution of about 10% sulfuric acid in water used for cleaning silver and gold items, especially after soldering) can be used for a long time. When it turns blue, you should dump it (not in the sink but at a chemical waste collection point). When only light blue it can still be used for cleaning. Extend its life by filtering solid particles through an old coffee filter (Ditzhuyzen 2000, 3).

Figure 12-11. Basic equipment for making tools. Illustration courtesy of *The Complete Modern Blacksmith* by Alexander G. Weygers (Ten Speed Press, 1997).

FORGING

Village blacksmiths have provided wrought tools and architectural and ornamental iron to their communities for hundreds of years. When iron is heated red hot, it becomes comparatively easy to cut, bend, weld, thin, thicken, twist, punch holes through, or otherwise manipulate its shape and form. Accomplished blacksmiths can make their own tools such as files, hammers, tin snips, punches, chisels, anvils, and shears. Making custom hinges, horseshoes, or plows is no problem for the blacksmith.

The center of the blacksmith's shop is the forge and the anvil. The forge is where the metal stock is heated hot enough to work or temper. The anvil is the heavy chunk of steel that supports the heated work piece as it's beaten and manipulated into shape. Modern shops will often have several different types of forges and special forging presses. These presses accept forging dies to forge specific patterns and shapes in hot iron. An excellent introduction to blacksmithing basics is *The Complete Modern Blacksmith* by Alexander G. Weygers. This book is based on the popular beginning blacksmithing tool-making classes that Weygers taught for many years. It is copiously illustrated with beautiful pencil drawings for each step.

Low-Tech Heat Treating

CARBON CONTENT

Steels come in a myriad of alloys and grades, but the carbon content in nonstainless steels is the most important factor in determining its hardening characteristics. The science of metallurgy fills many volumes, so I can only provide a rudimentary introduction that barely scratches the surface. For a much better introduction that is clear and understandable, see the *New Edge of the Anvil: A Resource Book for the Blacksmith* by Jack Andrews.

When hot steel (cherry red and hotter) cools, the steel hardens into small crystals referred to as "grains" in metallurgy. Both the grain size and the type of crystal lattice affect the hardness and toughness of the finished product. Carbon in the steel acts as "nucleating" sites for crystals to grow from, so steel with more carbon has the potential for smaller grains and a harder finished condition. Harder isn't always better. A harder material holds a sharp edge longer, but tends to be more brittle and may be prone to chipping and fracture. Mild steels are the most easily welded and fabricated for general use, but they hold an edge poorly. A spring must be fairly hard to avoid taking a set, but tough enough so that it doesn't crack easily. A cold chisel must be tough to handle impact, not so hard that it chips easily, but not so soft that it quickly loses its edge. A razor must have maximum hardness to hold an edge as long as possible.

Carbon content in steels is referred to by the number of points. Each ten points is one-tenth of a percent of carbon. A steel with 40 points would have 0.4% carbon content. The amount of carbon affects the hardenability of the steel. Low-carbon steels are typically in the 6- to 30- point range and are not very hardenable by heat treating except for a process called "case hardening" or "carburizing." Case hardening introduces high carbon content into the surface layer resulting in good toughness due to internal ductility combined with high surface hardness from the thin carbon-rich outer layer. Medium carbon steels are typically in the 30 to 52 range and are somewhat hardenable. "High carbon" steels are in the 55 to 95 range and tool steels may range as high as 170 points.

STEEL HARDENABILITY TEST

When a steel is heated to a light cherry red condition and then quenched in cold water, the grain structure is frozen in a highly stressed maximum hard condition. To test for the hardenability of an unknown steel, heat the steel in a clean fire (smokeless and essentially invisible flame) to a light cherry red condition and then quench in cold water. The steel should be a pearl gray color. If the steel is a high carbon steel suitable for tools, the tip of a file should skate off the piece like a needle on glass.

TEMPERING

A piece of high carbon steel that has been rapidly quenched is in a highly stressed condition and is easily cracked or shattered. "Tempering" describes various processes that reheat the steel to moderate temperatures to allow the steel to partially soften so the crystal lattice can shift to relieve some of the internal stress. When the steel has reached the temperature required for a specific hardness, it is quenched to lock in the proper amount of hardness. By controlling the temperature of reheat and the rate of quench, the desired toughness and hardness are maintained. In general, thicker parts hold heat longer, so they must be quenched faster. Thinner parts lose heat faster, so they must be quenched slower. The boiling point of a quenching solution determines the temperature that the steel sees at its surface. Plain water boils at 212°F at sea level, so it quenches the fastest and is best for thick parts. A heavy brine solution boils at about 226°F, so it quenches a little slower than plain water. Oil or rendered fat boils around 290°F, so it quenches the slowest and is better for very fine blades.

Because the temperatures required for tempering are much lower than forging temperatures, the tempered part does not glow. Tempering temperatures can be estimated by the color of an oxide layer forming on a polished area of steel, located in the area to be tempered, when the part is reheated in the forge. Colors are somewhat subjective, but the table provides a general idea of the oxide layer's colors and corresponding temperatures for achieving a variety of useful tempers.

> *CAUTION: Do not heat high carbon steels to a light yellow or white hot range as this extreme heat will burn off the carbon and the steel will lose its hardenability (except for case hardening).*

ANNEALING

When steel is heated to a light cherry red condition and then allowed to cool slowly, internal stresses are relieved and the material cools to a relatively soft condition that is called "annealed."

CASE HARDENING

The old-fashioned, low-tech case hardening started by covering the steel tool with a layer of shaved animal horn, which provided a source of carbon that would readily absorb into the hot steel. Next, it was wrapped in a cloth and then covered with a 3"-thick layer of refractory mud or plaster reinforced with chicken fat. This refractory covering prevented heated air from burning off the carbon layer. Once the package was dried, it was left in glowing coals overnight, and then the casing was knocked off and the glowing steel part was quenched in water. The end result was a toughened steel with a hard brittle skin and a ductile center (Weygers 1997, 25).

ESTIMATION OF TEMPERATURES

Most backyard foundry workers and blacksmiths will not bother with a pyrometer for accurately measuring temperatures. With a little practice, you can estimate higher temperatures by the color of light coming off the furnace or a chunk of metal (the values are the same for all materials, including steel, brick, bronze, etc.). If you desire a more accurate temperature measurement than you get from judging hot steel's color, a thermocouple is a good measuring tool that is much less expensive than a pyrometer. The best one for the backyard foundry is a platinum/platinum-rhodium (Pt + 10% Rh) couple, which allows measuring temperatures to 2912°F (1600°C).

CAUTION: Contact between liquid metal and thermocouple wires may dissolve the wire.

Metal temperatures based on glow color:

- 900°F: Barely red in the dark (about the threshold temperature that an object emits visible light)
- 1075°F: Blood red
- 1175°F: Dark cherry
- 1275°F: Medium cherry
- 1375°F: Cherry
- 1450°F: Bright cherry
- 1740°F: Orange (barely visible in bright sunlight).
- 2000°F: Orange yellow (light yellow in the dark, fairly visible in bright sunlight)
- 2370°F: Light yellow, nearly blinding

  CAUTION: At 2370°F and above, dark (welding) goggles are required.

- 2730°F: Nearly white, blinding (Ditzhuyzen 2000, 4 and Weygers 1997, 26).

Metal tempering temperatures and their estimation based on oxidation layer color

Temper color	°F	Tool
Steel gray	650+	N/A
Greenish blue	630	Light springs
Light blue	610	Screw drivers, wood saws, punches
Dark blue	590	Springs
Blue	570	Picks, light-duty cold chisels, knives
Dark purple	550	Cold chisels for steel
Purple	540	Axes, center punches
Light purple	530	Hammers
Dark brown	510	Twist drills
Bronze	500	Rock drills, hot chisels
Dark straw	490	Wood chisels
Golden straw	480	Drift punches, leather dies
Straw	470	Pen knives
Straw yellow	460	Threading dies
Yellow	450	Planer tools
Light yellow	430	Paper cutters and lathe tools
Pale yellow	410	Razors and scrapers

Source: Adapted from the *New Edge of the Anvil: A Resource Book for the Blacksmith* by Jack Andrews (SkipJack Press, 1994).

REFERENCES

Casting

Building Small Cupola Furnaces, by Stewart Marshall. 1996, 100 pp. (paperback), No ISBN. Published by Marshall Machine and Engineering Works, P.O. Box 279, Lopez Island, WA 98261. Lists for $25.00.
This is a great book for building your own small low-cost cupola furnaces to melt iron for multiple castings. Use this book for practical diagrams, tips, procedures, and recipes from someone who has recreated these old-time technologies for use with his own business and hobbies. Available from Lindsay's Publications or from Stewart's web site at www.rockisland.com/~marshall.

The Charcoal Foundry, by David J. Gingery. 1983, 80 pp. (paperback), ISBN 1-878087-002. Published by David J. Gingery Publishing, P.O. Box 318, Rogersville, MO 65742. Lists for $7.95.
In this book, Dave Gingery shows you how to build a small, low-cost, charcoal-fueled crucible furnace for melting common metals such as aluminum and brass for castings. He also provides a basic introduction to sand casting, including pattern making and recipes for casting sand and refractory materials. Dave tells you all the other little things you need to know so you can set up your own small backyard foundry and start melting and casting metal. This is the first in Dave's series of seven "Build Your Own Metalworking Shop From Scrap" books that show you how to build a minifoundry, lathe, shaper, mill, drill press, accessories, and sheet metal brake.

U.S. Navy Foundry Manual. 1989, 291 pp. (paperback), ISBN 1-55918-007-2. Published by Lindsay Publications Inc., P.O. Box 538, Bradley, IL 60915. Lists for $19.95.

This 1958 reprint is a very thorough handbook for sand casting foundry techniques before the days of high-tech automated foundries. It is an excellent reference that will teach you probably more than you wish to know about casting, including good casting design, pattern making, molding sands and cores, casting metallurgy, troubleshooting, heat treatment, and process control.

Secrets of Green-Sand Casting, **by International Correspondence Schools.** 1983, 174 pp. (paperback), ISBN 0-917914-08-2. Published by Lindsay Publications Inc., P.O. Box 538, Bradley, IL 60915. Lists for $9.95.

This reprint of a 1906 International Correspondence School's vocational manual is a good companion text to the *U.S. Navy Foundry Manual.* Numerous illustrations provide an excellent introduction to the sand casting and mold preparation processes. It is less technical than the Navy manual, but better at providing instructions for the inexperienced foundry worker.

Forging/Blacksmithing

The Complete Modern Blacksmith, **by Alexander G. Weygers.** 1997, 301 pp. (paperback), ISBN 0-89815-896-6. Published by Ten Speed Press, P.O. Box 7123, Berkeley, CA 94707. Lists for $19.95.

The focus of this book is on making your own forged hand tools. Copiously illustrated with beautiful pencil drawings, this manual teaches you the fine points of blacksmithing techniques through the same series of tool-making projects that the author used to teach in his popular classes. If I ever had the need or desire to forge my own tools, I would definitely want this book on my shelf.

New Edge of the Anvil: A Resource Book for the Blacksmith, **by Jack Andrews.** 1994, 243 pp. (paperback), ISBN 1-879535-09-2. Published by SkipJack Press, Inc., #6 Laport Ct., Berlin, MD 21811. Lists for $25.00.

The *New Edge of the Anvil* offers good illustrations and descriptions of basic blacksmithing methods and has a section on blacksmithing metallurgy and low-tech heat treatment of steels that is more thorough than *The Complete Modern Blacksmith.* This book is less tool oriented and more focused on the use of blacksmithing techniques for sculpture, decorative iron, and general usage. Contains a pictorial portfolio of modern metalwork that is great for artistic inspiration. *New Edge of the Anvil* is reportedly the best-selling blacksmith book of all time.

Foxfire 5: Ironmaking-Blacksmithing-Flintlock Rifles-Bear Hunting, **edited by Elliot Wigginton.** 1979, 512 pp. (paperback), ISBN 0-385-14308-7. Published by Bantam Doubleday Dell Publishing Group, Inc., 1540 Broadway, New York, NY 10036. Lists for $15.95.

If you ever had to reconstruct metalworking technology from scratch, this text would be very helpful. From large-scale charcoal making to boring and rifling a forged gun barrel or forging a wagon wheel rim, *Foxfire 5* shows you how to do it yourself. In the Foxfire tradition, you get a fascinating glimpse into a selection of old-timers' lives as well as a look at how they used to make the things that most of us have always bought from the store. Many of these folks never received a paycheck from a "straight" job. For an entire lifetime they traded, bartered, and sold what they made with their own two hands. It even shows you how to make a flintlock rifle from scratch or process saltpeter from nitrate-rich cave soil for making your own gunpowder.

Machining

Machinery's Handbook, 26th ed. **edited by Erik Oberg, Franklin D. Jones, Holbrook L. Horton, Henry H. Ryffel, and Christopher J. McCauley.** 2000, 2,640 pp. (hardcover), ISBN 0-8311-2625-6. Published by Industrial Press, Inc., 200 Madison Ave., New York, NY 10016. Lists for $85.00.

I have yet to see a highly skilled professional machinist who did not have a copy of this book on his workbench. This is not an instruction manual on how to machine metal, but it contains crucial information on millions of details that are important to draftsmen, engineers, designers, and machinists. Want to cut a spur gear, calculate the strength of a steel I-beam, figure out the size and thread system for a broken screw on some piece of obscure machinery (or machine a new one)? This book will provide the details, dimensions, and other specifications that you need to make proper hardware and components.

Machining Fundamentals: From Basic to Advanced Techniques, by John R. Walker. 2000, 640 pp. (hardcover), ISBN 1-56637-662-9. Published by Goodheart-Willcox Publisher, 18604 West Creek Dr., Tinley Park, IL 60477-6243. Lists for $49.28.
This comprehensive text provides instruction on all facets of machining work, including setup, cutting speeds, safety, mills, lathes, and drilling machines. A great guide for the beginning machinist and a fine reference for those with prior machining experience.

The Shop Wisdom of Frank McLean by Frank McLean and Joe D. Rice, ed. 1992, 240 pp. (hardcover), ISBN 0-941653-06-4. Published by Village Press, 2779 Aero Park Drive, Traverse City, MI 49686. Lists for $36.
Let master machinist Frank McLean teach you 47 valuable machining techniques and how to make 41 shop tools and mill/lathe accessories in your own home shop. This book may be difficult to find except through the Village Press web site at www.villagepress.com.

The Shop Wisdom of Rudy Kouhoupt, by Rudy Kouhoupt and Joe D. Rice, ed. 1989, 240 pp. (hardcover), ISBN 0-941653-06-4. Published by Village Press, 2779 Aero Park Drive, Traverse City, MI 49686. Lists for $36.
Tips and tricks from Rudy Kouhoupt contained in 15 micromachining articles plus precise plans for six scale engines. This book may be difficult to find

except through the Village Press web site at www.villagepress.com.

General

Metalworking: A Book of Tools, Materials and Processes for the Handyman, by Paul N. Hasluck. 1994, 760 pp. (hardcover), ISBN 1-55918-126-5. Published by Lindsay Publications Inc., P.O. Box 538, Bradley, IL 60915. Lists for $29.95.
This is a reprint of a remarkable 1907 how-to book that covers most facets of early 1900s metalworking including casting, machining, blacksmithing, spinning, sheet metal, metal finishing, and heat treating. Contains plans for numerous projects to teach yourself these skills, including how to build a lathe and a working steam engine. This is a great reference that provides the information you would need to build both metalworking skills and tools from scratch.

Welder's Handbook: A Complete Guide to Mig, Tig, Arc & Oxyacetylene Welding, by Richard Finch. 1997, 170 pp. (paperback), ISBN 1-55788-264-9. Published by Penguin Putnam, 345 Hudson St., New York, NY 10014. Lists for $17.95.
This is an excellent welding guide and instruction manual for the home shop welder. It is just right for someone like myself, who wants to do it right but only welds on an occasional basis. *Welder's Handbook* is far simpler and easier to understand than the serious welding manuals aimed at certified welders

De re Metallica, by Georgius Agricola, trans. by Herbert Clark Hoover and Lou Henry Hoover. 1950, 638 pp. (paperback), ISBN 0-486-60006-8. Published by Dover Publications, Inc., 31 E. Second St., Mineola, NY 11501. Lists for $21.95.
Former president Herbert Hoover and his wife translated the original Latin text into English. This treatise on medieval mining, metallurgy, and metalworking is commonly acknowledged as one of the most highly respected scientific classics of all time. It tells you things such as how to make nitric acid and refine silver using crude technologies. Lavish woodcuts offer a glimpse into another time and place.

The Pirotechnia of Vannoccio Biringuccio: The Classic Sixteenth-Century Treatise on Metals and Metallurgy, **by Vannoccio Biringuccio.** 1990, 477 pp. (paperback), ISBN 0-486-26134-4. Published by Dover Publications, Inc., 31 E. Second St., Mineola, NY 11501. Lists for $16.95. *The Pirotechnia of Vannoccio Biringuccio* was the first clear comprehensive work on metallurgy. It predates *De re Metallica* by many years and is a bit more difficult to understand, having a heavier alchemy influence with less premodern chemistry. If you are a history of technology buff, don't miss this one.

A Diderot Pictorial Encyclopedia of Trades and Industry: Manufacturing and the Technical Arts in Plates Selected from "L'Encyclopedie, ou Dictionnaire Raisonne des Sciences, des Arts et des Metiers," Volume One, **by Denis Diderot.** 1987, 936 pp. (paperback), ISBN 0-486-27428-4. Published by Dover Publications, Inc., 31 E. Second St., Mineola, NY 11501. Lists for $19.95. First printed in 1751, the plates contained in this historical encyclopedia offer a unique look at manufacturing techniques just prior to the industrial revolution. Volume One covers agriculture, articles of war, iron foundry and forge, mining, and metalworking. Another fine book for techno-history buffs. Want to cast a larger-than-life bronze statue of Napoleon riding his favorite horse? How about a 20-foot canon? The *Encyclopedia* will show you how.

On Divers Art: The Foremost Medieval Treatise on Painting, Glassmaking and Metalwork, **by Theophilus, trans. by John G. Hawthorne and Cyril Stanley Smith**. 1979, 216 pp. (paperback), ISBN 0-486-23784-2. Published by Dover Publications, Inc., 31 E. Second St., Mineola, NY 11501. Lists for $9.95. Another one for the history of technology buffs. *On Divers Arts* is acknowledged as the foremost medieval treatise on painting, glassmaking, and metalworking. It was the first technical manuscript on painting, glass, and metalwork that came from an actual artisan who practiced and observed firsthand what he wrote about, rather than a scholarly treatise written by persons with no real experience.

Magazines

Machinist's Workshop. Subscription: $23.00 per year for 6 issues. Village Press, 2779 Aero Park Drive, Traverse City, MI 49686; phone: (231) 946-3712; web site: www.machinistsworkshop.com. This is an excellent magazine for the novice to intermediate home shop machinist. From lathe work to milling and drilling, grinding, and casting, *Machinist's Workshop* pursues every technique it takes to transform raw stock into machining success.

The Home Shop Machinist. Subscription: $27.50 per year for 6 issues. Village Press, 2779 Aero Park Drive, Traverse City, MI 49686; phone: (231) 946-3712; web site: www.homeshopmachinist.net. More technical than *Machinist's Workshop* and with more difficult projects, this magazine is devoted to the serious home shop machinist. Many professional machinists contribute articles to this magazine and like to tinker around with its projects in their spare time.

Anvil Magazine. Subscription: $49.50 per year for 12 issues. Anvil Magazine, P.O. Box 1810, 2770 Sourdough Flat, Georgetown, CA 95634-1810; phone: (530) 333-2142; web site: www.anvilmag.com. This is a blacksmithing magazine with a heavy leaning toward farriers (horseshoeing). It is billed as "The voice of the American Farrier and Blacksmith."

The Anvil's Ring. This is the premier U.S. magazine for the modern artist-blacksmith. Get this magazine by joining ABANA (see below).

RESOURCES

Centaur Forge, 117 N. Spring Street, P.O. Box 340-AFN, Burlington, WI 53105-0340; phone: (262) 763-9175; fax: (262) 763-8350; web site: www.anvilfire.com/centaur. This is a fantastic source! Centaur Forge carries a large inventory of blacksmithing tools, forges, supplies, videos, and books. Centaur offers an unparalleled selection of books and videos on blacksmithing, casting, machining, horseshoeing, carriages, saddlery, gunsmithing, knives, and miscellaneous other crafts and trades. Check out www.anvilfire.com for great links into the blacksmithing world.

ABANA (Artist-Blacksmiths' Association of North America), P.O. Box 816, Farmington, GA 30638-0816; phone: (706) 310-1030; fax: (706) 769-7147; web site: www.abana.org.

For creative inspiration and to keep up with the latest tips, tricks, and news in the rapidly expanding field of modern blacksmithing, join the ABANA. Membership includes a subscription to their quarterly magazine, *The Anvil's Ring*, and their monthly newsletter, *Hammer's Blow*. My friends in the blacksmithing business say this is a must.

MIFCO (McEnglevan Industrial Furnace Company), 700 Griggs St., Danville, IL 61832; phone: (217) 446-0941; fax: (217) 446-6013; web site: www.mifco.com.

This company makes and sells furnaces for foundry work, in addition to all kinds of foundry accessories. Their web site also has links to a subsidiary company, Danville Industrial Machinery, which distributes a variety of metal fabricating machinery such as shears, brakes, and sheet metal rollers.

W.W. Grainger, Inc., 100 Grainger Parkway, Lake Forest, IL 60045-5201; phone: (847) 535-1000; fax: (847) 535-9221; web site: www.grainger.com.

Grainger offers a huge selection of industrial hardware, supplies, and tools. The company has a couple hundred branches, so I suggest you call or use their web site to locate the nearest branch. I use Grainger to supply many of the off-the-shelf components for the custom machinery that I design. Their catalog is encyclopedia-sized. They are great for things like motors, compressors, blowers, tanks, wheels, fittings, regulators, and so on.

Village Press, 2779 Aero Park Drive, Traverse City, MI 49686; phone: (231) 946-3712; fax: (231) 946-9588; web site: www.villagepress.com.

The Village Press publishes several magazines in addition to numerous books on machining, metalworking, and steam engines.

XIII Utensils & Storage

*Good pots elude their critics and analysts—
even the potters who formed them—by being
more than the sum of their quantifiable parts.
Nowhere are these indefinable elements more
evident than in pots taken from the cold ashes
of a wood fire. Whether they challenge or reinforce the beholder's values, these pots have a
strong presence born of their many days' trial
in the fire.*

—Jack Troy, *Wood-Fired Stoneware
and Porcelain*

For thousands of years, humankind has fabricated useful utensils and storage items, such as jars, baskets, pots, and pans. Archeological artifacts of common everyday items left behind by ancient tribes and civilizations exhibit levels of art and craft that range from downright ugly to exquisite. In this chapter I present several low-tech methods for making useful household utensils and storage items. Many of the books on primitive survival skills listed in the *References* section of Chapter 4 offer further instructions for constructing rudimentary utensils and containers. If you wish to travel beyond the basics to a higher level of proficiency, artistry, or mastery, the recommended references at the end of this chapter could provide very helpful instruction and inspiration.

MAKING A SIMPLE WOODEN CUP OR BOWL

You can make a simple cup or bowl by burning out the center of a chunk of wood using hot coals. Thomas Elpel, author of *Participating in Nature*, suggests cutting thick roots from downed trees to use as raw materials for wooden containers. Regular wood from logs usually burns slowly and tends to split easily, but Elpel finds that using root stock avoids these problems. Roots are naturally porous, so

they burn easily, plus their flexibility makes them resistant to splitting from the heat and dryness of the burning process, the moisture from contained fluids, or the combined heat and moisture from use as a primitive stewing pot.

Figure 13-1. Burning out a wooden container.

Begin by cutting your chosen chunk of wood to the desired length. Next, either burn the ends of some sticks in a fire until they become glowing coals, or simply scoop coals directly from the fire. Apply the burning stick ends or loose coals to the face of your chunk of wood and gently blow on the coal to start the face smoldering. Continue the process of burning to hollow out the inside of your chunk of wood. As the charring progresses, stop every now and then to dig out the larger chunks of charred wood, and then resume burning. Dribble water onto thin wall sections to prevent burning through. When you have hollowed out your container to nearly the finished inside dimensions, use a knife to scrape away most of the remaining charred wood. Polish the container by rubbing it with a stick or stone and some loose sand. You can waterproof your container with pitch or rendered fat.

To cook in your wood container, heat several stones in a fire, then drop them one at a time into your container. The liquid should boil surprisingly fast.

> **CAUTION: Never place stones from a creek bed into a fire. The stones may explode due to steam from trapped internal moisture.**

BASKET BASICS

Indigenous peoples everywhere on the planet make beautiful and functional baskets in a variety of shapes, styles, and materials that are truly astounding. The basic concepts and techniques for basket weaving are very simple, yet many examples of native baskets are marvels of intricate weaving and exquisite graphic design. Here are a few directions to help you create rather mundane but useful baskets.

Materials

The most common basket making materials are flat, round, and flat-oval reeds found growing in marshy areas. Baskets can also be woven from sticks, grasses, pine needles, cordage, roots, or long slender pieces of split wood—essentially any material that is somewhat flexible. A common North American combination of materials is to use slender willow sucker branches for basket "spokes" and to weave cattail reeds around these spokes. The original *Foxfire* book has a decent section on splitting freshly cut white oak and making strong heavy-duty baskets from "splits." To make splits, the old-timers recommend starting with a 4- to 6-inch-diameter white oak sapling, with at least a 7-foot section of unmarred straight trunk having no branches. They typically felled and split this sapling on the same day, or weighted it in a creek to stay wet until it could be worked. The bark was peeled from the straight section of trunk, and then it was split with wedges into quarters, followed by eighths. After this, each eighth was split further with a hand knife, until reaching the desired thickness. When I was a child, my father often carried a picnic lunch and extra clothing for our family of seven in a Native American style pack-basket made from woven splits.

When weaving reeds, dry reeds are typically soaked in hot water to make them more flexible and easier to work. Green summer reeds may be directly woven into baskets, but they will shrink considerably and cause the basket to loosen up. Bend each reed over your finger to feel for the "wrong" side of the reed. Rough fibers and splinters will extend from the "wrong" side while the "right" side will stay smooth. Weave basket bodies with the "right" side to the outside.

Making a Basket

The basket "spokes" are the elements that cross in the center of a circular basket pattern and extend outward like the spokes on a wheel.

Figure 13-2. Starting a circular basket with "spokes."

TWINING

In the case of interweaving cattails around long slender willow branch spokes, you may prefer to "twine" the cattails. "Twining" refers to a weave where two strands are woven around the spokes and given a 180° twist after each weave between each spoke. Twining helps hold the weave tight and give body to a basket, but requires either a round or very flexible flat weaving material.

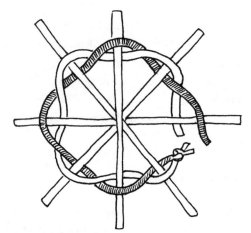

Figure 13-3. "Twining" weave around the spokes.

ADDING SPOKES

As the basket gets larger, additional spokes may be added. Thread new spokes alongside existing spokes, inside at least two weaves, and then spread the spokes apart and start separating them with additional rows of weave. When the base of the basket has reached the desired diameter, bend the spokes upward to start forming the basket's sides.

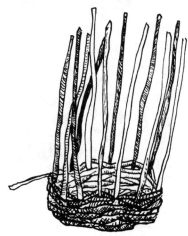

Figure 13-4. Bend the spokes and weave the sides.

When the spokes are not flat, but are round reeds or sticks, finish the last row by cutting the spoke tips to about 2 to 3 inches above the last weave. Next, bend each spoke into a "U" shape, and then tuck it down into the weaves beside the nearest spoke, trapping the last weave beneath the bent spoke end.

Figure 13-5. Finishing off the last weave ("rim row").

Alternately, a rectangular pattern is woven out of "stakes" that are then bent upwards to provide a structure, similar to the spokes, that the basket rows are woven around.

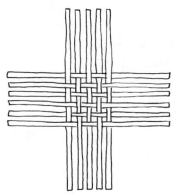

Figure 13-6. Woven base of "stakes" for a rectangular basket.

WEAVE BASICS

Baskets are typically woven as a "continuous weave" or "start-stop weave." Continuous weave is where the weaves are continuously spiraled around the basket until the top of the basket wall (the rim) is reached. In the continuous weave, when one length of reed or other weaving material is reached, a new length of weave is overlapped by a few inches with the tail of the last weave, and then the weave is continued on its spiral path. You can taper or shave reeds and other materials at the overlap to avoid undesired bulges.

> NOTE: For a continuous weave, you must have an odd number of staves or spokes for the weave to work out properly.

For the start-stop weave with reeds or splits, stagger the start of each row from the start of the last one. Finish the row by overlapping the same weave to the third stave after the start. Overlap the finish of each weave on the outside of the start.

> NOTE: For a start-stop weave, you must have an even number of staves or spokes for the weave to work out properly.

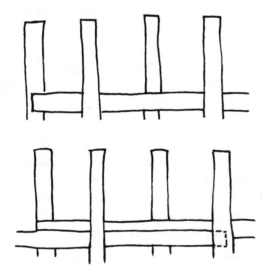

Figure 13-7. Start and finish of the "start-stop" weave.

BASKET RIM

Many baskets are finished with a thickened rim both for aesthetics and to make them more durable. Before you make the basket rim, you must finish off the top edge of the wall. Round reeds and sticks are commonly folded and tucked into the slot beside the next spoke over, as shown in Figure 13-5. Flat reeds

and splits are typically "trimmed and tucked" by folding over the last weave and being tucked beside themselves through several weaves to hold the ends in place. This prevents the last weave from unraveling and provides a secure weave to lash the rim to.

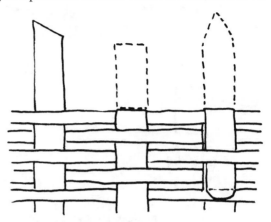

Figure 13-8. "Trim and tuck" to secure the staves and the last weave.

A common rim is made by encircling the last wall weave with two loops of reed or splits, one on the inside and one on the outside, and then lashing the rim in place with a thinner weaving material.

Figure 13-9. Lashing the rim.

BASKET HANDLES

There are many different styles of handles. Probably the most common handles are full hoops that replace one of the staves or spokes and extend all the way through the base. Partial hoops are also very common. These types of handles extend through the center of the rim and thread down through several weaves until they are trimmed and tucked around one of the lower weaves to secure the ends. Another alternative is to carve notches and ridges into thicker handle material, or loops for a drop handle, and then lock this thicker notched material between the upper weaves and/or rim.

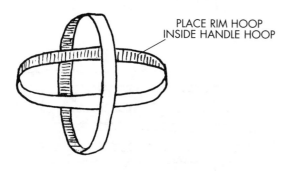

PLACE RIM HOOP INSIDE HANDLE HOOP

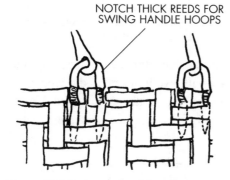

NOTCH THICK REEDS FOR SWING HANDLE HOOPS

Figure 13-10. A couple of handle options.

GOURDS

The gourd plant has been described as one of nature's greatest gifts to mankind. Of all the known plants, the gourd is the only one experts believe spanned the entire globe in prehistoric times. It appears as one of the first cultivated plants in regions throughout the world and was used by every known culture in the Temperate and Tropical Zones.

—Ginger Summit and Jim Widess, *The Complete Book of Gourd Craft*

The botanical definition of gourds is somewhat vague and can include all of the squash-melon-cucumber family and tropical calabash tree, but most people think of gourds as hard-shelled squash-like fruits that grow on vines. Once cured and cleaned, gourds can be fashioned into water containers, kitchen utensils, musical instruments, dry food containers, and ornamental objects.

Growing Gourds

Most gourds will grow like weeds when provided with decent soil, twice weekly watering (once established), and a hot two months of growing season or at least four months without frost. You may prefer to grow them on a trellis, because many gourds grown on the ground have a tendency to rot. Plant on mounds like melons, and thin to two to three plants per mound once the vines are established. Pinch the end bud of each vine's central stalk to force more growth into the fruit-producing lateral branches (Summit and Widess 1996, 19).

Curing Gourds

Pick brightly colored ornamental gourds when the stem next to the gourd is brown and the adjacent tendrils are dry. Ornamental gourds will eventually lose their beautiful colors and will fade more quickly in the sunlight. Leave at least one inch of stem on the gourd. Hard-shelled gourds should be left on the vine until autumn, when they are fully mature and the vine has turned brown and dry. At this point the gourd is about 90% water.

It will take from six weeks to more than a year to fully dry a gourd, depending on the gourd and local conditions. As the gourd's juices evaporate through its skin, the outer layer (epidermis) will probably mold and it may start to rot. Mold will not destroy the gourd's usefulness but rot will. The curing process can be accelerated by carefully scraping off the epidermis with a dull knife or scraper. Occasionally scrubbing the gourd with a cloth soaked in a mild bleach or disinfectant solution will discourage mold from forming on the gourd. Shortly after harvesting, when the epidermis has begun to change color and to soften (test with a fingernail scratch to the stem), it is ready to scrape. Experience is the best way to tell when the gourd is fully dried. The seeds of some gourds rattle when fully cured, but others don't. Some gourds are extremely light when cured, but thick-walled gourds may retain significant weight even when completely dry.

Cleaning Gourds

Mold on the epidermis may provide interesting patterns and colors that you wish to preserve. If this is the case, several coats of clear varnish will seal in the color and prevent the outer epidermis from flaking off with use. If you wish to clean the outer surface, you can loosen the mold by soaking in water with a little bleach until the mold is loosened enough to remove with a stiff scrub brush or pot scrubber. Alternately, wrap in a wet towel or place inside a dark plastic bag along with some water, then set in the sun for several hours, turning occasionally.

Cut the gourd with a knife or saw to provide access for cleaning the inside surface. Scrape the pulp and seeds from the inside. You can improvise your own scraping tools or use knives, spoons, ice cream scoops, potter's trimming tools, and so on. Save the seeds if you wish to plant more of the same gourds. After scraping, you may wish to sand or wire brush the inner surface for a smoother finish. An alternate method, particularly useful for long, narrow-necked gourds, is to fill the dry gourd with water until the pulp has become mushy and is easy to scrape out (may take as long as a month). After the pulp and seeds have been removed, fill with gravel and water, and then shake to scour the inside surface.

Sealing Gourds

For thousands of years, gourds have been used as eating utensils and for cooking or storing liquids and foods. To prevent a gourd from imparting a bitter taste to foods, soak the cleaned gourd for several days. Change the water daily until the soaking water has lost all bitterness. Some cultures prefer soaking in salt water or in boiling hot water. A tablespoon of baking soda in the soak water can help to remove bad tastes (Summit and Wildess 1996, 38). Gourds can be sealed or decorated with a variety of paints, oils and varnishes, but many of these are not compatible with foods. Repeated curing with warm kitchen oils, such as safflower or soybean oil, will seal the gourds with a nontoxic varnish-like surface. Coatings of hot beeswax or paraffin are common nontoxic gourd sealants. Pine pitch is a natural sealant that lends a sweet taste to water. Mixing some powdered charcoal into the pitch can give it more body and help to create a more stable bond to the substrate. If you wish to store water in a gourd, you can seal the gourd or leave it unsealed. Evaporative cooling from water slowly seeping through the walls will keep an unsealed gourd water container cooler than a sealed one.

NOTE: A pine pitch coating can also seal baskets or boats, making them watertight.

STORING FLUIDS IN SKINS AND OTHER ANIMAL PARTS

You can make water containers from rawhide and animal bladders. Probably the most important thing to remember is that these containers will rot if water is left in them continuously. If a wineskin is stitched with a long skinny neck, rolling the neck tightly, like a roll of dollar bills, will seal it watertight. The alcohol in the wine likely helps prevent wineskins from rotting.

A piece of rawhide will do for a stewing pot if nothing else is available. Simply dig a shallow hole in the ground and line it with a piece of rawhide. Fill the rawhide pot with your liquids and other ingredients. Heat rocks in a fire and drop them into your rawhide cooking pot to boil and cook the ingredients. Dry your rawhide pot between uses to prevent rot.

PRIMITIVE POTTERY

Pottery making, one of the earliest commercial technologies, is a skill that could make your life considerably easier if you were deprived of access to modern goods for a considerable period of time. Fired clay pots provide vermin-proof storage containers, watertight containers for liquids, and fireproof utensils for cooking. The use of clay to make useful objects is older than recorded history. Archeologists have dated the earliest known pottery shards at more than 12,000 years old and speculate that some Ice Age clay figurines may be as old as 37,000 years (Speight 1999, 3).

Clay

Clay is composed of tiny, fine-grained, flat "platelets," mostly consisting of silica and alumina oxides from naturally occurring finely ground rocks. Moisture in the clay lubricates these tiny platelets, but also has a binding reaction similar to the way a few water drops cause two plates of glass to stick together. This binding action gives moist clay its plastic characteristics and sticky feel. Potters refer to the particular types of clays that they use as "clay bodies." To be useful for making pottery, clay bodies must contain a certain amount of material, referred to as "flux," that lowers the melting point of the clay's silica and alumina oxides to the point where the clay will fuse into a rock-like material when heated in a fire or kiln. Additionally, a clay body must contain suitable refractory material to hold up to the high heat of firing. The modern-day potter has a plethora of commercially available clay bodies to choose from, each having well-documented and consistent characteristics.

Primitive potters had to rely upon clay bodies that were locally available. Clays are typically found in riverbeds, road cuts, and ponds where the surface soil has been stripped away. Not all clays are suitable for making pottery. Some clays are not plastic enough to hold together when modeled. Other clays will crack or fracture when fired. A good preliminary test for a potential clay is to first moisten and mash a lump of clay with your fingers to work it to an even consistency, then roll it between your hands into a pencil-thick piece. Twist this clay "rope" around your finger. If it cracks or breaks easily, it is probably not suitable for making pottery. The next step is to pinch some of your clay into a small pot, let it dry completely, and then bake it in the coals of a hot fire for several hours (this process is called "firing"). If your local clay survives the firing without cracking and hardens into a rock-hard material that does not soften when soaked in water, it is probably suitable for making pottery.

Clay bodies with very fine particles are not very porous, making them prone to cracking or fracturing during the drying or firing processes. Primitive potters often found that they had to add "temper-ing" materials to reduce shrinkage, slumping, or cracking in their pottery. Some common tempering materials are sand, chopped straw, mica, volcanic ash (pumice), or crushed shards of fired pottery (grog). See *Low Fire: Other Ways to Work in Clay* by Leon I. Nigrosh for a description of more extensive tests and procedures for using local clays.

PREPARING CLAY

If you're lucky, your clay bed will provide moist clay suitable for making pottery with minimal processing. If your clay is moist and fairly consistent, simply remove the surface layer to minimize the amount of debris contamination, and then proceed to "wedging" the clay. Most beds yield clays that require more processing before use. If your clay bed is dry or contains lumps of hard material such as small gravel, it is best to fully dry your clay chunks and then pound them into finely grained clay powder. If you have screens available, sift the dry powdered clay through the screens. If not, use the following process to remove lumps and debris.

Mix your clay powder with water to make a wet slurry. Mix this well and then let it sit for a couple of minutes to allow the stones to settle to the bottom. Pour the thin, soupy clay slurry into a second container, leaving the debris on the bottom of the first container. You may need to do this a few times. Once you have removed the debris and impurities, let the container sit for a few days, decanting or siphoning the clear water that rises to the surface. You can recycle your clay scraps from making pottery by dumping them back into your slurry buckets. Next, spread this clay out on some rocks, wooden boards, or plaster slabs to partially dry. Plaster works great for this purpose. Being porous, plaster rapidly draws moisture from the clay, releasing this moisture to the air once the clay is removed. Clay for pots must not be too wet or too dry. Clay that is too wet is excessively sticky and too soft to hold a shape without slumping. Clay that is too dry is not very workable. The next step is to "wedge" the clay.

WEDGING CLAY

Wedging clay is a process that removes trapped air bubbles and thoroughly mixes the clay to the point where it has an even consistency throughout the clay body. Clay is wedged with motions that are similar to kneading bread. To avoid tiring quickly, while wedging your clay on a table-high flat surface, stand so that you can lean your whole body into the motion. Wedge quantities of clay that are easily manageable (i.e., 2 to 15 lbs.). Draw your clay into a loaf or ball shape, and then lean into it and push a portion of it forward, giving the clay about a quarter twist as it distorts. As you keep repeating this process, your lump of clay will form into a spiral shape, thoroughly mixing each layer and releasing air bubbles through tiny cracks in the spiral. You can check the consistency by cutting the clay on a taught wire and examining the cut surface for any evidence of layers indicating that it needs more wedging. You can choose to add tempering materials either while you wedge or when the clay is still a slurry. My high school pottery teacher encouraged us to dry overly wet clays by adding powdered clay while wedging, but this is poor practice, because it takes several days for dry clay to completely assimilate moisture and become fully plastic.

Pinch Pots

The simplest form of pottery is the "pinch pot." Simply take a lump of clay and use your fingers to pinch it into the shape that you desire. Do not leave walls thicker than about ½" as these will trap moisture that may cause your pot to crack or explode when fired. Unfired clay pottery is referred to as "greenware." Dry your greenware slowly to prevent cracking. If you have some pieces of old garbage bags, drape them over your greenware while drying to slow the process. Otherwise, simply dry your pottery in a cool spot in the shade. Sprinkling the surfaces with water, or spraying with a fine mist, can help slow the drying process. Lips and handles tend to dry faster than the main body of the pot. Draping a moistened cloth or paper towel over a lip or handle will retard the drying process in these areas.

Figure 13-12. Making a pinch pot.

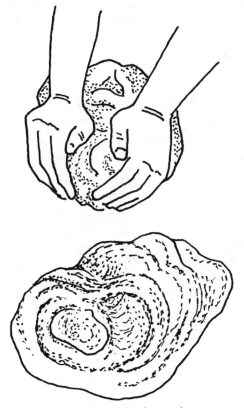

Figure 13-11. Wedging clay.

A variation on the pinch pot is to press your clay into a form such as an existing bowl.

Coil Pottery

A very common method for making pottery is to build pots from coils of clay. Most classic Greek pottery was first built from coils. The pots were then attached to a turntable and turned against a trimming template to give the pottery its classic outer profile and a smooth surface texture. Start by rolling out a flat slab of clay and cutting it to the size of the base of your pot. Roll ropes of clay coils either between each of your hands or between your hands and a smooth flat surface.

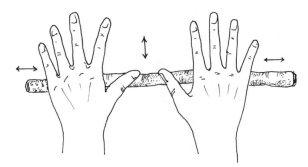

Figure 13-13. Rolling clay ropes for coil pots.

Build your coil pot by spiraling rolled clay ropes into the desired shape of your pot. Using your fingers, or a smooth wooden tool, mush one coil ridge into the coil below to smooth the surface and to join each coil together. It is important to distort enough clay from one coil into the next to prevent coils from separating or cracking during drying or firing.

Figure 13-14. Making a coil pot.

You can use a smooth wooden tool (called a "rib" tool) to smooth the outer profile. Support the inside of the pot with one hand while you smooth the outside with a scraping action using the rib. Many fine Southwestern Pueblo style pots are further finished by burnishing with a smooth stone. Repetitive rubbing with the stone burnishes a polished finish that is both beautiful and less porous than unburnished earthenware.

Figure 13-15. A burnished pit-fired coil pot by Renee Roybal, San Ildefonso Pueblo. Photo © Marcia Keegan.

Slab Pottery

Slab pots are made from joining semi-hardened slabs of clay that are first cut to the desired shape and then joined together. Start by rolling out slabs of clay using a rolling pin or a similar round object. The use of thin spacing strips, such as yardsticks, can facilitate rolling slabs of consistent thickness.

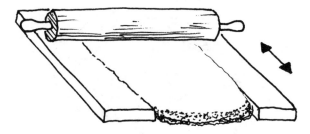

Figure 13-16. Rolling slabs.

You can either drape slabs into or over a form to give it a smoothly curved shape or allow them to dry until they reach a semi-hardened state referred to as "leather hard." Leather-hard slabs are the stiffness of full-grained leather. Cut leather-hard slabs to size using a knife or sharp stick. To join leather-hard slabs to each other, first score the edges with a sharp tool, and then coat the scored edges with a layer of thick clay slip. Press the scored and slip covered edges together with a slight sliding or twisting motion to ensure that no air bubbles are trapped. After cleaning excess slip from the joints, you can reinforce the inside of each joint with a tiny rope of clay worked into the sides with a wooden tool or your fingertips.

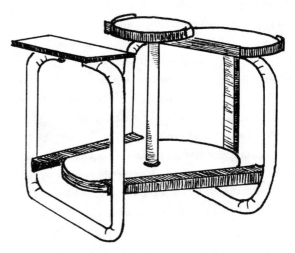

Figure 13-18. Low-tech kick wheel.

The following sections will give you some idea of the basic techniques for making pottery on the wheel. These instructions are the bare minimum necessary for learning this craft on your own. For more complete instructions, and a beautiful guide to the ceramic arts in general, I highly recommend *Hands in Clay* by Charlotte F. Speight and John Toki (see *References* section). I must admit that I am very partial to hand-thrown pottery. At one time, I seriously considered becoming a professional potter. There is something deeply satisfying in the act of transforming a shapeless lump of clay into the basis for an artful utensil in just a few minutes.

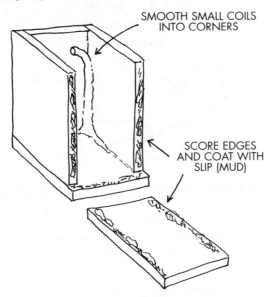

Figure 13-17. Joining slabs to make a pot.

Throwing on the Wheel

The invention of the potter's wheel made it possible for potters to turn out large quantities of consistent pots in a short period of time. "Thrown pottery" refers to pottery that has been made on a potter's wheel. You can make your own homemade kick wheel from a couple of bearings, a shaft, a round wheel head, and a flywheel made of cast concrete or a wooden form filled with bricks, sand or rock. Old-fashioned potter's wheels were foot powered, but modern electric wheels have powerful variable speed motors controlled by a foot pedal. Many different pottery books present well-illustrated instructions on the basics of wheel throwing.

CENTERING THE CLAY

After an appropriate-sized chunk of clay has been wedged, pat the clay into a smooth ball, or rounded cone shape, with a flattened bottom. Lightly moisten the wheel head and slap your chunk of clay onto the center of the wheel head. Pat it firmly in place. The idea is to get the ball of clay firmly stuck to the center of the potter's wheel. The next step takes some practice and developing a feel to get it right. Have a bucket of water at your side so you can regularly dip your hand into it to lubricate the interface between your hand and the clay. A small sponge is useful both for adding water to lubricate the clay or for soaking up excess water.

The object of centering is to use your hands to push against a spinning lump of clay until it is molded into a smooth mound of perfectly centered clay with almost no trace of wobble. The wheel should be spinning rapidly while centering clay. When learning to center, start with fairly soft clay. You will need to anchor and steady your arms as you center the clay. Pinching your elbows tight against your body or your upper legs can help brace them. Focus your attention not so much on pushing against the clay, but on holding your arms steady and "seeing" the clay as perfectly centered. Your body will make the necessary movements and compensations to center the clay. Bracing one hand against the side, bear forward and downward with the palm of your other hand, trying to smooth this lump into a hemispherical mound of clay perfectly centered on the wheel. If this action does not perfectly center your clay, place each hand on opposite sides of the mound and pinch the spinning clay to draw the mound up into a more elongated somewhat conical shape. Repeat the process of pushing down and drawing up until the mound is perfectly centered.

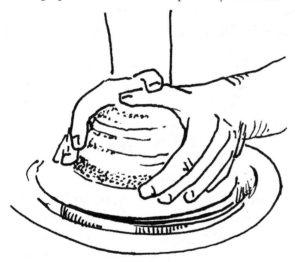

Figure 13-19. Centering the clay.

OPENING

Once the clay has been centered, the next step is "opening" the clay mass. Begin by flattening and pushing a dimple into the top of the spinning centered mound of clay. Brace your arms to keep the next motions steady and stable. Push your thumb or finger into this depression and continue driving downwards until it is about a half-inch above the wheel head, leaving enough thickness for the bottom wall of the pot plus a raised rim (foot) for the pot to stand on. You should now have a ring-shaped mound. Place your fingers in the center hole and cup the top of the ring with the palm of your hand(s) as you draw the ring downward and outward until it reaches an outer diameter that is slightly wider than the eventual base of your pot.

Figure 13-20. Opening the clay.

DRAWING UP THE WALLS OF A CYLINDER

During this stage, you will draw the thickened ring of clay into a tall, straight-walled cylinder. Do not try to neck or widen your pot toward its final form until it has been drawn into a uniform cylinder with a fairly thin wall. In the drawing process, one hand will be on the inside of the pot while the other hand is on the outside. Start at the bottom of your doughnut of centered clay. Exert an even squeezing pressure between the fingers of both hands. The clay will neck inwards between your fingers, creating a thickened ridge directly above your fingers. With the wheel spinning at moderate speed, continue exerting a steady squeezing pressure between the fingers of both hands as you draw this thickened ridge upward until your hands pass the top or the cylinder of clay. Repeat this process until you have transformed your low doughnut ring of clay into a uniform cylinder with the desired wall thickness. When the lip of your cylinder becomes uneven, insert a needle tool through the spinning wall to cut off the uneven lip. Thin wires and needle tools act like knives to cut clay, but do not adhere to the sticky clay as a knife would.

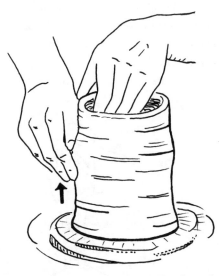

Figure 13-21. Drawing up the walls of a cylinder.

GIVING THE CYLINDER FORM

In this stage, you will either bow the wall of the spinning cylinder outwards, neck it inwards, or use a combination of both. Sometimes a wooden or metal rib helps to smooth the surface or provide support to the walls as you stretch the walls toward their final shape. A thin metal rib can be bent to match the desired outer curvature. Lubricate the walls as necessary with water, but avoid the use of too much water or taking too long since the walls may become overly softened and collapse. When you neck a wall inward, the wall will thicken and may need further drawing upwards to thin the wall back to the desired thickness. When the lip of your pot becomes uneven, insert a needle tool through the spinning wall to cut off the uneven lip.

Figure 13-22. Giving your cylinder form (collaring the neck).

Once the outer shape has its final form and the lip has been trimmed even, you may choose to thicken the lip, give it a decorative shape, or add a ridge to help trap a lid. Pour spouts for pitchers can be joined to the lip or formed from the existing lip. Handles and knobs are usually added after your pot has dried to the "leather hard" stage using the same techniques as for joining leather-hard slabs.

REMOVING THE POT FROM THE WHEEL

Using a wooden tool, with the wheel spinning slowly, trim excess clay from the perimeter of the base of your pot.

Figure 13-23. Trimming excess clay from the base.

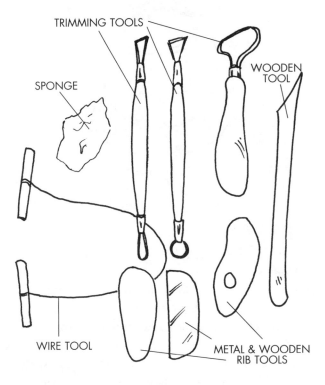

Figure 13-24. Basic pottery tools for throwing.

Using your sponge, dribble water on the wheel platter. With a taught wire or fishing line, cut the pot from the wheel head, drawing water under the pot as you slide the wire between the wheel head and the pot several times. With the side of your hand, slide the pot along the wheel head and onto a waiting tray to dry.

LIDS AND PLATES

Shallow lids and plates are thrown by opening up the mound of centered clay into a low, thick walled ring of clay. Push your palm against this clay, driving it to the inside shape of the shallow cover or plate. With your forearm or fist, flatten the clay and then use your fingers to give the lip a finished look. Once the plate has been drawn to near its final form, extra compression of the flat center with a rib tool helps to prevent cracking during firing or drying. Use a simple caliper to measure the lips of your pot and lid to ensure that they will fit well. The back of the plate or lid is trimmed into the pot after it has dried leather hard.

Figure 13-25. Measuring with simple calipers for proper fit.

PULLING A HANDLE

Pulled handles are popular due to their typically fluid graceful curves. Start with a thick rolled slug of moderately stiff, fine-grained clay (low on grog or other coarse tempering materials). Wet your hands and repeatedly draw the handle into a lengthened shape that is of the desired width and thickness. Stick the thick end of the pulled handle onto a shelf until it has dried enough to bend it into its final

form without slumping. Attach the handle to the pot. If the pot and handle have dried to the leather hard stage, first score the attachment areas and then cover the score marks with slip before attaching the handle. Smooth the joint with a wooden tool and small coils of clay for filler.

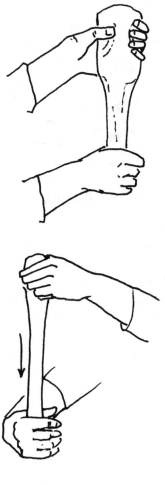

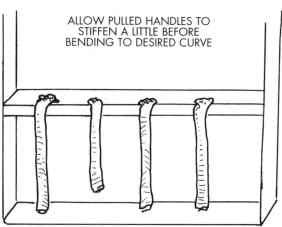

ALLOW PULLED HANDLES TO STIFFEN A LITTLE BEFORE BENDING TO DESIRED CURVE

Figure 13-26. Pulling a handle.

TRIMMING

After your pot has dried leather hard, flip it over onto its lip on top of the wheel head. Spin the wheel slowly and tap the pot to center it on the wheel. Once centered, attach it to the wheel with three or more pieces of soft clay. Using sharpened loops of flat steel wire attached to handles (trimming tools), gradually trim away excess clay from the base of the pot, and trim a raised lip ("foot") for the pot to rest upon. Do not leave thick walls at the base, or the pot will feel heavy and may explode when fired.

Figure 13-27. Trimming the base.

FIRING POTTERY

Until your greenware has been transformed into rock-hard pottery by extreme heat, it is very fragile and fairly useless. Pottery is often divided into three main categories—earthenware, stoneware, and porcelain. Earthenware is pottery that has been fired at a low temperature (below 2100°F or cone 1). It is usually porous, relatively soft, and red or brown in color. Stoneware is a type of clay body fired to temperatures where it becomes vitrified (glassy), dense and nonporous, but not translucent. Stonewares are typically fired between 2192° and 2419°F (cone 4 to 12) and are usually brown, but may be white. Porcelain is a translucent white clay body traditionally fired in the 2370° to 2640°F range (cone 9 to 13) (Speight 1999, 492–495). Firing earthenware is what we concentrate on here. Earthenware requires lower firing temperatures than either stoneware or porcelain. These lower temperatures are more easily achieved with crude technologies.

Greenware must be thoroughly dried before firing. Pottery handbooks usually describe firing temperatures in terms of "cone" numbers corresponding to carefully formulated pyrometric cones that soften and slump over when the kiln reaches specific temperatures. They are a mechanical sort of thermometer that indicates when a kiln firing has reached a specific temperature.

ABOVEGROUND FIRING

The simplest method of primitive firing, but also the one liable to lose the most pots to fracturing, is firing in an open bonfire. Place your greenware around the perimeter of a large pile of fuel and ignite the fuel. Once the fuel has burned to a bed of coals, place your preheated greenware upside down on top of the coals then carefully stack more fuel around and above the pots. At between 30 minutes and four hours, the pottery should blacken and appear to have sintered (hardened) and the firing is done. Either cover the pots with more fuel to generate reduction coloration effects, or simply allow the fire to burn out. Aboveground firing temperatures reach around 1085°F (cone 022) (Nigrosh 1980, 10).

PIT FIRING

Pit firing is a definite improvement over aboveground firing. The walls of the pit contain the fire and help to hold the heat in, making a rudimentary kiln. Start by digging a pit roughly 1½ to 3 feet deep by 2 to 5 feet in length and width. The extra dirt can be used to berm a raised rim around the pit. Line the bottom and sides of the pit with a layer of fuel such as kindling, corn cobs, or dried dung. Place the greenware on top of this layer and fill the spaces between the pots with more fuel. Finish with a layer of fuel on top of the pots, and then light the fuel on top. The fuel will slowly ignite downwards, ensuring that the pots are heated slowly. Once the fire is burning well, add more fuel until the pit is filled to the top with glowing coals. When the pots are glowing red, either allow the fire to burn out for oxidation colors or cover and smolder with wet leaves, straw, ashes, or dung for reduction effects. Open pit firing temperatures can reach 1285° to 1679°F (cone 018 to 09). You can increase the temperature of a pit firing by covering it. Build the downward or windward end of the pit wider to make a "fire mouth." Line the pit with fuel and then place your greenware on top of the fuel, starting a couple feet back from the fire mouth. Cover the pit with a nonflammable covering, such as corrugated sheet metal, leaving a small opening at the opposite end to act as a flue. Insulate this covering with dirt. Ignite the fuel in the pit and continue to stoke the fire from the fire mouth as the pit fuel burns to coals. Covered pit firing temperatures can exceed 1888°F (cone 05) in just a few hours (Nigrosh 1980, 11–14).

Primitive Kilns

To generate the higher temperatures required for stoneware or porcelain, or to protect the surface of glazed pots, a kiln must be constructed for firing the pottery. In the Southwest, Native Americans often fire pots in a sheet-metal box supported on bricks in a fire pit. A variation on this theme is the double-drum kiln of Figure 13-28.

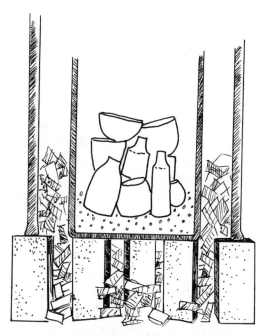

Figure 13-28. Double drum kiln.

Large multichamber kilns have been traditionally built into hillsides to take advantage of the natural upwards draft of hot air. The predecessors of these multichamber kilns were early Chinese and Japanese kilns dug into hillsides to channel hot air from a fire pit past the pottery.

Figure 13-29. Japanese snake kiln.

Hands in Clay contains numerous illustrations and descriptions for different kiln designs, but for the definitive book on kilns, ranging from ancient to modern, see *The Kiln Book: Materials, Specifications & Construction* by Frederick L. Olsen.

WATERPROOFING EARTHENWARE

Earthenware is naturally porous. Water will tend to seep through the walls of an earthenware jar, keeping the water cool by evaporative cooling, but eventually emptying the jar. Traditional unglazed jars were made waterproof by holding milk in them for several days, seasoning with vegetable oils, or coating with resinous materials such as pine pitch or bitumen. Probably from observing the natural glazing action occurring from wood ashes falling on pots during wood firings, it was discovered that a glassy material could be formed on the surface of pots. A typical ash glaze is formulated from about 40% ash, 40% feldspar, and 20% clay. The ash fluxes the clay and feldspar allowing them to melt into a glassy layer. Prepare ashes for glazes by soaking them in water to leach out the lye. Use rubber gloves and glasses to protect yourself from the caustic lye. Drain the water off and sieve the ashes before mixing with the other ingredients.

Most glazed pottery is fired twice. The first firing, referred to as a "bisque firing," fires unglazed greenware to a relatively low temperature (1661° to 1915°F, cone 010-05) to partially sinter the clay and to remove latent moisture and chemically combined water from the greenware. Liquid glazes adhere well to the porous surface of bisque fire pottery. Glazes are typically applied by dipping, pouring, brushing, or spraying. After the glaze has dried completely, glazed bisque pottery is fired a second time, usually at a higher temperature, to fuse the glaze into a glassy surface.

REFERENCES

The books on primitive survival skills listed in the *References* section of Chapter 4 offer some instructions for constructing rudimentary utensils and containers without the use of modern tools. The following references provide more detailed instructions to help you achieve a higher level of proficiency. The photographs, drawn from the best of modern and ancient artisans, are a great source of inspiration for their craft.

Baskets

Addicted to Baskets: 20 Original Baskets with Step-By-Step Instructions, **by Elizabeth Wheeler Clark.** 1997, 124 pp. (paperback), ISBN 0-9663737-0-7. Published by Griffin & Tilghman Publishing, 2605 Trent Road, New Bern, NC. Lists for $16.98.

This is an excellent beginner's introduction to basket weaving. It offers clear step-by-step instructions to get you started, including patterns, suggested tools, and materials. Patterns are for mostly basic baskets, with some intermediate ones.

The Basket Book: Over 30 Magnificent Baskets to Make and Enjoy, **by Lyn Siler.** 1988, 144 pp. (paperback), ISBN 0-8069-6830-3. Published by Sterling Publishing Company, 387 Park Avenue South, New York, NY 10016. Lists for $13.95.

Do you have a desire to make truly outstanding baskets? If you have patience and can pay attention to detail, the illustrations and instructions in this book will get you weaving baskets that are more than simply functional—they are truly works of art! Covers quite a variety of basket designs, ranging from simple to complex.

Gourds

The Complete Book of Gourd Craft: 25 projects, 55 Decorative Techniques, 300 Inspirational Designs, **by Ginger Summit and Jim Widess.** 1996, 144 pp. (paperback), ISBN 1-887374-55-8. Published by Lark Books, 50 College Street, Asheville, NC 28801. Lists for $18.95.

I never knew that gourds could be crafted into such an incredible array of beautiful, functional items. This book is a visual treat. In addition to providing excellent instructions for crafting gourds into useful and artful products, it displays hundreds of color photos of inspirational designs.

Ceramics

Hands in Clay, **by Charlotte F. Speight and John Toki.** 1999, 518 pp. (paperback), ISBN 0-7674-0501-3. Published by Mayfield Publishing Co., 1280 Villa Street, Mountain View, CA 94041. Lists for $43.95.

My college ceramics instructor, now head of the department at Cabrillo College, has adopted *Hands in Clay* as the main classroom text. This is a terrific comprehensive guide to ceramics. It covers the history of ceramics, excellent instructions for basic through advanced techniques, materials, tools and recipes. *Hands in Clay* is graced with hundreds of photographs for instruction and artistic inspiration.

Low Fire: Other Ways to Work in Clay, **by Leon I. Nigrosh.** 1980, 101 pp. (hardcover), ISBN 0-87192-120-0. Published by Davis Publications, Inc., 50 Portland Street, Worcester, MA 01608. Lists for $17.95.

This classic text is still in print. Of all the ceramic books that I reviewed, it is still the best introduction to a variety of low-fire methods and materials, particularly applicable to low-tech ceramics.

Wood-Fired Stoneware and Porcelain, **by Jack Troy.** 1995, 174 pp. (hardcover), ISBN 0-8019-8484-X. Published by Krause Publications, 700 E. State Street, Iola, WI 54945. Lists for $34.95.

If you have a desire to produce high quality, wood-fired stoneware or porcelain, this is the book for you. Contains a nice mixture of photos of inspirational works and actual wood-fired kilns from around the world.

The Kiln Book: Materials, Specifications & Construction, **by Frederick L. Olsen.** 1983, 291 pp. (hardcover), ISBN 0-8019-7071-7 Published by Krause Publications, 700 E. State Street, Iola, WI 54945. Lists for $40.00.

Still the definitive book on kiln construction. *The Kiln Book* covers everything from classic wood fired kilns to modern gas and electric kilns. Shows you how to build and operate kilns from scratch.

XIV Better Living Through Low-Tech Chemistry

Only a few decades ago most people used their own formulas to perform useful and essential tasks, inside the house and out. Every home was a workshop, a chemical laboratory, a factory, and a pharmacy. Today that rich culture of largely pure, organic remedies has been replaced by the huge pre-packaged store-bought formula business. But the convenience of buying premixed, premade potions has a high cost: preservatives, some of them harmful, are added to keep products fresh throughout shelf life; packaging creates litter and raises the product price; and perhaps most important, knowledge is lost.

—Paula Dreifus Bakule, editor of *Rodale's Book of Practical Formulas*

This chapter provides a basic introduction to a few old-fashioned recipes, procedures, and apparatus for making useful household products. These are the little things that we take for granted in our society—items like soap, ointments, glue, and cooking oils. They are simple items that make our lives a lot more pleasant than they would be without them, yet most of us don't have the foggiest idea how to make any of these products on our own.

For thousands of years, humankind has sought to extract, refine, or otherwise modify the chemical nature of natural materials. Who knows when humans first discovered that natural fermentation of vegetable and fruit sugars would produce alcohol? Certainly the practice of turning grape juice into wine was well established by early biblical times. The ancient practice of making soap from goat tallow and lye is described on 4,500-year-old Sumerian clay tablets. More than 5,000 years ago, ancient Greek and Chinese metallurgists were smelting, purifying, and alloying different metals to make bronze. In some cases, humankind has taken advantage of

nature's own chemical processors, such as the silkworm that eats the leaves of mulberry trees and then spins a cocoon of remarkably strong, yet luxuriously soft, organic polymer.

SOAP

There is something inherently satisfying about making soap. Maybe it relates to the 4,500+ year history of human soap making; maybe it simply reflects a desire to keep the jungle at bay and put our stamp on our personal environment. For pioneer women, soap making was an annual event, often lasting for days while lye was leached from wood ashes saved from the winter fires and then cooked with fat as the spring thaw began.

—Dr. Robert S. McDaniel, *Essentially Soap*

Soaps and detergents are both known as *surfactants*. Surfactants reduce the surface tension of water, causing the water to fully wet both the object to be cleaned and the debris, encouraging the debris to wash away. According to Susan Miller Cavitch, author of *The Soapmaker's Companion*, soap molecules also have a distinct head and tail, one end having an attraction to water and the other end having an attraction to dirt. This property helps soap molecules to connect the dirt to the water, further enabling the water to wash away the dirt.

Soapy Plants

There are a number of plants that can be used as a substitute for soap without any chemical processing. These plants contain naturally occurring soap-like substances, called saponins. Bouncing bet (also called soapwort), clematis, and yucca are three common North American plants with significant saponin content. It has been said that Native Americans bathed regularly and were often appalled by the smell of white pioneer men. To use any of these plants for soap, chop up the appropriate part of the plant and rub it between your hands with some water or dry it for future use. Before trying a full dose on your body, test for allergic reactions by rubbing a bit onto the inside of your wrist and waiting one day to make sure there is no adverse reaction. Because saponins are somewhat poisonous, and Native Americans have used them to paralyze fish, you do not want to eat these plants, except perhaps for the edible fruits and flowers of the yucca family (Brill 1994, 134).

BOUNCING BET

Do not use bouncing bet on your face, because it is very irritating to the eyes. Collect bouncing bet in the late summer to fall. Found nationwide, it is easiest to identify by its pretty white or pink flowers with five petals. You can use the entire plant (Blankenship and Blankenship 1996, 142).

Figure 14-1. Bouncing bet. Illustration courtesy of *Earth Knack: Stone Age Skills for the 21st Century* by Bart and Robin Blankenship (Gibbs Smith, 1996).

CLEMATIS

Clematis is a common climbing vine with white or purple flowers, and is often found dominating the tops of trees. Collect the leaves and flowers for use as soap (Blankenship and Blankenship 1996, 142).

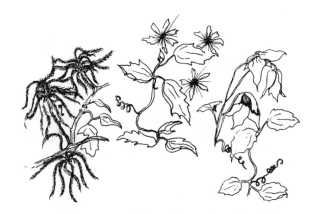

Figure 14-2. Clematis. Illustration courtesy of *Earth Knack: Stone Age Skills for the 21st Century* by Bart and Robin Blankenship (Gibbs Smith, 1996).

YUCCA, AGAVE, SPANISH BAYONET, SOTOL, AND JOSHUA TREE

These traditional desert-dwelling plants also contain saponins. The root contains the most saponins, but use of the root kills the plant, so please don't use this plant frivolously. If you are pounding and soaking the leaves for fiber to make cordage, the soaking water will contain sufficient saponins for bathing (Blankenship and Blankenship 1996, 143).

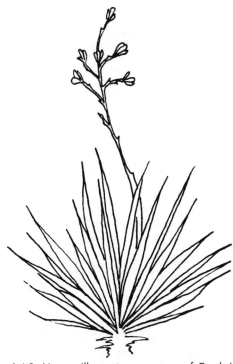

Figure 14-3. Yucca. Illustration courtesy of *Earth Knack: Stone Age Skills for the 21st Century* by Bart and Robin Blankenship (Gibbs Smith, 1996).

Lye Soap

Most of the specialty soaps that you find in trendy gift shops and bath stores are made from a mixture of lye and vegetable oils combined with scenting ingredients and perhaps a few additives, such as ground oatmeal or clay. Soap making is a chemical process, called saponification, that combines a caustic watery liquid (lye) with warm fats and considerable agitation to encourage their chemical reaction. Making lye soap with modern processed ingredients from your local supermarket or craft store is an easy, satisfying, present-day pastime, but due to the dangers of lye burns it's not a proper craft for kids. If you wish to explore the wonderful world of cottage industry soap making, the recommended references will give you plenty of recipes to keep you busy for a few years.

For our pioneering ancestors, the process of extracting lye from hardwood ash and rendering tallow from animal fat was considerably more difficult and involved than the modern-day equivalent. The spring soap making process was usually a multi-day affair.

> **CAUTION: Lye is poisonous and very caustic. See the following section for guidelines to deal with lye.**

Lye, also known by the chemical name *sodium hydroxide*, was originally derived from hardwood ashes, but is now made by a chemical process starting with plain salt. When soap is made properly, all of the lye is chemically combined with animal or vegetable fats, leaving no trace of lye in the finished process. A quick test for homemade soap is to cut the soap and taste the cut with your tongue. If the soap has a "bite" to it (makes the tongue tingle), it contains some pockets of lye and may be suitable for use on clothes and floors, but will probably burn your skin and eyes. You can "rebatch" soap with excess lye by melting it in a double boiler and adding more fat as necessary to react with all remaining traces of lye.

If you use purchased lye, it should be pure sodium hydroxide without aluminum or other drain-cleaning additives. Squeeze and shake the container to make sure that the lye granules have not solidified into an unusable solid chunk. If you don't use the entire container, cover it tightly or the lye will absorb moisture from the air and become useless. Some lye containers include a recipe for soap on the label.

COLD PROCESS SOAP

Most modern soap making books focus on the "cold process" for soap making. This name is a bit misleading, because you start by preheating the fats, but it distinguishes this process from traditional soap making with homemade lye, which requires cooking the soap solution for a considerable period of time to thicken the solution and encourage saponification. The cold process used in most modern soap making recipes requires store-bought lye and eliminates the need for the long cooking stage. Accurate measurements are one of the keys to success. If the ratio of lye to fat is too high, not all of the lye will react and you will get a soap that burns the skin and eyes. If there is more than enough fat to react with all of the lye, the condition is known as "superfat." Too much superfat and your soap will be greasy, will not clean well, and the excess fats may turn rancid over time. Susan Miller Cavitch likes to calculate lye content in her soap recipes at 10% below the theoretical amount required to fully react with the fat content. This guarantees enough fat to fully react with all of the lye and leaves a modest superfat safety margin. To prevent the excess fat from turning rancid, Susan recommends using grapefruit seed extract (available at health food stores and from craft suppliers) to preserve the soap.

Equipment

Lye is caustic and will react with (corrode) most metals. The lye solution should be mixed in a clear glass Pyrex-type container, with plenty of extra room for mixing. Plastic will do only if it is microwave safe, because the lye solution will get very hot. Wood containers are suitable, but will absorb lye and should not be used for anything else once contaminated with lye. Stainless steel is the preferred material for the soap pot, but enameled iron, Pyrex, or ceramic pots will do. In the old days, soap was usually made in cast iron pots, which corroded slightly and contributed rust, giving the bars of soap a reddish-brown color. *Do not* use aluminum, copper, or tin pots! Stirrers and dippers can be made of wood, heat resistant plastic, or stainless steel. An accurate scale and measuring cup are important for getting the best results. Rubber spatulas are helpful for getting the last bit of soap out of the pot. A floating stainless steel dairy thermometer is recommended for accurate temperature measurements. Goggles, safety glasses, and/or a face shield are important to protect your eyes from lye splashes. Keep a cup of vinegar on hand as a safety precaution for instantly neutralizing any lye splashes. Use rubber gloves and an apron to protect your hands and clothing.

Molds

Prepare your mold(s) and workspace ahead of time. A cardboard box lined with wax paper makes a good mold for a batch of soap. When the soap is semi-hard, it can be easily cut into individual bars. Milk cartons, PVC pipe, Tupperware, or small candle molds can also work well. When you pour your soap, it will be hot, but the saponification process may require continued warmth to complete the curing of the soap. If you choose to pour your soap into small molds, you may want to insulate the molds or otherwise keep them warm for a day or two to assist with the curing process.

Fats

Weigh or measure fats and oils per your recipe, and then add them to the pot and heat to the desired soap making temperature. Each soap making book gives a different recommended temperature, so it probably is not very critical. Robert McDaniel recommends heating the fats to around 140°F. Susan Miller Cavitch recommends 80° to 100°F for most of her recipes (she says she has tried numerous temperatures and they all worked). Carla Emery recommends vegetable oils at 110° to 115°F; bear and goose fats at 115°F; pork at 120°F; and beef, deer, and sheep at 130°F. Take your pick!

A Note on Water

The water used should be soft. Your tap water may be fine, but excessive dissolved minerals will hamper the soap making process by combining with the lye. The use of rainwater, distilled water, or deionized water (run through a reverse osmosis filter) will avoid any potential problems due to hard water.

Lye Solution

Measure the water (room temperature, never hot) and add to the glass container for dissolving lye. In a well-ventilated area, carefully weigh the lye granules and slowly add to the water.

> **CAUTION: Always add lye to water, not the other way around, and always use eye protection. An eye blinded by lye is an ugly sight, reminiscent of a cheap horror movie.**

Use a stovetop fan and/or plenty of ventilation to avoid breathing the fumes. Stir until solution is completely dissolved and clear. Solution will get very hot as the lye dissolves in the water, which is why you never start with hot water (it could boil over).

Add Lye to Oils

Some like to cool the lye solution to 80° to 100°F before adding to the warm fats, but McDaniel simply adds it once it is fully dissolved and clear. Wearing goggles and gloves, pour your lye solution into the fat, taking care to not splash any of the solution. Stir the mixture. You can add borax and most colorants at this point, but you probably should wait to add scents and essential oils. Continue stirring the solution until it becomes soap. This usually happens within 30 minutes, but could take 5 minutes to several hours, depending on temperatures and ingredients. The solution will thicken and become opaque as the soap crystals form. When it reaches the stage where the oil and lye are fully emulsified (no longer separated into oil and lye) and it "traces," it is ready to pour. "Trace" is described as the stage when some of the soap mixture drizzled off a spoon back into the soap pot leaves a "trace" of an image for a second or two before blending back into the pot.

Pouring

Add fragrance, herbs, colorants, and so on. Stir well and pour into molds.

Initial Cure

Cover the molds and keep warm for a day or two to assist with further saponification.

De-Molding and Bars

If you molded a large block in a carton, once it is partially hardened you can cut it into bars with a taught wire or knife. Molds can be dipped in hot water to help you get the soap out of the mold. Rest the soap on waxed paper until it is firm and somewhat dry.

Final Cure

Rest the soaps on paper bags, wicker, and so on in a warm well-ventilated place for two to four weeks, turning once, until the soap is fully cured. Wrap completely cured soap as you wish.

> *CAUTION: If a white powdery film appears, you may have some unreacted lye in your soap.*

LAUNDRY SOAP

The addition of borax to soap will enhance its cleansing properties, especially in areas with hard water. In a primitive situation, unless you happen to be near Death Valley or another salt flat, I guess you will be out of luck on this one.

Use the cold process to make your soap with 11 cups of water, 9 cups of rendered fat, and 1 can (18 oz.) of pure lye. In the curing stage, cure the soap in a vat, stirring occasionally for a few days, breaking chunks of soap with a potato masher or mallet. After 2 or 3 days, the soap should be a dry crumbly mass. When completely dry, grate or mash the soap and mix with 2 cups of borax (Rodale 1991, 272).

SIMPLE SOAP

Use 6 pounds of melted tallow (rendered fat), 5 cups of water, and one can (18 oz.) of lye. Make according to the cold process. (Emery 1994, 600).

SOFT SOAP WITH HOMEMADE LYE

In a soap kettle, mix 8 pounds of melted fat with 18 quarts of lye solution (strong enough to float an egg). Bring this mixture to a boil, and then pour into a barrel. Store the barrel in a warm area. It should be ready in a few weeks. Alternately, keep boiling the solution until completely saponified. Put a drop on a cool plate to test for clarity and saponification. If clear when cooled, the soap is done. If too much grease, the drop of soap will be weak and gray. If too much lye, a gray skin will spread over the soap drop. Taste test for "bite" (a drop tingles on the tongue), which indicates too much lye. Correct batch with additional lye or fat, as indicated by the tests (Hobson 1974, 14).

DR. BOB'S BASIC THREE-OIL SOAP

This is a simple soap made with readily available oils found in grocery stores. The coconut oil gives this soap a rich foamy lather. Use 26½ ounces of coconut oil (usually hard at room temperature), 26½ ounces olive oil, 31¾ ounces of shortening, and 12 ounces of lye. Make according to the cold process. (McDaniel 2000, 85).

Lye Precautions

- Lye is a caustic substance that is highly poisonous and burns the skin and eyes on contact.
- Keep lye out of reach of children and animals. Clearly label containers as **POISON**.
- Never mix lye with hot water or hot oil; splattering may occur.
- Keep poison control number handy when working with lye. If ingested, lye will burn the throat and may be fatal. Do not induce vomiting. Drink milk or eat ice cream to help neutralize the lye's action. Do not take vinegar or orange juice, as the reaction with the lye will generate heat and may further burn the stomach. Seek medical attention immediately.
- If splashed with lye, flush eyes immediately with copious quantities of water for 15 minutes. Seek immediate medical attention.
- Always add lye to water, not the other way around.
- Only mix lye with water in well-ventilated areas. **Do not breath the fumes!**
- Wear rubber gloves and goggles when working with lye. Use of a face shield is a good idea.
- When working with lye, keep a cup of vinegar handy to neutralize any splashes on skin, and then flush with water. Keep newspapers on hand to sop up spills.
- Dispose of lye properly. Small amounts (less than ½ cup) can be poured down the drain with

copious amounts of water. Lye can be neutralized with vinegar.

CAUTION: This reaction may release considerable heat.

- Use lye in glass (preferably Pyrex to take the heat), ceramic, stainless steel, or enameled iron containers. Never mix lye in aluminum, copper, or tin containers.

MAKING LYE FROM ASHES

You can make your own lye solution the way the pioneers did. For your leaching container, use a plastic bucket with a bottom turn spout or an old-fashioned wooden barrel. Lye will corrode metals. Over time, it will even corrode most stainless steels, though to a lesser degree. If you have a barrel, drill a hole in the bottom of a size that you can plug with a cork or tapered wooden plug, and cover the hole with a few rocks. Line the bottom of the bucket or barrel with a few inches of straw or sand to strain the ashes out of the lye solution. Fill the bucket with ashes from hardwoods, and then cover with rainwater or soft water. Unless you have no other choice, don't bother with softwood ashes, such as those from pines and firs, because they make a much weaker lye solution. Once the water begins to flow from the tap, plug the leaching barrel and let it soak for a few days. Drain the lye into a wooden, glass, enameled iron, or ceramic container.

Test the lye for strength by floating a raw egg or potato in the solution (crude specific gravity test). If the egg sinks, the solution is too weak and must be either run through ashes again or boiled down to increase its concentration. The egg should float with roughly a quarter-sized area showing above the lye. If a large amount of the egg floats above the lye, dilute the solution with water until the egg floats properly.

MAKING SOAP WITH HOMEMADE LYE

It takes experience to determine how much homemade lye to use with rendered fat (usually tallow or lard) to make soap. Traditionally, the fat and lye were boiled together in a pot until the mixture formed a thick frothy mass that didn't "bite" when a small amount was placed on the tongue. Homemade lye is primarily a potassium-based alkali that tends to make a softer soap than those made with sodium-based lye, which is made by the LeBlanc chemical process discovered in the nineteenth century. Soft lye soaps were stored in vats and barrels until needed. To make hard soap from soft lye soap, the soft soap was boiled longer and a considerable amount of salt was added to the pot. This removed more moisture from the soap mixture and turned some of the potassium-based soft soap into a layer of sodium-based soap that hardened into a cake on top of the soap pot. Most settlers left their soap soft, because salt was hard to get and was needed more for curing food and feeding to livestock than for hardening soap. When you have the proper lye-to-fat ratio, hard soaps will cut into a smooth curl of soap when shaved with a knife. Excess lye in the soap makes a coarse soap that bites the tongue and crumbles when cut into a shaving.

RENDERING FAT FOR SOAP AND CANDLES

The rendering process removes impurities and traces of meat from fats, making them suitable for use in soap and candle making. Rendered beef fat is known as tallow and rendered pig fat is called lard. When made with store-bought lye, tallow makes a hard soap without much lather. Sheep and goat fat makes the hardest soaps. Lard makes a soft, creamy bar of soap. You can mix different fats together to custom tailor the qualities of your soap (see recommended references). For example, the addition of coconut oil makes for a rich foamy lather. Grease collected from cooking can also be rendered, though it may retain undesirable odors.

Rendering is an odorous process best done outdoors or under a strong vented hood. Melt the fat in a large pot with somewhere between 1 quart of water for every 10 pounds of fat ranging to equal amounts of fat and water. Adding 3 tablespoons of salt for every pound of fat seems to help the process. Boil the fat for about half an hour, and then cool to room temperature. Either skim the fat off the top and strain it into another container or refrigerate to harden the fat layer. Scrape the crud off the bottom of the hardened fat layer. Your soap and candles won't smell much better than your fat, so you might want to repeat this process two or three times. When repeating the process, replace the salt with 2 to 3 tablespoons of baking soda per pound of fat to improve the smell (McDaniel 2000, 82). Rancid fat is no longer any good for food but can be used for soap or candles. Boil rancid fat in a mixture of five parts water to one part vinegar. Use 1 quart of liquid for each gallon of fat and repeat the process until you are satisfied with the fat purity (Emery 1994, 597).

CANDLES

Lamps and candles have lit the night for humankind throughout the ages. Eskimos extended the extremely short (or nonexistent) arctic winter's day with soapstone lamps that burned oil and fat rendered from the animals they hunted. Beeswax makes wonderful natural candles that smell great and burn slowly, but the scarcity of beeswax makes for costly candles. In the past, most common folk settled for candles made from tallow, which burns quicker and doesn't smell as nice. Of the common farm animal fats, mutton (sheep) is best for candles, followed by beef tallow. Pork lard is rather smelly and burns with a thick smoke.

Before the advent of braided wicking, old-fashioned candle snuffers were used to keep wicks trimmed to about a ½" length to prevent wicks from smoking excessively as the candle burned down. A candle snuffer looks like a pair of scissors with a small cup attached to catch the burning pieces of trimmed wicks. Sometime in the 1800s, someone figured out that a braided wick would tend to curl to the side, burning the excess wick length as the candle burned lower, eliminating the need for a candle snuffer.

Wicking

A fast-burning, easy-to-make candle substitute is a "rush light." To make a rush light, first strip the skin from mature rushes (cattails), and then dip the pulpy core in melted tallow. Cool and dip again to thicken the tallow layer. Carla Emery says that you can also roll dried mullein leaves and dip these in melted fat to make primitive candles. You can make your own wicks from pieces of cotton string or hand spin and braid wicks out of hemp, dogbane, milkweed, cotton, and so on (see Chapter 4 section on cordage). Wicks that are too thick will smoke excessively. Wicks that are too thin will burn a craterlike depression in the candle and drown themselves in melted wax.

Soaking wicks in a "mordant" solution before making them into candles promotes proper burning. There are numerous mordant formulas. Betty Oppenheimer, author of *The Candlemaker's Companion*, has used a mordant formula consisting of one part common table salt, two parts borax, and ten parts water. Carla Emery suggests soaking wicks in lime water, vinegar, saltpeter, or a mixture of lime water and saltpeter. Phyllis Hobson recommends the following mordants: turpentine; 2 ounces of borax, 1 ounce of lime chloride, 1 ounce of ammonia chloride, and 1 ounce of saltpeter dissolved in 3 quarts of water; or ½ pound of lime and 2 ounces of saltpeter dissolved in 1 gallon of water. Allow wicks to dry before dipping in wax or tallow. Machine-made commercial wicks generally yield far more consistent and superior results than most homemade ones.

Making Candles

Homemade candles are usually hand-dipped, rolled, or molded. Hand-dipped candles are made by dipping a wick repeatedly into a pot of melted candle wax (keep it just above the melting point) building the candle layer by layer. If you wish to make many candles, it is best to attach a number of wicks to a rod or rack for simultaneous dipping. The use of molds considerably speeds the process of making tallow candles, but sticky beeswax candles can be hard to get out of molds. Rolled candles were made by pouring melted wax onto a wick on a flat surface. The melted wax spreads out to a thin layer, and then it's hand rolled into a candle while the wax is still warm and pliable.

Figure 14-4. Dipping candles.

In the 1800s, a process was developed to refine tallow with alkali and sulfuric acid to produce stearin. Stearin is a hard nongreasy substance that is mixed with molten tallow, at about a 1:9 ratio, to make a tallow candle that is harder, burns longer, and does not give off the usual smoke and unpleasant odors of ordinary tallow. To make your own stearin, melt tallow in a glass or enameled iron pot and stir in 3 ounces of slaked lime for each 1¼ pounds of tallow. Boil over low heat until a thick substance forms (lime soap). Add 4 ounces of concentrated sulfuric acid for each 1¼ pounds of tallow and stir until the fat separates. When cool, remove the solid cake of stearin and melt over low heat, stirring constantly until all the remaining moisture is evaporated out of the stearin (Hobson 1974, 39).

> **CAUTION: Sulfuric acid is very dangerous and can cause severe burns. Dispose of properly!**

I'm not quite sure if stearic acid and stearin are the same thing or just closely related. Stearic acid is a dry, flaked, or powdered material that is mixed into melted tallow or paraffin to harden the wax and make a better burning candle. Stearic acid is available from suppliers of candle-making materials.

Paraffin is a wax made from refined petroleum. It is much cheaper than beeswax and makes good candles when mixed with stearic acid. Betty Oppenheimer likes to use about 15 percent stearic acid in her paraffin candles. *Wagner's Chemical Technology* (see *References* section) has a detailed section on stearin, candles, and other forms of artificial lighting, but most of the chemistry and processes are beyond the scope of this book.

In a primitive situation, unless you happen to be a chemical engineer, you will probably have to settle for tallow candles with perhaps a little beeswax mixed in. Even small amounts of beeswax will improve a tallow candle, although a half-and-half mixture of tallow and beeswax makes a superior all-natural candle. If you happen to live in an area with bayberry plants, you can extract candle wax from the sage-green-colored bayberries by boiling in water and skimming the wax from the pot. One pioneer-era recipe for candles was to boil 5 pounds of alum in 10 gallons of water until dissolved, and then add 20 pounds of tallow and boil for another hour. The wax was skimmed off the top and strained through muslin into candle molds or pots for dipping candles (Emery 1994, 38). I'm not quite sure how you would make alum in primitive conditions, but *Wagner's Chemical Technology* might give you a good start.

ALCOHOL

Even with all the chemical wizardry of modern science, the easiest way to make alcohol is to promote the actions of naturally occurring, microscopic, single-celled fungi, called yeast, which digest simple sugars and turn them into alcohol and carbon dioxide through a process called fermentation. When you drink an alcoholic beverage, you are consuming the excrement of yeast—how does that grab you? Alcohol is more than just a mind- and mood-altering substance, it is also a valuable fuel, preservative, antiseptic, and a powerful agent for extracting essential oils and other valuable compounds from medicinal and pungent plants (see herbal section of Chapter 9). Alcohol possesses the properties for dissolving a large number of materials that are not water soluble, making it an important solvent for many different chemical reactions and extractions. With minor carburetor modifications, you can run any carbureted gasoline engine on alcohol. The fumes from evaporated alcohol are not as toxic as evaporated kerosene; it also burns cleaner, making alcohol lamps a relatively clean source of artificial light. Used in a homemade blowpipe, alcohol provides a concentrated heat source for soldering metals or blowing small pieces of glass tubing into useful shapes.

The maximum concentration of alcohol in a fermented solution is about 12 percent (24 proof). At this concentration, the alcohol kills the yeast and stops the alcohol-making process. To obtain higher concentrations of alcohol, fermented alcohol-bearing solutions are "distilled." An alcohol still takes advantage of the fact that alcohol boils at a lower temperature than water. In the still "kettle," an alcohol-bearing fermented liquid is heated to the boiling point. At this elevated temperature alcohol and some water is evaporated from the liquid, and then these vapors are piped to a cooled coil where they are condensed back into a liquid containing a much higher concentration of alcohol. At the start of the process, the vapors contain mostly alcohol, but as most of the alcohol gets boiled out of the kettle, the concentration of water in the vapors increases.

Due primarily to its commercial value and secondarily to its social influences, alcohol production and distillation has a long and somewhat messy history of being controlled by government via taxes and regulatory laws. If you wish to distill ethyl alcohol (grain alcohol) for fuel, I encourage you to apply to the Bureau of Alcohol, Tobacco and Firearms (ATF) for a free permit. It is a serious legal offense to distill alcohol without a permit, but since the energy crisis of the 1970s, it has become very easy to obtain a permit to distill alcohol for personal use as a fuel. In the following sections, I outline the alcohol-making process, from malting through fermentation to distillation. If you wish to pursue the distillation of alcohol, I suggest that you look to the recommended references for more details that will improve your chances for a safe and successful venture.

Malt

Yeast requires simple sugars to create alcohol. The juices of sweet fruits, such as grapes and apricots, can be directly fermented with no further processing. Before fermentation, starchy roots (potatoes, etc.) and grains must be processed to convert starches into sugars. Malting is the process of sprouting grain, which converts grain starches into sugars. Enzymes in the malted grain will also act on the starches in unmalted grains and roots (called the "adjunct"), converting their starches into sugars. Barley is the most common grain for malting, providing superior malt with good flavor, but any other whole grain can be malted through the same process. You can purchase barley malt or make your own.

The first step in malting is to soak the grain in water. Fill the basin to a level about 6" above the grain and soak for at least 24 hours until the grains are soft to the core and easily crushed. Change the water whenever it starts to smell foul. At this point you want to avoid fermentation. When fully softened, drain the water from the grain. The grain requires dampness and warmth to sprout. You can sprout the grain in screened sprouting trays or in piles on a clean floor. If using sprouting trays, pile soaked grain in each tray about 1½" deep. Stack trays and twice daily sprinkle water onto the top tray to trickle down and rinse all the trays. Once a day, rotate the bottom tray to the top (Gingery 1994, 18). If you are sprouting your grain on the floor, spread it into a layer a few inches thick and partially dry the grain for a few hours, and then pile it into a heap until it is warm to the touch (12 to 24 hours). Spread the grain into a layer 8 to 20 inches thick (the "wet couch") and turn every 6 to 8 hours to keep evenly moist and warm (Wright 1994, 106). If the small white sprouts begin to lose their shiny white appearance, sprinkle the grain with more water. The grain is ready when the sprouts are roughly equal in length to the long dimension of the grain.

Next you must dry the sprouted grain. A food dehydrator works best, but malt can also be dried in any clean well-ventilated area. Spread the grain on a clean floor and turn it often until dried. Shake the dried grain in a burlap bag to knock the sprouts off the grain, and then sift the sprouts out of the grain by shaking in screened trays. The dried sprouted grain is now called malt and is stored whole until ready for use. You can crush or grind malt into coarse meal a day or two before use.

Mash

Mashing converts all the starches in the grain or vegetable matter into sugars. All home distillers have their own special recipes for mashing and fermentation, so I will just give you a quick summary of one process. The process is typically altered a bit to optimize for different grains or vegetables. In *The Secrets of Building an Alcohol-Producing Still*, Vince Gingery provides a detailed recipe for corn mash and offers several old moonshiners' tips for dealing with primitive conditions and grains. *Practical Distiller* offers tips and recipes for quite a variety of spirits. *Distillation of Alcohol & De-Naturing* provides good tips and recipes for mashes and ferments of grains, potatoes, and beets. According to the *Practical Distiller*, the usual proportions are one part malt for every four to seven parts of adjunct (unmalted coarsely ground grain), and 18 gallons of water for every bushel of adjunct/malt mixture (9:4 ratio).

FIRST STAGE

This is the premalt stage. Two different enzymes in the malt, protease and diastase, change the chemical structure of the mash. Diastase is the enzyme that converts starches into sugars. Protease is the enzyme that digests proteins and converts them into nutrients that the yeast feed on during fermentation, and operates best around 122°F. Both protease and diastase work together in the premalt stage. While the protease breaks down the proteins, the diastase helps the mash to liquefy by converting the sticky starches into sugars.

Take about one quarter of the water to be used and add it to the mash pot (or tub). Heat the water to between 130° and 140°F and add all of the adjunct and about one-fourth of the malt, stirring constantly to break up lumps and cakes of grain. Try to keep the temperature between 122° and 130°F for 30 minutes until the mash starts to thin and liquefy.

Do not allow the temperature to drop below 120°F (the solution may turn to vinegar).

SECOND STAGE

This is the gelatinization stage. Starch granules are covered by a protective cellulosic wall and are not easily reached by the diastase unless that wall is broken down. In this stage, the solution is cooked to break down the cellulose. Slowly raise the temperature to the boiling point. When the mash gets hot and thickens, you can thin it with another one-fourth of the total water. Hold the temperature at boiling for about 15 minutes to break down the cellulose. Allow to cool to 155°F.

THIRD STAGE

This is the saccharifying stage that converts the remaining starches into sugars. Temperature is critical in this stage. The diastase works best at 155°F. Its action is greatly reduced below 150°F and totally stops above 170°F. Add the rest of the malt (three-fourths of the full amount) to the mash solution. Preheat the rest of your water to 170°F for rinse water. Let the mash stand for a couple of hours until saccharification is complete. Saccharification is complete when the mash loses its mealy white look and turns dark brown, becomes thin and easily stirred, tastes sweet, and smells like fresh bread. If you remove a bit of mash and add a drop of iodine, it will turn purple if any starch is still present (you may not be able to get rid of all the starch). Heat the mash to 170°F to halt the enzyme action, and then strain the liquid from the mash into a vat (or large jars). Rinse the strained mash thoroughly with the hot rinse water and add the rinse to the vat. This strained solution is called the "wort." The strained mash makes great chicken feed or compost. Loosely cover the wort vat and let it cool to around 80°F.

Fermentation

The next step is to ferment the solution. In the old days, fermentation relied on hit-or-miss luck from airborne yeasts, resulting in a significant number of batches being spoiled by undesirable airborne organisms. By reserving a portion of mix from batches that fermented well, you get a more reliable starter for new batches. Cool the wort to 80°F and add either a starter batch of yeast or straight brewers yeast. To "proof" the yeast, I recommend beginning a starter batch about a day before the wort is ready for fermentation. Dissolve a tablespoon of sugar and a packet of wine or beer yeast (or brewer's yeast) in a couple cups of warm (about 80°F) sweet juice. Cover loosely and place in a warm spot for several hours, until very foamy. Cool another couple cups of wort to 80°F and add, along with another tablespoon of sugar, to the starter. After another few hours, the starter should be very frothy and ready to "pitch" (throw into the wort vat).

Cleanliness is very important, because undesirable microorganisms can spoil the wort by turning it into vinegar or causing it to putrefy. It is a good idea to sanitize vats, containers, and any utensils that might contact the ferment with a solution of 2 cups of liquid chlorine bleach mixed in 5 gallons of water. The ferment should be kept around 80°F, but no hotter than 85°F and no cooler than 65°F. As the yeast making process continues, the ferment will get very foamy, emit a hissing sound, and form a crusty yeast layer on the top surface. When the fermenting process is coming to a close, the hissing sound ceases and the fluid starts to clear. The yeast layer is skimmed and the fluid is immediately run into the still for distillation. The fermented liquid is called the "wash." When the vinous fermentation is complete, the yeasty crust will sink to the bottom, and the bacterial process of turning the alcohol into vinegar will begin. If unchecked, you will end up with vinegar instead of alcohol.

Distillation

The equipment for distillation ranges from crude moonshine stills to very sophisticated equipment designed for commercial alcohol production. A simple still is shown in Figure 14-5. The boiler (A),

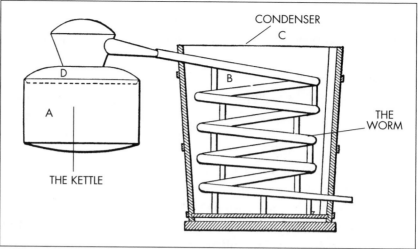

Figure 14-5. Simple still. Illustration courtesy of *Distillation of Alcohol & De-Naturing* by F. B. Wright (Lindsay Publications, 1994).

also known as the "kettle," is equipped with a snug-fitting cover (D) that allows for cleaning and charging between uses. To prevent the loss of steam, the joint between the cover and kettle is sealed with a packing of moist flour mixed with a little salt. A mixture of alcohol and water vapors flows into the "worm" (B) where it is condensed back into a liquid. The worm is cooled by cold water in the cooling tank (C). In a primitive still of this type, the liquid is usually run through the still two or three times until the alcohol level reaches the desired concentration.

If the still is boiled too rapidly, the liquid will boil up into the worm, building considerable back pressure, and the top will blow off the kettle. To guard against this calamity, rap with a wrench or metal pipe against the connection pipe running between the kettle and the worm. If it sounds hollow, it is okay, but if it gives off a dull thud, douse the fire immediately to prevent blowing the top off the kettle. If the distilled liquor is for consumption, charcoal is added to soak up "fusel" oil floating on top of the distillate. This oil tastes lousy and may make a person sick. More sophisticated stills incorporating rectifying stacks will usually eliminate the fusel oil.

Various improvements on the simple still design result in a highly concentrated alcohol processed in a single pass through the still. One such improvement is the "doubler" (shown in Figure 14-6), located between the kettle and the condenser. In the doubler tank (A), hot vapors from the kettle condense in the

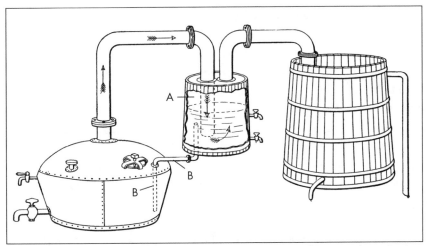

Figure 14-6. Still with a "doubler." Illustration courtesy of *Practical Distiller* by Leonard Monzert (Lindsay Publications, 1987).

will pass through the doubler, but most of the water vapors will be condensed and return to the kettle through the return pipe (B).

In his book, *The Secrets of Building an Alcohol-Producing Still*, Vince Gingery provides details for building the small electric powered still shown in Figure 14-7. In this still, Gingery incorporates a simple rectifying column to condense water vapor out of the gaseous output from the kettle. The water vapor condenses on the surface of the marbles held within the rectifying column, flowing back into the kettle. The result is a highly concentrated alcohol (170 to 190 proof) suitable for fuel.

doubler until it is heated to the boiling point of alcohol (roughly 173°F). At this point, the alcohol vapors

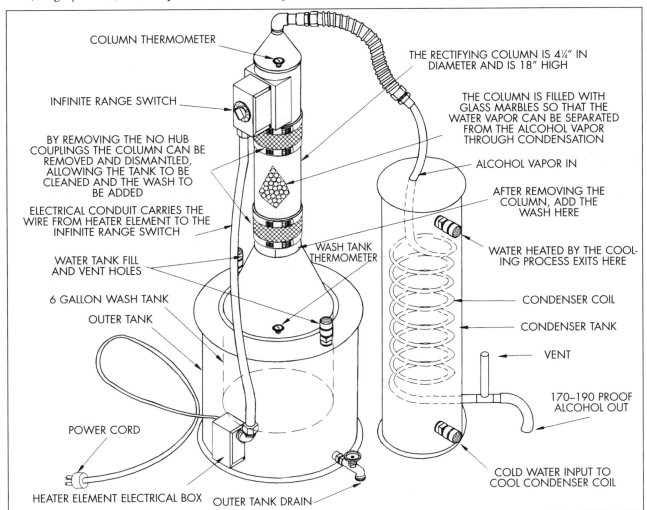

Figure 14-7. Vince Gingery's homemade electric still. Illustration courtesy of *The Secrets of Building an Alcohol-Producing Still* by Vincent R. Gingery (David J. Gingery Publishing, 1994).

VINEGAR

Vinegar is another valuable product that is made by natural fermentation. In this case, vinegar is made by the acetic bacteria, which digest alcohol and turn it into mild concentrations of acetic acid. Vinegar is useful for preserving foods (pickling), and as an ingredient in salad dressings and various sauces. Commercial vinegar is made by aerating properly cultured alcoholic liquids. Apple cider vinegar was traditionally made by filling clean barrels with pressed apple cider. The barrels were covered with cloth and stored in a place that was not too hot or cold. The cider first fermented, and then the alcoholic cider was converted into vinegar by acetic bacteria carried on the feet of vinegar flies. If your ferment does not have a high concentration of alcohol, it may putrefy from the wrong kind of bacteria culturing in the solution (a high alcohol content will kill the undesirable bacteria). See Carla Emery's *Encyclopedia of Country Living* for several old-time vinegar recipes. See *Practical Distiller* by Leonard Monzert for instructions on building and operating a mid-sized vinegar generator.

NATURAL GLUES

Pitch Glue

Pitch is nature's hot-melt adhesive. Using a knife, scrape dry or oozing pitch from pine and fir trees. The pitch should be slowly melted in a pot. Debris floats to the top or settles to the bottom. To reduce brittleness and improve its body, you can add finely ground charcoal or wood ashes in quantities up to one half the volume of the pitch. Use the pitch glue while hot, just like hot-melt glue, to repair cracks in pots, haft arrows, waterproof baskets, and so on. Make pitch sticks to store extra pitch. Repeatedly dip sticks into pitch until the pitch forms into a hotdog shaped lump. Pitch glue is waterproof. You can cover the surface of pitch-glued objects with finely ground charcoal to remove excessive stickiness. You can make your own pitch varnish by dissolving about one part of crushed pitch in four parts of rubbing alcohol.

Hide Glue

Hide glue is almost four times stronger than airplane cement and a third stronger than five-minute epoxy.
—Bart and Robin Blankenship, *Earth Knack: Stone Age Skills for the 21st Century*

Hide glues are surprisingly strong, but use them with caution since they are water soluble. To extract the natural glue from hides, steep hide shavings and/or slender strips in very hot water for several hours. Jim Riggs likes to boil his hide and water combination to extract the glue, but Bart and Robin Blankenship state that the strength of the glue is considerably weakened by boiling and recommend that you keep the temperature below 180°F. After an hour or two of boiling, or 12 to 24 hours of steeping, remove the gelatinous hide scraps and strain the fluid into another pot for concentrating the glue. Add more water to the first pot and cook for another hour before straining the fluid and squeezing the scraps to extract the remaining glue. This is an odorous process that is best done outdoors or under a strongly vented hood. You can also make glues from boiling down different fish skins and bladders, sinews, cartilage, hoofs, and horns.

Steep or boil the strained fluid until it thickens to a syrupy consistency. Apply like Elmer's glue. Hide glue works well on wood and for bow backing. It is not waterproof, but can be waterproofed with fat, oil, or a layer of pitch varnish (see *Pitch Glue* section). Liquid hide glue will quickly spoil. To store excess hide glue, continue cooking until it has reached the consistency of Jell-O. Cut the gelled hunk of hide glue into ¼"-thick strips and dry these strips until completely hard. To reconstitute, grind dried strips into a fine powder and mix with two parts of water to one part powdered glue. Let mixture sit for about one-half hour, and then heat (Blankenship and Blankenship 1996, 159–63 and Wescott 1999, 183–90).

VEGETABLE OILS

Extracting oil from nuts and vegetables can be somewhat involved. The easiest way to get oil is to grind your seeds into a butter and allow the oil to separate to the top, like it does in natural peanut butter. In her *Encyclopedia of Country Living*, Carla Emery describes two other processes for home extraction of olive oil. A brief summary is provided here.

In the first process, olives are dipped for about 30 seconds in a boiling solution of a half-pound of lye per gallon of water. Leave the olives to drain until the lye has nearly dissolved their skins, and then plunge the olives into cold water to stop the lye softening. Rub the softened olives against the screens in screened trays until the pits separate from the flesh and the flesh sieves through the screens. Simmer this pulp for about a half-hour in two to three parts of water, and then allow it to sit for several days. Skim the oil from the top.

In the second process, olives are placed in a burlap sack and smashed with a mallet. The burlap sack is placed in either a homemade press or a commercial press to expel the juices. The pressed pulp is combined with an equal part of water, boiled for a while, and then pressed again. The process is repeated to about the fourth pressing, when all the juices are collected, and the oil is allowed to settle out and skimmed as before.

For a makeshift home press, Emery suggests using a strong watertight tray for the press base. Place the burlap bag filled with crushed olives in the center of this tray and cover it with a thick board. Place a car jack on top of this thick board and attach it with ropes tied to each corner of the tray. Raise the jack to press the olives.

Both processes will produce a bitter-tasting olive oil. To improve the taste of the oil, mix the oil with an equal quantity of warm water. Stir for several minutes then allow to settle for several hours. Draw the water off the bottom of the container then repeat the process several times until the oil no longer tastes bitter. Filter the final product to remove cloudiness.

REFERENCES

***The Encyclopedia of Country Living: An Old-Fashioned Recipe Book,* by Carla Emery.**
This is a great all-around reference containing a wealth of information and resource lists. It includes good sections on soap and candle making; home remedies; cold pressed oils; formulas for homemade nontoxic cleansers; and tons of directions, guidance, and recipes for everything having to do with growing, raising, processing, and cooking animal and vegetable foods. Voluminous, thorough, entertaining, and practical. See the description in the *References* section of Chapter 1 for more details.

***The Soapmaker's Companion: A Comprehensive Guide with Recipes, Techniques & Know-How,* by Susan Miller Cavitch.** 1997, 281 pp. (paperback), ISBN 0-88266-965-6. Published by Storey Books, Schoolhouse Road, Pownal, VT 05261. Lists for $18.95.
This is a very comprehensive guide to soap making by the "cold process" using vegetable fats and lye (sodium hydroxide and water). Covers a broad range of recipes from basic to advanced. Excellent coverage of soap making, both in depth and breadth. It is illustrated with clear instructional line drawings. The main complaint about this book is that it has no color pictures of a medium that can be so colorful and artistic. If you just want a more basic beginner's book, try *The Natural Soap Book: Making Herbal and Vegetable-Based Soaps* by the same author.

***Essentially Soap: The Elegant Art of Handmade Soap Making, Scenting, Coloring & Shaping,* by Dr. Robert S. McDaniel.** 2000, 125 pp. (paperback), ISBN 0-87341-832-8. Published by Krause Publications, 700 East State St., Iola, WI 54990-0001. Lists for $19.95.
This is a beautifully illustrated and well-organized book on soap making. Though the focus is on the "cold process," it also covers "melt and pour rebatching" soaps, which are fun and don't use lye, so they are suitable for kid's craft projects. If I wanted to break into the cottage industry soap making business, I would buy both McDaniel's book and

Susan Miller Cavitch's book, *The Soapmaker's Companion*. If you just want to make some wonderful homemade soap, either book is fine. Carla Emery's book has instructions for several basic soaps and is more than adequate for occasional soap making and for soap making under primitive conditions.

The Candlemaker's Companion: A Complete Guide to Rolling, Pouring, Dipping, and Decorating Your Own Candles, by Betty Oppenheimer.
1997, 164 pp. (paperback), ISBN 0-88266-994-X. Published by Storey Books, Schoolhouse Road, Pownal, VT 05261. Lists for $18.95.

An excellent guide to making candles by a variety of processes. Includes clear line drawings and a good list of suppliers, but no photographs.

Rodale's Book of Practical Formulas, edited by Paula Dreifus Bakule. 1997, 464 pp. (hardcover), ISBN 1-56731-046-X. Published by Fine Communications, P.O. Box 0930, Planetarium Station, New York, NY 10024-0540. Lists for $12.98.

This is an interesting collection of practical, useful, do-it-yourself recipes for the average home. Lots of great ideas for making your own home and health care products from basic ingredients readily available in local stores. Sections include car care, cooking, gardening, beauty, health, home repair and remodeling, housekeeping, crafts, pet care (with pet food recipes), and outdoor life. More focused on practical modern healthy products made from commercially available materials than on frontier-type formulas made from scratch.

Henley's Formulas for Home and Workshop, by Gardner D. Hiscox, M.E. 1979, 809 pp. (hardcover), ISBN 0-517-293072. Published by Crown Publishing Group, 201 E. 50th St., New York, NY 10022. (Out of print.)

This is a very interesting reference that could come in handy if central services went down for a considerable period of time or if you simply wanted to become more self-reliant. Unfortunately, it is also out of print, but you may be able to find a good used copy floating around (I did). Originally published in 1907 and last revised in 1927, *Henley's Formulas* is a compilation of recipes, formulas, and processes for making thousands of items that we take for granted. It covers a wide range of goods, including adhesives, brushes, candles, soap, cosmetics, disinfectants, inks, dyes, paints, solders, fertilizers, explosives, and varnishes; shows how to do your own photography, metallurgy, and leather tanning; and discusses many other things. Many of the formulas require raw chemical ingredients. A significant portion of these are potentially quite dangerous. Exercise caution and realize that some of the remedies and ingredients might be hazardous to your health.

Wagner's Chemical Technology 1872, by Rudolf Wagner, Ph.D., trans. William Crookes, F.R.S. 1988, 762 pp. (hardcover), ISBN 0-917914-99-6. Published by Lindsay Publications Inc., P.O. Box 538, Bradley, IL 60915. Lists for $33.95.

This reprint of the state-of-the-art, 1872 manual on chemical technology is another one for the techno history buffs. Want to know how to make your own sulfuric acid so you can turn bones into glue? How about transforming bones into phosphorous for matches, beets into sugar, or corn into starch? Chances are that most of us wouldn't stand a chance of reproducing twentieth-century technology on our own, but a good team of industrious folks might be able to use this book to recreate a significant portion of late nineteenth-century technology. Includes information on soap, sugar, starches, salts, acids, explosives, vegetable fibers, silk, leather, limes and mortars, glass, stoneware, steel and other ferrous metals, nonferrous metals, paper, vinegar, dyeing, and more.

Practical Distiller, by Leonard Monzert. 1987, 156 pp. (paperback), ISBN 0-917914-58-9. Published by Lindsay Publications Inc., P.O. Box 538, Bradley, IL 60915. Lists for $8.95.

This reprint of a classic 1889 text on distilling alcohol tells you pretty much everything you need to know about how to make malt, ferment mash, and build and operate your own distillery. Even though distilling your own alcoholic beverages without a permit is illegal, this book shows you how to do it right without poisoning yourself, and with simple equipment. When made for use as a fuel, you can easily obtain a free permit from the Bureau of Alcohol, Tobacco and Firearms (ATF), making it a totally legal process.

***Distillation of Alcohol & De-Naturing,* by F. B. Wright.** 1994, 271 pp. (paperback), ISBN 1-55918-142-7. Published by Lindsay Publications Inc., P.O. Box 538, Bradley, IL 60915. Lists for $14.95.

If your goal is fuel-grade alcohol, this reprint of a 1918 text will help you get there. As compared to *Practical Distiller,* this book contains apparatus diagrams that are more modern and provides more detailed information about most of the processes, but does not offer as much practical wisdom for making consumable spirits.

***The Secrets of Building an Alcohol Producing Still,* by Vincent R. Gingery.** 1994, 82 pp. (paperback), ISBN 1-878087-16-9. Published by David J. Gingery Publishing, P.O. Box 318, Rogersville, MO 65742. Lists for $12.95.

This book provides practical detailed instructions for making a compact, portable, electric-powered still to distill fermented grain into 170 to 190 proof ethanol for use as fuel. It covers step-by-step instructions for the entire alcohol making process, including fermentation. With less effort and attention, this simple still produces a higher grade of purified alcohol than old-fashioned moonshine stills. Gingery also includes an interesting mini-history of alcohol, old-fashioned moonshining tips, and some rough guidelines for converting carburetors to run on alcohol. Available from Lindsay Publications.

Lindsay Publications Inc., P.O. Box 538, Bradley IL 60915; phone: (815) 935-5353; fax: (815) 935-5477; web site: www.lindsaybks.com.

Lindsay Publications reprints and distributes a huge variety of older manuals on how to make and build almost anything, including numerous reprints of older technology handbooks and recipes.

XV Engineering, Machines & Materials

Engineering: *1. a) the science concerned with putting scientific knowledge to practical uses, divided into different branches, as civil, electrical, mechanical, or chemical engineering; b) the planning, designing, construction, or management of machinery, roads, bridges, buildings, waterways, etc.*

—*Webster's New World Dictionary of the American Language*, Second College Edition

Thinking back on my past, I find it amusing that when I started undergraduate school I didn't really know what a mechanical engineer was, even though I had a strong sense that it would become my vocation. Once upon a time, engineering was more art than science, depending mostly upon the engineer's experience, intuition, and brute force tests to ensure the success of a design. Modern engineers draw upon a wealth of experience and analytical tools compiled and developed by engineers and scientists over centuries of manufacturing, building, and design. Much of this vast array of knowledge is available to the lay designer or engineer in the form of engineering handbooks. These encyclopedic volumes provide recommendations, charts, basic information about materials and process, and "cookbook" formulas that don't require an engineering degree to apply (although I admit that it can be helpful).

In this chapter, I provide an introduction to a few valuable concepts that the lay designer or inventor can apply to certain situations. Should the need arise and there is not an available engineer to consult with, a basic understanding of these concepts will help the lay designer to properly apply "cookbook" equations from engineering manuals. I will also include a few equations, a bit of practical math, and several minireviews for recommend texts that might come in handy someday, even if you aren't an engineer. Perhaps the discussions and diagrams in the following sections will help you to make sense out of some concepts that baffled you in school. If they still don't make sense, don't worry about it, just move on. If you wish to make practical calculations to check the strength of a design, I recommend that you pick up at least one of the mechanical engineering references.

ENGINEERING

Forces and Statics

In physics, a force is defined as the cause or agent that puts a stationary object into motion, or changes the direction or speed of a moving object. The popular seventeenth century, anecdote says that Sir Isaac Newton formulated the basis of the laws of mechanical physics (mechanics) after being struck by a falling apple. He realized that an object at rest will stay at rest until acted upon by a force, and similarly an object in motion will maintain the same speed and direction unless compelled by a force to change speed or direction. In the English system, forces are typically measured in "pounds" or "ounces."

SUM OF FORCES EQUALS ZERO

You might think of numerous times when you exerted a large force upon an object and it did not move. For example, push against a brick wall and chances are slim that you will be able to move it, unless you happen to be driving a bulldozer. The case of pushing against a brick wall with your hands is an example of "statics." Statics means that even though there are forces applied to an object (the brick wall), none of the objects is accelerating (no change in motion = statics), so the sum of all the forces must be zero. If you push hard against a brick wall, your feet are pushing equally hard in the opposite direction, so the sum of the forces acting on your body is zero and your body stays stationary.

call these components a vertical component and a horizontal component.

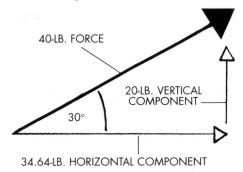

Figure 15-2. Components of a force.

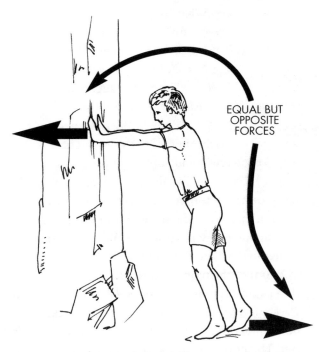

Figure 15-1. Static push (sum of forces equals zero).

Another example of statics is a bathroom scale. When you stand on a bathroom scale, the mass of your body is acted upon by the earth's gravitational pull. The scale measures the force caused by the acceleration due to gravity acting upon the mass of your body and the result is your weight. If you flew to the moon, your mass would remain the same, but your weight (a force) measured on the same bathroom scale would be one-sixth of your weight on earth because the moon's gravitational acceleration is one-sixth of the earth's. In terms of statics, your weight pushes against the scale and the scale pushes back with an equal and opposite force, which is measured by the spring on the scale, so the sum of the forces is zero.

For analyzing a static situation, engineers use something called a "free-body diagram." They take an object, or group of objects, and draw all the forces acting upon this object (or group). If the object is static, the sum of all these forces must be zero. Forces are not always pointed in the same direction. When a second force is going off at an angle to a first force, the second force can be considered to have a portion (component) in line with the first force and a different component at right angles (perpendicular) to the first force. For simplicity, let's

Scientists and engineers like to describe forces in terms of "vectors," which sounds complex and technical, but it's really pretty simple. A vector is simply something that has both a quantity and a direction and is typically shown graphically by an arrow. In the case of Figure 15-2, a force of 40 pounds of push is applied in a direction that is 30° above horizontal. The "magnitude," or quantity, of this vector is 40 pounds. The direction is 30°. This force can be divided into a vertical component and a horizontal component. Through simple trigonometry (see the *Mathematics* section of this chapter), if you multiply the force F (40 pounds) times the sine 30°, you get a vertical component of 20 pounds. Similarly, multiplying the force F (40 pounds) times the cosine 30°, you get a horizontal component of 34.64 pounds.

The sum of all the forces acting on a static object, or cluster of objects (a "free body"), must add up to zero in all directions. For ease of analysis, forces going off in different directions are separated into their horizontal and vertical components. In a static situation (no change in motion), all the horizontal components must add up to zero (i.e., they must cancel each other out). Similarly, all the vertical components must add up to zero. For a practical application of this knowledge, let's say that you were rock climbing in Yosemite Valley and you anchored yourself to a taught sling strung between two anchors. Your buddy is climbing up from below and he happens to fall. Now suddenly the combined weight of both you and your buddy (300 pounds) is hanging on your rope clipped to the center of the taught sling (now it's very, very taught). With your lives depending on these two anchors, you start to wonder if perhaps you should have tied into your anchors a little differently? Let's say that the taught sling only sags to 5° below horizontal (see Figure 15-3).

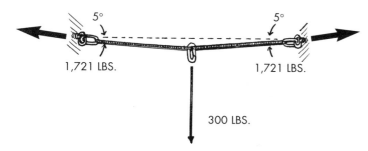

Figure 15-3. "Free body diagram" for two 150-pound rock climbers hanging on a couple of anchors.

The horizontal components of the sling forces on each anchor are equal but in opposite directions, so they cancel each other out. The vertical components are equal, and the sum of the vertical forces on both slings must be equal but opposite to the 300 pound weight of the two climbers. This means that the vertical force on each anchor is equal to 150 pounds. Using simple trigonometry, the sling tension on each anchor multiplied times sine 5° must be equal to the vertical force of 150 pounds. The result is that tension on each sling is over 1,700 pounds to hold only 150 pounds of climber's weight per sling. Pretty scary!

Now let's say that the first climber had understood this concept and tied into his anchors with a nice loose sling that hung down at 60° below horizontal instead of 5°. The tension is now multiplied by sine 60° instead of sine 5°, so the tension is now only 173 pounds per anchor. Much better! Even if you don't understand the math, just remember the concept.

MOMENT (TWIST)

Forces are not always nice clean pushes or pulls. Sometimes forces give a twisting action. These are called "moments" and "torque." Picture a child's playground merry-go-round in your mind. If you set a bunch of kids on the merry-go-round, nothing happens (static) until someone starts to pull or push on the outside of the merry-go-round, then it starts to spin. Imagine that two children are pulling on the outer rim of the merry-go-round with equal but opposite forces. What happens? The merry-go-round is in static balance and doesn't spin. The second rule of statics is that the sum of moments (torque) must also be equal to zero. Torque (also known as "moment") is defined as the product of a force multiplied by a distance. In the English system, torque and moment are typically measured in "foot-pounds" or "inch-ounces." Let's say you have a 1½-foot–long wrench and apply a 50-pound push to the end of the wrench. In this case, you are applying 75 foot-pounds of torque (50 pounds x 1½ feet).

Both a lever and a screw thread (such as in a vise) act on this same principle. When you slowly lift an item with a lever, it is considered a static problem. The sum of the moments around the fulcrum (lever's pivot point) must be equal to zero. In Figure 15-4, a lever is used to lift a 300-pound rock. The horizontal distance from the rock to the fulcrum is 2 feet. The horizontal distance from the fulcrum to your hand is 10 feet. Since the sum of the moments around the fulcrum must be equal to zero, 300 pounds multiplied by 2 feet must be equal to the force on your hand multiplied times 10 feet. This means that you only have to apply 60 pounds of force to the lever to lift the 300-pound rock. Archimedes once said that if you gave him a big enough lever, he could lift the whole world.

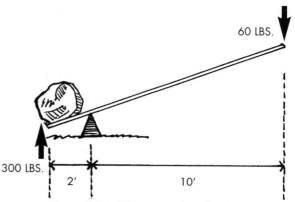

Figure 15-4. Lifting a rock with a lever.

One more concept that is very helpful in static analysis is "center of gravity." Every object or cluster of objects has a center point where it is perfectly balanced around that point in all directions. When an object spins in the air, it spins around its center of gravity. For the purpose of performing a static analysis of a body with significant mass, the force of grav ity pulling on the mass is assumed to act on the center of gravity. Imagine that you try to push against a wall with a force of 50 pounds. Naturally, you will lean forward while you exert this push. Why do you do this? If you stood straight up, as soon as you pushed against the wall, you would start to topple backwards. Leaning forward to brace yourself balances the moments as well as the forces to create a static situation.

In Figure 15-5, when you lean forward to get your center of gravity 1 foot in front of your feet, you will be able to push with a horizontal force of only 30 pounds at a distance of 5 feet above the ground (5' x 30 lbs push = 1' x 150 lbs weight). If you hunker down and push at a 3-foot distance above the ground, you can now push with a force of 50 pounds. If you simultaneously lean forward further and hunker down, placing your center of gravity 2 feet in front of your feet, you will be able to push with a force of 100 pounds (3 feet x 100 lbs push = 2 feet x 150 lbs weight).

Stress and Strength (Mechanics)

TENSION AND TENSILE STRENGTH

Now that you understand a little bit about forces and moments, we can begin to talk about the strength of materials and beams. Simple tension is when you pull on an object without giving it any twisting or bending forces. "Stress" is the engineering term to describe the amount of force acting on an object (or portion of an object) per unit area. When trying to figure out if something is strong enough, the most common material property that engineers refer to is the "tensile strength," which is the amount of stress that a material can handle before it breaks. In the English system, this is usually figured

in terms of pounds per square inch (psi). To determine the tensile strength of a material, a sample with a known cross-sectional area is pulled apart on a tensile test machine that records how much force it took to break the sample, and then that force is divided by the cross-sectional area to determine the breaking stress ("ultimate tensile strength"). Some of the properties of tensile strength are pretty intuitive. For example, if you make a rectangular chunk of wood twice as thick, its strength in tension will be twice as much. Another useful engineering term is "yield stress." The yield stress is the point where a material has reached its maximum stress before starting to plastically deform (yield) and take on a permanent deformation.

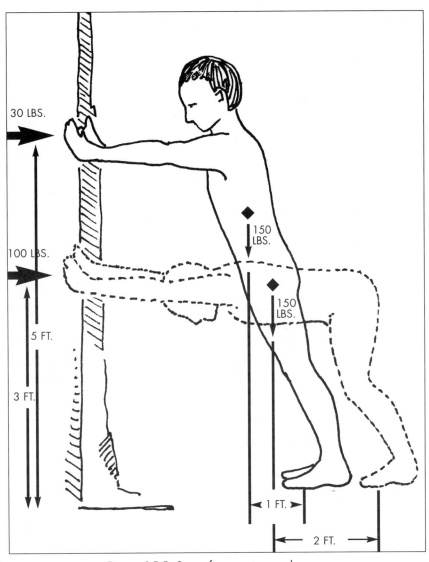

Figure 15-5. Sum of moments equals zero.

COMPRESSION

Compression can get a lot more complicated than simple tension. In short squat columns, compression behaves pretty similarly to tension, and you can usually figure compression strength based on the tensile strength, but in long slender columns, something very different happens. Imagine a simple wooden yardstick. If you could grip the ends tightly, you could probably hang more than your full body weight on it without breaking. Now stand that same yardstick on end and push on it. With very little force, the slender yardstick will bow in the middle and snap. This is called "buckling," and there are engineering formulas to calculate the buckling strength of slender beams, but they are beyond the scope of this book. Some materials, such as concrete, have much higher compression strengths than their tensile (pulling) strengths. The main reason that concrete structures are generally reinforced with steel rebar is to carry most of the tensile bending stresses in the steel rebar instead of the concrete, because concrete typically has poor tensile strength.

BENDING

Bending is very different from simple tension. When you bend a beam, the side on the inside of the curve gets compressed while the opposite side gets tensioned. There is a line through the center of a beam, called the "neutral axis" that is neither compressed nor tensioned.

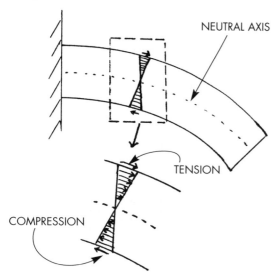

Figure 15-6. Beam bending.

Whereas the strength of a beam in tension is directly proportional to the cross-sectional area of the beam, the strength and stiffness of a beam in bending is heavily dependent on the geometry of its cross section, not just the area. For example, if you double the width of a rectangular beam, you double its tensile strength, stiffness, and bending strength. If you double its height, you still just double the tensile strength, but its bending stiffness and strength go up by a factor of 8.

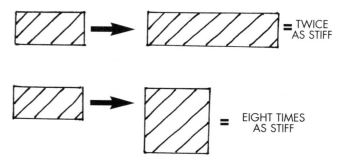

Figure 15-7. Rectangular beam stiffness versus cross section.

It turns out that the top and bottom areas of beams make by far the most difference in beam strength and stiffness. That is why most steel beams have a cross section like a classic capital "I." In fact, to conserve wood, modern engineered floor joists are now fabricated with narrow plywood vertical runners capped by a wider section on the top and bottom, much like a steel I-beam. Tubular beams also save considerable material over solid round beams of similar stiffness, though not as efficiently as an I-beam. When calculating beam bending strengths and deflections, there is an important factor known as the "area moment of inertia." This is a stiffness factor that is highly dependent on the cross-sectional geometry and dimensions, and is commonly shown as the letter "I" in engineering equations. For example, the area moment of inertia for a rectangular beam is $\frac{1}{3}$ x b x h^3, where "b" is the width and "h" is the height of the beam. In the case of a round beam, such as a tree trunk, $I = (\pi\, d^4)/64$. From this equation you can see that doubling the diameter of a round beam diameter increases its stiffness and bending strength by a factor of 16! To calculate the I values for I-beams and cylinders that are symmetric about the neutral axis, first calculate the I value for the solid shape and then subtract the I values for the areas of space.

Mechanical engineering and machinery handbooks carry charts for numerous beams of different geometry that enable one to quickly calculate the area moment of inertia for a wide variety of cross sections. They also offer charts for many different simplified beam loading configurations that make it relatively easy to calculate the strength of your design by simply matching it up with the figure that most closely represents this design, and then plugging your load and distance numbers into the equation.

BASIC BEAM EQUATIONS

When I am analyzing beam strength, stresses, and deflections, I usually use the handbook formulas in *Machinery's Handbook* or *Roark's Formulas for Stress and Strain*. In case you ever need to ensure that a simple hoist or bridging beam is strong enough for a particular application, and you don't have access to an engineering handbook, I provide equations for maximum stress in three of the simplest beam cases (*Machinery's Handbook* gives full stress and deflection equations for 24 different cases of beam loading, and *Roark's Formulas* has many more).

Case 1. Beam Supported at Both Ends with a Load in the Center

You can assume that one-half the weight of the beam adds to the sum of other loads applied to the center of the beam. Loads that move from one end to the other, such as a truck crossing a bridge, cause the most stress when they are at the center point. "Simply supported" means that the ends of the beam are free to rotate as the beam flexes under load.

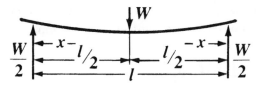

Figure 15-8. Diagram for case 1. Illustration courtesy of *Machinery's Handbook*, 26th ed., edited by Erik Oberg, Franklin D. Jones, Holbrook L. Horton, Henry H. Ryffel, and Christopher J. McCauley (Industrial Press, 2000).

The maximum stress, *s* is at the center of the beam. In the formula, s = (y x W x L)/4 I, *y* is equal to the maximum distance from the beam's neutral axis. For symmetric beams, the neutral axis runs along the center of the beam, so for a rectangular beam or I beam, *y* is equal to one-half the beam height. For beams with a circular cross section, *y* is equal to the radius of the beam. *I* is the area moment of inertia. See the previous section for equations for *I* for simple shapes, or see a mechanical engineering handbook to calculate *I* for more complicated beam cross sections.

Case 2. Beam Consisting of Built-In Ends with a Load in the Center

This case is the same as case 1, except that the ends of the beam are constrained to stay horizontal, either by being built into something, or because the beam is just a section of a long beam with multiple supports.

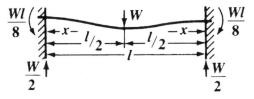

Figure 15-9. Diagram for case 2. Illustration courtesy of *Machinery's Handbook*, 26th ed., edited by Erik Oberg, Franklin D. Jones, Holbrook L. Horton, Henry H. Ryffel, and Christopher J. McCauley (Industrial Press, 2000).

The maximum stress, *s*, is at the center of the beam and at the ends by the built-in supports in the following formula: s = (y X W X L)/8 I.

Case 3. Cantilevered Beam with a Load at the End

For simplicity, assume that one-half the weight of the beam adds to the sum of other loads applied to the end of the beam. The anchored end of the beam is considered "built-in."

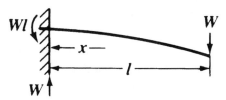

Figure 15-10. Diagram for case 3. Illustration courtesy of *Machinery's Handbook*, 26th ed., edited by Erik Oberg, Franklin D. Jones, Holbrook L. Horton, Henry H. Ryffel, and Christopher J. McCauley (Industrial Press, 2000).

The maximum stress, s, is at the end by the built-in support in the following formula: $s = (y \times W \times L)/I$.

NOTE: The source for all beam and area moment of inertia equations is Machinery's Handbook, 21st ed., edited by Erik Oberg, Franklin D. Jones, and Holbrook L. Horton (Industrial Press, 1982).

SAFETY FACTOR

Whenever I calculate the strength of a design, I employ a safety factor. The size of the safety factor chosen depends on several other factors, including my level of confidence in the accuracy of the analysis, the importance of other factors such as corrosion and fatigue (many repeated cycles), how expensive/difficult it is to add material to make the design safer, and the severity of the consequences of failure. A narrow safety factor might be on the order of 1.5. For instance, if I wanted to carry a load of 1,000 pounds, I would design my construction to carry at least 1,500 pounds. In general, I like to see a safety factor of at least 2.5, preferably 4, and sometimes as high as 10.

FLUIDS

For practical handbook calculations of fluid flows through pipes, I almost always use Lindeburg's *Mechanical Engineering Reference Manual for the PE Exam*. It is very clear and has all the information I need in one area of the book, plus sample problems that help me remember what to do if it's been years since I last calculated a similar fluid flow. To calculate pressure losses for fluids flowing through pipes, you can go through a fairly involved chain of steps using one of the recommended engineering handbooks or you can estimate these losses using the water pipe sizing chart in the *Micro-Hydropower* section of Chapter 11. Due to friction losses in pipe fittings, figure that each threaded elbow or tee counts for about as much pressure loss as 6 feet of the same sized pipe (this is called "equivalent length"). Handbooks give you a chart with specific values of equivalent lengths for most sizes and types of standard pipe fittings and valves.

Water pressure, pump output, and piping pressure losses are often specified by the number of feet of "head." In a static situation, water pressure increases with the depth. Head is the depth of static water that corresponds to a certain pressure. Multiply the number of "feet of head" by .433 to convert head into psi (pounds per square inch). For example, at ground level beneath a 50-foot-high water tower, the static pressure in the water pipe is 50 feet of head, or 50 x .433 = 21.65 psi.

When you pump water, the amount of work it takes to pump the water is a direct function of the water pressure, flow rate, and pump efficiency. Disregarding pump efficiency losses, the pump horsepower (work) is equal to the flow rate (Q in gallons per minute) multiplied times the pressure (in feet of head) divided by 3,960: $W = (Q \times H)/3960$.

Similarly, if you are generating power off a fluid flow, this same equation tells you the theoretical maximum power available from a fluid flow (efficiency losses will reduce the actual amount of power that you can generate). At a given pressure, if you double the flow rate, you double the horsepower. At a given flow rate, if you double the pressure, you double the horsepower.

MATERIALS

Materials at the disposal of preindustrial societies were mostly limited to those that could be grown, foraged, or hunted. Modern society has a huge variety of materials at our beck and call. Both *Mark's Standard Handbook for Mechanical Engineers* and the *Machinery's Handbook* contain numerous charts depicting various properties for hundreds of modern materials. On the next page is a chart with a few properties of some common materials. Unless otherwise specified, assume that tensile and compression strengths are roughly equal. See the recommended handbooks for more complete information.

MATHEMATICS

Both *Mark's Handbook* and the *Machinery's Handbook* contain extensive sections devoted to mathematics. Lindeburg's engineering review manuals have decent sections devoted to math that are more instructive, but not as extensive. Appearing below are a few simple rules and equations that I use on a regular basis for mechanical design. Also included are old-

Properties of some common materials

Material	Tensile strength (10³ psi)	Modulus of elasticity (10⁶ psi)	Compressive Strength (10³ psi)	Density (lbs/in³)	Notes
Cast iron, gray	20–60	12–18			Cast iron is a brittle material
Cast steel	60–100	30			Yield stress 30,000–70,000 psi
Cast iron, malleable	40–100	25			Yield stress 30,000–80,000 psi
Cast iron, ductile	60–120	23			Yield stress 40,000–90,000 psi
Mild steel (A 36)	58–80	30		.283	Yield stress 36,000 psi min
Steel, low carbon (1018)	60–103	30		.283	Yield stress 45,000 7" rod, turned. Yield stress 70,000 1" cold rolled
Steel, medium carbon (1045)	80–182	30		.283	Yield stress 55,000 5" rod, turned. Yield stress 85,000 1" cold rolled
Steel, high carbon (1095)	90–213	30		.283	Yield stress 20,000–150,000 psi (depends on heat treat)
Steel, stainless (302)	85–125	28		.283	Yield stress 35,000–95,000 psi
Aluminum, sand cast	19–35	10.3		.098	Yield stress 8,000–25,000 psi
Aluminum, wrought (1100)	13–24	10–11.4		.098	Annealed condition yield 5,000 psi, H18 temper yield 22,000
Aluminum, wrought (2024)	27–68	10.6		.1	T4 temper yield 47,000 psi
Red brass	39–105	16		.316	Yield stress 10,000–63,000 psi
Yellow brass	46–128	16		.316	Yield stress 14,000–62,000 psi
Copper, wrought	32–57	17			Yield stress 10,000–53,000 psi
Die cast zinc (Alloy 3)	41			.24	Yield stress 32,000 psi
Pewter	7.6			.263	
Brickwork, common	.05		1		
Concrete	.2–.6	3–5	1.5–8	150 1b/ft³	Average strength is 2,000–3,000 psi, High is 6,000–8,000. Strength depends on how much cement and water are used in mix.
Granite	.7	4–16	13–55	160–190 1b/ft³	
Marble	.5	5–11.5	8–27	165–179 1b/ft³	
Slate	.5	6–16	9–10	168–180 1b/ft³	
Sandstone	.3	.7–10	5–20	119–168 1b/ft³	
Limestone	.3	3–9	2.5–28	117–175 1b/ft³	
Oak, red northern	8.5	1.82		44 1b/ft³	Working stress approximately 25% of tensile. (See *Mark's Handbook*)
Oak, white	8.2	1.78		48 1b/ft³	Working stress approximately 25% of tensile. (See *Mark's*)
Birch, yellow	10.1	2.01		43 1b/ft³	Working stress approximately 25% of tensile. (See *Mark's*)
Douglas fir	7.8	1.95		34 1b/ft³	Working stress approximately 25% of tensile. (See *Mark's*)
Pine, ponderosa	6.3	1.29		28 1b/ft³	Working stress approximately 25% of tensile. (See *Mark's*)
Spruce, white or red	6.5	1.34		28 1b/ft³	Working stress approximately 25% of tensile. (See *Mark's*)

Source: *Machinery's Handbook,* 26th ed., edited by Erik Oberg, Franklin D. Jones, Holbrook L. Horton, Henry H. Ryffel, and Christopher J. McCauley (Industrial Press, 2000); *Mark's Standard Handbook for Mechanical Engineers,* 10th ed., edited by Eugene A. Avalone and Theodore Baumeister III (McGraw-Hill, 1996); *Steel and Aluminum Stock List,* from Earl M. Jorgensen Co., 1984; and *Elements of the Mechanical Behavior of Solids* by Nam P. Suh and Arthur L. Turner, 1975.

CONVERSIONS

The following table provides handy English-metric and English-English conversion factors.

MULTIPLY	BY	TO OBTAIN
Atmospheres (physics)	.76.0	cms mercury
atm	1.013	bar
atm	29.92	ins mercury
atm	33.90	ft water
atm	1.0333	kps/sq cm
atm	14.70	lbs/sq in
atm	1.058	tons/sq ft
Atmosphere (technical)	1	kp/sq. cm.
at	0.9681	atm
at	0.9807	bar
at	14.233	psi
Bar	10^5	newtons/sq m
bar	.9869	atm (physics)
bar	1.0197	at (tech.)
bar	14.504	psi
Barrels-Oil	42	gals-oil
BT Units	0.2520	kp-calories
BTU s	777.9	ft-lbs
BTU s	3.927×10^{-4}	hp-hrs
BTU s	107.5	kps-meters
BTU s	2.928×10^{-4}	kw-hrs
BTU/Min	12.96	ft-lbs/sec
BTU/min	0.02356	hp
BTU/min	0.01757	kw
BTU/min	17.57	watts
Centimeters	0.3937	inches
cm	0.01	meters
cm	10	mm
Cms Mercury	0.01316	atm
cms mercury	0.4461	ft water
cms mercury	136.0	kps/sq meter
cms mercury	27.85	lbs/sq ft
cms mercury	0.1934	lbs/sq in
Cms/Second	1.969	ft/min
cms/sec	0.03281	ft/sec
cms/sec	0.036	km/hr
cms/sec	0.6	meters/min
cms/sec	0.02237	miles/hr
cms/sec	3.728×10^{-4}	miles/min
Cms/Sec/Sec	0.03281	ft/sec/sec
Cubic Cms	3.531×10^{-5}	cu ft
cu cms	6.102×10^{-2}	cu in
cu cms	10^{-6}	cu meters
cu cms	1.308×10^{-6}	cu yds
cu cms	2.642×10^{-4}	gals
cu cms	10^{-3}	liters
cu cms	2.113×10^{-3}	pints (liq)
cu cms	1.057×10^{-3}	quarts (liq)
Cubic Feet	2.832×10^4	cubic cms
cu ft	1728	cu inches
cu ft	0.02832	cu meters
cu ft	0.03704	cu yds
cu ft	7.48052	gals
cu ft	28.32	liters
cu ft	59.84	pints (liq)
cu ft	29.92	quarts (liq)
Cu Ft/min	472.0	cu cms/sec
cu ft/min	0.1247	gals/sec
cu ft/min	0.4720	liters/sec
cu ft/min	62.43	lbs w/min
cu ft/sec	448.831	gals/min
Cu Inches	16.39	cc
cu ins	5.787×10^{-4}	cu ft
cu ins	1.639×10^{-5}	cu meters
cu ins	2.143×10^{-5}	cu yds
cu ins	4.329×10^{-3}	gals
cu ins	1.639×10^{-2}	liters
cu ins	0.03463	pints (liq)
cu ins	0.01732	quarts (liq)
Cu Meters	10^6	cc
cu M	35.31	cu ft
cu M	61,023	cu ins
cu M	1.308	cu yds
cu M	264.2	gals
cu M	10^3	liters
cu M	2113	pints (liq)
cu M	1057	quarts (liq)
Cu Yards	7.646×10^5	cu cms
cu yds	27	cu ft
cu yds	46,656	cu ins
cu yds	0.7646	cu meters
cu yds	202.0	gals
Decimeters	0.1	meters
Degs (Angle)	60	minutes
degs (angle)	0.01745	radians
degs (angle)	3600	secs
Degrees/Sec	0.01745	radians/sec
degs/sec	0.1667	revs/min
degs/sec	0.002778	revs/sec

MULTIPLY	BY	TO OBTAIN
Feet	30.48	cms
ft	12	ins
ft	0.3048	meters
ft	1/3	yds
Ft of Water	0.02950	atms
ft of w	0.8826	ins mercury
ft of w	0.03048	kps/sq cm
ft of w	62.32	lbs/sq ft
ft of w	0.4328	lbs/sq in
Feet/Min	0.5080	cms/sec
ft/min	0.01667	ft/sec
ft/min	0.01829	kms/hr
ft/min	0.3048	ms/min
ft/min	0.01136	miles/hr
Ft/Sec/Sec	30.48	cms/sec/sec
ft/sec/sec	0.3048	Ms/sec/sec
Ft-Pounds	1.286×10^{-3}	BTUs
ft lbs	5.050×10^{-7}	hp-hrs
ft lbs	3.241×10^{-4}	kp-calories
ft lbs	0.1383	kpm
ft lbs	3.766×10^{-7}	kw-hrs
Ft-lbs/Min	1.286×10^{-3}	BTUs/min
ft-lbs/min	0.01667	ft-lbs/sec.
ft-lbs/min	3.030×10^{-5}	hp
ft-lbs/min	3.241×10^{-4}	kp-calories/min
ft-lbs/min	2.260×10^{-5}	kws
Ft-Lbs/Sec	7.717×10^{-2}	BTUs/min
ft-lbs/sec	1.818×10^{-3}	hp
ft-lbs/sec	1.945×10^{-2}	kg-calories/min
ft-lbs/sec	1.356×10^{-3}	kws
Gallons	3785	ccs
gals	0.1337	cu ft
gals	231	cu ins
gals	3.785×10^{-3}	cu meters
gals	3.785	liters
gals	8	pints (liq)
gals	4	quarts (liq)
Gallons, Imp	1.20095	US gals
gallons, US	0.83267	imp gals
Gals Water	8.3304	lbs water
Gallons/Min	2.228×10^{-3}	cu ft/sec
gal/min	0.06308	liters/sec
gals/min	8.0208	cu ft/hr
Horse-Power	42.44	BTUs/min
hp	33,000	ft-lbs/min
hp	550	ft-lbs/sec
hp	1.014	hp (metric)
hp	10.70	kp-calories/min
hp	0.7457	kws
hp	745.7	watts
Hp-Hours	2547	BTUs
hp-hrs	1.98×10^6	ft-lbs
hp-hrs	641.7	kp-calories
hp-hrs	2.737×10^5	kp-meters
hp-hrs	0.7457	kw-hrs
Inches	2.540	cms
Ins Mercury	0.03342	atms
ins mercury	1.133	ft water
ins mercury	0.03453	kps/sq cm
ins mercury	70.73	lbs/sq ft
ins mercury	0.4912	lbs/sq in
Ins of Water	0.002458	atms
ins of w	0.07355	ins mercury
ins of w	0.002540	kps/sq cm
ins of w	5.202	lbs/sq ft
ins of w	0.03613	lbs/sq in
Kilopond	980,665	dynes
kps	2.205	lbs
kps	1.102×10^{-3}	tons (short)
kps	10^3	ponds
Kps/Sq Cm	0.9678	atms
kps/sq cm	32.81	ft water
kps/sq cm	28.96	ins mercury
kps/sq cm	2048	lbs/sq ft
kps/sq cm	14.22	lbs/sq in
Kilometers	10^5	cms
kms	3281	ft
kms	10^3	meters
kms	0.6214	miles
Kms/Hr	27.78	cms/sec
kms/hr	54.68	ft/min
kms/hr	0.9113	ft/sec
kms/hr	16.67	meters/min
kms/hr	0.6214	miles/hr
Kms/Hr/Sec	27.78	cms/sec/sec
kms/hr/sec	0.9113	ft/sec/sec
kms/hr/sec	0.2778	Ms/sec/sec

MULTIPLY	BY	TO OBTAIN
Kilowatts	56.92	BTUs/min
kws	4.425×10^4	ft-lbs/min
kws	737.6	ft-lbs/sec
kws	1.341	hp
kws	14.34	kp-calories/min
kws	10^3	watts
Kilowatt-Hrs	3415	BTUs
kw-hrs	2.655×10^6	ft-lbs
kw-hrs	1.341	hp-hours
kw-hrs	860.5	kp-calories
kw-hrs	3.671×10^5	kp-meters
Liters	10^3	ccs
liters	0.03531	cu ft
liters	61.02	cu ins
liters	10^{-2}	cu meters
liters	0.2642	gals
liters	1.057	quarts(liq)
Liters/Min	4.403×10^{-3}	gals/sec
Meters	100	cms
meters	3.281	ft
meters	39.37	ins
meters	10^{-3}	kms
meters	10^3	mms
meters/min	1.667	cms/sec
meters/min	3.281	ft/min
meters/min	0.05468	ft/sec
meters/min	0.06	kms/hr
meters/min	0.03728	miles/hr
Meters/Sec	196.8	ft/min
meters/sec	3.281	ft/sec
meters/sec	3.6	kms/hr
meters/sec	0.06	kms/min
meters/sec	2.237	miles/hr
meters/sec	0.03728	miles/min
Microns	10^{-6}	meters
microns	39×10^{-6}	in
Miles/Hr	44.70	cms/sec
miles/hr	88	ft/min
miles/hr	1.467	ft/sec
miles/hr	1.609	kms/hr
miles/hr	26.82	meters/min
Millimeters	0.1	cms
mms	0.03937	ins
Mins (Angle)	2.909×10^{-4}	radians
Newton	0.1020	kps
Ounces	0.0625	lbs
ozs	28.349527	pond
Ozs (Fluid)	1.805	cu in
ozs (fluid)	0.02957	liters
Ponds	980.7	dynes
ponds	10^{-3}	kps
ponds	10^3	milliponds
ponds	0.03527	ozs
ponds	2.205×10^{-3}	lbs
Ponds/Cm	5.600×10^{-3}	lbs/in
Ponds/Cu Cm	62.43	lbs/cu ft
ponds/cu cm	0.03613	lbs/cu in
Ponds/Liter	58.417	grains/gal
ponds/liter	8.345	lbs/1000 gals
ponds/liter	0.062427	lbs/cu ft
ponds/liter	1000	parts/million
Pounds	16	ozs
lbs	0.0005	tons (short)
lbs	4.44	newtons (N)
lbs	453.5924	ponds
Lbs of Water	0.01605	cu ft
lbs of water	27.73	cu in
lbs of water	0.1204	gals
Lbs of w/Min	2.679×10^{-3}	cu ft/sec
Pounds/Cu Ft	5.787×10^{-4}	lbs/cu in
Pounds/Cu In	1728	lbs/cu ft
Pounds/Sq In	0.06804	atms
lbs/sq in	2.311	ft water
lbs/sq in	2.036	in mercury
lbs/sq in	0.07031	kps/sq cm
Radians	57.29578	degrees
Tons (Long)	1016	kps
tons (long)	2240	lbs
tons (long)	1.12000	tons (short)
Tons (Short)	2000	lbs
tons (short)	907.18486	kps
tons (short)	0.89287	tons (long)
tons (short)	0.90718	tons (metric)
Watts	0.05692	BTUs/min
watts	44.26	ft-lbs/min
watts	0.7376	ft-lbs/sec
watts	1.341×10^{-3}	hp
watts	0.01434	kp-calories/
watts	10^{-3}	kws
Watt/Hours	3.415	BTUs
watt-hrs	2655	ft-lbs
watt-hrs	1.341×10^{-3}	hp-hrs
watt-hrs	0.8605	kp-calories
watt-hrs	367.1	kp-meters
watt-hrs	10^{-3}	kw-hrs

Table courtesy of *Mechanical Engineering Reference Manual for the PE Exam* by Michael R. Lindeburg, P.E. (Professional Publications, 1998).

fashioned trigonometry and logarithm tables just in case you need to perform calculations someday without access to a hand-held calculator or computer. In the days before electronic calculators, log and trig tables and/or a slide rule were considered essential equipment for every engineer. The slide rule enabled engineers to rapidly perform complex calculations to three significant digits (three digits of accuracy). A slide rule contains built-in trigonometry and logarithm tables for quick reference and easy calculation with accuracy that is adequate for most engineering solutions, but not for bookkeeping.

On the facing page, you will find a handy chart for converting from English to metric measures.

RECTANGLES

Area of a rectangle = length x width

Volume of a rectangular solid = length x width x height

CIRCULAR FORMS

Perimeter of a circle = π x diameter

> **NOTE: Pi (π) equals 3.14159 and is a very handy number that corresponds to a fixed ratio that relates the radius and diameter of circular forms to their circumference, area, and volume.**

Area of a circle = π x r² (r is the radius)

Volume of a sphere = 4/3 x πr³

Volume of cylinder = π x r² x l (l is the length of the cylinder)

Trigonometry

When you add the sum of the three internal angles of any single triangle, they always total 180°. A "right triangle" is any triangle that has a 90° angle. In any right triangle, the two shorter legs are next to the 90° angle, and the longest leg, called the "hypotenuse," is the leg opposite the 90° angle. "Similar triangles" are triangles that have exactly the same size angles. No matter how large or small similar triangles are, they always have the exact same proportions. These ratios may be looked up in trig (short for trigonometry) tables or found with the trig functions on a calculator. Figure 15-11 illustrates a typical right triangle. The little box drawn inside one corner indicates that it is a 90° angle.

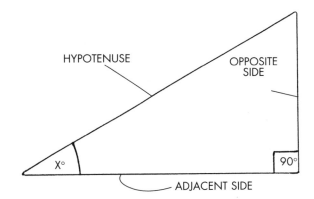

Figure 15-11. Typical right triangle.

Basic Trigonometric Ratios for Right Triangle Angles

Sine x = opposite side/hypotenuse (sine is abbreviated "sin")

Cosine x = adjacent side/hypotenuse (cosine is abbreviated "cos")

Tangent x = opposite side/adjacent side (tangent is abbreviated "tan")

Cotangent x = adjacent side/opposite side (cotangent is abbreviated "cot")

Secant x = hypotenuse/adjacent side (secant is abbreviated "sec")

Cosecant x = hypotenuse/opposite side (cosecant is abbreviated "cosec")

> **NOTE: In each of the above cases, insert the value of the angle that you are using in place of x.**

When I design most anything (even an addition to my house), I almost always use basic trigonometry. Since I left engineering school (with the exception of engineering exams), I believe that I have used calculus only twice, but I have used trigonometry thousands of times. This is very useful math and it's not hard to understand once you realize that it is just a bunch of fixed ratios for a right triangle with any specific angle.

"LAW OF SINES" AND "LAW OF COSINES"

The law of sines and the law of cosines provide handy tools for calculating the unknown angles or lengths of sides for triangles that don't have a right angle, provided that you already know a combination of any three angles and sides (except for all

TRIGONOMETRY

Trigonometric Functions of Angles from 0° to 15° and 75° to 90°

Angle	sin	cos	tan	cot	Angle	sin	cos	tan	cot	
0° 0′	0.000000	1.000000	0.000000	—	90° 0′	7° 30′	0.130526	0.991445	0.131652	7.595754	82° 30′
10	0.002909	0.999996	0.002909	343.7737	50	40	0.133410	0.991061	0.134613	7.428706	20
20	0.005818	0.999983	0.005818	171.8854	40	50	0.136292	0.990669	0.137576	7.268725	10
30	0.008727	0.999962	0.008727	114.5887	30	8° 0′	0.139173	0.990268	0.140541	7.115370	82° 0′
40	0.011635	0.999932	0.011636	85.93979	20	10	0.142053	0.989859	0.143508	6.968234	50
50	0.014544	0.999894	0.014545	68.75009	10	20	0.144932	0.989442	0.146478	6.826944	40
1° 0′	0.017452	0.999848	0.017455	57.28996	89° 0′	30	0.147809	0.989016	0.149451	6.691156	30
10	0.020361	0.999793	0.020365	49.10388	50	40	0.150686	0.988582	0.152426	6.560554	20
20	0.023269	0.999729	0.023275	42.96408	40	50	0.153561	0.988139	0.155404	6.434843	10
30	0.026177	0.999657	0.026186	38.18846	30	9° 0′	0.156434	0.987688	0.158384	6.313752	81° 0′
40	0.029085	0.999577	0.029097	34.36777	20	10	0.159307	0.987229	0.161368	6.197028	50
50	0.031992	0.999488	0.032009	31.24158	10	20	0.162178	0.986762	0.164354	6.084438	40
2° 0′	0.034899	0.999391	0.034921	28.63625	88° 0′	30	0.165048	0.986286	0.167343	5.975764	30
10	0.037806	0.999285	0.037834	26.43160	50	40	0.167916	0.985801	0.170334	5.870804	20
20	0.040713	0.999171	0.040747	24.54176	40	50	0.170783	0.985309	0.173329	5.769369	10
30	0.043619	0.999048	0.043661	22.90377	30	10° 0′	0.173648	0.984808	0.176327	5.671282	80° 0′
40	0.046525	0.998917	0.046576	21.47040	20	10	0.176512	0.984298	0.179328	5.576379	50
50	0.049431	0.998778	0.049491	20.20555	10	20	0.179375	0.983781	0.182332	5.484505	40
3° 0′	0.052336	0.998630	0.052408	19.08114	87° 0′	30	0.182236	0.983255	0.185339	5.395517	30
10	0.055241	0.998473	0.055325	18.07498	50	40	0.185095	0.982721	0.188349	5.309279	20
20	0.058145	0.998308	0.058243	17.16934	40	50	0.187953	0.982178	0.191363	5.225665	10
30	0.061049	0.998135	0.061163	16.34986	30	11° 0′	0.190809	0.981627	0.194380	5.144554	79° 0′
40	0.063952	0.997953	0.064083	15.60478	20	10	0.193664	0.981068	0.197401	5.065835	50
50	0.066854	0.997763	0.067004	14.92442	10	20	0.196517	0.980500	0.200425	4.989403	40
4° 0′	0.069756	0.997564	0.069927	14.30067	86° 0′	30	0.199368	0.979925	0.203452	4.915157	30
10	0.072658	0.997357	0.072851	13.72674	50	40	0.202218	0.979341	0.206483	4.843005	20
20	0.075559	0.997141	0.075775	13.19688	40	50	0.205065	0.978748	0.209518	4.772857	10
30	0.078459	0.996917	0.078702	12.70621	30	12° 0′	0.207912	0.978148	0.212557	4.704630	78° 0′
40	0.081359	0.996685	0.081629	12.25051	20	10	0.210756	0.977539	0.215599	4.638246	50
50	0.084258	0.996444	0.084558	11.82617	10	20	0.213599	0.976921	0.218645	4.573629	40
5° 0′	0.087156	0.996195	0.087489	11.43005	85° 0′	30	0.216440	0.976296	0.221695	4.510709	30
10	0.090053	0.995937	0.090421	11.05943	50	40	0.219279	0.975662	0.224748	4.449418	20
20	0.092950	0.995671	0.093354	10.71191	40	50	0.222116	0.975020	0.227806	4.389694	10
30	0.095846	0.995396	0.096289	10.38540	30	13° 0′	0.224951	0.974370	0.230868	4.331476	77° 0′
40	0.098741	0.995113	0.099226	10.07803	20	10	0.227784	0.973712	0.233934	4.274707	50
50	0.101635	0.994822	0.102164	9.788173	10	20	0.230616	0.973045	0.237004	4.219332	40
6° 0′	0.104528	0.994522	0.105104	9.514364	84° 0′	30	0.233445	0.972370	0.240079	4.165300	30
10	0.107421	0.994214	0.108046	9.255304	50	40	0.236273	0.971687	0.243157	4.112561	20
20	0.110313	0.993897	0.110990	9.009826	40	50	0.239098	0.970995	0.246241	4.061070	10
30	0.113203	0.993572	0.113936	8.776887	30	14° 0′	0.241922	0.970296	0.249328	4.010781	76° 0′
40	0.116093	0.993238	0.116883	8.555547	20	10	0.244743	0.969588	0.252420	3.961652	50
50	0.118982	0.992896	0.119833	8.344956	10	20	0.247563	0.968872	0.255516	3.913642	40
7° 0′	0.121869	0.992546	0.122785	8.144346	83° 0′	30	0.250380	0.968148	0.258618	3.866713	30
10	0.124756	0.992187	0.125738	7.953022	50	40	0.253195	0.967415	0.261723	3.820828	20
20	0.127642	0.991820	0.128694	7.770351	40	50	0.256008	0.966675	0.264834	3.775952	10
7° 30′	0.130526	0.991445	0.131652	7.595754	82° 30′	15° 0′	0.258819	0.965926	0.267949	3.732051	75° 0′
	cos	sin	cot	tan		Angle	cos	sin	cot	tan	Angle

For angles 0° to 15° 0′ (angles found in a column to the left of the data), use the column labels at the top of the table; for angles 75° to 90° 0′ (angles found in a column to the right of the data), use the column labels at the bottom of the table.

TRIGONOMETRY

Trigonometric Functions of Angles from 15° to 30° and 60° to 75°

Angle	sin	cos	tan	cot		Angle	sin	cos	tan	cot	
15° 0′	0.258819	0.965926	0.267949	3.732051	**75° 0′**	**22° 30′**	0.382683	0.923880	0.414214	2.414214	**67° 30**
10	0.261628	0.965169	0.271069	3.689093	**50**	**40**	0.385369	0.922762	0.417626	2.394489	**20**
20	0.264434	0.964404	0.274194	3.647047	**40**	**50**	0.388052	0.921638	0.421046	2.375037	**10**
30	0.267238	0.963630	0.277325	3.605884	**30**	**23° 0′**	0.390731	0.920505	0.424475	2.355852	**67° 0′**
40	0.270040	0.962849	0.280460	3.565575	**20**	**10**	0.393407	0.919364	0.427912	2.336929	**50**
50	0.272840	0.962059	0.283600	3.526094	**10**	**20**	0.396080	0.918216	0.431358	2.318261	**40**
16° 0′	0.275637	0.961262	0.286745	3.487414	**74° 0′**	**30**	0.398749	0.917060	0.434812	2.299843	**30**
10	0.278432	0.960456	0.289896	3.449512	**50**	**40**	0.401415	0.915896	0.438276	2.281669	**20**
20	0.281225	0.959642	0.293052	3.412363	**40**	**50**	0.404078	0.914725	0.441748	2.263736	**10**
30	0.284015	0.958820	0.296213	3.375943	**30**	**24° 0′**	0.406737	0.913545	0.445229	2.246037	**66° 0′**
40	0.286803	0.957990	0.299380	3.340233	**20**	**10**	0.409392	0.912358	0.448719	2.228568	**50**
50	0.289589	0.957151	0.302553	3.305209	**10**	**20**	0.412045	0.911164	0.452218	2.211323	**40**
17° 0′	0.292372	0.956305	0.305731	3.270853	**73° 0′**	**30**	0.414693	0.909961	0.455726	2.194300	**30**
10	0.295152	0.955450	0.308914	3.237144	**50**	**40**	0.417338	0.908751	0.459244	2.177492	**20**
20	0.297930	0.954588	0.312104	3.204064	**40**	**50**	0.419980	0.907533	0.462771	2.160896	**10**
30	0.300706	0.953717	0.315299	3.171595	**30**	**25° 0′**	0.422618	0.906308	0.466308	2.144507	**65° 0′**
40	0.303479	0.952838	0.318500	3.139719	**20**	**10**	0.425253	0.905075	0.469854	2.128321	**50**
50	0.306249	0.951951	0.321707	3.108421	**10**	**20**	0.427884	0.903834	0.473410	2.112335	**40**
18° 0′	0.309017	0.951057	0.324920	3.077684	**72° 0′**	**30**	0.430511	0.902585	0.476976	2.096544	**30**
10	0.311782	0.950154	0.328139	3.047492	**50**	**40**	0.433135	0.901329	0.480551	2.080944	**20**
20	0.314545	0.949243	0.331364	3.017830	**40**	**50**	0.435755	0.900065	0.484137	2.065532	**10**
30	0.317305	0.948324	0.334595	2.988685	**30**	**26° 0′**	0.438371	0.898794	0.487733	2.050304	**64° 0′**
40	0.320062	0.947397	0.337833	2.960042	**20**	**10**	0.440984	0.897515	0.491339	2.035256	**50**
50	0.322816	0.946462	0.341077	2.931888	**10**	**20**	0.443593	0.896229	0.494955	2.020386	**40**
19° 0′	0.325568	0.945519	0.344328	2.904211	**71° 0′**	**30**	0.446198	0.894934	0.498582	2.005690	**30**
10	0.328317	0.944568	0.347585	2.876997	**50**	**40**	0.448799	0.893633	0.502219	1.991164	**20**
20	0.331063	0.943609	0.350848	2.850235	**40**	**50**	0.451397	0.892323	0.505867	1.976805	**10**
30	0.333807	0.942641	0.354119	2.823913	**30**	**27° 0′**	0.453990	0.891007	0.509525	1.962611	**63° 0′**
40	0.336547	0.941666	0.357396	2.798020	**20**	**10**	0.456580	0.889682	0.513195	1.948577	**50**
50	0.339285	0.940684	0.360679	2.772545	**10**	**20**	0.459166	0.888350	0.516875	1.934702	**40**
20° 0′	0.342020	0.939693	0.363970	2.747477	**70° 0′**	**30**	0.461749	0.887011	0.520567	1.920982	**30**
10	0.344752	0.938694	0.367268	2.722808	**50**	**40**	0.464327	0.885664	0.524270	1.907415	**20**
20	0.347481	0.937687	0.370573	2.698525	**40**	**50**	0.466901	0.884309	0.527984	1.893997	**10**
30	0.350207	0.936672	0.373885	2.674621	**30**	**28° 0′**	0.469472	0.882948	0.531709	1.880726	**62° 0′**
40	0.352931	0.935650	0.377204	2.651087	**20**	**10**	0.472038	0.881578	0.535446	1.867600	**50**
50	0.355651	0.934619	0.380530	2.627912	**10**	**20**	0.474600	0.880201	0.539195	1.854616	**40**
21° 0′	0.358368	0.933580	0.383864	2.605089	**69° 0′**	**30**	0.477159	0.878817	0.542956	1.841771	**30**
10	0.361082	0.932534	0.387205	2.582609	**50**	**40**	0.479713	0.877425	0.546728	1.829063	**20**
20	0.363793	0.931480	0.390554	2.560465	**40**	**50**	0.482263	0.876026	0.550513	1.816489	**10**
30	0.366501	0.930418	0.393910	2.538648	**30**	**29° 0′**	0.484810	0.874620	0.554309	1.804048	**61° 0′**
40	0.369206	0.929348	0.397275	2.517151	**20**	**10**	0.487352	0.873206	0.558118	1.791736	**50**
50	0.371908	0.928270	0.400646	2.495966	**10**	**20**	0.489890	0.871784	0.561939	1.779552	**40**
22° 0′	0.374607	0.927184	0.404026	2.475087	**68° 0′**	**30**	0.492424	0.870356	0.565773	1.767494	**30**
10	0.377302	0.926090	0.407414	2.454506	**50**	**40**	0.494953	0.868920	0.569619	1.755559	**20**
20	0.379994	0.924989	0.410810	2.434217	**40**	**50**	0.497479	0.867476	0.573478	1.743745	**10**
22° 30	0.382683	0.923880	0.414214	2.414214	**67° 30**	**30° 0′**	0.500000	0.866025	0.577350	1.732051	**60° 0′**
	cos	sin	cot	tan	Angle		cos	sin	cot	tan	Angle

For angles 15° to 30° 0′ (angles found in a column to the left of the data), use the column labels at the top of the table; for angles 60° to 75° 0′ (angles found in a column to the right of the data), use the column labels at the bottom of the table.

TRIGONOMETRY

Trigonometric Functions of Angles from 30° to 60°

Angle	sin	cos	tan	cot		Angle	sin	cos	tan	cot	
30° 0′	0.500000	0.866025	0.577350	1.732051	60° 0′	37° 30′	0.608761	0.793353	0.767327	1.303225	52° 30′
10	0.502517	0.864567	0.581235	1.720474	50	40	0.611067	0.791579	0.771959	1.295406	20
20	0.505030	0.863102	0.585134	1.709012	40	50	0.613367	0.789798	0.776612	1.287645	10
30	0.507538	0.861629	0.589045	1.697663	30	38° 0′	0.615661	0.788011	0.781286	1.279942	52° 0′
40	0.510043	0.860149	0.592970	1.686426	20	10	0.617951	0.786217	0.785981	1.272296	50
50	0.512543	0.858662	0.596908	1.675299	10	20	0.620235	0.784416	0.790697	1.264706	40
31° 0′	0.515038	0.857167	0.600861	1.664279	59° 0′	30	0.622515	0.782608	0.795436	1.257172	30
10	0.517529	0.855665	0.604827	1.653366	50	40	0.624789	0.780794	0.800196	1.249693	20
20	0.520016	0.854156	0.608807	1.642558	40	50	0.627057	0.778973	0.804979	1.242268	10
30	0.522499	0.852640	0.612801	1.631852	30	39° 0′	0.629320	0.777146	0.809784	1.234897	51° 0′
40	0.524977	0.851117	0.616809	1.621247	20	10	0.631578	0.775312	0.814612	1.227579	50
50	0.527450	0.849586	0.620832	1.610742	10	20	0.633831	0.773472	0.819463	1.220312	40
32° 0′	0.529919	0.848048	0.624869	1.600335	58° 0′	30	0.636078	0.771625	0.824336	1.213097	30
10	0.532384	0.846503	0.628921	1.590024	50	40	0.638320	0.769771	0.829234	1.205933	20
20	0.534844	0.844951	0.632988	1.579808	40	50	0.640557	0.767911	0.834155	1.198818	10
30	0.537300	0.843391	0.637070	1.569686	30	40° 0′	0.642788	0.766044	0.839100	1.191754	50° 0′
40	0.539751	0.841825	0.641167	1.559655	20	10	0.645013	0.764171	0.844069	1.184738	50
50	0.542197	0.840251	0.645280	1.549715	10	20	0.647233	0.762292	0.849062	1.177770	40
33° 0′	0.544639	0.838671	0.649408	1.539865	57° 0′	30	0.649448	0.760406	0.854081	1.170850	30
10	0.547076	0.837083	0.653551	1.530102	50	40	0.651657	0.758514	0.859124	1.163976	20
20	0.549509	0.835488	0.657710	1.520426	40	50	0.653861	0.756615	0.864193	1.157149	10
30	0.551937	0.833886	0.661886	1.510835	30	41° 0′	0.656059	0.754710	0.869287	1.150368	49° 0′
40	0.554360	0.832277	0.666077	1.501328	20	10	0.658252	0.752798	0.874407	1.143633	50
50	0.556779	0.830661	0.670284	1.491904	10	20	0.660439	0.750880	0.879553	1.136941	40
34° 0′	0.559193	0.829038	0.674509	1.482561	56° 0′	30	0.662620	0.748956	0.884725	1.130294	30
10	0.561602	0.827407	0.678749	1.473298	50	40	0.664796	0.747025	0.889924	1.123691	20
20	0.564007	0.825770	0.683007	1.464115	40	50	0.666966	0.745088	0.895151	1.117130	10
30	0.566406	0.824126	0.687281	1.455009	30	42° 0′	0.669131	0.743145	0.900404	1.110613	48° 0′
40	0.568801	0.822475	0.691572	1.445980	20	10	0.671289	0.741195	0.905685	1.104137	50
50	0.571191	0.820817	0.695881	1.437027	10	20	0.673443	0.739239	0.910994	1.097702	40
35° 0′	0.573576	0.819152	0.700208	1.428148	55° 0′	30	0.675590	0.737277	0.916331	1.091309	30
10	0.575957	0.817480	0.704551	1.419343	50	40	0.677732	0.735309	0.921697	1.084955	20
20	0.578332	0.815801	0.708913	1.410610	40	50	0.679868	0.733334	0.927091	1.078642	10
30	0.580703	0.814116	0.713293	1.401948	30	43° 0′	0.681998	0.731354	0.932515	1.072369	47° 0′
40	0.583069	0.812423	0.717691	1.393357	20	10	0.684123	0.729367	0.937968	1.066134	50
50	0.585429	0.810723	0.722108	1.384835	10	20	0.686242	0.727374	0.943451	1.059938	40
36° 0′	0.587785	0.809017	0.726543	1.376382	54° 0′	30	0.688355	0.725374	0.948965	1.053780	30
10	0.590136	0.807304	0.730996	1.367996	50	40	0.690462	0.723369	0.954508	1.047660	20
20	0.592482	0.805584	0.735469	1.359676	40	50	0.692563	0.721357	0.960083	1.041577	10
30	0.594823	0.803857	0.739961	1.351422	30	44° 0′	0.694658	0.719340	0.965689	1.035530	46° 0′
40	0.597159	0.802123	0.744472	1.343233	20	10	0.696748	0.717316	0.971326	1.029520	50
50	0.599489	0.800383	0.749003	1.335108	10	20	0.698832	0.715286	0.976996	1.023546	40
37° 0′	0.601815	0.798636	0.753554	1.327045	53° 0′	30	0.700909	0.713250	0.982697	1.017607	30
10	0.604136	0.796882	0.758125	1.319044	50	40	0.702981	0.711209	0.988432	1.011704	20
20	0.606451	0.795121	0.762716	1.311105	40	50	0.705047	0.709161	0.994199	1.005835	10
37° 30	0.608761	0.793353	0.767327	1.303225	52° 30	45° 0′	0.707107	0.707107	1.000000	1.000000	45° 0′
	cos	sin	cot	tan	Angle		cos	sin	cot	tan	Angle

For angles 30° to 45° 0′ (angles found in a column to the left of the data), use the column labels at the top of the table; for angles 45° to 60° 0′ (angles found in a column to the right of the data), use the column labels at the bottom of the table.

Table courtesy of *Machinery's Handbook*, 26th ed., edited by Erik Oberg, Franklin D. Jones, Holbrook L. Horton, Henry H. Ryffel, and Christopher J. McCauley (Industrial Press, 2000).

three angles). See Figure 15-12 for an understanding of the assignment of letters to specific sides and angles used in the equation for the law of cosines or the law of sines.

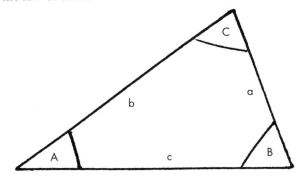

Figure 15-12. Triangle conventions for the law of sines or cosines.

Law of Sines

$a/b = (sin\ A)/(sin\ B)$ or $b/c = (sin\ B)/(sin\ C)$ or $a/c = (sin\ A)/(sin\ C)$

Law of Cosines

$c^2 = a^2 + b^2 - 2ab\ cos\ C$

Logarithms

Logarithms are one of those things that many people had to learn in high school. When I have a modern calculator at my fingertips, I only use logarithms for dealing with either huge or extremely tiny numbers. But, if I didn't have access to a calculator, logarithms would be indispensable for almost any complex calculation. Logarithms tremendously simplify hand calculations that involve multiplying or dividing large numbers, and any calculations that involve raising a number to a power beyond 2 (beyond the "square" of a number). They are especially useful for raising a number to a fractional power. I have absolutely no idea how I would calculate a fractional exponent, such as the value of $120^{.35}$ without either a calculator or a log table.

WHAT IS A LOGARITHM?

The logarithm (abbreviated as "log") of a number is the power that the number 10 would be raised to equal that number. For example, the log of 100 is equal to 2, since $10^2 = 100$. The log of .01 is equal to –2, since $10^{-2} = 1/10^2 = .01$. Similarly, the log of 10,000 equals 4, and the log of a million equals 6. Log tables typically provide logarithms for numbers between 1 and 10. To find numbers less than 1 or greater than ten, you convert the number into a number between 1 and 10 multiplied by 10 raised to some power. For instance, to find the log of 13,500,000, you would first convert this number to 1.35×10^7. Next, find the log of 1.35 using a log table, which is equal to .1303. The log of 13,500,000 is equal to .1303 + 7, or 7.1303. To find the anti-log of a logarithm, simply reverse this process. If you don't understand any of this, don't worry about it. If the need arises to perform a complex calculation, and you don't have access to a modern electronic calculator, hopefully you can find someone who understands logarithms.

WHAT IS AN ANTI-LOGARITHM?

An "anti-log" is the opposite of a logarithm. To convert a log back into a number, you raise 10 to the power of the log and you get a regular number again. The easy way to do this is to subtract out the whole number from the log and use a log table to find the anti-log of the remaining decimal (or fraction) between 1 and 0. Raise 10 to the whole number of the log and multiply by the anti-log of the fraction and you have converted the log back into a regular number. The whole reason for using logs is to simplify complex calculations, but you need to convert the logs back into regular numbers again (this is called finding the "anti-log") to get a meaningful answer. For example, the anti-log of 3 is equal to 1,000 because $10^3 = 1,000$. The anti-log of 2.49 is 309 because the anti-log of .49 is 3.09, and the anti-log of 2 is $10^2 = 100$, and $100 \times 3.09 = 309$. This will become clearer in the following sections.

MULTIPLICATION WITH LOGARITHMS

When multiplying large numbers, you would simply add the logs of the numbers and then convert the sum back (take the anti-log) into a regular number. It is easier to add large numbers, especially a string of numbers, than to multiply them, so logs simplifies complex string calculations.

LOGARITHMS

Table of Common Logarithms

	0	1	2	3	4	5	6	7	8	9
10	000000	004321	008600	012837	017033	021189	025306	029384	033424	037426
11	041393	045323	049218	053078	056905	060698	064458	068186	071882	075547
12	079181	082785	086360	089905	093422	096910	100371	103804	107210	110590
13	113943	117271	120574	123852	127105	130334	133539	136721	139879	143015
14	146128	149219	152288	155336	158362	161368	164353	167317	170262	173186
15	176091	178977	181844	184691	187521	190332	193125	195900	198657	201397
16	204120	206826	209515	212188	214844	217484	220108	222716	225309	227887
17	230449	232996	235528	238046	240549	243038	245513	247973	250420	252853
18	255273	257679	260071	262451	264818	267172	269513	271842	274158	276462
19	278754	281033	283301	285557	287802	290035	292256	294466	296665	298853
20	301030	303196	305351	307496	309630	311754	313867	315970	318063	320146
21	322219	324282	326336	328380	330414	332438	334454	336460	338456	340444
22	342423	344392	346353	348305	350248	352183	354108	356026	357935	359835
23	361728	363612	365488	367356	369216	371068	372912	374748	376577	378398
24	380211	382017	383815	385606	387390	389166	390935	392697	394452	396199
25	397940	399674	401401	403121	404834	406540	408240	409933	411620	413300
26	414973	416641	418301	419956	421604	423246	424882	426511	428135	429752
27	431364	432969	434569	436163	437751	439333	440909	442480	444045	445604
28	447158	448706	450249	451786	453318	454845	456366	457882	459392	460898
29	462398	463893	465383	466868	468347	469822	471292	472756	474216	475671
30	477121	478566	480007	481443	482874	484300	485721	487138	488551	489958
31	491362	492760	494155	495544	496930	498311	499687	501059	502427	503791
32	505150	506505	507856	509203	510545	511883	513218	514548	515874	517196
33	518514	519828	521138	522444	523746	525045	526339	527630	528917	530200
34	531479	532754	534026	535294	536558	537819	539076	540329	541579	542825
35	544068	545307	546543	547775	549003	550228	551450	552668	553883	555094
36	556303	557507	558709	559907	561101	562293	563481	564666	565848	567026
37	568202	569374	570543	571709	572872	574031	575188	576341	577492	578639
38	579784	580925	582063	583199	584331	585461	586587	587711	588832	589950
39	591065	592177	593286	594393	595496	596597	597695	598791	599883	600973
40	602060	603144	604226	605305	606381	607455	608526	609594	610660	611723
41	612784	613842	614897	615950	617000	618048	619093	620136	621176	622214
42	623249	624282	625312	626340	627366	628389	629410	630428	631444	632457
43	633468	634477	635484	636488	637490	638489	639486	640481	641474	642465
44	643453	644439	645422	646404	647383	648360	649335	650308	651278	652246
45	653213	654177	655138	656098	657056	658011	658965	659916	660865	661813
46	662758	663701	664642	665581	666518	667453	668386	669317	670246	671173
47	672098	673021	673942	674861	675778	676694	677607	678518	679428	680336
48	681241	682145	683047	683947	684845	685742	686636	687529	688420	689309
49	690196	691081	691965	692847	693727	694605	695482	696356	697229	698101
50	698970	699838	700704	701568	702431	703291	704151	705008	705864	706718
51	707570	708421	709270	710117	710963	711807	712650	713491	714330	715167
52	716003	716838	717671	718502	719331	720159	720986	721811	722634	723456
53	724276	725095	725912	726727	727541	728354	729165	729974	730782	731589
54	732394	733197	733999	734800	735599	736397	737193	737987	738781	739572
55	740363	741152	741939	742725	743510	744293	745075	745855	746634	747412
56	748188	748963	749736	750508	751279	752048	752816	753583	754348	755112
57	755875	756636	757396	758155	758912	759668	760422	761176	761928	762679
58	763428	764176	764923	765669	766413	767156	767898	768638	769377	770115
59	770852	771587	772322	773055	773786	774517	775246	775974	776701	777427

LOGARITHMS

Table of Common Logarithms

	0	1	2	3	4	5	6	7	8	9
60	778151	778874	779596	780317	781037	781755	782473	783189	783904	784617
61	785330	786041	786751	787460	788168	788875	789581	790285	790988	791691
62	792392	793092	793790	794488	795185	795880	796574	797268	797960	798651
63	799341	800029	800717	801404	802089	802774	803457	804139	804821	805501
64	806180	806858	807535	808211	808886	809560	810233	810904	811575	812245
65	812913	813581	814248	814913	815578	816241	816904	817565	818226	818885
66	819544	820201	820858	821514	822168	822822	823474	824126	824776	825426
67	826075	826723	827369	828015	828660	829304	829947	830589	831230	831870
68	832509	833147	833784	834421	835056	835691	836324	836957	837588	838219
69	838849	839478	840106	840733	841359	841985	842609	843233	843855	844477
70	845098	845718	846337	846955	847573	848189	848805	849419	850033	850646
71	851258	851870	852480	853090	853698	854306	854913	855519	856124	856729
72	857332	857935	858537	859138	859739	860338	860937	861534	862131	862728
73	863323	863917	864511	865104	865696	866287	866878	867467	868056	868644
74	869232	869818	870404	870989	871573	872156	872739	873321	873902	874482
75	875061	875640	876218	876795	877371	877947	878522	879096	879669	880242
76	880814	881385	881955	882525	883093	883661	884229	884795	885361	885926
77	886491	887054	887617	888179	888741	889302	889862	890421	890980	891537
78	892095	892651	893207	893762	894316	894870	895423	895975	896526	897077
79	897627	898176	898725	899273	899821	900367	900913	901458	902003	902547
80	903090	903633	904174	904716	905256	905796	906335	906874	907411	907949
81	908485	909021	909556	910091	910624	911158	911690	912222	912753	913284
82	913814	914343	914872	915400	915927	916454	916980	917506	918030	918555
83	919078	919601	920123	920645	921166	921686	922206	922725	923244	923762
84	924279	924796	925312	925828	926342	926857	927370	927883	928396	928908
85	929419	929930	930440	930949	931458	931966	932474	932981	933487	933993
86	934498	935003	935507	936011	936514	937016	937518	938019	938520	939020
87	939519	940018	940516	941014	941511	942008	942504	943000	943495	943989
88	944483	944976	945469	945961	946452	946943	947434	947924	948413	948902
89	949390	949878	950365	950851	951338	951823	952308	952792	953276	953760
90	954243	954725	955207	955688	956168	956649	957128	957607	958086	958564
91	959041	959518	959995	960471	960946	961421	961895	962369	962843	963316
92	963788	964260	964731	965202	965672	966142	966611	967080	967548	968016
93	968483	968950	969416	969882	970347	970812	971276	971740	972203	972666
94	973128	973590	974051	974512	974972	975432	975891	976350	976808	977266
95	977724	978181	978637	979093	979548	980003	980458	980912	981366	981819
96	982271	982723	983175	983626	984077	984527	984977	985426	985875	986324
97	986772	987219	987666	988113	988559	989005	989450	989895	990339	990783
98	991226	991669	992111	992554	992995	993436	993877	994317	994757	995196
99	995635	996074	996512	996949	997386	997823	998259	998695	999131	999565
100	000000	000434	000868	001301	001734	002166	002598	003029	003461	003891
101	004321	004751	005181	005609	006038	006466	006894	007321	007748	008174
102	008600	009026	009451	009876	010300	010724	011147	011570	011993	012415
103	012837	013259	013680	014100	014521	014940	015360	015779	016197	016616
104	017033	017451	017868	018284	018700	019116	019532	019947	020361	020775
105	021189	021603	022016	022428	022841	023252	023664	024075	024486	024896
106	025306	025715	026125	026533	026942	027350	027757	028164	028571	028978
107	029384	029789	030195	030600	031004	031408	031812	032216	032619	033021
108	033424	033826	034227	034628	035029	035430	035830	036230	036629	037028
109	037426	037825	038223	038620	039017	039414	039811	040207	040602	040998

Table courtesy of *Machinery's Handbook*, 26th ed., edited by Erik Oberg, Franklin D. Jones, Holbrook L. Horton, Henry H. Ryffel, and Christopher J. McCauley (Industrial Press, 2000).

DIVISION WITH LOGARITHMS

When dividing large numbers, you would simply subtract the log of the divisor (the number on the bottom) from the log of the number on the top, and then convert this value back (take the anti-log) into a regular number. It is easier to subtract large numbers, especially a string of numbers, than to multiply them, so logs simplify complex string calculations. In complex strings, you can both add logs of multiplied numbers and subtract logs of divisors all in one calculation, before taking the anti-log to convert it back into a regular number.

EXPONENTS (POWERS) WITH LOGARITHMS

The real beauty of logarithms comes into play when you start calculating numbers raised to powers (exponents), especially when exponents are large or fractional numbers (most fractional exponents are almost impossible to calculate by hand). When you raise a number to a power (exponent), the same operation in logs simply multiples the log of the number by its exponent, and then you use anti-logs to convert the answer back into a regular number. For instance, finding the value of 127^7 would probably take me at least an hour with hand multiplication, but only a couple of minutes with logarithms. First, convert the number into $(1.27 \times 10^2)^7$. Next, using a log table, find that the log of 1.27 is equal to .1038, so the log of 127 is equal to 2.1038. Now multiply 2.1038 x 7 and you find that the log of 127^7 is equal to 14.726. Next, taking the anti-log of .726 = 5.32 (.726 is the non-whole number portion), you find that the answer is the rather large number 5.32 x 10^{14}. Finding this number by manual multiplication would have been an extremely tedious task.

REFERENCES

Engineering

Mark's Standard Handbook for Mechanical Engineers, **10th ed., edited by Eugene A. Avalone and Theodore Baumeister III.** 1996, 1792 pp. (hardcover), ISBN 0-07-004997-1. Published by McGraw-Hill Companies, 1221 Avenue of the Americas, New York, NY 10020. Lists for $150.00.

"Broad in its coverage, yet concise in its treatment of each topic, the handbook is a virtual encyclopedia—covering all aspects of the multifaceted field of mechanical engineering and related disciplines....With more useful information than any other single source, this is the most practical and reliable handbook on mechanical engineering ever published." (*Canadian Metalworking and Machinery*)

This is a great reference to have for your personal technology library. It contains a huge amount of practical information about materials, machines, processes, and engineering principles. From basic math to calculus, patent law to economic analysis, strength of steel beams to wooden trusses, pouring concrete to piping water, burning coal to solar energy, you can find it in *Mark's Handbook*. Mechanical engineering is the mother of most engineering disciplines and the mechanical engineer often ties together widely varying technologies to make things work. *Mark's Handbook* includes a 91-page chapter on electrical engineering and basic electronics, because mechanical engineers often need to understand electronics well enough to design simple circuits or to properly interface with electrical engineers.

FE Review Manual: Rapid Preparation for the General Fundamentals of Engineering Exam **by Michael R. Lindeburg, P.E.** 2000, 864 pp. (paperback), ISBN 1-888577-53-3. Published by Professional Publications, Inc., 1250 Fifth St., Belmont, CA 94002-3863. Lists for $52.95.

Most people buy this book to help them study for the Fundamentals of Engineering exam (FE, used to be called EIT), which is a prerequisite for taking any of the professional engineering exams required for certification as a professional engineer. I recommend it as an excellent study guide and source for practical engineering information covering a broad range of fields, including mathematics, electronics, computers, controls, heat transfer, thermodynamics, fluids, mechanics, statics, dynamics, materials science, chemistry, physics, and engineering economics. Unlike most engineering handbooks, Lindeburg's study guides include solved examples of common engineering problems, so that you can figure out similar problems even if you have been out of school for years or don't have an engineering degree (but do have an aptitude for this sort of thing). This book contains only practical material that covers real-world engineering (no advanced theory or deriving of equations).

Mechanical Engineering Reference Manual for the PE Exam, by Michael R. Lindeburg, P.E. 1998, 1232 pp. (hardcover), ISBN 1-888577-13-4. Published by Professional Publications, Inc., 1250 Fifth St., Belmont, CA 94002-3863. Lists for $89.95.

This is one of the most valuable reference texts that I own. It has most of the charts and equations that I need to solve the real-world engineering problems that I regularly come across in my design practice. Most people buy this book to help them study for the Professional Engineering exam (PE) in mechanical engineering, and then continue to refer to it on a regular basis because it is such a wonderful practical reference. Because I have been out of school for over twenty years, and I'm not an analysis guru, the examples and solved problems help me to solve similar real-world problems, and would be invaluable to a nonengineer trying to apply the information in the manual.

Roark's Formulas for Stress and Strain, by Warren C. Young and Richard G. Budynas. 2001, 832 pp. (hardcover), ISBN 0-07-072542-X. Published by McGraw-Hill Companies, 1221 Avenue of the Americas, New York, NY 10020. Lists for $89.50.

Want to know if your steam boiler can take the pressure? How about if that steel I-beam can support a 30-foot bridge across the river? With this stress/strain "cookbook," engineers and even lay designers can perform accurate stress (strength) analysis of fairly sophisticated designs without resorting to complex numerical methods or computer-aided finite element analysis. Just scan the simple diagrams to find the case closest to yours, and then plug the numbers into the equations. No calculus required, just high school algebra. I've used an earlier edition of this handbook for about twenty years.

Civil Engineering Reference Manual for the PE Exam, by Michael Lindeburg, P.E. 1999, 1472 pp. (hardcover), ISBN 1-888577-40-1. Published by Professional Publications, Inc., 1250 Fifth St., Belmont, CA 94002-3863. Lists for $99.95.

Civil engineering is based upon most of the same disciplines as mechanical engineering, but applied on a larger scale, like buildings, roads, bridges and dams. Most people buy this book to help them study for the Professional Engineering exam (PE) in civil engineering, and then continue to refer to it on a regular basis because it is such a wonderful practical reference.

Standard Handbook for Civil Engineers, 4th ed., edited by Frederick S. Merritt, M. Kent Loftin, and Jonathan T. Ricketts. 1995, 1600 pp. (hardcover), ISBN 0-07-041597-8. Published by McGraw-Hill Companies, 1221 Avenue of the Americas, New York, NY 10020. Lists for $150.00.

A giant one-stop review of the field of civil engineering, this book gives you access to everything from the fundamentals of civil engineering to the most recent planning, design, and construction techniques related to twenty-three different disciplines—including systems design; geotechnical engineering; structural design with steel, wood and concrete; and community and regional planning. Definitely not the best text for advanced structural analysis and seismic design, but a good overall reference guide.

Electrical Engineering Reference Manual for the PE Exam, by Raymond B. Yarbrough. 1997, 520 pp. (hardcover), ISBN 1-888577-04-5. Published by Professional Publications, Inc., 1250 Fifth St., Belmont, CA 94002-3863. Lists for $69.95.

Like the mechanical equivalents, this is a good reference for practical electrical engineering and design. It won't help you to design the latest microprocessor chip, but it will give you guidance for power systems, motors, circuit design, logic circuits, amplifying circuits, and so on.

Machinery

Machinery's Handbook, 26th ed., edited by Erik
Oberg, Franklin D. Jones, Holbrook L. Horton,
Henry H. Ryffel, and Christopher J. McCauley.
2000, 2640 pp. (hardcover), ISBN 0-8311-2625-6.
Published by Industrial Press, Inc., 200 Madison
Ave., New York, NY 10016. Lists for $85.00.
I have yet to see a highly skilled professional
machinist who did not have a copy of this book on
his or her workbench. Most design engineers also
have a copy. This is not an instruction manual on
how to machine metal, but it contains crucial information on millions of details that are important to
drafting technicians, engineers, designers, and
machinists. Want to cut a spur gear, calculate the
strength of a steel I-beam, or figure out the size and
thread system for a broken screw on some piece of
obscure machinery (or machine a new one)? This
book will provide the details, dimensions, and other
specifications that you need to make proper hardware and components.

Electric Motor Repair, by Robert Rosenberg. 1987,
750 pp. (paperback), ISBN 0-03-059584-3.
Published by Saunders College Publishing,
Division of Harcourt Brace, 150 S.
Independence Mall West, Suite 1250,
Philadelphia, PA 19106-3412. Lists for $107.00.
This is a terrific nontheoretical book on electric
motor repair and control. It is a complete hands-on
approach to the repair and control of AC and DC
motors, written by a long-term vocational instructor
of electric motor repair. If you ever needed to scavenge together the parts and wire to rewind an arma-
ture, or otherwise repair an alternator or motor, this
is the book you would want to have on hand. It is
arranged in a double spiral-bound layout where the
illustrations are in a volume on one side and the text
on the opposite side. The unique binding ties both
volumes together yet they can be opened and laid
flat on a workbench for easy simultaneous viewing
of both the text and illustration volumes. This way
you don't have to flip pages with greasy hands while
in the middle of a repair. This latest edition features
a chapter on solid state and microprocessor controls.

Ingenious Mechanisms for Designers and Inventors,
by Franklin D. Jones, John A. Newell, and
Holbrook L. Horton. 1977, 2103pp. (Hardcover
in 4 volumes), ISBN 0-8311-1084-8. Published
by Industrial Press, Inc., 200 Madison Ave., New
York, NY 10016. Lists for $115.00.
Prior to the current electronics age, where micro-
processors and servomechanisms have taken over
most aspects of motion control, ingenious mechanisms were developed to control a wide variety of
machine motions and special functions. Much of
this knowledge has disappeared from current engineers' and machinists' curriculums due to replacement by electronic controls. These texts record the
functional details of ingenious mechanisms from
the past few centuries. Volume I was first
published in 1930, Volume II in 1936, Volume III
in 1951, and Volume IV in 1977. Among the
mechanisms described and illustrated by working
diagrams are cam applications and special cam
designs, intermittent motions from gears and
cams, interlocking devices, valve diagrams, revers-
ing mechanisms of special design, tripping or stop
mechanisms, drives of crank type for reciprocating
driven members, feeding mechanisms and auxil-
iary devices, feeding and ejecting mechanisms, and
many, many more.

Standard Handbook of Machine Design, edited by
Joseph E. Shigley and Charles R. Mischke. 1996,
1700 pp. (hardcover), ISBN 0-07-056958-4.
Published by McGraw-Hill Companies, 1221
Avenue of the Americas, New York, NY 10020.
Lists for $125.00.
A fine book for the serious designer of machinery.
The *Standard Handbook of Machine Design* offers
quick, reliable solutions to just about any machine
design problem you'll ever face—whether it involves
problems with wear, strength, usability, or safety.

***A Diderot Pictorial Encyclopedia of Trades and
Industry: Manufacturing and the Technical
Arts in Plates Selected from "L'Encyclopedie, ou
Dictionnaire Raisonne des Sciences, des Arts et
des Metiers,"*** Volume One, by Denis Diderot.
1987, 936 pp. (paperback), ISBN 0-486-27428-4.

Published by Dover Publications, Inc., 31 E. Second St., Mineola, NY 11501. Lists for $19.95. First printed in 1751, the plates contained in this historical encyclopedia offer a unique look at machines and technologies just prior to the industrial revolution. Volume 1 covers agriculture, articles of war, iron foundry and forge, mining, and metalworking. Volume 2 covers glassworks, printing, masonry, goldsmithing/jewelry, leatherworks, carpentry, and more. Both are fine books for techno-history buffs. Want to make an authentic nineteenth-century windmill to grind grain? The *Encyclopedia* will show you how.

Industrial Press, 200 Madison Ave., New York, NY 10016; phone: (212) 889-6330; fax: (212) 545-8327; web site: www.industrialpress.com.
Industrial Press publishes the well-known *Machinery's Handbook* plus about a hundred other technical books about machines, manufacturing, engineering, and technology.

RESOURCES

Appearing below are a few catalogs (among hundreds) that are particularly useful and carry a broad range of items.

W.W. Grainger, Inc., 100 Grainger Parkway, Lake Forest, IL 60045-5201; phone: (847) 535-1000; fax: (847) 535-9221; web site: www.grainger.com.
Grainger is an industrial supply company offering a huge selection of industrial hardware, supplies, and tools. I would be willing to bet that at least nine out of ten industrial maintenance specialists in the United States have a Grainger catalog in their bookcases. Grainger has a couple hundred branches, so I suggest you call or use their web site to locate the nearest branch. I use Grainger to supply many of the off-the-shelf components for the custom machinery that I design. Their catalog is encyclopedia-sized. Grainger is great for things like motors, compressors, blowers, tanks, wheels, fittings, fasteners, bearings, regulators, and so on.

McMaster-Carr Supply Company, P.O. Box 54960, Los Angeles, CA 90054-0960; phone: (562) 692-5911; fax: (562) 695-2323; web site: www.mcmaster.com.
Similar to Grainger, McMaster-Carr is an industrial supply company that seems to stock nearly everything under the sun. A sampling of the items they stock includes pumps, compressors, plumbing items, fasteners, machine tools, motors, controllers, hand tools, conveyors, instrumentation, and HVAC. Over 340,000 are items packed into their 3,200-page catalog. Available from five locations spread across the country.

Stock Drive Products/Sterling Instrument, P.O. Box 5416, New Hyde Park, NY 11042-5416; phone: (516) 328-3300; fax: (800) 737-7436; web site: www.sdp-si.com.
A great source for small quantities of precision parts for the inventor, engineer, or home shop. This company stocks a huge quantity of hardware, bearings, small motors, and various drive components.

Steven Engineering, 230 Ryan Way, South San Francisco, CA 94080-6730; phone: (800) 258-9200; fax: (650) 588-9300; web site: (in process).
Steven Engineering is a huge supplier of industrial controls, switches, controllers, enclosures, and so on—anything related to wiring and electronic control of machines and industrial processes. This company has a giant catalog.

Edmund Scientific, 101 East Gloucester Pike, Barrington, NJ 08007-1380; phone: (800) 728-6999; fax: (856) 547-3292; web site: www.edsci.com.
A fine source for optics, microscopes, telescopes, and lab supplies. Want to cook up some of the recipes in *Henley's Formulas* or *Wagner's Chemical Technology*? Edmund's could supply some of the necessary equipment.

Afterword

With all my being, I know that humankind cannot continue behaving as if the world was an infinite reservoir of natural resources that we may do with as we wish, consumed in ever-increasing amounts by an ever-increasing population. One of the things that defines humanity is the dual power of creativity and free will. We have the power to choose wisely or foolishly, but choose we must. To choose to do nothing is still making a choice.

We may choose a planetary future from two paths traveling in opposite directions. We may choose to accept our responsibility in the co-creation of ourselves along with planet Earth—the source of everything around us and everything that we have come to be over the millennia. This type of responsibility requires a fully conscious and compassionate awareness of the consequences of our actions for the long-term health of both the Earth and our humankind.

On the other hand, like lemmings rushing to the ocean, we can proceed toward famines, collapsing ecosystems, wars, and plagues. This is the path of business as usual, waiting for science and technology to come up with solutions, and ultimately suffering the consequences of the collapse of natural systems that took thousands of years or even more to evolve.

Throughout human history, great changes have followed actions that began at a grassroots level before blossoming into large-scale movements. Individuals, households, and communities changed their attitudes and behaviors and made sacrifices. The choice is ours. For our own sakes and those of our children to the seventh generation and beyond, we must choose a path with a future that we can all look forward to. In the words of Robert Muller, former assistant to the Secretary General for the United Nations:

> *Nothing but happiness is good enough for the genial and proud human race on planet Earth. Maximum peace, beauty, and happiness and not maximum economic welfare must be the objectives of the coming World Renaissance. The beauty of flowers is due to the care of the gardener. The beauty of the world will depend on the care of its gardeners. Let us therefore all become living gardeners of the world.*

Bibliography

Note: The following includes references used in this book as well as additional recommended works.

AAA Solar. "Design Guide." Available at http://www. aaasolar.com. Accessed April 2000.

ABC TV. "Over a Barrel." Transcript of program televised on February 9, 1999. Available at http://www. abc.net.au/lateline/stories/s49069.htm. Accessed une 2, 2000.

Agricola, Georgius. *De re Metallica.* Mineola, NY: Dover Publications, Inc., 1950.

AEI (Alternative Energy Institute), "Report on the World Oil Forum: October 30, 1998, in Denver, Colorado, USA," February 14, 1999. Available at http://www.altenergy.org/2/nonrenewables/fossil_fuel /depletion/denver_energy_meeting/denver_ener-gy_meeting.html. Accessed May 1999.

Alexander, R.F. "Beginning Considerations for Passive Solar Design: Comments on the Page 36 House Plan." *Adobe Builder,* Spring 1997.

Andrews, Jack. *New Edge of the Anvil: A Resource Book for the Blacksmith.* Berlin, MD: SkipJack Press, Inc., 1994.

A'o, Lono Kahuna Kupua. *Don't Drink the Water (Without Reading This Book): The Essential Guide to Our Contaminated Drinking Water and What You Can Do About It.* Pagosa Springs, CO: Kali Press, 1998.

ARM (Atmospheric Radiation Measurement program of the U.S. Department of Energy). "Methane Gas" and "Carbon Dioxide." Available at http://www.arm/gov/docs/education/ globwarm/methexpert.html and http://www. arm.gov/docs/education/globwarm/carbexpert. html, respectively. Accessed April 2000.

AtKisson, Alan. *Believing Cassandra: An Optimist Looks at a Pessimist's World.* White River Junction, VT: Chelsea Green Publishing Company, 1999.

Avalone, Eugene A., and Theodore Baumeister III, eds. *Mark's Standard Handbook for Mechanical Engineers.* 10th ed. New York: McGraw-Hill Companies, 1996.

AWEA (American Wind Energy Association). "1999 Global Wind Energy Market Report." Available at http://www.awea.org/news/news991223glo.html. Accessed April 2000.

Bakule, Paula Dreifus, ed. *Rodale's Book of Practical Formulas.* New York: Fine Communications, 1997.

Balch, James F., M.D., and Phyllis A. Balch, C.N.C. *Prescription for Nutritional Healing: A Practical A–Z Reference to Drug-Free Remedies Using Vitamins, Minerals, Herbs & Food Supplements.* New York: Avery Publishing Group, 1997.

Baldwin, William J., D.D.S., Ph.D. *Spirit Releasement Therapy: A Technique Manual.* Terra Alta, WV: Headline Books, 1995.

Banks, Howard. "Cheap Oil: Enjoy It While It Lasts." *Forbes,* June 15, 1998.

Baranowski, Zane, C.N. *Colloidal Silver: The Natural Antibiotic Alternative.* New York: Healing Wisdom Publications, 1995.

Barker, Jennifer Stein. *The Morning Hill Solar Cookery Book.* Canyon City, OR: Morning Hill Associates, 1999.

Barlow, Russ. "Residential Fuel Cells: Hope or Hype?" *Home Power Magazine,* #72, August/September 1999.

Barrow, C.J. *Land Degradation.* Cambridge: Cambridge University Press, 1991.

Bartholomew, Mel. *Square Foot Gardening.* Emmaus, PA: Rodale Press, 1981.

Beard, D.C. *Shelters, Shacks and Shanties and How to Build Them.* New York: The Lyons Press, 1999

Beeby, John. *Future Fertility: Transforming Human Waste into Human Wealth.* Willits, CA: Ecology Action, 1995.

————. *Test Your Soil with Plants!* Willits, CA: Ecology Action, 1995.

Bell Jr., Frank A. "Review of Effects of Silver-Impregnated Carbon Filters on Microbial Water Quality." *Journal AWWA*, August 1991.

Benson, Tedd. *Building the Timber Frame House: The Revival of a Forgotten Craft.* Newtown, CT: Taunton Press, 1986.

————. *The Timber Frame-Home: Design, Construction, Finishing.* Newtown, CT: Taunton Press, 1997.

————. *Timberframe: The Art and Craft of the Post-and-Beam Home.* Newtown, CT: Taunton Press, 1999.

Berger, Steve. "Ancient Arts, Modern Technology." *Natural Home Magazine*, July/August 2000.

Biringuccio, Vannoccio. *The Pirotechnia of Vannoccio Biringuccio: The Classic Sixteenth-Century Treatise on Metals and Metallurgy.* Mineola, NY: Dover Publications, Inc., 1990.

Blankenship, Bart, and Robin Blankenship. *Earth Knack: Stone Age Skills for the 21st Century.* Layton, UT: Gibbs Smith, 1996.

Blumenthal, Betsy. *Hands On Dyeing.* Loveland, CO: Interweave Press, 1988.

Bower, John. *The Healthy House: How to Buy One, How to Build One, How to Cure a Sick One.* Bloomington, IN: The Healthy House Institute, 1998.

Bradley, Fern Marshall, and Barbara W. Ellis, eds. *Rodale's All-New Encyclopedia of Organic Gardening: The Indispensable Resource for Every Gardener.* Emmaus, PA: Rodale Press, 1997.

Brennan, Barbara Ann. *Hands of Light: A Guide to Healing Through the Human Energy Field.* New York: Bantam Doubleday Dell Publishers, 1993.

Brill, Steve, and Evelyn Dean. *Identifying and Harvesting Edible and Medicinal Plants in Wild (And Not So Wild) Places.* New York: Hearst Books, 1994.

Brinker, Francis, N.D. *Herb Contraindications and Drug Interactions.* Sandy, OR: Eclectic Medical Publications, 1998.

Brower, Michael, Ph.D. and Warren Levon, Ph.D. *The Consumer's Guide to Effective Environmental Choices: Practical Advice from the Union of Concerned Scientists.* New York: Three Rivers Press, 1999.

Brown, Lester R. "Climate Change Has World Skating on Thin Ice." *Worldwatch Alert*, Issue #7, August 29, 2000.

Brown, Lester R., Christopher Flavin, and Sandra Postel. *Saving the Planet: How to Shape an Environmentally Sustainable Global Economy.* New York: W.W. Norton & Company, 1991.

Brown, Lester R., Michael Renner, and Christopher Flavin. *Vital Signs 1998: The Environmental Trends That Are Shaping Our Future.* New York: W.W. Norton & Company, 1998.

Brown, Lester R., Michael Renner, and Brian Halweil. *Vital Signs 1999: The Environmental Trends that Are Shaping Our Future.* New York: W.W. Norton & Company, 1999a.

Brown, Lester R., Christopher Flavin, and Hillary French. *State of the World 1999: A Worldwatch Institute Report on Progress Towards a Sustainable Society.* New York: W. W. Norton & Company, 1999b.

————. *State of the World 2000.* New York: W.W. Norton & Company, 2000a.

Brown, Lester R., Michael Renner, and Brian Halweil. *Vital Signs 2000: The Environmental Trends That Are Shaping Our Future.* New York: W.W. Norton & Co., Inc., 2000b.

Brown, Rachel. *The Weaving, Spinning and Dyeing Book.* New York: Alfred A. Knopf, 1983.

Brown, Tom Jr. *Tom Brown's Field Guide to Nature Observation and Tracking.* New York: Berkley Publishing Group, 1988.

Brown, Tom, Jr., with Brandt Morgan. *Tom Brown's Field Guide to Wilderness Survival.* New York: Berkley Publishing Group, 1987.

Bryant, Edward A., George P. Fulton, and George C. Budd. *Disinfection Alternatives for Safe Drinking Water.* New York: Van Nostrand Reinhold, 1992.

Bubel, Mike, and Nancy Bubel. *Root Cellaring: Natural Cold Storage of Fruits and Vegetables.* Pownal, VT: Storey Publishing/Garden Way Publishing, 1991.

Buchanan, Rita. *A Weaver's Garden: Growing Plants for Natural Dyes and Fibers.* Mineola, NY: Dover Publications, 1999.

Buhner, Stephen Harrod. *Herbal Antibiotics: Natural Alternatives for Treating Drug-Resistant Bacteria.* Pownal, VT: Storey Books, 1999.

Burns, Max. *Cottage Water Systems: An Out-of-the- City Guide to Pumps, Plumbing, Water Purification, and Privies.* Toronto, Ontario: Cottage Life Books, 1999.

Campbell, Colin J. *The Coming Oil Crisis.* Geneva, Switzerland: Petroconsultants S.A., 1997.

————. "The Twenty-First Century: The World's Endowment of Conventional Oil and Its Depletion," January 1996. Available at http://www.hubbertpeak. com/campbell/camfull.htm. Accessed March 2000.

Campbell, Stu. *The Home Water Supply: How to Find, Filter, Store and Conserve It.* Pownal, VT: Storey Publishing/Garden Way Publishing, 1983.

Carpenter, Bob. "Cast Earth: A New Form of Earthbuilding Takes Shape." *Adobe Builder,* Spring 1997.

Carroll, Ricki, and Robert Carroll. *Cheesemaking Made Easy.* Pownal, VT: Storey Books, 1995.

Cash, John D., and Martin G. Cash. *Producer Gas for Motor Vehicles.* Bradley, IL: Lindsay Publications, 1997.

Cavitch, Susan Miller. *The Soapmaker's Companion: A Comprehensive Guide with Recipes, Techniques & Know-How.* Pownal, VT: Storey Books, 1997.

CDIAC (Carbon Dioxide Information Analysis Center). "Frequently Asked Global Change Questions." Available at http://cdiac.esd.ornl.gov/pns/faq.html. Accessed April 2000.

Chambers, Robert. *Log Building Construction Manual.* River Falls, WI: Robert Chambers, 1999.

Chandler, Deborah. *Learning to Weave.* Loveland, CO: Interweave Press, 1995.

Chappell, Steve, ed. *The Alternative Building SOURCEBOOK: Traditional, Natural & Sustainable Building Products and Services.* Brownfield, Maine: Maple Press, 1998.

————. *A Timber Framer's Workshop: Joinery, Design & Construction of Traditional Timber Frames.* Brownfield, Maine: Maple Press, 1998.

Charney, Len. *Build a Yurt: The Low-Cost Mongolian Round House.* New York: Sterling Publishing Company, 1981.

Chatfield, Kimball, L.Ac., O.M.D. *Medicine from the Mountains: Medicinal Plants of the High Sierra Nevada.* South Lake Tahoe, CA: Range of Light Publications, 1997.

Chilton, Pamela, C.H.T., and Hugh Harmon, Ph.D. *Odyssey of the Soul, A Trilogy: Book I, Apocatastasis.* Rancho Mirage, CA: Quick Book Publishing, 1997.

Chopra, Deepak, M.D. *Quantum Healing: Exploring the Frontiers of Mind/Body Medicine.* New York: Bantam Doubleday Dell Publishing Group, 1989.

Clark, Elizabeth Wheeler. *Addicted to Baskets: 20 Original Baskets with Step-by-Step Instructions.* New Bern, NC: Griffin & Tilghman Publishing, 1997.

Clark, Hulda Regehr, Ph.D., N.D. *The Cure for All Diseases.* Chula Vista, CA: New Century Press, 1995.

————. *The Cure for All Advanced Cancers.* Chula Vista, CA: New Century Press, 1999.

Clark, Sam. *Independent Builder: Designing & Building a House Your Own Way.* White River Junction, VT: Chelsea Green Publishing Company, 1996.

CNN News. "Sagging Power Lines, Hot Weather Blamed for Blackout," August 11, 1996. Available at http://www.cnn.com/US/9608/11/power.outage. Accessed June 2000.

CNR (Center for Nutritional Research). "All About Colostrum." Available at http://www.bovinecolostrum. com/info/allabout.htm. Accessed June 2000.

Cobleigh, Rolfe. *Handy Farm Devices and How to Make Them.* New York: The Lyons Press, 1996.

Coffee, Hugh L. *Ditch Medicine: Advanced Field Procedures for Emergencies.* Boulder, CO: Paladin Press, 1993.

Cohen, Mark Nathan. *Health and the Rise of Civilization.* New Haven, CT: Yale University Press, 1989.

Coleman, Eliot. *Four-Season Harvest.* White River Junction, VT: Chelsea Green Publishing, 1992.

————. *The New Organic Grower: A Master's Manual of Tools and Techniques for the Home and Market Gardener.* White River Junction, VT: Chelsea Green Publishing, 1995.

Covey, Stephen R. *The 7 Habits of Highly Effective People.* New York: Fireside Books, 1990.

Cowens, Deborah, and Tom Monte. *A Gift for Healing: How You Can Use Therapeutic Touch.* New York: Crown Publishing Group, 1996.

Cox, Carol, and Staff. *Learning to Grow All Your Own Food: One-Bed Model for Compost, Diet and Income Crops.* Willits, CA: Ecology Action, 1991.

Crook, William G. *The Yeast Connection: A Medical Breakthrough.* New York: Vintage Books, 1986.

Cummings, Stephen, M.D., and Dana Ullman, M.P.H. (contributor). *Everybody's Guide to Homeopathic Medicines: Safe and Effective Remedies for You and Your Family.* New York: J. P. Tarcher, 1997.

Damerow, Gail. *A Guide to Raising Chickens: Care, Feeding, Facilities.* Pownal, VT: Storey Books, 1996.

Dankoff Solar. "Solar Water Pumping: A Practical Introduction." Available at http://www.dankoffsolar.com/reference/briefintro. Accessed May 2000.

Danks, Lisa Marie. *Building Your Ark: Your Personal Survival Guide to the Year 2000 Crisis.* West Fork, AR: DAL Enterprises, 1998.

Davis, Elizabeth. *Heart and Hands: A Midwife's Guide to Pregnancy and Birth.* Berkeley, CA: Celestial Arts, 1997.

Day, Laura. *Practical Intuition: How to Harness the Power of Your Instinct and Make It Work for You.* New York: Broadway Books, 1997.

De Bairacli-Levy, Juliette. *Complete Herbal Handbook for Farm and Stable.* New York: Faber & Faber, 1991.

Del Porto, David, and Carol Steinfeld. *Composting Toilet System Book: A Practical Guide to Choosing, Planning and Maintaining Composting Toilet Systems.* White River Junction, VT: Chelsea Green Publishing Company, 1999.

Desert Research Institute (DRI). "Fuel Cells." Available at http://www.dri.edu/Projects/Energy/Fuelcells. Accessed May 2000.

Dickson, Murray. *Where There Is No Dentist.* Berkeley, CA: The Hesperian Foundation, 1999.

Diderot, Denis. *A Diderot Pictorial Encyclopedia of Trades and Industry: Manufacturing and the Technical Arts in Plates Selected from "L'Encyclopedie, ou Dictionnaire Raisonne des Sciences, des Arts et des Metiers,"* Vol. 1. Mineola, NY: Dover Publications, Inc., 1987.

Ditzhuyzen, Klaas van. "A Metal Melting Furnace." Available at wuarchive.wustl.edu/edu/arts/metal/TOC/proces/cast/ag_cast.html. Accessed May 2000.

Donelan, Peter. *Growing to Seed.* Willits, CA: Ecology Action, 1999.

Dossey, Larry, M.D. *Healing Words: The Power of Prayer and the Practice of Medicine.* San Francisco, CA: Harper San Francisco, 1995.

Duke, James A., Ph.D. *The Green Pharmacy: New Discoveries in Herbal Remedies for Common Diseases and Conditions from the World's Foremost Authority on Healing Herbs.* Emmaus, PA: Rodale Press, 1997.

————. "Nature's Medicine: The Green Pharmacy." *Mother Earth News,* December/January 2000.

————. "Half the Story Is Worse than No Story at All: Dr. Duke Responds to the Washington Post." Unpublished letter sent to author, April 18, 2000.

Earl M. Jorgensen Co. *Steel and Aluminum Stock List.* Chicago, 1984.

Eastman, Wilbur F. *The Canning, Freezing, Curing and Smoking of Meat, Fish and Game.* Pownal, VT: Storey Books, 1983.

Easton, David. *The Rammed Earth House.* White River Junction, VT: Chelsea Green Publishing Company, 1996.

Ecology Action. "Worldwide Loss of Soil." Available at http://www.growbiointensive.org/biointensive/soil.html. Accessed January 2000.

Ecosystems. "The Hubbert Peak of Oil Production." Available at http://www.hubbertpeak.com.

Eddy, Mary Baker. *Science and Health with Key to the Scriptures.* Boston: The First Church of Christ, Scientist, 1991.

Edwards, David A., M.D. H.M.D. *Theory and Practice of Biological Medicine.* San Juan, Manila: MG Reprographics, 1995.

Einstein, Patricia. *Intuition: The Path to Inner Wisdom.* Rockport, MA: Element Books, Inc., 1997.

Ekarius, Carol. *Small-Scale Livestock Farming: A Grass-Based Approach for Health, Sustainability, and Profit.* Pownal, VT: Storey Books, 1999.

Eliade, Mircea. *Shamanism*. Princeton, NJ: Princeton University Press, 1986.

Elias, Thomas S., and Peter A. Dykeman. *Edible Wild Plants: A North American Field Guide*. New York: Sterling Publishing Co., 1990.

Elliot, Doug. *Wild Roots: A Forager's Guide to the Edible and Medicinal Roots, Tubers, Corms, and Rhizomes of North America*. Rochester, VT: Healing Arts Press, 1995.

Ellis, Barbara W., and Fern Marshall Bradley, eds. *The Organic Gardener's Handbook of Natural Insect and Disease Control: A Complete Problem-Solving Guide to Keeping Your Garden and Yard Healthy Without Chemicals*. Emmaus, PA: Rodale Press, 1996.

Elpel, Thomas J. *Participating in Nature: Thomas J. Elpel's Guide to Primitive Living Skills*. Pony, MT: HOPS Press, 1999.

Emery, Carla. *The Encyclopedia of Country Living: An Old Fashioned Recipe Book*. Seattle, WA: Sasquatch Books, 1998.

Energy Systems & Design. "The Stream Engine." Available at http://www.microhydropower.com. Accessed April 2000.

Environmental Building News. "Cement and Concrete: Environmental Considerations." *Environmental Building News*, 2:2, March/April 1993.

Epstein, Gerald, M.D. *Healing Visualizations: Creating Health Through Imagery*. New York: Bantam Doubleday Dell Publishing Group, 1989.

Farber, Dr. M. Paul. *The Micro Silver Bullet*. Houston, TX: Professional Physicians Publishing & Health Services Inc., 1998.

Farnham, A. B. *Home Tanning and Leather Making Guide*. Columbus, OH: Fur-Fish-Game, 1959.

Feltwell, Ray. *Small-Scale Poultry Keeping: A Guide to Free-Range Poultry Production*. New York: Faber & Faber, 1992.

Finch, Richard. *Welder's Handbook: A Complete Guide to Mig, Tig, Arc & Oxyacetylene Welding*. New York: Penguin Putnam, 1997.

Forgey, William W., M.D., ed. *Wilderness Medical Society Practice Guidelines*. Guilford, CT: Globe Pequot Press, 1995.

Foster, Steven, Roger Torey Peterson, and James A. Duke, Ph.D. *A Field Guide to Medicinal Plants: Eastern and Central North America*. Peterson Field Guide Series. Boston: Houghton Mifflin Co., 1998.

Fukuoka, Masanobu. *The One-Straw Revolution*. Emmaus, PA: Rodale Press, 1978.

————. *The Road Back to Nature: Regaining the Paradise Lost*. Tokyo and New York: Japan Publications, 1987.

Garten, M.O., N.D., D.C. *The Health Secrets of a Naturopathic Doctor*. West Nyack, NY: Parker Publishing, 1967.

————. *The Natural and Drugless Way for Better Health*. NY: Arco Publishing, 1973.

————. *The Magic of Advanced Body Manipulation for Home and Professional Use*. San Jose, CA: Maximillian World Publishers, 1983.

Gelbspan, Ross. *The Heat is On*. Reading, MA: Perseus Books, 1998.

Gill, Paul G., Jr. *Pocket Guide to Wilderness Medicine & First-Aid*. Camden, ME: Ragged Mountain Press, 1997.

Gingery, David J. *The Charcoal Foundry*. Rogersville, MO: David J. Gingery Publishing, 1983.

Gingery, Vincent R. *The Secrets of Building an Alcohol-Producing Still*. Rogersville, MO: David J. Gingery Publishing, 1994.

Gipe, Paul. *Wind Power for Home and Business: Renewable Energy for the 1990s and Beyond*. White River Junction, VT: Chelsea Green Publishing Company, 1993.

————. *Wind Energy Basics: A Guide to Small and Micro Wind Systems*. White River Junction, VT: Chelsea Green Publishing Company, 1999.

Golden Genesis Corporation. *Solar Electric Design Guide*, 1999.

Grant, Bruce. *How to Make Cowboy Horse Gear*. Centreville, MD: Cornell Maritime Press, 1956.

Grant, Bruce. *Encyclopedia of Rawhide and Leather Braiding*. Centreville, MD: Cornell Maritime Press, 1972.

Gugliotta, Guy. "Health Concerns Grow Over Herbal Aids." *Washington Post*, March 19, 2000.

Hadley, Josie, and Carol Staudacher. *Hypnosis for Change*. New York: New Harbinger Publications, 1996.

Halacy, Beth, and Dan. *Cooking with the Sun: How to Build and Use Solar Cookers*. Lafayette, CA: Morning Sun Press, 1992.

Hammond, D. Corydon, ed. *Handbook of Hypnotic Suggestions and Metaphors*. New York: W.W. Norton & Company, 1990.

Handal, Kathleen A., M.D. and the American Red Cross. *The American Red Cross First Aid & Safety Handbook*. New York: Little, Brown and Company 1992.

Harner, Michael J., Ph.D. *The Way of the Shaman*. San Francisco: Harper San Francisco, 1990.

Harney, Corbin. *The Way It Is: One Water…One Air…One Mother Earth*. Nevada City, CA: Blue Dolphin Publishing, Inc., 1995.

Harrington, H.D. *Edible Native Plants of the Rock Mountains*. Albuquerque, NM: University of New Mexico Press, 1998.

Hartmann, Thom. *The Last Hours of Ancient Sunlight: Waking up to Personal and Global Transformation*. New York, NY: Crown Publishing Group, 2000.

————. *The Prophet's Way: Touching the Power of Life*. Northfield, VT: Mythical Books, 1997.

Hasluck, Paul N. *Metalworking: A Book of Tools, Materials and Processes for the Handyman*. Bradley, IL: Lindsay Publications Inc., 1994.

Havens, Ronald A., and Catherine R. Walters. *Hypnotherapy Scripts: A Neo-Ericksonian Approach to Persuasive Healing*. New York: Brunner/Mazel Publishers, 1989.

Hawken, Paul, Amory Lovins, and L. Hunter Lovins. *Natural Capitalism: Creating the Next Industrial Revolution*. Boston: Little Brown and Co., 1999.

Haynes, N. Bruce, D.V.M. *Keeping Livestock Healthy: A Veterinary Guide to Horses, Cattle, Pigs, Goats & Sheep*. Pownal, VT: Storey Books, 1994.

Heede, Richard, and the Staff of Rocky Mountain Institute. *Homemade Money: How to Save Energy and Dollars on Your Home*. Amherst, NH: Brick House Publishing Company, 1995.

Hellweg, Paul. *Flintknapping–The Art of Making Stone Tools*. Canoga Park, CA: Canyon Publishing Company, 1984.

Henderson, Donald R., M.D., MPH, and Deborah Mitchell. *Colostrum, "Nature's Healing Miracle."* Salt Lake City, UT: CNR Publications, 1999.

Hiscox, Gardner D., M.E. *Henley's Formulas for Home and Workshop*. New York: Avenel Books, 1979.

Hobson, Phyllis. *Making Homemade Soaps and Candles*. Charlotte, VT: Garden Way Publishing, 1974.

Hoffman, David. *The Complete Illustrated Holistic Herbal: A Safe and Practical Guide to Making and Using Herbal Remedies*. Rockport MA: Element Books, 1996.

Hogue, John. *The Millennium Book of Prophecy: 777 Visions and Predictions from Nostradamus, Edgar Cayce, Gurdjieff, Tamo-san, Madame Blavatsky, the Old and New Testament Prophets and 89 Others*. San Francisco, CA: Harper San Francisco, 1997.

Home Energy Magazine editors. *No Regrets Remodeling: Creating a Comfortable, Healthy Home that Saves Energy*. Berkeley, CA: Energy Auditor and Retrofitter, Inc., 1997.

Honervogt, Tanmaya. *The Power of Reiki: An Ancient Hands-On Healing Technique*. New York: Henry Holt and Co., 1998.

Hunter, Roy C. *The Art of Hypnosis: Mastering Basic Techniques*. Kendall/Hunt Publishing Company, 1996.

Hupping, Carol. *Stocking Up III: The All-New Edition of America's Classic Preserving Guide*. Emmaus, PA: Rodale Press, 1986.

Hutchins, Alma R. *Indian Herbology of North America*. Boston: Shambala Publications, 1991.

Hutton, Primrose, and Jerry Ongerth, Ph.D. "Performance Evaluation of Ten Commercially Available Portable Water Filters." Department of Water Engineering, University of New South Wales, Australia, February 1997.

Hutton, William. *Coming Earth Changes: The Latest Evidence.* Virginia Beach, VA: A.R.E. Press, 1996.

Ibarra, Corazon D.M.D., H.M.D., and David A. Edwards, M.D., H.M.D. *A Primer of Biotoxicology.* San Juan, Manila: MG Reprographics, 1996.

Ingerman, Sandra. *Soul Retrieval: Mending the Fragmented Self.* San Francisco: Harper San Francisco, 1991.

Ingram, Colin. *The Drinking Water Book: A Complete Guide to Safe Drinking Water.* Berkeley, CA: Ten Speed Press, 1991.

International Correspondence Schools. *Secrets of Green-Sand Casting.* Bradley, IL: Lindsay Publications Inc., 1983.

Inversin, Allen R. *Micro-Hydropower Sourcebook: A Practical Guide to Design and Implementation in Developing Countries.* Arlington, VA: NRECA International Foundation, 1986.

Jacob, Stanley W., M.D., Ronald M. Lawrence, M.D., and Martin Zucker. *The Miracle of MSM: The Natural Solution for Pain.* New York: Berkley Publishing Group, Division of Penguin Putnam, 1999.

Jeavons, John. *The Complete 21-Bed Biointensive Mini-Farm.* Willits, CA: Ecology Action, 1987.

—————. *How to Grow More Vegetables: Fruits, Nuts, Berries, Grains, and Other Crops Than You Ever Thought Possible on Less Land Than You Can Imagine.* Berkeley, CA: Ten Speed Press, 1995.

Jeffrey, Kevin. *Independent Energy Guide: Electrical Power for Home, Boat and RV.* Ashland, MA: Orwell Cove Press, 1995.

Jenkins, Joseph C. *The Humanure Handbook: A Guide to Composting Human Manure.* White River Junction, VT: Chelsea Green Publishing, 1996.

Johnson, Dusty. *Saddlemaking: Lessons in Construction, Repair, and Evaluation.* Loveland, CO: Saddleman Press, 1993.

Jonas, Wayne B., M.D. and Jennifer Jacobs, M.D., M.P.H. *Healing with Homeopathy: The Doctor's Guide.* New York: Warner Books, Inc., 1996.

Jones, Franklin Day, John A. Newell, and Holbrook L. Horton. *Ingenious Mechanisms for Designers and Inventors.* New York: Industrial Press, Inc., 1977.

Joy, Brugh, M.D. *Joy's Way: A Map for the Transformational Journey: An Introduction to the Potentials for Healing with Body Energies.* New York: J. P. Tarcher, 1979.

Kachadorian, James. *The Passive Solar House: Using Solar Design to Heat & Cool Your Home.* White River Junction, VT: Chelsea Green Publishing Company, 1997.

Kemper, Donald W. *Healthwise Handbook: A Self-Care Guide for You.* Boise, ID: Healthwise Publications, 1999.

Keyes, Ken, Jr. *The Hundredth Monkey.* St. Mary, KY: Vision Books, 1981.

King, Bruce, P.E. *Buildings of Earth and Straw: Structural Design for Rammed Earth and Straw-Bale Architecture.* White River Junction, VT: Chelsea Green Publishing Company, 1996.

King, Doug. *The Emergency–Disaster Survival Guidebook.* Sandy, UT: ABC Preparedness Co., 1994.

Klober, Kelly. *A Guide to Raising Pigs: Care, Facilities, Breed Selection, Management.* Pownal, VT: Storey Books, 1998.

Komp, Richard J., Ph.D. *Practical Photovoltaics.* Ann Arbor, MI: Aatec Publications, 1995.

Koppel, Tom. *Powering the Future: The Ballard Fuel Cell and the Race to Change the World.* New York: John Wiley & Sons, 1999.

Kouhoupt, Rudy, and Joe D. Rice, eds. *The Shop Wisdom of Rudy Kouhoupt.* Traverse City, MI: Village Press, 1989.

Krieger, Dolores, Ph.D., R.N. *The Therapeutic Touch: How To Use Your Hands to Help or Heal.* New York: Simon & Schuster, 1992

Kubler-Ross, Elizabeth. *On Death and Dying: What the Dying Have to Teach Doctors, Nurses, Clergy and Their Own Families.* New York: Simon and Schuster, 1997.

Laubin, Reginald, and Gladys. *The Indian Tipi: Its History, Construction, and Use.* Norman, OK: University of Oklahoma Press, 1989.

Leadbeater, Eliza. *Handspinning.* Mountain View, MO: Select Books, 1983.

Le Baron, Wayne. *Preparation for Nuclear Disaster*. Commack, NY: Nova Science Publishers, 1998.

Lenz-Porter, Louisa. *Growing Medicinal Herbs in as Little as Fifty Square Feet*. Willits, CA: Ecology Action, 1995.

Levine, Stephen and Ondrea. *Who Dies? An Investigation of Conscious Living and Conscious Dying*. New York: Anchor Books/Doubleday, 1989.

Ley, Beth M. *The Forgotten Nutrient MSM: On Our Way Back to Health with Sulfur*. Detroit Lakes, MN: B.L. Publications, 1998.

———. *Immune System Control: Colostrum and Lactoferrin*. Detroit Lakes, MN: B.L. Publications, 2000.

Ligon, Linda, ed. *Homespun Handknit: Caps, Socks, Mittens & Gloves*. Loveland, CO: Interweave Press, 1988.

Lindeburg, Michael R., P.E. *Mechanical Engineering Reference Manual for the PE Exam*. Belmont, CA: Professional Publications, Inc., 1998.

———. *Civil Engineering Reference Manual for the PE Exam*. Belmont, CA: Professional Publications, Inc., 1999.

———. *FE Review Manual: Rapid Preparation for the General Fundamentals of Engineering Exam*. Belmont, CA: Professional Publications, Inc., 2000.

Loon, Dirk Van. *The Family Cow*. Pownal, VT: Storey Books, 1983.

Lowenhaupt, Harris. "A Revolutionary Innovation in Traditional Earth Construction," Phoenix, AZ. Available at http://www.castearth.com/cedesc.html. Accessed March 17, 2000.

Lucas, Rex A. *Men in Crisis: A Study of a Mine Disaster*. New York: Basic Books, 1969.

Lucas, Winafred B. *Regression Therapy: A Handbook for Professionals*. Vol. 1, Past-Life Therapy. Crest Park, CA: Deep Forest Press, 1993.

———. *Regression Therapy, a Handbook for Professionals*. Volume 2, Special Instances of Altered State Work. Crest Park, CA: Deep Forest Press, 1993.

Ludwig, Art. *Create an Oasis with Greywater: Your Complete Guide to Managing Greywater in the Landscape*. Santa Barbara, CA: Oasis Design, 2000.

Mackenzie, David, and Ruth Goodwin, eds. *Goat Husbandry*. New York: Faber & Faber, 1996.

Marshall, Stewart. *Building Small Cupola Furnaces*. Lopez Island, WA: Marshall Machine and Engineering Works, 1996.

Mastny, Lisa. "Melting of Earth's Ice Cover Reaches New High." Worldwatch News Brief #00-02, 2000.

Mazria, Edward. *The Passive Solar Energy Book: Expanded Professional Edition*. Emmaus, PA: Rodale Press, 1979.

McClure, Susan, and Sally Roth, eds. *Companion Planting: Rodale's Successful Organic Gardening Series*. Emmaus, PA: Rodale Press, 1994.

McDaniel, Dr. Robert S. *Essentially Soap: The Elegant Art of Handmade Soap Making, Scenting, Coloring & Shaping*. Iola, WI: Krause Publications, 2000.

McHenry, Paul Graham, Jr. *Adobe: Build it Yourself*. Tucson, AZ: The University of Arizona Press, 1998

McKibben, Bill. *The End of Nature*. New York: Anchor Books, Bantam Doubleday Dell Publishing Group, Inc., 1989.

McLean, Frank, and Joe D. Rice, eds. *The Shop Wisdom of Frank McLean*. Traverse City, MI: Village Press, 1992.

McPherson, John. *"How To" Build This Log Cabin for $3000*. Randolph, KS: Prairie Wolf, 1993.

McPherson, John and Geri McPherson. *Primitive Wilderness Living & Survival Skills*. Randolph, KS: Prairie Wolf, 1999.

Meadows, Donella H., Dennis L. Meadows, Jorgen Randers, and William W. Behrens III. *The Limits to Growth*. New York: Signet Books, 1975.

———. *Beyond the Limits: Confronting Global Collapse, Envisioning a Sustainable Future*. White River Junction, VT: Chelsea Green Publishing Co., 1993.

Mehl-Madronna, Lewis, M.D. *Coyote Medicine: Lessons from Native American Healing*. Fireside Books, 1998.

Meitzner, Laura, and Martin Price. "Amaranth to Zai Holes: Ideas for Growing Food Under Difficult Conditions." North Fort Meyers, FL: ECHO Publications, 1996.

Merritt, Frederick S., M. Kent Loftin, and Jonathan T. Ricketts, eds. *Standard Handbook for Civil Engineers*, 4th ed. New York: McGraw-Hill Companies, 1995.

Metcalf, Mark. *Colloidal Silver: Making and Using Your Own*. Forest Grove, OR: Silver Solutions, 1998.

Mettler, John J. and Elayne Sears. *Basic Butchering of Livestock and Game*. Pownal, VT: Storey Publishing/Garden Way Publishing, 1989.

Michael, Valerie. *The Leatherworking Handbook: A Practical Illustrated Sourcebook of Techniques and Projects*. Strand, UK: Cassell Wellington House, 1995.

Miller, Emmet E., M.D. *Deep Healing: The Essence of Mind/Body Medicine*. Carlsbad, CA: Hay House Inc., 1997.

Mindell, Earl L., R.Ph., Ph.D. *The MSM Miracle: Enhance Your Health with Organic Sulfur*. Lincolnwood, IL: Keats, 1997.

Mollison, Bill. *Permaculture: A Designer's Manual*. Tyalgum, NSW, Australia: Tagari Publications, 1999.

Monzert, Leonard. *Practical Distiller*. Bradley, IL: Lindsay Publications Inc., 1987.

Mowat, Farley. *People of the Deer*. Boston: Little Brown and Company, 1952.

Muller, Brigitte, and Horst Gunther. *The Complete Book of Reiki Healing*. Mendocino, CA: Life Rhythm, 1995.

Muller, Robert. *Most of All, They Taught Me Happiness*. Garden City, NY: Doubleday & Company, 1978.

Mullin, Ray C. *House Wiring with the National Electrical Code: Based on the 1999 National Electrical Code*. Albany, NY: Delmar Publishers, 1999.

Murray, Michael T., and Joseph E. Pizzorno, N.D. *The Encyclopedia of Natural Medicine*, Rev. 2nd ed. Rocklin, CA: Prima Publishing, 1997.

Myhrman, Matts, and S.O. MacDonald. *Build It with Bales: A Step-by-Step Guide to Straw-Bale Construction*, Version two. White River Junction, VT: Chelsea Green Publishing Company, 1998.

Myss, Caroline, Ph.D. *Anatomy of the Spirit: The Seven Stages of Power and Healing*. New York: Harmony Books, 1996.

———. *Why People Don't Heal and How They Can*. New York: Harmony Books, 1997.

NAIHC (North American Industrial Hemp Council). "Hemp Facts." downloaded from http://naihc.org/hemp_information/hemp_facts.html March 2000.

New England Solar Electric Inc. *The Solar Electric Independent Home Book*. Worthington, MA: New England Solar Electric Inc., 1995.

Nigrosh, Leon I. *Low Fire: Other Ways to Work in Clay*. Worcester, MA: Davis Publications, Inc., 1980.

Northrup, Christiane M.D. *Women's Bodies, Women's Wisdom: Creating Physical and Emotional Health and Healing*. New York: Bantam Books, 1998.

Oberg, Erik, Franklin D. Jones, and Holbrook L. Horton. *Machinery's Handbook*, 21st ed. New York: Industrial Press, Inc., 1982.

Oberg, Erik, Franklin D. Jones, Holbrook L. Horton, Henry H. Ryffel, and Christopher J. McCauley, eds. *Machinery's Handbook*, 26th ed. New York: Industrial Press, Inc., 2000.

Ody, Penelope. *The Complete Medicinal Herbal*. New York: Dorling Kindersley, 1993.

Olkowski, William, Sheila Daar, and Helga Olkowski. *Common-Sense Pest Control: Least-Toxic Solutions for Your Home, Garden, Pets and Community*. Newtown, CT: Taunton Press, 1991.

———. *The Gardener's Guide to Common-Sense Pest Control*. Newtown, CT: Taunton Press, 1996.

Olsen, Cynthia. *Essiac: A Native Herbal Cancer Remedy*. Pagosa Springs, CO: Kali Press, 1998.

Olsen, Frederick L. *The Kiln Book: Materials, Specifications & Construction*. Iola, WI: Krause Publications, 1996.

Oppenheimer, Betty. *The Candlemaker's Companion: A Complete Guide to Rolling, Pouring, Dipping, and Decorating Your Own Candles*. Pownal, VT: Storey Books, 1997.

Patagonia. "Rag Seller" (archive article). Available at http://www.patagonia.com. Accessed March 2000.

Pearson, David. *The Natural House Catalog: Everything You Need to Create an Environmentally Friendly Home*. New York: Simon & Schuster, 1996.

Pelletier, R. Kenneth. *Mind as Healer, Mind as Slayer: Discover the Life and Death Link Between Stress and Serious Illness…and What You Can Do About It.* New York: Dell Publishing, 1992.

Perkins, John. *Shape Shifting: Shamanic Techniques for Global and Personal Transformation.* Rochester, VT: Destiny Books, 1997.

Peterson, Roger Tory, and Lee A. Peterson. *Field Guide to Edible Wild Plants: Eastern and Central North America.* Boston, Houghton Mifflin Co., 1982.

Platt, Anne McGinn. "Water-borne Killers." *Worldwatch*, March/April 1996.

Plug Power. "Benefits for Consumers." Available at http://www.plugpower.com/about. Accessed May 2000.

Poole, William, ed. *The Heart of Healing.* Atlanta GA: Turner Publishing, 1993.

Population Information Network (POPIN) of the United Nations Population Division. "World Population Growth from Year 0 to Stabilization," June 7, 1994. Available at gopher://gopher.undp.org:70/00/ungophers/popin/wdtrends/histor. Accessed April 2000.

Postel, Sandra. *Pillar of Sand: Can the Irrigation Miracle Last?* New York: W. W. Norton & Company, 1999.

Prend, Ashley Davis, A.C.S.W. *Transcending Loss: Understanding the Lifelong Impact of Grief and How to Make It Meaningful.* New York: The Berkley Publishing Group, 1997.

Pyle, Walter, ed. *Solar Hydrogen Chronicles.* Richmond, CA: H-Ion Solar Inc., 1999.

Rahme, Lotta. *Leather: Preparation & Tanning by Traditional Methods.* Portland, OR: Caber Press, 1996.

Raven, Lee. *Hands On Spinning.* Loveland, CO: Interweave Press, 1987.

Read, Piers Paul. *Alive: The Story of the Andes Survivors.* New York: Avon Books, 1992.

Reader's Digest. *The New Complete Do-It-Yourself Manual.* Pleasantville, NY: Reader's Digest Association, 1991.

————. *Complete Guide to Sewing: Step-By-Step Techniques for Making Clothes and Home Furnishings.* Pleasantville, NY: Reader's Digest Association, *1995.*

————. *Back To Basics: How to Learn and Enjoy Traditional American Skills.* Pleasantville, NY: The Reader's Digest Association, 1999.

Reilly, Harold J.D., Ph.T., D.S., and Ruth Hagy Brod. *The Edgar Cayce Handbook for Health Through Drugless Therapy.* Virginia Beach, VA: A.R.E. Press, 1975.

Renders, Eileen, N.D. *Food Additives, Nutrients & Supplements A-To-Z: A Shopper's Guide.* Santa Fe, NM: Clear Light Publishers, 1999.

Rheingold, Howard, ed. *The Millennium Whole Earth Catalog: Access to Tools & Ideas for the Twenty-First Century.* San Francisco: Harper San Francisco, 1994.

Richards, Matt. *Deerskins into Buckskins: How to Tan with Natural Materials.* Rexford, MT: Backcountry Publishing, 1998.

Righetti, Maggie. *Crocheting in Plain English.* New York: St. Martin's Press, 1988.

————. *Knitting in Plain English.* New York: St. Martin's Press, 1986.

Ritter, Keith. *The Residential Hydropower Book.* Nevada City, CA: Sierra Solar Systems, 1986.

Robbins, John. *Reclaiming Our Health: Exploding the Medical Myth and Embracing the Source of True Healing.* Tiburon, CA: H. J. Kramer Inc., 1996.

————. *Diet for a New America: How Your Food Choices Affect Your Health, Happiness and the Future of Life on Earth.* Tiburon, CA: H.J. Kramer Inc., 1998.

Robertson, Dougal. *Survive the Savage Sea.* New York: Bantam Books, 1973.

Robinson, Raoul A. *Return to Resistance: Breeding Crops to Reduce Pesticide Dependence.* Davis, CA: AgAccess, 1996.

Rocky Mountain Institute. *Green Developments* (CD-ROM, Vers. 1.0). Snowmass, CO: Rocky Mountain Institute, 1997.

Rolling Thunder, with editing by Carmen Sun Rising Pope. *Rolling Thunder Speaks: A Message for Turtle Island.* Santa Fe, NM: Clear Light Publishers, 1999.

Rosen, Sidney, ed. *My Voice Will Go With You: The Teaching Tales of Milton H. Erikson.* New York: W.W. Norton & Company, 1991.

Rosenberg, Robert. *Electric Motor Repair*. Philadelphia: Saunders College Publishing, Division of Harcourt Brace, 1987.

Runyon, Linda. *A Survival Acre*. Phoenix, AZ: A.P.O.A. Books, 1995.

Sachs, Allan, D.C., C.C.N. *The Authoritative Guide to Grapefruit Seed Extract: A Breakthrough in Alternative Treatment for Colds, Infections, Candida, Allergies, Herpes, and Many Other Ailments*. Mendocino, CA: LifeRhythm, 1997.

Salaman, R.A. *Dictionary of Leather-Working Tools, c. 1700–1950: And the Tools of Allied Trades*. Mendham, NJ: Astragal Press, 1996.

Salatin, Joe. *Pastured Poultry Profits: Net $25,000 in 6 Months on 20 Acres*. White River Junction, VT: Chelsea Green Publishing Company, 1996.

———. *Salad Bar Beef*. White River Junction, VT: Chelsea Green Publishing Company, 1996.

———. *You Can Farm: The Entrepreneur's Guide to Start and Succeed in a Farming Enterprise*. Swoope, VA: Polyface Inc., 1998.

Salvato, Joseph A. *Environmental Engineering and Sanitation*. New York: John Wiley & Sons, 1982.

Schaeffer, John (introduction) and Douglas R. Pratt, ed. *The Real Goods Solar Living Sourcebook: The Complete Guide to Renewable Energy Technologies and Sustainable Living*. White River Junction, VT: Chelsea Green Publishing Company, 1999.

Sheldrake, Rupert. *A New Science of Life: The Hypothesis of Morphic Resonance*. Rochester, VT: Park Street Press, 1995.

Shell, Scott. "Environmental Impacts of Cement and Flyash" as reported in "Concrete, Flyash and the Environment—Proceedings." *Environmental Building News*. Available at http://www.ebuild.com/Archives/Features/Flyash/shell.html. Accessed March 16, 2000.

Shigley, Joseph E., and Charles R. Mischke, eds. *Standard Handbook of Machine Design*. New York: McGraw-Hill Companies, 1996.

Shurtleff, William, and Akiko Aoyagi. *Book of Tofu*. New York: Ballantine Books, 1992.

Siebert, Al, Ph.D. *The Survivor Personality: Why Some People are Stronger, Smarter, and More Skillful at Handling Life's Difficulties ...and How You Can Be Too*. New York: The Berkeley Publishing Group, 1996.

Siegel, Bernie, M.D. *Love, Medicine & Miracles: Lessons Learned About Self-Healing from a Surgeon's Experience with Exceptional Patients*. New York: Harper Collins Publishers, 1986.

Sierra Solar. "Design Center." Available at http://www.sierrasolar.com/design/design. Accessed April 2000.

Siler, Lyn. *The Basket Book: Over 30 Magnificent Baskets to Make and Enjoy*. New York: Sterling Publishing Company, 1988.

Silverman, Harold M., Pharm.D., ed. *The Pill Book: The Illustrated Guide to the Most Prescribed Drugs in the United States*. New York: Bantam Books, 1996.

Simmons, Paula. *Raising Sheep the Modern Way*. Pownal, VT: Garden Way Publishing, Storey Communications, 1989.

Simonton, O. Carl, M.D., Stephanie Matthews-Simonton, and James L. Creighton. *Getting Well Again*. NY: Bantam Books, 1992.

Smythe, Benjamin R. *Killing Cancer: The Jason Winters Story*. Las Vegas, NV: Vinton Publishing Co., 1993.

Sobon, Jack A. *Build a Classic Timber-Framed House*. Pownal, VT: Storey Books, 1994.

Sobon, Jack, and Roger Schroeder. *Timber Frame Construction: All About Post-and-Beam Building*. Pownal, VT: Storey Books, 1984.

Speight, Charlotte F., and John Toki. *Hands in Clay*. Mountain View, CA: Mayfield Publishing Co., 1999.

Steen, Athena Swentzell, Bill Steen, and David Bainbridge, with David Eisenberg. *The Straw Bale House*. White River Junction, VT: Chelsea Green Publishing Company, 1994.

Stein, Diane. *All Women Are Healers: A Comprehensive Guide to Natural Healing*. Watsonville, CA: The Crossing Press, 1990.

———. *Essential Reiki: A Complete Guide to an Ancient Healing Art*. Watsonville, CA: The Crossing Press, 1995.

Stein, Kathy. *Beyond Recycling: A Re-User's Guide: 365 Practical Tips [to] Save Money and Protect the Environment.* Santa Fe, NM: Clear Light Publishers, 1997.

Stevens, James Talmage. *Making the Best of Basics: Family Preparedness Handbook.* Seattle, WA: Gold Leaf Press, 1997.

Strong, Steven J., with William G. Scheller. *The Solar Electric House: Energy for the Environmentally Responsive, Energy-Independent Home.* Still River, MA: Sustainability Press, 1993.

Suh, Nam P,. and Arthur L. Turner. *Elements of the Mechanical Behavior of Solids.* New York: McGraw-Hill Companies, 1975.

Summit, Ginger, and Jim Widess. *The Complete Book of Gourd Craft: 25 projects, 55 Decorative Techniques, 300 Inspirational Designs.* Asheville, NC: Lark Books, 1996.

Sun Bear and Waban Wind. *Black Dawn, Bright Day: Indian Prophecies for the Millennium That Reveal the Fate of the Earth.* New York: Fireside Books, 1992.

Susanka, Sarah. *The Not So Big House: A Blueprint for the Way We Really Live.* Newtown, CT: Taunton Press, 1998.

Sustainable Agriculture Network. *Sustainable Agriculture Directory of Expertise,* 3rd Edition. Burlington, VT: Sustainable Agriculture Publications, University of Vermont, 1996

Tawrell, Paul. *Camping & Wilderness Survival: The Ultimate Outdoors Book.* Self-published, 1996.

Theobald, Robert. *Reworking Success: New Communities at the Millennium.* Gabriola Island, British Columbia: New Society Publishers, 1997.

Theodosakis, Jason, Barry Fox, and Brenda D. Adderly. *The Arthritis Cure : The Medical Miracle That Can Halt, Reverse, and May Even Cure Osteoarthritis.* New York: St. Martin's Press, 1997.

Theophilus. *On Divers Art: The Foremost Medieval Treatise on Painting, Glassmaking, and Metalwork,* trans. by John G. Hawthorne and Cyril Stanley Smith.Mineola, NY: Dover Publications, Inc., 1979.

Thomas, Sharon, and Marcia Zalbowitz. "Fuel Cells: Green Power." Los Almos, NM: The Los Alamos National Laboratory. Available at http://www.education.lanl.gov/resources/fuelcells. Accessed May 2000.

Thompson, Frank Charles, D..D, Ph.D, ed. *The Thompson Chain Reference Bible: New International Version.* Indianapolis, IN, 1983.

Tebbetts, Charles. *Self-Hypnosis and Other Mind Expanding Techniques.* Glendale, CA: Westwood Publishing Company, 1997.

Tibbets, Joe M. "Adobe Surfing the Chinese Way." *Adobe Builder,* Spring 1997.

Tierra, Michael, L.Ac., O.M.D. *The Way Of Herbs.* New York: Pocket Books, 1998.

————. *The Way Of Chinese Herbs.* New York: Pocket Books, 1998.

Troy, Jack. *Wood-Fired Stoneware and Porcelain.* Iola, WI: Krause Publications, 1995.

Union of Concerned Scientists (UCS). "World Scientists' Warning to Humanity," Cambridge, MA, 1992. Available at http://www.ucsusa.org/resources/warning.html. Accessed September 4, 2000.

U.S. Bureau of Census, International Data Base. "Total Midyear Population for the World: 1950-2050." Available at http://www.census.gov/ipc/www/worldpop.html. Accessed December 29, 1999.

U.S. Navy. *US Navy Foundry Manual.* Bradley, IL: Lindsay Publications Inc., 1989.

Van Auken, John. *The End Times: Prophecies of the Coming Changes: Including Prophecies and Predictions from the Bible, Nostradamus, Holy Mother, Edgar Cayce.* Virginia Beach, VA: A.R.E. Press, 1996.

Vanderhaeghe, Lorna R., and Patrick J. D. Bouic, Ph.D. *The Immune System Cure: Optimize Your Immune System in 30 Days—The Natural Way.* New York: Kensington Publishing Co., 1999.

Van Loon, Dirk. *The Family Cow.* Pownal, VT: Storey Books, 1983.

Vogue Knitting Magazine Editors. *Vogue Knitting.* New York: Pantheon Books, Division of Random House, 1989.

Vorhis, Dan. "Portable Water Filters: A Designer's Perspective," Seattle, WA, 1997. Available at http://www.marathonceramics.com/designrev.html. Accessed December 2, 1999.

Wagner, Rudolf, Ph.D. *Wagner's Chemical Technology,* trans. by William Crookes. Bradley, IL: Lindsay Publications Inc., 1988.

Walker, John R. *Machining Fundamentals: From Basic to Advanced Techniques.* Tinley Park, IL: Goodheart-Willcox Publisher, 2000.

Weil, Andrew, M.D. *8 Weeks to Optimum Health: A Proven Program for Taking Full Advantage of Your Body's Natural Healing Power.* New York: Alfred A Knopf, Inc., 1997.

Weiss, Eric A., M.D. *A Comprehensive Guide to Wilderness and Travel Medicine.* Oakland, CA: Adventure Travel Kits, 1997.

Werner, David, Carol Thuman, and Jane Maxwell. *Where There Is No Doctor: A Village Health Care Handbook.* Berkeley, CA: Hesperian Foundation, 1992.

Wescott, David, ed. *Primitive Technology: A Book of Earth Skills.* Layton, UT: Gibbs Smith, 1999.

Weygers, Alexander G. *The Complete Modern Blacksmith.* Berkeley, CA: Ten Speed Press, 1997.

Whittaker, John C. *Flintknapping: Making and Understanding Stone Tools.* Austin, TX: University of Texas Press, 1994.

Wigginton, Eliot, ed. *The Foxfire Book: Hog Dressing, Log Cabin Building, Mountain Crafts and Foods, Planting by the Signs, Snake Lore, Hunting Tales, Faith Healing, Moonshining.* New York: Anchor Books, Doubleday. 1972.

—————. *Foxfire 2: Ghost Stories, Spring Wild Plant Foods, Spinning and Weaving, Midwifing, Burial Customs, Corn Shuckin's, and Wagon Making.* New York: Anchor Books, Doubleday, 1973.

—————. *Foxfire 5: Ironmaking, Blacksmithing, Flintlock Rifles, Bear Hunting.* New York: Anchor Books, Doubleday, 1979.

Wilkerson, James A., M.D., ed. *Medicine for Mountaineering & Other Wilderness Activities.* Seattle, WA: The Mountaineers, 1992.

Wiseman, John. *The SAS Survival Handbook: How to Survive in the Wild, in Any Climate, on Land or at Sea.* London: Harper Collins Publishers, 1996.

Wright, F. B. *Distillation of Alcohol & De-Naturing.* Bradley, IL: Lindsay Publications Inc., 1994.

Yarbrough, Raymond B. *Electrical Engineering Reference Manual for the PE Exam.* Belmont, CA: Professional Publications, Inc., 1997.

Young, Warren C., and Richard G. Budynas. *Roark's Formulas for Stress and Strain.* New York: McGraw-Hill Companies, 2001.

Zimmerman, Elizabeth. *Knitting Without Tears.* New York: Fireside Books, 1995.

Worldwatch Institute. "Melting of Earth's Ice Cover Reaches New High." *Worldwatch News,* Brief 00-02, 2000.

Index